# FUNCTIONAL MANAGEMENT



**Prof. (Dr.) Parimal H. Vyas**
*Dean, Faculty of Commerce,*
*Head, Department of Commerce & Business Management,*
*The M.S. University of Baroda, Vadodara.*

**Dr. (Ms) Priti V. Nigam**
*Assistant Professor,*
*Department of Commerce & Business Management,*
*Faculty of Commerce,*
*The M.S. University of Baroda, Vadodara.*

**Dr. Madhusudan N. Pandya**
*Faculty Member,*
*Department of Commerce and Business Management,*
*Faculty of Commerce,*
*The M.S. University of Baroda, Vadodara.*

**Ms Neha Tiwari**
*Faculty Member,*
*Department of Commerce and Business Management,*
*Faculty of Commerce,*
*The M.S. University of Baroda, Vadodara.*

**Ms Drishti Joshi**
*Faculty Member,*
*Department of Commerce and Business Management,*
*Faculty of Commerce,*
*The M.S. University of Baroda, Vadodara.*

**Ms Yamini K.K.**
*Faculty Member,*
*Department of Commerce and Business Management,*
*Faculty of Commerce,*
*The M.S. University of Baroda, Vadodara.*

**Shri Parag Shukla**
*Faculty Member,*
*Department of Commerce and Business Management,*
*Faculty of Commerce,*
*The M.S. University of Baroda, Vadodara.*

**Ms Hetal Pandya**
*Faculty Member,*
*Department of Commerce and Business Management,*
*Faculty of Commerce,*
*The M.S. University of Baroda, Vadodara.*

Himalaya Publishing House

MUMBAI • NEW DELHI • NAGPUR • BENGALURU • HYDERABAD • CHENNAI • PUNE • LUCKNOW • AHMEDABAD • ERNAKULAM • BHUBANESWAR • INDORE • KOLKATA • GUWAHATI

First Edition : 2013

**Published by** : Mrs. Meena Pandey for **Himalaya Publishing House Pvt. Ltd.,** "Ramdoot", Dr. Bhalerao Marg, Girgaon, **Mumbai - 400 004.** Phone: 022-23860170/23863863, Fax: 022-23877178 **E-mail: himpub@vsnl.com; Website: www.himpub.com**

**Branch Offices** :

**New Delhi** : "Pooja Apartments", 4-B, Murari Lal Street, Ansari Road, Darya Ganj, New Delhi - 110 002. Phone: 011-23270392, 23278631; Fax: 011-23256286

**Nagpur** : Kundanlal Chandak Industrial Estate, Ghat Road, Nagpur - 440 018. Phone: 0712-2738731, 3296733; Telefax: 0712-2721216

**Bengaluru** : No. 16/1 (Old 12/1), 1st Floor, Next to Hotel Highlands, Madhava Nagar, Race Course Road, Bengaluru - 560 001. Phone: 080-22286611, 22385461, 4113 8821, 22281541

**Hyderabad** : No. 3-4-184, Lingampally, Besides Raghavendra Swamy Matham, Kachiguda, Hyderabad - 500 027. Phone: 040-27560041, 27550139

**Chennai** : 8/2 Madley 2nd street, T. Nagar, Chennai - 600 017. Mobile: 09320490962

**Pune** : First Floor, "Laksha" Apartment, No. 527, Mehunpura, Shaniwarpeth (Near Prabhat Theatre), Pune - 411 030. Phone: 020-24496323/24496333; Mobile: 09370579333

**Lucknow** : House No 731, Shekhupura Colony, Near B.D. Convent School, Aliganj, Lucknow - 226 022. Mobile: 09307501549

**Ahmedabad** : 114, "SHAIL", 1st Floor, Opp. Madhu Sudan House, C.G. Road, Navrang Pura, Ahmedabad - 380 009. Phone: 079-26560126; Mobile: 09377088847

**Ernakulam** : 39/104 A, Lakshmi Apartment, Karikkamuri Cross Rd., Ernakulam, Cochin - 622011, Kerala. Phone: 0484-2378012, 2378016; Mobile: 09387122121

**Bhubaneswar** : 5 Station Square, Bhubaneswar - 751 001 (Odisha). Phone: 0674-2532129, Mobile: 09338746007

**Indore** : Kesardeep Avenue Extension, 73, Narayan Bagh, Flat No. 302, IIIrd Floor, Near Humpty Dumpty School, Indore - 452 007 (M.P.). Mobile: 09303399304

**Kolkata** : 108/4, Beliaghata Main Road, Near ID Hospital, Opp. SBI Bank, Kolkata - 700 010, Phone: 033-32449649, Mobile: 7439040301

**Guwahati** : House No. 15, Behind Pragjyotish College, Near Sharma Printing Press, P.O. Bharalumukh, Guwahati - 781009, (Assam). Mobile: 09883055590, 08486355289, 7439040301

**DTP by** : HPH, Editorial Office, Bhandup (Megha, Hansa)

Printed at : M/s. Jayalakshmi Enterprises Offset Printers, Hyderabad. On behalf of HPH.

# Preface

It gives us great pleasure in presenting our efforts in the form of this publication for the benefit of students starving for the conceptual understanding of the management. This publication contains a comprehensive discussion on the elements of basic management areas in various parts.

**Part – I has included six chapters (chapter number one to six)** and deals with topics such as, *viz.*, Personnel Management, Human Resource Management and Human Resource Development. Human beings are important resources to an organisation. Like other resources, they represent an investment whose development and utilisation require managing (i.e., planning, organisation, leadership and evaluation). In every organisation, human resources are a pivotal variable without which the assets are worthless. Therefore, human resources need to be understood and utilised effectively to achieve the goals of an organisation. The discipline of personnel management has gained importance since professionalisation of management and is now regarded as a 'must' for the successful running of a business.

**Part – II has offered detailed discussion on (chapter number seven to thirteen)** concerning marketing as a business function that identifies customer needs and wants, determines which target markets the organization can serve best, and designs appropriate products, services, and programmes to serve these markets. The goal of marketing is to create customer satisfaction profitably by building value-laden relationships with important customers. The marketing department cannot accomplish this goal by itself. It must team up closely with other departments in the company and partner with other organizations throughout its entire value-delivery system to provide superior value to customers. Thus, marketing calls upon everyone in the organization to "think customer" and to do all they can to help create and deliver superior customer value and satisfaction. Discussion on marketing is followed by important areas of Marketing Research, Channels of Distribution and Advertising. It also includes discussion on Production and Material Management.

**Part – III has covered in one chapter (chapter number fourteen)** the topics on the Portfolio Management and Stock Exchanges which takes into consideration emerging requirement of present scenario of business.

**Part – IV has dealt with (chapter number fifteen to sixteen)** Office Management, Management of Information System.

**Part – V has focused upon (chapter number seventeen and eighteen)** coverage of topics such as Banking and Negotiable Instruments.

**Part – VI includes two chapters (chapter number nineteen and twenty)** covering Basics of Insurance and Transportation, and ISO 9000.

Each chapter ends with a case study, giving a practical mental exercise to the students. The publication gives a comprehensive, innovative, managerial, and practical introduction of Functional Areas of Managements. Extensive use of illustrations, cases, objective questions and descriptive questions make the book straightforward, easy to read, and enjoyable.

In this changed environment, new concepts of managements are being introduced. This publication has incorporated the new approach and we hope that readers will find this publication very useful which will meet their needs. Management is now a subject of study in almost all universities and this publication will be useful to all management students.

**Authors**

# Acknowledgements

We sincerely express a deep sense of gratitude and respectfully acknowledge the contributions and publications offered by the authors which have helped us immensely in the preparation of this publication. We are equally thankful to the management and staff of the Himalaya Publishing House Pvt. Ltd. Ahmedabad.

We welcome the esteemed readers to offer their comments and valuable suggestions on this publication.

You may reach us via e-mail: *parimalvyasmsu@yahoo.co.in.*

We hope that fellow academia and the students shall certainly find this publication useful.

**Authors**

# Contents

## PART-I :
## Personnel Management



## PART- II :
## Marketing and Production Management



## PART-III :
## Portfolio Management

## PART-IV :
## Office Management



## PART-V :
## Banking and Negotiable Instrument



## PART-VI :
## Insurance and ISO 9000

# Detailed Contents

## PART-I : Personnel Management

## PART-II : Marketing and Production Management

# PART-III : Portfolio Management



# PART-IV : Office Management

## PART-V : Banking and Negotiable Instrument



## PART-VI : Insurance and ISO 9000

# Part–I

# Personnel Management

CHAPTER 1

# Personnel Management

## LEARNING OBJECTIVES

- *Personnel Management*
- *Evolution of Personnel Management*
- *Important Roles Played by a Personnel Manager*
- *Line-staff Aspects of the Personnel Functions*
- *Describe the Scope of Personnel Management*
- *Meaning of HRM*
- *Definition of HRM*
- *Describe the Scope of HRM*
- *Draw the Distinction between Personnel Management and HRM*
- *Meaning of HRD*
- *Functions of HRD*
- *Distinction between HRM and HRD*

## INTRODUCTION TO PERSONNEL MANAGEMENT

Personnel management is concerned with managing people. It covers all levels of personnel, including blue-collared employees (craftsman, foreman, labourers), and white-collared employees (professionals, managers, clerical workers, salesmen). It is concerned with employees, both as individuals and a group with collaboration and involvement in the organisation's activity. Personnel management is concerned with helping the employees to develop their capabilities and potentiality to the maximum possible extent. Personnel management attempts at getting the willing cooperation of the people for the attainment of the desired goal. Organization is nothing without personnel. Preferring to work with human rather than objects is still important. What is IBM without its employee? Personnel constitute an integral part of the organization. The knowledge skills, imaginativeness, abilities and commitment of the members of the organization constitute the most critical factor in the development and implementation of work plan and the delivery of product and services. Without the full commitment of its employees, an organization cannot accomplish its objectives. Consequently, the attention, development, motivation and coordination of employees are essential responsibilities of all levels of management (top, middle, lower). Personnel manager must be greatly concerned with the expectations of both employees and societies in general. Today, personnel manager is attaining more importance because of rapid change in management process and other technological advancement. Personnel administration is the code of the ways of organising and treating individuals at work and the calculated use of resources so that they will each get the greatest possible realization of their intrinsic (inner) abilities thus, attaining maximum efficiencies for themselves and their group and thereby giving to the enterprise of which they are a part of its determining competitive advantage and its optimum or effective results. For example, ONGC's oil exploration capabilities, and Dell's ability to deliver low cost, high quality computers at an amazing speed.

Personnel administration help an organization in the management of personnel resources with the use of well thought out principles, practices, programmes, functions, activities and rationalise techniques in selecting, retaining, and developing personnel for the fulfilment of organizational objectives systematically and scientifically. It is an art and science of planning, organising, evaluating and implementing the personnel resources in any organization so that the organization derives maximum benefits in terms of performance and efficiency as well as achievement of the objectives, goals, and targets.

Day-by-day, it is becoming complex until and unless we understand all the implications of such an administration. For example, two professional bodies were formed namely Indian Institute of Personnel Management (IIPM) at Kolkata and the National Institute of Labour Management (NILM) at Mumbai.

In 1980s, these two professional bodies merged together and formed the National Institute of Personnel Management (NIPM) headquartered at Kolkata.

In the year 1990, another milestone was achieved by renaming of American Society for Personnel Administration (ASPA) as Society for Human Resource Management (SHRM). Over the year, a new approach — the Human Resource Management has emerged which focuses on developmental aspects of human resource with a pragmatic (positive) and flexible approach.

## Definitions of Personnel Management

- According to Edwin B. Flippo, "Personnel management is the planning, organising, directing and controlling of the procurement, development, compensation, integration, maintenance and separation of human resource to the end that individual organizational and social objectives are accomplished".
- According to Indian Institute of Personnel Management "Personnel Management, Labour Management, or Staff Management means, quite simply, the task of dealing with human relationship within an organization. Academically, the three aspects of personnel management are as follows:
  - (i) The welfare aspect concerned with working conditions and amenities such as canteens, crèches, housing, personal problems of workers, schools and recreations,
  - (ii) The labour of personnel aspect concerned with recruitment, placement of employees, remuneration, promotion, incentives, productivity, etc.
  - (iii) The industrial relations aspects concerned with trade union negotiations, settlement of industrial disputes, joint consultation and collective bargaining. All these aspects are concerned with human element in industry as distinct from the mechanical."
- The Institute of Personnel Management in UK defined personnel management (1966) as "that part of the management function which is concerned with people at work and with their relationships within an enterprise. Its aim is to bring together and develop into an effective organization, the man and woman who make up an enterprise and having regard to the well being of an individual and of working groups, to enable them to make their best contribution to its success."
- General Definition of Personnel Management:

  "Personnel management is the administrative discipline of hiring and developing employees so that they become more valuable to the organization. It includes, conducting job analysis; planning personnel needs and recruitment; selecting the right people for the right job; orienting and training; determining and managing wages and salaries; providing benefits and incentives; appraising performance; resolving disputes; and communicating with all employees at all levels."

## EVOLUTION OF PERSONNEL MANAGEMENT

With this shift in business dynamics, the realization dawned on companies that people and their knowledge is the only source of sustainable competitive advantage, as other resources related to materials, equipment, technology, finance etc have proved short lived in the absence of human capital capable of deploying this resources effectively and efficiently.

The history of personnel management begins around the end of 19th century, the origins of personnel management can be traced to the concerned about exploitation of people within the factories and was introduced through law of the land in most countries to deal with issues pertaining to grievances and the welfare of the women.

As the dynamics in relations between trade unions and management changed the personnel management responsibilities grew beyond welfare to other areas such as ensuring amicable (friendly) industrial relations and effective personnel administration.

Although the field of personnel administration as a discipline of study is relatively recent, the precepts (order) upon which its current concepts are based had their origins deep in history. For example, "The minimum wage rate" was included in the Babylonian code of Hammurabi around 1800 BC. The Chinese, as early as 1650 BC, had originated the principle of "division of labour" and they understood the meaning and implications of labour turnover even in 400 BC.

The "Span of management" was well originated by Moses around 1200 BC and the Caldrons had incentive wage plans around 400 BC. The ancients, with their stone axes, adages and other flint tools, may not have appreciated the principle of "transfer of skill from the humans to the machine", but they were nevertheless applying the principle of "Transfer of skill from the humans to the machine", and this separated them from large number of other human beings.

In India, Kautilya has observed that there existed a sound base for systematic management of human resource as early as fourth century BC. The government then took active interest in the operation of public and private sector enterprises and provided systematic procedure for regulating employee-employer relationship. Charm has described the contribution of Kautilya in the field of "Staffing and Personnel Management" in the form of table displayed below:

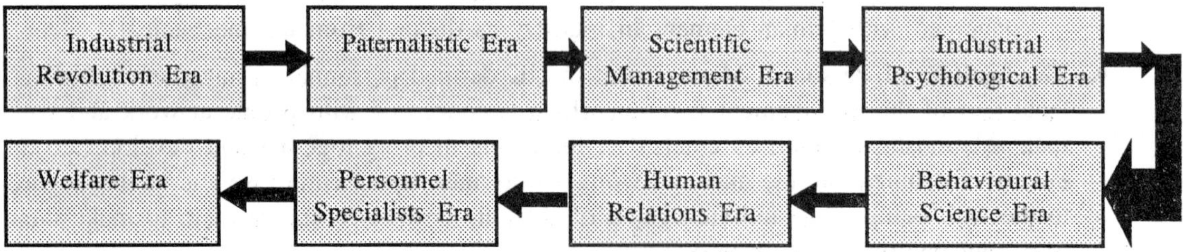


## STAGES OF THE EVOLUTION OF PERSONNEL MANAGEMENT

This classification is rather very broad. We would like to describe the chronological growth of the science of personnel management somewhat on the following lines:

1. Era of Industrial Revolution;
2. Era of Trade Unionism;
3. Era of Social Responsibility;
4. Scientific Management Era;
5. Industrial Psychology Era (including Human Relations Era);
6. The Behavioural Science Era, and
7. The Personnel Specialists and Welfare Era.

**1. Era of Industrial Revolution:** Modern personnel management has evolved from a number of significant interrelated developments which date back to the beginning of what is popularly known as the Industrial Revolution, we call it Evolution. There were several types of relationships involving employers and employees, which were distinctly termed as "slaver", "serfdom" and the "guild system". The initial stage of the guild system is said to be early beginnings of personnel management, for the three classes — the masters, the travelling journey man, and apprentices and the system involved "selecting, training, developing, rewarding and maintaining workers".

Wage and salary administration and collective bargaining over wage and conditions of work were in evidence. Gradually, economic and social changes brought about a change in the old economic, social and political system.

These changes were precipitated in manufacturing by a new economic doctrine (theory) and by inventions and utilization of new tools, process and machines. The economic doctrine, French concepts of *laissez faire* and *laissez passer* which meant that a person should be permitted to make what he wanted and to go where he pleases.

The industrial revolution consisted essentially in the development of machinery, the use of mechanical energy and the consequent establishment of factories employing large number of people — the productive power of man. The factory system gradually replaced the "cottage" system. This system arose out of the ability of factory owners to pay a family higher wages than he would be earned by it, primarily because of the speed of machines and efficiencies gained through the further subdivision of labour (specialised in one task).

The industrial revolution greatly expanded the mass production of goods. Science and technology began to be applied to all aspects of the working of modern industrial corporations. It has affected the Personnel Administration System in many ways.

(i) The place of work changed to a central work area, where people worked under common roof.

(ii) The method of production changed from manual to machine.

(iii) The migration from rural areas to urban areas started with the decline of cottage industries because there was no land to fall back upon for employment. On the other hand, there was heavy concentration of industry in certain areas.

(iv) Not only was geographical mobility facilitated but occupational and industrial mobility also increased. Jobs were more simplified with the result that the labour force readily adapted itself to a variety of positions.

(v) As a result of separation, it was difficult to maintain the close relationship which owners had with their employees in the past.

(vi) Mass production, which calls for a continuous flow of materials, was made possible by complex, integrated, automatic and electrically controlled equipment.

(vii) Mechanization made the work so simple that a large number of women and children began to be employed, and this replaced men.

(viii) With the introduction of machines, heavy physical labour was eliminated, work now become easy enough but on the other side, it reduced the opportunities of employment for unskilled labour.

(ix) Because of the complexity of the process of production and advanced technology, a new class of professional employees had developed in the industry who exercised tremendous power in the affairs of the company.

(x) Production control, method control, inventory control, financial control and manpower control have all become more effective because of the introduction of computerised techniques and procedures.

(xi) More new jobs are of the nature best suited to the white collar and executive groups who guide, regulate and coordinate production process. Formerly, this coordination was either the responsibility of blue collar production workers or artisans.

(xii) Specialization has developed in mechanical, electrical and civil engineering research; there are development and production engineers and such personnel specialist as labour relations managers, wage analysts, training directors and safety engineers.

(xiii) There had been a decline in the number of semiskilled and unskilled workers but an increase in professional and skilled workers, who handled a vast quantity of records, reports and data needed by the management.

(xiv) There has also been an increasing participation of women in the labour force for secretarial and other clerical jobs.

However, these results were achieved at a great price because of the following:

- There were a great concentration of people amongst many machines in small, dingy, dirty factories;
- The increased use of machinery resulted in changes in the employment situation. Since their operations called for specialised knowledge, and unskilled workers found it difficult to adjust themselves to the new equipment, large number of them could not find gainful employment;
- Working and living conditions were unsatisfactory and very unhygienic;
- Adults had to work from 9 to 11 hours a day and children from 14 to 15 hours as a day, and they were all treated harshly by the owners of the factories;
- Labour was looked upon as a commodity, could be bought and sold, and the government, because of the prevailing political philosophy of *laissez faire*, did little to protect the workers;
- Monotony and boredom were the results of division of labour and they felt no pride in their accomplishment;
- A shut down in one sector of the industry threw the entire system out of gear, bringing about great economic suffering;
- The worker was required to follow strict discipline, and
- They had to live by the clock or else would be fired or punished.
- At last, "the new Industrial Era brought about materialism, discipline, monotony, boredom, job displacement, impersonality ,work interdependence and related behavioural phenomena. The benefit of Industrial revolution, however, has far outweighed the costs of increasing industrialization". Economically, the Industrial Revolution brought about great increase in output and in the accumulation in the goods and capital in turn, business and commerce were greatly accelerated, owners and entrepreneurs did well, but the average citizen fared poorly.

**2. Era of Trade Unionism:** After the advent of factory system, groups of employees began to get together to discuss their common problems. The basic philosophy underlying the trade unionism was that "through strength and collective support, the management could be forced to listen to the workers and redress their grievances". The weapon used was that of strikes, slow downs, walkouts, picketing, boycotts and sabotage. Later, economic problems, including the question of employee's benefits and services became the major concern. Workers joined together on the basis of their common interest to improve their lot. This trade unionism, however, did influence the personnel management in such fields of activity as "the adoption of employee grievances handling system, the acceptance of arbitration as a means of resolving conflicts of rights, disciplinary practices, the expansion of employee benefit programmes, the liberalisation of holiday and vacation time, clear job duties, job rights through seniority and the installation of rational and defensible wage structure". Organisational units were created by the companies to deal with union relationships and representatives. In some cases, unions were sponsored by the companies as a means of controlling their activity. Where unions brought about wage increases, greater attention was paid to the study of jobs, methods improvements, connecting wages to performance, and the more careful selection of personnel. Trade union dilution accepting unskilled women into craftsman's job and changing manning levels.

**3. Era of Social Responsibility Feeling:** Robert Owen (1913), for the first time adopted a somewhat paternalistic attitude towards his employees. He was a British business man, reformer and humanitarian. He believed that "the principle, social and economic environments influence the physical, mental and psychological development of workers". In order to increase productivity, it was necessary to improve the conditions of employees by moving them from adverse environment or by changing the environment with the provision of more satisfactory living and working conditions. Owen implemented this philosophy by organising model villages next to his cotton mills in Scotland; by introducing shower baths and toilets into the factories, which were cleaned and painted, in which windows were installed for light and ventilation; by organising day schools for the children and night schools for the workers; and by raising the minimum age for the employment of children to 11 years and shortening their work day to 10 hours.

Later, he abolished child labour entirely. He regarded the workers like children who must be cautiously guided, trained and protected. He, therefore, advised his brother manufacturers to devote as much attention to their vital machine. By doing so, profit would be maximised. Adam Smith emphasised "if each individual worked or his own economic self-interest, the society would gain". These views were supported by Charles Babbage.

He observed that "the emphasis should be on mutuality of interests between employer and workers and on the division of labour, for such division for labour would reduced the waste in raw materials, achieve savings through more effective placement of workers, produced economies through a different wage skilled based on skill levels, save time by not switching from task-to-task, gained efficiencies stemming from familiarisation with special tools and stimulate workers' inventions pertaining to tools and methods". He held the view that "hard work and high productivity were a source of good wages for the worker and higher profits for the employer". But he denounced any unionisation of workers.

**4. The Scientific Management Era:** This era began in 1900, reached at its peak approximately in 1930. It has remained alive somewhat even to the present times. The scientific movement owes its origin to Frederick W. Taylor (1856-1955) who is known as "the father of scientific management". He started his experiments in the steel industry in the Midvale and Bethlehem plants in 1885. He developed the four great principles of management.

(i) The development of a true science of each job;

(ii) A scientific selection of the right person for the job;

(iii) Training a person to perform his job in scientific manner, and

(iv) Friendly cooperation between the management and the men.

Taylor believed that "planning should be the result of cooperation between the management and workers and that a provision should exist for compensating the personnel with financial incentives". He also believed that workers were "sources of untapped {unused} energy", which could be properly utilised if they are trained and fairly treated. He strongly recommended that when workers failed to respond to initial training, they should not be brutally (directly) discharged but given more time to familiarise themselves with their job or be transferred to a job for which they were better suited. The value of workers, ideas and anticipated the modern suggestions system by recommending cash bonuses for developed suggestions. He believed that by a scientific measurement of work, that is, by time study, method's study, job classification and method improvement, functional foremanship, standardisation of tools, specifications of the best methods, a different piece rate system, instructional cards for workman and a control system — most of the sources of conflict between labour and management would disappear.

The scientific movement has had a great influence on employee-employer relationships. It has greatly contributed to the professionalization of management. The use of his approach improved management methods, procedures and standards and strengthened production and supervision. Taylor's approach emphasis on the mutual benefits of productivity: the organization produced more and thus increased its profits, while workers made more money and lived better lives, so it was accepted by labour and the management. One name given to his outlook is Welfare Capitalism. Taylor's idea lead to a separate discipline called "Human Engineering". It is the study of people at work and of work methods, it includes a study of equipment design, pacing (speed) of work, hours of work, and environment conditions of work, its purpose are to improve productivity and job satisfaction.

But, after 30 years, this approach has begun to lose its popularity, for it has been discovered that many of the management problems are the result of "human" and not "mechanical factors". Taylor's approach stressed the need for techniques which ensure higher performance at the work place and estimate unnecessary movements and gave greater importance to "technology" than to the "men" at work.

Fragmentation (part) of an operations so that each man did only one little job encouraging a mechanistic conception of "man at work", ultimately lead to a times symptoms of alienation (separation), frustration, conflict, etc., leading to loss of production. This knowledge brought about a new thinking in recent years.

Such as those of Douglas McGregor in the USA, and Eric Trist in UK, who pointed out that "the best results were obtained in industrial occupations when human beings were treated in the totally of their physical and psychological characteristics".

Among others who modified Taylor's views were Henry Gantt and Frank and Lillian Gilbreth. Henry Gantt propounded "Task and Bonus Wage" system which removed the penalties provided under Taylor's wage system. Under Gantt's system, the worker was paid a guaranteed hourly rate, a bonus of 20 per cent if he reached the standard output and a high piece rate for output that was above the standard output. Further, the foreman was given a bonus for each man who was successful.

Frank Gilbreth made an extensive use of motion pictures of tasks being performed in order to analyse body movements. From these studies, he formulated the "laws of efficient motion".

Lillian Gilbreth worked closely with her husband and is credited with the publication of Psychology of Management (1914), the first book relating to the application of psychology to the principles of Scientific Management.

**5. Industrial Psychological Era:** During this period, psychologists were introduced to the field of industrial management to study systematically many personnel problems. The development of industrial psychology owes a great deal to Hugo Munsterberg's book, *Psychology and Industrial Efficiency*, which was published in 1913. He is regarded as the Father of Industrial Psychology. His contributions to industrial management were particularly notable in respect of his analysis of jobs in terms of their mental and emotional requirements and in terms of the development of testing devices (the Alpha and Beta tests). Advances were made in selection, placement, testing, and training and research practices. Industrial psychology introduced the "matching of employees to jobs, for different jobs require different skills and abilities". It emphasised the use of psychology in the field of personnel testing, interviewing, attitude measurement, learning theory, training, failure, and monotony study, safety, job analysis and human engineering. Of these, the major applications of the knowledge and techniques of industrial psychology have been in the field of recruitment, testing for employment, job replacement, promotion and training. The tools and practices of industrial psychology are applied through education, publication and consultation services.

The human relations movement is an outcome of the reaction against the impersonality of scientific management. Top management personnel began to realise that "human resources are the most valuable assets that any organisation possesses and that, without these, other resources are useless". Experiments were conducted at the Hawthorne Works of the Western Electric Company in Chicago during the late 1920s and early 1930s by Elton Mayo (1818-1949), F. Roethlisberger and W.J. Dickson of the Harvard Graduate School of Business Administration. They concluded that "human and social factors, not physical variables, accounted for the productivity phenomenon". As a result of this experiment, employee productivity began to be analysed in such behavioural terms as "teamwork, participation, cohesiveness, loyalty and *esprit de corps*, instead of in terms of engineering alternative".

The findings of the Hawthorne studies put emphasis on the importance for an understanding of the needs of both, management and workers of the special aspects of work performances. The message was that interpersonal relationships (between the workers and their supervisors) should be nurtured for the fullest realisation of the potential of individuals and groups. The basic conclusion was the "sociological and psychological phenomena often-exerted even greater influence on output than physical measurable conditions of work did". Accordingly, concepts such as the "social system, informal, organisation, group control of behaviour, equilibrium and logical and non-logical behaviour entered the field of Human Relations and Personnel Management specialists". Therefore, there was a swing from the "scientific management" with standards of performance, impersonal engineering by efficiency experts towards the new "human relations approach". The human relations movement was mainly concerned with the informal, spontaneous behaviour of work groups and the sentiments and attitudes of employees. The scientific management movement was mainly concerned with an organisation as a technical, economic system; the human relations movement viewed it as a social system.

**6. The Behavioural Era:** The behavioural science movement is an outgrowth of human relations studies and began around 1955; and its major impact lasted some 10 to 15 years. The behavioural sciences include anthropology, human, economics, history, physiology, mathematical, biology, medicine, social psychology. The research in these disciplines has provided the subject matter for personnel management. Behavioural scientists are concerned with the impact of various methods of pay and individual performance with the effect of different styles of leadership and different philosophies on total organisation's performance; with job design and its relationship to personality growth; with the impact of different appraisal system, with group influences and the effect of organisation's communications on productivity and change.

The method of research made use of data obtained from experiments, observations, survey, programme-or-action research and the theory of model-building.

Abraham Maslow (1954) propounded a theory regarding an individual "hierarchy of needs" also known as "Deficit Theory Motivation". He stated that there is a series of needs some of which are lower in the scale or system or values in individual or social and some are higher. Herzberg advanced a two factor theory of motivation. Some of hygiene considerations: money, supervision, job, and the physical aspects of work to motivate people; but these factors served only human "maintenance needs" rather than the job itself. Another consideration, motivators provided opportunities for personal realization.

Douglas McGregor formulated two contrasting kinds of management beliefs or views about the nature of man at work. McGregor's Theory X stands for the set of traditional beliefs generally held while Theory Y concerned with a different philosophy or understanding of man at work. Theory X involves strict supervision coercion and threat which might breed organised worker protest, restriction of output, etc., and his theory Y might be exploited by the subordinates and therefore he suggested a via media that of the Carrot and Stick approach to motivate work people.

Rensis Likert stated that assumptions like these reflect themselves in two basic system of organizations namely system I and system IV. System I of organisation is based upon theory X assumption, while system IV on theory Y assumptions. This type of approach is also known as the Human Relations approach. It is an aid to the process of integration of employees, however partial with their organization. This type of approach tries to understand human behaviour of employees, however partial with their organization. It tries to understand human behaviour at workplace.

**7. Personnel Specialist and Welfare Era:** With the introduction of the factory system, thousands of persons began to be employed under one roof, and had to be controlled if the goals of an organization were to be achieved. For work in the administrative office, clerks or manual employees had to be recruited. These were entrusted with the responsibility of hiring men to work of an organization. Later, they were concerned with the recruitment, placement and selection of personnel. With the increase in the size of the organization, and further increase in the number of employees, separate personnel executive had to be appointed to develop systematic methods, determine wage rates, and develop job discipline and descriptions and job specification. Later his duties were enlarged to cover additional responsibility of looking after the benefits and services provided for the employees. In the course of time, arrangements had to be made to train the existing personnel and hence, a manager for training was also provided. For administrative and organizational effectiveness, it was then found feasible to merge these different functions into a single position, like the personnel manager and welfare officer.

Subsequently, organisational planning, manpower planning, manpower selection and other allied problems regarding the management of managers and high talent manpower assumed significance in the organization. High talent personnel emerged as the key human resource and personnel management was turned to the existing economic structure. The emphasis now is on "management of human resource". So that personnel management has now passed through vast changes. Beginning with "Welfare Work", its responsibilities have grown wider and deeper.

The present day personnel management has been entrusted with three main responsibilities, *viz.*, First, to assist the line management in planning the organization and to maintain the workforce at optimum efficiency through recruitment, induction and placement, salary and wage administration, training for key non-management personnel, development of employee communication programmes.

Second, to provide task force to render services to the management in the field of labour relations with particular references to union-management relations, management of staff development functions, training for key non-management personnel, development of grievance procedure and development of personnel policies and procedure.

Third, to control functions regarding employee services such as housing and transport, promotion, recreational facilities, financial aids to employees and educational facilities.

It will thus be noted that personnel management is entrusted to undertake a multiple of personnel jobs. In sum, it may be noted that personnel management functions has been historically associated with the times and events of social, economic, political and technological factors that influence the nature and scope of personnel administration. Further, the historical evolution of the personnel functions is evolutionary and not revolutionary, that is the changes have occurred in the personnel field have been caused mostly by gradual cultural changes.

The last three decades saw the changes in the competitive environment, brought about the growing competition, which resulted in wide choice for customers and new dimensions for market place and innovations.

We can analyze how the organization would look like when it was really humming, really succeeding. Translating that back into culture, working practices, learning motivation, reward, and selection — those are the strategic choices that we have to equip our members to make.

As the 21st century advances, there seems no reason to suppose that the various roles and traditions will disappear, although their relative importance will change and evolve, depending on the political, legislative and intellectual climate of the time and organizational needs and culture. For the immediate future, the change agent and business partner roles seem likely to grow in importance, although they will continue to be a part of the function which, if it is not about implementing rules and legislation, it is about ensuring that line managers are enabled to do so competently.

## IMPORTANT ROLES OF A PERSONNEL MANAGER

The role of personnel manager in the industry, it may be said that by and large, reflects the top management's concept of personnel function and the methods of managerial control they believe in. For example, Police Agency, a legal defender of rights and a negotiator, a catering man meeting the welfare needs of the employees. The role of a personnel manager has changed through time. At first, the dominant role was to satisfy top management in procuring and maintaining a workforce that would be instrumental to organizational productivity as knowledge expanded in executing this role, the manager began to understand the necessary for ascertaining and accommodating to the needs of workforce. He or she constantly searches for the programme which would support the accomplishment of organizational and individual objectives. The job was made more difficult by rise in the modern labour union, the increasing educational level of societal members, the increasing size and complexity of the organization and its technology and sometimes violent demand of less privileged segments of our society. These factors has led to the final major alteration of the personnel manager's role. Though society permits and encourages the use of its citizens as means to organizational ends it is difficult precisely to relate the present day functions of personnel to his role as conceptualized earlier. If the personnel managers are what the personnel managers do, the picture that emerges is indeed confusing, for what personnel managers do, can be compared to a Sunday morning jumble sale — a collection of incidental chores, firefighting tasks, welfare functions and a watchdog functions.

As the workers were organizing themselves into strong unions and industrial conflicts were multiplying, the employer used the personnel man as a kind of trouble shooter or firefighter — either to advise him on how to find loopholes in the labour laws, or other statues so that the union demands could be resisted with a measure of legitimacy, or, to come to a settlement where concessions were inescapable. There was tendency, at this stage, to make him responsible for handling all kinds of labour trouble.

In this newly expanded role, the personnel manager will, at worst, act as the organization's social conscience, and at best, will work as an informed specialist with all members of the organizations in determining and meeting the demand of the social role.

A personnel manager therefore, requires a broad background in fields such as psychology, sociology, philosophy, economy and management. In the modern era, the personnel manager typically performs a variety of roles as follows:

1. The conscience role is that of a humanitarian who reminds the management of its moral and ethical obligations to its employees.
2. As a mediator, he plays the role of a peace-maker, offering to settle the disputes that may arise among individuals or groups. He acts as a liaison and communicating link between an individual and a group and between labour and management.
3. The personnel manager plays the role of a counsellor to whom the employees frequently go for consultation and with whom they discuss their marital, health, mental, physical, financial, social, career problems.
4. The personnel manager has always been a frequent spokesman for or a representative of the company because he has a better overall picture of his company's operations, since he deals intimately with many key organizational activities and functions.
5. The personnel manager also act as a problem-solver with respect to the issues that involve human resource management and overall long range organizational planning.
6. He helps line managers learn to detect and solve their problems.
7. He works as a change agent within the organization because he is best suited to introduce and implement major institutional changes. He takes initiative for installing organizational development programmes and convinces the top management of their need. It is he who alerts the top management regarding managerial obsolescence in his organization.

It has been now fully recognized that the basic role of the personnel manager is the management of manpower resources. Such management is concerned with leadership both in the group and individual relationship, and labour-management relations. It effectively describes the process of planning and directing the application, development and utilization is now considered as one of the four main function, *viz*., planning, production, marketing, and human relations.

The personnel manager undertakes all those functions which are concerned with human elements or relations in organizations as well as in material elements listed therein (as the function) the main objective is to see that human resources are purposefully utilized for the optimum good of the organization and there should be meaningful cooperation for achieving the objectives of management. The major role of personnel manager is given as under:

## 1. Personnel Role or Operational Role

(a) *Advisory:* Advising management on effective use of human resources.

(b) *Manpower Planning:* Recruitment, selection and performance appraisal.

(c) *Trainer and Developer:* Apart from talent, acquisition and retention, personnel manager find skilled efficiencies from time-to-time and offer meaningful opportunities and bring out the latent (inner) potential of people through intrinsic and extrinsic rewards.

(d) *Coordinator or Mediator,* and

(e) *Measurement and Assessment of Individual or Group Behaviour*

## 2. Welfare Role

(a) *Managing Services:* Canteen, crèches, cooperatives, transport, grain shops

(b) *Group Dynamics:* Group counselling, motivation, leadership, communication, and

(c) *Research in personnel and organizational problems*

## 3. Administrative Role

(a) *Policy Maker:* Policy governing talent, acquisition and retention, wage and salary administration, welfare activities and personnel records.

(b) *Human Engineering:* Man machine relationship.

(c) *Administrative Expert:* Recordkeeping like files and database, processing employee benefit claims, answering queries, regarding leave, medical facilities, transport submitting required report to regulating agencies, and

(d) *Housekeeper:* Recruiting, preemployment testing, reference checking, employee surveys, and timekeeping.

## 4. Firefighting Legal Role

(a) *Grievance Handling:* Conflict Resolution,

(b) *Settlement of Disputes.*

(c) *Handling Disciplinary Actions.*

(d) *Collective Bargaining:* This centred on dealing with trade union, to which might be added the development of strategies for dealing or handling industrial relations.

(e) *The Implementer of Legislation Role:* Implying, understanding and implementing of growing amount of legislations, and

(f) *Joint Consultations:* A formal system of communication between the management of an organization and the employees' representatives used prior to taking decisions affecting the workforce, usually affected through a joint consultative committee.

The bureaucratic role consists of implementing a series of roles about behaviour at work dealing with recruitment and managing actions. The social conscience of business role is all about integrating the personnel functions with business needs and taking a more strategic view. Human dynamics play a pivotal (basic) role in surmounting (to come over from) obstacles, defusing complex situations and achieving organizational goals.

The role of personnel manager is ever expanding and is strengthened by greater interest shown in human relations problems by specialists such as behavioural scientists, industrial engineers, social psychologists, labour and legal advisers, industrial and computer technologists, all of whose researches have enriched the field of personnel management, its functions and changed their nature making them wide and humanitarian.

In any enterprise, it is these "line men" who determine the personnel climate for the entire organisation. If the personnel man can meet the challenge of staff role, he would make the most effective contribution to industry.

## FUNCTIONS OF PERSONNEL MANAGER

The functions of the personnel manager are very comprehensive and varied and are determined and influenced by such factors as the size, nature and location of the organization, its short-term and long-term objectives, nature of industry and product, market conditions, degree of competitiveness among rivals, economic, cultural, political and legal environment, the structure of the administrative officers, the mental make-up of the personnel managers and overall organizational philosophy of business.

There are two categories of personnel management functions, managerial and operative.

### 1. Managerial Functions of Personnel Management

A manager is the one who exercises authority and leadership over other personnel, the president of a firm is certainly a manager and so also is the department head or supervisor.

Lawrence Appley said that "Management is the accomplishment of results through the efforts of other people" in the opinion of Harold Koontz, "it is the art of getting things done through people and with informally organised groups".

Management may be thought of as the process of allocating and organization's inputs (human and economic resources) by planning, organising, directing and controlling for the purpose of producing outputs (goods and services) desired by its customers so that organization's objectives are accomplished. In the process, work is performed with and through organization personnel in an ever-changing business environment.

***(a) Planning*:** This functions deals with the determination of the future course of actions to achieve the desired results. Planning of personnel today prevent crisis tomorrow. The process of goal establishment will involve the active and enlightened participation of the personnel manager with his or her expertise in the area of human resources.

Planning is defining goals for future organisational performance and deciding on the tasks and use of resources needed to attain them. For example, Komatsu, Japan's leading manufacturer of construction equipment and heavy machinery, president Satoru announced a long ranged plan called "G" 2000 which include moving the company into high-tech initiative such as lasers and 3D software as well as more traditional goals such as advances in heavy machineries and finding more environmentally friendly technologies.

Terry is of the view that "planning is the foundation of most successful actions of the enterprise". Planning is the determination of the plans, strategies, programmes, procedures, policies and standard needs to accomplish the desired objectives by recruiting, selecting and trained the employees in the organisations.

It involves the ability to think, to predict, to analyse and to come to decisions, to control the actions of personnel and to cope with the complex, dynamic fluid environment. They bridge the gap between where they are and where they want to go. The two most important features of planning are research and forecasting. Personnel administration should be able to predict trends in wages, in labour market, in union demands, in other benefits, in personnel policies and programmes, changes in production or seasonal variations and the levelling out of differences in productions. Therefore, planning and decision making has to be undertaken of an action so that anticipated problems and events may be handled properly. This is also stressed by the saying "Good Managers Make Things Happen".

***(b) Organising*:** Organising typically follows planning and reflects how the organization tries to accomplish the plan. Organising in fact, is considered to be the wool of the entire management fabric, and hence cannot be ignored.

According to J.C. Massie, "An organisation is a structure, a framework and a process by which a cooperative group of human beings allocates its tasks among its members, identifies relationships and integrates its activities towards common objectives". This is done by designing the structure of authority and responsibilities among jobs, personnel and physical factors because in its essentials, it consists of the assignments of the specific functions to designated person or departments with authority to have them carried out, and their accountability to management for the result obtained. It seeks to achieve the maximum return with minimum efforts by decentralization, whereby the power of decisions is brought down as near as possible to the individual concerned. In the words of Drucker: "The right organisational structure is the necessary foundation; without it, the best performance in all other areas of management will be ineffectual and frustrated.

For example, SEMCO, a Brazilian company making industrial pumps, mixtures, propellers and other products recognized from a highly structured, autocratic business into a company run on trust, freedom and democracy.

***(c) Directing (Motivating, Actuating, Commanding, and Leading)*:** Directions then consist of motivating, supervising, guiding and leadership. Without direction, there is no destination. According to McGregor, "many managers would agree that the effectiveness of their organization would be at least doubled if they could discover how to tap the unrealised potential present in their human resources. Directing is involved with getting persons together and asking them to work willingly and effectively for the achievement of designated goals.

Directing deals with not only the dissemination of the orders within an organization units and departments but also with the acceptance and execution of this order by the employees. The review or checking of the safety instalments, wage rate ranges, disciplinary actions and general wage changes are all the responsibility of personnel departments. Leading means creating a shed culture and values, communicating goals to employees throughout the organizations and infusing employees with the desire to perform at a high level. Leading involves motivating entire department, divisions as well as those individuals working immediately with the managers. An era of uncertainty, international competition and diversity of the workforce, the ability to shape culture, communicate goals and motivate employees is critical to business success.

***(d) Coordination and Control*:** In the words of Terry, "Coordination deals with the task of lending efforts in order to ensure a successful attainment of an objective, coordinating refers to balancing, timing and integrating activities in organization, so that a unity of action in pursuit of a common purpose achieved". Coordination in the supervisor and those for whom he is responsible. The personnel department has to coordinate the task of devēloping, interpreting and reviewing personnel policies, practices, and programmes such as safety programmes, employee benefits, job evaluation, training, development and communication. These activities are generally put into operation by and through the line people; but it is the personnel department which follows them through, unifies them and checks to see how they work.

Control is the managerial function concerned with regulating activities in accordance with personnel plan which in turn was formulated on the basis of analysis on fundamental organizational goals. Controlling is the act of checking, regulating and verifying whether everything occurs in conformity with the plan that has been adopted, the instructions issued and the principles established. It is the course and getting location reports; rather than it is steering the ship. By check, analysis, and review, the personnel department assist in realising the personnel objectives, auditing, training programme, analysing labour turnover records, directing morale surveys, conducting separation interviews, interviewing new employees, comparing various features of the programme with other organization programme. This monitoring process provides management with actual performance information for comparison with free determined performance standards, if there are unavoidable deviations from the planned performance, corrective actions can be taken immediately.

Management must ensure that the organization is moving towards its goals. New trends towards empowerment and trust of employees have led many companies to place less emphasis on top down control and more emphasis on training employees to monitor and correct themselves. For example, at ISS (International Service System), the Danish company, grew from a local office cleaning contractor to Billion Multinational Business, the entire control system is build on the belief that people at all levels will make the right decisions if they are provided with appropriate information. Frontline employees are thoroughly trained to measure their own performance against company standards and make corrections as needed.

## 2. Operating Functions of Personnel Management

An operative is the one who has no authority over others but has been given a specific task or duty to perform under managerial supervision. The operative functions of personnel management are concerned with the activities dealing with procuring, developing, compensating, integrating, maintaining, and separating an efficient workforce. These functions are also known as service functions.

**(a) Procurement:** The first operative function of personnel management is procurement. It is concerned with procuring and employing people who possess necessary skill, knowledge and aptitude. Under its purview, you have job analysis, manpower planning, recruitment, selection, placement, induction and internal mobility.

*(i)* ***Job Analysis:*** It is a systematic exploration of the activities within a job. It is a basic technical procedure, one that is used to define the duties, responsibilities and accountabilities of a job.

*(ii)* ***Human Resource Planning:*** It is the process by which an organisation ensures that it has the right number and kinds of people, at the right places, at the right time, capable of effectively and efficiently completing those tasks that will help the organization to achieve its overall objectives.

*(iii)* ***Recruitment:*** It is the process of searching for prospective employees and stimulating them to apply for jobs in the organization.

*(iv)* ***Selection:*** It is the process of ascertaining qualifications, experience, skill and knowledge of applicant with a view to appraising his or her suitability to the job.

*(v)* ***Placement:*** It is the process that ensures a fit, matching the employee's qualifications, experience, skills and interest with the job on offer. It is the personnel manager's responsibilities to position the right candidate at the right level.

*(vi)* ***Induction and Orientation:*** Those are the techniques by which a new employee is rehabilitated in his new surrounding and introduced to the practices, policies and people. He must be acquainted with the principles which define and drive the organization, its mission statement and values which form its backbone.

*(vii)* ***Follow-up:*** To measure and identify whether the performance is according to the plans or not.

*(viii)* ***Internal Mobility:*** The movement of employees from one job to another through transfer and promotions is called internal mobility. Some employees leave an organization due to various reasons leading to lay-off, resignation, retirement and even termination. These movements are known as external mobility. In the best interest of an organization and its employees, such job changes should be guided by well-conceived principles and policies.

**(b) Development:** It is the process of improving, moulding (shaping), changing and developing the skills, knowledge, aptitude, commitment, attitude, creativeness, etc., based on present and future job and organizational requirements. This functions includes:

*(i)* ***Performance Appraisal:*** It is the systematic evaluation of individuals with respect to their performance on the job and their potential for development.

*(ii)* ***Training:*** Training is a systematic process by which employees learn skills, knowledge, abilities or attitudes to further organizational and personal goals.

*(iii)* ***Management or Executive Development:*** It is the process of designing and conducting suitable executive development, programmes so as to develop the managerial and human relation skill of employees.

*(iv)* ***Career Planning and Development:*** It is the planning of one's career and implementation of career plans by means of education, training, job search and acquisition of work experiences. It includes internal and external mobility.

*(v)* ***Human Resource Development [HRD]:*** HRD aims at developing the total organisation. It creates a climate that enables every employee to develop and use his capabilities in order to further both individuals and organizational goals.

**(c) Compensation:** It is concerned with securing adequate and equitable remuneration to personnel for their contribution to the attainment of organizational objective.

*(i)* ***Job Design:*** Organising tasks and responsibilities towards having a productive unit of work is called job design. The main purpose of job design is to integrate the needs of employers to suit the requirements of the organization.

*(ii)* ***Work Scheduling:*** Organizations must realize the importance of scheduling the work to motivate employees through job enrichment, shorter work weeks, flexible times, work sharing and homework assignment.

*(iii)* Employees needs to be challenged at work and the job itself must be one that everyone value. Work scheduling is an attempt to structure work, incorporating the physical, physiological and behavioural aspects of work.

*(iv)* ***Job Evaluation:*** Organization formally determines the value of jobs through the process of job evaluation. Job evaluation is a systematic process of determining the relative worth of job in order to establish which job should be paid more than others within the organization. Job evaluation helps to establish internal equality between various jobs.

*(v)* ***Performance Appraisal:*** After employees has been selected for a job, has been trained to do it and has worked in it for a period of time, his performance should be evaluated. Performance evaluation is the process of deciding how employees do their jobs. It is the method of evaluating the employees at the workplace and normally includes both quality and quantity aspects of job performance. It is the process that involves determining and communicating to an employee how he or she is performing and ideally, establishing a plan of improvement.

*(vi)* ***Compensation Administration:*** It is the process of dividing how much an employee should be paid. The important goal of compensation administration is to design a low cost pay plan that will attract, motivate and retain competent employees which is also perceived to be fair by these employees.

*(vii)* ***Incentives and Benefits:*** In addition to a basic wage structure, most organizations now-adays offer incentive compensation based on actual performance. Unlike incentives, benefits and services are offered to all employees as required by law including — social security, insurance, workman's compensation, welfare amenities, maternity benefits to women employees, sickness benefits, medical benefits, disablement benefits or allowances, dependant benefits, retirement benefits like provident fund, pension, gratuity, etc. Organizations have been offering a plethora of other benefits and services as well as a means of "sweetening the pot". (Employees stock options, anniversary gifts, paid holidays, birthday gifts, and club membership).

Functions related to wage surveys, establishment of job classifications, job descriptions, job analysis and merit ratings, the establishments of wage rate and structure, wage plans and policies, wage systems, incentives and profit sharing plans, etc., fall under this category.

**(d) Integration:** With the employee procured, developed and reasonably compensated, the next step that follows is one of the most difficult challenges to the management. This tries to integrate the goal of an organization with employee aspirations through various employee-oriented programmes, like redressing grievances promptly, instituting proper disciplinary measures, empowering people to decide and think independently, encouraging a participative culture, offering constructive help to trade unions, etc.

*(i)* ***Grievance Redressal:*** A grievance is any factor that involves wages, hours or conditions of employment that is used as a complaint against the employer. Constructive grievance handling depends largely on manager's ability to recognize, diagnose and correct the causes of potential employee dissatisfaction before it convert into formal grievance.

*(ii)* ***Discipline:*** It is the force that prompt an individual or a group to observe the rules, regulations and procedures which are deemed necessary for the attainment of an objective.

*(iii)* ***Teams and Teamwork:*** Self-managed team have emerged as the most important formal groups in today's organizations. They enhance employee involvement and have the potential to create positive synergy. They encourage individuals to sublimate (to make high) their individual goals for those of the group. Teams have inherent strength which ultimately leads to organisational success at various levels. It rests upon the premise that significant overlapping of interest do exist in the organization in which programmes as job enlargement, job evaluation, variable compensations plans. The greater the overlap, the more productivity would coincide with employees that they would prefer to avoid. For example, assignment to narrow and repetitive tasks, meeting his output standards, acceptance of managerial decisions.

*(iv)* ***Collective Bargaining:*** It is the process of agreeing on a satisfactory labour contract between management and union. The contract contains agreement about conditions of employment such as wage, hours, promotions, disciplines, and lay-off benefits, vacations, rest pauses and grievance procedure.

*(v)* ***Employee Participation and Empowerment:*** Participation means sharing the decision making power with the lower rank of an organization in an appropriate manner. When workers participate in organization's decision, they are able to see the big picture clearly and also how their actions would impact the overall growth of the company. They can offer feedback immediately based on experience and improve the quality of decisions greatly. Since they are now treated with respect, they begin to view the job and the organization as their own and commit themselves to organizational objectives whole heartedly.

*(vi)* ***Industrial Relations:*** Harmonious relations between labour and management are essential to achieve industrial growth and higher productivity. When the relationship between the parties is not cordial (hearty), discontentment develops and conflicts erupt abruptly (hasty). It is not always easy to put out the fires with the existing dispute, settlement machinery created by government. Hence, both labour and management must appreciate the importance of openness, trusts and collaborations in their day-to-day dealings. This programme tends to decrease accidents, absenteeism, turnover and operating errors while raising morale, quality and productivity. Such programmes also prevents sabotage (an intentional damage to plant), undesirable behaviour such as insubordination, strike, etc.

At last, after the employee has been procured, his skill and ability developed and monetary compensation determined, the most important yet difficult of the personnel management is to bring about integration of human resource with organizations and to cope with inevitable conflicts that ensue. Integration is concerned with the attempt to effect a reasonable reconciliation of individual, societal and organizational impact. On the other hand, there are certain things that employees desire which the compensation is reluctant to provide. For example, increase in wages, safe working conditions, time off with pay, shorter hours of work, premium pay for overtime work.

**(e) Maintenance:** If we have executed the foregoing functions well, we now have a willing and able workforce. The maintenance of willingness is heavily affected by communications with employees, physical conditions of employees including health and safety and employee service programme are the responsibility of personnel departments.

1. ***Health and Safety:*** Managers at all levels are expected to know and enforce safety and health standards throughout the organizations. They must ensure a work environment that protects employees from physical hazards, unhealthy conditions and unsafe acts of their personnel. Through proper safety and health programmes, the physical and psychological well-being of employee must be preserved and even improved.
2. ***Employee Welfare:*** It includes the services, amenities offered to employees within or outside the establishment for their physical, psychological and social well-being. Housing, transportation, educations and recreational facilities are all included in the employee welfare package.
3. ***Social Security Measures:*** It includes employees in addition to fringe benefits. These measures include workman's compensation to those workers who are involved in accidents, maternity benefits, sickness and medical benefits, disablement benefits dependent benefits, provident funds, pensions, gratuity, etc.

**(f) Separation:** Some employees leave the organization due to various reasons like resignation, retirement, death, discharge and lay-off.

Personnel management cannot afford to lay greater emphasis on one and neglect the other two major functions. In this connection the observations of John F. Mee merits mention. "It is essential to grasp the significance of this dual division of personnel functions of the mistake of becoming preoccupied with the demand of detail problems to the neglect of managerial duties is to be avoided".

It is easy as more executives have learned to their regret, to become so busy with such tasks as hiring, transferring, counselling and training that they fail to foresee the shifting conditions which call for changes in operative functions; they fail to recognise the work of subordinates satisfactorily and they fail to keep a good check-up on the work conditions.

## SCOPE OF PERSONNEL MANAGEMENT

The scope of personnel management is very wide and it is as follows:

1. Organizational Planning and Development
2. Staffing and Employment
3. Training and Development
4. Compensation, Wage and Salary Administration
5. Employee Services and Benefits
6. Employee Records
7. Labour Relations, and
8. Personnel Research and Personnel Audit

**1. Organizational Planning and Development:** Organisational planning relates with the division of all the works to be performed at various position, department and division in such a way that they become manageable and efficient units. The integration and the coordination among the various departments and employees are the prerequisitions. Differentiation and integration are necessary for the achievement of organisational predetermined objectives.

(i) The determination of an organisations' needs in terms of long-term and short-term objectives, development of technology (industrial psychology and mechanical engineering) of production, deciding about the nature of product, keeping in mind the external environment.

(ii) Designing of an organisational structure by providing the authority and responsibility among the employees so that organisational goals can be effectively and efficiently achieved, and

(iii) Developing interpersonal relationship through a division of task and the formation of a homogeneous, cohesive and interactive informal group.

**2. Staffing and Employment:** The staffing process is a series of events which leads to a continuous filling of positions at all levels in the organisation. This process includes manpower planning, recruitment, selection, placement, induction and orientation, promotion, upgradation, transfer, demotion and separations (resignation, retirement, discharge, disability, death, etc.).

(i) Manpower planning is a forward looking function. Manpower planning is a process of analysing the present and future vacancies that occur, may be due to sick leave, leave of absence, discharge, retirement, promotion, transfer, and an analysis of present and future expansion or contraction in the various departments. Plans are then formulated for internal shifts or contraction in manpower for advertising openings, or for recruiting and selecting new personnel, or for the training and development of present employees.

(ii) Recruitment is concerned with the process of attracting qualified and competent personnel for different jobs. This consist the identification of existing sources of the labour màrket, the development of new sources and the need for attracting a large number of potential applicants for a good selection.

(iii) Selection process is concerned with the evaluation of potential employees in terms of job specification. This process includes the reception of application, development of application bank, psychological test, comprehensive interview, background investigation, physical examination, final employment decision, placement and induction.

(iv) Placement is concerned with providing the position according to job description; his/her job specification and personality needs.

(v) By induction/orientation it means the introduction of an employee to the organisation and the job by giving him all the possible information about the organisation's history, philosophy, objectives, policies, and procedures, methods of production, future development opportunities, goodwill of the company in the market, authority and responsibility as well as superior and subordinates of that particular employee.

(vi) Transfer process is concerned with the shifting of an employee from one position to another in which his ability can be best utilised. This is done by developing transfer policy, counselling employees and line management on transfers and evaluating transfer policies and procedures.

(vii) Promotion is concerned with rewarding capable employees by providing them higher position, responsibility and high pay scale. They are providing promotion either on merit basis or on performance basis. For this, a fair, just and equitable promotion policy and procedure have to be developed. Line managers and employees have to be advised on these policies; and

(viii) Separation process is concerned with the resignation; lay-off, disability, discharge or retirement. Exit interviews of employees are arranged and advice is given to the line management on the causes of reduction in labour turnover.

**3. Training and Development:** It is a very difficult process and it is concerned with increasing knowledge, capabilities, skills, talent, thinking power, decision making ability, logical ability of individuals and groups so that they may contribute effectively and efficiently to the achievement of an organisational goals.

This process covers the following aspects:

(i) Training is a learning experience, in that it seeks a relatively permanent change in an individual that will improve his or her ability to perform on the job.

(ii) Management development activities attempt to instil sound reasoning process to enhance one's ability to understand and interpret knowledge rather than imparting a body of serial facts or teaching a specific set of motor skills. So, development focuses more on the employee's personal growth.

(iii) The determination of training needs at all levels, employee counselling and communication and programmes for managerial, professional and employee development, and

(iv) Self-initiated developmental activities (formal education), reading and participation in the activities (seminar and conference), school/college/professional institutions.

This area covers the training needs of the company that are identified at each level, suitable training programmes are developed, the services of trainers are enlisted, workers and executives are identified for training, motivation and guidance are provided for joining training programmes, the line manager is advised in conducting training programmes. The effectiveness of training programmes has to be evaluated by follow-up.

**4. Compensation, Wage and Salary Administration:** It is concerned with the remuneration to the employees for services rendered and motivating them to attain the performance.

The components of these processes are as follows:

(i) Job evaluation through which the relative worth of a job is determined. This is done by selecting perfect job evaluation technique, analysing and dividing jobs into various categories and then determines their relative value in various categories.

(ii) Wage and salary programme consists of developing and conveying a suitable wage and salary programme. There are several factors influencing wage and salary administration such as organisation's ability to pay, supply and demand of labour, the cost of living, prevailing market rate, the living wage, productivity, trade union's bargaining power, job requirement, managerial attitudes, skill levels available in the market and psychological and social factors. On the basis of these factors, wage and salary rates have to be determined and implemented and their effectiveness evaluated.

(iii) The incentive plan includes non-monetary incentives which have to be developed, administered and reviewed time-to-time for motivating the employee. Non-monetary incentives include housing facility, canteens, school and recreational facility, transportation facility, etc.

(iv) The performance appraisal is related with evaluating employee performance at work in terms of predetermined standards in order to develop a sound and effective system of rewards, punishment and identifying employees' eligibility for promotions. For this purpose, performance appraisal plans, programmes and techniques are identified, their implementation evaluated and reports are submitted to the concerned authorities.

(v) Motivation is concerned with motivating employees by creating such a condition that they may get social and psychological satisfaction. For that, a programme for non-monetary incentives (like higher responsibility, recognition, symbol of status) is formulated, communication system is developed to solve the problems and for building of a healthy interpersonal relationship, morale and attitude surveys are undertaken and the health of human organisation diagnosed. The line management has to be advised on the implementation of the plan and the way of improving the morale of employees.

**5. Employee Services and Benefits:** These aspects are concerned with the process of sustaining and maintaining the workforce in an organisation. They include the following areas:

(i) Safety provision inside the factory. For this purpose, policies, techniques, procedures for the health and safety of the employees are developed, the line management is advised on implementation of safety programmes, and training has to be given to workers in safety practices, the causes of accidents have to be investigated and the effectiveness of the safety programmes evaluated periodically.

(ii) Employee counselling and communicating are the process through which employees are given counsel in solving their work-related problems, mental problems and personal problems. The line management has to be advised on the problems which may occur frequently.

(iii) The medical services include the provision of preventive medical, safety and health improvement facilities for employees. A periodical medical check-up of employees, training in hygienic and preventive measures are undertaken. Safety measures are also provided like glove, goggles, helmet, etc.

(iv) The welfare facilities include recreational services like entertainment activities, sports and games, film show, etc. Welfare facilities also covers housing, educational facility, canteen, transport. Suitable policies and programmes are framed and efforts are made to administer these services satisfactorily. The effectiveness of such programmes has to be assessed.

(v) Fringe benefits and other additional items are made available to employees are as follows:

1. Old-age benefit like pension, gratuities, provident fund, unemployment and women's maternity compensation,

2. Sickness benefit, accident benefit, insurance, medical facility, hospitalisation facility, voluntary retirement benefits,

3. Paid rest periods, travel time, etc.,

4. Paid vacation or bonus in lieu of vacation, paid sick and maternity leave, payment for holidays, and
5. Profit-sharing benefits, employees' educational and training expenditure and special wage payments ordered by the labour courts.

These benefits are given to employees for maintaining employees, to provide them social security and to reduce absenteeism and labour turnover. Policies and programmes for implementing these have to be properly assessed.

**6. Employee Records:** Complete and up to date information is maintained about employees so that these records may be utilised at the time of transfer, promotion, demotion, giving merit pay or sanctioning leave at the time of termination of service/retirement.

Such records covers information regarding education and qualification, performance of psychological test and interviews, job performance, leave, present, absent, number of hours worked, promotions, rewards and punishments.

**7. Labour Relations:** Labour relations means the maintenance of healthy and peaceful labour-management relations in order to run smooth and uninterrupted flow of work/production.

Labour relations area covers the following aspects:

(i) Grievance handling policy and procedures are developed, after finding out the nature and causes of grievances/problems and locating the area of dissatisfaction. Collective bargaining has to be developed so that all the grievances may be settled through mutual understanding and discussion. Such bargaining and administering agreement relating to wages, working conditions and living conditions, leave, non-monetary facilities and employee-employer relationship.

(ii) Rules and regulations are framed for the maintenance of discipline in the organisation and a proper system of reward and punishment can be developed.

(iii) Efforts are made to acquire knowledge of the labour laws of the country and acquaint the line management with the provisions which are directly concerned with organisation.

**8. Personnel Research and Personnel Audit:** These aspects are concerned with the following areas:

(i) A systematic inquiry into any aspect like how to enhance an organisation's personnel programmes consisting of recruitment, selection, placement, training and development, wages and salary, etc.

(ii) Data relating to quality, productivity, labour turnover, grievances, absenteeism, strike, lockout, wages, accidents, etc., which are observed and supplied to the top managements.

(iii) Policy, procedures, findings and feedback submitted to the top executives so that it may alter or improve existing personnel policies and procedures.

(iv) Morale, attitude and interest surveys.

In large organisations, some of these functions are performed by persons other than personnel department.

# HUMAN RESOURCE MANAGEMENT

## Meaning and Concept

Human resource management is the process of bringing people and organization together so that the goals of each are met. It tries to secure the best from people by winning their whole-hearted cooperation. HRM is concerned with the development and integration of strategies which are integrated with corporate strategies and ensure that the culture, values, and structure of the organizations and the quality, motivation and commitment of its members contribute to the achievement of its goals.

Over the past few years, with the rapidly changes in the business environment, human resource have taken the centre stage. Consider the following example

1. ***Adi Godrej:*** It is really important for me to spend more time with my people. We have had a number of HRD consultants, but HRD initiatives are time-consuming and one has to be patient for cultural and mindset changes.
2. ***Philips:*** According to Rama Chandra, MD, Philips India, "Human resource department is the centre of competency".
3. ***HLL:*** "At Hindustan Lever, the accent is on hiring people who are even better than the ones at HLL. HLL is now is a people and strategy company."

HRM has come to be recognized as an inherent part of management. Its objective is the maintenance of better human relations in the organization by the development, application and evaluation of policies, procedures and programmes relating to HR to optimize their contribution towards the realization of organizational objectives.

HRM is the function within an organization that focuses on recruitment of, management of and providing direction for the people who work in the organization. HRM deals with issues related to people such as compensation, hiring, performance management, organizational development, safety, wellness, benefits, employee motivation, communication, administration and training. HRM is emerged with getting better results with collaboration of people at work and relationship within an enterprise.

## Definitions of HRM

1. According to J.M. Ivancevich and W.G. Gulick, "Human resource management is the function performed in the organization that facilitates the most effective use of people (employees) to achieve organizational and individual goals".
2. L.L. Byars and L.W. Rue state that, "Human resource management encompasses those activities designed to provide for, and coordinate the human resources of an organization".
3. According to Dale Yorder, "The management of human resources is viewed as the system in which participants seeks to attain both individual and group goals".
4. According to Edwin Flippo, "HRM is the planning, organising, directing, and controlling of the procurement, development, compensation, integration, maintenance, and separation of human resources to the end that individual, organizational and societal objectives are accomplished".
5. In the words of Michael J. Jucious, "HRM may be defined as that field of management which has to do with planning, organising and controlling the functions of procuring,

developing, maintaining and utilising a labour force, such that: (a) Objectives for which the company is established are attained economically and effectively, (b) Objectives of all levels of personnel are served to the highest possible degree, (c) Objectives of society are dully considered and served".

6. According to George Milkovich and Johri W. Boudreau, "HRM is a series of integrated decisions that form the employment relationship, their quality contributes to the ability to the organizations and the employees to achieve their objective".
7. According to David A. Decenzo and Stephen P. Robins, "HRM is concerned with the people dimension in management. Since every organisation is made up of people, acquiring their services, developing their skills, motivating them to higher levels of performance and ensuring that they continue to maintain their commitment to the organization are essential to achieving organizational objectives. This is true regardless of the type of organization, government business, education, health recreation or social action."
8. "HR may be defined as the total knowledge, skills, operative abilities, talents, and attitudes of an organisation's workforce as well as the values, attitudes, approaches and beliefs of the individuals involved in the affairs of the organizations."

## SCOPE OF HRM

The scope of HRM is indeed vast. Any HR department and personnel executives typically perform a variety of roles in accordance with the needs of a situation. The HR manager plays multiple roles such as those of a researcher, a counsellor, bargainers, a mediator, a peace-maker, a problem-solver, and so on. All major activities in the working life of an employee — from the time of his entry into an organization until he leaves the organizations — come under the purview of personnel management. The functional areas of HRM as outlined by Northcott are (a) Employment, (b) Selection and training, (c) Employee services, (d) Wages, (e) Industrial relations, (f) Health and safety, and (g) Education.

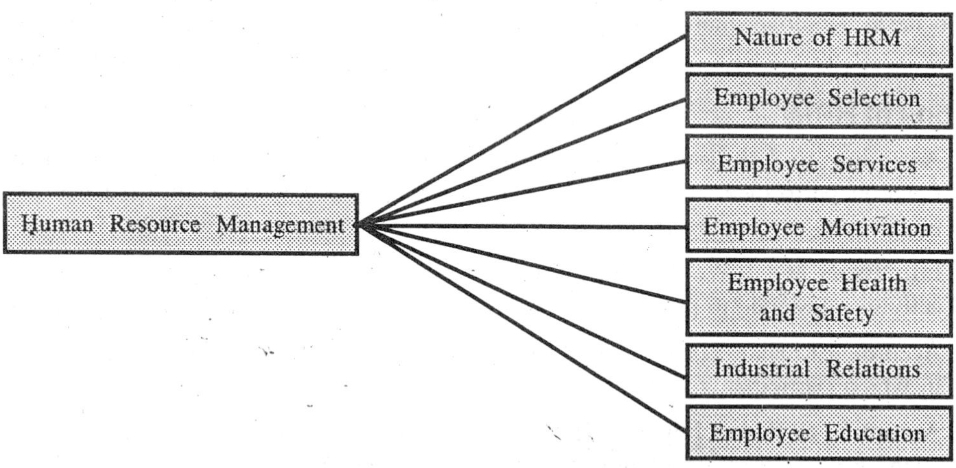


## SCOPE OF HUMAN RESOURCE MANAGEMENT

It has, therefore, been rightly observed by Peter Drucker that "Management is a multipurpose ( h has three jobs, two of which are directly related to personnel: Managing a business, m nanagers, and managing workers and the work".

They not only help in determining the rules of the organization but also play a powerful role in interpreting and applying the rules of the system itself. They are expected to enjoy the confidence of both management and employees, which is crucial for effective and efficient operations of the business organization. The focus of HRM is on people at work. It is indeed a wide area and covers a broad spectrum of activities. A manager, whether he is in charge of production or a marketing function deals with human beings and gets his job done through and with people.

At last, HRM comprises of three aspects:

1. **Personnel Aspects:** This is concerned with manpower planning, recruitment, selection, placement, transfer, promotion, training and development, lay-off and retrenchment, remuneration, incentives, productivity, etc.
2. **Welfare Aspects:** It deals with working conditions and amenities such as canteen, crèches, rest and lunchrooms, housing, transport, medical assistance, education, health and safety, recreational facilities, etc.
3. **Industrial Relations Aspects:** This covers union-management relations; join consultation, collective bargaining, grievance and disciplinary procedures, settlement of disputes, etc.

## EMERGING ISSUES IN HUMAN RESOURCE MANAGEMENT

Effective management of human resources depends on refining HRM practices to changing conditions. Hence, the need to look at other important issues that can motivate people to give their best in a dynamic and ever-changing environment.

- **Personnel Records:** Personnel records such as papers, files, cards, cassettes and films are maintained to have tangible records of what is actually happening in an organization and to formulate appropriate HR policies and programmes (based on historical records, actual experience and future trends) from time-to-time. **Human Resource Audit:** Human resource audit refers to an examination and evaluation of policies, procedures and practices to determine the effectiveness of HRM. Personnel audit: (a) measures the effectiveness of personnel programmes and practices, and (b) determines what should or should not be done in future. **Human Resource Research:** It is the process of evaluating the effectiveness of human resource policies and practices and developing more appropriate ones.
- **Human Resource Accounting (HRA):** It is a measurement of the costs and value of human resources to the organization. Human resource management is said to be effective if its value and contribution in any organization is more than its cost.
- **Human Resource Information System:** HRIS is an integrated system designed to improve the efficiency with which HR data is compiled. It makes HR records more useful to the measurement by serving as a source of information.
- **Stress and Counselling:** Stress is the psychological and physical reaction to certain life, events or situations. At an organizational level, stress results in burn out, substance abuse in the form of alcohol or drug use/dependence reduced job satisfaction, increased absenteeism and increased turnover. Companies therefore, are closely looking at what should be done to promote the physical and mental well-being of employees through proper counselling and employee development programmes.

- **International Human Resource Management:** International business is important to almost every business today and so firms must increasingly be managed with a clear global focus. This of course, poses many challenges before management including co-coordinating production, sales and financial operations on a worldwide basis. International HRM places greater emphasis on number of responsibilities and functions such as relocations, orientation and training services to help employees adapt to a new and different environment outside their own country.

## DIFFERENCE BETWEEN PERSONNEL MANAGEMENT AND HUMAN RESOURCE MANAGEMENT

1. Personnel management is more administrative in nature, dealing with payroll, complying with employment law and handling related tasks. While HR on the other hand, is responsible for managing a workforce as one of the primary resource that contributes to the success of an organization.
2. Human resource is described as much broader in scope than personnel management. HR is said to incorporate and develop personnel management task while seeking to create and develop teams of workers for the benefit of the organization. A primary goal of HR is to enable employees to work to maximum levels of efficiency. Personnel management can include administrative task that are both traditional and routine. It can be described as reactive, providing a response to demand and concerns as they are presented, while by contrast, HRM involves ongoing strategies to manage and develop and organisation's work force. It is proactive as it involves the continuous development of functions and policies for the purpose of improving a company's work force.
3. Personnel management deals with careful description of written contracts HRM aims to go beyond contract.
4. Personnel management is often considered as an independent function of an organization. HRM on the other hand, tends to be an integral part of overall capacity function.
5. Personnel management are rules dominated, while HRM are culture and value dominated.
6. Speed of decisions is very slow in personnel management, while it is fast in case of HRM.
7. Personnel management requires negotiation skills, while HRM requires facilitation skills.
8. In personnel management, training and development are controlled and limited, while in HRM, it is always, improving-learning.
9. Personnel management is typically the sole responsibility of an organisation's personnel department while in HR, all of an organisation's managers are often involved in some manner and a chief goal may be to have managers of various departments and develop the skills necessary to handle personnel related tasks.
10. Personnel management requires direct communications, while HRM requires indirect communications.
11. In personnel management, labour is treated as a tool which is expendable and replicable while, HRM people are treated as assets to be used for the benefit of organization. Its employees and the society at large.

12. Personnel management focus on division of labour, while HRM focus on team work.
13. As far as conflict handling is concerned, personnel management reach temporary solutions, while HRM manage climate, culture, and everlasting solutions.
14. Personnel management is collective bargaining contracts, while HRM is individual contracts.
15. Personnel management precedes HRM, while HRM is latest in the evolution of the subject.
16. In personnel management, fixed grades of pay are to be given, while in HRM, performance related pay are to be given.
17. Job categories and grades are many in personnel management, while it is few in HR.
18. Personnel management's role is transactional, and HRM role is transformational leadership.
19. As far as motivators are concerned, personnel management typically seeks to motivate employees with things such as compensation, bonuses, rewards and the simplification of work responsibilities. From the personnel management's point of view, employee satisfaction provides the motivation necessary to improve job performance. HRM holds that improved performance leads to employee satisfaction with HR work groups, effective strategies for meeting challenges and job creativity are seen as primary motivators.
20. Personnel management deals with labour management, while HRM deals with customers.
21. Personnel management guide to procedures, while HRM guide to business need.
22. In case of personnel management, managerial task and labour tasks are monitoring while in case of HRM, managerial task and labour tasks are nurturing.
23. In case of personnel management, nature of relations is pluralist, and in case of HRM, it is neo-unitarist.
24. Perception of conflict is institutionalising in personnel management, while it is pathological.

## MEANING AND DEFINITION OF HUMAN RESOURCE DEVELOPMENT

Organisations depend on people for their survival and growth. HRD is concerned with providing learning and development of opportunities, making training interventions and planning-conducting training programme. It is essentially a strategic process, which is concerned with meeting both business and individual needs.

Human resource development is a positive concept in human resource management. It is based on the belief that an investment in human beings is necessary and will invariably bring in substantial benefits to the organization in the long run. It aims at the overall development of human resource in order to contribute to the well being of the employees, organization and the society at large. HRD is rooted in the belief that human being has potential to do better. It therefore, places a premium on the dignity and tremendous latent energy of people. It is a set of systematic and planned activities designed for an organization to provide its members with the necessary skills to meet current and future job demands.

| | |
|---|---|
| HRD a humanistic Concept | People can do better, they can do wonders, involve them, trust them and empower them; treat them as resources as assets. |
| | Focus on strengths of people and help them overcome their weaknesses. |
| | Integrate the needs and aspirations of individuals into the strategic goals and the mission of an organisation – for better results. |
| | Encourage individual initiative and response by providing a fostering culture (openness, trust, collaboration, mutuality, etc.) |

HRD is the framework for helping employees to develop their personal and organizational skills, knowledge and abilities. HRD includes such opportunities as employee training, career development, performance management and development coaching, counselling, monitoring, succession planning, key employee identification, feedback, assistance, rewards, job rotation, and organizational development. According to Prof. T. V. Rao, "HRD is the process of helping people to acquire competencies. In an organizational context, HRD is a process by which the employees of an organization are helped in a continuous and planned way to:

- Acquire or sharpen capabilities required to perform various functions associated with their present or expected future roles;
- Develop their general capabilities as individuals and discover and exploit their own inner potential for their own and/or organisational development purposes;
- Develop an organisational culture in which superior-subordinate relationships, teamwork and collaboration among subunits are strong and contribute to the professional well-being, motivation and pride of employees."

## FUNCTIONS OF HUMAN RESOURCE DEVELOPMENT

1. HRD function has the expertise to diagnose problems in order to determine appropriateness of potential solution. Further analysis of the data divides responses under this critical event into three categories:

   (i) Expertise to diagnose organizational problems.

   (ii) Expertise to diagnose individual problems.

   (iii) Expertise to identify solution in terms of processes, product and resources and ultimately the expertise to recommend solution.

2. The HRD manager maintains an active network with other key managers in the organization.

3. There is a corporate training and development mission statement or corporate HRD policy and this competency based training leads to be behavioural change or organizational results.

4. The HRD manager routinely participates in corporate strategy sessions with other key staff persons and senior manager.

5. If the HRD manager is a part of the strategic thinking and planning process of the organization, then he/she will be a part of the change design process and will be able to identify and plan for the required training at the same time.

6. Allocation of HRD resources are based, at least in part, on the priorities of the organization HRD function must also engage in future thinking and planning and certainly a part of its resources must be targeted in some way to meeting the HRD needs of the organization for the next five to ten years as well as within the current fiscal year.

7. The HRD functions conducts needs assessments to determine organizational requirements like organizational planning, task analysis or organizational diagnosis to determine when training or other intervention may be required to improve productivity, the quality of work life or organizational functioning.

8. The roles, responsibilities and priorities of the HRD functions are clearly defined.

9. The HRD management and staff routinely meet to discuss problems and progress with current programmes. HRD manager is trying to anticipate and get ready with appropriate responses.

10. Their emphasis is on higher order needs such as how to design jobs with stretch, pull and challenge, how to improve creativity and problem-solving skills, how to empower people in all aspects, etc.

11. They try to develop the organization as a whole and its culture through better use of HR and improve satisfaction and morale.

## DIFFERENCE BETWEEN HUMAN RESOURCE MANAGEMENT AND HUMAN RESOURCE DEVELOPMENT

1. The HRM function is a routine, maintenance-oriented administrative function, while HRD is a continuous development function. The major attention of HRD is on improving human processes.

2. HRM is regarded essentially as a reactive function responding to the demands of the organization as and when they arise, while HRD is regarded as a proactive function. The function of HRD is not merely to cope with the needs of the organization but to anticipate them and act on them in advance in a continuous and planned way.

3. HRM is seen as an independent function with independent subfunctions, while HRD is viewed as a subsystem of a larger system. This means that the design of HRD cannot be considered in isolation.

4. HRM is supposed to be the exclusive responsibility of the personnel department, while HRD aims at developing the capabilities of all line managers to carry-out various personnel functions on their own.

5. The HRM function considers salary, economic rewards, job simplification and job specialisation as important motivators, while HRD emphasises the importance of higher needs in motivating individuals. It considers informal organisations, autonomous workgroups, job enrichment, job challenges and creativity as the main motivating forces.

6. HRM takes a very narrow view of its scope and aims only at developing and administering people, while HRD take a wider view of its scope and aims at developing the total organization.

7. HRM considers improved satisfaction and morale as the cause of improved performance, while HRD considers improved performance as the cause and improved satisfaction and morale as its results.

## SUMMARY


- Personnel management is concerned with the procurement and maintenance of a competent workforce and inspiring employees individually and in groups to give their most while realising organisational goals.
- Personnel management is concerned with two sets of functions, namely managerial and operative functions.
- Personnel policies are guides to actions and serve as road map for managers on a number of issues like manpower planning, recruitment, selection, training and development, and maintenance of human resources.
- Today the personnel manager performs a very crucial role. It is important for the HR manager to be a strategic business contributor in organizations.
- Personnel management as a profession has reached respectable heights, over the years, thanks to growing body of literature, mushrooming growth of management institutes and lucrative career prospects which are available to competent and committed individuals.
- HRM is responsible for the people dimension of the organization. It is a pervasive force, action-oriented, individually-oriented, development-oriented, future focused and integrative in nature and is a comprehensive function.
- HRM mainly covers three broad areas: Personnel aspect, welfare aspect and industrial relation aspect.
- HRM aims at achieving organizational goal meet the expectations of employees, develop the knowledge, skills, abilities, competence, talent of employees, improve the quality of working life and manage human resources in an ethical and socially responsible manner.
- HRD aims at helping people to acquire competencies required to perform all their functions effectively and make the organization do well. HRD improves the capabilities of people, promotes team spirit among employees and helps an organization achieve its goals efficiently.
- HRD is a proactive function as it prepares people to face future challenges with confidence. Many HRD mechanisms (performance appraisal, potential appraisal, career planning, training, organizational development, rewards, welfare amenities, etc.), are available to develop the competencies of people and improve the overall organizational climate. These mechanisms are designed to work together as an integrated system and deliver results.


## CASELET 1: CONCORD GENERAL

### 'The Times They are A-Changin'

John Michael was certainly convinced that he needed to hire a specialist to handle the myriad activities surrounding HRM. It was difficult to make the change, but he realized that the personnel job was too complicated for him to do alone.

- "It was a lot easier thirty years ago", he said, "One only needed to find a woman dedicated to helping people with their suffering, train her, and call her a nurse. Now there are so many conditions placed on this hospital that the work is insurmountable. I wish we could return to the way it was thirty years ago."

- "But John, remarked Jim Wilson, the new personnel specialist, "most of the changes have benefited the nurses and..."
- "Yes", said John, "but why should something that benefits the nurses is so much of a constraint on us? We always treated our nurses fairly, and they respected us for that."
- "They may be true, John, but in the short period of time since I've arrived, I've heard that some nurses are unhappy about their jobs. They are complaining that their pay is low and that there is neither upward mobility nor any incentive to motivate them."
- "But they're nurses, working here because they want to help those less fortunate. Their pay is adequate, and with unemployment running so high, their incentive should be that they are in a service career."
- "I see", said Jim. But what was Jim really thinking? "I've got my work cut out for me."

However, Jim felt confident. Even though he had had almost twelve years of experience in personnel matters since graduating from college, he had never worked for a hospital. The new constraints placed on him seemed unusual, but he was well aware of the politics involved in an organization. After serving as personnel assistant to Thomas Broady, personnel director at AT&T, he felt that not much more of a reality shock could come his way.

## ........ QUESTIONS FOR DISCUSSION

1. What impact has government legislation had on Concord General in the past thirty years of management practice?
2. What are the possible implications to Jim Wilson and the organization if he doesn't solve some of the HRM problems?
3. What advice and/or strategies would you give to help him solve these problems?

## Assignment and Questions for Discussions

1. "Personnel administration is not just a line responsibility, but a staff function." Discuss.
2. In your opinion, what is the most important role of personnel managers?
3. "The job of a personnel manager is one that is given to an individual who has trouble performing in the main stream of the organization's operations." Do you agree or disagree? Discuss.
4. Assuming that we want to alter personnel programmes in the direction of emphasising the role of the individual, what suggestions are made in the areas of job design, pay, fringe benefits, and freedom of speech?
5. Why is it important for a company to make its human resources into a competitive advantage? How can HR professionals contribute to doing so?
6. Suppose you manage a restaurant in a holiday resort near Dehradun. During the summer, it is profitable to keep the business open but in winters you need only one half of the cooks, servers, supervisors and cleaners. What actions would you take in October for the beginning of the peak tourist season?
7. Provide two examples of companies you are familiar with, which are not using their HRM programmers to maintain or create a competitive advantage. What specific suggestions would you offer to them?
8. What skills and competencies do HR professionals need to add more value to the HR function? How might these competencies and skills change in the future? How can HR professionals ensure that they are creating value for their organisations?

9. Why is a competitive advantage based on heavy investment in human resources more sustainable than investment in other types of assets?
10. Are people always organisation's most valuable assets? Why or why not?
11. Arrange yourself in small groups of four or five students and compare and contrast the difference among the organizations you investigated. Can you isolate any factors that appeared to influence how an organization perceives the value of its employees?
12. In small groups, find out the trends relating to technology and diversity that have significant bearing on the way businesses are managed in the 21st century. What challenges do these trends present? What initiatives have been taken by modern businesses to meet these challenges?
13. Retaining bright people especially at the middle and the top level — is one of the important concern of today's learner organization. How can human resource development efforts contribute to retention?
14. Today's organizations are flatter and offer fewer opportunities for advancement. How do you propose to develop the capabilities of employees in this type of organizational environment?
15. How can a teacher produce dysfunctional tension in a bright student (choose the most appropriate one)
    (i) Give difficult tests.
    (ii) Deliver boring lectures.
    (iii) Grade term papers on a curve.
    (iv) Demand oral presentation of a topic.
    (v) Assign grades in a random fashion for all written works.
16. Why is it correct to say that all managers are involved in the HRM functions?

## Subjective Questions

1. Contrast personnel management and human resource management.
2. Identify and distinguish among the four managerial functions and the six operative functions of personnel management.
3. What are the important stages in the growth of personnel management?
4. Describe the welfare and administrative role of personnel manager in achieving organizational goals.
5. The personnel manager is being paid by management. Is he or she therefore a representative of management or personnel? Discuss in detail.
6. How does the personnel function change as a firm grows in size? Briefly describe each stage of its development.
7. What do you mean by the term human resource management? And why the development, motivation and maintenance phases are important in HRM?
8. Define HRD and explain various functions of HRD.
9. Difference between HRM and HRD.

## Fill in the Blanks

1. __________ deals with the task of blending efforts in order to ensure a successful attainment of an objective
   (a) Coordination (b) Planning (c) Maintenance (d) Procurement
2. __________is a process of analysing present and future vacancies.
   (a) Organisational planning (b) Manpower planning
   (c) Staffing (d) Selection
3. __________ is concerned with evaluating employee performance at work in terms of predetermined standards.
   (a) Performance appraisal (b) Training
   (c) Job evaluation (d) Personnel audit

4. __________ deals not only with the dissemination of orders but also acceptance and execution of these orders by the employees.
   (a) Planning (b) Organising (c) Directing (d) Controlling.
5. __________ through which the relative worth of a job is determined.
   (a) Job analysis (b) Job evaluation (c) Job description (d) Job specification.
6. _________ was the first person who adopted paternalistic attitude towards his employees.
   (a) Robert Owen (b) F.W.Taylor (c) Henry Fayol (d) Adam Smith.
7. _________ was the person who propounded the need hierarchy theory.
   (a) Herzberg (b) Abrahim Maslow (c) McGregor (d) Robins.
8. The basic role of the personnel manager is the management of _________.
   (a) Manpower resources (b) Production
   (c) Finance (d) Organizational resources
9. Hugo Munsterberg is regarded as the father of ____________.
   (a) Scientific management (b) Industrial revolution
   (c) Industrial psychology (d) Behavioural science.
10. Development of the organizational structure according to predetermined goals is known as ________.
   (a) Planning (b) Organising (c) Directing (d) Controlling

*Ans:* **1.** Coordination (a), **2.** Manpower planning (b), **3.** Performance appraisal (a), **4.** Directing (c), **5.** Job evaluation (b), **6.** Robert Owen (a), **7.** Abraham Maslow (b), **8.** Manpower resources (a), **9.** Industrial psychology (c), **10.** Organising (b)

## Multiple Choice Questions

1. Manpower planning, recruitment, selection, placement are the part of –
   (a) Organisational planning and development (b) Staffing and employment
   (c) Wage and salary administration (d) Training and development
2. Planning consist of –
   (a) Directing personnel (b) Policies, procedures, programmes
   (c) Doing actual performance (d) Personal development
3. Welfare role concerned with –
   (a) Moral obligation to its employees
   (b) Handling disciplinary actions
   (c) Research in personnel and organizational problems
   (d) Advising manager on effective use of human resources
4. As a spokesman, personnel manager plays the role of a –
   (a) Peace-maker (b) Counsellor (c) Mediator (d) Representative
5. Personnel role concerned with –
   (a) Measurement and assessment of individual and group behaviour
   (b) Research in personnel and organizational problems
   (c) Handling disciplinary actions and collective bargaining
   (d) Managing services and maintenance of records

*Ans:* **1.** Staffing and employment (b), **2.** Policies, procedures, programmes (b), **3.** Research in personnel and organizational problems (c), **4.** Representative (b), **5.** Measurement and assessment of individual and group behaviour (a)

## Choose the Correct One

(a) (a) As a mediator, he plays the role of a peace-maker and settles the disputes.
   (b) As a mediator, he plays the role of a spokesman and a representative of the company.

(c) As a mediator, he plays the role of a change agent within the organization.

(d) As a mediator, he plays the role of a counsellor and discusses physical and career problems.

(b) (a) Era of social responsibility consist development of true science of each job.

(b) The scientific management era developed the principle of friendly cooperation between man and management.

(c) Hawthorne experiment was linked with the behavioural era.

(d) Theory X and theory Y were formulated by Herzberg.

(c) (a) Era of social responsibility strongly emphasis on the mutual benefits of productivity.

(b) Robert Owen's ideas led to separate discipline called "Human engineering".

(c) F.W. Taylor developed the principle as friendly cooperation between the management and the man.

(d) Theory of motivation was formulated by Robins.

*Ans:* **1.** (a), **2.** (b), **3.** (c)

## Match the Following

1. (i) Personnel aspect — (a) Group dynamics
   (ii) Welfare role — (b) Human engineering
   (iii) Industrial relation aspect — (c) Recruitment and placement
   (iv) Administrative role — (d) Joint consultation

2. (i) Labour relation — (a) Time study
   (ii) Scientific measurement — (b) Grievance handling
   (iii) Human engineering — (c) Helping people
   (iv) HRD — (d) People at work

*Ans:* **1.** (1. c), (2. a), (3. d), (4. b), **2.** (1. b), (2. a), (3. d), (4. c)

## True or False

1. The ideal personnel manager is a counsellor and a good advisor.
2. The industrial revolution brought about mass production of goods.
3. Directing means to decide in advance to achieve a particular job.
4. Human resource management is not an end in itself.
5. The term "workforce" means people working at lower levels only.
6. Getting and keeping good people is critical to the success of every organization.
7. Human capital can be managed the way organisations manage jobs, products and technologies.
8. Downsizing is the planned elimination of jobs.
9. People have never been central to organizations.
10. A well designed strategy can fail if sufficient attention is not paid to the HR dimension.
11. HRD is a multidisciplinary concept.

*Ans:* **1.** True, **2.** True, **3.** False, **4.** True, **5.** False, **6.** True, **7.** False, **8.** True, **9.** False, **10.** True, **11.** True

☺☺☺

CHAPTER 2

# Recruitment and Selection

## LEARNING OBJECTIVES

- *Recruitment*
- *Sources of Recruitment.*
- *Selection.*
- *Sequence of a Typical Selection Process.*
- *Weighted Application Blank.*
- *Various Ways of Conducting an Employment Interview.*
- *Induction Procedure and Techniques of Induction Programme.*
- *Selection Diagram.*

## RECRUITMENT

The human resources are the most important assets of an organization. Successful human resource planning should identify our human resource needs. Once we know these needs, we will want to do something about meeting them. The next step in the acquisition function therefore is recruitment. This activity facilitates us to acquire the number and types of people necessary to ensure the continued operation of the organization. Their objective is to increase the selection ratio, that is, the number of applications per job opening. It can be seen both, from the short-term and the long-term application. The short range plans involves those activities which are carried on to meet current demands for personnel, such as that which continually exists in every organization when positions are vacated and cannot be fill from internal manpower sources. The long-term planning includes those activities designed to assure a continuous supply of qualified professionals and service personnel. The success or failure of an organization is largely depending on the calibre of the people working therein. Without positive and creative contributions from people, organizations cannot progress. In order to achieve the goal or activities of organizations, we need to recruit people with requisite skills, qualifications and experience. While doing so, we have to keep the present as well as future requirements of the organizations in mind. Recruitment is a "linking function" — which it tries to bring together jobs seekers and employer with a view to encourage the former to apply for a job with the latter.

The ideal recruitment effort will attract a large number of qualified applicants who will take the job if it is offered. The basic purpose of recruitment is to develop a group of potentially qualified people. The organization must communicate the position in such a way that the job seekers respond. To be cost-effective, recruitment process should attract qualified applicants and provide enough information for qualified persons to self-select themselves out, e.g., the recruitment advertisement of a foreign bank may invite applications from chartered accountants who have cleared the CA examination in the first attempt only.

Recruitment is the discovery of the potential candidates for actual or anticipated organizational vacancies. Recruitment is the process concerned with the identification of the sources from where the personnel can be employed and motivating them to offer themselves for employment. It is the process of exhausting all the sources for finding prospective employees.

### Definitions of Recruitment

Werther and Davis have defined this as follows:

"Recruitment is the process of finding and attracting capable applicants for employment. The process begins when new recruits are sought and ends when their applications are submitted. The result is a pool of applicants from which new employees are selected."

Lord has defined recruitment in terms of its competitive nature. He views that:

"Recruitment is a form of competition. Just as corporations compete to develop, manufacture, and market the best product or service, so they must also compete to identify, attract, and hire the most qualified people. Recruitment is a business, it is a big business."

As Yorder and others point out:

"Recruitment is the process to discover the sources of manpower to meet the requirements of the staffing schedule and to employ effective measures for attracting that manpower in adequate numbers. It facilitates effective selection of an efficient working force."

Flippo views recruitment both as "positive" and "negative" activity. He says:

"It is the process of searching for prospective employees and stimulating and encouraging them to apply for jobs in an organization. It is often termed positive in that it stimulates people to apply for jobs to increase the 'hiring ratio'. that is, a number of applicants for the jobs. Selection, on the other hand tends to be negative because it rejects a good number of those who apply, leaving only the best to be hired."

In the words of Mamoria,

"Recruiting is the discovery of potential applicants for actual or anticipated organizational vacancies."

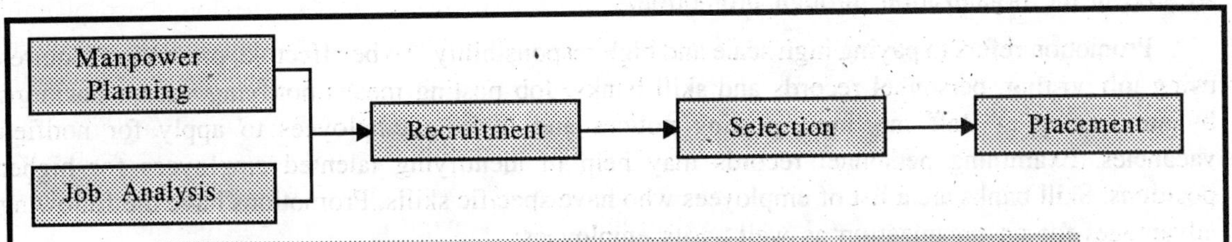


***Fig. 2.1: Linkage of Recruitment to Human Resource Acquisition***

## SOURCES OF RECRUITMENT

Normally, an organization can fill up its vacancies either through promotion of people available in the organization or through the selection of people from outside. Thus, there can be two sources of supply of manpower — external and internal.

### Internal Sources

Internal sources include personnel already on the payroll of an organization. Filling a job opening from within the organization has the following advantages:

- Stimulating for possible transfer or promotion.
- Increasing the general level of morale.
- Having more information about candidates through past performance appraisal.

A comprehensive programme of talent inventory and analysis, central coordination of recruitment and lay-offs in the personnel department and systematic posting of job openings will contribute much to the success of an internal recruitment programme. Retrenched employees, retired employees, dependence of deceased employees may also constitute the internal sources. Whenever any vacancies arise, someone from within the organization is upgraded, transferred, promoted, or even demoted.

The process of filling job openings by selecting from, among the pool of present workforce can be implemented by the following methods:

- Reviewing the personnel records.
- Job posting and job bidding.

Review of the personnel records and skills inventory provides adequate information for the personnel director to find suitable candidates for a particular position. Under job posting and bidding system, the organisation notifies its present employees of openings, using bulletin boards, and company publications, etc. This is more open approach where everyone gets the same right to apply for a job and bid for the same. If the labour shortage is of short-term nature and great amount of additional labour is not necessary, then organisation employs 'inside moonlighting'. It is a technique where organisation pays bonuses of various types to people not on a time payroll. Overtime procedures are, in many organisations, developed for those on time payroll.

Internal sources of recruitment are as follows:

**Promotion:** Filling up of positions through internal promotion has a favourable reaction among employees. They are likely to associate themselves with the organizations as they see their future secured in the organization through promotion.

Promotion refers to paying high scale and high responsibility. To be effective, promotion requires using job posting, personnel records and skill banks. Job posting means notifying vacant positions by announcing at staff meetings, posting notices and inviting employees to apply for notified vacancies. Examining personnel records may help in identifying talented employees for higher positions. Skill banks are a list of employees who have specific skills. Promotions have the following advantages for an organization as well as its employees:

- It builds morale among employees as organizations consider them for higher positions.
- It is cheaper than going for outside sources.
- Internal employees are familiar with the organization.
- Promotion when carefully planned acts as a training device for developing employees for higher level jobs.
- It improves the probability of good selection since the person is already known to the organization.
- It encourages competent individuals who are ambitious.

Here, it should be noted that promotions can be dysfunctional to the organization as the advantage of hiring outsiders who may be better qualified and skilled is denied. Promotion also results in inbreeding and discourage new employee from entering the organization which is not good for the organization.

**Upgradation:** It refers to giving higher responsibility to the internal employees.

**Transfer:** It refers to changing place from one position to another, but no change in pay scale and responsibility. A transfer is a change in a job assignment. A movement of an employee between equivalent positions at periodical intervals is called transfer. Transfers are normally made to place employees in positions where they are likely to be more effective or where they are likely to get greater job satisfaction. Transfer is often important in providing employees with a broad-based view of the organization. It is a lateral movement of employees.

**Demotion:** It refers to low pay scale and lower positions. However, it is a one kind of punishment.

**Former Employees:** Former employees can include those who have worked on part-time basis and now desire to work on a full-time employment, retired employees or those who have left the company for some reason but are now willing to come back. Former employees are a good internal source of recruitment. They have the advantage of knowing the organization and the organization knows the performance of these people. Typically, these are people who were laid off, although they may also have worked seasonally (during summer vacations or tax seasons). Forming online alumni at work could be a simple and cost-effective way to maintain a hiring pool of competitive candidates. Furthermore, a network of former employees can be a source of employee referrals because they are familiar with the company, its culture, and its values.

**Job Posting:** Job posting is a way of hiring people from within. In this method, the organization publicises job openings on bulletin boards, electronic media and similar outlets. For an example, Hindustan Lever introduced its version of open job posting in early 2002 and over 40 positions have since been filled through the process. HLL even allows its employees to undertake career shifts like from technical position to non-technical jobs such as marketing, market research, etc., through the open job posting system.

For example, the AV Birla group allows its employees an opportunity to apply not just for jobs within their own companies, but for jobs in any company in the Birla group, in India and in abroad.

One of the important advantages of this method is that, it offers a chance to highly qualified employees working within the company to look for growth, opportunities within the company without looking for outside.

**Suitability:** Suitable when internal candidate are good and well qualified.

## PROS AND CONS OF INTERNAL SOURCES OF RECRUITMENT

### Pros:

- It improves the morale of employees for they are assured of the fact that they would be preferred over outsiders when vacancies occur and it provides the company with more information about the candidate.
- Considerable savings can be made as individuals with inside knowledge of how a business operates will need a shorter period of training and time for "fitting in".
- The organization is unlikely to be greatly disrupted by someone who is used to working with others in the organizations.
- Internal promotion act as an incentive to all staff to work harder.
- The employer is in a better position to evaluate those presently employed than outside candidates. This is because the company maintains a record of the progress, experience and service of its employees.
- It promotes loyalty among employees, for it gives them a sense of job security and opportunities for advancement.
- They are tried people and can, therefore, be relied upon.
- It is less costly than going outside to recruit.
- It encourage good individuals who are ambitious.
- As the persons in the employment of the company are fully aware of and well acquainted with, its policies and know its operating procedures, they require little training, and the chances are that they would stay longer in the employment of the organization than a new candidate would.

- Current employees may also be more committed to the company.
- The organization can pick the right candidates having the requisites skills.
- The candidates can choose a right vacancy where their talents can be fully utilised.
- A policy of preferring people from within, offers regular promotional avenues for employees. It motivates them to work hard and earn promotions. They will work with loyalty, commitment and enthusiasm.
- It reduce labour turnover as it gives employees a sense of job security and opportunity for advancement.

**Cons:**

- It often leads to inbreeding, and discourages new blood from entering an organization.
- The organization is forced to select candidates from a limited pool. It may have to sacrifice quality and settle for less qualified candidates.
- There are possibilities that internal sources may "dry up" and it may be difficult to find the requisite personnel from within an organization (limits the choice).
- It discourages entry of talented people, available outside an organization. Existing employees may fail to bring in innovative ways and inject necessary dynamism to enterprise activities.
- It can be dysfunctional to the organization to utilise inferior internal sources. Promotions based on length of service rather than merit, may prove to be blessings for inefficient candidates. They do not work hard and prove their work.
- As promotion is based on seniority, the danger is that truly capable hands may not be chosen. The likes and dislikes of the management may also play an important role in the selection of personnel.
- Recruitment from within may lead to infighting among employees aspiring for limited, higher level position in an organization.
- You will have to replace the person who has been promoted.
- An insider may be less likely to make the essential criticisms required to get the company working more effectively.
- Promotion of one person in a company may upset someone else.

## EXTERNAL SOURCES

Inevitably (unavoidably), the companies must go to external sources for lower-entry jobs, for expansion and for positions whose specifications cannot be met by the existing manpower. Certain recruitment sources are found to be more effective than others. We therefore attempt to discuss each source in the following sections.

### 1. Advertising

Advertising in newspapers, trade journals, bulletins, publications and magazines is the most frequently used method. In order to be successful, an advertisement should be carefully written. If it is not properly written, it may not draw the right type of applicants, or it may attract too many a[illegible] who are not qualified for the job. By means of advertisement the organisation is able to communicate its requirement of people, some of whom may be its prospective employees. An advertisement contains brief statement of the nature of jobs, the type of people required, and procedure for applying for these jobs. There is a trend towards more selective recruitment in advertising. This can be affected in at least two ways. First, advertisements can be placed in media read only by particular groups.

For example: The tool engineer is ordinarily read by production engineers. Secondly, more information about the company, the job, and the job specification (age, education, experience) can be included in the advertisement to permit some self-screening. When time is limited, the daily newspaper, particularly the Sunday edition, will reach the maximum number in the shortest period.

Employment news in a leading government publication which serves as sources of recruitment. Sometimes, advertisements are placed in magazines read only by particular groups. For example, Data Quest for computer professionals, Business Today for management, etc. The advertisement is the most fragile contact between prospective candidates and the potential employer. Also, as each advertisement competes with many others for attention marketing people have a simple but effective guide — AIDA — for creating good advertisement.

**A:** Attract the reader's attention

**I:** Generate interest in the vacancy

**D:** Create desire for the job

**A:** Stimulate the reader to take action

Advertising is very useful for recruiting blue-collar and hourly workers, as well as scientific, professional, and technical employees. Local newspaper can be a good source of blue-collar workers, clerical employees and lower-level administrative employees.

The main point is that the higher the position in the organisation, or the more specialised the skills sought, the more widely dispersed advertisement is likely to be. The search for top executive might include advertisement in a national periodical, while the advertisement of blue-collar jobs is usually confined to the daily newspapers or regional trade journals.

Here, it's easy to place job ads without much of a lead-time. It has flexibility in terms of information and can conveniently target a specific geographic location. On the negative side, newspaper ads tend to attract only those who are actively seeking employment at that point of time, while some of the best candidates who are well paid and challenged by their current jobs may not be aware of such openings.

As a result, the company may be bombarded with applications from a large number of candidates who are marginally qualified for the job — adding to its administrative burden. To maintain secrecy for various reasons (avoiding the rush, sending signals to competitors, cutting down expenses involved in responding to any individual who applies, etc.), large companies with a national reputation may also go in for blind-box ads in newspapers, especially for filling lower level positions. In a blind-box ad, there is no identification of the advertising organisation. Job aspirants are asked to respond to a post office box number or to an employment firm that is acting as an agent between the job seeker and the organisation.

A number of factors influence the response rate to advertisements. There are three important variables: identification of the organization, labour market conditions, and the degree to which specific requirements are included in the advertisement.

The classified advertisement section of a daily newspaper or the Sunday weekly edition of the *Hindustan Times, The Times of India, The Tribune, Bharat Jyoti, The National Herald, The Free Press Journal, The Pioneer, Amrit Bazaar Patrika, The Economic Times, The Hindu, The Indian Express*, etc., carry advertisements for all types of positions. Such advertisements enable prospective candidates to screen themselves in order to find out whether they are fit for the job for which the advertisements has been issued.

According to advertisement tactics and strategy in personnel recruitment, three points need to be borne in mind before an advertisement is inserted. *First*, to visualise the type of applicant one is trying to recruit. *Second*, to write out a list of the advantages a company offers; in other words, why the reader should work for the company. *Third*, to decide where to run the advertisement, not only in which area but in which newspaper having a local, state or nationwide circulation.

**Television and Radio Ads:** These are more likely to reach individuals who are not actively seeking employment; they are more likely to stand out distinctly, they help the organisation to target the audience more selectively and they offer considerable scope for designing ads creatively. However, these ads are expensive. Also, television or radio is simply seen or heard, potential candidates may have a tough time remembering the details, making application difficult.

Advertisements can be used both for local recruitment effort and for regional, national and international searches. For example, clinical psychologist often finds jobs through listing in the American psychological association's monthly newsletter. For specialised employees, they can give an advertisement in trade and professional journals, like American psychologist, sales management, electronic news and travel trade.

**Internet Advertising and Career Sites:** Employees are increasingly turning to the web as a recruitment tool because online ads are relatively cheap, are more dynamic and can often produce faster results than newspaper help-wanted ads. It is also a convenient tool for job seekers. Thousands of career websites exist and almost all are free to people searching for job. For example, Monster.com. job seekers can search for jobs by industry, geographic location and in some case, by job description. The former practice of going through the Sunday help wanted ads with a highlighter in hand is rapidly becoming a theme of the past.

**Suitability:** We get qualified and experienced staff.

Clerk, peon and workers are recruited by giving advertisement in local newspapers.

Top executives are recruited by giving advertisements in newspapers, periodicals, bulletins, journals, magazines, etc.

## 2. Employment Agencies

As a statutory requirement, companies are also expected to notify (wherever the Employment Exchanges Act, 1959, applies) their vacancies through the respective Employment Exchanges, created all over India for helping unemployed youth, displaced persons, ex-military personnel, physically handicapped, etc. As per the Act, all employers are supposed to notify the vacancies arising in their establishments from time-to-time — with certain exemptions — to the prescribed employment exchanges before they are filled. The Act covers all establishments in public sector and non-agricultural establishments employing 25 or more workers in the private sector.

An employment exchange is an office set-up for bringing together as quickly as possible, searching for employment and employees looking for prospective employees. The main functions of employment exchanges are registration of job seekers and their placement in notified vacancies. Typically, the employment agencies are paid a fee-based on the salary offered to the new employees. Agencies can be particularly effective when the firm is looking for an employee with a specialised skills. Employment agency maintains separate database for nongraduates, graduates and postgraduates.

We will describe three forms of employment agencies: public or state agencies, private employment agencies, and management consulting firms.

- **Public Agencies:** In 1933, a public employment service was established as a federal state partnership. It was designed both to help job seekers find suitable employment and to help employers find suitable workers. There is employment exchange run by the government in almost all districts. The main function of these agencies is closely tied to unemployment benefits, since benefits in some states are given only to individuals who are registered with a state employment agency. These agencies provide a wide range of services — counselling, assistance in getting jobs, information about labour market, labour and wage rates. Normally, such exchanges provide candidates for lower positions like semi-skilled and skilled workers and lower level operatives like clerks, junior supervisors, etc. Most nonprofit professional and technical societies such as the institute for electrical and electronic engineers have units that help members find jobs. Many public welfare agencies try to place people who are in special categories, such as those who are physically disabled or are war veterans (experienced). The United States Training and Employment services provide general control of the state agencies through its power over federal tax rebates. Currently, USTES is developing nationwide computerized job bank to which all state employment offices can be connected. It is hoped that this job bank will be the link between job opportunities and applicants from all over the United States.
- **Private Agencies:** Private agencies are believed to offer positions and applicants of a higher calibre. Private employment agencies are widely used. They charge a small fee from an applicant. They specialise in specific occupation like salesman, technical workers, accountants, computer staff, engineers, and executives. These private agencies are brokers who bring employers and employees together. Private employment agency screen applicants against the criteria specified by employer and they usually provide a guarantee covering six months or a year as protection to the employer should the applicant not perform satisfactorily. The specialisations of these agencies enhance their capacity to interpret the needs of their clients, to seek out particular types of persons and to develop proficiency in recognizing the talent of specialised personnel. There are many consultancy and employment agencies like ABC Consultants, A.F. Ferguson and Company, Personnel and Productivity Services, S.B. Billimoria and Company, KPMG, etc., which provide employment services for selecting higher and middle level executives. This agency also undertakes total functions of recruiting and selecting personnel on behalf of various organizations. They charge fees for this purpose.

**Suitability:** Suitable to recruit skilled, semiskilled and unskilled workers.

### 3. Management Consultants

Agencies of this type are actually specialised private employment agencies. They specialise in middle level and top level executive placement. In addition to the level at which they recruit, the features that distinguish executive search agencies from most private employment agencies are their fees, their nationwide contacts, and the thoroughness of their investigations. In searching for an individual of vice-president calibre, whose compensation package may be far in excess of $ 1,00,000 a year, the potential employer is often willing to pay a very high fee to locate exactly the right individual to fill the vacancy. A fee amounting to 30% of the executive's first year salary is not unusual as a charge for finding and recruiting an individual.

They seek out highly effective executives who have the skills to do the job, can effectively adjust to the organization, and most important are willing to consider new challenges and opportunities. The executive search firm can act as a buffer for screening candidates and at the same time, keep the prospective employer anonymous. In the final stages, senior executives of the prospective firm can move into the negotiations and determine the degree of mutual interest.

## 4. Employee Referrals or Recommendations

Employee referral campaigns are an important recruiting option. Employee referral means using personal contacts to locate job opportunities. Employee recommendations can be considered to employ personnel particularly at the lower levels, manual and skilled workers. The idea behind employee recommendation as a source of potential applicants is that the present employees may have specific knowledge of the individuals who may be their friends, relatives or acquaintances. If the present employees are reasonably satisfied with their jobs and displayed better loyalty, they communicate these feelings to many persons in their communities. For example, some hospitals facing labour shortages and using employee referral. When the labour market is very tight, large employers frequently offers their employees bonuses or prizes for any referrals that are hired and stay with the company for a specific length of time. Some companies maintain a register of former employees with a good record to contact them when there are new job openings for which they are qualified. This method of recruitment however, suffers from a serious effect that it encourages nepotism. In the recruitment of sailors, in the navy, the candidates sponsored by the serving and retired armed forces personnel are given preferences over others, provided they meet the basic requirements.

For example, Citibank offers ₹ 50,000 to its employees for every vacancy filled up by the bank on the basis of their referral. Birla 3M also has an incentive based employee referral programme in place. InfoTech companies such as Polaris, Software Labs, Cognizant Technology Solutions, Cisco Systems, etc., have even discovered that the turnover of employees joining through referral system is quite low.

**Suitability:**

1. Suitable to recruit lower level personnel.
2. The existing employees are better at judging the degree of fitness between the organization and employee.

## 5. Schools, Colleges and Universities

Sometimes, recruiters go to educational institutions where they meet the placement officer or the faculty members who recommended suitable candidates. The companies that need employees maintain contact with the guidance counsellors of employment bureaus and teachers of business and vocational subjects. This source is quite useful for selecting people to the post of management trainees, technical supervisor, scientist and technicians. The organization holds preliminary interviews on the campus on the predetermined date and candidates found suitable are called for further interviews at specified places. High school diploma, specific vocational training or a college background with a bachelor's or master's or doctoral degree, educational institutions are an excellent source of potential employees for entry level positions in organizations. You might think that college recruiting may change in its nature and shift from face-to-face meeting to webbased interactions for an example Hewlett Packard has a website specifically focused on college recruiting at www.jobs.hp.com

**Suitability:**

1. Employer select apprentice trainee from such source.
2. Employer gives project work to student and then absorb him or her.
3. Technical and professional institutions provide blue-colour applicant and white-colour managerial professionals.

## 6. Labour Unions

In many organizations, labour unions are used as source of manpower supply, though at the lower levels. Many such union leaders whose styles are cooperative and constructive can be promoted to supervisory level. In many organizations, unions are asked to make recommendations for employment of people as a matter of goodwill and cooperation. But in case of adverse IR, these techniques may create difficulty.

**Suitability:**

1. Suitable to recruit manual and skilled workers.
2. Large and medium-scale firms use these sources.

## 7. Casual Labour

Most industrial units rely, to some extent on the casual labour which presents itself daily at the factory gate or employment office. However, this source is uncertain and the candidates cover a wide range of abilities. Even then, many of our industries make use of this source to fill up casual vacancies. This can be developed through provision of attractive employment office facilities and prompt and courteous replies to unsolicited letters. It can be effective by prompt disposal of applications by providing information about the organization's policy and procedure regarding such hiring and providing facilities to such gate callers.

Casual applicants will depend on economic conditions, the organization's image, and the job seeker's perception of the types of jobs that might be available; this source does provide an excellent supply of applicants. Unsolicited applications made by unemployed individuals, however, generally have a short life.

**Suitability:**

1. Suitable to fill up casual (accidental) vacancies.
2. Suitable for unskilled and semiskilled workers.
3. Suitable at the initial stage of the organization where large number of such people may be required by the organization.
4. Sometimes people may directly approach the organization and inquire about the vacancies.

## 8. Unconsolidated Applications

For positions in which large numbers of candidates are not available from other sources, the companies may gain in keeping files of applications received from candidates who make direct inquiries about possible vacancies on their own. The information may be indexed and filled for future uses when there are opening for these jobs. Sometimes, the candidates may be requested to keep the organization posted with any change in their qualifications, experience, or achievement made. Some candidate send their applications without any invitation from the organization.

**Suitability:** When large number of candidates are not available from other source.

## 9. Computer Data Banks

When a company desires a particular type of employee, job specifications and requirements are fed into a computer, where they are matched against the resume data stored therein. The output is a set of resumes of individuals who meet the requirements. Which particular source is to be tapped will depend on the policy of a firm, the position of labour supply, government regulations and agreements with labour organizations? However, the personnel managers must be in close touch with these different sources and use them in accordance to his needs.

**Suitability:** This method is very useful for identifying candidates for hard-to-fill positions which call for an unusual (uncommon) combination of skills.

## 10. Professional Organizations

Many professional organizations, including labour unions operate placement services for the benefit of their members. The professional organizations include such varied occupations as industrial engineers, psychologists and seafarers. These organizations publish rosters of job vacancies and distribute this list to members. It is also a common practice to provide placement facilities at regional and national meetings where individuals looking for employment and companies looking for employees can find each other. They maintain complete information record about employed executives. These same organizations may employ "executive search firms" to help them to find executive talent. This consulting firms recommended persons of high calibre for managerial, marketing and production engineers' posts. Indoctrination seminars for college professors are arranged to discuss the problem of companies and employees. Professors are invited to take part in these seminars. Visit to plants and banquets are arranged, so that the participant may be favourably impressed. They may later speak well of a company and help it getting the required personnel.

Professional organizations however can also apply sanctions to control the labour supply in their discipline.

## 11. Nepotism

The recruitment of relatives is an inevitable component of recruitment programme in family-owned firms. Such a policy does not necessarily coincide with hiring on the basis of merit, but the interest and loyalty, trust, confidence to the enterprise and the offsetting advantages.

## 12. Leasing

To adjust to short-term fluctuations in personnel needs (to meet fluctuating demand); the possibility of leasing personnel should be considered. In leasing, the company not only gets well trained personnel, but also avoids any obligations in pension, insurance and other fringe benefits. Every company cannot afford to develop every source of manpower to the fullest extent. Sources utilised should be evaluated and judged in terms of the degree of success in obtaining competent personnel. For each major category of jobs, present personnel can be evaluated for job successes. If a correlation is discovered between successful personnel and particular sources, those sources should be further developed.

It is a part-time or temporary job and payment may be on daily, weekly, or hourly basis. Here organization can get well trained and experienced persons. Success in recruitment can be judged by utilising a number of criteria. Some of them are the number of applications received, number of offers made, number of personnel recruited and number of successful placements. And here, the number of job applicants has least value in determining the effectiveness of the programme. The number of offers made is a better indication of the quality of recruitment. The number of personnel recruited is indicative of getting closer to the real objective of securing an adequate number of qualified personnel. But the real test of recruitment programme's effectiveness lies in the follow-up. Answers to the questions such as "Was the placement successful?", "Is he a good employee in terms of productivity and attitude?", and "Did the employee quit because he misunderstood the nature of the job and the company?" will provide the necessary inputs for taking any corrective actions.

### 13. Deputation

At the initial development of public sector organizations, this source was quite common for filling managerial vacancies in these organizations. Many organisations take people on deputation from other organizations. Such people are given choice either to return to their original organization after a certain time or to opt for the present organizations. People from civil and defence service were on deputation in this organizations. Organizations promoted by various industrial groups also use these sources to fill up higher managerial position. People working in one organization are deputed in another belonging to the same industrial house.

**Suitability:** Suitable in public sector organizations and to fill up higher managerial positions.

### 14. Field Trips

An interviewing team makes trips to towns and cities which are known to contain the kinds of employees required. In this method of recruitment, carefully prepared brochures describing the organization and the job it offers are distributed to the candidates before the interviewer arrives. The arrival date and the time and venue of interview are given to the candidates in advance.

### 15. Customers

An innovative recruitment source is the organization's customers, who are already familiar with the organization and what it offers. Customers can be more valuable than simply as buyers and consumers of product or service. These people, who must be happy with the organization's product or services because they remained customers, may bring more enthusiasm to the workplace than other applicants and as the recipients of the firm's product or service may have valuable insights into how the organization could be improved.

Finding qualified and motivated employees is a key concern for small businesses, as two-thirds of small businesses report their difficulty in finding the qualified employees. Bad hires can be catastrophic for small businesses, which do not have the luxury of reassigning workers who are not well suited for their positions.

## 16. Internet Recruiting

In recent years most companies have found it useful to develop their own website and list job openings on it. The website offers a fast, convenient and cost-effective means for job applicants to submit their resume through the internet. Infosys Technologies Ltd., for example, gets over 1,000 resumes a day from prospective candidates through the net. The resumes are then converted into a standard format using the software that the company has developed for short listing candidates according to a set criteria such as *alma mater*, qualifications, experience, etc. The HR manager has to key in his or her requirements and 'profiles' of candidates from the company's database get generated. There are a variety of websites available — in addition to a company's own website — where applicants can submit their resumes and potential employers can check for qualified applicants. Such as: (i) www.jobsahead.com; (ii) www.naukri.com; (iii) www.monsterindia.com; (iv) www.timesjobs.com internet recruiting, as mentioned earlier, generates fast, cost-effective, timely responses from job applicants from different parts of the world. And that's where the problem lies: the websites might be flooded with resumes from unqualified job seekers. Applications may also come from geographic areas that are unrealistically far away.

## 17. Voluntary Organizations

Like private clubs, social organizations might also provide employees who are handicapped, widowed or married women, old persons, retired hands, etc., in response to advertisements.

# PROS AND CONS OF EXTERNAL SOURCES OF RECRUITMENT

### Pros:

1. Fresh talent and skill come into the organization.
2. Highly qualified and experienced employees may help the organization to boost performance.
3. External sources provide the requisite type of personnel for an organization, having skill, training and education up to the required standard.
4. In the long run, this source proves economical, because potential employees do not need extra training for their jobs.
5. It helps in motivating internal employees to work hard and compete with external candidates while selecting career growth. Such a competitive atmosphere would help an employee to work to the best of his abilities.
6. Talented people could join the ranks, new ideas could find meaningful expression, a competitive atmosphere would compel people to give their best and earn rewards, etc.
7. Since, people are recruited from a large market; the best selection can be made without any distinctions of caste, gender, or colour and no personal bias.
8. It is in tune with the principle of democratic values and norms as it ensures equal opportunities for entry to public office to everyone.
9. This method can help able young men from universities to public service careers.
10. The public services are kept attuned to the changing socio-economic conditions of the country through the constant flow of young persons. It also checks stagnation in services.

11. In technical fields, the latest knowledge is required which the young man can easily supply.
12. Direct recruitment motivates the persons in service to keep themselves up to date in knowledge least they may not qualify in competitions for higher posts.

**Cons:**

1. This system suffers from what is called "brain drain", especially when experienced persons are raided or hunted by sister concerns.
2. Hiring costs could go up substantially. Tapping multifarious sources of recruitment is not an easy task.
3. It takes time to advertise, screen, to test and to select suitable employees. When suitable ones are not available, the process has to be repeated.
4. There is no guarantee that the organization, ultimately, will be able to hire the services of suitable candidates. It may end up hiring someone who does not "fit" and who may not be able to adjust in the new set-up.
5. Existing employees who have put in considerable service may resist the process of filling up vacancies from outside. The feeling that their services have not been recognised by the organization, forces them to work with less enthusiasm and motivation.
6. This reduces the morale of existing employees because outsiders are preferred to fill up superior vacancies.
7. They deny career advancement for existing employees.
8. Proper evaluation may not be possible due to the time constraint resulting in faulty selection.
9. Outsiders not being acquainted with the policies and the procedures of the organizations need training, before they can deliver.
10. Direct recruitment places younger persons over the older and experienced employees. This creates jealousy which is not good for the services.
11. An extensive outside recruitment at the higher grades is the poor reflection on the ability and the talent available within the service and undermines the career ideas.

## SELECTION

In human resource planning, we identified our personnel needs. Once these needs were established a job analysis was conducted, which clarified the characteristics of jobs being done and the individual qualities necessary to do these jobs successfully. This information was then used to recruit a pool of qualified applicants. Effective selection decisions are those where the candidate was predicted to be successful and later did prove to be a successful performer on job.

Selection is the process of discovering the qualifications and characteristics of the job applicant in order to establish their likely suitability for the job position.

Selection, either internal or external, is a deliberate effort of organization to select a fixed number of personnel from a large number of applicants. The primary aim of employee selection is to choose those persons who are most likely to perform their jobs with maximum effectiveness and remain with the company. Thus, an attempt is made to find a suitable candidate for the job. In doing so, naturally many applications are rejected. This makes selection a negative function. Having identified the potential applicants, the next steps are to evaluate their experience and qualifications and make a selection. For a sales position, for example: the criteria should be able to predict which applicants will generate a high volume of sales, for a teaching position as a university professor, they should predict which applicants will get high student evaluation or generate many high quality publications or both.

According to Yoder, "the hiring process is of one or many 'go-on-go' gauges. Candidates are screened by the employer and the short-listed applicants go on to the next hurdle, while the unqualified once are eliminated".

## Selection Process

High performing employees not only make the organization look good, they make the person who hired them look good. To avoid stressful situation, you need to use a systematic selection process. One "good hire" will more than reimburse you for the investment of your time. For example, based on the functions and responsibilities of the open position, you may determine that you want someone with intellectual curiosity or you need a person with superb organisational skills. Basic idea is to solicit maximum possible information about the candidates to ascertain their suitability for employment. It is possible that selection process may have different steps for various positions because their selection practices may differ. For example, some organizations conduct selection tests of various types, while others may not use these.

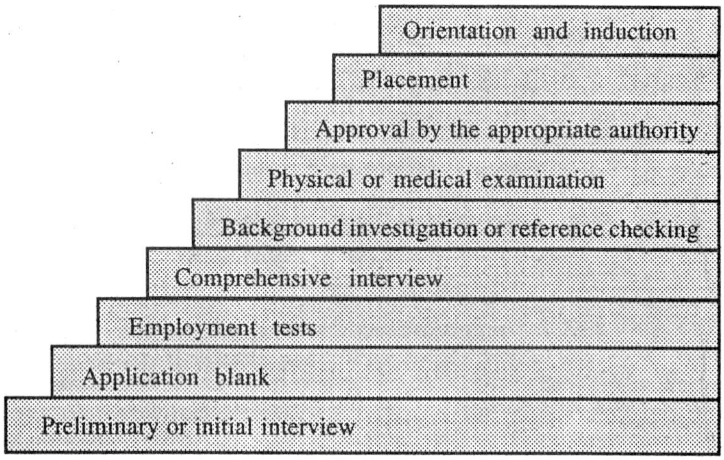


## 1. Preliminary or Initial Interview

It is conducted by high calibre receptionists. It is a "stand up" interview conducted at a desk or railing. The initial interview is usually very short and has as its object the elimination of the unqualified candidates. Preliminary interview is generally planned by large organizations to cut the cost of selection by allowing only eligible candidates to go through the further stages in the selection. A junior executive from the HR department may elicit response from applicants on important items determining the suitability of an applicant for a job such as age, education, skills, experience, pay expectations, nature of job, aptitude, location choice, etc. This "courtesy interview", as it is often called, helps the department screen out obvious misfits. If the department finds the candidate suitable, a prescribed application form is given to the applicants to fill and submit.

Guidelines for preliminary screening

| Name of Candidate: .............................................................................. | |
|---|---|
| (a) Personality: Grade* | A .......... B ............ C............ D ........... |
| (b) Expression (in English) | A .......... B ............ C............ D ........... |
| (In Hindi) | A .......... B ............ C............ D ........... |
| (c) Technical knowledge | |
| Theory: | A .......... B ............ C............ D ........... |
| Application: | A .......... B ............ C............ D ........... |
| (d) General knowledge | A .......... B ............ C............ D ........... |
| (e) Any other remarks | A .......... B ............ C............ D ........... |
| Selected for employment Test | Yes ........ No .......... |
| Date of Interview...................... | Signature of Interviewer ............................................... |

* Grade A ----- Outstanding; B ----- Good; C ----- Average; D ----- Poor

The most appropriate screening method will depend on the type of the job to be filled and seniority of the likely applicants.

## 2. Application Blank

Organizations often use application forms as screening devices to determine whether a candidate satisfies minimum job specifications, particularly for entry level jobs. The forms typically ask for information regarding past jobs and present employment status. In a sense, the application blank is a highly structured interview, in which, the questions are standardised and determined in advance. Application forms are for data gathering only. For example: on the quality of their handwriting or creativity of their replies. Application blank is a brief history sheet of an employee's background, usually containing the following things:

Contents of application blank

- Personal data (name, address, gender, date and place of birth, identification marks, age, nationality, number of dependants)
- Marital data (single or married, children)
- Physical data (height, weight, health condition)
- Educational data (levels of formal education, marks, distinctions, any training acquired by professional or technical institutions or correspondence courses)
- Employment data (past experience, promotions, nature of duties, reasons for leaving previous jobs, salary drawn, etc.)
- Extra-curricular activities data (sports or games, NSS, NCC, prize won, leisure-time activities)
- References (names of two or more people who certified the suitability of an applicant to the advertised position)

In general terms, the application form gives a synopsis of what applicants have been doing during their adult life, their skills and their accomplishments.

**LONG APPLICATION BLANK**

**Form for Application**

**Note:**

(a) All entries must be made in candidate's handwriting.

(b) All subsequent change in the particulars given in the application must be intimated to the personnel department within a week of such change.

(c) If space against any query is not adequate a separate sheet should be attached.

(d) Canvassing in any form will disqualify a candidate.

(e) The candidate will render himself liable to summary dismissal, if it is found that any information given by him is incorrect or any relevant information has been suppressed.

1. Full Name (with surname) in Block Letters: ..........................................................................
2. Nationality: .................... Cast: .................... Religion: .................. Sex: ......................
3. Father's Name and Occupation: ..........................................................................
4. Present address: ..........................................................................
5. Permanent address: ..................................Village: ............... Mohalla..........................

   H. No: .........................P.O ...................... Dist. ....................... State: ........................
6. Age: .................. Date of birth: ........................... Place of birth: .............................
7. Academic/Technical qualifications stating examinations passed from High school SLC/ Hr. Secondary onwards:

| Name of University | Examinations passed | Subjects offered | Years of passing | Division class (Marks obtained if there is no Division of class) |
|---|---|---|---|---|
| (a) | | | | |
| (b) | | | | |
| (c) | | | | |

8. Apprenticeship/Practical Training:

| Nature of Apprenticeship Training | Organization in which served | Duration From (date) | To (date) | Result |
|---|---|---|---|---|
| | | | | |

9. Language: (a) Can speak: Hindi, English/Gujarati, Marathi, any other

   (b) Can speak, read and write:
10. Physique: Games played: .........................

    (a) Height: (in cms) ...................... Hobbies: ..................................

    (b) Weight: (in kgs) ......................

    (c) Strength of glasses (if worn) .................

(d) Any disability: (current): ......................

(e) Any major disability or ailment suffered in the past: ..............................

(f) Identification marks: ........................................

11. Past Experience:

| | Name of Employer with complete address | Total number of staffs and workers | Post held and exact nature of duties | Period | | Salary | |
|---|---|---|---|---|---|---|---|
| | | | | Date of joining | Date of leaving | Basic and allowances | Reason for leaving |
| 1. | | | | | | | |
| 2. | | | | | | | |
| 3. | | | | | | | |

Information regarding specialization in a particular subject and other matters of interest
.........................................................................................................

12. (a) Have you ever been removed from your job. If so, state where and why........................
.........................................................................................................

(b) Have you been convicted by a court of law? If so, give particulars..............................
.........................................................................................................

13. (a) Have you ever applied to been interviewed by this company before?..........................
.........................................................................................................

(If yes, please state the name of the post and the date of interview)

14. References (other than relations) (Name and full address to be given)
.........................................................................................................
.........................................................................................................

15. Minimum salary acceptable (including all allowances):
.........................................................................................................

16. Time required for joining (if selected):

17. Number of dependants:..................... Male ...................... Female .........................

18. Marital status: Married/Bachelor/Divorced/Widowed/Separated

19. (a) Children ...............................................

(b) Ages of children .................................... Sons ...............................................

Daughter ............................................... Name of relative ..................................

Department ........................................... Relationship ..........................................

20. Any acquaintance in our company or at Udaipur? If so, give name and full particulars of each acquaintance:
.........................................................................................................
.........................................................................................................

21. Copies of Testimonials attached.

1.

2.

Place ........................

Date ........................ Signature of Applicant

**(TO BE FILLED IN BY THE PERSONNEL DEPARTMENT)**

Examined by 1. ............................................................................ (on date)

2. ............................................................................

3. ............................................................................

Remarks: ............................................................................................................................

............................................................................................................................

............................................................................................................................

Appointed by:. ............................................................................................................

Date of Appointment: ..................................................................................................

Salary fixed: ..................................................................................................................

Post to which appointed: ..........................................................................................

Nature of vacancy: Temporary/Permanent: ..............................................................

Period of Probation: ......................................................................................................

For THE ARAVALI PUBLISHING COMPANY PVT.LTD.

CHAIRMAN

---

To be filled in by the selected candidates only.

I have read and understood the company's service rules and agree to abide by them including any changes made therein by the management from time-to-time.

Specimen Signature:

Specimen Initials:

---

## 3. Employment Tests

For further assessment of a candidate's nature and abilities, some tests are used in the selection procedure. If the tests are properly conducted, they can reduce the selection cost by reducing the large number of applicants to manageable levels. A test is a standardised, objective measure of a person's behaviour, performance or attitude. It is standardised because the way the test is carried out, the environment in which the test is administered and the way the individual scores are calculated — are uniformly applied. The objective is to measure individual differences in a scientific way, giving very little room for individual bias and interpretation.

Various tests measure a wide range of ability, from verbal and qualitative skills to perceptual speed. Over the years, employment tests have not only gained importance but also a certain amount of inevitability in employment decisions. Since, they try to objectively determines how well an applicant meets job requirements, most companies do not hesitate to invest their time and money in selection testing in a big way. Some of the commonly used employment tests may be stated thus:

**(a) Intelligence Tests:** Intelligence tests tries to measure the level of intelligence of a candidate. They measure the incumbent's learning ability and also the ability to understand instructions and make judgements. The basic objective of intelligence tests is to pick-up employees who are alert and quick at learning things so that they can be offered adequate training to improve their skills for the benefit of the organization. Intelligence tests do not measure any single trait but rather several abilities such as memory, vocabulary, verbal fluency, numerical ability, perception, spatial visualization, inductive reasoning, mathematical ability, etc. Stanford-Binet test, Binet-Simon test, The Wechsler Adult Intelligence Scale is examples of standard intelligence test. Some of these tests are increasingly used in competitive examinations while recruiting graduates and postgraduates at entry level management position in banking, insurance, and other financial services sector.

The scores on the test are usually expressed numerically as Intelligence Quotient (IQ) which can be calculated as follows:

$$IQ = \frac{\text{Mental Age}}{\text{Actual Age}} \times 100$$

It means that the IQ is derived by converting actual age into mental age and multiplying it by 100 in order to facilitate comparison. Higher is the figure, higher is the level of intelligence. Intelligence tests are designed on the basis of age groups.

**(b) Aptitude Tests:** These tests measure whether an individual has the capacity or latent ability to learn a given job if given adequate training. The use of aptitude test is advisable when an applicant has had little or no experience along the line of the job opening. Specific aptitudes which are usually tested are mechanical, clerical, musical and academic aptitudes, dexterity (finger, hand), hand-eye coordination, etc. Some of the tests under this category are:

- MATRIX (Management Trial Exercise) designed by Procter and Gamble.
- CAT (Clerical Aptitude Test) to assess vocabulary, spelling, arithmetical ability, details checking, etc.
- PAT (Pilot Aptitude Test) to access coordination between hands and feet movements.
- Computer Aptitude Test to assess power of reasoning and analysis.

This tests measure an individual's potential to learn certain skills like clerical, mechanical, mathematical, problem-solving ability, technical vocabulary, etc. These tests indicate whether or not an individual has the ability to learn the job quickly and efficiently. Clerical tests for an example may measure the incumbent's ability to take notes, perceive thing correctly and quickly locate things, ensure proper movements of files, etc. Another example: for semiskilled workers the knowledge of assembling, packaging, testing, inspection is important. These tests may take one of the following forms:

(i) Mental or intelligence test measure the overall intellectual ability or the IQ of a person and enable us to know whether he has the mental capacity to deal with the new problems. They are useful for selection purpose and determine the future of an employee's word fluency, memory, inductive reasoning, speed of perception, and spatial visualization.

(ii) Mechanical aptitude test measure the capacity of a person to learn a particular type of mechanical work and measure a person's capacity for spatial visualization, perceptual speed, visual-motor coordination or integration, manual dexterity, visual insights, etc. They also measure specialised knowledge and information of techniques, arithmetical problem-solving ability and technical vocabulary. They are useful when apprentices, mechanists, mechanics, maintenance workers and mechanical techniques are selected.

(iii) Psychomotor or scales tests are those tests which measures a person's ability to do a specific job. They are administered to determine mental dexterity or motor ability and similar attributes involving muscular movement, control and coordination.

Examples of this type of tests are the McQuarril Test for mechanical ability, the Purdue Mechanical Adaptability Test, and the O'Connor Finger and Tweezer Dexterity Tests.

**(c) Personality Tests:** The importance of a personality to job success cannot be denied. These tests aim at measuring those basic make-up or characteristics of an individual, which are non-intellectual in nature. In other words, they probe deeply to discover clues to an individual's value system, his emotional reactions, and maturity, and his characteristic mood. They assess his motivation, interests, his ability to adjust himself to the stresses of everyday life, and his capacity for interpersonal relations and self-image. The definition of personality, methods of measuring personality, factors and the relationship between personality factors and actual job criteria have been the subject of much discussion. Researchers have also questioned whether applicants answer all the items truthfully or whether they try to respond in a socially desirable manner. Personality tests are used to measure basic aspects of an applicant's personality such as motivation, emotional balance, self-confidence, interpersonal behaviour, introversion, emotional stability, neuroticism, submissiveness, compulsion, delusions, self-image, aggressiveness, dominance, fear, distrust, objectivity, pressure, and stress, etc.

Examples of such tests are: Bell Adjustment Inventory, the California Test of Personality scale, Minnesola Multiphasic, Personality Inventory, Thermatic Appreciation Tests, etc.

These tests are of three types:

(a) Objective tests measure neurotic tendencies, self-sufficiency, dominance-submission, and self-confidence.

(b) Projective tests are those in which a candidate is asked to project his own interpretation into certain standard stimulus situations. The way in which he responds to these stimuli depends on his own values, motives, personality, frustrations, aspirations, attitude, and idea about life, etc. The most widely used tests of this type are the Roschach Blot Test and the Thematic Appreciation Test.

(c) Situation tests measures an applicant's reaction when he is placed in a peculiar situation, his ability to undergo stress and his demonstration of ingenuity under pressure. Such tests usually relates with leaderless group situation in which some problem is posed to a group and they are asked to reach to some conclusion without the help of a leader.

**(d) Achievement Tests:** These are designed to measure what the applicant can do on the job currently. Achievement is concerned with what one has accomplished. When a candidate claims to have certain knowledge and the know-how, the achievement test may be conducted to measure how well the candidates know these. For an example, a typing test may measure the typing performance of a typist in terms of speed, accuracy and efficiency. Performance test may be administered for selecting employees at operative level as well as junior management level. Examples of such test are: General Aptitude Test Battery; the Abstract Reasoning Test, The Millar Analogies Test, The Standford Binet Scales, the Adaptability Tests. Achievement tests are of two kinds.

(i) Test for measuring job knowledge, which may be oral or written. These tests are administered to determine proficiency in short hand and in operating calculation, adding machines, dictating and transcribing machines, and simple mechanical equipment. Such tests are useful for office workers, mill supervisors, stenographers, public utility employees, sales girls, inspector, and so on.

(ii) Work sample tests are miniature replicas of actual job requirements, they are difficult to fake. They offer concrete evidence of the proficiency of an applicant as against his ability to do the job. However, work sample test are not cost-effective, as each candidate has to be tested individually. A typing test provides the material to be typed and notes the time taken and the mistakes committed.

**(e) Interest Tests:** Interest test is designed to discover a person's area of interest and identify the kind of jobs that will satisfy him. It is assumed that a person who is interested in a job can do much better than the person who is not interested. Interest test generally measure interest in outdoor activities, mechanical, computational, scientific, persuasive, artistic, literacy, musical, clerical, social activities, etc. They are inventories of the likes and dislikes of the people of some occupation, hobbies and recreational activities. Two of the most widely used tests are:

- Strong vocational interest blank and kidder preference record.

**(f) Simulation Test:** Simulation exercise is a test which duplicates many of the activities and problems that an employee faces while at work. Such exercises are commonly used for hiring managers at various levels. To assess the potential of a candidate for managerial positions, assessment centres are commonly used.

**(g) Performance Simulation Test:** To avoid the criticism and potential liability that may result from the use of psychological, aptitude, and other types of written tests, there has been increasing interest in the past decade in developing performance simulation tests. The singular identifying characteristic of these tests is that they require the applicant to engage in specific behaviours which based on job analysis data, have been shown to be key behaviours necessary for doing the job successfully.

**(h) Assessment Centres:** In assessment centres, line executive, supervisors and/or qualified psychologist evaluate candidates as they go through two to four days of exercises that simulate real problems that the candidates are likely to encounter on the job. Based on the requirement that the actual job incumbent has to meet activities might include interviews, in-basket problem-solving exercises, group discussions, and business games. The evidence on the effectiveness of assessment centres is extremely impressive. Initially, a small batch of applicants comes to the assessment centre (a separate room). Their performance in the situational exercises is observed and evaluated by a team of six to eight trained assessors. The assessor's judgements on each exercise are complied and combined to have a summary rating for each candidate being assessed. The assessment centre approach thus, evaluates a candidate's potential for management on the basis of multiple assessment techniques, standardised methods of making inferences from such techniques, and pooled judgements from multiple assessors.

**(i) Other Tests:**

***(a) Graphology Test:*** Graphology involves a trained evaluator to examine the lines, loops, hooks, strokes, curves and flourishes in a person's handwriting to assess the person's personality and emotional make-up. The recruiting company may, for example, ask applicants to complete application forms and write about why they want a job. The use of graphology, however, is dependent on the training and expertise of the person doing the analysis.

***(b) Polygraph (Lie-detector):*** The polygraph records physical changes in the biological movement as the test subject answers a series of questions. It records fluctuations in respiration, blood pressure, skin sensitivity, and perspiration on a moving roll of graphpaper. The polygraph operator forms a judgement as to whether the subject's response was truthful or deceptive by examining the biological movements recorded on the paper. Polygraphs, despite strong resistance by many applicants, are increasingly being used by companies which have problems with inventory and security of funds. Government agencies have begun to use the polygraph especially for filling security, police, fire, and health positions. Critics, however, question the appropriateness of polygraphs in establishing the truth about an applicant's behaviour. Is it possible to prove that the responses recorded by the polygraph occur only because a lie has been told? The fact of the matter is that polygraphs are neither reliable nor valid. Since they invade the privacy of those tested, many applicants vehemently oppose the use of polygraph as a selection tool.

## 4. Comprehensive Interview

Interview is probably the most widely used selection tool. It is most complex selection technique because its scope includes measuring all the relevant characteristics and integrating and classifying all other information about the applicant. In practically all organisations interviewing is used for a variety of purposes, including selection, appraisal, disciplinary action, counselling and general problem-solving. Interviews are designed to probe into areas that cannot be addressed by the application form or tests. Interview seems to carry a great deal of weight. There is no doubt that the interview is the most widely used selection device that organizations rely on to differentiate candidates.

According to Scott and others, "an interview is a purposeful exchange of ideas, the answering of questions and communication between two or more persons". An eminent author defines an interview as "a conversation with a purpose", and the purpose may be to "Get information", "to give information", and "to make a friend". In other words, an interview is an attempt to secure maximum amount of information from the candidate concerning his suitability for the job under consideration. In this step, the interviewer tries to obtain and synthesise information about the abilities of interviewee and the requirement of the job. Interview gives the recruiter an opportunity to —

- Size of the interviewee's agreeableness (personally),
- Ask questions that are not covered in tests,
- Obtain as much pertinent information as possible,
- Assess subjective aspects of the candidate like personality, attitude, facial expression (gestures, postures, smiling, eye-contact, appearance, interest, nervousness, family background, ability to work under stress situations, ability to speak, previous experience, interpersonal skill, ability to "fit in" the organization, and problem-solving ability, etc,

- Make judgements on interviewee's enthusiasm and intelligence,
- Give facts to the candidate regarding the company, its policies, programmes, procedures, etc., and promote goodwill towards the company.

Richard Calhoon observes: "The interview makes three unique contributions to the selection process. *First*, it is the only way to see an applicant in action – how he looks, his manner, his bearing. *Second*, it is the only way to witness how he interacts and how he responds; his way of thinking, the effects of his personality on another. *Third*, it is perhaps the best way to get at the 'will do' features of a performance – motivation, initiative, stability, perservance, work, habits, and judgements. The so-called 'can do' aspect can be examined by application, test and reference checks.

Under the 'can do' factors, Dr. McMurray includes these elements: appearance, manners, education as required by the job, intelligence, ability to solve problems, experience in the field knowledge of the project, physical conditions and health.

Under the 'will do' factors are listed character traits, *viz*., stability, industry, willingness to work, perservance, ability to get along with others, loyalty — that is, identifying with employer — reliance, that is, standing on one's own feet and making one's own decisions and leadership.

Besides, "Motivation factors" are also taken into consideration. These are vigorous initiative and drive, need for income, need for security, need for statue, need for power, need for investigate, need to excel, need for perfection, even the need to starve.

From assessing 'emotional maturity', the factors to be taken into consideration are: freedom from dependence, regard for consequences, capacity for self-discipline, freedom from destructive tendencies and freedom from wishful thinking.

## 5. Reference Checking or Background Investigation

Every personnel administrator has the responsibility to investigate each potential applicant. Candidates are required to give their names of two or three references in their application forms. These references may be from individuals who are familiar with the candidate's academic achievements, or from applicant's previous employer, who is well versed with the applicant's job performance, and from coworkers. In case, reference check is from the previous employer, information in the following area may be obtained. They are job title, job description, period of employment, pay and allowances, benefits provided, rate of absence, etc. Further information regarding candidate's regularity at work, character, past behaviour, progress, ability to do the work, potentiality, his or her performance, etc., can be obtained. A personal visit is superior to the mail and telephone methods and is used where it is highly essential to get detailed information which can be secured by observation. Reference checks are taken as a matter of routine and treated casually or omitted entirely in many organizations.

A survey of 122 private and public organizations revealed that 90 per cent checked the applicant's work references, 84 per cent verified his or her educational background, 28 per cent checked personal references on a regular basis, and only 4 per cent ran regular credit checks. The most common method of checking was a combination of letters and telephone calls. A good reference check when used sincerely, will fetch useful and reliable information to the organization. Reference checking requires the same use of skills as required by the interviewer and some amount of diplomacy. The main difficulty is ascertaining the accuracy of the information given.

**A Sample Reference Form**

---

Mr..............................has applied to us for the post of...............

He claims to have been in your employ from ........... to ........ having had an opportunity to observe the above candidate as an employee your frank answers to the questions on the reverse side of this card will be valuable to us, and would be greatly appreciated. We assure you that your replies will kept strictly confidential.

REVERSE SIDE

1. When was the applicant in your employ? From ........ to ............
2. Positions held.....................................................................
3. Attendance regular? Yes ............ No ........... If not, what was the cause of absence?
4. Liked by his coworkers (well-liked, acceptable, sometimes criticised)?
   .......................................................................
5. Rate of progress (slow, average, above average)? .....................
6. Asked to resign or resigned voluntarily? ................................
7. Would you re-employ him in a similar position? Yes ...............
   No............... If not why?
8. What is your knowledge of the applicant's character, ability and dependability, how? ..................................... what? .......................................................................
9. If you prefer, we shall call you on the Telephone No. ................

---

## 5. Physical/Medical Examination

The step prior to the final "go-no-go" decision may consist of having the applicant take a physical examination. For most jobs, this is a screening device in the selection process. The majority of physical examinations are currently required to meet the minimum standards for the organization's group life and medical insurance programmes and to provide base data in case of future worker's compensation claims. Such jobs as police officer where rigorous, physical qualifications are required, physical examination is carried out to ascertain the physical standards and fitness of prospective employees. The practice of physical examination varies a great deal both in terms of coverage and timings. Certain jobs require unusual stamina, strength or tolerance of hard working conditions. A physical examination reveals whether or not a candidate possesses these qualities. It brings out deficiencies not as a basis for rejection but as a positive aid to selective placement and as indicating restrictions on his transfer to other positions.

Physical examination serves the following purposes:

- It gives us an indication whether a candidate is physically able to perform the job,
- It discovers existing disabilities and obtains a record of the employee's health at the time of hiring, so that the question of the company's responsibilities may be settled in the event a workman's compensation claim for an injury is referred,
- It prevents the employment of those who suffer from some type of disease,

- It helps the right placement of those people who are employable but physically handicaps may necessitate assignment only those specific job,
- The basic purpose of physical examination is to place people in jobs which they can handle without injury or damage to their health,
- Candidates are medically examined by company's physician or by a medical officer approved by the company for the purpose.

**Content:** Usually, a medical check-up involves quick examination of the eyes, acute hearing, throat, tolerance of arduous (hard) working conditions, stamina, clear tone of voice. Heart and lungs may also be thoroughly examined.

Stone and Kendall have outlined the following contents of physical examination.

(a) The applicant's medical history is obtained by interviews between the applicant and the medical officer.

(b) Physical measurements such as height, weight, chest and the abdominal circumferences.

(c) General examination, including an examination of skin, musculature and joints.

(d) Examination of special senses of the applicant-visual and auditory activity to be checked closely.

(e) Clinical examination of eyes, ears, nose, throat and teeth.

(f) Examination of chest and lungs.

(g) Check-up of blood pressure and heart.

(h) Laboratory tests to urine, blood, etc.

(i) X-ray examination of chest, and other parts of the body.

(j) Specialist's test, such as basal metabolic rate or consultation by a specialist.

(k) A neuron-psychiatric examination particularly when medical history or physician observations indicate an adjustment problem.

Another objective of the examination is to protect the company against unwarranted claims under worker's compensation laws, or against law suits for damages.

**Specimen of a Medical Report**

---

Name: .......................................... Age .................................... Sex: ...............................

Address: ........................................................................................................................

General Appearance: .................... Height: .............................. Weight: .........................

Eyes (R): .................................. Ears (R): ...............................................................

(L): .................................. (Hears with) (L): ..................................................

Nose: .......................................... Throat: ..............................................................

Neck: .......................................... Teeth: ...............................................................

Pulse: .......................................... Blood pressure: ...................................................

Chest contour: ........................... Lungs: ..................................................................

Abdomen: .................................... Urine: ....................................................................

Spine: ........................................ Stool: ....................................................................

Blood group: .............................. Skin: .....................................................................

Identification mark: ...............................................................................................

Past medical history: ..............................................................................................

Notes: ....................................................................................................................

Place: ........................................ Date: ..................................

(Signature of the doctor)

---

## 7. Approval by the Appropriate Authority

In executing the personnel unit screening functions, the emphasis tends to be more on formal qualifications and general suitability. At this point in the process, a third interview is conducted. First, the organizational relationship often requires that the supervisor be given the right to pass upon personnel, otherwise he or she cannot be held accountable for their performance. Second, the qualities that are generally appraised in the interview are highly intangible such as personality, ability to get along with others and leadership potential.

On the basis of the above steps, suitable candidates are recommended for selection by the selection committee. For personnel department, though such a committee or personnel department may have authority to select the candidates finally. Often, it has staff authority to recommend the candidates for selection to the appropriate authority. Organizations may designate the various authorities for approval of final selection of candidates for different categories of candidates. The personnel specialists together with line management will now have to weigh the strength and weaknesses of each candidate. Thus, for top level managers, board of directors may be approving authority; for lower levels, even functional heads concerned may be approving authority. For example, in university, it may be syndicate/executive committee. When the approval is received, the candidates are informed about their selection and asked to report for duty to specified persons. When the supervisor takes over, the emphasis tends to switch towards more specifically job-oriented worker characteristics such as training and relevant past experience. He is formally appointed by issuing him an appointment letter or by concluding with him a service agreement. The appointment letter contains the terms and conditions of the employment, policies, duties, responsibilities of applicants, future opportunities, pay scale, and other benefits associated with the job.

## 8. Placement

After selecting a candidate, he should be placed on a suitable job. It involves assigning a specific rank and responsibility to an employment. Most organizations put new recruits on probation for a given period of time (say six months or one year) after which their services are confirmed after successful completion of the probationary period. During this period, they are observed keenly, and when they complete this period successfully, they become the permanent employee of the organization.

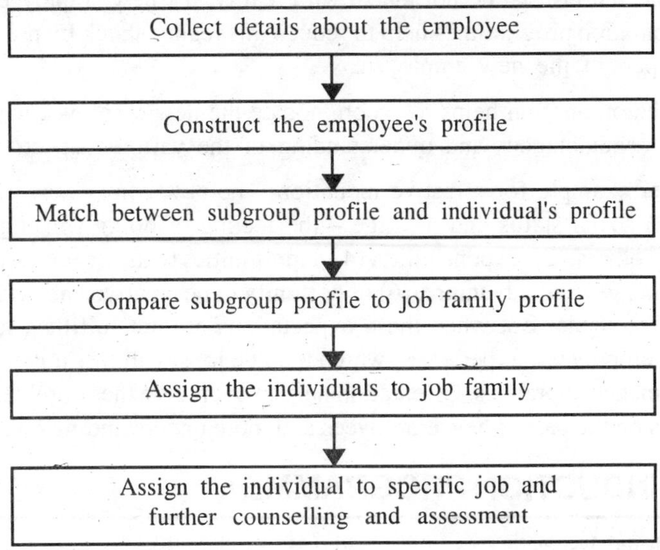


*Fig. 2.2: Employee Placement Process*

Placement is an important HR activity. If neglected, it may create employee adjustment problems leading to absenteeism, turnover, accidents, poor performance, and so on. Proper placement is important to both employee and the organization. Pigors and Myers have defined placement as the determination of the job to which an accepted candidate is to be assigned and his assignment to that job. It is matching of what the supervisor has reason to think he can do with the job demands; it is a matching of what he imposes in terms of strain, working conditions, etc., and what he offers in the form of payroll, companionship with others, promotional possibilities, etc. Proper placement helps to improve employee morale. If a candidate adjusts himself to the job and continuous to perform as per the expectations, it might mean that the candidate is properly placed. However, if the new employee has problems in adjusting himself to the job and he continues to perform below expectations, he might be misplaced. Such new recruits should be assigned some other more suitable jobs or they must be given further training to make them fit for the job.

## 9. Orientation, Induction or Indoctrination

Induction is a technique by which a new employee is rehabilitated into his surroundings and introduced to the practices, policies, rules and regulations, purposes of the organisation. In other words, it is a welcoming process — the idea is to welcome a newcomer, make him feel at home, generate in him a feeling that his own job and to introduce the new employee and the organisation to each other. A formal orientation tries to bridge the information gap of the new employee.

When a new comer joins an organisation, he is a stranger to the people, workplace and work environment. He may feel insecure, shy and nervous. The first few days may be anxious and disturbing ones for him. He may have anxiety caused by not following the usual practices prevalent in the organisation or the haphazard procedures, and lack of information. These may develop discouragement, disillusionment or defensive behaviour. Introduction leads to reduction of such anxieties, dispels the irrational fears of present employees and hold colleagues responsible for assisting the new comer so that he may feel confident. When employee joins an organisation with certain assumptions and expectations that do not match with reality; the new employee experiences a reality shock. Effective orientation programmes help to reduce this reality shock by providing a more realistic expectation on the part of the new employee.

Proper employee orientation helps to accommodate the new employee with existing employees by developing new acquaintances and understanding of the various aspects of the job.

There is another example for effective induction. The new comer may expect: (1) opportunity for advancement, (2) social status and prestige – the feeling of doing something important and the recognition of this by others, (3) responsibility, (4) opportunities to use special aptitude and educational background, (5) challenges and adventure, (6) opportunity to be creative and original, and (7) lucrative salary, and (8) current status. But when these expectations are not fulfilled, it results in frustrating experiences for new employees, experiences which include jobs with low initial challenge, inadequate feedback and performance appraisals. Orientation help to overcome these problems by providing more realistic expectations on the part of new employees and more understanding on the part of supervisors.

## CONTENT OF INDUCTION PROGRAMME

1. Organisational Issues:
   - History of the company
   - Names and title of key executives
   - Employees' title and department
   - Layout of physical activities
   - Products and services offered
   - Medical absence
   - Probationary period
   - Overview of induction process
   - Company policies and rules
   - Disciplinary procedures
   - Safety steps, welfare plans
   - Employees' handbook, material, manuals, house journals, etc.
2. Employee Benefits:
   - Pay scale and pay days
   - Vacations and holidays
   - Rest pause, overtime, hours of work, lunch period, restroom and locker facility
   - Training avenues
   - Counselling
   - Insurance, medical, recreation, and retirement benefits
3. Introductions:
   - To supervisors
   - To coworkers

— To trainers
— To employee counsellors

4. Job or Duties:
— Job location
— Job tasks
— Job safety needs
— Overview of jobs
— Job objectives
— Relationship with other job

## WEIGHTED APPLICATION BLANK, INTERVIEW AND INDUCTION

### Weighted Application Blank

To make the application form more job related, some organization assign numeric values or weights to response provided by applicants. Generally, the items that have a strong relationship to job performance are given high scores. For example, for a medical representative's position, items such as previous selling experience, medical status, age, commission earned on sales previously, etc., may be given high scores when compared to other items such as gender, place of birth, religion, language, etc. Another example to create such a form, individual form items like number of years of schooling, number of previous jobs, number of months on last job, reason for leaving last job, salary increase overall previous job and military experience are validated against performance and turnover measures and given appropriate weights. The total score of each applicant is obtained by summing the weights of the individual item responses. The resulting scores are then used in selection decision. It is best suited for jobs where there are many workers especially for sales and technical jobs and it is particularly useful in reducing turnover. It takes time to develop such a form. Cost of developing a weighted application blank could be prohibitive if the organization has several operating levels with unique features. The WAB must be "updated every few years to ensure that the factors previously identified are still valid predictors of job success". And finally the organization should be careful not to depend on weight of a few items while selecting employees.

Its objectives should be clearly determined. For example, there may be a selection of more stable employees to decrease labour turnover or increase job efficiency. The factors that bring about success may also be taken into account. For this purpose, the varying conditions in an organization should be noted. The blank should be continually updated. Finally, no firm should try to select an employee solely on the basis of one or two important facts.

*Weighted Application Blank for the Post of Secretary*

| Items | Percentage | | Weight |
|---|---|---|---|
| | Short-term | Long-term | |
| **Age** | | | |
| 20 or under | 10 | 0 | 0 |
| 21-25 | 50 | 12 | 4 |
| 26-30 | 20 | 12 | 0 |

| | | | |
|---|---|---|---|
| 31-35 | 20 | 23 | 0 |
| Over 35 | 10 | 53 | 5 |
| **Marital Status** | | | |
| Married | 20 | 47 | 2 |
| Unmarried | 63 | 41 | 1 |
| Widowed | 0 | 0 | 0 |
| Divorced | 10 | 6 | 0 |
| Separated | 7 | 6 | 0 |
| **Education** | | | |
| Attendance grade school | 0 | 0 | 0 |
| Grade school graduate | 0 | 0 | 0 |
| Attended high school | 0 | 12 | 0 |
| High school grade | 33 | 41 | 0 |
| Attended college | 40 | 41 | 0 |
| College graduate | 27 | 6 | 1 |
| Business school | 10 | 29 | 0 |
| **Years on last Job Less than 1** | 50 | 0 | -5 |
| 1 to 1.5 | 7 | 35 | 2 |
| 1.5 to 2.5 | 37 | 12 | -1 |
| 2.5 to 3 | 0 | 6 | 0 |
| More than 3 | 10 | 35 | 2 |
| **Years of Experience** | | | |
| 0 | 3 | 18 | 0 |
| Less than 1 | 20 | 0 | -1 |
| 1 to 2 | 20 | 0 | -1 |
| 2.5 to 3 | 30 | 0 | -3 |
| Over 3 | 27 | 71 | 5 |

## Interview

### Types of Interview

Several types of interviews are commonly used, depending on the nature and the importance of the position to be filled within an organization.

**(i) Patterned or Structured Interview:** It is based on the assumption that, to be more effective, every patient detail bearing on what is to be accomplished, what kind of information is to be sought or given, how the interview is conducted, and how much time is to be allotted to it, must be worked out in advance. Questions would be asked in a particular order, with every little deviation. In the directive interview, the recruiter uses a predetermined set of questions that are clearly job related. Structured questions improve the reliability of the interview process, eliminate biases and errors and may even enhance the ability of a company to withstand legal challenges. On the negative side, the whole process is somewhat mechanical, restricts the freedom of interviewers and may even convey disinterest to applicants who are used to more flexible interviews. Also designing a structured interview may take a good amount of time and energy.

McMurray explains why the patterned interview is likely to improve the judgement of the interviews; *First*, the interviewer works from definite, job specifications; he knows what qualities and each job requires. *Second*, he has a plan, he knows what questions to ask. *Third*, he has been trained in the techniques of conducting an interview, i.e., he knows how to put the candidate at ease, how to make him talk and how to extract pertinent information. *Fourth*, prior to interview, he has checked with outside sources (previous employers, schools, etc.), and already knows a great deal about the applicant. *Fifth*, he has a series of clinical concepts, i.e., that of emotional immaturity — which provides him with a yardstick for interpreting and evaluating the information obtained from the candidate. *Sixth*, the interviewer himself has been carefully selected "to assure that he has adequate intelligence and is emotionally well adjusted".

**(ii) Non-directive Interview:** In a non-directive interview, the recruiter asks questions as they come to mind. And there is no specific format to be followed. The interviewer asks broad, open ended questions such as "tell me more about what you did on your last job" and allows the applicant to talk freely with a minimum interruption and obtaining comparable data on various applicants. In other words, the interview is not directed by questions or comments as to what the candidate should be asked. Generally, the candidate is encouraged to express himself on a variety of subjects, on his expectations and motivations, background and upbringing, interest, political predictions, etc. The interviewer looks for threats of character and nature of his aspirations and his strengths and weakness esmanifest or potential. The purpose of such interview is to determine what kind of person a candidate really is.

**(iii) Situational Interview:** One variation of the structured interview is known as the situational interview. In this interview candidate is asked specific questions about what may happen on a job. The candidate is asked to assess a situation and to provide solutions on how he or she would handle it.

**(iv) Depth or Action Interview:** It is semi-structured in nature and utilities questions in key areas which have been studied in advanced by the interviewer. The typical subjects discussed at such interviews include the candidate's home life, education, previous experience, aptitude, recreational interests, and hobbies. The interviewer provides instructional information about his organization, the nature of work, pay, opportunities for advancement, and demand likely to be made on the employee. The basic objective of this interview is to get a true picture of the interviewee by intensively examining his background and thinking so that a correct evaluation and decision may be made. This type of interviews demands more mature understanding of human behaviour and development therefore, more careful selection of the interviewer.

**(v) Group Discussion Interview:** In this type of interview, the groups are interviewed. The interviewees are given certain problems and are asked to reach a specific decision within a particular time limit. The applicants entered into group discussions, knowing that the interview is a test, but do not know which qualities are being measured or tested. A few observers watch the activities of the interviewees — those who take a lead in the discussion, those who try influencing others, those who summarise and clarify issues, and those who speak effectively the assumptions underlying this type of interview is that "the behaviour displayed in the solution of the problem is related to potential success in the job. The object is to see how well individuals perform on a particular task or in a particular situation." In this type of interview, the emphasis is on the analysis of the interviewers' impressions from discussions rather than factual information.

**(vi) Panel or Board Interview:** In this type of interview, a candidate is interviewed by a number of interviewers. Questions may be asked in turn or asked in random order as they arise on any topic.

**(vii) Stress Interview:** In the stress interview, the interviewer assumes a hostile role toward the applicant. He deliberately puts him on the defensive by trying to annoy, embarrass or frustrate him. The interviewer in such a situation, asks questions rapidly, criticizes the interviewee's answers, interrupts him frequently, keeps the candidate waiting indefinitely and then subjects him to a barrage of interrogations. Questioning whatever he might state, ask too many questions at a time by many interviewers, make derogatory remarks about the candidate or puts him in an awkward situation, e.g., dropping something on the floor and asking him to pick it up, accusing him that he is lying and so on. The purpose is to find out how a candidate behaves in a stress situations – whether he loses his temper or gets confused. Moreover, the stressful interview situations may not necessarily review, how a candidate will behave in real life stressful situations on a job. Yet its judicial application may reveal many characteristics of an applicant.

## Induction

### Induction Procedure

The HR department may initiate the following steps while organizing the induction programme:

- Welcome to the organization.
- Explain about the company.
- Show the location/department where the new recruit will work.
- Give the company's manual to the new recruit.
- Provide details about various workgroups and the extent of unionism within the company.
- Give details about pay, benefits, holidays, leaves, etc., emphasise the importance of attendance or punctuality.
- Explain about future training, opportunities and career prospects.
- Clarify doubts by encouraging the employee to ask questions.
- Take the employee on a guided tour of buildings, facilities, etc., hand him over to his supervisor.

### Techniques or Types of Induction Programmes

**(i) General Induction Programme:** Once an offer of employment has been extended, and accepted, the final stage in procurement function is concluded. The individual has then to be oriented towards the job and the organization. It gives the necessary general information about the history and operations of the firm — the purpose of which is to help an employee to build-up some pride and interest in the organization. Information is also given on specific employee services, such as pension, health and welfare plans, safety programmes, etc. Induction, is a welcoming process, the idea is to welcome the candidate, make him feel at home in the changed surroundings and introduce him to the practices, policies, and purposes of the organizations. The necessity of an induction programme is that when a person joins an organization, he may feel, shy, insecure and nervous, induction helps to reduce such anxieties.

**(ii) Specific Orientation Programme:** Specific orientation is conducted by the foreman. Induction is specific and requires skill on the part of the foreman. A new employee must be pro operational knowledge that is specific to the position and location. The immediate boss is responsible for such induction and training. Every new employee should know:

- The people he or she works with.
- The work he is responsible for..
- The result to be accomplished.
- The current status of the work.
- His relationships with the organizations.
- Reports and records he must understand and maintain.
- Operating policies, procedures and rules.
- The service group available to help him.

The employee is shown the department and his place of work, introduced to other employees inform about the location of the bathrooms, canteens, time clock and told about the organization's specific practices and customs (whether the personnel bring their lunch or whether lunch is supplied to them at concessional rates, the timings and length of rest period, the work dress, etc.). The purpose of specific induction is to enable an employee to adjust himself in his work environment.

**(iii) Follow-up of Induction:** It is done sometime within one week to six months from the time of the initial hiring and orientation. It is conducted either by a foreman or a specialist. Its purpose is to find out whether the employee is reasonably wellsatisfied. The employee may be asked whether his hours of work and his pay are as represented to him before employment; now he feels about his fellow-workers: how he feels about his boss: and whether he has any suggestions to make for changes in the induction procedure or in other company practices. The interviewer records the answers as well as his own comments on the employee's progress. At the same time, the line supervisor completes an evaluation of the employee indicating his strong and weak points, indicating also whether he is doing well.

So by this way, personal talks, guidance and counselling efforts are made to remove the difficulties experienced by the new comer.

## SUMMARY

- With personnel needs projected, the next step is to build a pool of qualified applicants. **Recruitment** is the process of locating and encouraging potential applicants to apply for existing or anticipated job openings. Certain influences restrain (the freedom of) managers while choosing a recruiting source such as: image of company, attractiveness of the job, internal policies, budgetary support, government policies, etc.
- Recruitment is influenced by a variety of environmental factors — economic, social, technological, political, legal, etc.
- The source of recruitment may be broadly divided into two categories: internal sources and external sources. Both have their own merits and demerits.
- A firm may choose a particular recruitment method such as job posting, campus hiring, advertisements, private search firms or internal promotions and transfers, etc., depending upon the skills required the nature of the job and budgetary support, etc.

- Alternatives such as overtime, subcontracting, temporary employees, employee leasing and outsourcing could also be employed to cut down recruiting costs.
- Recruiters these days expect B-school graduates to possess certain special skills such as ability to work in a team, problem-solving, and creativity and communication skills, in addition to strong leadership potential.
- Basing your hiring decision on past performance and behaviours, will result not only in selecting candidates who are the best fit for your organization but also in selecting candidates who will be more likely to stay with your organization on a long-term basis.
- Finding candidates who is the perfect mix of attitude and aptitude can be tough. If you go about the selection process haphazardly, you will never be able to track a successful candidate on board.
- **Selection** is the process of choosing individuals who have relevant qualifications to fill jobs in an organisation. The primary purpose of selection activities is to predict which job applicant will be successful if hired.
- Selection is usually a series of hurdles or steps. Each one must be successfully cleared before the applicant proceeds to the next.
- In this chapter, we will carefully evaluate through initial screening, application, testing, interview, medical and reference checking — must be handled by trained, knowledgeable individuals.
- The application blank is effective for acquiring hard biographical data; the weighted application blank can provide relevant information for predicting job success.
- Selection tests include intelligence and aptitude tests, achievement tests, assessment centres and general psychological or personality tests. The value of tests should not be discounted, since they are objective and offer a broader sampling of behaviour.
- Performance simulation tests require the applicant to engage in specific behaviours that have been demonstrated to be job related. Work sampling and assessment centre receive high marks for their predictive capability.
- The interview is an important source of information about job applicants. Several types of interview are used, depending on the nature and importance of the position to be filled within an organisation. Interview can be conducted by a single individual or by a panel of interviewers who are generally trained for the purpose. The training helps interviewers to be more objective and not get carried away by biases and errors of various kinds.
- Physical examinations are valid when certain physical characteristics are required to be able to perform a job effectively.
- References and medical evaluations are common aspects of the selection process of many employers these days.
- **Recruitment and selection** is a vital function of HR in the organization. Slightest mistake will lead to a square peg in round hole. In the long run, these people would be a liability to their organization. The role of HR manager is very crucial in selecting and recruiting the right kind of people who can be an asset for the company. Instead of following a blind elimination process, focus should be on selecting people based on the skills and competencies required for the job.

## CASELET 1

### Which is More Important — Recruitment or Retaining?

Uptron Electronics Limited, is a pioneering and internationally reputed firm in the Electronics industry. It is one of the largest firms in the country. It attracted employees from internationally reputed institutes and industries by offering high salaries, perks, etc. It has advertised for the positions of an Electronics Engineer recently. Nearly 150 candidates applied for the job. Mr. Sashidhar, an Electronics Engineering Graduate from Indian Institute of Technology with five years working experience in a medium-sized electronics firm, was selected from among the 130 candidates who took tests and interview. The interview board recommended an enhancement in his salary by ₹ 5,000 more than his present salary at his request. Mr. Sashidhar was very happy to achieve this and he was congratulated by a number of people including his previous employer for his brilliant interview performance, and wished him good luck.

Mr. Sashidhar joined Uptron Electronics Ltd., on 21st January, 2002, with great enthusiasm. He also found his job to be quite comfortable and a challenging one and he felt it was highly prestigious to work with this company during the formative years of his career. He found his superiors as well as subordinates to be friendly and cooperative. But this climate did not live long. After one year of his service, he gradually learnt about a number of unpleasant stories about the company, management, the superior-subordinate relations, rate of employee turnover, especially at higher level. But he decided to stay on as he had promised several things to the management in the interview. He wanted to please and change the attitude of management through his diligent performance, firm commitment and dedication. He started maximising his contributions and the management got the impression that Mr. Sashidhar had settled down and will remain in the company.

After sometime, the superiors riding rough-shod over Mr. Sashidhar. He was over-loaded with multifarious jobs. His freedom in deciding and executing was cut down. He was ill-treated on a number of occasions before his subordinates. His colleagues also started assigning their responsibilities to Mr. Sashidhar. Consequently there were imbalances in his family life, social life and organisational life. But he seemed to be calm and contented. Management felt that Mr. Sashidhar had the potential to bear with many more organisational responsibilities.

So the general manager was quite surprised to see the resignation letter of Mr. Sashidhar along with cheque equivalent to a month's salary one fine morning on 18th January, 2004. The general manager failed to convince Mr. Sashidhar to withdraw his resignation. The general manager relieved him on 25th January, 2004. The general manager wanted to appoint a committee to go into the matter immediately, but dropped the idea later.

**Questions:**

1. What prevented the general manager from appointing a committee?
2. Why did Mr. Sashidhar's resignation surprise the general manager?
3. What is wrong in the recruitment part of the company?

## CASELET 2

### "You Call This Selection Interview"

Suresh Kumar was production manager for Singer Industries Limited; a Noida based electrical appliances company near Delhi. Suresh had to approve the hiring of new supervisors in the plant. The HR manager performed the initial screening.

On Friday afternoon, Suresh got a call from Anil Dhavan, Singer's HR director. 'Suresh' Anil said, "I have just talked to a young engineering graduate from a regional engineering college who may be just who you're looking for to fill that supervisor job you asked me about. He has some good work experience in a multinational firm located in Pune, but at a lower salary level. He wants to come over to Noida where his parents live". Suresh replied, "Well, Anilji, I would take care of the boy". Suresh hesitated a moment before replying, "Great Sir, I am certainly busy today but I can't afford to displease you either. Sir, please send him immediately".

A moment later, Ranga Rao, the new applicant arrived at Suresh's office and introduced himself. "Come on in Rao", said Suresh. "I'll be right with you after I make a few urgent phone calls". Fifteen minutes later, Suresh finished the calls and began interviewing Rao. Suresh was quite impressed. The merit certificates, the best suggestion award from previous multinationals firm and Rao's quick responses revealed the candidate's potential. Meanwhile, Suresh's door opened and a supervisor yelled, "We have a small problem on line number 5 and need your help".

"Sure", Suresh replied, "Excuse me a minute, Rao". Fifteen minutes later, Suresh returned and the dialogue continued for another few minutes before a series of phone calls again interrupted him.

The same pattern of interruption continued for the next forty minutes. Rao looked at the watch embarrassedly and said, "I am sorry, Suresh, I have to go now. I have to catch the train to Pune at 9 p.m".

"Sure thing, Rao", Suresh said as the phone rang again. "Call me after a week".

**Questions:**

1. What specific policies might a company follow to avoid interviews like this one?
2. Explain why Suresh and not Anil should make the selection decision?
3. Is it a good policy to pick-up candidates through 'employee referral method'? Why? Or Why not? Explain keeping the case in the background.

## CASELET 3

Optimizing the supply and demand match: putting the right people with the right skills in the right place at the right time.

Matching the supply with the demand for labour has relied on forecasting techniques that examine employer needs and availability of workers. However, workers are not necessarily interchangeable: They bring with them different backgrounds, skills, and interests. Further, the demand for labour with particular skills is shifting all the time. What managers need is a way to allocate labour so that the competencies best match the various demands. Current developments now hold the promise of making this match a reality.

In a new trend, labour is viewed from a supply chain perspective, in which the demands of various customers, projects, or tasks are matched with workers who have the appropriate skills.

For example, the US Department of Defence is working with PeopleSoft (now owned by Oracle) HRM software to develop an integrated system that will cut across all branches of the military. The system will include information about the skills, knowledge, and experiences of all military personnel that the department can immediately access to match available members to various assignments. The plan is to enable the efficient allocation of close to 1.5 million personnel scattered across the world by 2007. The demand of the military can change at a moment's notice, but with the software being developed, the department of defence should be able to allocate the best people to the right place or projects at the right time.

IBM is another example of an organization that has developed software to manage the labour supply chain. The IBM system also catalogues employees' competencies and experiences. It has enabled IBM to reduce the average amount of time its consultants spend with their clients by approximately 4 per cent, because IBM is now able to assign talent that best matches the needs of the client. The system has been so successful that IBM is now marketing it to other businesses.

**Questions:**

1. How does the labour supply chain approach differ from traditional forecasting approaches? Is the labour supply chain preferable? Why or why not?
2. The labour supply chain approach is based on the notion that the best match is of people with the skills and experiences that most closely correspond to the task that needs to be done. Can you think of situations in which this assumption might be false? (For example, innovation might be improved when there is diversity of backgrounds and skill sets that may not best match the tasks)?

## ........ QUESTIONS FOR DISCUSSION

1. When you go looking for a job upon college graduation, what sources do you expect to utilise? Why?
2. How would you help a firm that wants to improve its campus hiring effort?
3. What background information should a recruiter have before beginning to recruit job seekers?
4. If you were responsible for hiring someone for your job, which recruitment source would you use? Why? Which recruitment sources would you avoid? Why?
5. Consider the scenario: you have a vacancy which you know can be filled internally by a suitable candidate related to the Managing Director. Is it ethical to try to encourage the candidate to apply and if so, how would you go about doing so?
6. Interviewing unqualified applicants can be a frustrating experience and a waste of time for managers, peers or whoever is responsible for interviewing. How can the HR department minimize or eliminate this problem?
7. You work for a medium-sized, high tech firm that faces intense competition on a daily basis. Change seems to be the only constant in your workplace, and each worker's responsibilities shift from project to project.
   Suppose you have the major responsibilities for filling the job openings at your company. How would you go about recruiting and selecting the best people? How would you identify the best people to work in this environment?
8. What is weighted application blank? How does one go about the process of setting one up? Is it legal?
9. Should applicants be selected primarily on the basis of ability or on personality/fit? How can fit be assessed?
10. Develop a resume for yourself. Give certain unique achievements that will make employers prefer you over other similar candidates for the post of Management Trainee.

11. If you were interviewing a promising candidate but he seemed nervous, what actions might you consider to calm the candidate?
12. You are starting a new manufacturing company. What phases would you go through to select your employees?
13. Prepare and give a short presentation titled, "How to orient new employees"?
14. What makes you effective when you are speaking before a group of people?
15. In your opinion, which is the most effective way of communicating an idea and persuading peers?
16. What difficulties have been encountered which were caused by overcommunication on your part or on the part of others?
17. Mega Corp. consists of a group of companies which manufacture and market diverse products including textiles, sugar, tyre, and pharmaceuticals. The policy of the group has been to recruit its management trainees from various engineering and management institutes. As an in charge of recruitment, how would you undertake this task?

## Questions for Review

1. What are the advantages and disadvantages of internal sources of recruitment?
2. Discuss some ways by which firms can make campus recruiting more effective.
3. What are the most popular recruiting sources for unskilled jobs? Discuss in detail.
4. What are the most popular recruiting sources for managerial jobs? Explain in detail.
5. Write notes on: (a) Personality tests, (b) Achievement tests, (c) Polygraph, (d) Graphology.
6. Explain the terms "Placement" and "Induction" in detail.

## Objective Questions

### Fill in the Blanks

1. ____________is helpful for adjust to short period fluctuations in personnel needs.
   (a) Deputation (b) Leasing (c) unconsolidated application (d) Professional organization.
2. ____________method of recruitment encourages nepotism.
   (a) Professional organization (b) Employee recommendation
   (c) Computer data bank (d) Casual labour.
3. Most industrial units rely on the ____________which are present daily at the factory gates.
   (a) Deputation (b) Internal recruitment (c) Labour union (d) Casual labour.

*Ans:* **1.** Leasing (b), **2.** Employee recommendations (b), **3.** Casual labours (d)

### Multiple Choice Questions

1. Unconsolidated applications are suitable in such a situation when
   (a) To recruit manual and skilled workers
   (b) Large number of candidate are not available from other source
   (c) An unusual combination of skills are required
   (d) To fill up higher managerial position
2. The most common constraints on recruiting including all but —
   (a) Image of a firm (b) Interviewing
   (c) Organizational policies (d) Government policies
3. The primary source of information for recruiting is:
   (a) Testing (b) Recruiters themselves
   (c) Interviews with applicants (d) Job analysis
4. A good source of hiring technical staff would be:
   (a) Private search firm (b) Vocational school
   (c) Employment exchange (d) Professional organization

5. A negative aspect of promotion from within is:
   (a) Lower morale (b) Employee turnover
   (c) Career prospects (d) Idea stagnation
6. Aptitude test covers:
   (a) Mental, mechanical and psychomotor test (b) Job knowledge and work sample test
   (c) Projective, objective and situation test (d) Interest test
7. An intelligent test covers:
   (a) Mathematical problem-solving ability (b) Job knowledge and work sample test
   (c) Projective and situation test (d) Inductive reasoning and speed of perception
8. Comprehensive interview consists of:
   (a) Review of potentially acceptable candidate (b) Ability to work under pressure
   (c) Investigation of applications (d) Actual hiring decision
9. Ultimately, selection decisions are based on:
   (a) Personal whims and fancies (b) Performance issues
   (c) Turnover potential (d) Human resource plans
10. The most reliable types of interview is:
   (a) Stress (b) Situational
   (c) Structured (d) Panel

*Ans:* **1.** (b), **2.** (b), **3.** (d), **4.** (b), **5.** (d), **6.** (a), **7.** (d), **8.** (b), **9.** (b), **10.** (c)

## Match the Following

| | | |
|---|---|---|
| 1. | 1. Recruiter | (a) Firm publishes job openings on bulletin board |
| | 2. Employee referral | (b) A lateral movement within the same grade |
| | 3. Job posting | (c) Acquire the number of people |
| | 4. Transfer | (d) Recommendation from a current employee. |
| 2. | 1. Employee leasing | (a) Evaluate employee potential by multiple types of groups |
| | 2. Walk-ins | (b) Hiring permanent employee from another firm |
| | 3. Search firm | (c) Casual unsolicited applicants |
| | 4. Assessment centre | (d) A private employment agency |
| 3. | 1. Test | (a) Perform a small portion of the job |
| | 2. Work sampling | (b) Indepth conversation |
| | 3. Selection interview | (c) Actual posting |
| | 4. Placement | (d) Measure of a person's behaviour or attitude. |

*Ans:* **1.** (1. c) (2. d) (3. a) (4. b), **2.** (1. b) (2. c) (3. d) (4. a), **3.** (1. d) (2. a) (3. b) (4. c)

## True or False

1. Hiring of blood relation in the organisation encourages nepotism.
2. Internal recruitment can be used as a technique of motivation.
3. Casual applicants as an external sources are suitable for higher level jobs.
4. The recruitment process begins with human resource planning and concludes with evaluation of recruiting efforts.
5. Recruitment is a mere vacancy-filling function.
6. Employment exchanges are important sources of clerical and managerial personnel.
7. In practice, recruitment methods seem to vary according to job level and skill.
8. Hiring costs could go up substantially when a firm hires candidates from within.

9. The basic source of information for recruiting is recruiters themselves.
10. Personality test is used to measure the candidates' level of knowledge and skill in a particular job.
11. Test often doesn't reflect on individual's true ability.
12. Interviews are one of the most reliable selection devices.
13. The most reliable type of interview is structured.
14. Ultimately, selection decisions are based on job performance issues.
15. Internal selection is based on data from job applicants.
16. Most benefits of orientation are due to reducing anxiety.
17. Orientation has a long-term benefit to the organisation.
18. Most organisations put new recruits on probation for a given period of time.
19. Good orientation programmes still require follow-up.
20. One advantage of seniority based promotions is that they are based on performance.
21. A transfer implies an ascending or descending change in status or responsibility.

*Ans:* **1.** True, **2.** True, **3.** False, **4.** True, **5.** False, **6.** False, **7.** True, **8.** False, **9.** False, **10.** False, **11.** True, **12.** True, **13.** True, **14.** True, **15.** False, **16.** True, **17.** False, **18.** True, **19.** True, **20.** False, **21.** False.

## Selection Diagram

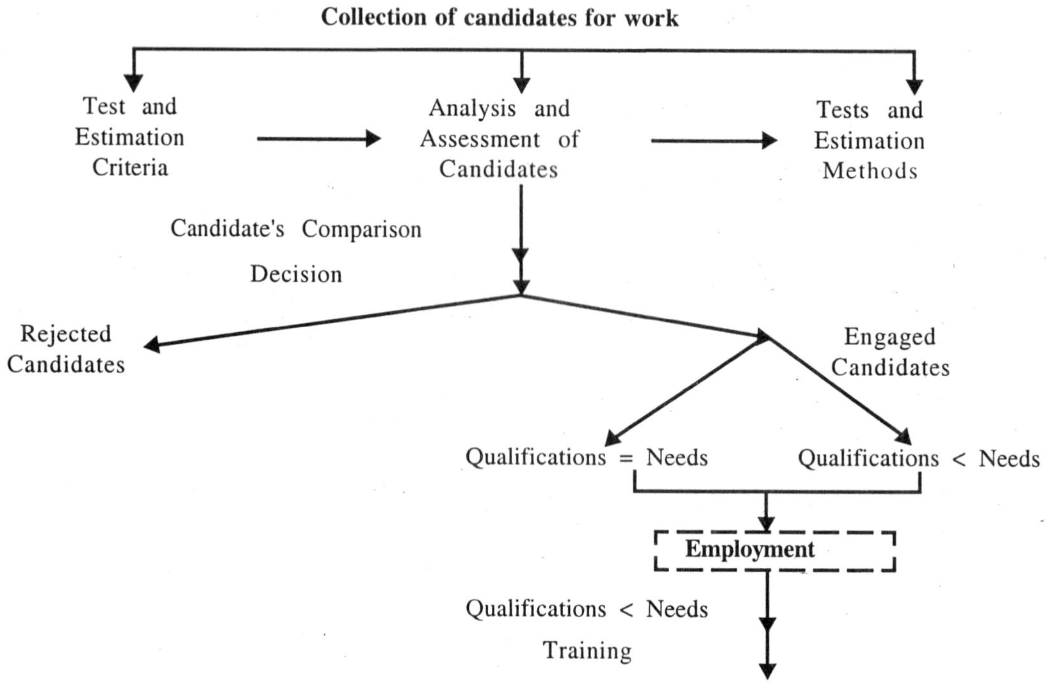


☺ ☺ ☺

CHAPTER 3

# Training and Development

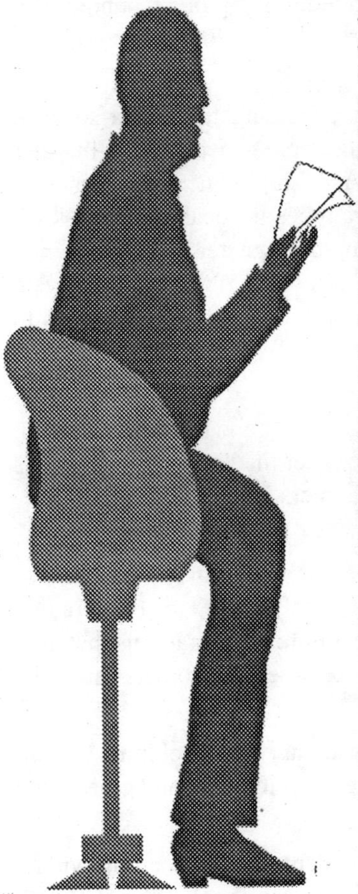

## LEARNING OBJECTIVES

- *Meaning and Definition of Training.*
- *Identify the Needs for Training.*
- *Advantages or Importance of Training.*
- *Objectives or Purposes of Training.*
- *The Various Training Methods that are Currently Employed.*
- *Meaning and Definition of Management Development.*
- *Discuss the Various Methods of Developing Managers.*
- *Difference between Training and Management Development.*

## INTRODUCTION TO TRAINING

After the employee has been recruited, selected, and inducted, he or she must next be developed to fit in the job and the organization. Training is a procedure of learning a series of programmed behaviour. To be able to achieve competitive growth, an organization needs to develop its manpower. Possessing knowledge and putting it into effective use are two different things. It is essential to help in developing skills and updating knowledge. Especially in a cut-throat competitive world, an organization must commit resources in employee training and development if it has to maintain a viable and knowledgeable workforce. Nowadays, training have an additional purpose of facilitating change. India, through a developing country, spends $ 50 billion on training each year, whereas wealthy USA spends nearly twice as much. Expenditures of such magnitude call for a periodic sharp look especially since organizations are expanding fast and there is a growing demand for finding benefits commensurate with the escalating costs of training. It provides skills and abilities that may be called on in the future to satisfy the organization's human resources needs. Inadequate job performance or a decline in productivity or changes resulting out of job redesigning or a technological breakthrough requires some type of training and development efforts. As the jobs become more complex, the importance of employee development also increases.

In 1964, The Economic Opportunity Act was directed towards providing training assistance for young entrants in the job market. In 1973, because of the confusion generated by literally thousands of publicly financed training programmes, the comprehensive Employment and Training Act was passed. Its objective was to decentralise the control of programmes to local and state level and to focus most funds on assisting the unskilled and long-term unemployed. After an experimental programme in the late 1970s, the Job Training Partnership Act of 1982 allocated $ 3 billion to private industry councils to implement training for the hardcore unemployed and attention will be given to developing skills that lead to long-term employment.

Planned development programmes will return values to the organizations in terms of increased productivity, heightened morale, reduced cost and greater organizational stability and flexibility to adapt to changing external environments. Such programmes will also help to meet the needs of individuals in their search for work assignments that can add up to life long careers.

What today's and tomorrow's training programmes must focus on, are soft-skills such as interpersonal communication, teamwork, innovation and leadership. Most importantly, the training has to be comprehensive, systematic and continuous and should be closely linked to the strategy with which the company is planning to fight the competition. In the future, it is training that will act as catalyst between people, between strategy and systems, between customers and the organization.

Training can help the organization to meet the challenges. It is necessary for developing overall personality. Expenditure on such training is an investment for manpower development and gives good dividend in the long run. It will increase employee's efficiency.

Training is a learning experience in that it seeks a relatively permanent change in an individual that will improve his or her ability to perform on the job. We say training can involve the changing of skills, knowledge, attitudes or social behaviour. It may mean changing what employees know, how they work, their attitudes towards their work, or their interactions with their coworkers or their supervisor. For example, new equipment may require workers to learn new ways of doing the job or a worker may have a deficient understanding of a work process. In both cases, training can be used to correct the skill deficit.

## Definition

According to Flippo, "Training is the act of increasing the knowledge and skills of an employee for doing a particular job".

## Needs for Training

After employees have been selected for various positions in an organisation, training them for the specific tasks to which they have been assigned assumes great importance. It is true in many organisations that before an employee is fitted into a harmonious working relationship with other employees, he is given adequate training. Training is the act of increasing the knowledge and skills of an employee for performing a particular job. The major outcome of training is learning. A trainee learns new habits, refined skills and useful knowledge during the training that helps him improve performance. Training enables an employee to do his present job more efficiently and prepare himself for a higher level job. Training is needed to serve the following purposes —

- Newly recruited employees require training so as to perform their tasks effectively and efficiently. Instructions, guidance, coaching help them to handle jobs competently without any wastage.
- Training is necessary to prepare existing employees for higher level jobs (promotion).
- Existing employees require refresher training so as to keep abreast of the latest developments in the job operations. In the phase of rapid technological changes, this is an absolute necessity.
- Instruction can help employees increase their level of performance on their present assignment. Increased human performance often directly leads to increased operational productivity and increased company profit.
- Better performing workers are less likely to make operational mistakes. Quality increases may be in relationship to a company product or services or in reference to the intangible organisational employment atmosphere.
- Training is necessary when a person moves from one job to another (transfer). After training, the employee can change jobs quickly, improve his performance levels and achieve career goals comfortably.
- Organisations that have a good internal educational programme will have to make less drastic manpower changes and adjustments in the event of sudden personnel alterations. When the need arises, organizational vacancies can be more easily staffed from internal sources, if a company initiates and maintains an adequate instructional programme for both its non-supervisory and managerial employees. So it will help company to fulfil its future personnel needs.
- Training is necessary to make employees mobile and versatile. They can be placed on various jobs depending on organizational needs.
- Training is needed to bridge the gap between what the employees have and what the job demands. Training is needed to make employees more productive and useful in the long run.
- An endless chain of positive reactions results from a well planned training programme. Production and product quality may improve, financial incentives may then be increased, there is a boost for internal promotions, less supervisory pressure and base pay rate

increases result. Increased morale may be due to many factors but one of them is current state of an organization's educational endeavour. Thus, it will improve overall organizational climate.

- Proper training can help to prevent industrial accidents. A safer work environment leads to more stable mental attitudes on the part of employees. Managerial mental state would also improve if supervisors know that they can better themselves through company designed development programmes. So it improves health and safety.
- Training and development programmes foster the initiative and creativity of employees and help to prevent manpower obsolescence, which may be due to age or temperament or motivation or the inability of a person to adapt him to technological changes.
- On a personal basis employees gain individually from their exposure to educational experiences. Again management development programmes seem to give participants a wider awareness, an enlarged skill and enlightened altruistic (kindness) philosophy and enhance personal growth.
- Training is needed for employees to gain acceptance from peers. (learning a job quickly and being able to pull their own weight is one of the best ways for them to gain acceptance).

### Advantages or Importance of Training

Training is the cornerstone of sound management, for it makes employees more effective and productive. It is actively and intimately connected with all the personnel or managerial activities. It is an integral part of the whole management programme, with all its many activities functionally inter-related.

There is an ever present need for training people so that new and changed techniques may be taken advantage of and improvements made (implemented) in the old methods, which are woefully inefficient.

The employee training in an organization has been emphasized because of the following advantages:

- Building a more efficient, effective and highly **motivated team** which **enhances the company's competitive positions.**
- Creating a pool of readily available and **adequate replacements for personnel** who may leave or move up in the organization.
- **Enhancing the company's ability** to adopt and use advances in technology because of a highly knowledgeable staff.
- Employees frequently develop a **greater sense of self-worth, dignity and well-being** as they become more valuable to the firm and to the society. They will receive **a greater share of the material gains** that result from their **increased productivity**. These factors give them a sense of satisfaction through the achievement of personal and company goals.
- Training **raises the efficiency, effectiveness and productivity** with minimum efforts. It also improves the performance of workers due to their motivation.
- It usually leads to **an increase in quality and quantity** of output by putting the materials, tools and equipment to optimum use.
- It helps management in **facing the challenges** of a changing environment.

- It **reduces accidents** as trained employees work systematically and avoid mistakes in the work assigned.
- Training **reduces expenditure on supervision** as trained employees take interest in the work and need limited supervision and control. Hence, trained workers need not be put under close supervision and they know how to handle operations efficiently.
- A **satisfactory organizational structure** is build-up.
- Training leads to **job satisfaction and higher morale** of the employee, for it helps in reducing dissatisfaction, complains and grievances.
- Trained workers help an organization **to face competition from rival organization.**
- Training **creates skilled and efficient manpower** which is an asset to an industrial unit.
- Training **helps employees in developing and growing** within the organization and **increasing their capacity of earning and job security**.
- Training **moulds attitude of employees** and develops cordial industrial relations and **become loyal** to the organizations. They will be less inclined to leave the unit where there are growth opportunities.
- Training results in employees making **better economic use of equipment and materials** thereby **reducing wastages and spoilage**. These **reduce cost of production and improve quality (superior performance).**
- Training helps workers in better job adjustment and interest in job and they prefer to remain present on all working days and thus **reduce the rate of absenteeism and labour turnover** and bring stability to labour force.
- It facilitates the **introduction of new management techniques** and also new production techniques including automation and computer technology.
- Training **creates a pool of trained and capable personnel** from which, replacements can be drawn to fill up the loss of key personnel due to retirement.
- Training **provides proper guidance and instructions** to newly appointed employees and assists them to adjust well with the job and the organization.
- Training makes an employee more useful to a firm. Hence, he will **find employment more easily**.
- Training creates a **feeling of confidence** among the employees. It gives them **personal safety and security** at the workplace.
- It **develops skills** which act as valuable personal assets of employees.
- Training enables employees to **secure promotions easily** and **opportunity to quick self-development**. They can realise their career goals comfortably.
- Training provides **attractive remuneration** and **other monetary benefits** to employees.
- Training **develops adaptability** among employees; **it updates their knowledge and skills.** It actually refreshes the mental outlook of employees.
- It **develops positive attitude towards work** assigned and thereby creates interests and attraction for the job and the workplace.

- Training creates **an attitude of mutual cooperation and understanding** among the workers and managers. Such attitude is useful not only at the workplace but also in the social life.

Thus, training can contribute to higher production, fewer mistakes, greater job satisfaction and lower labour turnover. It can enable employees to cope with organizational, social and technological change. Effective training is an invaluable investment in the human resources of an organization.

## Objectives or Purposes of Training

The overall objective of the training programme is designed to solve the problem. For example, Wyeth, pharmaceutical company, focuses its training on separate sets of companies for sales employees, and for managers. Training is the application of the knowledge. It makes people aware of the rules and procedures for guiding their behaviour. It attempts the improvement of their performance in the present job or prepares them for a future job. Training objectives are laid down keeping in view the company's goals and objectives. According to Edwin D. Flippo, "The purpose of training is to achieve a change in the behaviour of those trained and to enable them to do their jobs better". For achieving this objective, a training programme should try to bring positive change in:

- To impart to new entrants the basic **knowledge**, which helps a trainee in knowing the policies, facts, procedures and rules related to his job and enable them to perform their jobs well.
- **Skills**, which help a trainee in increasing his technical and manual efficiency necessary in doing in his job and to teach the employees new techniques and ways of performing the job or operations. It may suggest that skills need to be "fine-tuned".
- **Attitude**, which moulds a trainee's behaviour towards his supervisors and coworkers and creates a sense of responsibility in the trainee.
- To **equip the employee** to meet the changing requirements of the job and the organization.
- To **prepare employees** for higher level tasks and build-up a second line of competent managers.
- To broaden the minds of senior managers by **providing** them with **opportunities for an interchange of experiences** with others with a view to correcting the narrowness of the outlook that may arise from over specialisation.
- To impart customer education for the purpose of meeting the training needs of corporations which deal mainly with the public. For example, Hindustan Steel Ltd., Gujarat State Road Transport Corporation, Heavy Electrical, Gujarat State Fertilizer Corporation, Western Railway, All India State Road Transport Corporation, and B.E.S. & T. Mumbai.
- To **raise efficiency and productivity** of employees and the organization as a whole.
- To **create a pool of well trained, capable and loyal employees** at all levels and thereby to make arrangement to meet the future needs of an organization.
- To **provide opportunities of growth and self-development** to employees and thereby to motivate them for promotion and other monetary benefits. In addition, to give safety and security to the life and health of employees.
- To **avoid accidents and wastages** of all kinds. In addition, to develop balanced, healthy and safety attitudes among the employees.

- To **meet the challenges** posed by new developments in science and technology.
- To **improve the quality of production** and thereby to create market demand and reputation in the business world.
- To **develop cordial labour-management relations** and thereby to improve the organizational environment.
- To **develop positive attitude and behaviour pattern** required by an employee to perform a job efficiently. In other words, to improve the culture of the organization.
- To **prevent manpower obsolescence** in an organization.
- To **develop certain personal qualities** among employees which can serve as personal assets on long-term basis.
- It **improves administrative capability** for development involves the ability to mobilize, allocate and combine actions that are technically needed to achieve organizational objectives.

## TRAINING METHODS

It is difficult, if not impossible; to say which combination of methods is more useful than the other. The best technique for one situation may not be best for different groups or tasks. Care must be taken in adopting the method to the learner and job. An effective training technique fulfils these objectives; provides motivation to the trainee to improve job performance, develop a willingness to change, provide for the trainee's active participation in the learning process, provide a knowledge of results about attempts to improve (i.e., feedback), and permit practice where appropriate. There are mainly two kinds of training methods, i.e., on-the-job training and off-the-job training.

### On-the-job Training

Training can be carried out either on-the-job or off-the-job. In the very common on-the-job training approach, the trainee works in the actual work setting, usually under the guidance of an experienced worker, supervisor, or trainer. It is basically "Learning by doing while working". Training is imparted to employees while they perform their regular jobs. After a plan is developed for training, employees should be informed of the details. An experienced employee will act as a friend, philosopher and guide. The new employee follows the orders, carries out instructions and adopts the right technique while doing the job. In this way, he is able to learn the work practically. While doing so, he can ask questions, seek clarifications on various job-related matters and obtain guidance from his senior employees. A timetable should also be prepared with periodic evaluations to inform employees about their progress. On-the-job training include coaching, job instruction training, apprenticeships, job rotation, etc.

**1. On-the-job Training:** Virtually, every employee, from the clerk to company president gets some on-the-job training, when he joins a firm. That is why William call it, "The most common, the most widely used and accepted and the most necessary method of training employees in the skills essential for acceptable job performance. Trainees earn as they learn under the watchful eyes of a master mechanic or craftsman, receive immediate feedback and practice in the actual work environment. It is associated with the same people they will work with after training. Under this technique, an employee is placed in a new job and is told how it may be performed. It is primarily concerned with developing in an employee's skills and habits consistent with the existing practices of an organization and orienting him to his immediate problems. It is mostly given to unskilled and semi-skilled jobs-clerical and sales jobs.

Employees are coached and instructed by skilled coworkers, by supervisors, by special training instructors. They learn the job by personal observation and practice as well as occasionally handling it. It is learning by doing and most useful for jobs that are either difficult to stimulate or can be learned quickly by watching and doing. There is variety of OJT methods such as "Coaching" or "Understudy", "Job rotation" and "special assignments". Under coaching or understudy method, (which is also known as internship and apprenticeship methods) the employee is trained on-the-job by his immediate superior. "Internship" is usually applied to managerial personnel and provides wide variety of job experience, often involving job rotation, or an "assistant to" type of position. Internships or assistantships are usually a combination of classroom and on-the-job training and are often used to train prospective managers or marketing personnel. "Apprenticeship" is generally used to impart skills requiring long periods of practice as found in trade, crafts, and other technical fields. In "job rotation", a management trainee is made to move from job-to-job at certain intervals. "Special assignments or committees" are other methods used to provide lower level executives with firsthand experience in working with actual problems. Executives from various functional areas serve on "boards" and are required to analyze problems and recommend solutions to top management. On-the-job training is made more effective by the use of variety of training aids and techniques such as charts, lecture manuals, sample problems, demonstrations, tape recorders, oral and written explanation and other aids.

Training procedure involves following steps:

1. Instructor preparation,
2. Trainee preparation,
3. Present the task,
4. Try out performance,
5. Follow-up.

***Merits:*** The first advantage of on-the-job training is that the trainee learns on the actual equipment in use and in the true environment of his job. He gets a feel of the actual production conditions and requirements. In this way, a transfer from a training centre or school to the actual production conditions following the training period is allowed. Secondly, it is highly economical since no additional personnel or facilities are required for training. Thirdly, the trainee learns the rules, regulations and procedures by observing their day-to-day applications. He can, therefore, be easily evaluated by the management. Fourthly, this type of training is suitable alternative for a company in which there are almost as many jobs as there are employees. The fifth advantage is that, it has the advantage of strongly motivating the trainee to learn since it is not located in the artificial situation of a classroom. Finally, it is most appropriate for teaching the knowledge and skills which can be acquired in a relatively short period, say a few days or weeks.

***Demerits:*** The principle disadvantage of on-the-job training is that, instruction is often highly disorganized and haphazard. This is due to reasons such as the inability of the experienced employee to impart skills to the trainee, the break down of the job for the purpose of instructions and the lack of motivation on the part of the trainee to receive training. Moreover, learners are often subjected to distractions of a noisy shop or office. Further, the other demerit is the low productivity, especially when the employee is unable to fully develop his skills.

**2. Job Instruction Training:** The JIT method (developed during II World War) is a four-step instructional process involving preparation, presentation, performance try out, and follows-up. It is used primarily to teach workers how to do their current jobs. A trainer, supervisor or coworker acts as the coach. This method is very popular in the states for preparing supervisors to train operatives. The JIT method requires skilled trainers, extensive job analysis, training schedule and prior assessment of the trainee's job knowledge. This method is also known as "training through step-by-step learning". It involves listing all necessary steps in the job, each in proper sequence. This steps show what is to be done, how it is to be done and when it is to be done.

The actual training follows a four steps process, beginning with: *First*, the preparation of the trainee for instruction. This includes putting him at ease, emphasizing the importance of the task and giving a general description of job duties and responsibilities. *Second*, the preparation of the instructions, giving essential information in a clear manner. This includes positioning the trainee at work site, telling and showing him each step of the job, stressing why and how each step is carried out as it is shown. *Third*, having the trainee try out the job to show that he has understood the instructions. If there are any errors, they are corrected and *fourth*, encouraging questions and allowing the trainee to work along and the trainer follows-up regularly.

The JIT method provides immediate feedback on results, quick correction of errors, and provision of extra practice when required. However, it demands a skilled trainer and can interfere with production and quality.

***Merits:***

1. Trainee learns fast through practice and observation.
2. It is economical as it does not require any special settings. Also mistakes can be corrected immediately.
3. It is mostly suitable for unskilled and semi-skilled jobs where the job operations are simple, easy to explain and demonstrate within a short span of time.
4. The trainee gains confidence quickly as he does the work himself in actual setting with the help from supervisor.

***Demerits:***

1. The trainee should be as good as the trainer. If the trainer is not good, transference of knowledge and skills will be poor.
2. Experienced workers cannot use the machinery while it is being used for training.
3. While learning, trainee may damage equipment, waste materials, and cause accidents frequently.

**3. Vestibule Training:** The concept of vestibule school or training centre is that, people will learn and develop skills while working in the situations similar to what they will face after they are put on the actual job. In this method, actual work conditions are simulated in a classroom. This method attempts to duplicate on-the-job situations in a company classsroom. It is imparted with the help of equipment and machines which are identical to those in use in the place of work. This technique enables the trainee to concentrate on learning the new skills rather than on performing an actual job. This system sometimes creates critical line staff difficulties. Theoretical training is given in the class-room, while the practical work is conducted on the production line. It is very efficient method of training semi-skilled personnel, particularly when many employees have to be trained for the same kind of work at the same time. It is often used to train clerks, bank tellers, inspectors, machine operators, testers, typists, etc., it is most useful when philosophic concepts, attitudes, theories and problems solving abilities have to be learnt. Training is generally given in the form of lectures, conferences, case studies, role playing and discussion.

*Merits:*

1. As training is given in a separate room, distractions are minimised.
2. A trained instructor who knows how to teach can be more effectively utilised.
3. The correct method can be taught without interrupting production.
4. It permits the trainee to practice without the fear of supervisors, coworkers, observation and their possible ridicule (to laugh at).
5. Since, the training is away from the actual production process, it is not affected by the training process.

*Demerits:*

1. The splitting of responsibilities leads to organizational problems.
2. An additional investment in equipment is necessary, though the cost may be reduced by getting some productive work done by trainees while in the school.
3. This method is of limited value for the jobs which utilise equipment which can be duplicated.
4. The training situation is somewhat artificial.

However, this method of training can be adopted only when there are large numbers of trainees because it requires additional investments for creating training facilities. This method is suitable for those employees who are required certain specific technical skills before they are engaged in actual operations

**4. Training by Experienced Workmen:** By this method, training is imparted by experienced senior fellow-workers. It is particularly adaptable where experienced workmen need helpers. It is useful for departments in which workmen advance through successive jobs to perform a series of operations.

**5. Training by Supervisors:** Such training is imparted on the job by the workers immediate supervisors. It provides to the trainees opportunities for getting acquainted with their bosses. The bosses too, have an opportunity to judge the abilities and potential of trainees from the point of view of their job performance.

The success of both these methods depends upon the fact that:

(a) The experienced supervisors must be good teachers;

(b) They should have incentives and sufficient time for carrying out the training programmes; and

(c) They should be provided with an accurate account of the training needs of the trainees they are to teach.

**6. Demonstrations and Examples (Learning by Seeing):** In the demonstration method, the trainer describes and displays the job as when he teaches an employee how to do the job by actually performing the activity himself and by going through a step-by-step explanation of "why" and "what" he is doing.

Teaching by example is effective in mechanical operations or interpersonal relationships, for job duties and responsibilities, for informal group standards, supervisory expectations, and the like.

Demonstrations are very effective in teaching because it is much easier to show a person how to do a job than to tell him or ask him to gather instruction from the reading material. Demonstrations are often used in combination with lectures, pictures, text materials, discussions, etc.

Demonstrations are particularly effective in the training for the acquisition of skills; but their usefulness is limited when it is a question of training management personnel. In a demonstration, the emphasis is primarily on know-how, the principles and theory of a job must, therefore, be taught by some other method.

**7. Simulation:** Any training activity that explicitly places the trainee in an artificial environment that closely mirrors actual working conditions can be considered a simulation. Simulation activities include case exercises, experiential exercises, complex computer modelling, and vestibule training. Case present an in-depth description of a particular problem an employee might encounter on the job. Experiential exercises are usually short, structured learning experiences where individual learn by doing. It could be used to create a conflict situation where employees have to experience a conflict personally and workout its resolution. Computer modelling simulates the work environment by programming a computer to imitate some of the realities of the job. And in the vestibule training, employees learn their jobs on the equipment they will be using but the training is conducted away from the actual work floor.

Simulation techniques have been most widely used in the aeronautical industry. It is a mock-up real thing. Trainee interest and employee motivation are both high in simulation exercise because the actions of a trainee closely duplicate real job conditions. This training is essential, in cases in which actual on-the-job practice might result in a serious inquiry, a costly error, or the destruction of valuable materials or resources. It is for this reason that the technique is a very expensive one. It involves a particular procedure, simulated learning involves the following:

(a) In simulation, essential characteristics of a real-life situation are presented in an abstract form as whole characteristics are difficult to be simulated.

(b) A simulation often involves a telescopic, or compressing of time events; a single session may be equated with a month or many months of real-time situations. Further, the events and situations may be presented in brief, leaving out many details.

(c) Participants in the training programme are required to do according to the situation prescribed and to see the problem from the perspectives of various roles given in the situations.

(d) The role of instructor is quite restricted to allow the trainees to participate fully.

(e) After the exercise war, the instructor provides the feedback to the participants to evaluate themselves and to strengthen themselves by overcoming their weak points.

The trainee aids to develop diagnostic and decision making skills.

**8. Apprenticeship:** This includes decisions concerning course content, means of instruction and examination and allocation of time between organised group instruction and work on the job.

The Civil Right Act of 1964 specifically prohibits discrimination in all phases of employment including training. Apprenticeship programmes are available in a number of crafts such as mechanists, electricians, pipe fitters, welders, tinners, carpenters, and millwrights. For training in crafts, trades and in technical areas, apprenticeship training is the oldest and most commonly used method, especially when proficiency in a job is the result of relatively long training period of two years to tree years for persons of superior ability and from four years to five years for others. The field in which apprenticeship training is offered are numerous and range from the job of a draughtsman, a machinist, a printer, a tool-maker, a pattern designer, a mechanic, carpenters, weavers, tailor, bricklayers, iron workers, fitters, jewellers, die-sinkers, engravers, and electricians. A major part of training time is spending on the job productive work. Each apprentice is given a programme of assignments according to a predetermined schedule, which provides for efficient training in trade skills. In India, the Apprentices Act, 1961 (amended in 1973) makes it obligatory on the part of all employers in the specified industries to place apprentices in the designed trades in terms of standard laid down.The apprenticeship involves basic on-the-job training with related instructions embracing the entire period of training. During this period, each trainee is paid certain amount of stipend as stipulated in the Act.

Assistantships and internships are similar to apprenticeship because they also demand high levels of participation from the trainee. An internship is a kind of on-the-job training that usually combines job training with classroom instruction in trade schools, colleges or universities. Coaching is similar to apprenticeship because the coach attempts to provide a model for the trainee to copy.

***Merits:***

1. A skilled blue collar workforce is maintained.
2. Immediate returns can be expected from training.
3. The workmanship is good.
4. The hiring costs are lower because of reduced turnover and lower production costs.
5. The loyalty of employees is increased and opportunities for growth are frequent.
6. The organization can build a pool of technically trained personnel.
7. Apprenticeship programmes employ many of the principles of learning such as modelling, feedback, classroom training, etc., and are often quite effective.

***Demerits:***

1. Apprenticeship training include the period of training at which the employees are under paid may be quite long.
2. The uniform period of training is not suitable to all.
3. People have different abilities and learn at varied rates. Those who learn fast may quit the programme in frustration. Slow learners may require additional training time.
4. It is also likely that in these days of rapid changes in technology, old skills may get outdated quickly. Trainees who spend years learning specific skills may find, upon completion of their programmes that the job skills that they acquired are no longer required in the market.

**9. Job Rotation:** Job rotation is the process of training employees by rotating them through series of related tasks. This kind of training involves the movement of trainee from one job to another.

This helps him to have a general understanding of how the organisation functions. The purpose of job rotation is to provide trainees with a larger organisational perspective and a greater understanding of different functional areas as well as better sense of their own career objectives and interests. Apart from relieving boredom, job rotation allows trainees to build rapport with a wide range of individuals within the organization, facilitating future cooperation among departments. The cross-trained personnel offer a great amount of flexibility for organisation when transfers, promotions or replacements become inevitable. Job rotation is more broadly trained and skilled workforce for the employer. The job rotation has one main advantage; it makes flexibility possible in the department. For instance, when one employee of a work unit is absent, another employee can perform his job.

***Merits:***

1. It improves participant's job skills and job satisfaction.
2. It provides valuable opportunities to network within the organization.
3. It offers faster promotions and higher salaries to quick learners.
4. Lateral transfers may be beneficial in rekindling enthusiasm and developing new talents.

***Demerits:***

1. It increase workload for participants.
2. Constant job change may produce stress and anxiety.
3. Mere multiplication of duties does not enrich the life of a trainee. That is, it is very difficult to coordinate various assignments such as production, finance, marketing, etc.
4. Training costs may shoot up when trainees commit mistakes, handle tasks less optimally.
5. Some of the coaches may not be motivated to concentrate on trainees assigned only for short period.
6. Different coaches may espouse conflicting view points of company's policy and procedures.

**10. Coaching:** Coaching is a kind of daily training and feedback given to employees by immediate supervisors. It involves a continuous process of learning by doing. It may be defined as an informal, unplanned training and development activity provided by supervisors and peers. In coaching, the supervisor explains things and answers questions; he throws light on why things are done the way they are; he offers a model for trainee to copy; conducts lot of decision making meeting with trainees; procedures are agreed upon and the trainee is given enough authority to make decisions and even commit mistakes. Of course, coaching can be a taxing job in that the coach may not possess requisite skills to guide the learner in a systematic way. Sometimes, doing a full day's work may be more important than putting the learner on track.

When to use coaching usefully? Coaching could be put to use when:

- An employee demonstrates a new competency.
- An employee expresses interest in a different job within the organisation.
- An employee seeks feedback.
- An employee is expressing low morale, violating company policies or practices or having performance problems.
- An employee needs help with new skills following a formal training programme.

- Effective working, obviously, requires patience and communication skills. It involves:
- Explaining appropriate ways of doing things.
- Making clear why actions were taken.
- Starting observations accurately.
- Offering possible alternatives/suggestions.
- Following up.

**11. Special Courses:** Rapid changes in technology may force companies to go in for this kind of training. By organising short-term courses which incorporate the latest developments in a particular field, the company may keep its employees up to date and ready to take on emerging challenges. It is conducted at regular intervals by taking the help of outside consultants who specialise in a particular discipline. The teaching machine, a device originated by Sidney L. Pressey of Ohio State University in 1924, has become a popular technique in the past two decades. Programmed learning has been used in a number of ways, as in a textbook. But its adaptation to a machine has stimulated more widespread use. Advantages to trainee are that one can select a personal pace of learning, go back over materials when desired, and use the machine when it convenient. A slow learner will be forced to go through every portion in the programme, while correct responses by fast learners will permit more rapid completion. This method of instruction utilizes the basic learning concepts of: (1) establishing explicit goals, (2) breaking the subject into bits of logically sequenced knowledge, (3) requiring an active role on the part of the learner, (4) making learner self-pacing possible, and (5) providing immediate reinforcement of learning through feedback of results.

Concerning the relative effectiveness of programmed learning as compared with other more conventional methods, attention can be allocated to three factors: saving in learning time amounts of immediate learning, and long-term retention. A survey of over 150 studies reveals that programmed instructions are clearly superior in only the first factor, learning time. On the average, the time saved was approximately one-third of that normally taken by competitive methods. Time saved issues largely from individual flexibility in establishing one's own pace. In a survey of 193 films, 20 per cent used some form of programmed instruction.

**12. Orientation Training:** Orientation or induction training tries to put the new recruits at ease. Each new employee is usually taken on a formal tour of the facilities, introduced to key personnel and informed about company policies, procedures and benefits. To be effective, orientation training should be well planned and conducted within the first week of employment. Such a pre-job training helps the recruit to familiarise himself with the job and its settings.

**13. Committee Assignments:** In this method, trainees are asked to solve an actual organisational problem. The trainees have to work together and offer solution to the problem. Assigning talented employees to important committees can give these employees a broadening experience and can help them to understand the personalities, issues and processes governing the organisation. It helps them to develop team spirit and work united towards common goals. However, managers should very well understand that committee assignments could become notorious time wasting activities.

- The above on-the-job methods are cost-effective. Workers actually produce while they learn. Since immediate feedback is available, they motivate trainees to observe and learn the right way of doing things. Very few problems arise in the case of transfer of training because the employees learn in the actual work environment where the skills that are actually used. On-the-job methods may cause disruptions in production schedules. Experienced workers cannot use the facilities that are used in training. Poor learners may damage machinery and equipment. Finally, if the trainer does not possess teaching skills, there is very little benefit to the trainee.

## Off-the-job Training

Under this method, trainee is separated from the job situation and his attention is focused upon learning the material related to his future job performance. Since the trainee is not distracted by job requirements, he can place his entire concentration on learning the job rather than spending his time in performing it. There is an opportunity for freedom of expression for the trainees. "Off-the-job training" simply means that training is not a part of everyday job activity. The actual location may be in the company classroom or in places which are owned by the company or in universities or associations which have no connections with the company. These include classroom activities like lectures, special study, films, case studies, role-playing, programmed instructions, laboratory training, etc.

**1. Lecture (Classroom Instruction):** The lecture is a traditional and direct method of instructions. Lectures are regarded as one of the simplest way of imparting knowledge to the trainee, especially when facts, concept or principles, attitudes, theories and problem-solving abilities are to be taught. Lectures are formal organised talks by the training specialist.

The lecture method can be used for very large groups which are to be trained within a short-time for reducing the cost per trainee. It can be organised to rigorously promote company's ideas and principles. Lectures are essential when it is a question of imparting technical or special information of a complex nature. They are usually related with discussion, film shows, case studies, role playing and demonstrations, audio-visual aids enhance their values. The lecture method is not dead as some would believe. In the hands of able lectures, and for certain kinds of purposes and participants, it may turnout to be more interesting and effective than any other method.

In training, the most important uses of lectures include:

1. Reducing anxiety about upcoming training programmes or organisational changes by explaining their purposes.
2. Presenting basic material that will provide a common background for subsequent activities,
3. Introducing a subject and presenting an overview of its scope,
4. Illustrating the application of rules, principles; reviewing, clarifying and summarising.

The main advantage of the lecture system is that it is simple and efficient and through it more material can be presented within a given time than by any other method.

However, the lecture system suffers from some limitations:

1. The learners are passive instead of active participants. The lecture method violates the principle of learning by doing. It is one-way communication. There is no feedback from the audience.
2. A clear and vigorous verbal presentation requires a great deal of preparation for which management personnel often lack the time. Moreover, it calls for a substantial speaking skill,

3. The attention span of even a well-motivated and adequately informed listener is only from 15 minutes to 20 minutes, so that in the course of an hour, the attention of learners drifts.
4. It is difficult to stimulate discussion following a lecture, particularly if the listener is uninformed or awestruck by the lecture.
5. The presentation of material should be geared to common level of knowledge.
6. The untrained lecture either rambles or packs far too much information in the lecture, which often becomes unpalatable to the listener.
7. Though, a skilful lecturer can adapt his material to the specific group, he finds it is difficult to adjust it for individual differences within a group.
8. It tends to emphasise the accumulation and memorisation of facts and figures and does not stress on the application of knowledge.
9. The major limitation of the lecture method is that it does not provide for transfer of training effectively.

According to the conclusion reached at the Conference on Management Education and Training (held from January 22 to 24, 1954) at Pune, the essential prerequisites for a successful lecture method are:

(i) Group interest should be motivated and adapted to its needs;

(ii) It should be presented by an enthusiastic and animated speaker who has his listener's needs and interest in mind at all times;

(iii) A lecture should be well-planned as to the purpose; the main ideas and organisation should be clear and the development should be interesting;

(iv) It should not last less than 30 minutes and not more than an hour;

(v) A lecture should be made interesting and enlist the active participation of the learners with the aid of guided discussion, the lecture should pose leading questions, instead of giving out knowledge and information to which the listeners should provide answers.

**2. The Conference Method:** In this method, the participating individuals 'confer' to discuss points of common interest to each other. It is a formal meeting, conducted in accordance with an organised plan, in which the leader seeks to develop knowledge and understanding by obtaining a considerable amount of oral participation of trainees. It lays emphasis on small group discussions on organised subject matter and on the active participation of the members involved. Learning is facilitated by building up on the ideas contributed by the conferees. When big organisation use this method, the trainer uses audio-visual aids such as blackboards, mock ups, and slides; in some cases, the lectures are videotaped or audiotaped. Even the trainee's presentation can be taped for self-confrontation and self-assessment. There are three types of conferences. In the direct discussion, the trainer guides the discussion in such a way that the facts, principles or concepts are explained. In the training conference, the instructor gets the group to pool its knowledge and past experience and bring different point of view to bear on the problem. In the seminar conference, answer is bound to a question or a solution to a problem. For this, the instructor defines the problem, encourages and ensures full participation in the discussion.

*Merits:* The conference is ideally suited for the purpose of analysing problems and issues and examining them from different point of views. It is an excellent method for the development of conceptual knowledge and for reducing dogmatism and modifying attitudes because the participants develops solutions and reach conclusion which they often willingly accept.

*Demerits:*

1. It is limited to a small group of 15 to 20 persons because larger group often discourage the active participation of all the conferees.
2. The progress is usually slow because all those desiring to speak on a point are generally allowed to do so. Consequently, irrelevant issues easily creep in.

If the method is to be effective:

(a) Training issue must involve a problem or need that each individual is currently facing else interest in the conference results will wane (decrease in size).

(b) The size of the group should be small enough to allow each individual to participate and become personally involved in the deliberations of the group.

(c) The conferees should have some knowledge of the subject to be discussed at the conference.

(d) Good and stimulating leaders are needed for it is they who summarise material at appropriate times during a discussion and think along with the group to help it analyse and reach decisions; adopt a permissive point of view which encourages members to express themselves without fear to censure or ridicule.

**3. Seminar or Team Discussion:** This is an established method for training. A seminar is conducted in many ways:

(i) It may be based on a paper prepared by one or more trainees on a subject selected in consultation with the person in charge of the seminar. It may be part of a study or related to theoretical studies or practical problems. The trainees read their papers, and this is followed by a critical discussion. The chairman of the seminar summarises the contents of the papers and the discussions which follow their reading.

(ii) The person in charge of the seminar contributes in advance the material to be analysed in the form of required readings. The seminar compares the reactions of trainees, encourages discussion, defines the general trends and guides the participants to arrive at conclusion.

(iii) It may be based on the statement made by the person in charge of the seminar or on a document by an expert who is invited to participate in the discussion.

(iv) Valuable working material may be provided to the trainees by actual files. The trainees may consult the files and bring these to the seminar where they may study in detail and various aspects, ramifications and complexities of a particular job or work or task.

**4. Case Studies (Learning by Doing):** This method was first developed in the 1800s by Christopher Langdell at the Harvard Law School to help students to learn for themselves by independent thinking and discovering in the ever tangled skein of human affairs, principles and ideas which have lasting validity and general applicability. A collateral object is to help them develop skills in using their knowledge.

The case study is based upon the belief that managerial competencies can best be attained through the study, contemplation and discussion of concrete cases. The "case" is a set of data (real or fictional) written or oral miniature description and summary of such data that present issues and problems calling for solutions or action on the part of the trainee. When the trainees are given cases to analyse, they are asked to identify the problem and recommend solutions for it. This method offers to the trainees matter of reflection and brings home to them a sense of the complexity of life as opposed to theoretical simplifications of and practices in the decision making process. It diagnosis and deals with real life situations. This method is primarily useful as training technique for supervisors and is especially valuable as a technique of developing decision making skills and for broadening the perspective of the trainee.

The person in charge of training, makes out a case, provides the necessary explanations, initiates the discussion going and then once the discussion gets going he intervenes as little as possible. In the incident method, a full detailed description of a situation is not given. The trainer merely presents an outline often in the form of a complaint from a customer or a severe conflict in the management of a business. The trainee arrives at the facts in the issue by asking questions from the trainer or finding out a solution by "acting out" the situation in which a trainee plays a role. In this method, trainers from a particular business describe its development and some of its problems. After discussions, and detailed studies, the trainee prepares a report which contains analyses of the situation and their recommendations on the corrective actions to be taken.

In case study method, the trainee is expected to:

1. Master the facts and become acquainted with the content of the case.
2. Define the objectives sought in dealing with the issues in the case.
3. Identify the problem in the case and uncover their probable causes.
4. Develop alternative courses of action.
5. Screen the alternatives using the objectives as the criteria.
6. Define the controls needed to make the action effective, and
7. To "role play" the action to test its effectiveness and find conditions that may limit it.

***Merits:***

1. It promotes analytical thinking and develops a person's problem-solving ability.
2. It encourages open mindedness and serves as a means of integrating the knowledge obtained from different basic disciplines.
3. Since, cases are usually based upon real situations problem, the trainee's interest in them tend to be very great.
4. Although trainees quickly learn that there is no single answer to or solution of a case problem, they are never the less expected to arrive at usual generalisation and principles.
5. The method is accepted by everyone, for it deals with detailed description of real life situations.
6. If the problems faced by managers are described, the trainees become increasingly aware of obscurities, contradictions and uncertainties they encounter in their business careers and the need for remedial action.

*Demerits:*

1. It may degenerate into a mere dreary (gloomy) demonstration of dusty museum pieces, if it is taught only from books at developing centres of learning.
2. Instruction in the methods of analysis may not be given due importance. It may suppress the critical faculties of mediocre trainees and the habit of bunking by analogies may develop.
3. The cases become permanent precedents in their minds and may be used indiscriminately.
4. The preparation of cases is difficult, for it needs money and time and it is not quite certain that the outcome of this method would be worth the expenditure in money and men incurred on it.

The method is extensively used in professional schools of law and business administration in supervisory and executive training programmes in industry and in teaching personnel management, marketing, production management, human relations, labour relations, business policies and other disciplines. In India, cases are prepared by the Administrative Staff College at Hyderabad and other 18 institutes of higher learning in management.

For an effective use of this method, it is essential that:

1. The group of learners should be of such persons as are fairly well advanced in understanding the different concepts of management,
2. It should be comprehensive and well documented with a proper history, facts, and figures, thus enabling the students to see the organization and the historical setting in which the reported events took place,
3. The case should be a faithful representation of the issues involved as objectively as possible without any observations and comments from the case writer,
4. The case report should be realistic and based on first hand information. It should not contains opinions discussed as factual information,
5. The case situation should be reproduced in full and should be of the Harvard School type or a part of it may be presented in a film or on television or on tape or recreated through role playing.

**5. Role Playing:** This method was developed by Moreno, a Venetian Psychiatrist. He coined the terms "role playing", "role-reversal", "socio-drama", "psycho-drama", and a variety of specialised terms which emphasis on learning human relations skills through practice and insight into one's own behaviour and its effect upon others. It has been defined as, "a method of human interaction which involves realistic behaviour in the imaginary situations". As Norman Major has pointed out, a "role playing experience soon demonstrates the gap between 'thinking and doing'. The idea of role playing involves exchange, doing and practice." Role playing primarily involves employee, employer-relationships. Hiring, firing, discussing a grievance procedure, conducting a post appraisal interview or disciplining a subordinate or a salesman making a representation to a customer. In role playing, trainees act out a given roles as they would in a stage play. Two or more trainees are assigned parts to play before the rest of the class. These parts do not involve any memorisation of lines or any rehearsals. The role players are simply informed of a situation and of the respective roles they have to play. Sometime, after the preliminary planning, the situation is acted out by the role players.

*Merits:*

1. Learning by doing is emphasised,
2. Human sensitivity and interactions are stressed,
3. The knowledge of results is immediate,
4. Trainee interest and involvement tend to be high,
5. It is a useful method to project the living conditions between learning in the classroom and working on the job and creating a live business situations in the classroom,
6. It develops skills and abilities to apply knowledge particularly in areas like human relations,
7. It brings about desired changes in behaviour and attitude,
8. Role playing are the opportunities to attempt to create an environment similar to real situations without the high cost involved should the actions prove undesirable.

***Demerits:*** It is difficult to duplicate the pressure and realities of actual decision making on the job and individuals often act differently in real life situations than they do in acting out a role playing exercise.

- Thus, role playing is especially useful in providing new insight and in presenting the trainee with opportunities to develop interactional skills. Unless the trainer engages in coaching or unless someone states the criteria for behaviour, however, role playing may not adhere to the objectives of the training programme and the reinforcement of the desired behaviour may be somewhat lacking, that is the interpersonal relations could be faulty.

**6. Programmed Instructions (Teaching by The Machine Method):** Programmed instructions involves a sequence of steps which are often set up through a central panel of an electronic computer as guides in the performance of a desired operation or series of operations. It incorporates a pre-arranged, proposed or desired course of proceedings pertaining to the learning or acquisition of some specific skills or general knowledge. Programmed instructions involve breaking down information into meaningful units and then arranging these in proper way to form a logical and sequential learning programme or package.

In such a programme, knowledge is imparted with the use of a textbook or a teaching machine. The programme involves: presenting questions, facts or problems to the trainee to utilise the information given; and the trainee instantly receives feedback and sometime rewards or penalties on the basis of the accuracy of his answers.

The programmed instruction technique can be in the form of programmed texts or manuals while in some organizations teaching machines are utilised. All programmed instruction approaches have common characteristics: they condense the material to be learned into highly organised, logical sequences which require the trainee to respond. The ideal format provides for merely instantaneous feedback that informs the trainee if his or her response is correct.

*Merits:*

1. Instructors are not a key part in learning,
2. Trainees learn at their own pace,
3. The materials to be learned are broken down into small units,
4. Immediate feedback is available,

5. Active learner participation takes place at each step in the programme,
6. Individual differences can be taken into account,
7. Training can be imparted to odd times and in odd places,
8. There is a high level of learner motivation.

***Demerits:***

1. The instructional setting is impersonal,
2. An advanced study is not possible until preliminary information has been acquired,
3. Philosophical and attitudinal concepts and motor skills cannot be taught by this method,
4. Only factual subject matters can be programmed,
5. The cost of creating any such programme is very high and its a time-consuming method.

This method is primarily used in teaching factual knowledge such as mathematics, physics, foreign language, etc.

**7. Laboratory Training:**

**(i) Sensitivity Training** is an experimental approach to training. Sensitivity training is a group training method that uses intensive participation and gives immediate feedback for self-analysis and change. It provides participants an opportunity to actually experience some concepts of management just as a manager would experience them in his own organisational situation. This training has two advantage: (a) participants remain involved and enthusiastic, (b) the responsibility of learning experience lies with the participants. He would make positive efforts to derive many benefits from the exercise. The training attempts to develop the diagnostic ability of the participants — the ability to perceive reality. At a group level, one learns about normative structures and authority relationships leading to better team-work. It increases sensitivity, training aims at developing sensitivity within people towards thoughts, feelings and behaviour of other persons. Through this improves one's human interactions, the effectiveness of sensitivity training depends upon the ability of the participants to apply the concepts and awareness obtained in the laboratory or groups to his job, the transfer of his knowledge to the organisation is possible if the organisation has an open culture and an atmosphere for open discussion, encourage conflict resolution and promote mutual trust.

**(ii) T-groups:** One of the methods of the sensitivity training is the T-group. Bethel Maine of USA was the pioneer of the T-group. It was considered necessary that to change behaviour, imparting necessary skills is required. A change in a variety of skills and experiences like self-awareness, interpersonal relationships, group organisational process, teamwork and intergroup conflict resolution. Sensitivity training has developed to the status of an intervention in organizational development. T-group training is processed-oriented and not content-oriented where people operate on a feeling level of communication, observing, revealing, listening, and unravelling messages.

**8. Teletraining:** A training option that can be useful when trainees are dispersed across various physical locations is tele training. Satellites are used to beam live training broadcasts to employees at different locations. In addition to the video reception, the satellite link can allow trainees to ask questions of the instructor during the broadcast.

Two disadvantages of tele training are the need for an expensive satellite connection and the difficulty of scheduling the broadcast so that everyone will be able to attend. A company can solve the scheduling problems by videotaping the presentation and then offering the videotape to people in locations schedules conflicted with the live broadcast. The training instructor can be available via phone or computer to respond to questions. This method makes the trainer's expertise available to trainees without requiring him or her to redeliver the entire training programme.

**9. Computer-aided Instruction and Interacting Video:** All these have one thing in common. They allow the trainee to learn at his or her own pace. Also, they allow material already learned to be bypassed in favour of material with which a trainee is having difficulty. After the introductory period, the instructor need not be present and the trainee can learn as his or her time allows. These methods sound good, but may not be available with the resources of some small businesses.

Computer based training can range from the use of a CD-ROM to training over the Internet. Web-based training is fast becoming the training method of choice. Both small and large businesses are finding computer training to be a cost-effective medium. In particular, if a job requires extensive use of computers then computer-based training is highly job-related and provides for a high degree of transfer of training back to the job. Computers also have the advantages of allowing trainees to learn at a comfortable pace. As a trainer, the computer never gets tired, bored or short tempered. Further, computer can be a multimedia training option in which text can be combined with film, graphics and audio components.

Learnshare is a successful example of collaboration among companies to use e-learning. Members of Learnshare include General Motor Corp. Motorola Inc., Owens-Corning, Deere & Co., and 3M Corp., among others.

**10. Experimental Exercises:** Experimental exercises are usually short, structured learning experiences where individuals learn by doing. For instance, rather than talk about interpersonal conflicts and how to deal with them, and experiential exercise could be used to create a conflict situation where employees have to experience a conflict personally workout its resolution. After completing the exercise, the facilitator or trainer typically discusses what happened and introduces theoretical concepts to help explain the members' behaviour during the exercise.

## INTRODUCTION TO MANAGEMENT DEVELOPMENT

Management or executive development is a long-term educational future-oriented process. Managers are the indispensable resourcess, the priceless assets of an organization. They generate creative ideas, translate them into concrete action plans and produce results. The outcomes of managerial actions are going to be deep, profound and decisive. To get ahead in the race especially in a complex, dynamic and ever-changing world, managers need to develop their capabilities that go beyond those required by the current jobs. The managers have to deal not only with the staff but also with others outside his own group and has a decided influence on the organization. The major and more elusive task of management development is to mould and fashion the behaviour component into a virile and unmixed weapon of enterprise achievement. The secret of effective management lies in vitality, a conceptual attitude of mind concerned with profitable results matched by determination and integrity in management and managers. Management development activities attempt to instill sound reasoning processes to enhance one's ability to understand and interpret knowledge — rather than imparting a body of serial facts or teaching a specific set of motor skills. Development therefore focuses more on the employee's personal growth. Successful managers have analytical, human, conceptual and specialised skills and qualities. They are able to think and understand. Training parse cannot overcome a manager's or potential manager's inability to understand cause and affect relationship, to synthesis from experience to visualise relationships or to think logically. Manager's needs good listening skills, interviewing competency and the ability to read, analyse and classify types of employee behaviour. The methods for developing executives that we will consider are educational and are intended to foster the manager's analytical and conceptual abilities. Development is a related process that not only covers those activities that improve performance of jobs, but also those activities that lead to growth of the personality; help individuals to progress towards maturity and actualization of their potentials so that they become good employees as well as better human beings. In organizational terms, development plans are intended to prepare persons to gain promotion and hold greater responsibility. Managerial development ensures that as and when the demand for managers arises, suitably qualified persons are ready to fill vacancies. Managerial development consists of all means by which executives learn to improve their performance. It is designed to improve the effectiveness of managers in their present jobs and to prepare them for higher jobs in future. Managerial development aims at helping the managers to realise their full potential.

Management development is a way of improving the culture of the organization so that it could be geared to excellence. "People move organizations — not machines".

According to Edwin Flippo, "No organization has a choice of whether to develop employees or not; the only choice is that of method". The need for management development is well accepted in the present business, which is fast-changing due to technological and social developments.

## Meaning of Management Development

Management development or executive development is a systematic process of growth and development by which the managers develop their abilities to manage. It is the result of, not only participation in formal courses of instruction, but also of actual job experience. It is concerned with improving the performance of the managers by giving them opportunities for growth and development.

It is an effort to provide employees with the abilities that the organization will need in the future. Management or executive development is the long-term educational process that utilises a methodical and organised procedure that imparts conceptual and theoretical knowledge to managers.

## Definition of Management Development

- According to G.R.Terry, "Management development should produce change in behaviour which is more in keeping with the organizational goals than the previous behaviour. The change frequently consists of a number of small steps resulting from training but the cumulative effect is considerable. It is also basic that a terminal behaviour is identified before the development efforts start."
- According to P.N. Singh, "Management development is an activity designed to improve the performance of existing managers, provide a supply of managers to meet the need of organizations in future and extend the understanding of the management activity by drawing from the following three resource areas: (a) Knowledge, (b) Experience, and (c) Trainee himself".
- "Executive or management development is the planned, systematic and continuous process of learning and growth by which managers develop their conceptual and analytical ability to manage. It is the result of not only participation in formal courses of instruction but

also of actual job experience. It is primarily concerned with improving the performance of the managers by giving them stimulating opportunities for growth and development."

## METHODS OF MANAGEMENT DEVELOPMENT

### On-the-job Method

The object of manager's development is improving on-the-job behaviour, this method of training and education has its own value. It is inexpensive and saves productive hours. But the main drawback is that neither the trainer nor the trainee is free from the daily chores and the pressure of their respective routine jobs. A senior seldom has the time and the patience to impart training to the person. Most popular techniques under this type are:

**1. Coaching and Counselling Method:** When a manager takes an active role in guiding another manager, we refer to this activity as coaching. Just as track coaches observe, analyze and attempt to improve the performance of their athletes, "coaches" on the job can do the same. The effective coach, whether on the track or in the corporate hierarchy, gives guidance through direction, advice, criticism, and suggestions in an attempt to aid the growth of employee. Coaching is a method which is used in developing managerial thinking processes and operative skills. In coaching, the superior plays the role of the guide and the instructor. The coach should help by explaining the relevance of information. The coach sets some mutually agreed upon goals and tell the trainee what he wants to be done, suggest how it might be done, follow-up suggestions and correct errors. He helps the trainee live up to those goals through periodic reviews of the trainee's progress and by suggesting modifications in his behaviour where needed. The objective of coaching is not only to teach and guide a subordinate in the performance of his immediate assignments but also provide him with diversified work so that he may grow and progress. The learner cannot develop much beyond the limits of his own boss' ability.

The coaching method enjoys certain advantages:

1. It requires the least centralized staff coordination for every executive can coach his men even if no management development programme exists.
2. It provides quick feedback to the trainee as well as the trainer of what they lack and what measures can be taken to overcome their shortcomings.
3. It is learning by doing.
4. It provides an opportunity to a trainee to develop himself.

However, (1) the coaching technique is authoritarian for an executive tends to familiarize his subordinates with his own work habits and beliefs even though this may be faulty. In other words, it has the tendency to perpetuate the current managerial style and practices in the organization. (2) It relies heavily on the coach's ability to be a good teacher, which he may not necessarily be. (3) The training atmosphere is free from worries of the daily duties.

There is increased motivation for the trainee with minimization of the problem of learning transfer from theory to practice. The foremost disadvantages lie in frequent neglect by the superior, both in time and quality of teaching efforts. Trainer's styles of working which may not necessarily be suitable percolate in a trainee. Therefore, if this method is relied upon heavily, there is a chance for the development of organizational traditionalism which works as resistant to change. Further. the trainer may be preoccupied with his work and he may not be able to give sufficient time to the trainee concerned.

To be effective, coaching demands that the supervisor should render assistance when the subordinate seeks or needs it. The superior should have the ability to communicate and to stimulate and should have patience to help his subordinates. He should also set aside time for scheduling sessions. He should avoid being too dominating of the performance process, so that the trainee can experience things for himself and does not become completely dependent on the coach for decisions.

"Coaching will work well if the coach provides a good model with whom the trainee can identify, if both can be open with each other, if the coach accepts his responsibility fully, and if he provides the trainee with recognition of his improvement and suitable rewards."

**Counselling:** Under this method, the subordinate wanting advice approaches his superior. Counselling is provided in matters relating to the job. However, on request from the subordinate, counselling may also be offered on matters not directly related to the job. There is two-way dialogue between the subordinate and the superior to find solution to his problem. Counselling provides emotional stability to trainee-subordinate.

**2. Job Rotation or Channel Method of Development:** Job rotation presents an excellent method for broadening the manager or potential manager for fortuning specialists into generalists. It refers to the transfer or movement of executives from one job to another and from one plan to another on some planned basis for educational learning purposes. Job rotation is often designed for beginning level managers while planned progression is more likely to occur at higher managerial level. Such rotation may continue for a period ranging from 6 to 24 months. Method provides a great deal of job experience for those who are potential executives who need broadening of outlook and increased understanding of the various aspects of management. The emphasis is on diversified instead of specialized skills and knowledge. Job rotation as a means for management development offers certain positive contributions. It allows the managers to appreciate the intricacies involved in different jobs and how their own jobs are affected by such inerrancies. This way, they can develop more co-operative approach to different functions in the organization. Further, managers may develop broader horizon and perspective of a generalist rather than the narrower horizon of a specialist.

Under this method, the trainees are rotated over various routine jobs in a department, division or unit before they are due for promotions as managers. The idea is to impart an overall knowledge and familiarity with the different sectional jobs such as billing, issuing challans, preparing inspection notes, setting railway claims, handling customer accounts, etc., in the sales department before they are posted as manager in the department. This secures a compromise between over-specialization even from the lowest most routine level, and minimum of special skills and expertise necessary for middle level managers. These persons are moved from one job to another according to a schedule of rotation. It also includes moving people between line and staff positions.

Job rotations are mostly horizontal or lateral. Such rotations can be instituted: (i) on a planned basis, i.e., by means of training programme whereby the worker spends two or three months in an activity and is then moved on; or (ii) on a situational basis, i.e., by moving the person to another activity when the first is no longer challenging to him or to meet the needs of work scheduling.

*Merits:*

1. Boredom, monotony are reduced and since job rotation permits a greater understanding of other activities within the organization people are prepared more rapidly to assume greater responsibility, especially at the upper echelons.
2. It breaks down departmental provincialism for everyone is moved from one to another. It rather develops inter departmental cooperations.
3. Through this system, a man does not end up in just one place. He gets a chance to step into a higher position. In this way, an organization gains management strength in-depth.
4. Job rotation ensures the avoidance of the problem which arises when a newly promoted manager is required to supervise his former peers.
5. Job rotation injects new ideas into the older departmental personnel who may otherwise fall in a route. New concepts are infused into them and they are diffused throughout an enterprise.
6. It makes it possible for the management to compare one man with another, and gives everyone an equal chance for advancement.
7. It does not develop "specialists" but produces "generalists" that is men who take a broad, companywide point of view, men whose chief ability is to handle people and make decisions.
8. Awareness of what is happening elsewhere and familiarity with other tasks centres helps a balanced and informed attitude to enterprise goals and activities.
9. Each manager's abilities and talents are best tested in a variety of jobs so the enterprise can secure his best utilisation in the ultimate assignment.
10. The manager should provide a variety of job experiences for those judged to have the potential for higher ranks before they are promoted.
11. The benefit of wider exposure is available to trainee manager.

*Demerits:*

1. It upsets family and home life because many a time transfers are affected to different geographical areas.
2. The new incumbent is likely to bring a zeal for change while sound changes are good, ill-conceived and hasty innovations may lead to costly experiments and reduced productivity by moving workers.
3. It undermines organizational morale, efficiency since "executives may have little inducement to sink their teeth deeply into as assignments". Established options are disturbed and the manager is prone to error in a new seat.
4. It becomes difficult for a subordinate to adjust himself to his new bosses, interpersonal relationships takes time for adjustment and employees with frequent moves are apt to feel insecure.
5. It develops sharp cleavages, friction, jealousy and other non-cooperative and dysfunctional forms of human behaviour.
6. Job rotation can demotivate intelligent and aggressive trainees who seek specific responsibility in their chosen speciality. The system is like a highly competitive game of musical chairs.

whenever there are promotions and transfer. Some people are left behind. Therefore, smart young people avoid taking risks.

7. The system may easily become overcentralized, inflexible and closed.
8. Rotation sometimes leads to subtle class distinctions. Men who are not rotated develop defensive reactions. This lead to misunderstanding and poor communication.
9. The work of department is affected due to frequent changes of executives for training purpose.
10. Even the executives are not in a position to have specialized knowledge and training in one particular branch of work.
11. It may create confusion in the mind of a trainee and he may not be able to understand the rationale of job rotation if not properly counselled. These may affect his performance as well as that of others with whom he works.

— **Understudy Assignments:** The understudy system can be considered as somewhat different approach than those described above, in that a certain person is specifically designed as the heir apparent. An understudy is a person who is in training to assume at a future time, the full responsibility of the position currently held by his superior. This method supplies the organization a person with as much competence as the superior to fill his post which may fall vacant because of promotion, retirement or transfer. An understudy is usually chosen by the head of a particular department. The head will then teach him what his entire job involves. The superior involves him in decision making by discussing the daily operating problems as well. An understudy may be picked up by a manager from amongst a large number of subordinates, or several individuals. Such an understudy learns the complexities of the problems and how to solve them and investigates and making written recommendations to his superior. He is generally assigned a project which is closely related to the work in his section. He is deputed to attend executive meetings as a representative of his superior, at which he makes a presentation and proposals. The essence is that the senior route much of the departmental work through the junior; discusses problems with him and allows him to participate in decision making process as often as possible.

***Merits:***

1. It is practical and quick in training persons for greater responsibility for it lays emphasis on learning by doing.
2. The trainee manager is also not overburdened with work and responsibility at the same time he secures full participation in the running of the function and assignment of the job content.
3. The learner's interest and motivation are high and superior is relieved of his heavy work-load.
4. The trainee is able to continuously obtain guidance of the senior. The work passed through him opens up windows for him to appreciate different angles and views points related to the job. He receives an opportunity to see the job in total.
5. It ensures continuity of management facilities even when the superior leaves his position.

6. The chances of costly mistakes or upsetting relationship within the group are eliminated.
7. The understudy, in turn, gets an opportunity to learn the superior's job and get ready for challenging roles at a later date.
8. It is beneficial from the organization's point of view also as it will not be at the receiving end when an executive suddenly leaves his job.

***Demerits:***

1. The motivation of all the employees in the unit may decrease since the incentive to get ahead is partially destroyed when one particular subordinate is identified in advance as the one who will be the next occupant of a higher level managerial position.
2. Since the understudy is picked up by the superior often on the basis on favouritism, he tends to perpetuate the existing practices of in-breeding.
3. Under a competent senior, the junior trainee might lose his independence and his critical appraisal of the way of job is performed.
4. The subordinate employees might ignore him and withhold cooperation, they might tend to treat him as an intruding appendage to the function without authority and accountability.
5. Since, the understudy has been specially picked up, others who are left out in the race may get a feeling that competition for promotions is over. This would affect the motivation level of both the one who is designed and for those who tend to carry the bitter feelings for a long time.

While there are opportunities for sizeable errors, this technique is used predominantly in situation where major or critical decisions can be delayed till the manager returns or can be made in close consultation with the manager next in line. The whole exercise would be beneficial when trainees get a real opportunity to deal with challenging or interesting assignments.

**3. Participation in Deliberations of the Junior Board and Committees or the Multiple Management Techniques:** Managerial personnel may be developed through their participation in deliberations and decision making from group such as committees task forces, project assignment, etc., it is a technique whereby juniors are assigned to board or committees, by the chief executive. They are asked to participate in deliberations of these boards and committees. In these sessions, actual real life problems are discussed different views are debated and decisions are taken. The juniors get an opportunity to share managerial decision making to learn by watching others and to delve into specific organizational problems. Interdepartmental committees are normally created for bringing coordination in the activities of different departments. Managers from different departments are taken on such committees. Junior managers are also given membership of such committees so as to give them a broader exposure to the viewpoints of other departmental heads.

When committees are of "*ad hoc*" or temporary nature, they often take a task force activities designed to delve into a particular problem, ascertain alternatives solutions, and make a recommendation for implementing a solution. These temporary assignments can be both interesting and rewarding to the employee's growth. On the other hand, appointment to permanent committees increases the employees' exposure to other members of the organization, broadens his understanding and gives him an opportunity to grow and make recommendation under the scrutiny of other committee members.

Normally, group decision making passes through three stages: (i) At the initial stage, the group tries to acquire the largest pool of common information about the facts of the situation. (ii) The group tries to make inferences and evaluation of information and to form common opinions in a general way. (iii) It gets around more specific suggestions and solutions to the problem. After agreement is achieved on the essential facts of the situation, every member is given opportunities to express his views. At this level, there may be emotional tension in deliberations and the chairman should direct the group back to the facts and begin anew from there. This returning back to the facts of the problem works as cooling effect on the members and agreements may be arrived at because members may look at the problem in a sounder way.

***Merits:***

1. It permits a considerable number of managers to participate in certain activities within a reasonable period of time. Besides the Boards do make important contributions to efficiency, productivity and a better human relations, climate. In fact they assist in a better administration in the organization.
2. It is relatively inexpensive method of development.
3. It helps to identify those who have executive talent. Multiple managements are obtained on each individual to the Board rating system.
4. It gives Board members an opportunity to gain knowledge on various issues.
5. The members gain tactical experience of group decision making and of teamwork. As a result of the interaction process, they develop respect for the rights and view of their associates.

***Demerits:***

1. It does not permit any specific attention to training needs of the manager.
2. It is only suitable for middle and senior level managers.
3. The debates in these committees often tend to be discursive, lacking purposiveness or authority. The deliberations often degenerate into academic discussion without the participants feeling committed to the conclusions.

— **Syndicate:** Syndicate method of development has been introduced by Administrative Staff College at Henley — on Thames. The purpose of the syndicate technique is to "expose a participants to a milieu in which he is persuaded into reflecting upon his experiences as an executive, updating his knowledge, improving his executive skills and developing a greater insight into human behaviour. In other words, this method enables an executive to acquire a proper perspective on his job in relation to the activities in areas other than his own, and to give him practice in skills, techniques and procedures which he has to use in his day-to-day work as he rises higher up the ladder of management.

By this method, a team of persons of mature judgement and proven ability is set up with different functional representations so that there are an interchangeable ideas and experiences. The syndicate is given a task properly spelt out in terms of briefs and background papers. Large groups are split into small ones (consisting of 7 to 10 persons) and discussions are supplemented by short lectures. After the presentations of ideas, these are evaluated by group members with the help of the resource person and group members evaluate as to where they have lacked. Such exercises are repeated so as to enable the participants to look at the problems in right perspective. The teacher acts as a "resource person" rather than as a lecturer. Both the organization and participants must understand the mechanics of the utilization of this method; otherwise it would result in a lot of waste of time and frustration. Each syndicate prepares a report which is presented to the other groups of executives. An opportunity is provided for discussion, suggestions, criticism, comments and recommendations for action.

This method is used as a device not only for the study of a specific problem but also for other tasks. The syndicate method is quite helpful in developing analytical skills in the participants and their approach for understanding others, if conducted properly.

**4. Multiple Management:** It also known as 'Junior-board of executives', it is a system in which permanent advisory committees are constituted to study problems of the organizations and make recommendations to the top level management. In multimanagement, the constituted committees discuss actual problems and offer alternative solutions. The recommendations are made based on the best alternatives. Multiple management offers several advantages; it helps board members to gain first hand experiences in various important aspects of business; it becomes easy to spot people with talent; juniors get a chance to improve their problem-solving skills; and more importantly it is an inexpensive way of training a good number of executives to do things; on their own and develop fast.

**5. General Knowledge:** In addition to job knowledge and organizational knowledge, managers should possess general knowledge as the external environment interacts with and influences the business. The general knowledge includes the knowledge about the economic conditions of the country and the world in general, in respect of major areas such as prices, GNP per capita income, various other industries, other sectors of the economy, political conditions, social factors, etc. General knowledge can be acquired through special courses, special meetings and specific readings.

— **Special Courses:** Special courses – like the workshops or executives development programmes or organized by the institutes, universities and colleges — help the trainee to acquire general knowledge.

— **Special Meetings:** Special meetings organized in Consumers' Forums, Voluntary organizations, etc., help the trainees develop their general knowledge.

— **Specific Readings:** Specific articles published by various journals, specific portions of important books are provided to the trainees to improve their general knowledge.

**6. Delegation:** Delegation is one more internal method of management development. The performance of subordinates may not improve unless additional responsibility and authority are delegated to them. Making the subordinates achieve a particular target through delegation is one way by which subordinates will learn to grow and develop independently. They will develop leadership qualities and decision making skills, which are necessary for a good manager.

**7. Appointment as "Assistant to":** A junior executive may be appointed as 'Assistant to' senior executive for the purpose of training and practical experience. Here, the junior executive is given exposure to the job of senior executive and he teams new techniques while providing assistance to his boss. This broadens his viewpoint and makes him ready for future promotions. The superior executive also gets the benefit as he can delegate some of his responsibilities to the assistant and also acts as a guide to his assistant.

**8. Promotion and Transfer:** Promotions and transfers are two more internal methods of management development. Promotion gives an opportunity to a manager to acquire new skills required for the job at the higher level. It motivates him for self-improvement. Transfer also facilitates the broadening of viewpoint required for higher positions. It gives an opportunity to work at different positions and develop.

**9. Behaviour Modelling:** Though sometimes confused with role playing, behaviour modelling is a more structured approach to teaching specific supervisory skills. It is based on social learning theory insofar as the trainee is: (1) provided with specific model of behaviour. (2) informed in advance of the consequences of engaging in that type of behaviour.

This is an approach that demonstrates desired behaviour, gives trainees the chance to practice and role-play those behaviours and receive feedback. The basic behaviour modelling involves the following steps:

- **Learning Points:** At the beginning, the essential goals and objectives of the programme are stated. In some cases the learning points are a sequence of behaviours that are to be taught.
- **Modelling:** Trainees watch films or videotapes in which a model manager is portrayed dealing with an employee in an effort to improve his performance. The model shows specifically how to deal with the situation and demonstrates the learning points.
- **Role Playing:** Trainees participate in extensive rehearsal of the behaviours shown by the models.
- **Social Reinforcement:** The trainer offers reinforcement in the form of praise and constructive feedback based on how the trainee performs in the role playing situation.
- **Transfer of Learning:** Finally, trainees are encouraged to apply their new skills when they return to their jobs.

Behaviuor modelling can be effective. Several controlled studies have demonstrated success in helping managers interact with employees, handle discipline, introduce change and increase productivity. This method of learning in isolation may prove to be inadequate, but in combination with other off-the-job techniques may prove to be useful.

In the handling of interpersonal problems, the fundamental approach to all such situations involves: (1) description of the desired behaviour, (2) justification for the necessity of such behaviour, (3) active listening to employee responses, and (4) active involvement of the employee in the solution. As an example, the behaviour model in handling a complaining employee emphasizes the following key action steps:

1. Avoid responding to the complaint with hostility and defensiveness.
2. Ask for and listen properly to the complaint.
3. Restate the complaint to ensure thorough understanding.
4. Recognize and acknowledge the complainant's viewpoint.
5. State your position not defensively.
6. Set specific date for follow-up meeting.

**Limitations of on-the-job Techniques are:**

1. In a group of participants from different spheres of management and drawn from different enterprise cultures, the participants are exposed to new ideas, new ways to analyse and divergent enterprises of members of the group provoke introspection and generate impulses to behaviour change.
2. Modern tools and techniques of manager's development are more sophisticated and highly developed and their handling needs specialized field instructions.
3. Technological development demands that managers need to be placed in a highly manoeuvred (military movement) and stimulated atmosphere. It is not possible on-the-job training.
4. The management process has become complex, but on-the-job training does not allow adequate facilities, environment and teaching expertise.
5. Though the main objective of management development is to improve behaviour of the managers in different environment in actual practice, this objective is not well achieved.

## Off-the-job Method

There is a wealth of executive development techniques that managers can adopt in off-the-job. The more popular ones are:

**1. Case Study:** Case study method is an excellent medium for developing analytical skills. It was started by Harvard Business School. This method is increasingly being used by many other prestigious and not so prestigious management institutes in India. Case is "a written description of an actual situation", which provokes in the reader the need to decide what is going on, what the situation really is or what the problems are and what can and should be done. A case is an objective description of a "real life" business situation in which executives is required to take action and is responsible for results.

In this method, an actual business situation is described in writing, in a comprehensive manner. The trainees are asked to appraise and analyse the problem situation and suggest solutions. The actual decision taken in the subject case is known only to the executive and is disclosed only at the end of session when it is compared with the various solutions offered by the group.

The case method of development utilizes actual case example collected from various organizations for diagnostic purposes. The trainee must: (1) identify the major and minor problems in the case; (2) filter out the significant facts from the insignificant; (3) analyze the issues and use logic to fill in the gaps in the facts; (4) arrive at some means for solving the identifiable problem. Cases in personnel management are after each major section in the text. In ensuring group discussion, concerning the case, the trainee will usually see that other candidates differ from himself or herself about what is important and what action should be undertaken.

Case study is one of the most frequently used pedagogical tools in management education and development. Case method of learning has the following objectives:

1. The description of real business situation to acquaint the learner with the principles and practices obtained in work setting;
2. Demonstration of various types of goals, problems, facts, conditions, conflicts and personalities obtained in organisational settings;

3. Introduction of realism into formal instruction;
4. Development of decision-making ability; and
5. Development of independent thinking but cooperative approach to work in team situations.

Such case study may be related to any aspect of management such as production, marketing, personnel, finance and so on. The case presented is always incomplete.

Case study can provide stimulating discussions among participants as well as excellent opportunities for individuals to defend their analytical and judgemental abilities. It is rather an effective method for improving decision making abilities within the constraints of limited information. This method represents a dynamic and powerful approach to learning. Sometimes the case discussion, take place in a small syndicate before they are called upon to discuss before the whole class.

A case may be presented either in structured form or in unstructured form. In a highly structured case, there are leading questions at the end that indicate the focus and predetermined the direction with which the discussion will go. The sessions in the classroom can degenerate into a question answer session between instructor and participants. The participants search, through the process of analysis, what problem to choose as focus. This helps them to learn how to get on the real problems in a given situations. At the end of the discussion of the case, the instructor presents his own view on the case and provides feedback to the trainees about their performance.

***Merits:***

1. Improves problem-solving skills of participants.
2. Trainees can apply theory to practical problems and learn quickly. It is a way of learning by doing.
3. Case studies can provide interesting debates among trainees, as well as excellent opportunities for individuals to defend their analytical and judgemental abilities.
4. Trainees learn how others solve a situation in their own unique way. They get a feel of how others work at a problem and begin to appreciate each other's thinking.
5. If the case reflects a real life situation, participants take keen interest and examine the cross-currents with an open and inquisitive mind.
6. In-depth thinking about the matter by managers.
7. More perception in situations and greater respect for the opinion of others.

***Demerits:***

1. Good case studies do not originate easily. They are costly and time-consuming (collect data, analyse report, summaries) exercise.
2. Examining historical evidence may fail to develop the analytical and reasoning abilities of participants.
3. Cases sometimes are not sufficiently realistic to be useful.
4. Indiscriminate use of case studies may not help participants who are not mature enough to analyse and participate in discussions actively.
5. Cases may contain information inappropriate to the kinds of decisions that trainees would make in a real setting.

6. A trainee who is not skilled in this technique can undermine its usefulness.
7. The case study methods have little or nothing in common with the trainee's workplace, which may limit its effectiveness.

**2. Incident Method:** This method was developed by Paul and Faith Pigors. "The central aim of this method is to stimulate self-development in a blend of understanding that is essential for productive interaction. This blend combines intellectual ability (power to think clearly incisively and reasonably about specific facts and also about abstractions); practical judgement (capacity to modify conclusions arrived at intellectually, so that they meet the test of common sense); and social awareness (being able to appreciate the force of other people's feelings and willing to adjust or implement a decision so that it can be more acceptable to persons who are affected by it. Group work of each of these cases begins when a group meets. Each member working along for a couple of minutes, studies a written incident. He asks himself, what seems to be going on this incident? What lead can I find here toward facts or the case and issues that stirred people up? Appended to each incident is an invitation to make short-term decisions in the role of person who had to cope with an incident when it actually happened. A slight variation in this method may be in the form of incident method. In this method, trainee is given certain incidents and his reactions are noted down. Some trainees may even play surprise roles which interrupt the manager and give him two or more simultaneous problems more like real on-the-job pressures. Through the feedback of his behaviours, the trainee comes to know his behavioural pattern and tries to overcome the one which is not productive or functional. Thus, he can learn techniques of giving priorities to various problems faced by him.

Under this method, group members address questions to the discussion leader. The general trend of questioning is to find out about what, when, and how of the situation in which an incident developed, and who was present there at the time. Clues are also tracked down if they seem to offer reliable insight into the why of behaviour. Asking the collection of data, it is necessary to isolate the most important items for decision making.

— **Project:** In the project assignment method, a trainee manager is given a project that is closely related to the work of his department. Here, the executive has to study the project on his own and make recommendations for the consideration of the departmental head. Such assignment provides valuable experience to the trainee and develops problem-solving attitude, which is one essential requirement of an executive.

A project is a planned undertaking a proposed scheme, a definitely formulated piece of research or a mental projection. Students are assigned a specific problems area, depending on their specialisation, and professional work. Each student studies a problem of the organisation, studies the facts and makes recommendation in the light of his theoretical learning in the classroom and his experience in business. He prepares a report, which is evaluated in a viva examination to test the depth of his understanding. This method is useful in reinforcing learning and in exposing students to various problems of business organisation and teaches them how to tackle them.

**3. Role Playing:** Role playing, as a method of learning was introduced by Moreno, a Vatican psychiatrist. He introduced the terms 'role playing', 'role rehearsal', 'psychodrama' and a variety of specialized terms, with emphasis on learning human relations through insight into one's own behaviour and its impact on others. Role playing is a simulation in which the trainee is asked to play a part in a problem situation requiring integration with others. Basic mental sets are stated for all participants, but no dialogue is provided. For example, a supervisor, on the advice of a motion and time study engineer, has decided to change the work methods of subordinates. Role playing as a method of learning involves human interaction in imaginary situation and leadership learning. In drama, and play, actors play various roles. While playing these roles, they assume themselves as the persons whose role they play. Similar is the case in role playing training. Role playing technique is used in groups where various individuals are given the roles of different managers who are required to solve a problem or to arrive at a decision. Thus, it is spontaneous acting in a situation involving two or more persons under training situation. Dialogues grow spontaneously as the role playing proceeds. At the end of the role playing sessions, there is a critique session in which trainees are given feedback about their role playing.

Role playing is close to a laboratory situation in dealing with people in job situations. Playback of tape, if recorded, provides opportunities for the trainee to examine his or her performance with the additional insight of participants and experienced observers. Role playing helps the trainees to develop better perspectives in performing their jobs, because they may see the jobs from different angles. It also develops sensitivity among trainees which is quite helpful in maintaining better human relations.

The values of role playing are:

1. It requires the persons to carry-out a thought or decision he may have reached.
2. It permits the practice of carrying out an action and makes it clear that good human relations require skill.
3. Attitudinal changes are effectively accomplished by placing persons in specified roles. It becomes clear in role play that a person's behaviour is not only a function of his personality but also of the situation in which he finds himself.
4. It makes these person aware of the feelings of others.
5. It helps in developing a fuller appreciation of the important part played by feelings.
6. Each person gets an opportunity to discover his own personal faults.

Four types of learning can take place through role play: (a) learning by practice of desired skills, (b) learning through limitation of desirable behaviour, (c) learning through observation and feedback about the effectiveness and weaknesses, and (d) learning through analysis and conceptualization.

The merits and demerits of this method have been discussed in the previous method.

To this end, trainers should:

- Ensure that members of the group are comfortable with each other.
- Select and prepare the role players by introducing a specific situation.
- Help participants prepare; ask them to prepare potential situation.
- Realise that volunteers make better role players.
- Prepare observers by giving them specific tasks (e.g., evaluation, feedback)
- Guide the role play enactment over its bumps (since it is not scripted)
- Keep it short.
- Discuss the enactment and prepare bulleted points of what was learned.

Its objective is to raise the ability of manager trainee while dealing with others.

**4. In-basket Method:** In-basket is a popularly used device in identifying executive potential in executive assessment centres. In this method, each item of the trainees is given a file of correspondence bearing on a functional area of management. Each individual studies the file and makes his own recommendations on the situations. If further information is required by him, it is supplied by the members of the team. They are provided with an in-basket of assorted memoranda, requests, and data pertaining to the firm. The trainee must be sense out of his mass of paperwork and prepare memos, make notes and delegate tasks within a limited time period. Later, the observations of each individual member are compared and conclusions on different functional areas reached and these are put down in the form of a report. For this purpose, such teaching methods as the incident process, role playing, syndicate method, and conference method are used.

***Merits:***

1. The participants pay for the consequences of their decisions.
2. Decisions are rapid, feedback is objective and further decisions are based on the feedback of earlier decisions.
3. The consequences of many possible alternatives in a situation can be evaluated over a period of time.
4. Decision making is by a group which consists of managers, and specialists from different departments. Each member gets opportunities to participate in it. Because of emotional involvement without any strain, the participants play for hours with sustained interests.
5. By mixing with managers from different functional areas, managers get a better appreciation of other functional areas.
6. Teachers welcome management games since students' participation is excellent.
7. The efficiency of planning and systematic approach can be demonstrated.
8. Team cooperation can be fostered and departmental conflicts softened down or eliminated.
9. The effect of long-term policies can be demonstrated in the game.
10. The method is inexpensive and can be organised easily.
11. The specified time limit imposes the time constraint on the trainees which stimulates reality.
12. Promising young managers get a perspective on the company as a whole when they work with their senior colleagues in the game.
13. An abstract and complex situation is given the semblance of a real world situation and this illusion facilitates the learning process.

If the trainee is asked to decide issues within a timeframe, it creates a healthy competition among participants. The method is simple and easy to follow. Trainees learns quickly as they have to list priorities, make assumptions, assign work to others and get things done within a timeframe.

***Demerits:***

1. It sometimes discourages originality for teams have to adopt themselves to rigid situations.
2. The logical solutions suggested by the team to be abstracted from compulsions against which it had to be tackled in the actual situation.
3. The method is somewhat academic and removed from real life situation.

**5. Business or Management Game:** Business games are classroom simulation exercises in which teams of individuals compete against one another or against an environment in order to achieve a given objective. The game is close representation of real life conditions. Under these, an atmosphere is created in which the participants play a dynamic role and enrich their skills through involvement and simulated experience. Most business games are expressed in the form of mathematical model controlled and manipulated by an electric computer; while others can be played manually. In the former case, quicker feedback is available; clerical work is avoided and time is controlled. Some games are interacting types of games, while others are non-interacting in types. The interacting types of games are like a game of tennis; the decision of one team influence or affect the performance of the other teams. In the non-interacting types of games, each team is independent and do not affect others. A problem is provided to them along with all the necessary information and constraints. Team of trainees are formed to meet, discuss and arrive at a decisions concerning such subjects as production amounts, research and development, inventories, sales and a myriad of other activities for a simulated films. Games can be relatively simple, permitting rapid decision making to be effected, or extremely complicated, entailing long and detailed analysis of trends in cost, inventories and sales.

Usually, management games consist of several teams which represents competing companies. Each team consists of two to six members. Team take decisions regarding production, prices, research expenditure, marketing, advertising, and attempt to maximize hypothetical profits in this simulated environment. The decisions of a team are fed into a computer which has been programmed according to a particular model or of the market. The game continues for six to twelve periods. At the end of that period, the final results are worked out by each team and compared with those of others.

Business games are intended to teach trainees how to take management decisions in an integrated manner. The participants learn by analyzing problems and by making trial-and-error decisions. Such games illustrate the existence of various group processes, including communication, the resolution of conflicts, the emergence of leadership and the development of ties of friendship.

The processing of information is supposed to be guided by knowledge of the goals and policies of the Organisation. Even if mistake is made in the game, the trainee can learn a lot from his mistake. This avoids possible mistakes while taking decisions for his company. This method develops capacity to take rational decisions by managers.

***Merits:***

1. There is usually a great sense of excitement and enjoyment in playing games. This helps to develop problem-solving skills and helps focus attention on the need for planning than on "putting out fires".
2. As the company elect their own officers and develop their own organizational structures, they can be useful for developing leadership skills and for fostering cooperation and team-work.
3. It helps to analyse and select the significant and relevant data from mass of information and also helps ability to decide with incomplete data and amid conditions of uncertainty.
4. It helps in changing attitudes. The participants become more tolerant.
5. One can learn from mistakes, take a different course of action by looking at the consequences and improve performance.

6. They promote increased understanding of complex relationships among organizational units.
7. Prompt feedback facilitates quick learning.
8. The participants learn how to operate in a competitive environment, as each team competes as the same outcomes which may be in the form of win-lose situation.

***Demerits:***

1. A major problem with games is that, they can be very expensive to develop and implement particularly when the game itself is computerized.
2. Management games usually force decision maker to choose his alternatives from a "closed" list in real life managers are more often rewarded for creating new alternatives.
3. Though, games may be accurate, simulations, they are never totally realistic, for no evidence is available which may indicate that those who are successful in business games will also be successful in real job.
4. Creativity may take a back seat when unorthodox strategies advanced by innovative participants may not find acceptance from others in the race.

On the whole, the trainees almost always react favourably to a well-run game and it is a good technique for developing, problem-solving and leadership skills.

**6. Sensitivity, Laboratory, or T-group Training:** This becomes quite popular during 1950s. Sensitivity training also known as laboratory or T-groups with T-standing for training evolved from the group dynamics concept of Kurt Lewin, and the first sensitivity training session was held in 1946 in State Teachers College, New Britain, USA. Since then, it spread to numerous training centres in USA and other countries. Sensitivity training is a small group interaction processing the unstructured form which requires people to become sensitive to others' feelings in order to develop reasonable group activity. It is known by several names such as 'T-group training', 'action training', 'group dynamics', 'confrontation groups', 'awareness expertises', 'sensitivity retreats', 'human capacity movement', 'encounter sessions' and so forth.

It involves face-to-face learning about ongoing behaviour within a small group that needs continually for periods as long as one to two weeks. According to Chris Argyris, "sensitivity training is a group experience, designed to provide maximum possible opportunity for the individuals to expose their behaviour, give and receive feedback, experiment with new behaviour and develop awareness of self and of others". Specific result sought includes increased ability to emphasis with others, improved listening skills, greater openness, increased tolerance for individual differences, understanding group process and improved conflict resolution skills.

**Objectives:** Sensitivity training involves the use of development techniques which attempts to increase or improve human sensitivity and awareness.

1. Managers with increased awareness of their own behaviour and of how others perceive them;
2. A clarification and development of personal values and goals constant with a democratic and scientific approach to problem of social and personal decision and action;
3. Greater sensitivity to be behaviour of others, and increased understanding of group process;

4. Development of concepts, and theoretical insights that will serve as tool in linking personal values, goals and intentions to actions that are consistent with these inner factors and with the situation requirements; and
5. Achievement of greater behavioural effectiveness in transactions with one's various environments.
6. Changed attitudes toward own role, role of others, and organisational relationships, that is more respect for and willingness to deal with others on whom one is interdependent, greater willingness to achieve collaborative relationships with others based on mutual trusts.
7. Increased interpersonal competencies in handling relationship on own organisational role with superior, peers and subordinates.
8. Increased awareness of changed attitudes towards and increase in interpersonal competency about specific organisational problems existing in groups or in units which are interdependent.
9. Organizational improvement through the training of relationships or groups rather than individuals.

In sensitivity training, the actual technique employed is T-group. It is small group of ten to twelve people assisted by a professional behavioural scientist who act as a catalyst and trainee for the group. There is no specified agenda. He merely creates the opportunity for group members to express their ideas and feelings freely. Since, the trainer has no leadership role to play; the group must workout its own methods of proceeding. A leaderless and agendum-free group session is on. They can discuss anything they like. Individuals are allowed to focus on behaviour rather than on duties. As members engage in the dialogue, they are encouraged to learn about themselves as they interact with others. The aim is to achieve behaviour effectiveness in transactions with one's environment. The notable features of sensitivity training are:

- T-group training is based on the following philosophy: "open your eyes. Look at yourself. See how you look to others. Then decide what changes, if any, you want to make and in which direction you want to do."
- It emphasis the process rather than the content of the training and focuses upon emotional rather than conceptual training.
- It is an experience-based methodology aimed at changing behaviour through unstructured group interaction.
- It is not a set of hidden, manipulative processes, aimed at brainwashing individuals.
- It is not intended to suppress conflict, it is not a group therapy and of course, it does not guarantee change.

***Merits:***

1. A majority of the trainees feel that the experience gained during training is uniquely valuable, as it develops the personality.
2. Practically, there is no real hazard for the emotionally healthy participants, and sick participants are not admitted to the training.
3. Even hardheaded business managers have a softhearted appeal for sensitivity training because they acknowledge the positive value of the training. Many organizations have started paying impressive amounts for training.

4. Research on sensitivity training also strongly attests to the benefits of training to employees in an organization.

5. Research on sensitivity training also reveals that participants have developed added realism and honesty in their relationships before and after tests indicate significant changes in attitudes and behaviour and in personal growth.

***Demerits:***

1. The programme of sensitivity training is considered to be a waste of time. Even participants who are themselves favourably impressed cannot point out the specific benefits and neither can their associates.

2. T-group leaders are considered to be amateur headshrinkers; they are like children playing with fire.

3. The T-group experience is an immoral and unjustified invasion of privacy. Based on false assumptions about the nature of human relationship at work.

4. The process of sensitivity training involves an emotional blood bath; emotional buffering creates a frightening threat to an individual who is a trainee; it can shatter personal defenses and damage future capabilities. Sessions of sensitivity training may — as happens quite often – result in suicide of the interests in the organization. It may take months if not years, to repair the damage caused by sensitivity training.

5. Sensitivity training has a tendency to result in undesirable behaviour of employees for the trainee will find it easier to feel hostile without feeling guilty during training. The teamwork also gets affected adversely because of T-group training.

6. The weakest individual in the group bearing the brunt of the complaints can result.

7. Too much of it is attempted by people who are not trained professionals.

8. There is also considerable doubt as to whether the skills acquired are transferable to the workplace.

**7. Simulations:** It is a training technique which indicates the duplication of organizational situations in a learning environment. It is a mock-up of a real thing. This technique has been used for developing technical and interpersonal skills.

In simulation, the following procedure is adopted:

1. Essential characteristics of a real life organisation or activity are abstracted and presented as a case — not to be studied and analysed as in the usual case study method but to be experienced by the trainee as a realistic, life like circumstances.

2. Trainees are asked to assume various roles in the circumstances and to solve the problem facing them. They are asked to be themselves, not to act.

3. A simulation often involves a telescope of compressing of time events, a single hour may be equated with a month or a quarter or a year in real life and many events are experienced in a relatively brief period of time.

4. Simulated decisions games and role playing exercises put individuals in the role of acting out managerial problems. Games which are frequently played on an electronic computer

that has been programmed for the particular game, provide opportunities for individuals to make decisions and to consider the implications of a decision on other segments of the organization, with no adverse effect should the decision be a poor one.

5. Trainees are required to make decisions that have a real effect in the simulation and about which they receive rapid feedback. The simulation is followed by a critique of what went on during exercise.

For example, activities of an organisation may be simulated and the trainee may be asked to make a decision in support of those activities. The results of those decisions are reported back to the trainee with an explanation. The report illustrates what would have happened if that decision was taken. The trainee teams from this feedback and improves his subsequent simulation.

The advantages to simulations are the opportunities to attempt to create an environment, similar to real situations the managers incur, without high costs involved should the action prove undesirable. The disadvantages are that it is difficult to duplicate the pressure and realities of actual decision making on the jobs and individuals often act differently in real life situations when they do in acting out a simulated exercise.

**8. Grid Training:** The managerial grid is an organisational development technique developed by Robert R. Bloke and Jane S. Mouton. The grid represents several possible leadership styles. Each style represents a different combination of two basic orientations concern for people (1.9) and concern for production (9.1)

The management training programme is built around this managerial grid. It aims at developing open confrontation of organisational problems and high people high production (9.9) leaders.

Such programmes last for three to five years and usually involve the following steps:

1. ***Phase-1*** involves a weekend conference, where trainees are taught the fundamental of grid-training,
2. ***Phase-2*** comprises the discussion, analysis and solution of the units' problems and practices by the management and the subordinates.
3. ***Phase-3*** involves meeting with various groups with the aim of working out companywide problems and setting some development targets for the company as a whole,
4. ***Phase-4*** involves outlining specific procedures for accomplishing the company's development targets.
5. ***Phase-5*** includes evaluation of the units' accomplishments and beginning work on any remaining or new problems.

Managerial grid with concern for people is shown on the vertical scale and concern for output on the horizontal. A score of 1 indicates trainee low concern and score 9 indicates high concern. Such assessments are then followed by thorough group discussion of the meaning of the measured location of each trainee. Usually with the admonition that the group should move to a more balanced position of equal concern for both people and productivity.

**9. Conferences:** The conference method is another commonly used method of executive development. Topics such as human relations, safety education, customer relations, sales training, are often discussed, debated, spoken about at conference specially organised and designed for the purpose. A conference is a meeting of people to discuss a subject of common interest, problems, and doubts. The conference is structured around a small group meeting, wherein a leader helps the group indentify and define a problem, guides the discussion along desired lines and summarises the views that represents the consensus of the group in dealing with the problem. The participants exchange notes, opinions, and ideas on the subject in a systematic, planned way. A conference may be divided into small groups for focused discussions. Participants are expected to air their opinions and thoughts freely. In order to ensure its success: (i) participants are expected to come prepared for the conference, (ii) the conference leader should conduct the sessions according to a plan, giving enough room for healthy interchange of different viewpoints, (iii) the discussion should proceed along desired lines, and (iv) the size of the groups should not be too large. When big organizations use this method, the trainer uses audio visual aids such as black board, mock ups, and slides.

**10. Lecture:** In this method, the instructor organizes the material and gives it to trainees in the form of talk. Lectures are formal talk on a topic by an experienced and knowledgeable person. The presentation is generally supported by discussions, case studies, audio-visual aids and films shows. It is a simple and inexpensive way of imparting knowledge on a topic of special importance to a large audience. There could be a speedy interchange of ideas on a specific topic. The method may often degenerate into a kind of one-way traffic where the presenter tries to get ahead without paying attention to the reactions of the audience. If the lecture is not interesting enough, the audience may not participate and offer any feedback. The listeners play a largely non-participatory role. They may ask questions but they never get the feel of what is being talked about. Moreover, participants do not share each other's experiences and hence the learning is confined to what the presenter has to say.

An advantage of lecture method is that, it is direct and can be used for a large group of trainees. The method could be used effectively if the following things are to be kept in mind:

1. The presentation should be interesting, lively and leave enough room for healthy discussions.
2. The presenter must possess excellent communication and interpersonal skills. Adequate presentation must precede the actual presentation.
3. To enrich the presentation, audio-visual aids, examples, real life incidents, cases, books and periodicals should be used freely, encouraging the audience to participate freely. Better to set time limits to the lecture, since listeners tends to switch off completely beyond a point.

**11. Transactional Analysis:** When people interact with others, there is a transaction for which one person responses to another. The study of these social transactions between people is called transactional analysis (TA). It was popularized by Berne's book, *Games People Play* (1964) and Harris' book, *I Am Ok. You Are Ok* (1976). According to Berne, two people interact with each other from one of the three psychological positions known as ego states. These three states are called parent, adult and child. People, whose parent ego state is in control, may be protective, controlling, nurturing, critical, and instructive. They may dogmatically refer to the policies and standards. The parent state is made up of one's attitudes and behaviour incorporated from external sources. It is an ego state of authority and superiority. A person acting in a parent state is usually dominant, scolding and otherwise authoritative. The parent tends to be judgemental, condescending and punishing with frequent use of such words as "should", "ought", and "mustn't". The adult ego state will appear as calculative, factual and emotional behaviour. It tries to upgrade decisions by seeking facts, processing data, estimating probabilities and holding factual decisions. The adult state is objective and rational. It deals with reality, and objectively gathers information and open mind. Since it reasons and is reasonable, its actions are almost computer like — making decisions, give opinion. The child ego state reflects the emotions developed in response to childhood experiences. It may be spontaneous, dependent, creative, or rebellious. Like a child, this ego states desires approval from others and prefers immediate rewards. The child contains all the impulses that are natural to an infant. Acting in this state, the person can be obedient or manipulative, charming, at one moment and repulsive the next. Whereas the parent acts as he or she was taught, the child is emotional and acts according to how he or she feels at the moment.

In TA theory, the parent and child ego states feel and react directly while the adult state think or process transactional data logically before acting. In most situations, the ideal interaction is an adult stimulus, followed by an adult response. TA is based on intuitive feel rather than on hard evidence, the TA experience may help managers understand others better and assist them in altering their responses so as to produce more effective results. The objective of TA is to provide better understanding of how people relate to one another, so that they may develop improved communication and human relations.

**12. Management Institutions:** Along with the universities and colleges, there are management training institutions such as NITIE, Bombay Management Association, and Productivity Councils and so on. These institutes run special training courses for graduates interested in management education and also orientation programmes for existing managers from public and private sector enterprises. Companies can depute their managers for short orientation courses and update the knowledge and information of their managers in specific areas. Even seminars, workshops and conferences are arranged for the training of managers by various associations such as chambers of commerce and export promotion councils.

Mumbai University has its Bajaj Institute of Management for various management development courses. Colleges affiliated to the Universities also conduct DBM, MBA and other management development programmes for the executives from business sector. Candidates working at managerial levels in companies are normally selected for such training programmes.

Various methods of management development have been discussed above. However, it is difficult to suggest which of the training method will prove better, for the success of each method largely depend on:

(a) How it is employed;

(b) The instructor's ability and personality;

(c) The trainee's maturity, background and willingness to learn; and

(d) Company atmosphere and the extent to which there is an opportunity and encouragement to the trainee to apply to the job what he learnt in the class or the programme.

It may only be said that some methods may suit some training objective or group of participants better than others, but the acceptance and adoption of one or other of these methods will have to be done with caution and after careful thinking.

## KEY TERMS

- **Training:** Training is a planned programme designed to improve performance and to bring about measurable changes in knowledge, skills, attitude and social behaviour of employees.
- **Development:** Broadening an individual's knowledge, skills, and abilities for future responsibilities.
- **Modelling:** Copying someone else's behaviour.
- **Job Instruction Training:** Training received directly on the job.
- **Obsolescence:** A condition that results when an employee loses the knowledge or abilities to perform successfully due to changes in the field.
- **Feedback:** The process of providing trainees with information about their performance.
- **Job Rotation:** Moving a trainee from job-to-job so as to provide cross training.
- **Vestibule Training:** A training method involving creation of training facilities separate from the regular production area but with the same equipment.
- **Role Playing:** A development technique requiring the trainee to assume a role in a given situation and act out behaviours associated with that role.
- **On-the-job Training:** Any training technique that involves allowing the person to learn the job by actually performing it on the job.
- **Counselling:** The discussion of an employee's problem with the general objective of helping the employee cope with it.
- **Simulations:** Any artificial environment that tries to closely mirror an actual condition. These include case studies, decision games, role plays, etc.
- **Apprenticeship:** A training method that puts trainees under the guidance of a master worker, typically for two to five years.
- **Case:** An in-depth description of a particular situation an employee might encounter on the job.
- **In-basket:** A method where the trainee is required to examine a basket full of papers and files relating to his area and make recommendations on problems contained therein.
- **Executive Development:** The process in which executives acquire not only skills and competence in their present jobs but also capabilities for future managerial tasks of increasing difficulty and scope.
- **Management Game:** It is a learning exercise representing a real-life situation where trainees compete with each other to achieve specific objectives.
- **Simulation Method:** It is a method employed to develop a situation that is close to reality where people learn by doing things – in a controlled environment.
- **Programmed Learning:** A kind of individual study where trainees learn through a series of small steps, e.g., linear programming.
- **Understudy:** A development method whereby potential managers are given the chance to temporarily relieve an experienced manager of part of his jobs and act as his substitute

during the period, giving him vital insights into the overall job that would make him the automatic choice in the succession process.

- **Behaviour Modelling:** An approach that demonstrate desired behaviour and gives trainees the chance to practice and role-play those behaviours and receive feedback.

## SUMMARY

- Employee training has become increasingly important as jobs have become more sophisticated and influenced by technological changes.
- Training is a planned programme, designed to improve performance and to bring about measurable changes in knowledge, skills, attitude, and social behaviour of an employee.
- Training makes employees versatile, mobile, flexible and useful to the organization.
- An organization's training needs will evolve from asking these questions:
  (a) What is an organizational goal?
  (b) What tasks must be completed to achieve these goals?
  (c) What behaviours are necessary for each job incumbent to complete his or her assigned tasks?
  (d) What deficiencies, if any, of incumbents have in the skills, knowledge or attitude required to perform the necessary behavours?
- Formal methods can be classified as:
  (a) On-the-job training, including apprenticeships, job instruction training, vestibule training, simulation, training by supervisors and workmen, etc.
  (b) Off-the-job training, including lectures, conferences, firms, programmed instructions, seminar, case studies, role playing.

## CASELET 1

### Leading with One Voice: Training in a Global Organization

BP is a global energy company that doubled its size in four years through a series of mergers and acquisitions. Although BP has one name, it is actually comprised of a multitude of nationalities and corporate cultures. It had 35 different leadership development programmes taking place around the world. The sheer number of these training programmes pointed out a major problem: There was no common understanding, or model, of what it meant to be a leader at BP. How could people have a common understanding and work together toward shared goals without a common approach to how to lead?

Top management at BP decided to address this problem by training first-level leaders (the BP label for first-line supervisors). This is a large and diverse group of more than 10,000 people in every sector of the organization. Although their diversity and geographic dispersion would make the training effort more difficult, this group was too important to BP not to have a common understanding of how to be an effective BP manager.

A leadership training programme was developed on input from first-level leaders across the organization. Finally, BP would have a common management framework across the globe. The course was well received by first-level leaders, with 84 per cent reporting satisfaction with the programme. (The target satisfaction rated had been set at 80%). Demand for the programme was higher than expected, and additional courses had to be offered.

The team that developed the training realized that it did not have measures with which to demonstrate the value of the training programme. The satisfaction surveys given at the end of each course wouldn't answer what the team viewed as the critical issue: What happened when people got back to their jobs after the training was completed? Was the training applied in the workplace?

In order to address whether the training was being transferred back to the job, the team identified behavioural changes that should be evident in leaders who completed the programme. These behavioural changes were divided into six categories:

- **Organizational Awareness.** Understanding the BP organization and being able to network in it.
- **Communication Skills.** Ability to listen and take into account other's viewpoints.
- **Confidence and Self-awareness.** Ability to be objective and remain calm under pressure.
- **Management Skills.** Problem-solving, priortizing, delegation, and time-management ability.
- **Leadership Skills.** Ability to develop and maintain an effective team, generate commitment and overcome obstacles.
- **Team Performance.** Effective team leadership to achieve results.

Using the behaviour measures, BP surveyed managers and direct reports of first-level leaders in the first year after the programme. Performance on each of the six measures was significantly better for first-level leaders who had taken the training..Another survey the next year again found the same positive results for the training programme.

### Questions

1. Referring to Kirkpatrick's four levels of training evaluation discussed in the chapter, what level of evaluation was BP using before it devised the six measures of change?
2. What level of training evaluation is represented in the six measures of change identified by BP? Is this an adequate measure of training effectiveness? Explain.
3. If you oversaw the first-level leader training programme at BP? What major steps do you think should be undertaken next? Explain.

## CASELET 2

### Hotel Mangalore Private Ltd.

Hotel Mangalore Private Ltd., is located in Hampankatta, Mangalore. It is one km from Mangalore railway station. Though started about two years ago, it is now attracting business customers throughout the country. Mr. R. K. Shetty, who has served in five-star hotels in Mumbai and Chennai, wants to make it the number one hotel in Mangalore.

The staff and employees of this hotel are recruited locally. Since most of them do not have experience working in five-star hotels, they do not have the attitudes and skills to deal with the hotel's customers. In contrast, the supervisory staff are qualified having a degree in Hotel Management and have undergone intensive training in five-star hotels in Mumbai, before joining Hotel Mangalore.

However, their assistants in the front office, lobby, restaurant, kitchen and housekeeping, do not have any formal training in their respective jobs. The supervisory staff therefore finds it difficult to give them suitable instructions. The employees and staff are not of the standard expected of them from the business customers, who compares the service at Hotel Mangalore with other five-star hotels. Of late, there have been increasing number of complaints about general cleanliness, housekeeping, room service and service at the restaurant.

Mr. Shetty has called a number of meetings with departmental heads and supervisory staff. They recommended a formal training programme for staff and employees of the hotel. It was therefore agreed that suitable training to be given to the staff and employees. However, the supervisory staff do not wish to relieve the staff during working hours and the staff are not willing to attend the training programme after working hours.

You have been appointed as management consultant for Hotel Mangalore and have been asked to give a comprehensive training plan for the employees, starting the needs, duration of the training, contents, methodology, resource persons, and a formal appraisal method to evaluate the effectiveness of the training programme.

### Questions

1. How will you make a comprehensive training plan for all the staff who needs training?
2. What would the contents of the training programme be?
3. How will you assess the training needs?
4. How will you motivate the staff to attend the training programme?

## CASELET 3

### Unwanted Promotion

Kertar Singh, joined Lakshmi Bank, Meerut branch as a clerk after obtaining a postgraduate degree in chemistry from Delhi University in 1986. He did his work diligently and was generally rated as a hard working, ambitious young man. He obtained the professional qualification, CAIIB in 1992. Thereafter, he applied for the officers' post under the promotional quota. He could not get the promotion as his scores in the written test were low. Meanwhile, he was transferred to the Delhi University, campus branch, Delhi. His attempts to scale the career ladder did not succeed and after several frustrating trials, he consciously decided to join the ranks of the union as an active member. He became the president of the local branch of Bank Employees' Union in 1995. Through his interpersonal skills, he moved closer to most employees in the bank and was able to put out the fires between people quickly. Of late, he is considered a tough union activist to bargain with and management has developed a kind of negative attitude towards his career moves. In 1996, when the opportunity came, he was not considered for promotion as his interview scores, this time were found to be not satisfactory! The branch managers' confidential report about his union activities, it is rumoured, is said to be the major obstacle to his promotion. Meanwhile, Kartar Singh started a business of dealership in automobiles using a dummy name. He also succeeded, to a large extent, in diverting the deposits of nearby business community to other banks. Based on the recommendations of the new branch manager, management decided to promote Kartar singh to the office cadre in 1999. Kartar received the appointment order for the officer's post from the head office recently. The colleagues, along with the branch manager planned an evening tea party, congratulating his achievement. To their surprise, Kartar expressed his unwillingness to accept the offer and refused the promotion straightaway, citing medical reasons.

## Questions

1. Comment on the promotion policy of the bank, using inputs from the above case.
2. Do you think management's action of selecting Kartar as an officer after 13 years' of service is in the right direction? Why? Why not?
3. Why did Kartar refuse promotion?

## ........ QUESTIONS FOR DISCUSSION

### Assignments or Questions for Discussion

1. "You can't develop managers. People either have the ability to manage or they don't." Do you agree or disagree? Discuss.
2. "Management development should down play job knowledge and leadership abilities and emphasis the ethical issues in managerial decision making." Do you agree or disagree? Discuss.
3. How effective do you think training can be in raising employee motivation?
4. Human resource management is nothing but looking at the development of manpower of an organization in the light of its requirements. Do you agree with this statement? Give reasons for your answer.
5. "Training programmes are helpful to avoid personnel obsolescence." Discuss.
6. Suppose that you are the manager of an accounts receivable unit in a large company. You are switching to a new system of billing and recordkeeping and need to train you supervisors and 32 employees in the new procedures. What training method(s) would you use? Why?
7. Suppose you are providing a training to someone to use a new accounting software package in a medium-sized firm. What training method(s) would you use? Why?
8. How would you identify the training needs of a group of sales employees of a large public sector insurance company facing stiff competition from private sector insurance companies in recent times?
9. Training programmes are usually the first casualties when management decides to cut costs. Why do you believe this occurs?
10. How are external changes in the environment of business affecting the training and development function in human resource departments?
11. "Successful development requires top management support and an understanding of the relationship of development to other HR activities." Discuss.
12. Many companies spend considerable time and money on training interpersonal skills. Do you think such training really works? Explain your answer.
13. Performance problems seem all too common in your workplace. People do not seem to be putting forth the needed effort and interpersonal conflict on the work teams seems to be a constant. Is training the answer? If so, what kind of training should be done? What other actions may be approprite?
14. Training provides workers with skills needed in the workplace. However, many organizations have dynamic environments in which change in the norm. How can training requirements be identified when job duties are a moving target?

### Questions for Review

1. Define "Training". Distinguish between training and development. Explain the various methods of training.
2. Contrast apprenticeship programmes with job instructional training.

3. Contrast case studies and role plays as a training methods.
4. What are the reasons for the growing usage of external training in present day organizations?
5. What are the objectives of employee training? Explain the benefits of the training.
6. What do you mean by executive development? Discuss the various methods of executive development.

## Objective Questions

### Fill in the Blank

1. __________ is given to the employees in the area of developing their operational and technical skills.
   (a) Recruitment, (b) Selection,
   (c) Training, (d) Development
2. __________ is a technique which duplicates the actual conditions countered on a job.
   (a) Case study, (b) Simulation,
   (c) Demonstration, (d) Programmed instructions.
3. __________ is a set of data that present issues and problem for solutions on the part of trainee.
   (a) Case, (b) Conference,
   (c) Simulation, (d) Seminar
4. __________ is a method of human interaction which involves realistic behaviour in the imaginary situation.
   (a) Role playing, (b) Coaching,
   (c) Seminar, (d) Laboratory training
5. __________ is a meeting of several people to discuss the subject of common interest.
   (a) Case study, (b) Conference,
   (c) Seminar, (d) Simulation
6. __________ tends to emphasis the accumulation and memorization of facts and figures and does not stress on the application of knowledge.
   (a) Lectures, (b) T-group,
   (c) Programmed instruction, (d) Management game
7. __________ consists of steps which are often set up through the central panel of an electronic computer as guides in the performance of a desired operation or series of operation.
   (a) Programmed instruction, (b) Coaching method,
   (c) Simulation, (d) Case study
8. __________ training is an experimental approach to training.
   (a) Role playing, (b) Sensitivity,
   (c) Simulation, (d) Vestibule
9. Role playing was developed by __________ a venetian psychiatrist.
   (a) Moreno, (b) Robert Owen,
   (c) Hugo Munsterberg, (d) Henry Fayol.
10. In __________ method, a trainee is made to move from job-to-job at certain intervals.
    (a) Demonstration, (b) Job rotation,
    (c) Job instruction training, (d) Laboratory training.
11. __________ may be based on a paper prepared by one or more trainees on a subject selected.
    (a) Seminar, (b) Conference,
    (c) Case study, (d) Project.

**Ans: 1.** (c), **2.** (b), **3.** (a), **4.** (a), **5.** (b), **6.** (a), **7.** (a), **8.** (b), **9.** (a), **10.** (b), **11.** (a)

## Multiple Choice Questions

1. In on-the-job training:
   (a) Trainer learns on the actual environment; (b) Consist of groups discussions;
   (c) Discussed points of common interests; (d) Includes case study
2. Job instruction training is also known as:
   (a) Role playing (b) Learning by seeing
   (c) Apprenticeship training (d) Training through step-by-step learning
3. Vestibule training often imparted with:
   (a) Steps show what is to be done;
   (b) Learning the new skills;
   (c) The job by worker's immediate supervisors;
   (d) The training in crafts, trades and technical area.
4. Simulation is a technique which:
   (a) Duplicates as nearly as possible, the actual conditions encountered as jobs;
   (b) Going through a step-by-step explanation;
   (c) Based on a paper prepared by one or more trainees;
   (d) Emphasis on small group discussion.
5. Programmed instructions are also known as:
   (a) Teaching by the machine method; (b) Learning by doing;
   (c) Team discussion; (d) Classroom instructions
6. Development:
   (a) is short-term in nature
   (b) focuses on the employee's current job
   (c) is a luxury most organisations avoid
   (d) aims at improving the total personality of a manager
7. The advantage of the lecture method include:
   (a) Economy; (b) Feedback;
   (c) Participation; (d) Transference;
8. Role playing is often used to:
   (a) Model behaviour (b) Change results
   (c) Learn skills (d) Change attitudes
9. Business games:
   (a) Improve firefighting skills (b) Promote cooperation among participation;
   (c) Compress time; (d) Are easy to develop

**Ans: 1.** (a), **2.** (d), **3.** (b), **4.** (a), **5.** (a), **6.** (d), **7.** (a), **8.** (d), **9.** (c)

## Match the Following

1.

| | |
|---|---|
| 1. T-group | (a) Teaching in technical areas |
| 2. Demonstration | (b) vestibule training |
| 3. Apprenticeship | (c) Self-awareness |
| 4. On-the-job training | (d) Step-by-step explaination. |

2.

| | |
|---|---|
| 1. off-the-job training | (a) need refresher training |
| 2. training programme | (b) laboratory training |
| 3. old employees | (c) small group discussion |
| 4. conference | (d) prevent obsolescence of manpower |

3.

| | |
|---|---|
| 1. seminar | (a) moving employees to various positions |
| 2. case study | (b) similar to actual work environment |
| 3. job rotation | (c) issue and problem-solving techniques |
| 4. vestibule training | (d) paper preparation |

4.

| | |
|---|---|
| 1. job instruction | (a) an act of increasing skill |
| 2. training | (b) highly organised technique |
| 3. programmed instructions | (c) learn different identities and circumstances. |
| 4. role playing | (d) a systematic approach of preparing the trainees. |

**Ans:** **1.** (1. c), (2. d), (3. a), (4. b) **2.** (1. d), (2. c), (3. a), (4. b) **3.** (1. d), (2. a), (3. b), (4. c)

## True or False

1. Coaching is an effective on-the-job method depends upon the supervisor's ability.
2. In off-the-job training method, training is a part of everyday job activity.
3. In vestibule training method, training is imparted with equipments identical to those used in work, in a separate classroom.
4. Well trained employees need less guidance and controls.
5. Training objectives should be set in terms of changes needed in behaviour and performance.
6. Role playing is often used to learn skills.
7. Job rotation can be either horizontal or vertical.
8. T-group work on a specialised agenda focusing attention on duties rather than behaviour.
9. Job rotation is an excellent method for broadening individual's exposure to company operations and for turning specialists into generalists.
10. On-the-job training should be relatively structured.
11. Vestibule training easily transfers to the work setting.
12. Development is the long-term educational process.
13. Transfer of executives from one location to another is called job rotation.
14. Programmed instructions is a vital component of distance learning.
15. Development focuses more on the employee's personal growth.
16. Coaching involves a continuing flow of instructions, comments and suggestions from the manager to the subordinate.
17. The main job of the manager is to make routine decisions.
18. Executive development is a one shot deal.
19. Employee development is more future-oriented and more concerned with education than employee training.

**Ans:** **1.** True, **2.** False, **3.** True, **4.** True, **5.** True, **6.** False, **7.** True, **8.** False, **9.** True, **10.** True, **11.** True, **12.** True, **13.** False, **14.** True, **15.** True, **16.** True, **17.** False, **18.** False, **19.** True.

☺☺☺

CHAPTER 4

# Performance Appraisal

## LEARNING OBJECTIVES

- *Introduction to Performance Appraisal*
- *Meaning of Performance Appraisal*
- *Objectives of Performance Appraisal*
- *Contents of Performance Appraisal*
- *Process of Performance Appraisal*
- *Main Appraisers*
- *360 Degree Performance Appraisal*
- *Methods of Performance Appraisal*
- *Managerial Appraisal*
- *Problems of Performance Appraisal*
- *Recent Developments*
- *Chapter Summary*

## INTRODUCTION TO PERFORMANCE APPRAISAL

Despite the fact that employees are well educated and well trained, most of the learning takes place at workplace. For maintaining the quality and high performance level of employees, systematic appraisal of performance is very much required. Appraising the performance of others is a common practice in our society. We generally evaluate or appraise the behaviour of others in relations to our own needs or goals. Some appraisals are formal and structured while others are quite informal. Thus, teachers evaluate the performance of students, parents evaluate the performance of their children, and all of us, consciously or unconsciously evaluate our own action from time-to-time. For example, different course work and examinations are set to test your ability to perform; the grades you receive are the feedback of your performance.

## MEANING OF PERFORMANCE APPRAISAL

Performance refers to the degree of accomplishment of the tasks that make-up an individual's job. It indicates how well an individual is fulfilling the job demands. Often the term is confused with effort, but performance is always measured in terms of results and not efforts.

Performance appraisal is an objective assessment of an individual's performance against well defined benchmarks. It is a method of evaluating the behaviour of employees in the work normally including both the quantitative and qualitative aspects of job performance. In simple words, performance appraisal may be understood as the assessment of an individual's performance in a systematic way, the performance being measured against factors such as — knowledge, quality and quantity of output, leadership abilities, dependability, cooperation, judgement, adaptability, etc.

Some of the important features of performance appraisal are as follows:

- Performance appraisal is the systematic description of an employee's job-related strengths and weaknesses.
- The basic purpose is to find out how well the employee is performing the job and establish a plan for improvement.
- Appraisals are arranged periodically according to a definite plan.
- Performance appraisal is a continuous process.

Performance appraisal is not job evaluation. Performance appraisal refers to how well someone is doing the assigned job. Job evaluation determines how much a job is worth to the organisation and, therefore, what range of pay should be assigned to the job. Job evaluation is a technique to rank jobs in an organization on the basis of the duties and responsibilities assigned to the job.

## OBJECTIVES OF PERFORMANCE APPRAISAL

The main purpose of performance appraisal in an organization is as follows:

- To create and maintain a satisfactory level of performance by reviewing the current performance of the subordinate, rectifying the deficiencies and setting new standards of work.
- To take decisions regarding salary fixation, promotion, transfer and demotion based on competence and performance.

- To assess training and development needs.
- To contribute to the employee growth and development through management development programmes.
- To assist in career planning decision.
- To facilitate fair and equitable compensation based on performance.
- To assess the future potential of the employee.
- To interact closely with her/his superior and learn the job-related and behaviour-related aspects.
- To confirm the services of probationary employees upon completing their probation period satisfactorily.
- To let the employees know where they stand insofar as their performance is concerned and assist them by giving guidance and constructive criticism.

## CONTENTS OF PERFORMANCE APPRAISAL

Every organisation has to decide upon the content to be appraised which may vary with the purpose of appraisal and the type and level of employees to be appraised. Generally, the content to be appraised is determined on the basis of job analysis.

A job analysis is the process used to collect information about the duties, responsibilities, necessary skills, outcomes, and work environment of a particular job. For example, the job analysts may observe the workers performing their jobs, collect materials that directly or indirectly indicate the required skills (duty statements, instructions, safety manuals, quality charts, etc.).

### Contents to be Appraised for an Officer's Job

- Regularity of attendance.
- Self-expression: written and oral.
- Ability to work with others.
- Leadership styles and abilities.
- Initiative.
- Technical skill
- Ability to grasp new things.
- Ability to reason
- Originality and resourcefulness.
- Creative skills.
- Area of interest and suitability
- Judgement skills.
- Integrity.
- Capability to take responsibility

- Level of acceptance by subordinates.
- Honesty and sincerity.
- Thorough knowledge about the job and the organisation.
- Knowledge of systems and procedures.
- Quality of suggestions offered for improvement.

**Company Examples of Performance Appraisal**

| | |
|---|---|
| Xerox | Provide a core set of metrics for use across the organization |
| Toyota | Focus performance reviews on goals rather than numbers to ensure employee alignment |
| FedEx | Design a balanced scorecard performance measurement system |

## THE PERFORMANCE APPRAISAL PROCESS

**1. Establish Performance Standards:** The performance appraisal begins with the establishment of performance standards. Performance standard is fixed on the basis of job analysis. The performance standard should be clear and objective enough to understand and measure.

**2 Communicate to the Employees:** Key performance areas need to be identified and communicated to the employees to get an understanding of the level, nature and quality of performance expected, time allotted to complete the given task, etc. It is necessary to identify the behavioural dimensions that are critical for evaluating the performance effectiveness and should be included in the appraisal form.

**3. Analysis of Performance by Identifying Facilitating and Inhibiting Factors:** A good performance system should focus on identifying the factors that help or hinder the good performance from within and outside the organization and workout the action plan to strengthen the facilitating factors and weakening the inhibiting factors. To measure the actual performance, the most common information source used by the managers are personal observation, statistical reports, oral, and written reports, etc.

**4. Compare Actual Performance with the Standard:** Compare the actual performance with the standard performance and if there is any deviation take corrective action.

**5. Identify the Training and Development Needs and Draw an Action Plan:** Constant poor performance on certain dimensions need to be identified and training and development activities aimed at developing the employees on this dimensions are to be planned.

**6. Discuss the Performance Appraisal with the Employees:** One of the most challenging tasks facing by managers is to present an accurate appraisal of the subordinate and then have the subordinate accept the appraisal in a constructive manner.

**7. Take Corrective Action, if Necessary:** Corrective action can be of two types. One is immediate and deals predominantly with symptoms. The other one is basic and delivers into causes. Immediate corrective action is often described as "putting out fire", where as basic corrective action gets to the source of deviation and seeks to adjust the deviations permanently.

## THE MAIN APPRAISERS ARE

**Supervisors:** Supervisors include superiors of the employee, other superiors having knowledge about the work of the employee and the department head or the manager. General practice is that immediate superiors appraise the performance which in turn is reviewed by the departmental head/ manager.

**Peers:** Peer appraisal may be reliable if the workgroup is stable over a reasonably long period of time and performs task that require interaction. However, little research has been conducted to determine how peers establish standards for evaluating their coworkers.

**Subordinates:** The concept of having superiors rated by subordinates is being used in most organizations today, especially in developed countries. This method can be useful in other organisational settings too provided the relationships between superiors and subordinates are cordial.

**Self-appraisal:** If individuals understand the objectives they are expected to achieve and the standards by which they would be evaluated, they are to a great extent capable of appraising their own performance. Employees who appraise their own performance may become highly motivated. Escorts, Wipro, etc., use self-appraisal method.

**Users of Services/Customers:** Employee performance in service organizations relating to behaviours, promptness, speed in doing the job and accuracy can be better judged by the customers or users of services. For example, teacher's performance is better judged by the students and the performance of a doctor is judged by the patients.

**Consultants:** Sometimes consultants may be engaged for appraisal when employees or employers do not trust supervisor appraisal and the management does not trust self-appraisal, peer appraisal or subordinate appraisal.

## 360 DEGREE PERFORMANCE APPRAISAL

The appraiser may be any person who has thorough knowledge about the job contents to be appraised and who observes the employee while performing a job. The appraiser should be capable of determining what activities are more important and what are relatively less important. He should prepare reports and make judgements without bias. Typical appraisers are: supervisors, peers, subordinates, employees themselves, users of service and consultants. Performance appraisal by all these parties is called "360 Degree Performance Appraisal". For example, Ponds, General Electric, Hindustan Lever Limited, Grasim, Colgate-Palmolive, Hewlett-Packard, etc., practice 360 Degree performance appraisal.

### Maruti Adopts '360-Degree' Appraisal System

"Leading car makers Maruti Udyog is starting the '360-Degree feedback process' with employees in the top management such as Chief General Managers and General Managers, whose performance will now be assessed based on feedback from their peers and junior management employees within the same department. Earlier, their performance was being appraised only by the Directors and the Managing Director", says Maruti's Chief General Manager (HR), Mr. S.Y. Siddiqui. Ernst & Young, in consultation with Maruti, has listed a set of leadership competencies that are expected in a general manager. Based on that, it has prepared a questionnaire to which peers and subordinates can respond online.

Although acknowledged as an effective tool for leadership development in the West, Indian companies have been shy of introducing such a feedback system for fear of disturbing traditional hierarchical structures. HR consultants feel that the critical issues in implementing such a system include assuring respondents that their feedback will remain confidential and convincing the person receiving the feedback that this is a development tool and not an appraisal tool. Maruti has handled this by getting E&Y and other consultants to make detailed presentations to the senior management personnel before the process got underway. The company has a committee of general managers, called Human Resource Inter Divisional Committee (HRIDC), which is consulted on all major HR issues. The initiative has been unveiled with an e-mail by Maruti's Managing Director, Mr. Jagdish Khattar, asking people to support the online questionnaire process. The 360-Degree feedback system will also include a self-appraisal by the General Manager. At the end of the process, he can compare his self-appraisal with the assessment of his subordinates and peers. One of the benefits that Maruti is hoping to get out of the 360-Degree feedback process is the sense of empowerment and importance felt by subordinates, when they are asked to offer their feedback about their superiors. Maruti currently has over 4,000 employees on its rolls.

**When to Appraise?:** Informal Appraisals are conducted whenever the supervisor or personnel managers feel it necessary. However, systematic appraisals are conducted on a regular basis, say for example, every six months or annually.

## METHODS OF PERFORMANCE APPRAISAL

With the evolution and development of the appraisal system, a number of methods or techniques of performance appraisal have been developed. The important among them are as follows:

**A. Traditional Methods:** (i) Graphic Rating Scales, (ii) Ranking Method, (iii) Paired Comparison Method, (iv) Forced Distribution Method, (v) Checklist Method (Simple Check-list, Weighted Check-list, Critical Incident Method), (vi) Essay or Free Appraisal (vii) Group Appraisal, (viii) Confidential Reports.

**B. Modern Methods:** (i) Behaviourally Anchored Rating Scales, (ii) Assessment Centre, (iii) Human Resource Accounting, (iv) Management by Objectives, and (v) Psychological Appraisers.

### A. Traditional Methods

**(i) Graphic Rating Scales:** Graphic rating scales compare individual performance to an absolute standard. This is the oldest and widely used technique. This method is also known as Linear Rating Scale or Simple Rating Scale.

In this method, judgements about performance are recorded on a scale. The appraisers are supplied with printed forms, one for each employee. These forms contain a number of objectives, behaviour and trait-based qualities and characters to be rated like quality and volume of work, job knowledge, dependability, initiative, attitude, etc., in the case of workers and analytical ability, creative ability, initiative, leadership qualities, emotional stability in the case of managerial personnel.

These forms contain rating of scales. Rating scales are of two types: i.e., Continuous Rating Scale and discontinuous Rating Scales. In continuous scale ratings are in the form of 0, 1, 2, 3, 4, and 5 and in discontinuous scale, the appraiser assigns the points to each degree. Performance regarding each character is known by the points given by the rater. The points given by the rater to each character are added up to find out the overall performance. Employees are ranked on the basis of total points assigned to each one of them. This method takes less time to develop and administer and permit quantitative analysis and comparison. For example, 'Birla Jute' appraises employee performance using graphic rating scale.

**(ii) Ranking Method:** Under this method, the employees are ranked from best to worst on some characteristics. The rater first finds the employee with the highest performance and the employees with the lowest performance in a particular job category and rates the former as the best and the latter as the poorest. Then the rater selects the next highest and next lowest and so on until he rates all the employees in that group.

Ranking can be relatively easy and inexpensive, but may be affected by rater bias or varying performance standards. It is possible that the low ranked individual in one group may turnout to be a superstar in another group. One important limitation of the ranking method is that the size of the difference between individuals is not well defined. For instance, there may be little difference in performance between individuals ranked second and third. Bajaj Tempo uses this method of performance appraisal in their organization.

**(iii) Paired Comparison Method:** This method is relatively simple. Under this method, the appraiser ranks the employees by comparing one employee with all other employees in the group, on a one-to-one basis. Paired comparison method could be employed fairly easily where the number of employees is less. Where the number is fairly large the technique may be time-consuming. Another limitation of this technique is that employees are simply compared to each other on total performance rather than specific job criteria. Godrej Soaps follow this method of performance appraisal.

**(iv) Forced Distribution Method:** The rater may rate his employees at the higher or at the lower end of the scale under the earlier methods. Forced distribution method is developed to prevent the raters from rating too high or too low. Under this method, the rater after assigning the points to the performance of each employee has to distribute his ratings in a pattern to conform to normal frequency distribution.

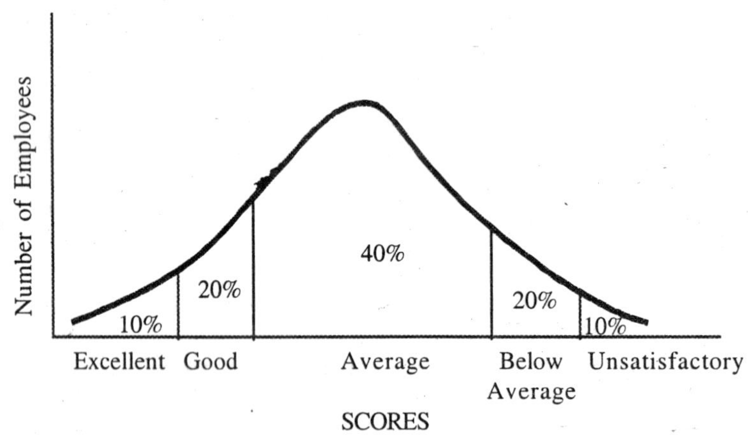


*Fig. 4.1: Forced Distributions on a Bell-shaped Curve*

Thus, similar to the ranking technique, forced distribution requires the raters (supervisors) to spread their employee evaluations in a prescribed distribution. This method eliminates central tendency and leniency bias. However, in this method, employees are placed in certain ranked categories . it not ranked within the categories. Quite often, workgroups do not reflect a normal distribution of individual performance.

This method is based on the assumption that all groups of employees will have the same distribution of excellent, average and poor performers. If one department has all outstanding employees, the supervisor would find it extremely difficult to decide who should be placed in the lower categories. Difficulties can also arise when the rater must explain to the employee why he was placed in one grouping and others were placed in higher groupings. Usha follows this method of performance appraisal in their organization.

**(v) Checklist Methods:** The checklist is a simple rating technique in which the supervisor is given a list of statements or words and asked to check statements representing the characteristics and performance of each employee. There are three types of checklist methods, namely, Simple Checklist, Weighted Checklist, and Forced Choice Method.

- ***Simple Checklist Method:*** The checklist consists of a large number of statements concerning employee behaviour. The rater checks the statements to know whether the behaviour of an employee is positive or negative to each statement. Employee performance is rated on the basis of the number of positive checks. The negative checks are not considered in this method. A difficulty may often arise because the statements may appear to be virtually identical in describing the employee. The words or statements may have different meanings to different raters.

- ***Weighted Checklist:*** The weighted checklist method involves weighting different items in the checklist, having a series of statements about an individual, to indicate that some are more important than others.

  The rater is expected to look into the questions relating to the employee's behaviour, the attached rating scale (or simply positive/negative statements where such a scale is not provided) and tick those traits that closely describe the employee behaviour. Often, the weights are not given to the supervisors who complete the appraisal process, but are computed and tabulated by someone else, such as a member of the personnel unit. In this method, the performance ratings of the employee are multiplied by the weights of the statements and the coefficients are added up. The cumulative coefficient is the weighted performance score of the employee. Weighted performance score is compared with the overall assessment standards in order to find out the overall performance of the employee. The weighted checklist is expensive to design, since the checklist for each different job in the organisation must be produced. This may also prove time-consuming in the end. Though the weighted checklist method is evaluative as well as developmental, it has the basic problem that the evaluator may not know the items which contribute most to successful performance.

- ***Forced Choice Method:*** This method was developed at the close of World War II. Under this method, a large number of statements in groups are prepared. Each group consists of four descriptive statements concerning employee behaviour. Two statements are most descriptive (favourable) and two are least descriptive (unfavourable). Sometimes, there may be five statements in each group out of which one would be neutral. The actual weightage of the statements are kept secret. The appraiser is asked to select one statement that mostly describes employee's behaviour out of the two favourable statements and one statement from the two unfavourable statements. The items are usually a mixture of positive and negative statements. The aim is to eliminate or greatly reduce the rater's personal bias, specifically the tendency to assign all high or low ratings. The items are designed to discriminate effective from ineffective workers as well as reflect valuable personal qualities.

It is difficult to construct and validate the statements under the forced choice method, especially for relatively small organizations. For raters who are not properly trained, it may be difficult to choose among statements that are equally desirable or equally undesirable. Further, it may be time-consuming to prepare statements that suit the demands of a particular job or company. Finally, it may be unpleasant and unacceptable for the raters to believe that they cannot make an objective evaluation and hence their freedom is curtailed. This method is followed in CEAT.

- ***Critical Incident Method:*** Under this method, the supervisor continuously records the critical incidents of the employee performance or behaviour relating to all characteristics (both positive and negative) in a specially designed notebook. The supervisor rates the performance of his subordinates on the basis of notes taken by him. Since the Critical Incident Method does not necessarily have to be a separate rating system, it can be fruitfully employed as documentation of the reasons why an employee was rated in a certain way. An employee was given a deposit mobilization target of 20 lakh, but mobilized 30 lakh is an example of Critical Incident. The college dean may write the following critical incident about one of his instructors, "Outlined the day's lecture on the chalkboard at the beginning of the class."

  The critical incident method has the advantage of being objective because the rater considers the records of performance rather than the subjective points of opinion, for example, mood, emotional balance, relationship between superior and subordinate. This certainly helps in reducing bias in the evaluation. However, the system is not without drawbacks. First, what constitutes a critical incident is not defined in the same manner by all the raters. Next, recording events (critical) continually over a period of time may not be preferred by the raters. The question of discounting precious time of the executive is also involved here.

  The employee might have done something 'critically good and excellent' but the supervisor concerned may not have been present and hence that incident was not recorded. Further, the method can result in employees becoming concerned about what the superior writes about them. Employee may begin to fear the manager's "black book". ITC, Voltas, etc., follow this method of performance appraisal.

**(vi) Essay or Free Form Appraisal:** This method requires the manager to write a short essay describing each employee's performance during the rating period. This format emphasises evaluation of overall performance, based on strengths or weaknesses of employee performance rather than specific job dimensions. By asking supervisors to enumerate specific examples of employee behaviour, the essay technique minimises supervisory bias and the Halo Effect.

The time involved in writing separate essays about each employee can be formidable. Essays are not amenable for evaluation and analysis; essays describing different employees' performance cannot be tied to merit increases and promotion possibilities because there is no common standard. Another inherent limitation of this method is that the evaluators may have unequal skills in writing the essays. Thus, the quality of the ratings depends, not actually on employee performance, but on the writing ability of the rater. BPL and Bata follow this method of performance appraisal.

**(vii) Group Appraisal:** Under this method, an employee is appraised by a group of appraisers. This group consists of the immediate supervisor of the employee, the other supervisors who have close contact with the employee's work, manager or head of the department and consultants. The head of the department or manager may be the chairman of the group and the immediate supervisor may act as the coordinator for the group activities. This group uses any one or multiple techniques discussed earlier. The immediate supervisor enlightens other members about the job characters, demands, standards of performance, etc. Then the group appraises the performance of the employee, compares the actual performance with standards, finds out the deviations, discusses the reasons therefore, suggests ways for improvement of performance, prepares action plans, studies the need for change in the job analysis and standards and recommends change, if necessary. This method is widely used for purposes of promotion, demotion and retrenchment appraisal. Kinetic Honda, Birla VXL and Blue Star follow this method of performance appraisal.

**(viii) Confidential Reports:** Assessing the employees' performance confidentially is a traditional method of performance appraisal. Under this method, the superior appraises the performance of his subordinates based on his observations, judgement and intuitions. The superior keeps his judgement and report confidentially. In other words, the superior does not allow the employee to know the report and his performance. The superior writes the report about his subordinates' strengths, weaknesses, intelligence, attitude to work, sincerity, commitment, punctuality, attendance, conduct, character, friendliness, etc. Though confidential report is a traditional method, most of the public sector organizations still follow this method in appraising the employees' performance.

## B. Modern Methods

**(i) Behaviourally Anchored Rating Scales (BARS):** The Behaviourally Anchored Rating Scales (BARS) method combines elements of the traditional rating scales and critical incident methods.

Using BARS, job behaviours from critical incidents — effective and ineffective behaviours — are described more objectively. The method employs individuals who are familiar with a particular job to identify its major components. They then rank and validate specific behaviours for each of the components.

**How to Construct BARS?**

*Step I* : *Collect Critical Incidents:* People who have knowledge of the work such as job holders and supervisors describe specific examples of effective and ineffective behaviour related to job performance.

*Step II* : *Identify Performance Dimensions:* Examples of performance dimensions include technical competence, customer handling, paperwork and meeting day-to-day deadlines. While developing varying levels of performance for each dimension, specific examples of behaviour should be used, this could later be scaled in terms of good, average or below average performance.

*Step III* : *Reclassification of Incidents:* Another group of job experts are instructed to reclassify the critical incidents generated previously. They are given the definition of job dimension and are told to assign each critical incident to the dimension that it best describes. At this stage, incidents for which there is not 75 per cent agreement are discarded.

*Step IV* : *Assigning Scale Values to the Incidents:* Each incident is then rated on a one-to-nine scale with respect to how well it represents performance on the appropriate dimension.

A rating of one represents ineffective performance; the top scale value indicates very effective performance. The second group of experts usually assigns the scale values. Means and standard deviations are then calculated for the scale values assigned to each incident. Typically, incidents that have standard deviations of 1.50 or less (on a 7-point scale) are retained.

*Step V* : ***Producing the Final Instrument:*** About six or seven incidents for each performance dimension will be used as behavioural anchors. The final BARS instrument consists of a series of vertical scales (one for each dimension) measured by the final incidents. Each incident is positioned on the scale according to its mean value.

**(ii) Assessment Centre:** This method of appraising was first applied in the German Army in 1930. Later, business and industrial houses started using this method. This is not a technique of performance appraisal by itself. In fact, it is a system, where assessment of several individuals is done by various experts by using various techniques. These techniques include all the methods which we are discussed in this chapter plus other methods like in basket, role playing, case studies, stimulation exercises, etc.

**(iii) Human Resources Accounting:** Human resources accounting deals with cost and contribution of human resources to the organisation. Cost of the employee includes cost of manpower planning, recruitment, selection, induction, placement, training, development, wages and benefits, etc. Employee contribution is the money value of employee service which can be measured by labour productivity or value added by human resources.

Cost of human resources may be taken as standard. Employee performance can be measured in terms of employee contribution to the organization. Employee performance can be taken as positive when contribution is more than the cost and performance can be viewed as negative if cost is more than contribution. Positive performance can be measured in terms of percentage of excess of employee contribution over the cost of employee. Similarly, negative performance can be calculated in terms of percentage of deficit in employee contribution compared to the cost of the employee.

These percentages can be ranked to 'Zero level'. This technique has not fully developed and is in the transitionary stage. Bank of Baroda, SAIL, ITC Limited, etc., made attempts to follow this method.

**(iv) Management By Objectives:** Management By Objectives (MBO) is "a process whereby the superior and subordinate managers of an organisation jointly identify its common goals, define each individual's major areas of responsibility in terms of results expected of him and use these measures of guides for operating the unit and assessing the contribution of its members". Thus, MBO focuses attention on participative goal setting that is tangible, verifiable and measurable. The emphasis is on what must be accomplished rather than how it is to be accomplished. Generally, the MBO process is undertaken along the following lines:

- The subordinate and superior jointly determine goals to be accomplished during the appraisal period and what level of performance is necessary for the subordinate to satisfactorily achieve specific goals.
- During the appraisal period, the superior and subordinate update and alter goals as necessary due to changes in the business environment.

Both superior and subordinate jointly discuss whether the subordinate achieved the goals or not. )t, they should identify the reasons for deviation like strike/lockout, market change, etc.

**(v) Psychological Appraisal:** Psychological appraisals are conducted to assess the employee's potential. Psychological appraisals consist of: (i) In-depth Interviews, (ii) Psychological Tests, (iii) Consultations and Discussions with the Employee, (iv) Discussions with the Superiors, Subordinates and Peers, and (v) Reviews of other Evaluations.

Evaluation is conducted in the areas of: (i) Employee's intellectual abilities, (ii) emotional stability. (iii) motivational responses, (iv) reasoning and analytical abilities, (v) interpretation and judgement skills, (vi) sociability, (vii) employee's ability to comprehend the events, and (viii) ability to foresee the future. The psychological appraisal results are useful for decision making regarding: (i) employee placement, (ii) career-planning and development, and (iii) training and development.

## Traditional vs. Modern Technique of Performance Appraisal

Traditional techniques of performance appraisal are appropriate for the stability and sustainable growth strategies. Modern performance appraisal techniques are suitable for growth strategies like expansion, diversification, joint ventures, mergers and acquisitions. These strategies help the company to meet competition, build competencies, acquire strengths, enhance market share, innovate and create new markets, new products and new technologies. Performance appraisal by the customers, subordinates and peers in addition to the superiors, help the employees to have a feedback from multiple directions, identify their deficiencies and acquire competencies through training and development.

In addition, the modern techniques of performance appraisal and 360 Degree Performance Appraisal enhances employee creativity which in turn contributes for the achievement of new product development, low cost leadership and differentiation strategies. Traditional performance appraisal techniques and appraisal by superiors are suitable for retrenchment strategies like turnaround, disinvestments and liquidation strategies.

### Difference between Traditional and Modern Method of Performance Appraisal

| Basis of Difference | Traditional Method | Modern Method |
|---|---|---|
| Terminology | Merit rating, performance evaluation and control. | Employee appraisal/Performance appraisal. |
| Purpose | Determine the basis for wage increase, transfer, promotion, lay-off, etc. | Employee development, Team building. |
| Application | For hourly paid casual or temporary workers. | For technical, professional and managerial employees. |
| Emphasis | Heavy emphasis on personal traits. | Emphasis on results, accomplishment and performance. |
| Techniques | Rating scales emphasis on scores, statistical manipulation of data for comparison purpose. | Management by objectives, mutual goal setting, critical incidents, group appraisal, mutual consultation , Performance analysis and human resource development, more qualitative standards. |
| Post-appraisal | Supervisor communicates his ratings to his employees. | Superior stimulates employees to analyse himself/herself and set own objectives in line with job requirements. Superior helps and guides subordinates. |

| | | |
|---|---|---|
| Appraisers | Only superiors. | 360 degree performance appraisal (appraisal by superiors, subordinates, peers, self, customers and consultants). |
| Nature | Completely confidential. | Open appraisal. |
| Leadership Style | Autocratic. | Participative and democratic. |

## MANAGERIAL APPRAISAL

It is relatively easy to appraise the performance of technical or operative employees compared to managerial personnel. This is because the performance of operative employees can be measured quantitatively, whereas the performance of managers cannot be measured in quantitative terms. Harold Koontz has developed a concept of managerial appraisal, i.e., appraising managers as managers. According to this concept, the managers attain organisational objectives by performing the basic managerial functions, *viz.* planning, organising, leading, motivating, staffing and controlling. Each of these functions can be done by performing a number of series of activities. For example, performing staffing function requires performing a series of activities like analyzing jobs of his department, planning for human resources, deciding upon internal and external recruitment, developing sources of recruitment techniques and so on. Thus, each function and sub-function of the manager is elaborated into a series of activities. These activities in this model are taken as behaviour and standards of performance.

The checklist containing the questions in these areas is prepared with a five degree rating scale, i.e., extremely poor performance, neither poor nor fair performance, fair performance and extremely fair performance. The appraisers rate performance of managers by assessing weights to the scale and appraise only those areas which are clear and are supported by adequate knowledge. Thus, this technique measures the performance of managers in managing organisational environment. But this technique does not seem to be a new one; it is only an extension of subjective areas of appraisal to the level of managers. Further, this technique is subject to fluctuations of performance and influence of various internal and external environmental factors.

## PROBLEMS OF PERFORMANCE APPRAISAL

The major problem in performance appraisal is:

**Rating Biases:** The problem with subjective measure (rating which is not verifiable by others) is that it has the opportunity for Rater Bias. The rater biases include: (a) Halo Effect, (b) the Error of Central Tendency, (c) the Leniency and Strictness Biases, (d) Personal Prejudice, and (e) the Recency Effect.

*(a)* ***Halo Effect:*** It is the tendency of the raters to depend excessively on the rating of one trait or behavioural consideration in rating all other traits or behavioural considerations. For example, if an employee tends to be conscientious and dependable, we might become biased towards that individual to the extent that you will rate him or her "high" on many desirable attributes. People who design performance appraisal form for college students to fill out in evaluating the effectiveness of their teacher also confront with halo effect. Students tend to rate a faculty member as outstanding on all criteria when they are particularly appreciative of a few things he or she does in the classroom. One way of minimizing the halo effect

is appraising all the employees by one trait before going to rate them on the basis of another trait.

(b) ***The Error of Central Tendency:*** Some raters follow play safe policy in rating by rating all the employees around the middle point of the rating scale and they avoid rating the people at both the extremes of the scale. They follow play safe policy because of answerability to the management or lack of knowledge about the job and person he is rating has least interest in his job. For example, a manager rates all the subordinates as 3, on a scale of 1 to 5, then no differentiation among the subordinates exists.

(c) ***The Leniency and Strictness:*** Lenient means showing mercy or tolerance. Every evaluator has his or her own value system which acts as a standard against which appraisals are made. Relating to the true and actual performance an individual exhibits, some evaluators give subordinate a high rating and some others give a low rating. The former is referred to as positive leniency error and the later negative leniency error. When calculators are positively lenient in their appraisal, an individual's performance becomes over rated. Similarly, a negative leniency error understates performance, giving an individual a negative appraisal.

(d) ***Personal Prejudice:*** If the rater dislikes any employee or any group, he may rate them at the lower end, which may distort the rating purpose and affect the career of these employees.

(e) ***The Recency Effect (rate on the basis of latest action only):*** The raters generally remember the recent actions of the employee at the time of rating and rate them on the basis of these recent actions — favourable or unfavourable — rather than on the whole activities.

— *Similarity Error (Rate All Employees in The Same Way):* When the evaluators rate the employees in the same way that the evaluators perceive themselves, they are making a similarity error. Based on the perception that evaluators have of themselves, they project these perceptions on others. For example, an evaluator perceives himself or herself aggressive may evaluate others by looking for aggressiveness. Those subordinates who demonstrate this characteristics tend to benefit, while others are penalized.

**Other Problems are:**

- Negative ratings affect interpersonal relations and industrial relations system.
- In some companies management uses performance appraisal results to punish the employee rather than using it for rectification of errors and development of an employee.
- Some ratings particularly about the potential appraisal are purely based on guess work.

The problems of performance appraisal can be minimized by conducting counselling meetings of appraises with the employees and let employees know their performance, its consequences and also how to take corrective action.

## RECENT DEVELOPMENTS

Performance appraisal to performance development and then to performance management: The approach of performance appraisal is changed significantly in recent times. The approach is shifted from controlling to development. Consequently, it is termed as performance analysis and development. Under this approach, performance of the employee on the job is analysed, weak areas are identified, and developmental activities are taken up to convert weak areas into strong areas. Further, the approach is changed from performance development to performance management.

Under performance management, performance of the employee is continuously monitored and developed in tune with the organizational requirements. Performance management is a process that consolidates goal setting, performance appraisal and performance development into a single common system, the aim of which is to ensure that the employee's performance is supporting the company's strategic performance.

Organizations started adopting customized performance management system where separate performance appraisal techniques are designed for each employees, separately based on employee skills, behaviour and his job needs. Nowadays, computer based performance management software is used for implementing the entire performance management process. However, some of the problems of performance appraisal (like personal bias) can be removed by appraising performance through computers.

## SUMMARY

Performance appraisal is a method of evaluating the behaviour of employees in the work normally including both the quantitative and qualitative aspects of job performance. Performance refers to the degree of accomplishment of the tasks that make up an individual's job. It indicates how well an individual is fulfilling the job demands. Traditional techniques of performance appraisal are appropriate for the stability and sustainable growth strategies. Modern performance appraisal techniques are suitable for growth strategies like expansion, diversification, joint ventures, mergers and acquisitions. The main purpose of performance analysis and development is to analyse the present performance of the employee from multiple viewpoints, observe the gap/developmental needs and develop the employee. Typical appraisers are: supervisors, peers, subordinates, employees themselves, users of service and consultants. Performance appraisal by all these parties is called "360 Degree Performance Appraisal". The use of performance appraisal is that it enables the management to make effective decisions and/or correct or modify their earlier decisions.: The problem with subjective measure (is that rating which is not verifiable by others) has the opportunity for bias. The rater biases include: (a) halo effect, (b) the error of central tendency, (c) the leniency and strictness biases, (d) personal prejudice and (e) the regency effect. The problems of performance appraisal can be minimized by conducting counselling meetings with the appraisees to appraise them of the reasons for their performance and its consequences.

## KEY TERMS

- Performance Appraisal,
- Traditional Methods,
- Graphic Rating Scale,
- Ranking Method,
- Paired Comparison Method,
- Forced Distribution Method,
- Checklist Method,
- Free Form Appraisal,
- Confidential Reports,
- Behaviourally Anchored Rating Scales,
- Assessment Centre,
- Human Resource Accounting,
- Management By Objectives,
- Halo Effect,
- Recency Effect.

## CASELET 1: PERFORMANCE APPRAISAL

Mr. Paresh is one of the mechanics working with Kiran Motors for the last fifteen years. Except the initial years, there was no consistency in Mr. Paresh's performance. His supervisor Mr. Alok Shah is a highly considerate person. He is highly respected by his subordinate for his humanitarian consideration. He not only guides his subordinates but also works with them if situation demands. He attends all the family functions of his subordinates and even helps them financially. He is well-known for his impartiality as well as strictness. The moment he arrives at the scene, there is only work and nothing else.

Mr. Paresh's wife was seriously ill. He has spent a huge amount of money for her treatment. He has borrowed money from the entire known source and has taken a loan from the company for which 20% of his salary is regularly deducted for the loan. He was very much depressed.

Mr. Shah is well acquainted with the declining performance of Paresh and wanted to help Paresh. When it was the time for performance appraisal, Mr. Shah decided to help him out. Although Paresh was an average mechanic, Mr. Shah rated him outstanding in virtually all respects. As the company's compensation system was solely based on the performance appraisal of superiors, Paresh become eligible for 10 per cent salary hike. Mr. Shah called Paresh and briefed him why he has done so. Paresh agreed that his performance has taken a beating. He promised Mr. Shah that he will reciprocate Mr. Shah's gesture in terms of performance from his side.

### Questions

1. What is the problem in this case?
2. How do you evaluate Mr. Alok Shah?
3. What would you have done if you are in the place of Mr. Alok Shah?
4. What is your opinion about the performance appraisal system followed by the company?

## ........ QUESTIONS FOR DISCUSSION

1. Describe in detail the process of performance appraisal.
2. "Performance appraisal is not merely for employee appraisal but for accomplishment and improvement of performance." Discuss
3. "Some of the so-called modern industries still follow traditional techniques of performance appraisal." Do you agree with this statement? if yes, defend your argument
4. Discuss the merits and demerits of critical incident techniques and graphic rating scale.
5. "Management By Objectives is not a technique of performance appraisal but it denotes a systematical process of performance appraisal," Explain critically.

### Objective Questions

#### (a) Fill in the Blanks

1. ________is a method of evaluating the behaviour of employees in the work.
2. _________refers to the degree of accomplishment of the tasks that make up an individual's job.
3. _________is the systematic description of an employee's job-relevant strength and weaknesses.
4. Performance appraisal by supervisors, peers, subordinates, employees themselves, users of service and consultants are called "___________."
5. Under ___________, the appraiser ranks the employees by-comparing one employee with all other employees in the group, one at a time.

6. ________is developed to prevent the raters from rating employees too high or too low.
7. __________ is a simple rating technique in which the supervisor is given a list of statements or words and asked to check statements representing the characteristics and performance of each employee.
8. Under ________________, the supervisor continuously records the critical incidents of the employee performance or behaviour relating to all characteristics (both positive and negative) in a specially designed notebook.
9. The __________ combines elements of the traditional rating scales and critical incident methods.
10. __________ deals with cost of and contribution of human resources to the organisation.
11. ____________ is a process whereby the superior and subordinate managers of an organisation jointly identify its common goals, define each individual's major areas of responsibility in terms of results expected of him and use these measures of guides for operating the unit and assessing the contribution of its members.
12. _______ is the tendency of the raters to depend excessively on the rating of one trait or behavioural consideration in rating all other traits or behavioural considerations.

***Ans:*** **1.** Performance appraisal, **2.** Performance, **3.** Performance Appraisal, **4.** 360 Degree Performance Appraisal, **5.** Paired Comparison Method, **6.** Forced Distribution Method, **7.** The Checklist, **8.** The Critical Incident Method, **9.** Behaviourally Anchored Rating Scales (BARS) Method, **10.** Human Resources Accounting, **11.** Management By Objectives, **12.** Halo Effect.

## (b) Multiple Choice Questions

1. Which of the following is not a type of performance appraisal?
   (a) Team based appraisal (b) 90 degree appraisal
   (c) Appraisal of managers (d) Customer appraisals
2. Performance management is believed to have originated from which country?
   (a) Japan (b) USA
   (c) France (d) Germany
3. Which of the following statements about performance appraisal is not true?
   (a) Employees may be appraised on both objective and subjective measures
   (b) Companies use appraisal to encourage employee loyalty and commitment
   (c) Performance appraisal has become a tool to motivate and control workers
   (d) Performance appraisal reduces managerial control
4. What is 360 Degree appraisal?
   (a) A system where line managers rates subordinates simultaneously.
   (b) A system where every employee rates another employee chosen at random.
   (c) A system where feedback is obtained from peers, subordinates and supervisors.
   (d) A system where a senior manager rates all line managers simultaneously.
5. Some raters follow play safe policy in rating by rating all the employees around the middle point of the rating scale and they avoid rating the people at both the extremes of the scale. This error is known as
   (a) Halo Effect, (b) The Error of Central Tendency,
   (c) The Leniency and Strictness, (d) The Recency Effect.
6. The raters generally remember the recent actions of the employee at the time of rating and rate them on the basis of these recent actions rather than on the whole activities. This problem is known as
   (a) Halo Effect, (b) The Error of Central Tendency,
   (c) The Leniency and Strictness, (d) The Recency Effect.

7. Under this approach, performance of the employee is continuously monitored and developed in tune with the organizational requirements.
   (a) Performance management, (b) Performance evaluation
   (c) Performance development, (d) Performance appraisal.
8. The systematic process of making job valuation determinations about a job based upon its content and the way in which it actually functions within the organization is called
   (a) Job Determination, (b) Job Analysis,
   (c) Job Grading, (d) Job Evaluation.
9. This format emphasises evaluation of overall performance, based on strengths/weaknesses of employee performance rather than specific job dimensions.
   (a) Critical Incident Method, (b) Essay or Free Form Appraisal,
   (c) Forced Choice Method, (d) Checklist Methods.

*Ans:* **1.** (b), **2.** (b), **3.** (d), **4.** (c), **5.** (b), **6.** (d), **7.** (a), **8.** (d).

## (c) State whether the following are TRUE or FALSE, justify your answer

1. Performance appraisal is not job evaluation.
2. Traditional performance appraisal techniques are suitable for growth strategies like expansion, diversification, joint ventures, mergers and acquisitions.
3. Performance analysis and development is a departure from the traditional and controlling approach.

*Ans:* **1. True.** Performance appraisal refers to how well someone is doing the assigned job. Job evaluation determines how much a job is worth to the organisation and, therefore, what range of pay should be assigned to the job.

**2. False.** Traditional techniques of performance appraisal are appropriate for the stability and sustainable growth strategies. Modern performance appraisal techniques are suitable for growth strategies like expansion, diversification, joint ventures, mergers and acquisitions.

**3. True.** It views from the development aspect of the employee. Therefore, the main purpose of performance analysis and development is to analyse the present performance of the employee from multiple viewpoints, observe the gap/developmental needs and develop the employee.

***Behaviourally Anchored Rating Scales (BARS):*** This method combines elements of the traditional rating scales and critical incident methods. Using BARS, job behaviours from critical incidents are described more objectively.

***Assessment Centre:*** This is not a technique of performance appraisal by itself. In fact, it is a system or organisation, where assessment of several individuals is done by various experts by using various techniques.

***Human Resources Accounting:*** It deals with cost of and contribution of human resources to the organisation. Cost of the employee includes cost of manpower planning, recruitment, selection, induction, placement, training, development, wages and benefits, etc. Employee contribution is the money value of employee service which can be measured by labour productivity or value added by human resources.

***Management By Objectives:*** MBO is a 'process whereby the superior and subordinate managers of an organisation jointly identify its common goals, define each individual's major areas of responsibility in terms of results expected of him and use these measures of guides for operating the unit and assessing the contribution of its members.

***Psychological Appraisal:*** Psychological appraisals are conducted to assess the employee's potential. Psychological appraisals consist of: (i) in-depth interviews, (ii) psychological tests, (iii) consultations and discussions with the employee, (iv) discussions with the superiors, sub-ordinates and peers, and (v) reviews of other evaluations.

***Managerial Appraisal:*** According to this concept, the managers attain organisational objectives by performing the basic managerial functions, *viz.*, planning, organising, leading, motivating, staffing and controlling. Each of these functions can be done by performing a number of or series of activities.

***Halo Effect:*** It is the tendency of the raters to depend excessively on the rating of one trait or behavioural consideration in rating all other traits or behavioural considerations.

***The Error of Central Tendency:*** Some raters follow play safe policy in rating by rating all the employees around the middle point of the rating scale and they avoid rating the people at both the extremes of the scale.

***The Leniency and Strictness:*** The leniency bias crops when some raters have a tendency to be liberal in their rating by assigning higher rates consistently.

***Personal Prejudice:*** If the rater dislikes any employee or any group, he may rate them at the lower end, which may distort the rating purpose and affect the career of these employees.

***The Recency Effect:*** The raters generally remember the recent actions of the employee at the time of rating and rate them on the basis of these recent actions — favourable or unfavourable — rather than on the whole activities.

CHAPTER 5

# Wage and Salary Administration

## LEARNING OBJECTIVES

- *Introduction to Wage and Salary Structure*
- *Basic Concepts of Wage and Salary Structure*
- *Nature and Purpose of Wage and Salary Structure*
- *The Wage Determination Process*
- *Wage Administration Rules*
- *Objectives of Wage and Salary Structure*
- *Factors Influencing Wage and Salary Structure*
- *Principles of Wage and Salary Structure*
- *Theory of Wages*
- *Types (Minimum, Fair and Living Wage)*
- *Elements or Ingredients of a Good Wage Plan*
- *Methods of Wage Payment*
- *Executive Compensation*
- *Components of Remuneration*
- *Chapter Summary*

## INTRODUCTION TO WAGE AND SALARY STRUCTURE

Organisation expects efficient performance from their employees in order to contribute to the attainment of organizational objective. It is possible only when employees are paid remuneration in accordance with their contribution. Many people regard compensation as a yardstick for measuring their success in the world of employment.

'Wage and Salary Administration' refers to the establishment and implementation of sound policies and practices of employee compensation. It includes such areas as job evaluation, surveys of wages and salaries, analysis of relevant organisational problems, development and maintenance of wage structure, establishing rules for administering wages, wage payment incentives, profit sharing, wage changes and adjustments, supplementary payments, control of compensation costs and other related items.

## BASIC CONCEPTS OF WAGE AND SALARY STRUCTURE

**Compensation** may be defined as money received in the performance of work, plus the many kinds of benefits and services that organizations provide to their employees. **'Money'** is included under direct compensation (popularly known as wages, i.e., gross pay); while **benefits** come under indirect compensation, and may consist of accident and health insurance, the employer's contribution to retirement, pay for vacation or illness, and employer's required payments for employee welfare as social security.

A **'wage'** (or pay) is the remuneration paid, for the service of labour in production, periodically to an employee/worker. "Wages" usually refer to the hourly rate or daily rate paid to such groups as production and maintenance employees ("blue-collar workers").

Indian Labour Organisation (ILO) defined the term wage as "the remuneration paid by the employer for the service of hourly, daily, weekly and fortnightly employees".

**'Salary'** normally refers to the weekly or monthly rates paid to clerical, administrative and professional employees ("white-collar workers").

**Earnings** are the total amount of remuneration received by an employee during a given period. This includes salary, dearness allowance, house rent allowance, city compensation allowance, other allowance, overtime payments, etc.

**Nominal Wage:** It is the wage paid or received in monetary terms. It is also known as money wage.

**Real Wage:** It is the amount of wage arrived after discounting nominal wage by the living cost. It represents the purchasing power of money wage.

**Take Home Salary:** It is the amount of salary left to the employee after making authorized deductions like contribution to the provident fund, life insurance premium, income tax and other charges.

**Cost to the Company (CTC):** The concept 'cost to the company' includes payment made to the employee including pensions, health insurance, death in service, gratuity, company car or own the car scheme, child care provisions, subsidized meals, etc. The CTC includes all the investments made by the employer to the employee including the monetary and non-monetary benefits.

The **'wage levels'** represent the money an average worker makes in a geographic area or in his organisation.

**Wage Rate:** It is the amount of remuneration to a unit of time excluding incentives, overtime pay, etc.

The term **'Wage Structure'** is used to describe wage/salary relationships within a particular grouping. The grouping can be according to occupation, or organisation, such as wage structure of craftsman (carpenters, mechanics, bricklayers, etc.)

**The Wage Structure or 'Grade'** is comprised of jobs of approximately equal difficulty or importance as determined by job evaluation.

**Job:** A "job is a group of positions that are similar as to the kind and level of work". In some instances, only one position may be involved, simply because no other position exists. For example, ,in a small organisation, there will be only one position of personnel manager. But in large organization, there may be ten employees with the same title, yet each may perform slightly different work.

**Job Analysis:** The US, department of labour defined job analysis as "the process of determining (by observation and study) and reporting pertinent information relating to the nature of a specific job. It is the determination of the task which comprises of the jobs and of the skills, knowledge, abilities and responsibilities required of the worker for a successful performance and which differentiate one job from all others". Job analysis include job description and job specification.

**Job Description:** "Job description is an organized, factual statement of the duties and responsibilities of a specific job." In brief, it should tell what is to be done, how it is done and why? It is a standard of function, in that it defines the appropriate and authorized content of a job.

**Job Specification:** A job specification is "a statement of minimum acceptable human qualities necessary to perform a job properly." It is a standard or personnel and designates the qualities required for acceptable performance.

**Job Classification:** A job classification is "a grouping of jobs on some specified basis such as the kind of work or pay". For example, a teacher, a doctor, an engineer, etc.

## OBJECTIVES OF WAGE AND SALARY ADMINISTRATION

A sound wage and salary administration tries to achieve these objectives:

**(i) To Acquire Qualified Competent Personnel:** Candidates decide upon their career in a particular organization mostly on the basis of the remuneration the organization offers. Qualified and competent people join the best paid organizations. As such, the organizations should aim at payment of salaries at that level, where they can attract competent and qualified people.

**(ii) To Retain the Present Employees:** If salary level does not compare favourably with that of similar other organizations, employees quit the present one and join the other organizations. The organisation must keep the wage level at the competitive level, in order to prevent such occurrence.

**(iii) To Secure Internal and External Equity:** Internal equity means payment of similar wages for similar jobs within the organization. External equity means payment of similar wages to similar jobs in comparable organizations.

**(iv) To Ensure Desired Behaviour:** Good rewards reinforce desired behaviour like performance, royalty, accepting new responsibilities and challenges, etc.

**(v) Control Costs:** To keep labour and administrative costs in line with the ability of organization to pay.

**(vi) Comply With Legal Regulations:** A sound wage and salary considers the legal challenges imposed by the government.

**(vii) To Protect the Company Image** in the eyes of the public.

**(viii) To Pay According to the Content and Difficulty of the Job** and in tune with the efforts and merits of the employee.

**(ix) To Facilitate Payroll Administration:** To facilitate payroll administration of budgeting and wage and salary control.

**(x) To Simplify Collective Bargaining** procedures and negotiations.

**(xi) To Promote Organizational Feasibility.**

**Benefits of a good compensation package to the employees:**

(i) Employees are paid according to requirements of their jobs, i.e., highly skilled jobs are paid more compensation than low skilled jobs. This eliminates inequalities.

(ii) The chances of favouritism (which creep in when wage rates are assigned) are greatly minimised.

(iii) Job sequences and lines of promotion are established wherever they are applicable.

(iv) Employees' morale and motivation are increased because a wage programme can be explained and is based upon facts.

**Benefits of a good compensation package to the employers:**

(i) They can systematically plan and control their labour costs.

(ii) In dealing with a trade union, they can explain the basis of their wage programme because it is based upon a systematic analysis of job and wage facts.

(iii) A wage and salary administration reduces the likelihood of friction and grievances over wage inequities.

(iv) It enhances an employee's morale and motivation because adequate and fairly administered wages are basic to his wants and needs.

(v) It attracts qualified employees by ensuring an adequate payment for all the jobs.

## THE WAGE DETERMINATION PROCESS

Usually, the steps involved in determining wage rates involves performing job analysis, wage surveys, analysis of relevant organisational problems, forming wage structure, framing rules of wage administration, explaining these to employees, assigning grades and price to each job and paying the guaranteed wage.

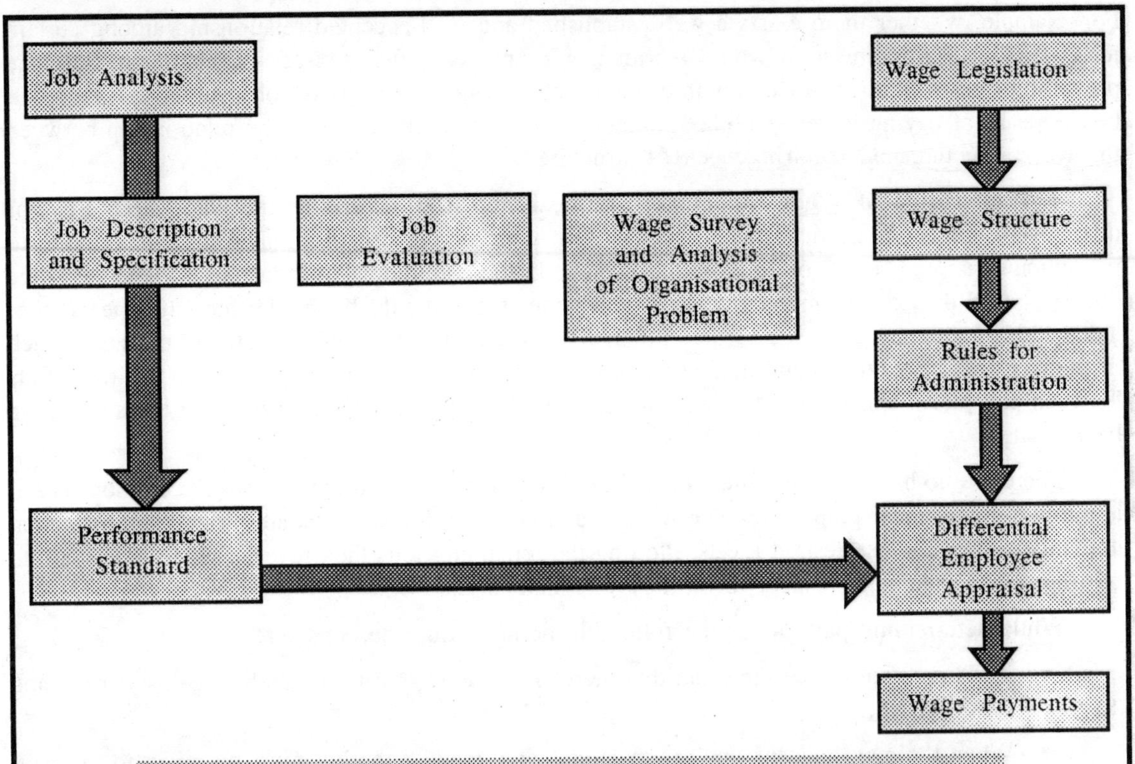


*Fig. 5.1: Steps Involved in the Determination of Wage Rates*

## The steps Involved in Determination of Wage Rate

**1. The Process of Job Analysis:** A job analysis describes the duties, responsibilities, working conditions and interrelationships between the job and the other jobs associated to it. It attempts to record and analyse details concerning the training skills, qualifications, abilities, experience, and responsibilities expected of an employee. After preparing a statement of the minimum acceptable qualities necessary to perform a job properly, the actual process of grading, rating or evaluating the job occurs. A job is rated in order to determine its value relating to all the other jobs in the organisation which are subject to evaluation. The next step is that of providing the job with a price. This involves converting the relative job values into specific monetary values or translating the job classes into rate ranges.

**2. Wage Surveys:** Once the relative worth of jobs has been determined by job evaluation, the actual amounts to be paid must be determined. This is done by making wage or salary surveys in the area concerned and by gathering information about 'benchmark jobs', which are usually known as good indicators. There are various ways to make such a survey. Most firms either use the results of "packaged surveys" available from the research bodies, employer's associations, Government Labour Bureaus, etc., or they participate in wage surveys and receive copies of results, or else they conduct their own. These surveys may be carried out by mailed questionnaire, telephone, or personal interviews with other managers and personnel agencies.

**3. Relevant Organisational Problems:** In addition to the results of job analysis and wage surveys, several other variables have to be given due consideration in establishing wage structure.

For example, whether there exists a well-established and well-accepted relationship among certain jobs, whether the organisation would recruit new employees after revised wage structure; are the prevailing rates in industry or community inconsistent with the results of job evaluation, what will be the result of paying lower or higher compensation; and what should be the relationship between the wage structure and the fringe benefit structure?

**4. Preparation of Wage Structure:** The next step is to determine the wage structure. For this, several decisions need be taken, such as: (a) whether the organisation wishes, or is able, to pay amounts above, below, or equal to the average in the community or industry; (b) whether wage ranges should provide for merit increases or whether there should be single rates; (c) the number and width of the 'pay grades' and the extent of overlap; (d) which jobs are to be placed in each of the pay grades; (e) the actual money value to be assigned to various pay grades; (f) differentials between pay plans; and (g) what to do with salaries that are out of line once these decisions have been made.

There are no hard and fast rules for making such decisions, and the procedure commonly used is the two-dimensional graph on which job evaluation points for key jobs are plotted against actual amounts paid or against desired levels. Plotting the remaining jobs then reveals which jobs seem to be improperly paid with respect to the key jobs and to each other.

While determining pay ranges the following points should be considered:

- It is important to keep in mind that there is an adequate differential between superiors and subordinates.
- When the pay-range of one group is changed, equal attention must be given to the pay-level of the other.
- The existing pay structure should be regularly reviewed and revised. This will make job evaluation programme more acceptable to employees.
- Regional differences in wages should invariably be maintained. Forces that favour regional differences are: low mobility; lower skill jobs; major cost of living differences between areas; added sources of income; or characteristics (rural versus urban or industrial); seasonal occupations as in agriculture versus stable occupations.

**5. Wage Administration Rules:** Rules have to be developed to determine to what degree advancement will be based on length of service rather than merit; with what frequency pay increases will be awarded; how controls over wage and salary costs can be maintained; what rules will govern promotion from one pay grade to another, etc.

**6. Explaining About Wage and Salary Programme to the Employees:** At the next stage, the employees are to be informed of the details of wage and salary programme. Although most hourly-paid workers are informed through the wage contract about the details of wage programme, a substantially smaller number of salaried employees have such information about their jobs. It is considered advisable, in the interest of the concern and the employees, that the information about average salaries and ranges in the salaries of group should be made known to the employees concerned; for secrecy in this matter may create dissatisfaction; and it may also weaken the potential motivating effects of disclosure.

**7.** Finally, the **employee appraisal takes place** and the **wage rate is fixed for the grade** for which the employee is found fit.

## FACTORS INFLUENCING WAGE AND SALARY STRUCTURE

The wage policies differ from organisation-to-organisation. Some units pay only the minimum wage rates required by labour legislation and recruit marginal labour. Some other units pay well above the going rates in the labour market to attract and retain the highest calibre of the labour market. A sound wage policy is to adopt a job evaluation programme in order to establish fair differentials in wages based upon differences in job contents. The factors that determine the determination of wage and salary structures are:

**(i) The Organizations' Ability to Pay:** Wage increases should be given by those organizations which can afford them. Companies that have good sales and, therefore, high profits tend to pay higher wages than those which are running at a loss or earning low profits because of the high cost of production or low sales pay low wages. All employers, irrespective of their profits or losses, must pay not less than their competitor's pay. Non-profit organizations (like hospitals and educational institutions) pay relatively low wages because of low or no profits.

**(ii) Supply and Demand of Labour:** The labour market conditions of supply and demand forces operate at the national, regional and local levels, determine organisational wage structure and level. If the demand for certain skills is high and the supply is low, the result is a rise in the price to be paid for these skills, these labour-market pressures probably force most organizations to "reclassify hard-to-fill jobs at a higher level" than that suggested by the job evaluation. The other alternative is to pay higher wages if the labour supply is scarce; and lower wages when it is excessive. Similarly, if there is great demand for labour expertise, wages rise; but if the demand for manpower skill is minimal, the wages will be relatively low.

**(iii) Prevailing Market Rate:** This is also known as the 'comparable wage' or 'going wage rate', and is the most widely used criterion. An organization's compensation policies generally tend to conform to the wage rates payable by the industry and the community.

This is done for several reasons.

- Competition demands that competitors adhere to the same relative wage level.
- Various government laws and judicial decisions make the adoption of uniform wage rates an attractive proposition.
- Trade unions encourage this practice so that their members can have equal pay, equal work and geographical differences may be eliminated.
- Functionally related firms in the same industry require essentially the same quality of employees, with the same skills and experience. This results in a considerable uniformity in wage and salary rates.
- If the same or about the same general rates of wages are not paid to the employees as are paid by the organization's competitors, it will not be able to attract and maintain a sufficient quantity and quality of manpower.

**(iv) The Cost of Living:** The cost-of-living pay criterion is usually regarded as an automatic minimum equity pay criterion. This criterion calls for pay adjustments based on increase or decrease in an acceptable cost of living index. When the cost of living increases, workers and trade unions demand adjusted wages to offset the erosion of real wages. However, the living costs are stable or decline, the management does not resort to this argument as a reason for wage reduction.

**(v) The Living Wage:** The wages paid should be adequate to enable an employee to maintain himself and his family at a reasonable level of existence.

**(vi) Productivity:** It is measured in terms of output per man-hour. It is not due to labour efforts alone. Technological improvement, better organization and management, better method of production, greater ingenuity and skill by labour are all responsible for increase in productivity. Actual productivity measures the contribution of all the resource factors — men, machine, methods, materials and management.

**(vii) Trade Union's Bargaining Power:** The wages are often influenced by the strength of the unions, their bargaining capacity and their strategies. Unions pressurise management through their collective bargaining strategies, political tactics and by organizing strikes, etc. Trade unions demand for hike in wages may be on the grounds of wages paid by the comparable industries, firms financial position, rising living cost, government regulations, etc.

**(viii) Job Requirements:** Generally, the more difficult a job, the higher are the wages. Measures of job difficulty are frequently used when the relative value of one job to another in an organization is to be ascertained. Jobs are graded according to the relative skill, effort, responsibility and job condition required.

**(ix) Managerial Attitude:** Top management plays a very important role in many areas of wage and salary administration like, whether a company should pay below average or above average rates, what job factors should be used to reflect job worth, etc. If the top management wants to keep prestige, improve the morale and reduce labour turnover ratio, improve living standards of employees and to attract high calibre persons to the organization, then it will pay high amount as compensation.

**(x) Psychological and Sociological Factors:** Psychologically, persons perceive the level of wages as a measure of success in life; people may feel insecure; have an inferiority complex, they may not feel pride in their work, if they feel that the wages paid are not adequate.

Sociologically and ethically, people feel that "equal work should carry equal wages", and that wages should commensurate with their efforts and that they are not exploited, and that no distinction is made on the basis of caste, colour, sex or religion". To satisfy the conditions of equity, fairness and justice, management should take these factors into consideration.

**(xi) Skill Levels Available in the Market:** With the rapid growth of industries, there is a shortage of skilled workers. The technological developments, automation have been affecting the skill levels at a faster rate. Thus, the wage levels of skilled employees are constantly changing and an organization has to take these factors into consideration while fixing wages and salaries of employees.

## PRINCIPLES OF WAGE AND SALARY ADMINISTRATION

The generally accepted principles governing the fixation of wage and salary are:

(i) There should be a definite plan to ensure that the difference in pay are on the basis of job requirements, such as level of skill required, the kind of responsibility one has to undertake, working conditions and the mental and physical requirements of the job.

(ii) The general level of wage and salary should be reasonably in line with that prevailing in the labour market. Labour market criterion is most commonly used.

(iii) The plan should carefully distinguish between jobs and employees. A job carries a certain wage rate, and a person is assigned to fill it at that rate. Exceptions sometimes occur in very high-level jobs in which the job holder may make the job large or small, depending upon his ability and contributions.

(iv) Equal pay for equal work, i.e., if two jobs have equal difficulty requirements, the pay should be the same, regardless of who fills them.

(v) An equitable practice should be adopted for the recognition of individual differences in ability and contribution. For some units, this may take the form of rate ranges, with in-grade increases, in others, it may be a wage incentive plan; in still others, it may take the form of closely integrated sequences of job promotion.

(vi) There should be a clearly established procedure for hearing and adjusting wage complaints. This may be integrated with the regular grievance procedure, if it exists.

(vii) The employees and the trade union, if there is one, should be informed about the procedure used to establish wage rates. Every employee should be informed of his own position, and of the wage and salary structure.

(viii) The wage should be sufficient to ensure for the worker and his family reasonable standard of living. Workers should receive a guaranteed minimum wage to protect them against conditions beyond their control.

(ix) The wage and salary structure should be flexible so that changing conditions can be easily met.

(x) Prompt and correct payments of the dues to the employees must be ensured and arrears of payment should not accumulate.

(xi) For revision of wages, a Wage Committee should always be preferred than the individual judgement of a manager no matter however unbiased he is in his judgement.

(xii) The wage and salary payments must fulfil a wide variety of human needs, including the need for self-actualization.

## WAGES

Wage means "any economic compensation paid by the employer under some contract to his workers for the services rendered by them". It includes family allowance, relief pay, financial support and other benefits. In the narrower sense wages are the price paid for the services of labour in the process of production and include only the performance wages.

They are composed of two parts – the basic wage and other allowances. The basic wage is the remuneration, by way of basic salary and allowances, which is paid or payable to an employee in terms of his contract of employment for the work done by him. Allowances, on the other hand, are paid in addition to the basic wage to maintain the value of basic wages over a period of time. Such allowances include holiday pay, overtime pay, and bonus and social security benefits. These are usually not included in the definition of wages.

However, in India, different Acts include different items under wages, though all the Acts include basic wage and dearness allowance under the term wages. For example, under the Workmen's Compensation Act, 1923, Section 2 (m), "wages for leave period, holiday pay, overtime pay, bonus, attendance bonus, and good conduct bonus" form part of wages.

Under the Payment of Wages Act, 1936, Section 2 (vi), "any award of settlement and production bonus, if paid, constitutes wages".

But under the Payment of Wages Act, 1948, "retrenchment compensation, payment in lieu of notice and gratuity payable on discharge constitute wages".

The following type of remuneration, if paid, does not amount to wages under any of the Acts:

(i) Bonus or other payments under a profit-sharing scheme which do not form a part of the contract of employment.

(ii) Value of any house accommodation, supply of light, water, medical attendance, travelling allowance, or payment in lieu thereof, or any other concession.

(iii) Any sum paid to meet special expenses entailed by the nature of the employment of a workman.

(iv) Any contribution to pension, provident fund, or a scheme of social security and social insurance benefits.

(v) Any other amenity or service excluded from the computation of wages by a general or special order of an appropriate governmental authority.

## Theory of Wages

Wages are fixed mainly as a result of individual bargaining, collective bargaining or by public or State regulation. How wages are determined has been the subject of several theories of wages. The main elements in these theories may be summed up as follows:

**Subsistence Theory:** This theory, also known as "Iron Law of Wages", was propounded by David Ricardo (1817). This theory states that: "The labourers are paid to enable them to keep alive in the race without increase or decrease". The theory was based on the assumption that if the workers were paid more than subsistence wage, their numbers would increase as they would procreate more; and this would bring down the rate of wages. If the wages fall below the subsistence level, the number of workers would decrease — as many would die of hunger, malnutrition, disease, cold, etc., and many would not marry, when that happened the wage rates would go up.

**Wages Fund Theory:** This theory was developed by Adam Smith (1723-1790). His basic assumption was that wages are paid out of a predetermined fund of wealth which lay surplus with wealthy persons — as a result of savings. This fund could be utilised for employing labourers for work. If the funds are large, wages would be high; if it is small, wages would be reduced to the subsistence level.

**The Surplus Value Theory of Wages:** This theory owes its development to Karl Marx (1818-1883).The price of any product was determined by the labour time needed for producing it. The labourer was not paid in proportion to the time spent on work, but much less, and the surplus went over, to be utilised for paying other expenses.

**Residual Claimant Theory:** Francis A. Walker (1840-1897) propounded this theory. According to him, there were four factors of production/business activity, *viz.*, land, labour, capital and entrepreneurship. Wages represent the amount of value created in the production which remains after payment has been made for all these factors of production. In other words, labour is the residual (left over) claimant.

**Marginal Productivity Theory:** This theory was developed by Phillips Henry Wicksteed (England) and John Bates Clark (USA). According to this theory, wages are based upon an entrepreneur's estimate of the value that will probably be produced by the last or marginal worker. In other words, it assumes that wages depend upon the demand for, and supply of, labour. Consequently, workers are paid what they are economically worth. The result is that the employer has a larger share in profit as he has not to pay to the non-marginal workers. As long as each additional worker contributes more to the total value than the cost in wages, it pays the employer to continue hiring; where this becomes uneconomic, the employer may resort to superior technology.

**The Bargaining Theory of Wages:** John Davidson propounded this theory. Under this theory, wages are determined by the relative bargaining power of workers or trade unions and of employers. When a trade union is involved, basic wages, fringe benefits, job differentials and individual differences tend to be determined by the relative strength of the organisation and the trade union.

**Behavioural Theories:** Many behavioural scientists — notably industrial psychologists and sociologists — like Marsh and Simon, Robert Dubin, Eliot Jacques have presented their views of wages and salaries, on the basis of research studies and action programmes conducted by them. Such theories are:

- ***The Employee's Acceptance of a Wage Level:*** This type of thinking takes into consideration the factors which may induce an employee to stay on with the company. The size and prestige of the company, the power of the union, the wages and benefits that the employee receives in proportion to the contribution made by him — all have their impact.
- ***The Internal Wage Structure:*** Social norms, traditions, customs prevalent in the organisation and psychological pressures on the management, the prestige attached to certain jobs in terms of social status, the need to maintain internal consistency in wages at the higher levels, the ratio of the maximum and minimum wage differentials, and the norms of span of control, and demand for specialized labour all affect the internal wage structure of an organisation.
- ***Wage and Salaries and Motivators:*** Money often is looked upon as means of fulfilling the most basic needs of man. Food, clothing, shelter, transportation, insurance, pension plans, education and other physical maintenance and security factors are made available through the purchasing power provided by monetary income — wages and salaries. Merit increases, bonuses based on performance, and other forms of monetary recognition for achievement are genuine motivators. However, basic pay, cost of living increases, and other wage increases unrelated to an individual's own productivity typically may fall into maintenance category.

## Types (Minimum, Fair, and Living Wage)

**Statutory Minimum Wage:** It is the wage determined according to the procedure prescribed by the relevant provisions of the Minimum Wages Act, 1948. Once the rates of such wages are fixed, it is the obligation of the employer to pay them, regardless of his ability to pay. Such wages are required to be fixed in certain employments where there is a great chance of exploitation of labour.

**Bare or Basic Minimum Wage:** It is the wage which is to be fixed in accordance with the awards and judicial pronouncements of Industrial Tribunals, National Tribunals and Labour Courts. They are obligatory on the employers.

The Report of the Committee on Fair Wages, set up by the Government in 1948 identifies three types of wages namely, minimum wage, fair wage and living wage. According to this Committee, the minimum wage should represent the lower limit of a fair wage. The next higher level is the fair wage, and the highest level of the fair wage is the living wage.

**A Minimum Wage:** It has been defined by the Committee as "the wage which must provide not only for the bare sustenance of (to support) life, but for the preservation of the efficiency of the worker. For this purpose, the minimum wage must provide for some measure of education, medical requirements and amenities". In other words, a minimum wage should provide for the sustenance of the worker's family, for his efficiency, for the education of his family, for their medical care and for some amenities. The principles for determining minimum wages were evolved by the Government and have been incorporated in the Minimum Wages Act, 1948.

**Living Wage:** Committee defined a Living Wage as "one which should enable the earner to provide for himself and his family not only the bare essentials of food, clothing and shelter but a measure of frugal comfort, including education for his children, protection against ill-health, requirements of essential social needs and a measure of insurance against the more important misfortunes, including old age". In other words, a living wage was to provide for a standard of living that would ensure good health for the worker, and his family as well as a measure of decency, comfort, education for his children, and protection against misfortunes.

**Fair Wage:** According to the Committee Fair Wages, "is the wage which is above the minimum wage but below the living wage". The lower limit of the fair wage is obviously the minimum wage; the upper limit is set by the "capacity of the industry to pay". Between these two limits, the actual wages should depend on considerations of such factors as: (a) The productivity of labour; (b) The prevailing rates of wages in the same or neighbouring localities; (c) The level of the national income and its distribution; and (d) The place of industry in the economy of the country.

**The Need-based Minimum Wage:** The Indian Labour Conference, at its 15th session held in July 1957, suggested that minimum wage fixation should be need-based, and should meet the minimum needs of an industrial worker. For the calculation of the minimum wage, the Conference accepted the following norms and recommended that they should guide all wage-fixing authorities, including the Minimum Wage Committee, Wage-Boards, and adjudicators:

(i) The standard working class family should be taken to consist of three consumption units for the earner; the earnings of women, children and adolescents should be disregarded;

(ii) The minimum food requirements should be calculated on the basis of the net intake of 2,700 calories, as recommended by Dr. Akroyd, for an average Indian adult of moderate activity.

(iii) The clothing requirements should be estimated at a per capita consumption of 18 yards per annum, which would mean, for an average worker's family of four, a total of 72 yards;

(iv) In respect of housing, the norms should be the minimum rent charged by the Government in any area for houses provided under the Subsidized Housing Scheme for low-income groups; and

(v) Fuel, lighting and other miscellaneous items of expenditure should constitute 20 per cent of the total minimum wage.

## ELEMENTS OR INGREDIENTS OF A GOOD WAGE PLAN

(i) It should be easily understandable,

(ii) It should be capable of easy computation,

(iii) It should be capable of effectively motivating the employees,

(iv) It should provide for remuneration to employees as soon as possible after the completion of the work

(v) It should be relatively stable rather than frequently varying so that employees are assured of a stable amount of money.

## BASIC KINDS OF WAGE PLANS

**The Different Methods of Wage Payments are:**

**1. Time Rate:** This is the oldest and the most common method of fixing wages. Under this system, workers are paid according to the work done during a certain period of time, at the rate of so much per hour, per day, per week, per fortnight or per month or any other fixed period of time. The essential point is that the production of a worker is not taken into consideration in fixing the wages; he is paid at the settled rate as soon as the time contracted for is spent.

***Merits:***

The merits of the system are:

(i) It is simple, for the amount earned by a worker can be easily calculated.

(ii) As there is no time limit for the execution of a job, workmen are not in a hurry to finish it and this may mean that they will pay attention to the quality of their work.

(iii) As all the workmen employed for doing a particular kind of work receive the same wages, jealousy among them are avoided.

(iv) Due to the slow and steady pace of the worker, there is no rough handling of machinery, which is a distinct advantage for the employer.

(v) It is the only system that can be used profitably where the output of an individual workman or groups of employees cannot be readily measured.

(vi) The day or time wage provides a regular and stable income to the worker and he can, therefore, adjust his budget accordingly.

(vii) This system is favoured by organised labour, for it makes for solidarity among the workers of a particular class.

(viii) It requires less administrative attention than others because the very basis of the time wage contract is good faith and mutual confidence between the parties.

***Demerits:***

The main drawbacks of this system are:

(i) It does not take into account the fact that men are of different abilities and that if all the persons are paid equally, better workmen will have no incentive to work harder and better. They will therefore be drawn down to the level of the least efficient workman.

(ii) The labour charges for a particular job do not remain constant. This puts the authorities in a difficult position in the matter of quoting rates for a particular piece of work.

(iii) As there is no specific demand on the worker that a piece of work needs to be completed in a given period of time, there is always the possibility of a systematic evasion of work by workmen.

(iv) This system permits a person to perform a task for which he has neither taste nor ability.

(v) As the employer does not know the amount of work that will be put in by each worker, the total expenditure on wages for turning out a certain piece of work cannot be adequately assessed.

(vi) As no record of an individual worker's output is maintained, it becomes difficult for the employer to determine his relative efficiency for purposes of promotion.

**2. Piece Rate:** Under this system, workers are paid according to the amount of work done or the number of units completed, the rate of each unit being settled in advance, irrespective of the time taken to do the task. This does not mean that a worker can take any time to complete a job because if his performance far exceeds the time which his employer expects he would take, the overhead charge for each unit of article will increase. There is indirect implication that a worker should not take more than the average time. If he consistently takes more time than the average time, he does it at the risk of losing his job.

Under this plan, a worker, working in given conditions and with given machinery, is paid exactly in proportion to his physical output. He is paid in direct promotion to his output, the actual amount of pay per unit of service being approximately equal to the marginal value of his service in assisting to produce that output.

This system is adopted generally in jobs of a repetitive nature, where tasks can be readily measured, inspected and counted. It is particularly suitable for standardized processes, and it appeals to skilled and efficient workers who can increase their earnings by working to their full capacity. In weaving and spinning sections of the textile industry and in the shoe industry, this system can be very useful. But its application is difficult where different shifts are employed on the same work or where a great variety of different grades of workers are employed on different and immeasurable services, as in the Gas and Electricity Industries.

A worker's earnings can be calculated on the basis of the following formula:

***Workers Earning = Number of pieces produced multiplied by the rate per piece***

## Merits of Piece Rate System

This system has many advantages:

(i) It pays the workman according to his efficiency as reflected in the amount of work turned out by him. It satisfies an industrious and efficient worker, for he finds that his efficiency is adequately rewarded. This gives him a direct stimulus to increase his production.

(ii) Supervision charges are not so heavy, as workers are not likely to waste their time since they know that their wages are dependent upon the amount of work turned out by them.

(iii) Being interested in the continuity of his work, a workman is likely to take greater care to prevent a break down in the machine or in the workshop and thereby reducing plant maintenance charges.

(iv) As the direct labour cost per unit of production remains fixed and constant, calculation of costs while filing tenders and estimates becomes easier.

(v) Not only the output and wages are increased, but the methods of production too are improved, for the worker demands materials free from defects and machinery in perfect running conditions.

(vi) The total unit cost of production comes down with a larger output because the fixed overhead burden can be distributed over a greater number of units.

### Demerits of Piece Rate System

The demerits of the system are:

(i) In spite of the advantages accruing to the management as well as to the workmen, the system is not particularly favoured by workers. The main reason for this is that the fixation piece rate by the employer is not done on a scientific basis. In most cases, he determines the rate by the rule-of-thumb method.

(ii) As the workers wish to perform their work at breakneck speed, they generally consume more power, overwork the machines, and do not try to avoid wastage of materials. This results in a high cost of production and lower profits.

(iii) There is a greater chance of deterioration in the quality of work owing to over enthusiasm on the part of workers to increase production. This may affect their health, resulting in a loss of efficiency.

(iv) Excessive speeding of work may result in frequent wear-and-tear of plant and machinery and frequent replacement.

(vi) Trade unions are often opposed to this system, for it encourages rivalry among workers and endangers their solidarity in labour disputes.

**3. Balance or Debt Method:** This is a combination of time and piece rates. The worker is guaranteed an hourly or a day-rate with an alternative piece rate. If the earnings of a worker calculated at the piece rate exceed the amount which he would have earned if paid on time basis, he gets credit for the balance, i.e., the excess piece rate earnings over the time rate earnings. If his piece rate earnings are equal to his time rate earnings, the question of excess payment does not arise. Where piece rate earnings are less than time rate earnings, he is paid on the basis of the time rate; but the excess which he is paid is carried forward as a debt against him to be recovered from any future balance of piece work earnings over time work earnings. This system presupposes the fixation of time and piece rates on a scientific basis.

The obvious merit of this system is that an efficient worker has an opportunity to increase his wages. At the same time, workers of ordinary ability, by getting the guaranteed time wage, are given a sufficient incentive to attain the same standard, even though the excess paid to them is later deducted from their future credit balance.

## EXECUTIVE COMPENSATION

For the higher levels of management, salaries are influenced by the size of a company, performance of the company, and the contribution of the manager in the process of decision making. The more profitable the organisation, the better is the compensation paid to the executives. The industries that are more highly constrained by governmental regulation (banks, life insurance, rail/roads, public utilities) pay relatively less than those that are more free to carry on their business (private firms).

Executive remuneration has certain unique features, such as:

- It cannot be compared to the wage and salary schemes meant for other employees in organizations.
- Executives are denied the privilege of having unionized strength.
- Secrecy is maintained in respect of executive remuneration.
- Executive pay is not supposed to be based on individual performance measure but rather on unit or organisational performance.
- Executive remuneration is subject to statutory ceilings in some respects.

## COMPONENTS OF EXECUTIVE REMUNERATION

Executive remuneration generally comprises four elements: (i) salary and allowance, (ii) bonus, (iii) incentives, and (iv) perquisites (financial and other benefits apart from salary).

Salary is the first component of executive remuneration. Salary is supposed to be determined through evaluation and serves as the basis for other types of benefits. Bonus plays an important role in today's competitive executive payment programmes. There are almost as many bonus systems as there are companies using this form of executive remuneration. If bonus constitutes short-term benefit, stock options are long-term benefits offered to executives. Stock options are attractive to shareholders too. Perquisites contribute a major source of income for executives.

Straight salaries, bonuses, stock purchase plans and profit-sharing are used to compensate major executives. Of these, the straight salary is the most common method. The salary is determined by mutual agreement between the individual and the employer. The effective sales, the cost of production, reduction in expenses and the profits made are also taken into account.

Bonuses related to performance are also paid to executives at a certain percentage of the profits. The bonuses may average from 30 per cent to 50 per cent of the basic salary.

These bonuses motivate employees, if the following conditions are met:

(i) The amount paid is closely related to the level of individual performance;

(ii) The amount paid after taxes represent a clearly noticeable rise above the base salary level;

(iii) The amount paid is closely related to the level of company performance;

(iv) The amount paid is tied into the base salary in such a way that the combined earnings are equitable both in relation to internal and external standards;

(v) The amount paid is based on an easily understandable system of allocation, and the individual is provided with complete information on the relationship between bonus and performance.

Moreover, executives are compensated for the various expenses incurred by them, for taxation takes away a major portion of their salary. Such payments are in the form of:

(a) Medical care;

(b) Counsel and accountants to assist in legal, tax and financial problems;

(c) Facilities for entertaining customers and for dining out;

(d) Company recreational area (swimming pool and gymnasium);

(e) The cost of the education and training of executives, scholarships for their children, and allowances for business magazines and books; and

(f) Free well-furnished accommodation, conveyance and servants. All these go under the head of perquisites.

## SUMMARY

'Wage and Salary Administration' refers to the establishment and implementation of sound policies and practices of employee compensation. Compensation may be defined as money received in the performance of work, plus many kinds of other benefits and services that organizations provide to their employees. A 'wage' (or pay) is the remuneration paid, for the service of labour in production, periodically to an employee/worker. "Wages" usually refer to the hourly rate or daily rate paid to such groups as production and maintenance employees (blue-collar worker). On the other hand, 'Salary' normally refers to the weekly or monthly rates paid to clerical, administrative and professional employees (white-collar workers). The steps involved in determining wage rates are: performing job analysis, wage surveys, analysis of relevant organisational problems, preparation of wage structure, framing rules of wage administration, explaining these to employees, assigning grades and price to each job and paying the guaranteed wage. The basic factors determining wage and salary administration are: The organization's ability to pay; Supply and demand of labour; The prevailing market rate; The cost of living; Living wage; Productivity; Trade Union's Bargaining power; Job requirements; Managerial attitudes; Psychological and Sociological factors and the levels of Skills available in the market. A Minimum Wage has been defined by the Committee as "the wage which must provide not only for the bare sustenance of life, but for the preservation of the efficiency of the worker. A living wage was to provide for a standard of living that would ensure good health for the worker, and his family as well as a measure of decency, comfort, education for his children, and protection against misfortunes. There are three methods of wage payment time rate, piece rate and balance or debt method. Under time rate system, workers are paid according to the work done during a certain period of time, at the rate of so much per hour, per day, per week, per fortnight or per month or any other fixed period of time. Under Piece Rate system, workers are paid according to the amount of work done or the number of units completed, the rate of each unit being settled in advance, irrespective of the time taken to do the task. Balance or Debt Method is a combination of time and piece rates. For the higher management, salaries are influenced by the size of a company, performance of the company and the specific industry and in part by the contribution of the incumbent to the process of decision making. The more profitable is the organisation or the firm, the better is the compensation paid to the executives.

## CASELET 1

Sunil Shinde senior IT employee with Digital Computers discovered that his company has hired a fresh university computer graduate for the post of system analyst — with a starting salary almost as high as of Mr. Shinde. Although Shinde was of good nature, he was totally shocked and upset.

It had taken him almost five years to become senior system analyst and attain his current salary level in Digital Computers. He was generally pleased with the company for its present work environment and professional culture. He has been thoroughly enjoying his job in the company.

Next day he met the chief of HR department, Mr. Ramamurthy and enquired about the news. Mr. Ramamurthy apologically admitted that it was true and tried to explain the company's situation. He told Mr.Shinde that the market for system analyst is very tough these days and it is difficult to find a right person after so many advertisements. In order to attract qualified personnel to the company, he was forced to offer a premium on starting salary. The company desperately needed another analyst and this was the only way they could get one. Since Mr. Shinde was too much overloaded, company wanted to reduce his burden.

Mr. Shinde asked Mr. Ramamurthy whether his salary would be adjusted accordingly now. He has assured Mr.Shinde that his salary would be revalued periodically and praised him for his commitment towards the organization. Mr.Shinde thanked Mr.Murthy but left the office shaking his head and thinking about his future in the company. He is seriously thinking to quit the company and has to examine various lucrative offers he has with him.

### Questions

1. What is the problem in this case?
2. Was it wrong on the part of Mr. Murthy to give a different package to a new system analyst? If yes, why? If no, why?
3. Do you think Mr. Ramamurthy's explanation was satisfactory? Discuss.
4. How can you motivate Mr, Shinde and persuade him to continue in the company?

## CASELET 2

A private insurance company has opened a branch in an interior village of Anand district, Gujarat. Company has decided to hire local people for clerical job. The company has to determine an appropriate wage structure for this staff. After doing a small survey, the company came to know that the 'going rate in that area is in the range of 2,000 to 3,000 a month. The cost of living in the area is comparatively high and very few people are qualified for the post.

### Questions

1. Suggest an appropriate salary structure for this employees.
2. What factors need to be considered in the fixation of salary?

### Assignments

- Examine the reward system of a private insurance company; outline the positive and negative aspects of compensation package. If reward system is inappropriate suggest an alternative package.

## ........ QUESTIONS FOR DISCUSSION

1. Distinguish between Minimum Wage, Fair Wage and Living Wage.
2. What are the methods of wage payment? Explain any one method in brief.
3. Explain the factors influencing Wage and Salary Structure.
4. Explain briefly: (a) Piece rate system, (b) Balance or debt method

## Objective Questions

### A. Fill in the Blanks

1. _______ is the remuneration paid for the service of labour in production, periodically to an employee or worker.
2. A sound wage policy is to adopt a ___________ programme in order to establish fair differentials in wages based upon difference in job contents.
3. The _______ pay criterion is considered as an automatic minimum equity pay criterion.
4. _______ is that wage which must provide not only for the bare sustenance of life, but for the preservation of the efficiency of the worker.
5. _________is determined by keeping in view the national income and the capacity of firm to pay.
6. ______is the wage which is above the ______ but below the ______.
7. The lower limit of the fair wage is the _______.
8. ______ system is generally adopted when the job is of a repetitive nature.
9. In piece rate system the workers earning is calculated as workers earning (WE) = NR, where N stands for _________ and R stands for ___________.
10. __________ is based on the principle of **"equal pay for equal work".**
11. _______ is paid to maintain the standard of living that should ensure a good health for the worker.
12. The ______ system discourages the efficient workers.
13. The ____________ system is not appreciated by the trade union.
14. __________ rate is also known as going wage rate or comparable wage rate.
15. In the labour market if the labour is in short supply, wage rate would be _________.
16. A wage system in which workers are paid according to the time spend at the workplace is known as ____________ system.
17. Wage system in whic.. wages are paid to the workers according to their output is known as ________.
18. _______ comes under direct compensation, while _______ come under indirect compensation.
19. __________ is all forms of direct and indirect compensation paid or provided to the employee in recognition of employment status and performance.
20. Life and medical insurance or reimbursement of medical bills is considered as a part of _______ .
21. Piece workers come under ___________ class of workers.
22. _______ is that portion of dearness allowance which Government declares to be paid for all purposes.
23. Basic purpose of wage and salary administration is to establish and maintain an equitable ________.

*Ans:* **1.** Wage, **2.** job evaluation, **3.** cost of living, **4.** Minimum wage, **5.** Living wage, **6.** Fair wage, minimum wage, living wage, **7.** minimum wage, **8.** Piece rate, **9.** number of piece/units, rate per piece, **10.** Fair wage, **11.** Living wage, **12.** time rate, **13.** piece rate, **14.** Prevailing wage, **15.** high, **16.** time rate, **17.** piece rate system, **18.** Wages, benefits, **19.** Total compensation, **20.** Perks, **21.** semi-skilled, **22.** Dearness pay, **23.** wage and salary structure.

### B. Multiple Choice Questions

1. The basic purpose of wage and salary administration is to establish and maintain an _______ wage and salary structure.

   (a) attractive (b) equitable (c) unequal (d) offerable

2. _______ is money received in performance of work plus many kinds of benefits that the organization provides to its employees.

   (a) Compensation (b) Funds (c) Minimum Wage (d) Finance

3. _______ is the remuneration paid for the service of labour in production, periodically to an employee.

   (a) Salary (b) Wage (c) Pension (d) Gratuity

4. ________ refers to weekly or monthly rates paid to clerical or administrative staff.
   (a) Provident Fund (b) Benefits (c) Salary (d) Wages
5. Minimum Wage Act was passed in the year________.
   (a) 1926 (b) 1947 (c) 1948 (d) 1958
6. ___________ is determined by keeping in view the national income and capacity of industry to pay.
   (a) Maximum wage (b) Minimum wage (c) Fair wage (d) Living wage
7. In ________ method the production of workers is not taken into consideration while fixing the wages.
   (a) daily rate (b) time rate (c) monthly rate (d) piece rate
8. In ________ method, workers pay attention to the quality of work.
   (a) time rate (b) piece rate (c) standard rate (d) monthly rate
9. ________ method provides regular and stable income to the workers.
   (a) Minimum rate (b) Monthly rate (c) Piece rate (d) Time rate
10. In ___________ method a worker is paid wages, exactly in direct proportion to his physical output.
    (a) piece rate (b) standard rate (c) time rate (d) minimum rate
11. Total compensation is all forms of direct and indirect compensation paid or provided to the employee in recognition of employment status and performance. All of the following are forms of direct compensation except
    (a) Base Pay (b) Variable Pay
    (c) Statutory Benefits (d) Stock Benefits
12. Benefits that are required by law to provide to all employees are called
    (a) Medical Benefits (b) Direct Benefits
    (c) Indirect Benefits (d) Statutory Benefits
13. All of the following are statutory benefits except
    (a) Social Security (b) Unemployment Insurance
    (c) Workers Compensation (d) Medical Insurance
14. Which of the following factors may influence compensation?
    (a) Health care costs (b) Taxation
    (c) Cost of living (d) All of the above

*Ans:* **1.** (b), **2.** (a), **3.** (b), **4.** (c), **5.** (c), **6.** (d), **7.** (b), **8.** (a), **9.** (d), **10.** (a), **11.** (c), **12.** (d), **13.** (d), **14.** (d).

## C. States by Giving Reasons Whether the Following Statement are True or False:

1. The wage and salary administration is concerned with the financial aspects of needs, motivation and rewards.
2. Fair wage is the wage which is above living wage but below minimum wage.
3. In time wage system the quality of product is not maintained.
4. When wages are paid based on the length of time devoted by a worker is known as piece-wage system.
5. In short-run the firm's ability to pay may be practically zero.
6. Productivity as one of the factor influencing wage and salary administration is due to labour efforts alone.
7. Supply and demand of labour influences the wage and salary level.

*Ans:* **1. True**

Wage and salary is significant to most of the employees as it constitutes a major share of their income pay in one form or another and is certainly one of the main springs of motivation. Salary provides more than means of satisfying the physical needs. It provides recognition, a sense of accomplishment and determines social status. It is said that people do what they want to do to satisfy some need, before doing anything they look for a reward.

2. **False**

 Fair wage is the wage which is above the minimum wage but below the living wage. The lower limit of fair wage is the minimum wage and the upper limit is set by the capacity of industry to pay between these two limits the actual wage depends upon various factors such as productivity of labour, prevailing rate of wages, the level of national income and its distribution and the place of the industry in the economy, etc.

3. **False**

 In time rate system quality of product is maintained. As such there is no time limit for the completion of job so workers pay attention to the quality of work.

4. **False**

 When wages are paid based on the length of time devoted by a worker is known as time rate system.

5. **True**

 In short run all the factors of production cannot be changed and in short run it is difficult to increase the profit because apart from profitability there are various expense that the firm has to bear, which should be taken into consideration in determining the ability to pay. Thus, whatever the influence of other factors may be the organisation cannot pay more than its ability to pay in the short run.

6. **False**

 When productivity increases the wage will also increase, but increase in productivity is not due to the labour efforts alone. There are other factors which contribute to increase in productivity such as technological improvement, better management, the development of better methods of production, etc.

7. **True**

 If the demand for certain skills is high the supply is low, the result is a rise in the price to be paid for these skills and *vice versa*.

☺ ☺ ☺

CHAPTER 6

# Trade Union

LEARNING OBJECTIVES

- *Introduction*
- *Definition and Characteristics*
- *Why do Workers Join Trade Unions?*
- *Functions and Role of Trade Unions*
- *Growth of Trade Union Movement*
- *Federations of Trade Unions*
- *Objectives of Important Indian Trade Unions*
- *Union Structure*
- *How Trade Union Objectives are Achieved*
- *Factors Affecting Growth of Trade Unions*
- *Weakness of Trade Union*
- *Measures to Strengthen Trade Union Movement in India*
- *Recommendations of the National Commission on Labour*
- *Chapter Summary*

## INTRODUCTION

A trade union or labour union is an organization of workers who have come together to achieve common goals such as better working conditions. The trade union, through its leadership, bargains with the employer on behalf of union members and negotiates labour contracts (Collective Bargaining) with employers. This may include negotiation of wages, work rules, complaint procedures, rules governing hiring, firing and promotion of workers, benefits, workplace safety and policies. The agreements negotiated by the union leaders are binding on the rank and file members and the employer and in some cases on other non-member workers.

Originating in Europe, trade unions became popular in many countries during the Industrial Revolution (which disrupted the older way of life and created a new society forged by the shop, the factory, the mine and the industry) when the lack of skill necessary to perform most jobs shifted employment bargaining power almost completely to the employers' side, causing many workers to be mistreated and underpaid. Trade unions are formed to protect the interests of the employees. There are some 164 million trade union members' worldwide, making trade union the world's largest 'social movement'. This number represents only one in twenty of the world's three billion workers, the rest remain unrepresented.

## DEFINITION AND CHARACTERISTICS

The term trade union has been defined variously by different authors. Some view that there are only associations of employees or persons working in the industry and wage earners engaged in one or more professions, undertaking or business while others view that these also include employer's organisations and friendly societies.

According to G.D.H. Cole, a trade union means "an association of workers in one or more professions — an association carried on mainly for the purpose of protecting and advancing the members' economic interests in connection with their daily work".

Dale Yoder defined a trade union as "a continuing long-term association of employees, formed and maintained for the specific purpose of advancing and protecting the interest of the members in their working relationship".

According to S.D. Punekar, "a union is a continuous association of persons in the industry — whether employer or independent workers — formed primarily for the purpose of the pursuit of the interests of its members of the trade they represent".

According to Section 2(b) of the Trade Unions Act of 1926, "a trade union is any combination of persons, whether temporary or permanent, primarily for the purpose of regulating the relations between workers and employers, or between workers and workers, and for imposing restrictive conditions on the conduct of any trade or business, and includes the federation of two or more trade unions".

An analysis of the above definitions on trade unions reveals the following characteristics of trade unions:

- It may be observed that the trade union is an association, either of employees or employers or of independent workers.
- It is a relatively permanent combination of workers and is not temporary or casual.

- It is an association of workers engaged in securing economic benefits for its members.
- The character of trade union has been constantly changing.
- Its origin and growth has been influenced by a number of ideologies.
- It achieves its objectives through collective action and group effort.
- It includes federations of trade unions also.

On the basis of the above characteristics, trade union can be defined as:

"A continuous and voluntary association of the salary or wage-earners and engaged in whatever industry or trade, formed for safeguarding the interests of its members, maintaining and improving the conditions of their working lives, raising their status and promoting their vocational interests; and securing better relations between them and their employees, through collective bargaining."

Thus, a trade union is a device which enables a group, a class in industry or trade to bargain with any other class or group on equal footing. Such a union is: (i) economically oriented; (ii) an instrument of defense against exploitation; (iii) an outcome of industrialization and implies class distinction and women should receive equal remuneration for work of equal value.

## WHY DO WORKERS JOIN TRADE UNIONS?

Workers join trade unions to achieve" their objectives which they could not achieve individually specifically, workers join trade unions due to the following reasons:

**(i) To Get Economic Security:** That is, they want steady employment with an adequate income; which is possible with the help of trade union.

**(ii) To Have Greater Bargaining Power:** Workers would like to resist the management's irrational, illogical and discriminatory actions. The individual employee possesses very little bargaining power as compared to that of his employer. Workers can resist the management by improving their bargaining power which in turn requires joining in trade unions.

The threat or actuality of a strike by a union is a powerful tool that often causes the employer to accept the demands of the workers for better conditions of employment. Management's decisions regarding promotion, transfers, work assignment, grievance redressal and disciplinary issues can be challenged by a group of workers rather than any individual worker.

**(iii) Make Their Voices Heard:** The desire for self-expression is a fundamental human drive for most people. A trade union provides such a forum where the feelings, ideas and opinions of the workers could be discussed. It can also transmit the feelings, ideas, opinions and complaints of the workers to the management. The collective voice of the workers is heard by the management and given due consideration while taking policy decisions.

**(iv) Minimise Discrimination:** The decisions regarding pay, work, transfer, promotion, etc., are highly subjective in nature. Similarly, the personal relationships existing between the supervisor and each of his subordinates may influence the decision making process. Thus, there are chances of favouritisms and discriminations.

**(v) To Satisfy Their Social and Psychological Needs.** To get along with their fellow-workers in a better way and to gain respect in the eyes of their peers;

**(vi) To Secure Power:** Employees believe unionization fetch them power.

**(vii)** To resist schemes of the management which reduce employment, e.g., rationalization and automation.

**(viii) Sense of Security:** The employees may join the unions because of their belief that it is an effective way to secure adequate protection from various types of hazards and income insecurity such as accident, injury, illness, death, disability, unemployment, old age, etc. The trade union secure retirement benefits of the workers and compel the management to invest in welfare services for the benefit of the workers.

**(ix) Sense of Participation:** The employees can participate in management of matters affecting their interests only if they join trade unions. They can influence the decisions that are taken as a result of collective bargaining between the union and the management.

**(x) Sense of Belongingness:** Many employees join a union because their coworkers are the members of the union. At times, an employee joins a union under group pressure; if he does not, he often has a very difficult time at work. On the other hand, those who are members of a union feel that they gain respect in the eyes of their fellow workers. They can also discuss their problem with' the trade union leaders.

## FUNCTIONS OF TRADE UNIONS

The basic functions of unions are to protect and promote the interest of the workers and conditions of their employment. The other factors are:

(i) Achieving higher wages and better working and living conditions for the members;

(ii) Acquiring the control of industry by workers;

(iii) Minimizing the helplessness of the individual workers by making them stand collectively and increasing their resistance power through collective bargaining; protecting the members against victimization and injustice of the employers;

(iv) Raising the status of the workers as partners of the industry and citizens of society by demanding increasing share for the workers in the management of industrial enterprises;

(v) Instilling self-confidence and a feeling that the worker is not simply a clog in the machine;

(vi) Imbibing sincerity and discipline in workers;

(vii) Taking up welfare measures for improving the morale of the workers, and

(viii) To protect the right to be consulted on all the matters affecting the worker's interest.

The National Commission on Labour has pointed out the following basic functions on which the trade unions have to pay greater attention:

(i) To secure fair wages for workers;

(ii) To safeguard security of tenure and improve conditions of service;

(iii) To enlarge opportunities for promotion and training;

(iv) To improve working and living conditions;

(v) To provide for educational, cultural and recreational facilities;

(vi) To cooperate and facilitate technological advance by broadening the understanding of a workers on its underlying issues;

(vii) To promote identity of interests of the workers with their industry;

(viii) To offer responsive cooperation in improving levels of production and productivity, discipline and high standard of quality; and generally

(ix) To promote individual and collective welfare.

Besides these basic functions of the trade unions, the Commission also entrusted the following responsibilities upon the trade unions:

(i) Promotion of national integration;

(ii) Generally influencing the socio-economic policies of the community through active participation in their formulation at various levels, and

(iii) Instilling in their members a sense of responsibility towards the industry and the community.

The functions of Trade Union can be divided into five categories, *viz.*:

(a) Militant or protective or intra-mural functions,

(b) Fraternal or extra-mural,

(c) Social functions,

(d) Political functions, and

(e) Ancillary functions.

(a) **Militant or Protective or Intra-mural Functions:** These functions include protecting the workers interests, i.e., hike in wages, providing more benefits, job security, etc., through collective bargaining and direct action such as strikes, gheraos, etc.

(b) **Fraternal or Extra-mural Functions:** These functions include providing financial and non-financial assistance to workers during the periods of strikes and lockouts, extension of medical facility during sickness and casualties, provision of education, recreation, recreational and housing facility provision of social and religious benefits, etc.

(c) **Social Functions:** These functions include carrying out social service activities, discharging social responsibilities through various sections of the society like educating the customers.

(d) **Political Functions:** These functions include affiliating a union to a political party, collecting donations, canvassing during the election pain seeking the help of political parties during the strikes and lockouts.

(e) **Ancillary Functions:** Ancillary functions of trade unions include:

*(i) Communication:* Trade unions communicate its activities, programmes, decisions, achievements, etc., to its members through publication of newsletters or magazines.

*(ii) Welfare Activities:* Trade unions undertake welfare activities like acquiring of house sites, construction of houses, establishment of cooperative housing societies, cooperative credit societies, organising training activities, etc.

*(iii) Education:* Trade unions provide educational facilities to its members and their family members.

(iv) *Research:* Trade unions arrange to conduct research programmes. They systematically collect and analyse data and information for collective bargaining, preparing of notes for union officials, for court cases, etc. They also arrange to analyse macrodata about the economy, industry and different sectors, etc.

## GROWTH OF TRADE UNION MOVEMENT IN INDIA

The trade union movement in India started rather late, though the industrialization of the country began about 1850. The first trade union was founded by Mr. N.K. Lokhande in 1890, and was known as the Bombay Mill Hands Association. This was followed by the Amalgamated Society of Railway Servants in India, 1897, the Printers' Union of Calcutta, 1905, the Madras and Calcutta Postal Union, 1907, and the Kamgar Hitwardhak Sabha 1910. All these trade unions aimed at promoting welfare activities for workers, spreading literacy among them and redressing their grievances by constitutional methods. They were, however, not trade unions in the true sense of the phrase but rather social unions, and they were completely free from even the most rudimentary touch of radicalism. The movement was for the workers rather than by the workers, and was generally confined to the somewhat educated class of workers. As a result, it did not make much headway among those employed in the textile, mining and plantation industries. The leadership in this movement was provided mostly by social reformers, careerists and politicians-cum-nationalists.

The movement developed somewhat during the First World War, although it began to take roots in the country only after the end of this catastrophic conflict. Frequent rise or fall in prices, the Swaraj Movement, the Russian Revolution and the setting up of the International Labour Organisation (ILO) — all these affected the ideas of the workers, and intensified the sense of class-consciousness among them. By 1920, there was a fairly large class of industrial employees, many of whom joined the various unions — the Indian Seamen's Union, the Madras Textile Labourers Union, the Jamshedpur Labour Association, the G.I.P. Workers' Union, and the Colliery Employees Association of Jharia. The Ahmedabad Textile Labour Association came into being following the initiative taken for that purpose by Mahatma Gandhi, which was the forerunner of the Indian National Trade Union Congress set up in 1947.

National leaders provided the political climate in which the trade union movement thrive. At the same time, the manner in which it was conducted generated a mounting sense of bitterness among the employers, for trade unions formed for the purpose of getting higher wages for workers.

In 1928, when the Communists gained influence in the trade union movement, one of the longest and costliest trials of strength ensued between the Communists and others, which continued for about four-and-a-half years. On the questions of the boycott of the Whitley Commission, the affiliation of the All-India Trade Union Congress with the League against Imperialism (The Pan-Pacific Trade Union Secretariat, a camouflaged Communist Organisation) and the sending of a delegation to the ILO Conference, the moderates, headed by N.M. Joshi, broke away from the AITUC and formed another organisation, the All-India Trade Union Federation. In 1931, following fundamental differences between the Communists and left-wing unionists, there was another rift in the AITUC, and the Communists, led by B.T. Ranadive and others formed the Red Trade Union Congress. Two years later, the National Federation of Labour was formed, which attempted to facilitate the unity of all the left-wing organizations of labour. The AITUF and NFL joined together to form the National Trade Union Federation (NTUF). The AITUC and the RTUC, however, remained aloof. In 1935, the RTUC merged into the AITUC.

During the Second World War, the Indian National Congress was in power in seven provinces. There were big strikes, which made it possible for labour to organise a larger number of trade unions. After nine years of split, the NTUF was dissolved and the organisation merged into the AITUC (in 1940), which became the sole representative of organised labour. In the following year, however, there was another split, when the radicals in the organisation broke away from the parent body to form the Indian Federation of Labour, which was recognised by the government as a representative organisation of Indian labour. By the end of the war, the Communists dominated the AITUC, while the Royists controlled the IFL. As a result of these developments, a qualitative change came about in the trade union movement, which made it possible for labour to participate in negotiations with employers and in tripartite deliberations.

When attempts to restructure the AITUC failed, those who favoured the ideals of socialism and shared the views of the Indian National Congress separated from the labour organisation, and set up the Indian National Trade Union Congress in 1947. When, in the following year, the Socialists broke away from the Indian National Congress, they formed the Praja Socialist Party, whose supporters in the labour movement established what came to be known as the Hindustan Mazdoor Panchayat (HMP). Later, this organisation and IFL merged to form the Hind Mazdoor Sabha. In 1949, a group of left wing Socialists, who were dissatisfied with the policies and attitude of the Socialist Party, established the United Trade Union Congress. These moves and counter moves in favour of a split or unity continued to dominate the labour scene for a number of years.

After 1952, a number of efforts were made for bringing about unity in the movement such as in 1953, and 1958. In 1959, a few unions led by the members of the socialist party seceded from the H.M.S. and formed Hind Mazdoor Panchayat (H.M.P.). It became the organ of Samyukta Socialist Party and was launched in 1962. In 1962, a new organisation called Confederation of Free Trade Unions (CFTU) was formed as a result of the active interest taken in its formation by the International Confederation of Christian Trade Union and the support of the Swatantra Party.

There was again a rift in the AITUC in 1970, when the Communists divided themselves into the CPI and CPM. The AITUC came under the control of the CPI and the CPM started a new organisation — the Centre of Indian Trade Union (CITU).

The split in the Indian National Congress in two separate groups in 1972 also resulted in a change in the INTUC. The ruling Congress party retained its control on the INTUC and the (Organisation Congress) severed itself from the INTUC and formed a new union — National Labour Organisation (NLO).

In September 1972, a new development took place. With the formation of National Council of Central Trade Union (NCCTU), providing a common platform for trade union activities of the AITUC, INTUC and HMS, CITU was isolated. It, therefore, formed a United Council of Trade Union (UCTU) as rival body of NCCTU. Since then, both these bodies have ceased to exist.

After the declaration of the emergency, again the INTUC, AITUC and HMS combined and joined with employers' representatives on what was called National Apex Body. With the lifting of emergency and the installation of the Janata Government at the Centre, this body ceased to exist.

There were 28,924 registered trade unions of which 8,177 were submitting returns and these had a membership of 54.47 lakh in 1977, as against 14,370 registered unions, 7,086 submitting returns with a membership of 43.69 lakh in 1966.

At present, there are five major central trade union organizations, namely, INTUC, BMS, HMS, AITUC and CITU. Other trade unions are Hind Mazdoor Kisan Panchayat (HMKP), Indian Federation of Free Trade Union (IFFTU), National Front of Indian Trade Union (NFITU), National Labour Organization (NLO), Trade Unions' Coordination Centre (TUCC), United Trade Union Congress (UTUC) and United Trade Union Congress-Lenin Sarani (UTUC-LS)

## FEDERATIONS OF TRADE UNIONS

1. All-India Bank Employees' Association.
2. National Federation of Indian Railwaymen.
3. All-India Post and Dock Workers' Federation.
4. National Federation of Post and Telegraph Workers.
5. All-India Mine Workers' Federation.
6. Indian Federation of Working Journalists.

## OBJECTIVES OF IMPORTANT INDIAN TRADE UNIONS

### All-India Trade Union Congress

The most important year in the history of Indian Trade Union Movement is 1920, when the All-India Trade Union Congress (AITUC) was formed, consequent upon the necessity of electing delegates for the International Labour Organisation (ILO). This is the first All-India Trade Union in the country. The first meeting of the AITUC was held in October 1920 at Bombay under the Presidentship of Lala Lajpat Rai. Formation of AITUC led to the establishment of All-India Railwaymen's Federation (AIRF) in 1922. Many company Railway Unions were affiliated to it. Signs of militant tendency and revolutionary ideas were apparent during this period.

**The Basic Objectives of the AITUC are:**

(i) To establish a socialist state in India;

(ii) To socialize and nationalize means of production, distribution and exchange;

(iii) To ameliorate the economic and social conditions of the working class;

(iv) To watch, promote and further the interests, rights and privileges of the workers in all matters relating to their employment;

(v) To secure and maintain for the workers the freedom of speech, freedom of press, freedom of association, freedom of assembly, the right to strike and the right to work and maintenance;

(vi) To coordinate the activities of the labour unions affiliated to the AITUC;

(vii) To abolish political or economic advantage based on caste, creed, community, race or religion; and

(viii) To secure and maintain for the workers the right to strike.

## Indian National Trade Union Congress

The efforts of the Indian National Congress resulted in the establishment of Indian National Trade Congress (INTUC) by bringing the split in the AITUC. INTUC started gaining membership from its inception itself.

**The Objectives of INTUC are:**

(i) To place industry under national ownership and control in a suitable form;

(ii) To secure increasing association of workers in the administration of industry and their full participation in that control;

(iii) To organise society in such a manner as to ensure full employment and the best utilization of its manpower and other resources;

(iv) To promote social, civic and political interest of the working class;

(v) To establish just industrial relations;

(vi) To secure redressal of grievances, without stoppage of work, by means of negotiation, conciliation and failing these, arbitration and adjudication;

(vii) To take other legislative methods, including strikes or any suitable form of satyagraha where adjudication is not applied and settlement of disputes within reasonable time by arbitration is not available for the redressal of grievances;

(viii) To make necessary arrangements for the efficient conduct and satisfactory and speedy-conclusion of authorized strikes of satyagraha;

(ix) To foster the spirit of solidarity, service, brotherhood, cooperation and mutual help among the workers;

(x) To develop in the workers a sense of responsibility towards industry and the community; and

(xi) To raise the worker's standard of efficiency and discipline.

## Other Central Unions

Socialists separated from AITUC had formed Hind Mazdoor Sabha (HMS) in 1948. The Indian Federation of Labour merged with the HMS. Radicals formed another union under the name of United Trade Union Congress in 1949. Thus, the trade union movement in the country was split up into four distinct central unions during the short span of 1946 to 1949.

Some other central unions were also formed. They are Bharatiya Mazdoor Sangh (BMS) in 1955. The Hind Mazdoor Panchayat (HMP) in 1965, The Centre of Indian Trade Union (CITU) in 1970. Thus, the splinter group of INTUC formed trade union — the split in the Congress particularly in 1969 resulted in the split in INTUC and led to the formation of National Labour Organisation (NLO).

**The Objectives of Hind Mazdoor Sabha are:**

(i) To organise and promote the establishment of a democratic socialist society in India and to further the economic, political, social and cultural interests of the Indian working class;

(ii) To provide full opportunities for the development of mental and physical personality of the workers;

(iii) To strive for getting a living wage to all workers;

(iv) To guarantee work to every worker;

(v) To get full social security measures and comprehensive medical care introduced by the industry for workers;

(vi) To get adequate leisure for the workers in the form of reasonable hours of work and holidays with pay;

(vii) To arrange for adequate housing facilities;

(viii) To arrange for the introduction of free and compulsory education and facilities for vocational guidance;

(ix) To get effective recognition of the right of collective bargaining;

(x) To cooperate with other organizations in the country and outside, having similar aims and objectives, and

(xi) To secure and maintain for workers freedom of association, freedom of assembly, freedom of speech, freedom of press and the right to strike.

**The Objectives of Bharatiya Mazdoor Sangh are:**

(i) "To establish the Bharatiya order of a classless society in which there shall be secured full employment; replacement of profit motive by service and establishment of economic democracy; development of autonomous industrial communities — with each one of them consisting of all the individuals connected with the industry as partners";

(ii) To assist workers in organising themselves in trade unions as a medium of service to the motherland irrespective of faiths and political affinities;

(iii) The right to strike, and

(iv) To inculcate in the minds of the workers the spirit of service, cooperation and dutifulness and develop in them a sense of responsibility towards the nation in general and the industry in particular.

**The Objectives of Hind Mazdoor Panchayat are:**

(i) "To organise and promote the establishment of a democratic socialist society in India and to further the economic, political, social and cultural interests of the Indian working class";

(ii) To provide full opportunities for the development of mental and physical personality of the workers;

(iii) To strive for getting a living wage to all workers;

(iv) To guarantee work to every worker;

(v) To get full social security measures and comprehensive medical care introduced by the industry for workers;

(vi) To get adequate leisure for the workers in the form of reasonable hours of work and holiday with pay;

(vii) To arrange for adequate housing facilities;

(viii) To arrange for the introduction of free and compulsory education and facilities for vocational guidance;

(ix) To get effective recognition of the right of collective bargaining;

(x) To cooperate with other organizations in the country and outside having similar aims and objects; and

(xi) To secure and maintain for workers freedom of association, freedom of assembly, freedom of speech, freedom of press and the right to strike.

**The Objectives of the UTC are:**

(i) To establish a socialist society in India;

(ii) To establish a workers' and peasants' State in India;

(iii) To nationalize and socialize pertaining the means of production, distribution and exchange;

(iv) To safeguard and promote the interests, rights and privileges of the workers in all matters, social, cultural, economic and political;

(v) To secure and maintain workers' freedom of speech, freedom of press, freedom of association, freedom of assembly, right to strike, right to work or maintenance and the right to social security, and

(vi) To bring out unity in the trade union movement.

**The Objectives of National Front of Indian Trade Unions (NFITU) are:**

(i) To organise and unite trade unions with the object of building up a National Central Organisation of trade unions, independent of political parties, employers and the government, to further the cause of labour and that of national solidarity, security and defense of India, and to make the working people conscious of their rights as well as of obligations in all spheres of life;

(ii) To secure to members of trade unions full facilities of recognition and effective representation of interest of workers and to ensure for the working people fair conditions of life and service and progressively to raise their social, economic and cultural state and conditions;

(iii) To help in every possible way member trade unions in their fight to raise real wages of the workers; and

(iv) To endeavour to secure for members of affiliated trade unions adoption of progressive legislation for their welfare and to ensure the effective enforcement of the rights and interests of members of affiliated trade unions and for the working people in general.

**The Policies of Centre of Indian Trade Union (CITU) are:**

(i) The CITU believes that the exploitation of the working class can be ended only by socialising all means of production, distribution and exchange and establishing a socialist state, that is. It stands for the complete emancipation of the society from all exploitation.

(ii) The CITU fights against all encroachments on the economic and social rights of the workers and the enlargement of their rights and liberties including the right to strike, for winning defending and extending the freedom of the democratic trade union movement.

(iii) In the fight for the immediate interest of the working class, the CITU demands: (a) nationalization of all foreign monopoly concerns who exploit the working class; (h) nationalization of all concerns owned by Indian monopolists and big industry which garner huge profits at the expense of the workers, who exploit the people by pegging prices at a high level and who dictate the anti-labour and anti-people policies of the Government.

(iv) The CITU fights against the repressive policy of the Government towards the democratic and trade union movement; it fights against its economic policy of safeguarding the interests of capitalists and landlords and piling burdens of the common man and the working class through increasing taxation and inflation. It fights for replacing the present bourgeois-landlord regime by a democratic regime. It finally adheres to the position that no social transformation can be brought about without class-struggle and shall constantly repel attacks to take the working class along the path of class-collaboration.

## UNION STRUCTURE

The structure of trade unions in India varies from organisation-to-organisation. However, the structure can be classified into four types, *viz.*: (l) Craft Unions; (2) General Unions; (3) Industrial Unions, and (4) Federations.

1. **Craft Unions:** If the workers of the same craft or category of the job form into a union, that union is called Craft Union. These unions are called as horizontal unions. The basic logic behind the formation of such unions is that the workers belonging to the same craft do face similar problems — mostly non-managerial personnel form such unions. Examples of Craft Unions are Drivers' Associations, Signalling Staff Union in Indian Railways.

2. **General Unions:** If the workers of any industry, any region and of any job or occupation form into one union in order to protect the overall interests of the workers, such unions are called General Unions.

3. **Industrial Unions:** If the workers of different categories form into a union, that union is called Industrial Union. These unions are also called "vertical" unions. The logic behind the formation of these unions is that workers of the same industry have the common aim and they are governed by same rules and regulations and are administered by the same management. Moreover, the problems of all in the same industry are more or less common. The importance of these unions has been increasing in recent times.

4. **Federation and Confederation:** Industrial unions, either of the same industry or of the different industry may form into an association in order to improve trade union unity/ strength. Such a union of unions is called Federations. During the critical situations, Unions/ Federations in different industries may resort to concerted action without losing their individuality. In such situations, the Federations form into an Association and such an association is called Confederation. For example, Federation of Indian Railways, Central Government Employees may form into a Confederation.

## HOW TRADE UNION OBJECTIVES ARE ACHIEVED?

The objectives of a trade union are achieved by a pursuit of traditional methods. These are:

(i) The organisation of a trade union on the basis of the craft or industry in which its members are employed, such as general unions and professional employees' organizations;

(ii) Recognition of a trade union as the only bargaining agent; that is, it is only a representative union which is entitled to advocate the interests of its members. This recognition may be voluntarily forthcoming from a management or forced upon it by its employees; or it may be gained by secret ballot, each member voting in favour of the trade union which he wants to be recognised by the management. In these circumstances, the trade union which is favoured by a majority of the workers in an industry is the one which is recognised by the management;

(iii) Collective bargaining, which is the essence of industrial relations, for it is through collective bargaining that the terms and conditions of employment are determined and under which work is performed satisfactorily;

(iv) Union security, which is achieved through a closed shop or a union shop or an agency shop arrangement or some such similar arrangement which gives a trade union control of the hiring, the supervision and the discharge of workers.

(v) Grievance processing and handling procedures, under which grievances are redressed or dealt with by a correction of the situation or by a channeling up of these "up the line". When a grievance reaches the chief executive officer, it has to be satisfactorily dealt with by him or sent to an outside statutory agency for settlement.

(vi) Negotiated agreements with the management. These negotiations deal with wages, hours of work, other terms and conditions of employment, personal and job security, increased employee benefits, medical assistance, retirement benefits, and so on;

(vii) Arbitration, by which unsettled or unresolved disputes can be settled by an outside agency;

(viii) Political pressure exercised through legislators who are capable of bringing about changes in labour laws; and

(ix) Mutual insurance thorough common contributions to meet the financial needs of workers when there are stoppages of work.

Most of the trade unions have not effectively participated in achieving these objectives because:

(a) Of lack of awareness on their part of the importance of mutual insurance;

(b) Till recently, most trade unions have been "resistance organisation", and have been looked upon by employers with hostility and distrust;

(c) They suffer from class conflicts, divergent interests, inter-union and intra-union rivalries, multiplicity, financial weakness, outside leadership, and ignorance of the needs of the rank and file of their members; and

(d) Of the lack of education, cultural backwardness, and social and linguistic heterogeneity of their membership.

## FACTORS AFFECTING GROWTH OF TRADE UNIONS

The Trade Union Movement has gathered momentum in the post-independence period. The factors governing its rapid growth are: International influences, the pressure of trade union rivalries which are often the result of political or ideological differences, the government's industrial relations policies which have provided for compulsory adjudication and conferred special privileges on registered Trade Unions, and the desire of the workers for unity so that their interest may be safeguarded particularly when managements resort to discharges, dismissals, retrenchment, lockouts, lay-offs, etc.

It may be pointed out here that many trade unions have come up because of the stresses and strains of industrial development. They are, therefore, the direct offshoots of the industrial situation in the country. In the early stages of their development, trade unions were looked upon as trouble-makers and renegades in the context of the prevailing norms of society. Now they are considered to be an essential part of the industrial scene, and are an important socio-economic institution in the country. To begin with, trade unions were agitation, threatening and unreasonable organizations. They have now developed — at least most of them have so developed — into persuasive and peaceful organizations.

## WEAKNESSES OF TRADE UNION

The problems and weaknesses of trade unionism in India are as follows:

**(i) Uneven Growth:** The trade unionism in India is characterized by uneven growth, both industry-wise and area-wise. Trade unions are popular in big industries and the degree of unionization varies widely from industry-to-industry. Besides, trade union activities are concentrated in a few states and in bigger industrial centres mainly due to concentration of industries in that place. Here again, it is the manual workers who are covered by trade union activity.

**(ii) Limited Membership:** The number of trade unions in India has increased considerably. But this has been followed by the declining membership per union. This is due to the reason that any seven workers can form a union under the Trade Unions Act, 1926 and get it registered. The total membership of trade unions is only a small part of the total number of wage-earners. As a result, the trade union movement has touched only a small member of the working class population.

**(iii) Rivalry Among the Union Leaders:** Because of rivalry among leaders workers lose interest in unionism. The employers also get an opportunity to play unions against each other. They are able to take advantage of infighting among unions and may refuse to bargain on the plea that there is no strong representative union. They can argue saying that they don't know that with whom they should bargain with.

**(iv) Outside Leadership:** Trade unions in India are led largely by people who themselves are not workers. These outsiders are politicians, intellectuals and professionals having no experience of work in industry. Outsiders continue to dominate the trade unions to advance their personal interests. Since outsiders have links with political parties, they give greater importance to the interest of their political parties. At times, they don't mind sacrificing the interest of their followers for the achievement of political ends. Their approach towards labour problems is coloured by political considerations. This hampers the growth of healthy employer-employee relations.

**(v) Financial Problems:** The financial position of the trade union is weak because their average yearly income is very low and inadequate. The workers are apathetic towards trade union and do not want to contribute from their hard earned money. The subscription rates are very low. Due to multiplicity of unions, a union interested in increasing its membership figures keeps the subscription rate unduly low. As a result, the funds with the unions are inadequate and they cannot undertake welfare programmes for their members. Another reason for the weak financial position of union is that large amounts of subscription dues remain unpaid by the workers. Besides this, unions do not have an appropriate system to collect subscriptions.

**(vi) Lack of Expert Guidance:** Many trade unions have small number of members and therefore, not in a position to engage the services of experts to advise and guide them, and help them to face the challenge of employers. In other words, their financial position is weak; their bargaining power is weak; and they are not able to make their influence felt.

**(vii) Indifferent Attitude of Workers:** In India, a large number of workers have not joined any union. Moreover, all the members of the trade unions do not show interest in their affairs. The attendance at the general meetings of the unions is very low. Under such circumstance, trade unionism cannot be expected to make much progress. The control which political leaders have acquired over trade unions, the backwardness of the workers and their fear of victimization has discouraged them from actively participating in trade union activities.

**(viii) Lack of Education:** Lack of education makes the workers narrow-minded, and prevents them from taking long-term views. Thus, anything, which does not result in an immediate reward, becomes unattractive to them. This attitude is responsible for many strikes and lockouts in industrial concerns. When labour unions go on strike on illogical grounds, incalculable losses occur to producers, community and the nation.

**(ix) Slow Growth of Trade Union:** Trade unions, which have grown very slowly, have not developed as effective voluntary organizations because of the unrealistic labour policies of the Government.

**(x) Lack of Unity Among Workers:** The loose and amorphous nature of trade union organizations, the majority character of labour, casteism, regionalism and linguism which have divided the workers into heterogeneous groups, and the hostile attitude of the employers are some of the reasons for the weaknesses of trade union.

In short, the political involvement of trade union leaders and union rivalries has weakened the trade union movement. So have the proliferation of trade unions, the absence of functional unity among them, their irregular and small membership, the many unsuccessful strikes which they have sponsored, and the limited number of welfare programmes which they have sponsored and supported.

## Trends in Trade Union Movemnt

1. A major trend witnesses these days is the change in the attitude of unions towards management, industry, Government and the economy.
   (i) Unions are becoming increasingly matured, responsive and realistic in their thinking and action. Gone are the days for cat-call strikes, bandhs, gheraoes and violence.
   (ii) Unions are reconciled to economic reforms. They are now opposing the adverse impact of reforms and not the reforms.
   (iii) Now trade unions are discussing issues like productivity, total quality management, technology, competition, exports, etc. Major unions like that of the telecom employees, for example, are on line with the corporation plans of the department. They are now talking about issues like gearing up for competition, inculcating a customer-friendly approach, etc.
   (iv) Unions have accepted that there is surplus labour everywhere and it needs to be curtailed. They are now extending cooperation to schemes like voluntary retirement, golden handshake and the like. For example, 35,000 workers of National Textile Corporation have retired voluntarily.

2. Depoliticisation of Union is another trend witnesses these days. All the federations of union are affiliated to one party or the other. Being affiliated to one or the other political party, the unions are more interested to follow the instructions of their leaders than protecting the interests of the workers. Unions have now realized the uselessness of such affiliation and are now insulating themselves against political influences. Many leading companies such as Telco, Philips, Voltas, Hindustan Unilever Limited, Pfizer, etc., have unions not affiliated to any political party. For example, the Philips employee's union successfully prevented the entry of Tatas into the company. When the Philips management allegedly offered the Tatas a part of their rights cum preferential issue, at an unusually low premium, the union demanded that it should be allowed to examine the agreement and successfully moved to the Bombay High Court to settle the issue.

3. Worker's associations in our country are highly fragmented and the consequences have been the multiplicity of unions. Multiplicity is caused by ideological rifts, personal ambition of leaders, craft division among workers and the management's own myopia. The multiplicity of unions weakens the bargaining strength of employees. The futility of multiple unions is being realized by the government and the workers. The government proposes to amend trade Union Act of 1926 to prescribe minimum strength for the formation of the union as 100 or 10 per cent of the total staff, whichever is less. Of late, unions have presented a common front on issues like industrial sickness. At the 31st session of the Indian Labour Conference held in 1995, unions have demanded better utilization of the fund and felt that the amount should not be used merely for financing Voluntary Retirement Schemes.

4. One of the defects of Trade Union Movement in our country has been the phenomenon of outside leadership. Individuals who are not connected with the factory would assume the leadership mantle of the union. The Trade Union Act also permits outside participation to the extent of 50 per cent of the strength of the office bearers in a union. The Government is planning to reduce this percentage now.

5. The attraction towards central trade union, which peaked during the post-nationalization years, has decreased considerably now. The workers now are more educated and they gradually have realized that independent unions are more advantageous than national union.

## MEASURES TO STRENGTHEN TRADE UNION MOVEMENT IN INDIA

The following are some of the measures to minimize trade union problem and to strengthen the Trade Union Movement in India:

1. It should be the constant endeavour of policy makers to aim at the unity of trade union organizations, so that they may be brought together on the basis of a common programme. There should be legal provision for the recognition of the representative union. Due recognition should be given to trade unions as the legitimate bargaining agents of workers.

2. Outside political leadership has been developed due to the absence of internal leadership. Outside leadership is the main cause for the multiple problems of the trade union. The problems can be eradicated through the development of leadership talents from within. Management should encourage internal workers to lead their own movement. Management and trade union should provide educational and training facilities for the development of internal leadership.

3. The functions of trade unions should be widened and broadened. In addition to safeguarding the economic interests of their members, they should be encouraged to assume social responsibilities. As far as possible, trade unions should be drawn into participation in the development programme of the country.
4. The Trade Union Act of 1956 should be amended and the number of members required to a trade union should be increased from 7 per cent to 50 per cent of the employees of the organization. Similarly, the scope for outside leadership should be reduced from 50 per cent to 10 per cent.

   The membership subscription should be enhanced from 25 paise to 1 per cent of the monthly wages of the worker. The Trade Union Act should be amended in order to avoid dual membership.
5. Trade union should not unnecessarily involve in the management decision, where their interference reduces the organizational effectiveness.
6. Trade union should form a labour party and trade union in the country should be affiliated to it. It gives adequate strength to the trade unions both in the industry and in the Parliament.
7. Paid union officials should be employed, so that they may devote their whole time to union work.

## RECOMMENDATIONS OF THE NATIONAL COMMISSION ON LABOUR

The National Commission on Labour has made some very valuable suggestions to improve harmonious industrial relations in the country.

It has recommended that the formation of craft and occupation trade unions should be discouraged. As far as possible, the formation of industrial trade unions and industrial federations should be encouraged. The Trade Unions Act lays down that at least half the number of office-bearers of trade union should be its members. The National Commission has recommended that:

(a) The number of outsiders in a trade union should be limited to 30 per cent in the case of trade unions whose membership is drawn from a particular industry as well as in the case of those which have a membership of more than 10,000 as against 20 per cent in the case of those whose membership is between 1,000 and 10,000 and 10 per cent in the case of those which have a membership of less than 1,000.

(b) All ex-employees should be treated as insiders, for many resign their jobs in order to shoulder increasing responsibilities of trade union activity or because they have been victimized by their employers for their active participation in trade union activity. In both cases, it would be unfair to treat them as outsiders. The Trade Unions Act should, therefore, be amended with a view to excluding such persons from the definition of outsiders.

## SUMMARY

A trade union is an association of workers in one or more professions — an association carried on mainly for the purpose of protecting and advancing the members' economic interests in connection with their daily work. Workers join trade unions to achieve their objectives which they could not achieve individually like to get economic security, to improve their bargaining power, to ventilate the workers' grievances to the management, etc. The basic functions of unions are to protect and promote the interest of the workers and conditions of their employment. At present, there are five major central trade union organizations, namely, INTUC, BMS, HMS, AITUC and CITU. The objectives of a trade union are achieved by collective bargaining, negotiated agreements with the management, arbitration and the political pressure exercised through legislators. Some of the reasons for the weaknesses of trade union are the political involvement of trade union leaders and union rivalries, concentration of activities in metropolitan centres, small number of members, etc. It should be the constant endeavour of policy makers to aim at the unity of trade union organizations, so that they may be brought together on the basis of a common programme. In this way, they would become strong bargaining agents for their members.

## CASELET 1

The Ashoka Transport Company Ltd., has been providing transport facility to passengers since 1985. It has been extending its operation from one region to another by nationalizing the private passenger transport companies on a phased manner. Presently, it is offering its services in 80 per cent of the routes in Orissa and Madhya Pradesh. It nationalized its two routes in East Orissa in October 1995. Normally, it absorbs all the employees working in private passenger transport companies and fixes their salaries at par with the scales of similar categories of jobs in the state government transport corporation.

The pay scales in the corporation are determined on the basis of mutual agreement between the management and the recognized trade union. The scales are revised once in three years. The recent agreement came into force with effect from September 1997. There are two classes in the driver's category, i.e., class one (drivers working in long distance buses) and class two (drivers working in short distance routes). The pay scale of class two officers is enhanced from ₹ 1,600-2,200 to1,900-2,600 (with effect from September 1998) in consequence to the latest agreement. The agreement further says that the pay scales of the drivers drawing the scales of ₹ 1,600-2,200 will be fixed in the scale of ₹ 1,900-2,600.

The corporation absorbed 10 drivers in December 1998 who were with the private passenger transport companies consequent upon the recent nationalization of two routes. The personnel department fixed the scale of these 10 drivers in the scale of ₹ 1,600-2,200 and it rejected their plea of fixing their pay scale at ₹ 1,900-2,600 saying that only drivers in the scale of ₹ 1,600-2,200 are now eligible to draw the scale of ₹ 1,900-2,600. The company has set up both the grievance machinery and collective bargaining machinery to resolve employee's problem. Then these drivers submitted these issues to the foremen, their immediate superior. The foremen told them to raise this issue in collective bargaining with the help of trade union leaders and persuaded them to solve the issue. The trade union leaders included this item in the agenda to the collective bargaining committee to be held in January 1999 but the collective bargaining committee deleted this item from the draft agenda saying that this issue can be settled through grievance machinery as only 10 drivers out of 3,000 in the corporation are concerned with this issue.

### Questions

1. What is the problem?
2. What are the major issues of this problem?
3. Suggest the measures to handle this problem.

## ........ QUESTIONS FOR DISCUSSION

1. Define the term trade union. Why do workers join trade union?
2. Explain the functions of trade unions.
3. Compare and contrast the objectives of important trade unions in India.
4. Why do trade unions in India often fail to achieve their objectives? Suggest measures for the successful functioning of trade unions.
5. Define trade union. State the objectives and the weakness of Indian Trade Union.

## Objective Questions

### A. Fill in the Blanks

1. ________ is an association of workers formed with a purpose to protect and promote the common interest of the member.
2. The primary source of income to the unions is ________.
3. The unsound financial position is mostly due to ________ and low rate of ________.
4. Trade Union Act was passed in the year ________.

*Ans:* **1.** Trade Union, **2.** membership fee, **3.** low membership, membership fee, **4.** 1926.

### B. Multiple Choice Questions

1. The functions of a trade union are ________ and ________.
   (a) Managerial and Operative
   (b) Planning and Organising
   (c) Militant and fraternal
   (d) Recruitment and Selection

*Ans:* **1.** (c)

### C. State Whether the Following Statement are True or False. Justify Your Answer

1. Outside leadership undermined the purpose of trade union and weakened their authority.
2. There can be a dual membership of unions.
3. Trade union's bargaining power can be successful only when there is only one trade union in an industry.
4. The size of membership and successful functioning of trade union are interrelated and interdependent.
5. A trade union's bargaining power is often measured in terms of its membership, its financial strength and the nature of its leadership.

*Ans:* **1. True**

Due to the inability of insiders to lead their movement, they depend on some outside leader having dynamic personality and this outside leader cannot understand the workers problem as they don't live the life of a worker and due to personal benefits and prejudice sometimes weigh more than unions, as a result the main objective of trade union gets sidelined.

**2. False**

As per the code of conduct there cannot be a dual membership of unions, which will ultimately help in reducing the inter-union rivalry. The worker can be a member of any trade union of his own choice and if the worker is a member of a particular trade union then he cannot be a member of any other trade union at the same time.

**3. True**

The existence of a single strong union not only protects the employee's interest more effectively but also halts the various unproductive activities of the unions and forces the leader to concentrate on the strategic issues. Further, it helps to bring about congenial industrial relation by bringing about system of orderliness in dealing with the employees and by facilitating expeditious settlement of disputes. It is because of inter- and intra-union rivalries industrial dispute takes place and are responsible for weak bargaining power of trade union in collective bargaining.

4. **True**

Size of membership of trade unions determines their strength and financial soundness which in turn determines the activities undertaken by them and their ability to protect employee's interest. The size of membership and successful functioning of trade union are interrelated and interdependent.

5. **True**

Management on one side is highly diplomatic, so the union should hold a dynamic personality to deal with such management along with dynamic personality it should hold a good financial position which is possible if the membership is very high which will ultimately strengthen the trade unions bargaining power.

☺ ☺ ☺

# Part-II
# Marketing and Production Management

CHAPTER 7

# Marketing

## LEARNING OBJECTIVES

- *Meaning and Scope of Marketing.*
- *Core Concept of Marketing.*
- *Company Orientation Towards the Market-place or Philosophies of Marketing.*
- *Concept and Characteristics of Marketing Mix*
- *4Ps of Marketing, i.e,. the Marketing Mix.*
- *Meaning and Importance of Market Segmentation.*
- *Levels and Patterns of Market Segmentation.*
- *Steps in Market Segmentation Process.*
- *Bases for Segmenting Consumer and Business Markets.*

## MARKETING: AN INTRODUCTION

Marketing is an ancient art; it has been practiced since very long. Today, it has become the most important function in the world of business. The marketing concept holds that the key to achieving organizational goals consists in determining the needs and wants of target markets and delivering the desired satisfactions more effectively and efficiently than competitors. The emphasis of marketing concept is on selling satisfaction and not merely on the selling a product. The objective of marketing is not the maximization of profitable sales volume, but profits through the satisfaction of customers. The most important person in marketing is consumer, and all marketing activities operate around the consumer. It is, therefore, essential that the marketers identify their customers, establish a rapport with them, identify their needs and deliver the goods and services that would meet their requirements.

**The components of marketing concept are as under:**

(a) **Satisfaction of Customers:** In this competitive environment, where satisfying customer has become the main concern for almost all organisations, they should aim at producing those goods and services, which will lead to satisfaction of customers.

(b) **Integrated Marketing:** The various functions of production, finance and marketing should be integrated to satisfy the needs and expectations of customers.

(c) **Profitable Sales Volume:** Marketing can be successful only when it is capable of maximizing profitable sales and achieves long run customer satisfaction.

The digital revolution has placed a new set of capabilities in the hands of consumer. The consumer of 21st century have a substantial increase in buying power, greater variety of goods and services are available to choose from, lot of information about anything could be easily accessed from any corner of the world, it has become very easy to place and receive orders. The objective of all business enterprises is to satisfy the needs and wants of the society. Marketing is, therefore, a basic function of all business firms. When a salesperson sells air-conditioner, a doctor treats a patient or a Government asks parents to take their children for getting polio drops, each one of them is involved in the activity of marketing therefore, focusing on target markets. Traditionally, marketing was not given much importance by small firm owners as compared to the other functions such as accountancy, production and selling. Since, early 1990s there has been a drastic change in the thinking of businessman from product-orientation to consumer-orientation. Modern business concerns lay emphasis on 'selling satisfaction' and not merely on selling products. The activities have to be coordinated so as to develop the marketing mix, which provides maximum satisfaction to the customers. Marketing plays a major role in our daily lives. Each day is filled with consuming products made available by marketers. We pay for marketing each time we buy a product. The every dollar that we spent at the retail level goes to cover marketing costs. Marketing is responsible for satisfying customers, which in turn increases our standard of living and quality of life.

**Few benefits of good marketing are:**

1. It promotes the company, increases its visibility and exposure and makes people aware, about the company's products and services.
2. It differentiates products/services of the company by positioning it in a unique way.

3. It helps the company to acquire new business and retain old customers.
4. It generates income for the company and helps build networks with other professionals to further enhance company growth.

## WHAT IS MARKETING?

Marketing is the process of planning and executing the conception, pricing promotion, and distribution of ideas, goods, and services to create exchange that satisfy individuals and organizational goals. It is about identifying and meeting human and social needs. The shortest definition of marketing is "meeting needs profitably".

Marketing is a societal process by which individuals and group obtain what they need and want through creating, offering, and freely exchanging products and services of value with others.

The American Marketing Association defines marketing as "an organizational function and a set of processes for creating, communicating and delivering value to customers and for managing customer relationships in ways that benefit the organization and its stakeholders".

According to Kilter, "Marketing management is the art and science of choosing target markets and getting, keeping and growing customers through creating, delivering and communicating superior value".

According to Peter Drucker, "Exchange, a key concept in marketing is the process of obtaining a desired product from someone by offering something in return. When an agreement is reached in an exchange a transaction takes place". The key conditions for an exchange potential to exist are:

- There must be at least two parties.
- Each party must have something of value for the other party.
- Each party must be capable of communication and delivery.
- They should be free to accept or reject the offer.
- Each party should believe that it is appropriate to deal with the other party.

### Importance of Marketing

**Importance of marketing is as follows:**

Marketing is important for:

1. Society.
2. Business.
3. It offers outstanding career opportunities.
4. It affects our day-to-day life.

**1. Marketing Plays an Important Role in Society:** The total population of India is unimaginable; it is the second highest populated country. The numbers of transactions that take place to satisfy the needs such as food, clothing and shelter for the huge population are quite high. And yet it all works quite well, partly because the marketing makes food available when we want it, in desired quantities, at accessible locations, and in convenient packages and forms (such as instant and frozen foods).

**2. Marketing is Important to Business:** The fundamental objectives of most businesses are survival, profits, and growth. Marketing contributes directly to achieving these objectives. Marketing includes the following activities, which are essential to business organizations: identifying the needs and wants and then satisfying the potential customers, designing and managing product offerings, determining prices and pricing policies, developing ,distribution strategies and communicating with actual and potential customers.

Every manager, regardless of specialization or area of responsibility, needs to be familiar with the basics of accounting, finance, management, and marketing. So also people in all business areas need to be able to communicate with specialists in other areas. Furthermore, marketing is not just a job done by people in a marketing department. Marketing is a part of the job of everyone in the organization. According to David Packard of Hewlett-Packard put it, "Marketing is far too important to be left only to the marketing department". Marketing is not a department so much as a companywide orientation. Therefore, a basic understanding of marketing is important to all business people.

**3. Marketing Offers Outstanding Career Opportunities:** Marketing offers great career opportunities in the areas of professional selling, marketing research, advertising, retail buying, distribution management, product management, product development, and wholesaling. Marketing career opportunities also exist in a variety of nonbusiness organizations, including hospitals, museums, universities, the armed forces, and various government and social service agencies. The world has become a global marketplace and the job of marketer has become more challenging, companies all over the world and of all sizes have to become better marketers to compete.

**4. Marketing Affects Our Day-to-day Life:** Marketing plays a major role in our everyday life. Every rupee that we spend pays for marketing costs, such as marketing research, product development, packing, transportation, storage, advertising and sales expenses. Advertisement makes people aware about the new product in market; it also helps people to choose the best product which satisfies their needs. By developing a better understanding of marketing, one can become a better informed consumer.

## Scope of Marketing

Marketing is typically seen as the task of creating, promoting and delivering goods and services to consumers and businesses. Marketing managers are responsible for demand management. There can be eight possible demand states namely negative demand, nonexistent demand, latent demand, declining demand, irregular demand, full demand, overfull demand and unwholesome demand.

1. **Negative Demand:** Consumer dislikes product and may even pay price to avoid it. For example, heart surgery or any kind of operation, people may dislike it but they go for it.
2. **Nonexistent Demand:** Consumer may be unaware of or uninterested in the product. For example, school boys may not be interested in craft work and school girls may not be interested in physical training programme.
3. **Latent Demand:** Consumer may share a strong need that cannot be satisfied by an existing product. For example, cars in air and not on road.
4. **Declining Demand:** Consumers begin to buy the product less frequently or not at all. For example, decline in demand of desktop as compared with air laptop.

5. **Irregular Demand:** Consumers purchase varies on a seasonal, monthly weekly, daily, or even hourly basis. For example, theatres are under visited on regular days as compared to weekends.

6. **Full Demand:** Consumers are buying all products which are available at marketplace. For example, whatever is being produced is being sold.

7. **Overfull Demand:** More consumers would like to buy the product than they could be satisfied. For example, parks and museum are overcrowded during vacation.

8. **Unwholesome Demand:** Consumer may be attracted to products that are not desirable for society. For example, cigarettes, alcohol, etc.

## Marketing people are involved in marketing 10 types of entities

Marketing people market 10 types of entities such as: goods, services, events, experiences, persons, places, properties, organizations, information, and ideas.

These entities are as follows:

**1. Goods:** Physical goods constitute of almost most of the countries production and marketing efforts. Each Indian companies market, air-conditioned cars, LCD television set, machines, cosmetics, mobiles and various other products which are used in our day-to-day life.

**2. Services:** Services include the work of banking institution, airlines, hotels, insurance firms, barbers, beauticians, maintenance and repair people, and accountants, lawyers, doctors, software programers, and management consultants. At a restaurant, for example, the customer consumes both a product and a service, if marketing of school needs to be done it would market its education and service provided by a school.

**3. Experience:** By providing several goods and services a firm can create, stage, and market experience. An amusement park or a water park represents experiential marketing: customers, by taking different rides in the amusement park or the water park, enjoy the thrill from their own experiences.

**4. Person:** Celebrity marketing is a major business. Most of the products in India are being marketed through celebrity. Celebrities such as Amitabh Bachchan, Sachin Tendulkar, Shah Rukh Khan, Aishwarya Rai, Shilpa Shetty and M.S. Dhoni are big brands themselves. Most of the product is sold in the market very easily if sold through celebrity marketing. As Sachin Tendulkar being a brand ambassador of Boost "Is the power of my energy".

**5. Events:** Marketers promote time-based events, such as major trade shows, artistic perform and company anniversaries. Global events such as the Olympics and the World Cup are promoted aggressively to both companies and fans. For example IPL.

**6. Places:** Cities, states, regions, and whole nations compete actively to attract tourists, factories, company headquarters, and new residents. Place marketers include economic development specialists, real estate agents, commercial banks, local business associations, and advertising and public relations agencies. In tourism industry Kerala is marketed as "Gods own country" and has become one of the hot spots for tourism. The Government of India is marketing India as a tourist destination through the "Incredible India" advertisement campaign or as Attithi Devo Bhavoh.

**7. Properties:** Properties are intangible rights of ownership of either real property (real estate) or financial property and bonds. Properties are bought and sold, and these exchanges require marketing.

**8. Organizations:** They actively work to build a strong, favourable, and unique image in the minds of their target publics. Universities, museums, performing arts and nonprofits organizations all use marketing to boost their public images and to compete for audiences and funds. Corporate identity campaigns are the result of intensive research programmes. This is certainly the case with Philips "Sense and Simplicity" campaign.

**9. Information:** Information is essentially what books, schools, and universities produce, market, and distribute at a price to parents, students, and communities, e.g. Royal School of Business Management gives information about high quality service.

**10. Ideas:** Everything which is sold in the market includes a basic idea. Fair and handsome sell hopes by making men fairer just in few days. Social marketers are busy promoting ideas by creating awareness by discouraging smoking.

## KEY CUSTOMER MARKETS

**Markets:** Earlier, a "market" was a physical place where buyers and sellers gathered to buy and sell goods. A market is a place which allows the purchaser and the seller to invent and gather information and lets them carry-out exchange of various products and services. In other words, the meaning of market refers to a place where the trading of goods takes place. The essential markets and their connecting flows starts from manufacturers, they go to resource markets such as raw material markets, labour markets, money markets, etc., buy resources and turn them into goods and services, and then sell finished products to intermediaries, who sell them to consumers. Consumers earn money by working or by providing services to any company for which they receive money with which they pay for goods and services which they purchase. The government collects tax from manufacturer, and intermediary markets and uses these goods and services to provide public services. Every economy whether it is a nation's or global economy, consists of complex interacting sets of markets linked through exchange processes.

The term market has been used for grouping of customers. They view sellers as constituting the industry and buyers as constituting the market. The market is composed of various markets such as need markets (the diet-seeking market), product markets (the watch market), demographic markets (the education market), and geographic markets (the Gujarat market); or the concept of market could be extended to cover other markets, such as voter markets, labour markets, etc.

### Key Customer Markets

The consumer, global, business and nonprofit markets are said to be key customer markets which are as follows:

**1. Consumer Markets:** Companies who sell consumer goods and services such as soft drinks, cosmetics, air travel; they spend lot of time in trying to establish a superior brand image as compared with competitors. The strength of brands lies in creating a superior product and packaging, ensuring availability of the product with regular services without any problem.

**2. Global Markets:** The companies selling goods and services in global marketplace needs to be careful while taking decision and face challenge from different companies. The company w ch wants to enter any country must decide, which countries to enter; how to enter each (as an exporter, licenser, joint venture partner, contract manufacturer, or solo manufacturer) how to adopt product and service features of each country; to know that pricing strategy is different for different countries; and how to communicate to fit different cultures. The various decisions are made on the basis of different requirements for buying, negotiating, and disposing of property; different culture, language, and legal and political and currencies that might fluctuate in value.

**3. Business Markets:** The buyers in business markets are well trained, well-informed and skilled professional buyers who are competent of making an evaluation of competitive offerings made by the sellers. Business buyers buy goods for making and reselling a product to others by booking profit. Marketers must show that how their products would help buyers to achieve revenue at a lower costs.

**4. Nonprofit and Governmental Markets:** Companies selling to nonprofit organizations such as universities, churches, and charitable organizations and government agencies need to price their product or service carefully, as these buyers have limited purchasing power. Lower selling prices may affect the features and quality that seller may offer to nonprofit and governmental markets.

## CORE CONCEPTS OF MARKETING

The core concepts of marketing are as follows:

**Marketers and Prospects:** Anyone who seeks a response (attention, a purchase) from another party, called the prospect. If two parties are to sell something to each other, they are called as marketers.

**Marketplaces, Market Spaces, and Meta Market:** The marketplace is physical from where one does shopping or it is a place where buyer goes to shop, market space is said to be digital, as when people shop through the internet; meta market describes about complementary products and services that are closely related in the minds of consumers, but spread across a diverse set of industries. The real estate market consists of builders, contractors new and secondhand house dealers and financing companies, insurance companies, banks, agents, moneylender for loan to be taken for a number of years, etc. For purchasing a house, a buyer will get involved in many aspects of this meta market, and this gives an opportunity to meta market diaries to assist buyers in moving seamlessly through groups, although they are disconnected in physical space. For example, many companies through their website like www.magicbricks.com helps buyers and sellers for second-hand sell, buy, or exchange new and used houses. This website provides useful information that facilitates informed transactions for both buyers and sellers. There are many meta intermediaries for buying selling and renting products for example for booking air tickets (MakeMytrip.com, Yatra.com,) for purchasing books (e.g., Amazon.com).

**Needs, Wants and Demands:** The marketer must try to understand the target markets needs, wants, and demands. Needs are the basic human requirements. People need air, water, clothing, and shelter to survive. People also have strong needs for education, entertainment and junk food. These needs become wants when they are directed to specific objects that might satisfy the need. An Indian needs food but wants a burger, and a soft drink. A person in Goa needs food but wants a sea food. Wants are shaped by one's society. Demands are wants for specific products backed by an ability to pay. Many people want a Mercedes; only a few are able and willing to buy one. Companies must measure not only how many people want their product but also how many would actually be willing and able to buy it. Marketers do not create needs: needs pre-exist marketers. Marketers, along with other societal factors, influence wants. Marketers might promote the idea that a Mercedes would satisfy a person's need for status. They do not, however, create the need for social status.

**Target market, Positioning, and Segmentation:** A marketer cannot satisfy everyone in the market. Everyone has their own likes and dislikes for movie, hotels, cars or courses that a person opt in college. As marketers cannot serve everyone in the market they start dividing market .They identify groups of buyers who would like to require varying product mixes.

By examining demographic, psychographic and behavioural differences among buyers' market segments could be identified. The marketer identifies the segment with greatest opportunity which acts as their target markets. For each chosen target market the firm develops market offerings. The offering is then positioned in the minds of customer as giving some benefits. For example, Ford Ikon positioned its car as a josh machine. Ford Ikon therefore, positioned its car as a speedy car.

**Product, Offering and Brands:** Most firms address their needs by putting forth a value proposition, a set of benefits they offer to customers to satisfy their needs. The intangible value proposition is made physical by an offering, which can be a combination of products, services, information, and experiences.

A brand is an offering from a known source. A brand names such as Inox, Fame, etc., caries many associations in the minds of people such as entertainment, fun, fast food and friends. These associations make up the brand image. Every company work hard to build brand strength — that is, a strong, favourable brand image.

**Value and Satisfaction:** The offering would be of great success if it delivers value and satisfaction to the target buyer. The buyer try to choose between different offerings on the basis of their perception that a particular product would deliver the most value. Value could be seen as a combination of quality, service, and price (QSP), which is also called as a customer value triad. Value increases with quality and service and decreases with price. Value could be defined as a ratio between what the customer gets and what he gives. The customer gets benefits and incurs costs. The benefits that customer receive include functional benefits and emotional benefits. The costs which a person incurs are monetary costs, time costs, energy costs, and psychic costs.

**Exchange and Transaction:** There are four ways in which a person can obtain a product. 1. A person can self-produce the product or service, as in when he hunts, fishes, or gathers fruit. 2. One can use force to get a product, as in a hold up or burglary. 3. The person can beg, as it happens when a homeless person asks for food. 4. A person can offer a product, a service, or money in exchange for something he or she desires.

Exchange, which is the core concept of marketing, is the process of obtaining desired product from someone by offering something in return. For exchange to exist, five conditions must be satisfied:

1. There are at least two parties.
2. Each party has something that might be of value to the other party.
3. Each party is capable of communication and delivery.
4. Each party is free to accept or reject the exchange offer.
5. Each party believes it is appropriate or desirable to deal with the other party.

Whether exchange actually takes place depends on whether the two parties agree on terms that will leave them both better off (or at least not worse off) than before. Exchange is a value-creating process because it normally leaves both parties better. Two parties are engaged in exchange if they are negotiating — trying to arrive at mutually agreeable terms. When an agreement is reached, it is said that a transaction has taken place. A transaction is a trade of values between two or more parties: A gives X to B and gets Y in return. Radha sells Sita a television set and Sita pays ₹ 10,000 to Radha. This is a monetary transaction but transactions do not require money as one of the traded value. A barter transaction involves trading goods or services for other goods or services when lawyer Mitesh writes a will for physician Rakesh in return for a medical examination.

A transaction involves several dimensions: at least two things of value, agreed upon conditions, a time of agreement, and a place of agreement. Without a law of contracts, people would approach transactions with some distrust, and everyone would lose.

A transaction differs from a transfer. In a transfer, Ram Mohan gives X to Sunder but does not get anything tangible in return. Gifts, subsidies, and charitable contributions are all transfers. In this, the transferer expects to receive something in exchange for his or her gift example, gratitude or seeing a changed behaviour in the recipient. Professional fund raisers provide benefits to donors, such as thank you notes, donor magazines, and invitations to events. Marketers have broadened the concept of marketing to include study of transfer behavior as well as transaction behaviour.

**Relationship and Networks:** Transaction marketing is a part of a larger idea called relationship marketing. Relationship marketing aims at building mutually satisfying long-term relations with key parties-customers, suppliers, distributors in order to learn and retain their business. Marketers accomplish this by promising and delivering high quality products and services at fair prices to the customers over time. Relationship marketing builds strong economic, technical, and social ties among the parties to a business. It also reduces transaction costs and time by maintaining good relationship with the customer.

The result of relationship marketing is building a unique company asset called a marketing network. A marketing network consists of the company and its supporting stakeholders (customer's employees, suppliers, distributors, retailers, agencies, university, and others) with whom the companies build mutually profitable business relationships. The competition is between marketing networks, that companies make and a company which has a strong marketing network has an upper hand as compared to the other companies. The operating principle is simple: Building an effective network of relationship with key stakeholders, would lead to more profits.

**Marketing Channels:** The marketer uses three kinds of marketing channels to reach a target market. Communication channels deliver and receive messages from target buyers, such as newspapers, magazines, radio, television, mail, telephone, billboards, poster fliers, CDs, audiotapes and the Internet. Communications can also be made through facial expressions and clothing, the look of retail stores, and many other medias. Marketers are adding, (e-mail and toll-free numbers) to counterbalance the more normal advertisements.

The distribution channels are used by marketers to display, sell, or deliver the physical product or service(s) to the buyer or user which includes distributor, wholesalers, retailers and agents.

The service channels are used by marketers to carry-out transactions with potential buyers. Service channels include warehouses, transportation companies, banks and insurance companies that facilitate transactions. Marketers clearly face a design problem in choosing the best mix of communication, distribution, and service channels for their offerings.

**Supply Chain:** The marketing channels connect the marketer to the target buyers; the supply chain describes a longer channel stretching from getting raw materials to final products that are delivered to the final buyers. The supply chain for gents purses starts with hides, and moves through tanning operations, cutting operation, manufacturing, and the marketing channels bringing products to customers. The supply chain represents a value delivery system. Each company captures only a certain percentage of the total value generated by the supply chain.

**Competition:** Competition includes all the actual and potential rival offerings substitutes that a buyer might consider. Suppose a builder of Vishwanath Enterprise is planning to buy cements for its building. There are several competitors selling the same product or the substitute product. It must also consider whether to make substitute materials or stick only to applications where cement offers superior performance.

There are four levels of competition based on the degree of product substitutability:

1. **Brand Competition:** A company sees its competitors as other companies offering similar products and services to the same customers at similar prices. Honda might see its major competitor such as Volkswagen, Tata, etc.
2. **Industry Competition:** A company sees its competitors as all companies making the same product or class of product. Honda would see itself as competing against all other automobile manufacturers.
3. **Form Competition:** A company sees its competitors as all companies manufacturing products that supply the same service. Honda would see as competing against not only with other automobile manufacturer, but also against manufacturers of motor cycles, bicycles, and trucks.
4. **Generic Competition:** A company sees its competitors as all companies that compete for the same one rupee. Honda would see competing itself with companies that compete for the same consumer rupee. Honda would see itself as competing with companies that sell major consumer durables, homes, etc.

**Marketing Environment:** The marketing environment consists of task environment and the broad environment. The task environment is composed of the company, suppliers, distributors, dealers, and the target consumers. The supplier group includes advertising agencies, banking and insurance companies, transportation and telecommunication companies. It would also include dealer, broker and the manufacturer's representative. The broad environment is composed of demographic environment, economic environment, natural environment, technological environment, political-legal environment, and social-cultural environment. The broad environment can create an impact on the task environment of a company.

## MARKETING PROCESS

Marketing managers are responsible for a variety of activities which represents the marketing process. These include the following:

1. Understanding the organization's mission and the role marketing plays is by fulfilling that mission.
2. Setting marketing objectives.

3. Gathering, analyzing, and interpreting information about the organization's situation, including its strengths and weaknesses as well as opportunities and threats in the environment.
4. Developing a marketing strategy by deciding exactly which wants and whose wants the organization will try to satisfy (target market strategy) and by developing appropriate marketing activities (the marketing mix) to satisfy the desires of selected target markets. The marketing mix combines product, distribution, promotion, and pricing strategies in a way that creates exchanges that satisfy individual and organizational goals.
   — Implementing the marketing strategy.
   — Designing performance measures.
   — Periodically evaluating marketing efforts, and making changes, if needed.

## Company Orientation Towards the Marketplace (Philosophies of Marketing)

The philosophies of marketing are as follows:

1. The Production Concept
2. The Product Concept
3. The Selling Concept
4. The Marketing Concept
5. The Holistic Marketing Concept
6. The Consumer-oriented Marketing Concept

**1. The Production Concept:** In an organization that practices this concept, production dominates the thinking process. It is believed that marketing can be managed by managing production. This concept holds that consumers would, support those products that are produced in great volume at low unit cost. In this type of organization effort is focused on production. They achieve cost reduction through maximization of output. They assume that the lower cost would bring all the customers to their doors. The focus of marketing efforts should be on improving production and distribution efficiency. This works well when there is a great deal of unmet demand for a product or when the cost of the product is so high that it needs to be manufactured cheaper in order to get consumers to adopt it. However, a focus simply on production and distribution efficiency ignores an important factor, i.e., the needs of the customers. The product concept holds that consumers will favour those products that offer the most quality, performance or innovative features. Managers in these organizations focus on making superior products and improving them over time.

**2. The Product Concept:** The product concept is different from the production concept. The product concept focuses on the features of the product, whereas the production concept argues for the focus on production and distribution processes, the product concept assumes that consumers will buy the product with the best quality, performance and features.

In the production concept the marketer seeks to win markets and profits through high volume of production and low unit cost, the product concept seeks to achieve the same result via product excellence, improved products, new products and ideally designed and engineered products. It also places an emphasis on quality assurance. The product concept tries to achieve marketing success through product attributes. Organizations that subscribe to the product concept assume that consumers would buy products of high quality. The managers concentrate on product excellence; they spend their time and money on research and development, and bring out many new products. But, they failed in the marketplace. They do not bother to study the market and the consumer in detail. They paid more attention on the product and almost forgot the consumer for whom the product is actually meant. The concept called marketing myopia came into existence; it means people do not have long-term vision and suffered for a short-sightedness about business. Excessive attention to production or the product or selling aspects at the cost of the customer and their actual needs creates this myopia. It even leads to a wrong or inadequate understanding of the very nature of the business in which the organization is engaged.

**3. The Selling Concept:** The selling concept holds that consumers, and businesses if left alone, will ordinarily not buy enough of the organization's products. The organization must, therefore, undertake an aggressive selling and promotion effort. The selling concept is used when companies find themselves with an overabundance of products that they have to sell in order to sell all their stocks. Followers of the selling concept believe that consumers will not buy their products unless they undertake a large-scale selling and promotion effort. Their aim is to sell what they make rather than make what will sell in the market.

The selling concept maintains that the company has to aggressively promote and push its products; it cannot expect its products to get picked up automatically by the customers. Heavy advertising, high-power personal selling, large-scale sales promotion, heavy price discounts, and strong publicity and public relations are the normal tools used by organizations that rely on this concept. But, these organizations too, do not enjoy the best as; it also suffers from marketing myopia, just as the production concept and the product concept do.

The differences between marketing and selling are as follows:

- ***Selling:*** (1) Selling starts with the seller, and is preoccupied all the time with the needs of the seller. (2) Seller is the centre of the business; activities start with the sellers' existing products. (3) Emphasizes on saleable surplus available within the corporation. (4) Seeks to quickly convert 'products' into 'cash'. (5) Concerns itself with the tricks and techniques of getting the customers to part with their cash for the products available with the salesman. (6) Overemphasizes the 'exchange' aspect, without caring for the 'value satisfactions' inherent in the exchange. (7) Sellers' preference dominates the formulation of the 'marketing mix'. (8) The firm makes the product first and then figures out how to sell it and make profit. (9) Emphasis on staying with the existing technology and reducing costs. (10) Sellers' motives are to dominate marketing communications. (11) Transportation, storage and other distribution functions are perceived as mere extensions of the production function. (12) Emphasis is on 'somehow selling'; there is no coordination among the different functions of the total marketing task. (13) Different departments of the business operate as separate watertight compartments. (14) In firms practicing 'selling', production is the central function of the business.

- ***Marketing:*** (1) Marketing starts with the buyer and focuses constantly on the needs of the buyer. (2) Buyer is the centre of the business; activities follow the buyer and his needs. (3) Emphasizes on identification of a market opportunity. (4) Seeks to convert customer 'needs' into 'products' and also emphasizes on fulfilling the needs of the customers. (5) Buyer determines the shape the 'marketing mix' should take. (6) What is to be offered as a product is determined by the customer. (7) The firm makes a 'total product offering' that will match and satisfy the identified needs of the customer. (8) The 'product' is the consequence of the marketing effort; the marketing effort leads to products that the customers actually want to buy in their own interest. (9) Emphasis on innovation in every sphere; on providing better value to the customer by adopting better technology. (10) Marketing communications is looked upon as the tool for communicating the benefits/ satisfactions provided by the product. (11) Consumer determines price: price determines costs. They are seen as vital services to be provided to the customer, keeping customer's convenience in focus. Emphasis is on integrated marketing: an integrated strategy covering product, promotion, pricing and distribution. (12) All departments of the business operate in a highly integrated manner, the sole purpose being generation of consumer satisfaction. In firms practicing 'marketing', it becomes central function of the business: the entire company or business is organized around the marketing function.

**4. The Marketing Concept:** The main aim of marketing concept is that the key to achieving organizational goals needs the company to be more effective than competitors in creating, delivering, and communicating superior customer value to its chosen target markets.

Elements of the Marketing Concept are: (a) Customer Focus. (b) Target Market. (c) Integrated Marketing or Coordinate Marketing, and (d) Profitability.

The marketing concept was born out of the awareness that a business should start with the determination of consumer wants and end with the satisfaction of those wants. The concept puts the consumer at both the beginning and the end of the business cycle. It stipulates that any business should be organized around the marketing function and its task should be one of anticipating, stimulating and meeting customers' requirements. The customer has to be the centre of the business universe. A business cannot succeed by supplying products and services that are not designed to serve the needs of the customers. According to Drucker, 'the essence here is that the entire business has to be seen from the point of view of the customer'. In a company practising this concept, all departments will recognize that their actions have a profound impact on the company's ability to create and retain a customer. Every department and every worker and manager will think of customer and act for customer.

The marketing concept aims at satisfying the customer at a profit. Three features of the marketing concept are customer orientation, coordinated effort by all departments within the organization to provide customer satisfaction, and emphasis on long-term profit. The marketing concept describes an ideal state of affairs. It exists when an organization focuses all of its efforts on providing products that satisfy its customers. The customer is the focal point for running organization. Products are created with the goal of satisfying customers' needs and wants. All departments within the organization work together towards the goal of customer satisfaction. They closely coordinate their efforts both to satisfy customer wants and to achieve the organization's long-term goals. When an organization is attempting to implement the marketing concept, it has a market orientation. An organization is market-oriented when it generates market intelligence on its customer needs, disseminates the intelligence across departments, and then responds to the organizations information. Organizations adopting the marketing concept are committed to market-focused and customer-driven philosophies.

**Few examples are as follows:**

Finds wants and fill them

You are the boss

Love the customer not the product

Meeting need profitability

Hence, marketing is said to be much wider and dynamic concept than selling.

**5. The Holistic Marketing Concept:** It is based on the development, design, and implementation of marketing programmes, processes and activities that recognizes their breadth and interdependencies. It recognizes that "Everything Matters" with marketing and that a broad, integrated perspective is often a necessary aim to reconcile the scope and complexities of marketing.

**HMC consists of four components of marketing which are as follows:**

*(1)* ***Relationship Marketing:*** The main aim of relationship marketing is to build mutually satisfying long-term relationships with key parties — customers, suppliers, distributors, and other marketing partners so as to earn and retain their business. It builds strong economic, technical, and social ties among the parties. The ultimate outcome of relationship is building of a unique company asset called as a Marketing Network

***Marketing Network*** consists of the company and its supporting stakeholders with whom the company has to build mutually profitable relationships.

*(2)* ***Integrated Marketing:*** It focuses on integration of the marketing programmes, processes and activities to create, communicate and deliver value to consumers. It concentrates towards integration among communications, products/services, and channels. McCarthy classified these four broad tools called as Marketing Mix which includes four Ps: Product, Price, Place and Promotion.

Robert Lauterborn advocates a shift of 4 Ps to 4Cs as follows.

| Four Ps | Four Cs |
|---|---|
| Product | Customer Solution |
| Price | Customer Cost/Value |
| Place | Convenience |
| Promotion | Communication |

*(3)* ***Internal Marketing:*** The main idea of internal marketing is to embrace appropriate marketing principles in the organization. Its task is to hire, train, and motivate employees of an organization to serve customers well. It should take place at two levels. First, the various marketing functions must work together, and second, marketing must be followed by all other departments. Its main focus should be on customer.

*(4)* ***Socially Responsible Marketing:*** It is concerned with marketing activities in the context of the Social or Societal Marketing, and the Legal, Ethical and Environmental Marketing.

***The Societal or Social Marketing Concept:*** The societal marketing concept holds that the organisation's task is to determine the needs, wants and interests of target markets and to deliver the desired satisfaction more effectively and efficiently than the competitor in a way that preserves or enhances the consumer's and the society's well-being.

**(6) The Consumer-oriented Marketing Concept:** The consumer-oriented marketing concept can be defined as "A principle of an enlightened marketing that holds that the company should view and organize its marketing activities from the consumer's point of view. Marketers should work hard to identify, serve and satisfy the needs of a target markets. Marketers need to look from the eyes of customer, as what actually customer needs."

## MARKETING MIX

### Introduction

The basic task of marketing is the delivery of product(s) to consumers so that their needs are fulfilled and organizational objectives are also achieved. It involves several important decisions, e.g., deciding about the product or products which should be offered for sale, price of the product, markets where products may sell and the means of communication with the consumer for the sale of the product. All these decisions form part of marketing mix. The concept of marketing mix, its components and the relationship among various components of marketing mix are as follows:

Marketing mix is the process of designing and integrating various elements of marketing in such a way as to ensure the achievement of enterprise objectives. The elements of marketing mix have been classified under four heads — product, price, place and promotion which is pronounced by McCarthy. That is why marketing mix is said to be a combination of 4 Ps. Decisions relating to the product include product designing, packaging and labelling and varieties of the product. Decision on 'Price' is very important as sales depend, to a large extent, on product pricing. Whether similar price will be charged or different prices will be charged for the same product in different markets are examples of decision pertaining to the price of the product. The third important element is 'place', which refers to decision regarding the market where products will be offered for sale. 'Promotion' involves decisions bearing on the ways and means of increasing sales. Different tools or methods may be adopted for this purpose. The relative importance to be attached to the various methods is decided while concentrating on the element of 'promotion' in marketing mix. The marketing manager has to keep in mind the impact of external factors like consumer behaviour, competitors' strategy, and government policy on each element of marketing mix.

Marketing mix involves decisions regarding products which are to be made available in the market, the price to be charged for the product, the incentives which are required to be provided to the consumers in the markets where products could be made available for sale. These decisions are taken, keeping in mind the various marketing forces outside the organization.

### Characteristics of Marketing Mix

(i) **Marketing Mix is the Crux of Marketing Process:** Marketing mix involves many crucial decisions relating to each element of the mix. The impact of the marketing mix would be the best when proper importance is assigned to each element so that the combination in totality gives the best results.

(ii) **Marketing Mix has to be Reviewed Constantly in Order to Meet the Changing Requirements:** The marketing manager is required to constantly review the mix and conditions of the market, and try to make necessary changes in the marketing mix so as to cope up with the changes that are taking place in the market and the complexities that arise.

(iii) **Changes in External Environment Necessitate Alterations in the Mix:** The changes that take place in the external environment, would lead to change in the marketing mix of a product. For almost all industries, customer is the most fluctuating variable of environment. Customers' tastes and preferences keep on changing very fast. Brand loyalty and purchasing power too changes over a period of time. The marketing manager has to carry-out market analysis very frequently so as to make necessary changes, if required, in the marketing mix.

(iv) **Changes Taking Place Within the Firm too Necessitate Changes in Marketing Mix:** The changes that take place within the firm may be due to technological changes, or changes in the product-line, or changes in the size and scale of operation. Such changes call for immediate changes in the marketing mix.

In order to fulfil the requirements of identified market segment, a company has to develop an appropriate marketing mix. Marketing mix is a systematic and balanced combination of the four inputs which constitute the core of a company's marketing system — the product, the price structure, the promotional activities and the place or distribution system. These are popularly known as "Four Ps" of marketing.

An appropriate combination of these four variables will help to influence demand in the market. The problem that small firms face is that they do not feel that they are capable of controlling each of the four variables in order to influence the demand.

## MARKETING MIX: 4Ps OF MARKETING

| **Product** | **Price** | **Place** | **Promotion** |
|---|---|---|---|
| Features | List Price | Location | Advertising |
| Design | Discounts | Transport | Personal Selling |
| Variety | Allowances | Channels | Sales Promotion |
| Quality | Payment Period | Coverage | Publicity |
| Brand Name | Credit Terms | Delivery | |
| Packaging | | | |
| Availability Sizes | | | |
| Inventory | | | |
| Services | | | |

A brief description of the four elements of marketing mix is as follows:

**1. Product:** The first element of marketing mix is product. A product is anything that can be offered to a market for attention, acquisition, use, or consumption that might satisfy a want or need.

Products include physical objects, services, events, persons, places, ideas or mixes of these. This element involves decisions concerning features, product variety, product-line, quality, design, brand name, label, after-sales services, warranties, product range, etc. An appropriate combination of features and benefits by the small firm will provide the product with USP (unique selling proposition). It may also lead to customer loyalty. Products and services are broadly classified into consumer products and industrial products. Consumer products are purchased by the person for a final consumption; whereas industrial products are purchased by individuals and organizations for further processing or for use in conducting business.

**Other ways of classifying products are as follows:**

*(a)* ***Convenience Products:*** They are consumer products that the customer purchases very frequently, without much deliberation. The prices of these products are not very high and are widely available at many outlets. They may be further subdivided as:

— *Staple Products:* Items like juice, jam, milk, bread, butter, etc., which the family consumes on a regular basis. Once in the beginning the decision is programmed and it is usually carried on without change.

— *Impulse Products:* Purchase of these products is unplanned and impulsive. The consumer purchases these products mostly when they shop from a mall where the products are displayed in such a way which attracts our attention very quickly. Usually when the consumer is buying other products, he buys these spontaneously for e.g., magazines, toffees and chocolates. Usually these products are located where they can be easily noticed.

— *Emergency Products:* These products are purchased during emergency as a result of urgent and compelling needs. Often a consumer pays more for these. For example while travelling if someone has forgotten his toothbrush or soap; he will buy it at the available price.

*(b)* ***Shopping Products:*** These products are not purchased on frequent basis and the customer carefully checks suitability, quality, price and style. He spends much more time and effort in gathering information and making comparisons. E.g., durable products like LCD, double door refrigerator, furniture, clothing and used cars.

*(c)* ***Specialty Products:*** These products are consumer goods which have a unique characteristics/ brand identification for which a significant group of buyers is willing to make a special purchase effort. For example, two-wheeler of Honda such as Activa, Ray Ban glasses.

*(d)* ***Unsought Product:*** These are the products that potential buyers do not know that they exist or do not yet want. For example, life insurance, a lawyers services in making a will of property. These product decisions are very essential to ensure the sale of products. A product has both tangible and intangible components. While buying a product, the customer does not merely look for the physical product, but they also look for a bundle of satisfaction. There is a psychological dimension to all customer purchases; what a customer thinks about a product also influences its purchase behaviour by far more than the product itself. For example, the buyer of an air-conditioner is not purchasing a machine that gives a cooling effect in a room, but he also looks for attractive colour and design, durability, low noise,

quick cooling, etc. These influencing factors must be considered by the small firms to meet the requirements of different kinds of customers.

**2. Price:** The second element of marketing mix is the price, which affects the volume of sales one of the most difficult tasks of the marketing manager to fix the right price. The variables that influence the price of a product are: demand of the product, cost, competition and government regulation. The product mix includes: determination of unit price of the product, pricing policies and strategies, discounts and level of margins, credit policy, terms of delivery, payment, etc. Pricing decisions have direct influence on the sales volume and profits of the firm. Price, therefore, is an important element of the marketing mix. Right price can be determined through pricing research and by adopting test-marketing techniques.

Small firms should think of pricing as a method whereby prices are set with regard to costs, profit targets, competition and the perceived value of products. Because of their simplicity, cost-plus-pricing are attractive to small businesses, though this is not the only mode of pricing utilized by small firms. For example, the profit margin in the cost-plus approach may well be fixed after examining both the nature of the market and the competitor activity within it. It is a mistake for small firms to rely wholly on cost-plus of profits and market share.

The pricing policies mainly followed by the small firms are as follows:

*(a)* ***Competitive Pricing:*** This method is used when the market is highly competitive and the product is not much different from the competitor's products.

*(b)* ***Skimming-the-cream Pricing:*** Under this pricing policy, higher prices are charged during the initial stages of the introduction of a new product. The aim is to recover the initial investment quickly. This policy is quite effective when the demand for a product is likely to be more inelastic with respect to price in its early stages; to segment the market into segments that differ in price elasticity of demand and to restrict the demand to a level, which a firm can easily meet. Here, the firm earns much of profit in the very early stage of a product in the market.

*(c)* ***Penetration Pricing:*** Under this policy, prices are fixed below the competitive level to obtain a larger share of the market. Penetration pricing is likely to be more successful when the product has a highly elastic demand; in order to enjoy the economies of scale, i.e., when a firm produces on a large-scale, the outcome is low cost of production per unit; and there is strong competition in the market.

**3. Promotion:** Promotion refers to the various activities undertaken by the enterprise to communicate and promote its products to the target market. The different methods of promoting a product are through advertisement, personal selling, sales promotion and publicity.

**4. Place or Physical Distribution:** Place is the last marketing mix tool, which stands for the various activities the company undertakes to make the product available or reachable to target customers. Place mix or delivery mix is the physical distribution of products at the right time and at the right place. It refers to finding out the best means of selling, sources of selling (wholesaler, retailers, and agents), inventory control, storage facility, location, warehousing, transportation, etc. This includes decisions about the channels of distribution, which make the product available to target customers at the right time, at the right place and at the right price. By selecting wrong distribution channels or by using the ones it has traditionally used, a small firm may not get an opportunity to enter a new market. In a situation where a small firm has only one primary product, the general rise and fall of sales will lead to a rise and fall of the firm, unless the firm learns to consistently adjust its marketing mix to match consumer demand.

Marketing mix of a firm selling air-conditioner

*Target Market:* Urban households with high income and status consciousness.

*Product:* Latest technology, five-star rating, 1.5 ton, designer air-conditioner.

*Price:* High, but should not be beyond the low range high-income groups.

*Promotion:* Heavy advertising through high image magazines and television stressing the high cooling effect within a very less time.

**Place (distribution):** Through high image retailers.

A marketing mix must be consistent for any product. Pricing, for example, must be consistent with packaging and perceived product quality. If one of these is not in line with others, then sales might suffer as a result. Every company knows that there is no 'one best way' to mix the ingredients. Different combinations may be used depending upon one's needs and objectives. In the marketing as in cooking, there is no standard formula for a successful combination of ingredients. Marketing mixes vary from company-to-company and from situation-to-situation. The right marketing mix is important for any product to succeed and stay in the market for a long period of time.

## MARKET SEGMENTATION

### Meaning of Market Segmentation

A market consists of a large number of individual customers who differ in terms of their needs, choice, preferences and purchasing capacity. Therefore, it becomes necessary to divide the total market into different segments or homogeneous customer groups. Such division is called market segmentation. They may have uniformity in employment patterns, educational qualifications, economic status, preferences; etc. It is very difficult for a company to meet the needs of the entire market, so they select a market which can be served in a much better way. Market segmentation helps companies to match their marketing efforts to the requirements of the target market. Instead of wasting their efforts in trying to sell to all types of customers, a small-scale unit can focus its efforts on the segment most appropriate to its market.

To compete more effectively, companies are now adopting target marketing, which involves market segmentation, market targeting and market positioning. The four levels at which markets can be targeted are segments, niches, local areas and individuals.

Segmenting the market is done by identifying group of customers, who share a similar set of needs and wants.

### Importance of Market Segmentation

Market segmentation is the identification of portions of the market that are different from one another. Segmentation allows the firm to satisfy the needs of its potential customers in a better way.

The marketing concept calls for understanding customers and satisfying their needs better than the competitors. But different customers have different needs, and it is not possible to satisfy all customers by treating them alike. Mass marketing refers to treatment of the market as a homogeneous group and offering the same marketing mix to all customers. Mass marketing allows economies of scale to be realized through mass production, mass distribution, and mass communication. The drawback of mass marketing is that customer needs and preferences differ and the same offering is unlikely to be viewed as optimal by all customers. If firms ignored the differing customer needs, another firm would enter the market with a product that serves a specific group, and the incumbent firms would lose those customers. Target marketing on the other hand recognizes the diversity of customers and does not try to please all of them with the same offering. The first step in target marketing is to identify different market segments and their needs. Market segmentation makes it feasible for the firm to adapt the marketing mix for specific target markets, it will help the firm to satisfy the need of customer better, instead of offering the same marketing mix to the different customer with different needs.

## LEVELS OF MARKET SEGMENTATION

The starting point for segmentation is mass-marketing. In mass-marketing, the seller engages in the mass production, mass distribution, and mass promotion of one product for all buyers. For e.g., Coca-Cola, Parle-G also practised mass-marketing, by giving the same product to entire market.

**Segment Marketing:** A market segment consists of a group of customers who share a similar set of wants. So, we can differentiate between car buyers who want a low-cost basic transportation and those who would like to go for a luxurious driving experience. There is a difference between a segment and a sector. A car company it target young, middle-income car buyers, but, these car buyers differ about what they want in a car, some will want a low-cost car and others will want an expensive car. So, we can say that young, middle-income car buyer is a sector, not a segment.

The marketer's work is to identify the segments and decide which one(s) to target and not to create the segments so, that they can satisfy that segment. Segment marketing offers several benefits over mass-marketing. The company can create a more fine-tuned product or service offering and price it accordingly for the target segment. The company can more easily select the best distribution and communication channels, and so that they can get a clear picture of their competitors or the companies which are targeting the same segment.

Every consumer is different from others and has different needs and good sellers have to satisfy them by designing a separate marketing programme for each buyer. That is why market segmentation can be carried out at different level segments, niches, local areas, individuals and mass-marketing.

**Niche Marketing:** A niche is a more closely defined group, it is dividing the segment into subsegment and it can be divided by identifying the distinct trait of consumer which might need special combination of benefits, this subsegments are made for those consumers whose needs and wants are not satisfied with the product available in the market. A niche is a more narrowly defined group seeking a mix of benefits. Marketers usually identify niches by dividing a segment into sub-segments. For example, the segment of heavy smokers includes two niches: those trying to stop smoking and those who do not care. An attractive niche is characterized as follows: The customers will pay a premium price to the firm that best satisfies their needs. The nicher gains certain advantage through specialization; and the niche has size, profit, and growth potential. Whereas niches are fairly small and normally attract only one or two. Niche marketers understand their customers need so well, that customers are ready to pay a premium price for it for e.g., tennis shoes, tennis players are ready to pay a premium price for it and would not go for local shoes.

**Local Marketing:** Local marketing focuses on the needs and wants of local consumer and the marketers design marketing programme accordingly, so that the needs of local consumer, groups, cities, and of even specific stores are easily met.

In marketing products to the local customer, marketing programmes are tailored to the needs and wants of local customer groups. For example, Bank of Baroda provides different mixes of banking services in its branches, on the basis of neighbourhood demographics. The advertisement should be made in such a way, that it appeals to the need of local customer.

**Individual Marketing:** Individual marketing focuses on satisfying the needs and wants of individual customer it's also known as one-to-one marketing and customized marketing. Here, the seller tries to customize the product for a consumer so, that the products are made according to the needs and preference of consumer.

The ultimate level of segmentation leads to "segments of one", "customized marketing", or "one-to-one marketing". Every individual has a unique set of wants and preferences. For e.g., the tailor stitched a suit according to the requirement and specification of individual customer. In the era of Information Revolution, the growing number of companies preferred to go for mass-customization of their offerings. Mass-customization is the ability of a company to prepare individually designed products; today customers are taking more individual initiative in determining what and how to buy. They log on to the internet; look up information and evaluations of product or service offers; dialogue with suppliers, users, and product critics; and in many designs the product they want.

Customerization combines operationally driven mass customization with customized marketing in a way that empowers consumers to design the product and service offering of their choice. The firm no longer requires prior information about the customer, nor does the firm need to own manufacturing. The firm provides platform and tools and "rents" out to customers the means to design their own product.

## Patterns of Market Segment

The patterns of market segmentation are as follows:

Market segments can be built-up in many ways. One way is to identify preference segments. Suppose cake buyers are asked how much they value sweetness and creaminess as two product attributes. Three different patterns can emerge.

1. **Homogeneous Preferences:** In this market almost all consumers have same preferences. The market shows no natural segments. We may predict that existing brands would be similar and cluster around the middle of the scale in both sweetness and creaminess.

2. **Diffused Preferences:** The consumer preferences may be scattered throughout the space which indicates that consumers vary in their preferences. The first brand which enters the market is likely to position in the centre so as to appeal to most people. A second competitor which enters the market could locate near to the first brand and may fight for

market share, or it could locate in a corner so that a company can attract a customer group that was not satisfied with the centre brand.

3. **Clustered Preferences:** The market might reveal distinct preference clusters; called natural market segments. The firm which enters the market first, has three options. It might position in the inner, hoping to appeal to all groups. It might position in the largest market segment (concentrated marketing). It may develop several brands, each positioned in a different segment. If the firm which enters first in the market develops only one brand, competitors may enter and introduce brands in the other segments.

## STEPS IN SEGMENTING A MARKET

The market segmentation is done, in both consumer and business markets, so as to identify marketing opportunities. From the following steps in segmenting a market, it could be noted that steps 5 and 6 are actually marketing activities that follow market segmentation (steps 1 through 4).

**1. Select a Market or Product Category for Study:** Define the entire market or product category to be studied. It may be a market in which the firm already competes, a new but related market or product category, or a totally new one. For e.g., Kellogg's closely examined the snack market before introducing flavoured cornflakes and cornflakes which reduces two kgs. weight just in two weeks.

**2. Choose a Basis or Bases for Segmenting the Market:** This step requires managerial insight, creativity, and market knowledge. There are no scientific procedures for selecting segmentation variables. However, a successful segmentation scheme must produce segments that meet the four basic criteria for segmentation.

**3. Select Segmentation Descriptors:** After choosing one or more bases, the marketer must select the segmentation descriptors. Descriptors would identify the specific segmentation variables which are required to be used. For example, if a company selects demographics as a basis of segmentation, it may use age, occupation and income as description. A company that selects usage segmentation needs to decide whether to go after heavy users, nonusers, or light users or if a company wants to go geographically, it may use region, cities, state or climate.

**4. Profile and Analyze Segments:** The profile should include the segment size, expected growth, purchase frequency, current brand usage, brand loyalty, long-term sales and profit potential. This information can then be used to rank potential market segments by profit opportunity, risk consistency with organizational mission and objectives, and other factors important to the firm.

**5. Select Target Markets:** Selecting a target market is not a part of the segmentation process but, it is the natural outcome. It is a major decision that influences and often directly determines the firm's marketing mix.

**6. Design, Implement, and Maintain Appropriate Marketing Mixes:** The marketing mix has been described as product distribution, promotion, and pricing strategies that tend to bring about mutually satisfying exchange relationships with target markets.

### Effective Segmentation

All segmentation is not useful. For example, sugar buyers could be divided into blond and brunette customers, but colouring hair is not relevant to the purchase of sugar. Furthermore, if sugar b ers buy the same amount of sugar each month, believe all sugar is the same, and would pay only one price for sugar, this market would have a minimum segment from a marketing point of view.

Effective segmentation could be:

1. **Measurable:** The size, purchasing power, and characteristics of the segments can be measured.
2. **Substantial:** The segments are large and profitable enough to serve. A segment should be the largest possible homogeneous group worth going after with a tailored marketing programme. It would not pay, for example, for an automobile manufacturer who manufactures tall car to target people who are less than four feet tall.
3. **Accessible:** The segments can be effectively reached and served. It means that the customer should be easily approached and they could get the product wherever they want.
4. **Differentiable:** The segments are conceptually distinguishable and respond different to different marketing-mix elements and programmes. If married and unmarried women respond similarly to a sale of sarees, they do not constitute separate segments.
5. **Actionable:** Effective programmes can be formulated for attracting and serving the segments.

## BASES FOR SEGMENTING CONSUMER MARKETS

Bases for segmenting consumer market are geographic, demographic, psychographic and behavioural.

**1. Geographic Segmentation:** In geographical segmentation the market is divided into different geographical units such as nations, states, regions, counties and neighbourhoods. The company can operate in one or a few geographic areas, or operate in all but pay attention to local variations.

**2. Demographic Segmentation:** In demographic segmentation, the market is divided into groups on the basis of variables such as age, family size, family life cycle, income, occupation, education, religion, race, generation, nationality, and social class. Demographic variables are the most popular bases for distinguishing customer groups. The reason being that consumer wants, preferences, and usage rates are often associated with demographic variables as well as they are easier to measure. Demographic variables are as follows:

- ***Age and Life Cycle Stage:*** The wants and abilities of a consumer changes with the change in age. When a girl is two-year-old she would like to play with toys, when she grows up say of ten years she may like to play badminton. Marketers realized this and began expanding their choice of horizon. For example, Cerelac is a food for very small child and not for a youngster.
- ***Life Stage:*** A person may pass through different stages in their lifespan. Life stage may define a person's major concern, such as going through a divorce, going into a second marriage, taking care of an older parent, deciding to buy a new home, giving birth to a baby and so on. These life stages present opportunities for marketers who can help people cope with their major concerns.
- ***Gender:*** Men and women tend to have different attitude and behaviour which may partly depend on genetic make-up and partly on socialization practices. Women tend to be more

self-controlled and men tend to be more self-expressive and goal directed. Women tend to take as much data from immediate environment; men tend to focus on the part of the environment that helps them achieve a goal. Men are different from women in terms of clothing, hairstyling, choice for magazines. Some products have been positioned as more masculine or feminine. The automobile industry is beginning to recognize gender segmentation. There are now more women car owners, some manufacturers are designing features to appeal to women, although they stop short of advertising the cars as women's cars.

- ***Income:*** Income segmentation is practised more in case of product and service categories such as boats, clothing, automobiles, cosmetics, hotels and travel. Many companies target affluent consumers with luxury goods and convenience services. In case a company wants to segment the market on the basis of income, so as to get an idea that product or service is meant for which income level. However, income does not always predict the best customers for a given product. Blue-collar workers were among the first purchasers of colour television sets; it was cheaper for them to buy these sets than to go to movies and restaurants. People who feel they are poor do not purchase the most economical cars as compared to people who think of themselves as relatively poor to their status aspirations. Medium-priced and expensive cars tend to be purchased by privileged segments of each social class.
- ***Generation:*** Each generation is influenced by the times in which it grows up — the music, movies, politics, and events of that period in which they grow up. Demographers call these groups cohorts. Members of a cohort share the same major experiences and have the same statistical character. They have similar outlooks and values. There are of two types of generation X and generation Y as per Meredith Schewe and Karlovich. The generation X cohort are shaped by bad economic times, the Challenger explosion, and AIDS awareness; aged 24-34 in 2000. This cohort puts the quality of personal life ahead of work life; they are not team players, and do not like about advertising.

  The following are traits as described to Generation Y:

  — A heightened ability to multitask

  — Greater acceptance of racial and ethnic differences

  — Technological savvy

  — A strong sense of community and teamwork

  — Suspicious of advertising

  — Higher levels of stress

  — Media savvy

  — A wish to make money, but a need to give back

  — Busy schedules

  — Optimism and big expectations for the future
- ***Social Class:*** Social class has a strong influence on choice and preference of people in terms of cars, clothing, home furnishings, leisure activities, reading habits, and retailers. Many companies design products and services for specific social classes. The tastes of social classes may change with the change in time.

**3. Psychographic Segmentation:** In psychographic segmentation, buyers are divided into different groups on the basis of lifestyle or personality or values. People within the same demographic group may vary differently in their psychographic profiles.

- ***Lifestyles:*** People have different lifestyles, they differ in their attitudes, interests, and activities and it may affect the goods and services they consume. Lifestyles are shaped partly by whether consumers are time-constrained or money-constrained. Consumers who experience time-constrain usually go for multitasking, that is doing two or more things at the same time. They will talk with someone on phone or eat while driving, or reading while eating. They may also pay more money to quicker service anywhere. They prefer keeping cat as pet as compared to dogs as dogs are difficult to handle, and require more time as compared to cats. Companies aiming to serve them will create convenient services for this group. Those people who are always constrained of money would require lower-cost products and services. Companies making cosmetics, beverages, and furniture are always seeking opportunities in lifestyle segmentation. Leading computer makers such as Dell, Acer and Lenovo are putting their bet on a new product segment — the all-in-one PC. These companies are planning to position these computers as a lifestyle product and as a true convergence between the computer and television. Titan Watches segmented watch buyers on lifestyle, and a subbrand, Titan Fastrack.
- ***Personality:*** Marketers have used personality variables to segment markets. They give their products a personality with a brand personality that corresponds to a target consumer personality. Honda four-wheeler buyers were identified as independent, impulsive, masculine, alert and self-confident. A brand may wish to appear sincere (Lenevo Computer), exciting (Nike shoes), and Ray Ban glasses. A brand personality may have several attributes: Levi's suggests a personality that is youthful, rebellious rugged authentic, and American. The company utilizes product features, services, and image making to transmit the product's personality.
- ***Values:*** Few marketers segment on the basis of core values, the belief systems that underlie consumer attitudes and behaviours. Core values are much deeper than behaviour or attitude and determine, at a basic level, people's choices and desires over the long-term. Marketers who go for segmenting the market through values believe that by appealing to people's inner selves it is possible to influence their outer selves — their purchase behaviour.

**4. Behavioural Segmentation:** Market can also be segmented on the basis of buyer behaviour. In behavioural segmentation; buyers are divided into groups on the basis of their knowledge, attitude towards use of product, or response to a product. Many marketers believe that behavioural variables depends on several subfactors that can be tried as bases for example purchase occasions, can be one base or they can be segmented on the basis of whether they are regular buyers or special occasion buyers, degree of use could be another variable; buyers can be segmented on the basis of light, medium or heavy user of the product, buyers' attitude towards the product can be another base; buyers can be segmented on the basis of whether they are indifferent, enthusiastic, or negative in their attitude towards product. In brief, the best start for constructing market segments are benefits, user status, rate, loyalty status, buyer-readiness stage, and attitude.

- ***Occasion:*** Buyers can be distinguished according to the occasions when they develop a need, purchase a product, or use a product. For example, air travel is triggered by occasions related to business, vacation, or family. Some products or services are seen as being appropriate for a particular situation or occasion. Take orange juice as an example. Most of us think of it as a product that is mainly a breakfast drink. This limits the market for this product. Indeed, orange growers are trying to convince the public that orange juice is a beverage for any occasion. How about a pizza and orange juice for lunch? Or, burger and orange juice for dinner? If the orange growers are successful in this campaign, they can greatly expand the market for orange juice. Interestingly, Pepsi at one time was trying to market a cola product for breakfast (the name of the beverage they were testing was Pepsi AM). This makes sense since many people eat breakfast at a fast food restaurant such as McDonald's or Burger King. However, most people do not think cola beverages make sense for breakfast and the product did not succeed.

- ***Benefits:*** Buyers can be classified according to the benefits they seek. People vary considerably in the benefits they seek from the same product. The benefits that are sought by customers when buying the generic product are varied. Some benefits desired when purchasing shampoo include, dandruff prevention, making hair smell nice, making hair soft and manageable, inexpensive, preventing baldness, being mild and gentle, restoring lustre, etc. The reason that benefit segmentation is so popular is because it is the method that is the most consistent with the marketing concept for e.g.:

  How would you segment the market for vitamins? Some possibilities.

  By sex: vitamins for men and for women. Women need more iron and calcium than men.

  By age: older people have different needs than children. You might need several different products: for babies, growing children, teens, adults, and senior citizens.

- ***User Status:*** Consumers can be divided based on whether or not they are patronizing a product. Hence, a consumer can be a non-user, ex-user, potential user, first-time user or a regular user of a given product or service. You might have found that you are a regular user of a particular service provider, like your bank, and an ex-user of a chocolate you used to like, but not anymore. A young girl may not have ever used the pond's age miracle as she is young so, she is a nonuser of the product. Market share leaders tend to focus on attracting potential users because they have the most to gain. Smaller firms focus on trying to attract current users away from the market leader.

- ***Usage Rate:*** Consumers can be light, medium or heavy users. Although heavy users account for a very small percentage of a market, they are also responsible for a high percentage of the total buying. It is not surprising, to find that hotel chains like Holiday Inn offer special prizes to reward their frequent visitors. Marketers would rather attract one heavy user than several light users. The problem however, is that heavy user either is extremely loyal to one brand, or never stays loyal to a brand and is always looking for the lowest price.

- ***Loyalty Status:*** Consumers may have high degrees of loyalty to specific brands, stores and companies. According to Oliver, loyalty is "A deeply held commitment to rebuy or repatronize a preferred product or service in the future despite situational influences marketing efforts having the potential to cause switching behaviour".

Buyers can be divided into four categories according to brand loyalty status:

1. *Hard-core loyal:* Consumers who prefer to buy one brand all the time.
2. *Split loyal:* Consumers may make a choice between two or three loyal brands.
3. *Shifting loyal:* Consumers who very easily move from one brand to another.
4. *Switchers:* Consumers who are not loyal to any brand they keep on changing their brand on the basis of profit.

Each market consists of different numbers of the four types of buyers. A brand-loyal market consists of high percentage of hard-core brand-loyal buyers. The toothpaste markets are fairly high brand-loyal markets. New company's face a tough time in getting customers, if a customer is hard-core loyal, company can learn a great deal by analyzing the degrees of brand loyalty: (1) by studying their hard-core loyal customers, the company can identify its products' strengths. (2) By studying its split loyal customers, the company can pinpoint which brands are most competitive with their own. (3) By looking at customers who are shifting away from its brand, the company can learn about its marketing weaknesses and attempt to correct them.

**Buyer-readiness Stage:** Markets have different types of people in different stages of readiness to buy a product. Some people are unaware of the product, some are aware of the product, some have been just informed about the product, some are interested in product, some desire the product, and some intend to buy the product. Segments can be divided based on how ready, the consumers are to make a purchase. Consumers are typecast according to their state of readiness. For example, you might be aware that a tour operator provides excellent travel packages to India, your friend might be very well informed of its details, your father might be interested in this product, while your sister is not. This allows marketers to guide consumers through the many stages leading to a final purchase.

**Attitude:** Consumers can be segmented according to their attitudes towards products and services. For instance you can be enthusiastic, positive, indifferent, negative or hostile about a product or service. Door-to-door workers in a political campaign use the voters' attitude to determine how much time to spend with that voter. They thank enthusiastic voters and remind them to vote; they reinforce those who are positively disposed; they try to win the votes of indifferent voters; they spend no time trying to change the attitude of negative and hostile voters. To the extent that attitudes are correlated with demographic descriptors, the political party can more efficiently locate the best prospects.

## BASES FOR SEGMENTING INDUSTRIAL MARKETS

The segmentation strategy has been used for consumer product marketing as well as for industrial marketing. The bases for segmenting the industrial product markets are as follows:

Commonly used bases for segmenting industrial product markets:

**Size of the Customer:** This is one of the oldest methods of segmenting industrial market. It is based on the size and purchases, that customer makes, such as —

(a) Customer's — who are large buyers

(b) Customer's — who are medium sized buyers

(c) Customer's — who are small buyers

The firms have different terms and conditions for different customers, the payment terms, product packaging, and sales call frequencies for each of these customer groups are different. The firm can decide its sales potential and competitive position in that customer group on the basis of size of a customer. This type segmentation strategy could help the marketer to balance their selling efforts.

**Geographical Location:** The geographical location of a customer is another basis for segmenting the industrial products market. For example, firms located in the Nadiad district of Gujarat constitute one segment for a telecom firm, while firms located at Nariman Point in Mumbai constitute another market segment or plan.

**End Use:** By differentiating the end-users of the firm's product, the industrial market segmentation could be made. For a steel manufacturer, some of the end-user segments include automobiles, construction, office furniture, and cables. Each of these segments have their characteristics and requires a different marketing approach.

**Buyer Behaviour/Motivation or Purchase Criteria:** The market could also be segmented on any specific end use segment; it could further segment the market on the basis of purchase criteria. For example, using price as an input, the marketer can segment buyers as insensitive, sensitive and highly sensitive to price changes. Customers can also be categorized on the basis of needs of the customer — whether he wants standardized or customized products.

**Combining Purchase Criteria, Size, and Geography Matrix form of Market Segmentation:** The recent trends in marketing is that firms tend to combine size and buying criteria of the customer to segment the market and also to evolve their marketing strategy. A firm may even add a third dimension to it — the geographic location of the customer. The most important dimension of this kind of segmentation is the use of buying motives along with buyer characteristics.

Let us consider the case of an electrical power pump company that wishes to segment its market. Market survey showed that the company has the following customer segments.

**Segment I:** This type of segment consist of larger customers with an average order size of ₹ 2,00,000. The firm has only 20 per cent share in these customer purchases. For example, some customers want a standardized motor and are not particularly concerned about the vendor's service, as most have their own engineering and maintenance departments. However, some customers want a most competent priced, good quality product, which is delivered on time. These buyers generally buy on the basis of facts and not just emotions. Most of these buyers are located in western part of India.

**Segment 2:** This type of segment consists of large buyers, the characteristics and buying motives are same as compared to the above segment. The only difference is that they are highly price sensitive and generally not as quality conscious as the other group of customers. Most of these buyers are located in north India.

**Segment 3:** These are medium sized firms with an average order size of about ₹ 50,000. They want customized product, that is as per the specification given by them and are very price sensitive. They would pay only, when they consider the "value" for the product, would like to get goods and services from vendors, and are also particular about vendor credibility. They would also like to get extended credit periods, and the option that the vendor takes back a product if it fails. Most of these ...s are in south India.

**Segment 4:** The firms in this segment are small and are scattered all over India. They want tailor-made products, excellent and reliable after-sales service and delivery as per approved schedules. Firms in this segment face financial problem. They purchase the product at the vendor's price, they expect vendor to empathize with them and generally not insist on penalty clauses for a slight or occasional delay in payment. These firms are owner-managed. Their average order size never exceeds ₹ 5,000. The vendor firm has a 15 per cent share in this segment.

The marketing tasks of vendor firm changes with the change in segment. It also creates the need for focused strategies to penetrate different segments. It urges the marketer to forget the mass marketing approach and, instead adopt the niche marketing approach.

**Multiple Bases for Segmentation:** In a highly complex market environment no firm can possibly afford to use only one basis for segmenting the market. Today, multiple bases are used to segment the market. Geography, age, education, occupation, income, gender, lifestyle, loyalty status. Consumption behaviour and other product attitudes are used simultaneously to segment the market and design the marketing mix.

## Market Trgeting

After identifying the market-segment opportunities, the firm has to decide how many and which ones to target.

**Evaluating and Selecting the Market Segments:** The firm has to evaluate different market segments and while evaluating must look at two factors: the segment's overall attractiveness and the company's objectives and resources. Does a segment which a firm wants to target have characteristics that make it generally attractive, such as size, growth, profitability, scale economies, and low risk? Is it worth to invest in a segment and does it match with the firm's objectives, competencies, and resources? Some attractive segments may not match with the company's long run objectives, or the company may lack one or more necessary competencies to offer superior value. After evaluating different segments, the company can consider five patterns of target market selection.

**Single Segment Concentration:** Maruti Suzuki's concentrates on the small-car market, such as Alto and WagonR and Jaguar on the sports car market. Through concentrated marketing, the firm has a strong knowledge of these segment's needs and tries to achieve a strong presence in market. Furthermore, the firm enjoys economies of scale through specializing its production, distribution, and promotion. If a firm is a leader in particular segment, then the firm can earn a high return on its investment in that particular segment.

However, concentrated marketing involves risks. A particular market segment can turn sour. Many companies prefer to operate in more than one segment, as if one segment fails there are other segments to sell the product. It involves marketing one product to a single market segment. It may either be a rather large market segment or a small but very lucrative one (doctors, dentists, professional athletes, and so forth).

**Selective Specialization:** The firm selects a number of segments, each objectively attractive and appropriate. There may be little or no synergy among the segments, but each promises to be a moneymaker. This multisegment strategy has the advantage of diversifying the firm's risk. The business focuses on a number of segments in the market — there is no necessity of any relationship between the segments, however, each segment has a high degree of value for a business objectives and resources. Because the segments can standalone, the risk of failure is minimized by the diversification — the assumption is that at least one, or more, of your segments will be successful at any one time. Consider a Radio Mirchi that wants to reach to both younger and older listeners.

**Product Specialization:** The focus is on one product that it sells to a number of segments. For example, a coffee distributor might sell coffee to a retail store chain, to a number of coffee shops, and even directly to the end-user (through an online store). By expanding the market through product specialization one can build a very strong brand for a product and business. The risk is on the product's desirability itself — does the product have a long product life cycle or a short life cycle. One needs to be aware of that and plan accordingly (for example, have new products in development and be ready to take them to market quickly).

**Market Specialization:** The firm focuses on supplying many products to one market segment. For example, one might be supplying all types of sporting goods to sporting goods stores (e.g., soccer, tennis, snowboards, etc.). With this type of strategy, the business must focus on developing a strong reputation for service, quality, value and be respected for its knowledge of the industry. The type of reputation will allow the firm to be a leader in its market and its customers will rely on a firm to help introduce new products as necessary. This strategy is very dependent on the health of the industry and a specific customer group.

**Full Market Coverage:** The firm may decide to aim its resources at the entire market with one particular product. Coca-Cola's original marketing strategy was based on this form. One product aimed at the mass market in the hope that a sufficient amount of buyers would be attracted, although there are now changes in their product-line to cater for growing dietary and caffeine free needs of consumers. In undifferentiated marketing, the firm offers the same product to the entire market by ignoring segment differences. It designs a product and marketing programme that appeals to the large number of buyers. It relies on mass-distribution and mass-advertising. It aims to endow the product with a superior image in people's minds. Undifferentiated marketing is "the leads to standardization and mass-production in manufacturing". The narrow product-line keeps down the cost of research and development, production, inventory, transportation, marketing research, advertising, and product management. In undifferentiated marketing, the advertising costs are kept low. The company can turn its costs into lower prices to win the price-sensitive segment of the market.

In differentiated marketing, the firm operates in various market segments and has different products for each segment. The firm decides to target several segments and develops distinct products/services with separate marketing mix strategies aimed at varying groups. An example of this would be airline companies offering first, business (segment 1) or economy class tickets (segment 2) with separate marketing programmes to attract the different groups.

## SUMMARY

Target marketing involves three activities: market segmentation, market targeting, and market positioning. Markets can be targeted at four levels: segments, niches, local areas, and individuals. Market segments are large identifiable groups within a market. A niche is a more narrowly defined group. Marketers are localizing their campaigns for trading areas, neighbourhoods, and even individual stores. Finally, more companies now practice individual and mass-customization. The future is likely to see more self-marketing, a form of individual marketing in which individual consumers take the initiative in designing products and brands. The major segmentation bases variables for consumer markets are geographic, demographic, psychographic, and behavioural. These variables can be used singly or in combination. Business marketers use all these variables along with operating variables, purchasing approaches, and situational factors. To be successful and useful, market segments must be measurable, substantial, accessible, and differentiable and actionable.

Once a firm has identified its market-segment opportunities it has to evaluate the various segments and decide how many and which ones to target. In evaluating segments it must look at the segment's attractiveness indicators and the company's' objectives and resources. In choosing which segments to target, the company can choose to focus on a single segment, several segments, a specific market, or the full market, if it decides to serve the full market, it must choose between differentiated and undifferentiated marketing.

Marketers must choose target markets in a socially responsible manner. Marketers must also monitor segment interrelationships, and seek economies of scope and the potential for marketing to super segments. Marketers should develop segment-by-segment invasion plans. The market segment managers should be prepared to cooperate in the interest of overall company performance.

## CASELET 1

Showman Organisation Ltd., focuses on exploration and production of natural gas and crude oil in locations around the world. Its success depends on the network of customers, employees, suppliers, distributors, investors and other stakeholders. Yet, it focuses on social responsibility.

### Questions

1. Why would Showman Organization Ltd., advertise its socially responsible activities in a business magazine?
2. What effect does a company expect the advertisement would do on its relationship with various stakeholders?

## ........ QUESTIONS FOR DISCUSSION

1. Explain the demographic method of market segmentation.
2. Briefly describes the concept of marketing mix.
3. Explain the important steps in buying process.
4. Explain the contents of demographic method of market segmentation.
5. Discuss the significance of need arousal and post-purchase behaviour of a buyer with suitable example.
6. Define marketing and explain the philosophies of marketing.
7. Define marketing and explain what marketing mix is.
8. Describe the philosophies of marketing giving suitable example.
9. Define the term 'Marketing' and explain the core concepts of marketing.
10. Discuss the important steps in buying process.

## Objective Questions

### A. Fill in the Blanks

1. The ___________ segmentation means dividing the market into different areas such as nations, states and regions.
2. The ___________ concepts assume that the consumer will prefer those products which offer the best quality and features.

3. Marketing mix involves product, price, promotion and __________ .
4. In __________ segmentation market is divided into groups on the basis of variables such as age, gender, occupation, family size, religion, income, etc.
5. __________ is a human activity directed at satisfying the needs and wants through exchange process.
6. Wants become __________ when backed by purchasing power.
7. __________ refers to the set of actual and potential buyers of a product.
8. __________ is the value which a buyer passes on to the seller in lieu of the product/services.
9. __________ is a short-term incentive which helps the company in stimulating the sales.
10. __________ is an act of obtaining a desired product from someone by offering something in return.
11. For exchange to exist there should be at least __________ parties.
12. __________ is defined as the set of marketing tools; the firm uses to pursue its marketing objectives.
13. __________ propounded the concept of 4Ps of marketing.
14. Sellers who concentrate on the product instead of the customer's need are said to be suffering from __________.
15. __________ holds that consumer will prefer products that are "widely available and are inexpensive".
16. __________ refers to a consistent pattern of behaviour.
17. The act of dividing a market into distinct group of buyers having similar wants is called _______ as.
18. __________ refers to the set of norms, beliefs and values that are learned from the society.
19. __________ provides more specific identification and socialization for their members.
20. A __________ is a trade of values between two or more parties.

***Ans:*** **1.** geographic, **2.** product, **3.** place, **4.** demographic, **5.** Marketing, **6.** demand, **7.** Market, **8.** Price, **9.** Sales promotion, **10.** Exchange, **11.** two, **12.** Marketing mix, **13.** McCarthy, **14.** Marketing Myopia, **15.** Production concept, **16.** Personality, **17.** market segmentation, **18.** Culture, **19.** Subculture, **20.** transaction.

## B. State Whether the Following Statement is True or False:

1. The buying process starts when a customer recognizes a need.
2. Psychographic segmentation divides buyer into different groups based on age, gender, income, occupation, etc.
3. The selling concepts state that consumer will favour those products that are good in quality.
4. Production concept states that consumer will favour those products that are good in quality.
5. The selling concept is practised most aggressively with unsought goods. State one example for unsought goods.
6. F.W. Taylor gave the concept of 4Ps of marketing.
7. The organization undertaking selling concept does an aggressive selling and promotion effort.
8. Social class is indicated by a single factor called income.
9. In psychographic segmentation, buyers are divided into different areas like states, regions and countries.

***Ans:*** **1.** True, **2.** False, **3.** False, **4.** False, **5.** True e.g. insurance, **6.** False, **7.** True, **8.** False, **9.** False

☺ ☺ ☺

CHAPTER 8

# Product Positioning and Life Cycle

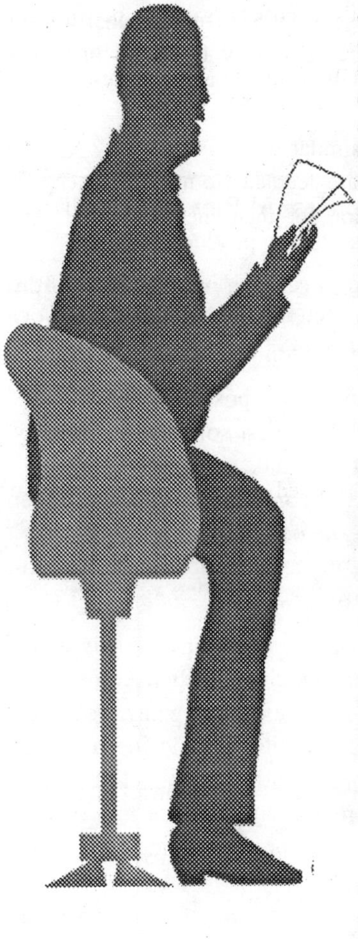

LEARNING OBJECTIVES

- *Meaning of Positioning.*
- *Positioning According to Rise and Trout.*
- *Positioning Errors.*
- *Positioning Possibilities.*
- *Various Differentiation Tools.*
- *Differentiation Variables.*
- *Meaning of the Product Life Cycle*
- *Product Life Cycle Stages and Strategies.*
- *Life Cycle Concept: Critique*

## POSITIONING: AN INTRODUCTION

All marketing strategy is built on STP Segmentation, Targeting, and Positioning. A company discovers people with different needs and groups them in the marketplace, targets those whose needs could be satisfied in a superior way, and then positions its offering so that the target market recognizes the company's distinctive offering and image. Positioning needs to be done in a careful way as entire market planning and strategy depends on it. A product's position is the way the product is defined by consumers on important attributes — the place the product occupies in consumers' minds relative to competing products. For e.g., Tide is positioned as a powerful, all purpose family detergent.

### Positioning Defined

According to management expert Philip Kotler, positioning is "the act of designing the company's offering and image to occupy a distinctive place in the mind of the target market". Thus, the objective of positioning is to create in the minds of firm's prospect, a predetermined favourable perception of both your personal brand (image) and your product (offering). Consequently, effective positioning results in a value proposition, a compelling reason offered to prospects to buy financial products and to buy them from your firm.

## POSITIONING ACCORDING TO RIES AND TROUT

The word positioning was popularized by two advertising executives, Al Ries and Jack Trout, according to them positioning is a creative exercise done with an existing product.

Positioning starts with a product. A piece of merchandise, a service, a company, institution, or even a person. . . . Positioning is not what we do to a product. Positioning is what firms do to the mind of the prospect. That is, firm positions the product in the minds of the prospect.

Ries and Trout argue that well known products generally hold a distinctive position in consumers' minds. Pizza Hut's pizza, McDonald's Berger, Coca-Cola as the world's largest soft-drink company, and Nano as the cheapest car. These brands own these positions, and it would be hard for a competitor to claim them. A competitor has three strategic alternatives such as a company has to strengthen its own current position in the consumer's mind. 7-Up capitalized on not being a cola drink by advertising itself as "the Uncola". The second strategy is to grab an unoccupied position. The third strategy is to de-position or re-position the competition in the customer's mind.

Developing a positioning strategy depends much on how competitors position themselves. Do organizations want to develop 'a me too' strategy and position themselves close to their competitors so consumers can make a direct comparison when they purchase? Or does the organization want to develop a strategy which positions themselves away from their competitors? Offering a benefit which is superior depends much on the marketing mix strategy the organization adopts. The pricing strategy must reflect the benefit offered and the promotion strategy must communicate this benefit. Ultimately positioning is about how you want consumers to perceive your products and services and what strategies you would adopt to reach this perceptual goal.

## POSITIONING ERRORS

A company must avoid four major positioning errors:

1. **Under Positioning:** A scenario in which customers have a blurred and unclear idea of the brand. This error takes place when customers don't identify the brand or the brands

features readily. The product must stand out in the minds of consumers. As per few companies, buyers have an unclear idea of the brand. Most brands are considered as another entry in a crowded marketplace. When Pepsi introduced its clear Crystal Pepsi in 1993, customers were distinctly unimpressed. They didn't see "clarity" as an important benefit in a soft drink. Consumer doesn't foresee anything special in the product.

2. **Over Positioning:** A scenario in which customers have too limited awareness of the brand. This error creates a picture in the minds of the audience which is hyper in character and does not fit in with the true product image, which the marketer is trying to communicate. Buyers may have too narrow an image of the brand. Thus, a consumer might think that diamond rings at Tanishq start at ₹ 25,000 when, in fact, Tanishq now offers affordable diamond rings starting at lower range also.
3. **Confused Positioning:** A scenario in which customers have a confused opinion of the brand. Buyers might be confused of image that brand holds, as the company's making too many claims or changing the brand's positioning too frequently. For e.g., Johnson & Johnson is into baby product market, but they are trying to move to female market also.
4. **Doubtful Positioning:** A scenario in which customers don't accept the claims of a brand. Buyers may find it hard to believe the brand claims in view of the product's features, price, or manufacturer.

## DIFFERENT POSITIONING POSSIBILITIES

The different positioning possibilities are as follows:

1. **Attribute Positioning:** A company positions itself on an attribute, such as size or number of years in existence. For e.g., positioning by attribute is common in the automobile industry — Volvo emphasizes safety and durability, while jeep emphasizes off-roading ability.
2. **Benefit Positioning:** The product is positioned as the leader in a certain benefit. Kellogg's may try to position itself as a food that reduces two kgs. of weight by taking two bowls of Kellogg's for two weeks.
3. **Use or Application Positioning:** Positioning the product as best for some use or application. When positioning by application, this means by what the product will be used for. For instance, Nescafe coffee is positioned as being the best choice for coffee.
4. **User Positioning:** Positioning the product as best for some user group. Product user positioning is demonstrated by Johnson & Johnson's baby shampoo.
5. **Competitor Positioning:** The product claims to be better in some way than a competitor. For example, Vatika claims that it is better in comparison to coconut oil.
6. **Product Category Positioning:** The product is positioned as the leader in a certain category. Colgate can position itself as a toothpaste which gives full protection to teeth.
7. **Quality or Price Positioning:** The product is positioned as offering the best value. Price is the easiest way for consumers to compare their product with that of competitors — people know the difference in clothing price when they're choosing between shopping at Pantaloons and Westside.

The number of differentiation opportunities varies with the type of industry. The Boston Consulting Group (BCC) has distinguished four types of industries based on the number of competitive advantages and on the basis of their size which are as follows:

**1. Volume Industry:** An industry characterized by few opportunities to create competitive advantages, but each advantage is huge and gives a high pay-off. In this industry companies can gain only a few, but rather large, competitive advantages. In the construction-equipment industry, a company can strive for the low-cost position or the highly differentiated position and win big on either basis. Profitability is correlated with company size and market share.

**2. Stalemated Industry:** An industry that produces commodities and is characterized by a few opportunities to create competitive advantages, with each advantage being small. The potential competitive advantages in this industry are few but small. In the steel industry, it is difficult to differentiate the product or decrease manufacturing costs. Companies can only try to hire good salespeople, so that they can treat customers in a better way, and the like, but the advantages from this are small. Profitability is not related to company market share.

**3. Fragmented Industry:** An industry characterized by many opportunities to create competitive advantages, but each advantage is small. The companies in this industry face many opportunities for differentiation, but each opportunity for competitive advantage is small. A restaurant can differentiate in many ways but do not gain a large market share. A profitable or unprofitable situation can occur for both small and large restaurants.

**4. Specialized Industry:** An industry where there are many opportunities for firms to create a competitive advantage that are huge or gives a high pay-off. Among companies making specialized machinery for selected market segments, some small companies can be as profitable as some large companies.

According to Lele, companies differ in their potential manoeuvrability along five dimensions: target market, product, place (channels), promotion, and price. The company's freedom is affected by the industry structure and the firm's position in the industry. For each potential, the company needs to estimate the return.

## DIFFERENTIATION VARIABLES

The differentiation variables are as follows:

**Product Differentiation:** It is the process of distinguishing a product or offering from others, to make it more attractive to a particular target market. This involves differentiating it from competitors' products as well as a firm's own product offerings. It is distinguishing one product or service from another that firm offers in comparison to the products of the competing business down the street. The firm is simply trying to make their product more desirable to a niche market by listing the differences between their product and those of competitors. Creating a value package that is better/different than competition's in a way that is meaningful to the customer. Different consumers have different tastes; same old product will not do for all the customers.

Physical products vary in their potential for differentiation. At one extreme the products that allow little variation: car, steel, crocin. The seller faces an abundance of design parameters, including form, features, performance quality, conformance quality, durability, reliability, repair, ability style, and design.

**Form:** The products can be differentiated in the form of the size, shape, or physical structure of a product. The products can take many possible forms such as two-wheeler of Honda, i.e., Activa. Although Activa is essentially a commodity it can be differentiated by mileage, size, shape, colour, coating, or action time.

**Features:** Most products can be offered with varying features that supplement the product's basic function. Being the first to introduce valued new features is one of the most effective ways to compete. For e.g., Whirlpool came with a refrigerator with a unique feature of 6th Sense cool system for superior cooling in the peak of summers and Unique Range of storage capacity refrigerator to suit the needs utility features so as to add "magic" to homemaking.

**Performance Quality:** Almost all products are based on one of four performance levels: low, average, high, or superior. Performance quality is the level at which the products' primary characteristics operate. The important question here is: Does offering "higher product performance produce higher profitability"? According to the Strategic Planning Institute, the impact of higher relative product quality found a significantly positive correlation between relative product quality and return on investment (RoI). High quality business units earned more because premium quality allowed them to charge a premium price; they benefited from more repeat purchasing, consumer loyalty, and positive word-of-mouth; and their costs of delivering more quality were not much higher than for business units producing low quality.

Quality's link to profitability does not mean that the firm should design the highest performance level possible. The manufacturer must design a performance level appropriate to the target market and competitors' performance levels. A company must manage performance quality through time and by continuously improving the product that may give high return and good market share. The second strategy is to maintain product quality at a given level. The third strategy is to reduce product quality through time. Some companies cut quality to reduce costs of production; others reduce quality deliberately in order to increase current profits, although this course of action often hurts long run profitability. For example, Procter & Gamble's Tide, performance sets them apart from others and Maruti 800 to some extent, HLL detergents for low level-Wheel, for average-Rin, high-Surf, superior-Surf Excel.

**Conformance Quality:** Buyers expect products to have a high conformance quality, it is the degree to which all the produced units are identical and meet the promised specifications. If the products have low conformance quality, buyers may be disappointed. For example, Yamaha Rx-100 pickup is 0-60 kmph in 7 seconds consistently. If a company claims to have zero defects in product and later on product is found to be defective, customers may be disappointed.

McDonald's conformance to reduce trans fat and salt thereby adding more of healthier food items to its menu such as premium salads for adults, and 1% fat milk and fresh apple slices as Happy Meal options for children.

**Durability:** The durability of many products will depend on regular maintenance. This class of products may have a short lifespan if not maintained or may have a very long life if properly maintained. A good example of this is wood products, which require repainting or refinishing at regular intervals to prevent moisture or ultraviolet damage and wear. Durability, a measure of the product's expected operating life natural or stressful conditions, is a valued attribute for certain products. Furthermore, the product must not be subject to rapid technological obsolescence, as is the case with personal computers and video cameras. For example, Asian Paints.

**Reliability:** Buyers normally will pay a premium for more reliable products. Reliability is a measure of the probability that a product will not malfunction within a specified time period. Panasonic home appliances India Company, which manufactures major home appliances, has an outstanding reputation for creating reliable appliances.

**Repair Ability:** Buyers prefer products that are easy to repair. Repair ability measures the ease of fixing a product when it malfunctions or fails. A mobile phone made with standard parts that are easily replaced, has high repair ability, would exist if users could fix the product themselves with little money or time. Some products include a diagnostic feature that allows a service to correct a problem over the telephone or advise the user how to correct it. Many computer hardware and software companies offer technical support over the phone, fax or e-mail.

**Style:** Style explains the product's look and feel to the buyer. Car buyers pay a premium for Mercedes Benz because of their extraordinary look and style. Piere Cardin pen is said to be the best pen in a market. Strong style does not always mean that it would show a high performance. When a product is no longer desirable because it has gone out of the popular fashion, its style is obsolete. One example is "acid-wash" jeans; although this article of clothing may still be perfectly functional, it is no longer desirable because style trends have moved away from the acid-wash look. For e.g., People would like to go for Designer wear and Rolex watches. We must include packaging as a styling weapon, especially in food products, cosmetics toiletries, and small consumer appliances. The package is the buyer's first encounter with the product and is capable of turning the buyer on or off.

**Design the Integrating Force:** As competition intensifies, design offers a way to differentiate and position a company's products and services. In increasingly fast-paced markets, price and technology are not enough. Design is the factor that often gives a company its competitive edge. Design is the totality of features that how a product looks and functions in terms of customer requirements.

Design is particularly important in making and marketing retail services, apparel, packaged goods, and durable equipment. All the qualities we have discussed are design parameters. The designer has to figure out how much to invest in form, feature development, performance, conformance, durability, reliability, reparability and style. To the company, a well-designed product is one that is easy to manufacture and distribute. To the customer, a well-designed product is one that is pleasant to look at and easy to open, install, use, repair, and dispose of. The designer has to take all these factors into account.

**Services Differentiation:** When the physical product cannot easily be differentiated, the key to competitive success may lie in adding valued services and improving their quality. The main service differentiators are ordering ease, delivery, installation, customer training, customer consulting, and maintenance and repair.

**Ordering Ease:** It refers to how easy it is for the customer to place an order with the company. For example, ATMs. Nowadays consumers are even able to order and receive groceries without going to the supermarket, concept of shop from home or with a click of mouse have come in existence.

**Delivery:** It refers to how well the product or service is delivered to the customer. It includes speed, accuracy and care attending the delivery process. Today customers have grown to expect delivery of pizza within half an hour. Attending delivery gave rise to Turbo marketing, i.e., doing things faster — innovation, manufacturing, logistics and retailing.

**Installation:** Installation refers to the work done to make a product operational in its planned location. Buyers of heavy equipment expect good installation service. Differentiating at this point in the consumption chain is particularly important for companies with complex products. Company may create policy to install equipment at customer's location to ensure smooth functioning of the product at a nominal cost. For example, Kelvinator the coolest one, used to install its refrigerator in such a way that the doors used to close by themselves when left open. This reduced hot air entering into refrigerator and thereby, making it the coolest one.

**Customer Training:** Customer training refers to training the customer's employee to use the vendor's equipment properly and efficiently. For example, Elpro, Siemens (medical equipment).

**Customer Consulting:** Customer consulting refers to data, information systems, and advice services that the seller offers to buyers. Software suppliers also give training about hardware.

**Maintenance and Repair:** Maintenance and repair describes the service programme for helping customer keep purchased products in good working order. For example, automobiles free service car/bike, widespread workshops of Maruti, low price of spares parts, i.e., Hero Honda.

**Miscellaneous Services:** Companies can find other ways to differentiate customer service. They can offer an improved product warranty or maintenance contract. Customers valued service more than price paid for it. For example, mobile service or petro card service.

**Personnel Differentiation:** Companies can gain a strong competitive advantage through having better-trained people. Better-trained personnel exhibit six characteristics: Competence: They possess the required skill and knowledge; courtesy: They are friendly, respectful, and considerate, credibility. They are trustworthy; reliability: They perform the service consistently and accurately; responsiveness: They respond quickly to customers' requests and problems; communication: They make an effort to understand the customer and communicate clearly.

**Channel Differentiation:** Companies can achieve competitive advantage through the way they design their distribution channel's coverage, expertise, and performance. Companies can achieve differentiation through the way they distribute their products, i.e., through distribution channel. For example, PC-Dell Computer.

**Image Differentiation:** Buyers respond differently to company and brand images. Identity and image need to be distinguished. Identity comprises the ways company aims to identify or position itself or its product. Image is the way the public perceives the company or its products. Image is affected by many factors beyond company's control, as the marketing versus Nike, and Adidas shows. For example, Cinthol has more male customers.

**Symbols, Colours, Slogans, Special Attributes:** Identity can be built by strong symbols. The company can choose a symbol such as the leaf (HLL) apple (Apple Computer); a brand can be built around famous person, as Amitabh Bacchan in thanda-thanda cool-cool oil Amrutanjan.

Every company would benefit by adopting and repeating a short slogan or tag line after every mention of its name. AT&T called itself "The Right Choice"; Ford "Quality is Our Number One Job".

**Physical Plant:** The seller's physical space can be another powerful image generator. Taj hotels developed a distinctive image through its service, location and its architectural building in Mumbai. A bank that wants to convey the image of a safe bank must communicate this through the building's architecture, interior design, layout, colours, materials, and furnishings.

**Events and Sponsorships:** A company can build its brand image through creating or sponsoring various events. Event marketers have favoured sports events and are using other venues such as art museums, zoos, or ice shows to entertain clients and employees. Companies are searching for better ways to quantify benefits of sponsorship and they are demanding greater accountability from event and organizers. Companies can also create events designed to surprise the public and create a buzz. The type of event the company is associated with /sponsors also create image. For examples, Femina Miss India.

**Using Multiple Image-building Techniques:** The Swatch watch provides an excellent example of how to use multiple image-building techniques to fetch a long-lasting image in the public's mind.

## PRODUCT LIFE CYCLE MEANING

We define a product as "anything that is capable of satisfying customer needs. This definition includes both physical products (e.g., cars, washing machines, DVD players) as well as services (e.g., insurance, banking, private health care).

Like human beings, products also have their own life cycle. From birth to death human beings pass through various stages, e.g., birth, growth, maturity, decline and death. A similar life cycle is seen in the case of products. The product life cycle goes through multiple phases, involves many professional disciplines, and requires many skills, tools and processes. Product life cycle (PLC) has to do with the life of a product in the market with respect to business/commercial costs and sales measures. To say that a product has a life cycle is to assert four things:

- that products have a limited life,
- product sales pass through distinct stages, each posing different challenges, opportunities, and problems to the seller,
- profits rise and fall at different stages of product life cycle, and
- products require different marketing, financial, manufacturing, purchasing, and human resource strategies in each life cycle stage.

The stages through which individual products passes over time, is commonly known as the "Product Life Cycle".

### Product Life Cycle

Most product life cycle curves are bell-shaped. It is divided into four stages: introduction, growth, maturity and decline.

1. **Introduction:** A time period in which sales growth is slow as the product is introduced in the market. Profits are nominal or do not exist because of the heavy expenses incurred, when products are introduced in the market.

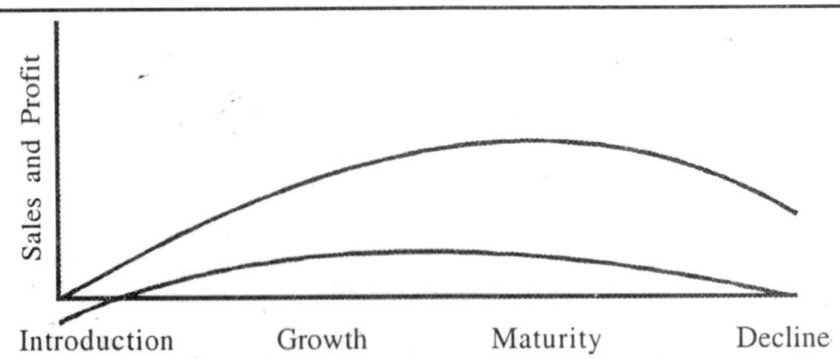

2. **Growth:** A period where product is rapidly accepted in market and slowly profit starts improving.
3. **Maturity:** A time period of a slow down in sales growth as the product has been accepted by most potential buyers. Profits stabilize or decline because of increased competition.
4. **Decline:** The period when sales show a downward slope and profits erode.

The concept of PLC can be used to analyze a product category (liquor), a product form (white liquor), a product (vodka), or a brand (Smirnoff). All products do not show a bell shaped outline.

## PATTERNS OF PLC

There are three common alternate patterns of PLC such as:

1. Growth-slump-maturity Pattern.
2. Cycle-recycle Pattern.
3. Scalloped PLC

**1. Growth-slump-maturity Pattern:** This type of pattern could be easily seen in small kitchen appliances. It may happen when the product is introduced in the market, sales of juicer mixer grew rapidly and then fell to a "petrified" level. The petrified level is sustained by late adopters buying the product for the first time and early adopters replacing the product.

**2. Cycle-recycle Pattern:** This type of pattern could be easily seen in the sales of new drugs. Mostly the pharmaceutical company aggressively promotes its new drug, and this produces the first cycle. With the passage of time the sales of drug starts declining and the company gives the drug another promotion push, which produces a second cycle.

**3. Scalloped PLC:** This type of pattern could be easily seen in when the sales pass through a succession of life cycles, based on the discovery of new-product characteristics, or users. Nylon's sales, for example, show a scalloped pattern because of the many new uses in hosiery, carpeting, automobile tyres, shirts, parachutes over a period of time.

### Special Categories of Product Life Cycle

There are three special categories of product life cycle which are as styles, fashions, and fads.

**Style:** A style is a basic and distinctive mode of expression appearing in a field of human endeavour. Styles in homes (carpet, LCD); clothing (formal, casual, funky); and art (realistic), etc. A style can last for generations, and can vanish without any reason.

**Fashion:** A fashion is a currently accepted or popular style in a given field. Fashions pass through four stages: distinctiveness, emulation, mass-fashion, and decline. For how long a particular cycle will continue is hard to predict. According to Chester Wasson fashion ends because they represent a purchase compromise, and consumers start looking for missing attribute.

For example, if automobiles turnout to be smaller with the period of time, they become less comfortable and then a number of buyers start demanding larger cars. According to William Reynolds the length of a particular fashion cycle depends on the extent to which the fashion meets a particular need, it is consistent with other trends that are taking place in the society, satisfies societal norms and values, and does not exceed technological limits as it develops.

**Fads:** Fads are fashion that are easily accepted by public, and are adopted with great enthusiasm, which is accepted very quickly and declines very fast. The period of acceptance is short and they tend to attract only a few people who are searching for excitement or want to be different from others. These people, to distinguish themselves from others, go for body piercing and tattooing. Fads do not survive for a long period of time as they do not satisfy a strong need.

## Marketing Strategies: Introduction Stage

In introduction stage, sales growth tends to be slow. According to Robert Buzz *et. al.*, there are several factors for slow sales and growth such as it leads to delays in the expansion of production capacity; technical problems, delays in obtaining adequate distribution through retail outlets; and customer reluctance. Sales of expensive new product are delayed due to product complexity and fewer buyers.

In introduction stage, profits are negative or low. Promotional expenditure is at their highest ratio to sales because of the need: (1) to make people aware about new product (2) to induce product trial, and (3) to secure distribution in retail outlets. Generally, most of the firms focus on those buyers who are ready to buy their product, usually people from high income groups. A price tends to be high as the costs of production are high.

Those companies that first reach practical solutions will enjoy "first-mover" advantages, in the market. Most studies indicate that the market pioneer gains the most advantage. Companies like Coca-Cola, Xerox, and Google.com developed and sustained market dominance.

What are the sources of advantage for the enterprise, which came first with a product (pioneer) in a market? Early users will recall the pioneers brand name if the product satisfies them. The pioneer's brand also establishes the attribute the product class should possess. The pioneer's brand normally aims at middle of the market and so captures more users. Customer inertia also plays a role; and there are producer advantages: economies of scale, technological leadership, patent, ownership of scarce assets, and other barriers to entry. The pioneer should have a strong vision about various product markets it could initially enter; as such it is difficult to enter all at once. Market segmentation analysis reveals the product market segments. The pioneer should analyze the potential of profit in each product market as separate and in combination and decide on a market expansion path.

## The Competitive Cycle

The company which enters the market first is aware that competitors would enter the market, which would lead to fall in market share and price of product. When will this happen? What should the pioneer do at each stage? Frey describes five stages of the competitive cycle that the pioneer has to anticipate.

1. In the beginning pioneer is the only supplier, with full production capacity and sales.
2. Competitive penetration starts when a new competitor has built production capacity and starts commercial sales. The leader's share of production capacity and share of sales falls. As more and more competitors enter the market and provide offers at different price, the perceived relative value of the leader's offer declines, forcing a reduction in the leaders price premium.
3. Capacity tends to be overbuilt during rapid growth. When a cyclical slow down occurs, industry overcapacity drives down margins to lower levels. New competitors decide not to enter, and existing competitors try to solidify their positions. This leads to share stability.

4. Stability is followed by commodity competition. The product is viewed as commodity, buyers no longer pay a price premium, and the suppliers earn only an average rate of return.
5. At this point, withdrawal begins. The pioneer might decide to build share further as other firms withdraw.

The strategies usually at this stage are they have one or few products relatively undifferentiated. Mostly, cost plus pricing should be used to set a price. Distribution is selective and scattered as the firm commences implementation of the distribution plan. Promotion is aimed at building brand awareness; sample or trial incentive may be directed towards the customers. Advertising is aimed to be high to build brand awareness. The companies in the introduction stage are Pepsi Tropicana, Clear shampoo.

## Marketing Strategies: Growth Stage

In growth stage there is a rapid climb in sales. Early adopters like the product and additional consumers start buying it. New competitors enter the market; they are attracted by the opportunities. They introduce new product features and expand distribution. There is no change or slight change in price of the product, it may remain same or fall slightly, depending on how fast demand increases. The promotional expenditures of the company remain same or increase slightly to meet competition and to continue to educate the market. Sales increases at a much faster rate than promotional expenditures, causing a decline in promotion sales ratio. Profits increase during this stage as promotion costs are spread over a larger volume and unit manufacturing costs fall faster than price declines owing to the producer learning effect. Firms have to watch for a change from an accelerating to a decelerating rate of growth in order to prepare new strategies.

The firm uses several strategies in growth stage to sustain rapid market growth:

- It increases its distribution coverage and enters new distribution channels.
- It shifts from product-awareness advertising to product-preference advertising.
- It lowers prices to attract the next layer of price-sensitive buyers.
- It improves product quality and adds new product features and improved styling.
- It enters new market segments.
- These market expansion strategies strengthen the firm's competitive position.
- It adds new models and flanker products (i.e., products of different sizes, flavours, and so forth that protect the main product.

In the growth stage the firm faces a trade-off between high market share and high current profit. The firm spends money on product improvement, promotion, and distribution; so that it can capture a top position. It forgoes maximum current profit in the hope of making even greater profits in the next stage. The products in this stage may be Mountain Dew and Lays.

## Marketing Strategies: Maturity Stage

This is the stage at which the rate of sales growth will be slow, and the product will enter a stage of relative maturity. This stage lasts longer as compared to the previous stages, and poses a challenge to marketing management. The problem that marketing manager face at maturity stage is the problem of marketing the mature product.

The maturity stage divides into three phases: growth, stable, and decaying maturity. In the growth phase, the sales growth rate starts to decline. There are no new distribution channels to fill. In the stable phase, sales flatten on a per capita basis because of market saturation. The most potential consumers have tried the product, and future sales are governed by population growth and replacement demand. In the decaying maturity phase, the absolute level of sales starts to decline, and customers begin switching to other product.

The sales in the maturity stage slow down and create overcapacity in the industry, which leads to intensified competition. Competitors try to find niches for their product. Increase in advertising and trade and consumer promotion takes place in this stage. Companies increase their budgets to improve their product and line extensions. If a company is not successful then the weaker firm withdraws from the market. The industry eventually consists of well-entrenched competitors, their main aim is to gain or maintain market share.

Few giant firms dominate the industry through quality, service and cost leadership, by making profit through high volume and lower costs. Surrounding these dominant firms is a multitude of market nichers, including market specialists, product specialists, and customizing firms. The challenge before a firm in a mature market is whether to become of the "big three" and achieve profits through high volume and low cost or to pursue a niching strategy and achieve profits through low volume and a high margin.

There are few companies who leave weaker products and concentrate on more profitable products and on new products. Industries widely thought to be mature like autos, motorcycles, television, watches, and cameras — were proved otherwise by the Japanese, who found ways to offer new values to customers.

The strategies that a company may adopt in this stage are:

1. Market modification
2. Product modification
3. Marketing mix modification

**1. Market Modification:** The company would try to expand the new horizon of market for its mature brand by working with the two factors that make-up sales volume which can be calculated as: volume = number of brand users × usage rate per user.

The company can expand the number of brand users by: (1) converting nonuser's into users: It means all those customers into users who have never tried our product. (2) Entering new market segments: Johnson & Johnson successfully promoted its baby shampoo to adult users. (3) Winning competitors' customers: PepsiCo is constantly tempting-Coca-Cola users to switch. (4) Volume can also be increased by convincing current users to increase their brand usage: (i) Use the product on more occasions. Kellogg's cornflakes for breakfast, dinner, lunch. (ii) Use more of the product on each occasion. Drink a larger glass of orange juice. (iii) Use the product in new ways. Use washing machine for making lassi.

**2. Product Modification:** The companies in this stage are trying to improve their existing product through quality improvement, feature improvement or style improvement.

(a) **Quality Improvement:** It aims at increasing the product's functional performance. A company may win over competition by launching a "new and improved" product. This strategy is effective to the extent that the quality is improved, buyers accept the claim of improved quality, and a sufficient of buyers will pay for higher quality. However, customers are not always willing to accept an "improved" product. As such when Pepsi came with a blue transparent Pepsi it was not accepted in the market.

(b) **Feature Improvement:** It aims at adding new features to an existing product. The improvement in product could be in the form of size, weight, materials additives, accessories that expand the product's versatility, safety, or convenience.

This strategy has several advantages it could create an image of company as an innovator and win the loyalty of market segments that value these features. It also provides an opportunity for free publicity and generates sales force and distributor enthusiasm. The major disadvantage is that feature improvements are easy to be copied unless there is a permanent gain from being first, the feature improvement might not pay-off in the long run.

A strategy of style improvement aims at increasing the product's aesthetic appeal. The periodic introduction of new car models is largely about style competition, as is the introduction of new packaging for consumer products. A style strategy might give the product a unique market identity. Yet style competition has problems. First, it is difficult to predict whether people and which people will like a new style. Second, a style change usually requires discontinuing the old style, and the company risk losing customers.

**3. Marketing Mix Modification:** The market mix modification may take place if following questions are answered:

- **Prices:** Would a price cut attract new buyers? If so, should the list price be lowered, should prices be lowered through price specials, volume or early purchase discounts, freight cost absorption, or easier credit terms? Or would it be better to raise the price to signal higher quality?
- **Distribution:** Can more outlets be penetrated? Can the company obtain more product support and display in existing outlets? Can the company introduce the product into distribution channels?
- **Advertising:** Should the media mix be changed? Should the timing, frequencies; or size of ads be changed? Should advertising expenditures be increased? Should the message or copy be changed?
- **Sales Promotion:** Should the company step up sales promotion — trade deals, cents off coupons, rebates, warranties, gifts, and contests?
- **Personal Selling:** Should sales territories be revised? Should the number or quality of salespeople be increased? Should sales force incentives be revised? Can sales-call planning be improved? Should the basis for sales force specialization be changed?
- **Services:** Can the company speed up delivery? Can it extend more technical assistance to customers? Can it extend more credit?

Marketers often debate which tools are most effective in the mature stage. For example, would the company gain more by increasing its advertising or its sales promotion budget? Sales promotion has more impact at this stage because consumers have reached an equilibrium in their buying habits and preferences, and psychological persuasion (advertising) is not as effective as financial persuasion (sales-promotion deals). Many consumer-packaged-goods companies now spend over 60 per cent of their promotion budget on sales promotion to support mature products. Others argue that brands should be managed as capital assets and supported by advertising. Advertising expenditures should be treated as a capital investment. Brand managers however, use sales promotion because its effects are quicker and more visible to their superiors. But excessive sales promotion activity can hurt the brand's image in long run profit performance.

## Marketing Strategies: Decline Stage

This is a stage where sales decline for many reasons such as; shift in consumer tastes, increased price cutting, technological advancement, and increased domestic and foreign competition and this would lead to overcapacity, and profit erosion. The decline might be slow or rapid, as in the case of automobile industry. Sales may come down to zero or they may petrify at a low level. Due to decline in sales and profits, some may leave the market. The firm which remains in the market may reduces the number of products they offer. They may withdraw from smaller market segments and weaker trade channels, and they may cut their promotion budgets and reduce prices further. Most companies have not tried the policy for handling aging products. If a strong reason does not exist, carrying a weak product is very costly to the firm — not just by the amount of uncovered overhead but also in terms of profit also, as there are many hidden costs. Weak products often consume a lot of time; require frequent price and inventory adjustments; generally involve short production runs in spite of expensive set-up times; require both advertising and sales force attention that might be better used to make the healthy products more profitable; and can cast a shadow on the company's image. The biggest cost might well lie in the future. Failing to eliminate weak products delays the aggressive search for replacement products.

In handling aging products, a company faces a number of tasks and decisions. The first task is to identify weaker products of the company. Many companies appoint a product-review committee with representatives from marketing, R&D manufacturing, and finance. The controller's office supplies data for each product showing trends in market size, market share, prices, costs, and profits. A computer program then analyzes this information. The product-review committee makes a recommendation for each product leave it alone, modify its marketing-strategy, or drop it.

The strategies for declining industries, by Kathryn Harrigan are as follows:

1. Increasing the firm's investment (to dominate the market or strengthen its competitive position.
2. Maintaining the firm's investment level until the uncertainties about the industry are resolved.
3. Decreasing the firm's investment level selectively, by dropping unprofitable customers while simultaneously strengthening the firm's investment in lucrative niches.
4. Harvesting ("milking") the firm's investment to recover cash quickly.
5. Divesting the business quickly by disposing its assets as advantageously as possible?

The appropriate strategy depends on the industry's relative attractiveness and the company's competitive strength in that industry. A company that is in an unattractive industry but possesses competitive strength should consider shrinking selectively. A company that is in an attractive industry and has competitive strength should consider strengthening its investment. If the company were choosing between harvesting and divesting, its strategies would be quite different. Harvesting calls for gradually reducing a product or business while trying to maintain its sales. The first step is to cut R&D costs and plant and equipment investment. The company might also reduce product quality, sales force size, marginal services, and advertising expenditures. It would try to cut these costs without letting customers, competitors, and employees know what is happening. Harvesting is an ethically ambivalent strategy, and it is also difficult to execute. Harvesting can substantially increase the company's current cash flow. When a company decides to drop a product, it faces further decisions. If the product, has strong distribution and residual goodwill, the company can probably sell it to another firm. If the company can't find any buyers, it must decide whether to liquidate the brand quickly or slowly. It must also decide on how much inventory and service to maintain for past customers.

## THE PLC CONCEPT: CRITIQUE

The PLC concept helps interpret product and market dynamics. It can be used for planning and control, but it is not much useful for forecasting. PLC theory undergoes a criticism. According to the critics, patterns of life cycle are too variable in shape as well as in duration.

PLC lacks what living organisms have, i.e., a fixed sequence of stages and a fixed length of each stage. It is also difficult for marketers to tell in which stage its product is in.

A product may appear to be mature when actually, it has reached a plateau prior to another upsurge. According to critics, PLC pattern is the result of marketing strategies and not because of inevitable course sales.

## SUMMARY

Positioning is "the act of designing the company's offering and image to occupy a distinctive place in the mind of the target market. Thus, the objective of positioning is to create in the minds of firm's prospect a predetermined favourable perception of both your personal brand (image) and your product (offering). Consequently, effective positioning results in a value proposition, a compelling reason offered to prospects to buy financial products and to buy them from your firm. The key to competitive advantage in positioning is based on Product differentiation, Services differentiation, Personnel differentiation, Channel differentiation, Image differentiation. There are various positioning errors that take place, such as underpositioning, overpositioning, confused positioning and doubtful positioning.

Product life cycle (PLC) has to do with the life of a product in the market with respect to business/commercial costs and sales measures. The general sequence of stages in product life cycle is introduction stage, growth stage, maturity stage and decline stage. Though many products have bell shaped product life but some have other patterns such as Growth-slump-maturity pattern, Cycle-recycle pattern, Scalloped PLC. The special categories of PLC are style, fashion and fad. Each stage of PLC has different marketing strategies to be the market leader, sustain in market to make profit or to minimize loss.

## CASELET 1

Intense competition is the rule in the fast paced and ever-changing IT business. By looking at their advertisements, practices and strategies, determine how IT companies are attempting to position themselves.

1. What market segments seem to be the most important targets?
2. What product differences are present between the major players? Are these really significant differences or only imagined ones?
3. What kind of strategies it would use if a company is in a mature stage?

## ........ QUESTIONS FOR DISCUSSION

1. Describe the introduction and growth stages of product life cycle with diagram.
2. Describe the growth and decline stages of product life cycle with diagram.
3. Explain the important stages in product life cycle.
4. Explain giving examples, the maturity and decline stages of product life cycle.
5. Explain giving examples the introduction and growth stages of product life cycle.
6. Describe the growth stage of product life cycle.
7. Explain the meaning of product life cycle.

## Objective Questions

### State Whether the Following Statement is True/False.

1. There is a greater acceptance of a product in growth stage as compared to introduction stage.
2. Customers entering into the market during the introduction stage of the product life cycle are called as innovators.
3. The objective of advertising at the introductory stage is to create a primary demand for the company's product.
4. During the introduction stage of product life cycle, sales start rising at a very fast rate.

*Ans:* **1.** True, **2.** True, **3.** True, **4.** True.

### Fill in the Blanks

1. ______ is the period of rapid market acceptance and substantial profit improvement.
2. In _______ stage of product life cycle, the sales start declining very rapidly.
3. There are ________ stages in product life cycle.
4. ________ stage is a period when sales show a downward shift and profit erodes.
5. In maturity stage of product life cycle the sales ________ but at a slow rate.

*Ans:* **1.** Growth stage, **2.** decline, **3.** four, **4.** Decline, **5.** increases.

☺ ☺ ☺

CHAPTER 9

# Consumer Behaviour

## LEARNING OBJECTIVES

- *Define What is Meant by Consumer Behaviour*
- *Understand its Role and Importance for a Marketer.*
- *Identify the Major Factors that Influence a Consumer's Purchase Decision and Behaviour.*
- *Study Each of the Major Influencing Factors in Detail to be able to Understand How it Affects Consumer Behaviour.*

## INTRODUCTION

One thing that we have in common is that we are all consumers. In fact, everybody in this world is a consumer. Everyday of our life we are buying and consuming a different variety of goods and services. However, we all have different tastes, likes and dislikes and adopt different behaviour patterns while making purchase decisions. Mr. 'X' may prefer to use Colgate toothpaste, Denim toilet soap and Halo shampoo while Mrs. 'X', the spouse may prefer to use Pepsodent toothpaste, Lux soap and Sun silk shampoo. Similarly, different types of people may have a different set of preferences in food, clothing, books, magazines, recreational activities, forms of savings and the stores from where one prefer to shop, which may be different not only from that of our family members but also from our friends, neighbours and colleagues. Each consumer is unique and this uniqueness is reflected in the consumption behaviour, pattern and process of purchase. The study of consumer behaviour provides us with reasons why consumers differ from one another in buying and using products and services.

'What' products and services do we buy, 'why' do we buy, `how often' do we buy, from 'where' do we buy, 'how' we buy, etc., are the issues which are dealt within the discipline of consumer behaviour.

Consumer behaviour can be defined as those acts of individuals (consumers) directly involved in obtaining, using, and disposing of economic goods and services, including the decision processes that precede and determine these acts. Understanding how consumers make purchase decisions can help marketing managers in several ways. For example, if a manager knows through research that gas mileage is the most important attribute for a certain target market, the manufacturer can design the product to meet this criterion. For example, an automobile manufacturer can advertise a car's maintenance-free features and sporty European style while downplaying gas mileage.

## IMPORTANCE OF CONSUMER BEHAVIOUR FOR MARKETERS

Consumer behaviour helps us to understand the purchase behaviour and preferences of different consumers. Consumers differ in terms of sex, age, education, occupation, income, family set-up, religion, nationality and social status. As different background factors have different needs, the consumer buys those products and services which he thinks will satisfy his needs. In marketing terminology, specific types or group of consumers buy different products (or variation of the same basic product) represent different market segments. To successfully market to different market segments, the marketing manager needs appropriate marketing strategies which he can design only when he understands the factors which account for these differences in consumer behaviour and tastes. In today's world, consumers' tastes are also characterized by frequent changes. To survive in the market, a firm has to be constantly innovating and understand the latest consumer trends and tastes. Consumer behaviour provides invaluable clues and guidelines to marketers on the new technological frontiers which they should explore. For example, the advent of colour television in India. When we switched over from black and white transmission to colour transmission in the early eighties, the consumers exhibited a desire to purchase colour TV for closer-to-life picture viewing and now consumer have moved on to purchase LCD.

Consumer behaviour is a process, and purchase forms one part of this process. There are various environmental factors which influence this process. All these factors and the type of influence which they exert on an individual's consumption behaviour can be understood and analyzed. Moreover, some of these factors can be further influenced by specific elements of the marketing strategy, so that the consumer behaviour process results in a definite purchase decision. To the extent that the marketer can understand and manipulate the influencing factors, he can predict the behaviour of consumers. Though prediction can never be absolutely accurate, it certainly reduces the risk associated with different marketing strategies. Thus, the importance of consumer behaviour lies in the fact that behaviour can be understood and influenced to ensure a positive purchase decision. The marketing manager's interest lies exactly here, i.e., to ensure that marketing strategy results into purchase of the product.

## Types of Consumers

All consumers can be classified into two types — personal and organizational. When a person purchases a shirt for his own use — he would purchase shirt as per his requirement. However, when a person purchase computer for his office use and the purchase is in capacity as per the requirement of the organization. Whenever a person purchases goods and services for his own or for family use, it is said to be personal consumer. All individuals thus, fall in the category of personal consumer. All business firms, government agencies and bodies, non-business organizations such as hospitals, temples, and trusts are organizational consumers of goods and services purchased for running the organization.

## Buyer Versus User

It is not necessary that a person who purchases the product is the actual consumer, the purchased product may be consumed by anyone. For example, a mother buys toys and clothes for her young children. The mother is the buyer but the actual consumers are the children. A car is purchased by the husband or the wife but is used by all the members of the family. Thus, in the family context, you may either have the situation where the buyer is distinct from the consumer or the buyer is only one of the many consumers. The question that arises is: Who should be the subject of study in consumer behaviour? Should we study the buyer or the consumer? To overcome this problem, in many instances it is the household or the family and not the individual who is considered the subject of the study.

However, a person involved in marketing, should have a very sharply defined focus for marketing strategy, especially promotional strategy. He must identify the best prospect for his products — whether it is the buyer or the user. But even when the consumer is distinct from the buyer, the consumer's likes and dislikes, taste, etc., influences the buyer's decision to purchase a specific product or brand. Thus, many companies play it safe and focus their promotion at both the user and the buyer. Consider the promotional message of Maggi noodles and Rasna Soft drink concentrate: the taste and fun aspects of both these products are meant to appeal to the children who are the major consumers, while, the convenience (in case of noodles) and economy (in case of Rasna) is meant to appeal to the mothers, who are the buyers.

Buying behaviour is the decision processes and acts of people involved in buying and using products.

Need to understand:

- Why consumers make the purchases that they make?
- What factors influence consumer purchases?
- The changing factors in our society.

Consumer buying behaviour refers to the buying behaviour of the ultimate consumer. A firm needs to analyze buying behaviour for: Buyers reactions to a firms marketing strategy has a great impact on the firm's success. The marketing concept stresses that a firm should create a Marketing Mix (MM) that satisfies (gives utility to) customers, therefore need to analyze the what, where, when and how consumers buy. Marketers can better predict how consumers will respond to marketing strategies.

## Stages in the Buyer Decision Process

In making a purchase decision the consumer goes through the five stages of:

(i) Problem/need recognition,

(ii) Prepurchase information search,

(iii) Evaluation of alternatives,

(iv) Purchase decision, and

(v) Post-purchase behaviour.

However, for purchase decision involving extensive problem-solving, the consumer is likely to go through all the five stages in the specified sequence.

It is important to note that the buying process starts much before the actual purchase and has implications even after the purchase has been made. This should give ideas to the marketer as to how he has to start designing his marketing strategy in order to achieve his specified marketing objectives.

Let us understand the stages in decision making process with the help of Mr. Tarak Mehta specific decision to purchase a briefcase.

**1. Problem/need Recognition:** It occurs when consumers are faced with an imbalance between actual and desired state. The buying process starts with the buyer recognizing a need or problem. For example, Tarak Mehta feels very uncomfortable carrying his papers, files and lunch packet in his hand or in a plastic bag to his workplace. Sometimes, the papers and even files from his hands get spoiled. Mr. Tarak Mehta feels the need for a suitable bag to carry papers to and fro from his office and has identified a briefcase as the solution to his problem.

A marketing manager's objective is to get consumers to recognize an imbalance between their present status and preferred state. Advertising and sales promotion often provides this stimulus. Surveying buyer preferences provides marketer with information about consumer wants and needs that can be used to tailor products and services. For example, Procter & Gamble frequently surveys consumers regarding their wants and needs.

**2. Prepurchase Information Search:** After recognizing a need or want, consumers search for information about the various alternatives available to satisfy it. An information search can occur internally and externally or both. An internal information search is the process of recalling information stored in the memory. This stored information stems largely from previous experience with a product. For instance, while travelling a person encounters a restaurant belonging to chain that a person might have tried somewhere else. By recalling his memory he can remember that whether the food was good and within his price range or not. In contrast, an external information search seeks information in the outside environment. There are two basic type of external environment source, i.e., a non-marketing controlled information source, it includes personal experience (trying or observing a new product); personal sources (family, friends, acquaintances, and coworkers)and public sources such as consumer reports, etc.

On the other hand, marketing controlled information source is based towards a specific product, as it originates with marketers promoting that product. Marketing controlled information sources include mass media advertising (radio, newspaper, television, and magazine advertising), sales promotion (contest, diplays, premiums and so forth), salespeople, product labels, packaging and the internet.

In response to the stimuli provided by the need for a briefcase, Mr. Tarak Mehta starts searching for information on the kinds of briefcases available in the market. Search can be of two types: internal and external.

Internal search refers to recalling relevant information stored in the memory. For instance, Mr. Tarak Mehta may recall having seen the different kinds of briefcases used by his colleagues. Or he may recall having seen some advertisements of briefcases on the television or in some magazines and newspapers.

External search refers to the deliberate and voluntary seeking of new information regarding the product/brand under consideration. Mr. Tarak Mehta can seek information from the following three sources:

- Personal sources : family, friends, colleagues, neighbours.
- Commercial sources : advertisements, retailers, salesmen.
- Public sources : seeing others, consumer information centres.

By tapping all these sources of information, Mr. Tarak Mehta is able to identify the different types of briefcase on the basis of material, branded versus unbranded, high-medium- low priced. A wide variety of materials are used for making briefcases ranging from the best leather to rexine to plastic. There are branded briefcases available and Mr. Tarak Mehta can choose from the well known VIP, Safari and Aristocrat and some less known local brands, or he can choose to buy an unbranded briefcase. The price ranges from ₹ 125 to ₹ 1,200. Also, there are a number of other features which can influence the choice, such as type of lock, and number of partitions and pockets for keeping different documents.

By the end of this stage, Mr. Tarak Mehta has gathered enough information about different kinds of briefcases available and has narrowed down his alternatives to moulded plastic, branded briefcase. Within this broad range there are various brands and price ranges to make the final choice from.

**3. Evaluation of Alternatives:** After getting information and constructing and evoked a set of alternative products, the consumer is ready to make decision. A consumer will use the information stored in memory and obtained from outside source to develop a set of criteria. These standards help the consumer evaluate and compare alternatives. One way to begin narrowing the number of choices in the evoked set is to pick a product attribute and then exclude all products in the set that don't have the attribute. For example, Mr. Tarak Mehta will make his final decision using certain evaluative criteria. The most commonly used criteria are: (i) product attribute, (ii) the relative importance of each attribute to the consumer, (iii) brand image, (iv) attitudes towards the different brands or alternatives under considerations. For instance, the product attributes of the (Plastic branded briefcase) alternatives identified by Mr. Tarak Mehta are: unbreakable, light weight, spaciousness, reliability of locking system, colour, and price. Mr. Tarak Mehta attaches maximum importance to the product attributes of light weight and spaciousness as compared to other attributes. He already has some kind of attitude towards the various brands developed in the stage of information search which will affect his final decision.

This stage of the buying decision process gives the marketer a chance to modify his product offering in keeping with the relative importance attached to each attribute by various consumer segments, altering beliefs and attitudes about his own brand, and calling attention to neglected product attributes.

**4. Purchase Decision:** In the evaluation stage, Mr. Tarak Mehta has ranked the various brands in terms of his first, second and third preference. In short, he has made up his mind about which brand he wants to buy. However, Mr. Tarak Mehta may finally end up buying a brand which is not his most preferred. This may happen because attitudes of others and situational factors.

For instance, when Mr. Tarak Mehta goes to the shop to make his purchase, the shopkeeper's negative remarks about his (Mr. Tarak Mehta) most preferred brand may make him change his mind. Also, it is possible that Mr. Tarak Mehta preferred brand is not available, or there is a very attractive price discount on the brand ranked third by him which eventually makes him change his mind.

**5. Postpurchase Behaviour:** After purchasing the briefcase, if Mr. Tarak Mehta finds that its performance or utility matches up to his expectation, he will feel satisfied with his purchase. The satisfaction will reinforce he perceived favourable image of the brand, which is likely to be extended to the entire range of products manufactured by the company. Also, he would strongly recommend the brand when his friends ask his advice for buying a new briefcase. A satisfied customer is thus a very powerful source of influence for potential customers. However, if he feels that the briefcase which he has purchased is not up to his expectation, then he is likely to feel dissatisfied. The gap between expected (or perceived) and the actual performances cause discomfort or dissonance to the buyer. As a result of this, Mr. Tarak Mehta may decide to stop buying other products sold by the same company and also warn his friends about the poor utility of his briefcase. To reduce his own state of discomfort or dissonance arising from the feeling that he has not made the right choice he can: (i) reevaluate the unchosen brands and downgrade their desirability by identifying some negative features, and (ii) search for information to confirm his choice.

## FACTORS INFLUENCING CONSUMER BEHAVIOUR

The consumer decision making process does not occur in a vacuum. On the contrary, underlying cultural, social, individual, and psychological factors strongly influence the decision process. They have an effect from the time consumer perceives a stimulus through post-purchase behaviour. Consumer behaviour is affected by cultural factors, which include culture and values, subculture, and social class, exert the broadest influence over consumer decision making. Social factors sum up the social interaction between a consumer and influential groups of people, such as reference groups, opinion leaders, and family members. Personal factors which include gender, age, family, family life cycle stage, personality, self-concept, and lifestyle play a major role in the type of products and service consumer want. Psychological factors such as individual consumer needs and motivations, perceptions, attitudes, the learning process and personality characteristics are the similarities which operate across different types of people and influence their behaviour.

The combinations of these various factors produce a different impact on each one of us as manifested in our different behaviour as consumers. We may think that the best way of utilizing our annual saving is to go for a holiday, but wife may think to invest in a house, while a close colleague considers buying shares as the best way of spending savings. Thus, we may find that each person has his or her own standards of judgements and distinct behaviour in every aspect of his role as a consumer. But at the same time, underlying the individual differences are similarities which help explain behaviour of specific types or groups of people. It is these similarities which make it possible for us to classify and analyze the behaviour of individual consumers. The factors influencing consumer behaviour are as follows:

**CULTURAL FACTORS:** It consists of culture and values, subculture, and social class, which are as follows:

**Culture:** It is the essential character of society that distinguishes it from other cultural groups. Culture is an extremely critical and all pervasive influence in our life. The study of culture encompasses all aspects of a society such as its religion, knowledge, language, laws, customs, traditions, music, art, technology, work patterns, products, etc. All these factors make-up the unique, distinctive 'personality' of each society. For our purpose of studying consumer behaviour, culture can be defined as the sum total of learned beliefs, values and customs which serve to guide and direct the consumer behaviour of all members of that society. It may also be defined as "The set of values, norms, attitudes, and other meaningful symbols that shape human behaviour and the artifacts, or products, of that behaviour as they are transmitted from one generation to the next".

Culture is learned through the following three ways:

***Determinations of Consumer Behaviour***

(a) **Formal Learning:** In which parents and elders teach children the proper way to behave; for instance a child may be taught that too many toffees and chocolates are bad for his teeth. This learning may influence his response, both as a child and adult, towards these products.

(b) **Informal Learning:** In which we learn by imitating the behaviour of our parents, friends, or by watching TV and film actors in action.

(c) **Technical Learning:** In which instructions are given about the specific method by which certain things have to be done such as painting, dancing, singing, etc. Though a marketer can influence all the three types of learning through his company's advertising strategy, it is informal learning which is most satisfying to such influences. Children learn much more about products and services through advertisements in mass media (especially TV) than they do either from their parents or teachers. Brand loyalties and images developed in the early, formative years of childhood tend to be deep-rooted and affect the child's consumer behaviour even in later years of adulthood. Marketers' interest lies in identifying the potential consumer segments and catching them young.

The kinds of products and advertising appeals that can work effectively in a society depend largely on its cultural background. In the American society, individualism, freedom achievement, success, material comfort, efficiency and practicality are values which are followed and imbibed by the younger children. Products and services which fulfil these values are most successfully marketed in America. In the Indian society, on the contrary, conformity, spiritualism, respect for the elderly, traditionalism and education are some of the dominant cultural values. However, our society is undergoing a cultural change and one can discern some major cultural shifts which have far reaching consequences for the introduction of a vast variety of new products and services. Some of these changes are as follows:

(i) **Convenience:** With more women joining the workforce there is an increasing demand for products that help lighten and relieve the daily household chores, and make life more convenient. This is reflected in the soaring sale of gas stoves, mixer-grinder, washing machines, vacuum cleaners, ready to eat/cook packets of dehydrated frozen/precooked foods, fast food outlets, etc.

Fifteen years ago when Hindustan Lever Ltd., first introduced the concept of dehydrated vegetables and marketed packet peas, the concept did not succeed. The cultural value was of eating fresh and freshly cooked food. But today, that cultural value does not have a strong hold, and frozen foods which can be kept up to 6-7 months are being successfully marketed.

(ii) **Education:** People in our society today wish to acquire relevant education and skills that would help improve their career prospects. This is evident from the fact that so many professional, career-oriented educational centres are coming up, and still they cannot seem to meet the demand. As a specific instance the number of institutions offering courses and training in computers that has opened in many cities have increased drastically.

(iii) **Physical Appearance:** Physical fitness, good health, and smart appearance are on premium today. Slimming centres and beauty parlours are growing in all major cities of the country. Cosmetics for both women and men are being sold in ever-increasing numbers. Exclusive shops retailing designer clothes at fancy prices are doing brisk business.

(iv) **Materialism:** There is a definite shift in the people's cultural value from spiritualism towards materialism. People are spending more money than ever before on acquiring products such as air-conditioners, cars, scooters, video cassette recorders, etc., which add to both physical comfort as well as status.

A company which wants to grow must keep a tab on such major cultural trends to ensure that its products fit in well with these new trends.

**Subculture:** A subculture is an identifiable distinct, cultural group, which, while following the dominant cultural values of the overall society also has its own beliefs, values and customs that set them apart from other members of the same society.

These subcultures offer ready-made market segments to the marketer who can position his product to meet the specific needs, motivation, perception and attitudes of each subculture. However, the marketer may need to modify, both his product and advertising appeal to suit their specialized needs.

Every member of a society is a member of several subgroups, (such as an elderly, Keralite, Christian, woman teacher) and the consumer's purchase decision is a result of the influence of these various subgroups. The marketer must understand how the specific subcultural groups interact with each other and exert their influence on the member's consumption behaviour.

**Social Class:** Social class is a concept based on distribution of status and the categories are usually ranked in a hierarchical order ranging from low status to high status. In every society there is inequality in social status amongst different people and the people are categorized into different social classes. Social class is an ideal basis for segmenting the market, as different social classes exhibit distinct product and brand preferences. Social classes can be defined as relatively permanent and homogeneous divisions in a society in which individuals or families sharing similar values, life-styles, interests and behaviour can be categorized. People belonging to a particular class tend to restrict their interaction to people belonging to the same class; unless it is for a very specialized purpose. Within a social class there are shared values, attitudes and behavioural patterns of consumption of certain products and services. But if we compare different social classes, we would find differences in values, attitudes and behaviour between each class, as also a pattern of consumption behaviour unique to each class.

Social class is a complex variable which is determined by persons' income, occupation, education; personal performance and possession of different types of products. Within the same social class, there is sharing of information on different products and brands, while between the different social classes there is little communication. Different social classes have different media exposure and habits. Let us take the instance of English women's magazines: If we study the profile of *Femina*, and *Woman's Era*, we would immediately realize the different class of readers each magazine is catering to. Social classes, thus, are market segments which are easily identified and also easy to reach. Social classes can be categorized on the basis of a number of different bases such as blue-collar workers and white-collar workers, educated and uneducated and so on.

**SOCIAL FACTORS:** Most consumers are likely to seek the opinion of others to reduce their search and evaluation efforts or uncertainty, especially as the perceived risk of the decision increases. Determinations of consumer behaviour are as follows:

**Reference Groups:** It is a group in society that influences an individual's purchasing behaviour. As a consumer, your decision to purchase and use certain products and services, is influenced not only by psychological factors, your personality and lifestyle, but also by the people around us with whom we interact and the various social groups to which we belong. The groups with whom we interact directly or indirectly influence our purchase decisions and thus their study is of great importance to marketers.

A group is defined as two or more people who interact to achieve individual or common goals. The three categories of groups which are important for the marketer to understand are:

(i) **Primary and Secondary Groups:** A primary group is one with which an individual interacts on a regular basis and whose opinion is of importance to him. Family, neighbours, close friends, colleagues and coworkers are examples of primary groups. Secondary groups are those with which an individual interacts only occasionally and does not consider their opinion very important.

(ii) **Formal and Informal Groups:** Rotary club, Lions club and Karnavati club are some of the well known social groups in our society. Labour unions, social clubs and societies are other types of formal groups to which individuals may belong. A formal group has a highly defined structure, specific roles and authority positions and specific goals.

(iii) In contrast, **an informal group** is loosely defined and may have no specified roles and goals. Meeting neighbours over lunch once in a month for friendly exchange of news is an instance of an informal group.

(iv) **Membership and Symbolic Groups:** A membership group is one to which a person belongs or qualifies for membership. All workers in a factory qualify for membership to the labour union. A symbolic group is one which an individual aspires to belong to, but is not likely to be received as a member. A head clerk in an office may act as if he belongs to the top management group by adopting their attitudes, values and modes of dress. Both membership and symbolic groups influence consumer behaviour but membership groups have a more direct influence. Primary, informal and small groups exert the maximum influence on consumers and are of great interest for marketers. Aspirational groups are those which a person wishes to join and nonaspirational or dissociative group influences our behaviour, but we try to maintain distance from it. Any of these groups can serve as a reference group for a consumer if it serves as a point of reference or comparison in the formation of the values, attitudes and behaviour. Different kinds of groups, whether small or large, formal or informal or symbolic qualify as a reference group. The concept of reference group is a very wide one and includes both direct and indirect individual and group influences.

Indirect reference groups comprise those individuals or groups with whom an individual does not have any direct face-to-face contact, such as film stars, TV stars, sportsmen, politicians. Reference groups are used in advertising to appeal to different market segments. Group situation with which potential customers can identify are used to promote products and services. Hidden in this appeal is the slight inducement to the customer to identify himself with the user of the product in question. The three types of reference group appeals most commonly used are: celebrities, experts, and the 'common man'.

Celebrities are well known people (in their specific field of activity) who are admired and their fans aspire to emulate their behaviour. Film stars and sports heroes are the most popular celebrities. Soft drinks (Sprite), shaving cream (Palmolive), toilet soaps (Lux), textiles (Raymond) are advertised using celebrities from the sports and film fields. Experts such as doctors, lawyers, accountants and authors are used for establishing the benefits of the product. Colgate and Babool toothpastes are examples of products which use the expert reference group appeal for promotion. Another reference group appeal is that which uses the testimonials of a satisfied customer. It demonstrates to the prospective customer that someone just like him uses and is satisfied with the product. Hindustan Lever Ltd., for Surf has used this appeal very effectively, using a stereo type upper middle-class housewife known as 'Lalitaji'. Direct reference groups which exert a significant influence on consumers purchase decisions and behaviour can be classified into six categories. These are:

(i) The family,

(ii) Friendship groups,

(iii) Formal social groups,

(iv) Formal shopping groups,

(v) Consumer action groups, and

(vi) Workgroups.

**Opinion Leaders:** Apart from the family, a consumer is influenced by the advice he receives from his friends, neighbours, relatives and colleagues about what products and services he should buy. This process of influencing is known as the opinion leadership process and is described as the process by which one person (the opinion leader) informally influences the actions or attitudes of others (opinion receivers). The influence is informal and the setting in which the influencing process takes place has nothing to do with the actual buying or selling of the product in question. For instance, during lunch hour, you may casually ask your colleague to recommend a good scooter mechanic. Or you discuss with your relatives and neighbours what brand of TV they possess and try to ascertain which is the brand recommended by most, before purchasing a TV for your own home. Further, the process often occurs between two persons rather than in a large group setting. Thus, the opinion leadership process can also be thought of as the 'word-of-mouth' communication. The advice of opinion leaders is sought in case of specific products. People who have acquired considerable knowledge and experience in a particular field are thought of as opinion leaders in that area.

Both opinion leaders and followers receive information on all kinds of products and services from the mass media. But the opinion receivers are more influenced by the opinion leaders rather than the media. In the eyes of the opinion receiver, the opinion leader has more credibility than the mass media. The opinion leaders become a sort of 'middleman' receiving information from mass media and passing it on to opinion receivers. Advertisers and marketers are concerned with reaching the opinion leaders and ensuring that they receive the intended information which they can, in turn, pass on to opinion receivers. Thus, the first task of the marketer is to identify the opinion leaders. In a particular society, persons who are members or participants in a number of social organizations and have high social activity participation are likely candidates for opinion leaders. Having identified the opinion leaders, the next task is to reach them through the media which they patronize. Direct mail pieces, magazines and journals of clubs and social organizations and special interest magazines (for specialty products) are some of the appropriate channels for this purpose.

Opinion leaders are usually innovators. They are always trying out new products and brands, and recommending them to the opinion receivers. The acceptance of new products, brands, and ideas is known as the diffusion of innovation. In a narrow sense, innovation is defined as something new or modified which has a relative advantage over the existing products. Marketers are concerned with the spread or diffusion of this innovation which is a two-step process. The first step is the spread of awareness of an innovation from its source to the consumers. The second step is the individual consumer decision making process which leads to the acceptance or rejection of the innovation.

**Family:** The family is the most important of all these groups. The family as a unit, is an important consumer for many products which are purchased for consumption by all family members. It is a source of major influence on the individual members' buying behaviour. We can identify two families which shape an individual's consumption behaviour. One is the family of orientation that is the family in which you are born and consists of your parents, brothers and sisters. It is from parents that we imbibe most of our values, attitudes, beliefs and purchase behaviour patterns. Long after an individual has ceased to live with his parents, their influence on the subconscious mind still continues to be great. In our country, where children continue to live with their parents even after attaining adulthood, the influence is extremely important. The second type of family is the family of procreation consisting of the consumer's spouse and children. Within the family, different members play different roles. Marketers are interested in finding out exactly the role played by individual members so that they can appropriately design their promotion strategy to suit these differing roles. Traditionally, it has been the wife's role to purchase food, clothing and other household sundries, while the husband played a dominant role in the purchase of automobiles and life insurance. But with the emergence of the working woman, these lines of traditional role demarcation have been getting increasingly blurred. Husbands now have to shoulder a greater part of the household duties while women are asserting themselves in areas so far treated as the husband's domain. Thus, the same decision, in different families may be made either by the husband or wife, or both may have an equal voice. Children are also beginning to exert their influence on the family's purchase decisions. This is especially true in case of products such as television, stereo music systems, records, personal computers, etc., where the children are likely to have more updated information about various brands and product attributes.

**Roles:** An individual may participate in many groups. His position within each group can be defined in terms of the activities he is expected to perform. You are probably a manager, and when in your work situation you play that role. However, at home you play the role of spouse and parent. Thus, in different social positions you play different roles. Each of these roles influences your purchase decisions.

As a manager, you would like to buy clothes which reflect your status within the organization, such as safari suit, three-piece suit, tie, leather shoes, etc. But at home where you are in a relaxed and informal situation you would prefer clothes which are comfortable rather than formal and you may wear shirts, jeans, kurta pajama, dhoti or shorts.

**Status:** Each role that a person plays has status, which is the relatively prestigious in society. Status is often measured by the degree of influence an individual exerts on the behaviour and attitude of others.

People buy and use products which reflect their status. The managing director of a company may drive a Mercedes to communicate his status in society. He may go to London or Switzerland for a holiday, rather than going to Shimla or Ooty.

**Group Norms:** The norms of a group are the implicit rules of conduct and behaviour that are expected of its member. For instance, in certain multinational companies in India, the norm for office wear includes a full-sleeved shirt and tie, notwithstanding the terrible heat conditions. If marketers can identify the various groups to which potential consumers belong, they can successfully market those products and services whose consumption is dictated by the group norms.

**PERSONAL FACTORS:** A consumer's purchase decisions are also affected by his personal characteristics such as age, sex, and stage in family lifecycle, education, occupation, income, life-style, his overall personality and overall self-concept. We shall now discuss some of the influences. The first factor influencing a buyer's decision is his age. The need for different products and services, changes with age. Babies and children have special needs for products such as milk powder, baby foods and toys. Young adults need clothes, recreational and educational facilities, transportation and a host of other age and fashion related consumption needs. There are certain physiological differences between men and women which result in their having different consumption needs. Their requirement of clothes and cosmetics is different from that of men. Each gender thus has its own need for specific products and services. Consumption behaviour is also influenced by the specific stage of the family life cycle. This family life cycle may be applicable in India only in the urban upper middle-classes.

**Education:** It widens a person's horizons, refines his tastes and makes his outlook more cosmopolitan. An educated person, as compared to less educated, is more likely to consume educational facilities, books, magazines and other knowledge-oriented products and services. For instance, in India, we find that educated families are more inclined towards adopting family planning than families which have no educational background.

**Occupation:** It also shapes the consumption needs. People following specialized occupations as photography, music, dance, carpentry, etc., need special tools and equipment. But, apart from this specific need, the status and role of a person within an organization affects his consumption behaviour. Chief executives would buy three-piece suits of the best fabric, handmade leather briefcase and use services of airlines and five-star hotels. A junior manager or blue-collar worker in the same organization may also buy a three-piece suit but he compromises on quality.

**Income:** The income which a person earns is an extremely important influence on his consumption behaviour. He may aspire to buy certain goods and services but his income may become a constraint. Income in this context really refers to the income available for spending (i.e., income after tax, provident fund and other statutory deductions). The person's attitude towards spending versus saving and his borrowing power are also important influencing factors. Small size packaging in sachets for products such as tea, shampoo, toothpaste are meant for the lower income customers who cannot afford a one time large outlay of money on such products. Products which are considered luxuries are more income sensitive than products which fall in the category of necessities. If marketers are marketing a luxury product then they must keep a close watch on income and saving trends to avoid decrease in sales resulting from recession. To avoid sales decline you may need to reposition the product, change the marketing mix or both.

**Personality:** Personality is the sum total of an individual's psychological traits, characteristics, motives, habits, attitudes, beliefs and outlooks. Personality is the very essence of individual differences. In consumer behaviour, personality is defined as those inner psychological characteristics that both determine and reflect how a person responds to his environmental stimuli. Personality is enduring and ensures that a person's responses are consistent over time.

There has been a great deal of research into the concept of personality with the objective of predicting consumer behaviour, in terms of product and brand choice. The assumption in all personality related research has been that different types of personalities can be classified and each type responds differently to the same stimuli, and personality can be used to identify and predict that response. In case of products such as cigarettes, beer and cars, personality has been used to segment the market. In contrast, surf detergent powder is promoted with the help of 'Lalitaji' — a middle-class traditional, forthright and objective housewife. These are just the right personality variables that would appeal to a potential customer of Surf. Personality research to predict consumer behaviour has either focused on total personality profile or a specific trait or attempted to find a correlation with product brand choice. But both these approaches assume that individuals with a given personality profile or trait are homogeneous in all other respects such as age, income, education, occupation, etc. We have seen how all these factors strongly influence a consumer's decisions. A much broader, more comprehensive approach for characterizing behavioural patterns is needed and this is provided by the concept of lifestyle.

**Lifestyle:** Lifestyles are defined as patterns in which people live, as expressed by the manner in which they spend money and time on various activities and interests. Lifestyle is a function of our motivations, learning, attitudes, beliefs and opinion, social class, demographic factors, personality, etc. It involves measuring consumers' responses to Activities, Interests and Opinions(AIO), along with collecting information on demographic factors. The different lifestyles are then used for market segmentation, product positioning and for developing promotional campaigns, including new products. Lifestyle is measured by a technique known as psychographics.

To get a good idea of marketing based on lifestyles, you only need to look at the promotional strategies of Garden Vareli, Raymonds and Dinesh Mill Textiles.

## Lifestyle Dimensions

| Activities | Interests | Opinions | Demographics |
|---|---|---|---|
| Work | Family | Themselves | Age |
| Hobbies | Home | Social issues | Education |
| Social | Job | Politics | Income |
| Vacation | Community | Business | Occupation |
| Entertainment | Recreation | Economics | Family size |
| Club Membership | Fashion | Education | Dwelling |
| Community | Food | Products | Geography |
| Shopping | Media | Future | City size |
| Sports | Achievements | Culture | Stage in life |

**PSYCHOLOGICAL FACTORS:** An individual buying decision is further influenced by psychological factors such as perception, motivation, learning, beliefs, and attitudes.

**Perception:** The major psychological factor that influences consumer behaviour is perception. Perception can be described as "how we see the world around us". All the time we are receiving messages through our five sense organs, *viz.*, eyes, ears, nose, mouth and skin. The different sights, sounds, smells, tastes and sensations that we feel are known as stimuli. Each person recognizes, selects, organizes and interprets these stimuli in his own individual manner based on his needs, values and expectations and this is known as perception. Since each individual's needs, motives and expectations are unique therefore each individual's perception is unique.

Perception helps to explain the phenomenon of why different individuals respond differently to the same stimulus under the same condition. As a marketing manager, we are providing stimulus to your consumers through the physical shape, colour, size, fragrance, and feel, taste of your product, its package, advertisements and commercials. Our interest is to understand why and what different types of perceptions are associated with each of the stimuli so that we can highlight that particular stimulus or combination of stimuli which evokes the most favourable perception in the maximum number of consumers. For example, generally consumers tend to perceive the quality of perfumes on the basis of package, brand name, price and manufacturer's image.

As a person involved in marketing, we would like to ensure that the stimuli which are provided are not ignored by the consumers, but rather they are recognized, interpreted and retained in the consumer memory. In this context, there are three aspects of perception which are of immediate interest to the marketer. These are selective exposure, selective distortion and selective retention.

**Selective Exposure:** If a person wants to purchase a specific product, be it camera, refrigerator, television or any other high value product or service, he comes across more than the usual number of advertisements pertaining to that specific product. People are more likely to notice stimuli which relate to their immediate needs. For the marketer, the implication is that he has to carefully and accurately identify his potential customers since other customers are not at all likely to notice the stimuli. Having identified the potential customers, the marketer has to ensure that the stimuli are interesting enough to attract and hold their attention.

**Selective Distortion:** If a person decided to purchase a specific brand 'X' of pressure cooker. Since the decision is already made the purchaser would seek only that information which reinforces the correctness of his decision.

If you hear some positive remarks made about brand 'X' you would tend to find some shortcoming or flaw in that brand, so that you do not feel that you have made a wrong decision by buying brand 'X'. When person attempt to fit information to suit his own ideas or personal meaning, the process is known as selective distortion. Thus, a marketer may find that his message is often not received in the intended manner but it is twisted in different ways by different consumers.

**Selective Retention:** People forget much of the stimuli which they receive and only retain that information which reinforces their values and decision. The person is more likely to remember the positive features of brand 'X' pressure cooker since they help reassure him that the decision which he made was correct.

**Motivations:** It is a driving force which leads to an action. We all have needs and we consume different goods and services with the expectation that they will help fulfils these needs. When a need is sufficiently pressing, it directs the person to seek its satisfaction. It is known as motive. All our needs can be classified into two categories — primary and secondary. Primary needs or motives are the physiological needs which we are born with, such as the need for air, water, food, clothing, shelter and sex. The secondary needs are our acquired needs which we have developed in response to the society and environment in which we live. The secondary needs are the result of the individuals' psychological make-up and his relationship with other members of the society. The secondary needs may include the need for power, prestige, esteem, affection, learning, status, etc. Clothing is a primary need for all of us; but the need for suit, or benarasee saree or silk patola are expressions of our acquired needs. The man wearing a suit may be seeking to fulfil his status need or his ego need by impressing his friends and family.

All human needs can be classified into five hierarchical categories and this hierarchy is universally applicable. The theory of hierarchy of needs was propounded by Abraham Maslow. According to Maslow's hierarchy all needs can be ranked in order of importance from the low biological needs to the higher level psychological needs. Each level of unfulfilled need motivates the individual's behaviour, and as each successive level of need is fulfilled people keep moving on to the next higher level of need. The different levels of needs have been depicted as being water tight compartments, but in reality there is always overlap amongst the different levels of needs, since no need is ever totally satisfied. There is always scope for further fulfilment.

Maslow's hierarchy of human needs helps us understand consumer motivations. It's useful for the marketer who can identify what generic level need his product is capable of fulfilling and accordingly position his product and back it up with relevant marketing inputs. Products such as food and clothing are bought to fulfils physiological needs; insurance, burglar alarms, security services are purchased because they fulfils safety needs; most personal care products such as soap, toothpaste, shaving cream, perfume are bought primarily because they serve social needs, and luxury products such as jewellery, expensive clothing, fancy house and cars are bought mainly to serve ego and self-actualization needs. The same product can be sold to entirely distinct customer segments provided the marketer can correctly identify the need which the product is fulfilling. For instance, a bicycle may be bought by different customer segments for entirely different reasons. One segment may buy to use it as a means of commuting. For another segment, a bicycle serves a recreational/leisure need while for a third segment, it fulfils the need of a health aid. Still another customer segment buys a bicycle for converting into a rickshaw or bicycle cart for selling fruits, vegetables, etc. A bicycle is also purchased for use in competitive sport.

**Learning:** Learning refers to the skill and knowledge gained from past experience which we apply to evaluate future decisions and situations. A marketer can build-up demand for his brand by associating it with strong motives, using the appropriate stimuli and cues and providing positive reinforcement, thus making the consumer 'learn' that the brand is good and worth patronizing.

Much of an adult's human behaviour is learned behaviour. This is a very significant fact for marketers, because it implies that consumers can be made to learn the desired behaviour through interplay of motives, stimuli, cues, responses and reinforcements. A housewife has the need for cutting down the time she spends for cooking in the kitchen. When this need is strong enough to propel her to take action it becomes a motive. The motive is directed towards the stimulus object — a pressure cooker. The stimuli are the various advertisements about the product which she sees and hears. Cues are minor stimuli that determine when, where and how the housewife responds. Positive feedback about pressure cooker from a friend, seeing it on display in a show-window, a special introductory price offer is all examples of cues which influence a housewife's response to the motive for buying a pressure cooker. Suppose the housewife buys the pressure cooker and is satisfied with its performance, then the chances are that she would like to use it as often as possible, and in the future may buy another one. The housewife's response to pressure cookers has been reinforced. At some later stage, the same housewife wants to buy an electric oven. Since she has had a positive experience with brand 'A pressure cooker, she may infer that the company manufacturing brand 'A' also makes good electric ovens and choose it over other brands. This is known as 'generalization' of response.

**Beliefs and Attitudes:** A belief is a descriptive thought that a person has about something. A person may believe that a certain cooking oil 'X' has the lowest fat content and is best for health. The beliefs constitute the brand image, and if the customer has the wrong beliefs he is likely to generate a negative image about the brand. The marketer must ensure that consumers have all relevant and correct information about the brand to facilitate formation of a positive brand image. This belief may be based on some real facts or it may merely be a notion or opinion that the person has. The belief that the customer has about a brand is important because it determines his behaviour towards buying and using it. Attitude is a person's enduring feeling, evaluation and tendency towards a particular idea or object. Starting from childhood, attitudes develop over the time with each fresh knowledge input, experience and influence. Attitudes get settled into specific patterns and are difficult to change. It is easier to market a product which fits in well with the existing patterns of attitudes rather than change the attitudes to fit a new product concept.

## SUMMARY

The study of consumer behaviour also provides an insight into how consumers arrive at the purchase decision and the variable which influences their decision. Once the influencing variables have been identified, the marketer can manipulate them so as to induce in his consumers a positive purchase decision.

If the marketer can correctly identify those stimuli that evoke a positive response in the consumer he can very easily design effective marketing strategies using these stimuli. A consumer's decision to purchase a product is influenced by a number of variables which can be classified into four categories, namely — psychological, personal, social, and cultural. Consumer behaviour is the study of why, how, what, when, where, and how often do consumers buy and consume different products and services. Knowledge of consumer behaviour is helpful to the marketer in understanding the needs of his different consumer segments and developing appropriate marketing strategies for each. It is also useful for the marketer in developing an understanding of, how consumers respond to the various marketing stimuli, which he provides in terms of the product, price, promotion and place. Man is a many faceted, complex psychological being. His consumer behaviour is influenced by his motives, perceptions, attitudes and learning. Each of these psychological factors provides a unique mental framework for each consumer within which he makes his purchase decisions. For the marketer it is essential to associate his product with the motives and positive perceptions of his consumers. Also he must ensure that the product concept fits in with the consumer's existing attitudes and beliefs.

Consumers differ from one another in terms of their sex, age, education, income, family lifecycle stage, personality and life style, and other personal characteristics which influence their buying behaviour. The needs of elderly consumers are different from those of young consumers. Newly married couples have needs which are totally different from older retired married couples. To successfully market to consumers with differing personal characteristics, the marketer must accordingly modify his marketing strategies.

Man is a social animal and is influenced by the people with whom he interacts. Each person interacts with and is a member of many groups. These groups provide a point of reference or comparison for the consumer and are known as reference groups and strongly affect his product and brand choices. Amongst the various groups such as family, friends, social organizations, professional associations, the strongest influence is exerted by the family.

Culture is the most pervasive influence on our lives and influences all aspects of our behaviour; consumers operate within the cultural framework of their society and purchase only those products which fit in with their cultural norms. Within each culture there exist many subcultures comprising distinct nationality groups, religious groups, racial groups, geographic groups that have their own unique values and lifestyle. Social classes are group of people who have similar income, education, and wealth, social-status, value and beliefs. The marketer must understand that people with different cultural, subcultural and social class background have different product and brand preferences and need suitably modified products and marketing strategies.

## CASELET 1

XYZ company operates a web filter service for public schools and libraries to protect students from inappropriate material on the internet. Like the industry as a whole; the company's market share has been stagnant for the past two years. Looking for new sources of revenue, the company is considering selling the data, it has collected from students surfing habits to marketers trying to learn more about students' behaviour on the web. The data is anonymous but privacy advocates are concerned about the precedent of selling information about children to marketers.

### Questions

1. What should XYZ do? Should it protect the students' data, or should it create an opportunity to create new revenues?
2. What else a company can do to increase its market share?

## ........ QUESTIONS FOR DISCUSSION

1. Explain the important steps in buying process.
2. Discuss the significance of need arousal and post-purchase behaviour of a buyer, with suitable example.
3. Discuss the important steps in buying process.
4. Explain: (i) evaluation of alternatives (ii) post-purchase feeling as a step in the buying process.

## Objective Questions

### State Whether the Following Statement is True/False.

1. The buying process starts when a customer recognizes a need.
2. The person who purchases the product is not always the user.
3. Consumer interprets the information that supports their preconception.
4. Reference groups influences buying decision.

*Ans:* **1.** True, **2.** True, **3.** True, **4.** True.

### Fill in the Blank

1. ______ group consist of those groups that have a direct or indirect influence on the persons attitude and behaviour.
2. _________ is a complex mental picture of us.
3. A group to which a person would like to belong is called __________.
4. __________consist of activities that a person is expected to perform according to the person around him/her.
5. A __________ is one whose values or behaviour an individual rejects.
6. The person within the group who exerts, influence and transmit information is known as the ____.
7. ______ is a process whereby, the individual interacts with his/her environment for the purpose of making marketplace decision on product/services.
8. ______ is relatively homogeneous divisions in a society having similar values, interests and behaviour.
9. ______ is a person's pattern of living in the world as expressed in his activities, interests and opinion.
10. ______ is a process in which an individual selects, organises and interprets information inputs to create a meaningful picture of the world.
11. A relatively permanent change in a behaviour as a result of experience is called as _______.
12. ______ is a descriptive thought that a person holds about something.
13. ______ is a person's favourable or unfavourable evaluations and tendencies towards some object or idea.
14. _______ developed a two factor theory of motivation.

*Ans:* **1.** Reference, **2.** Self-concept, **3.** aspirational group, **4.** Role, **5.** dissociative group, **6.** opinion leader, **7.** Consumer behaviour, **8.** Social class, **9.** Lifestyle, **10.** Perception, **11.** Learning, **12.** Belief, **13.** Attitude, **14.** Frederick Hertzberg.

☺ ☺ ☺

CHAPTER 10

# Channels of Distribution

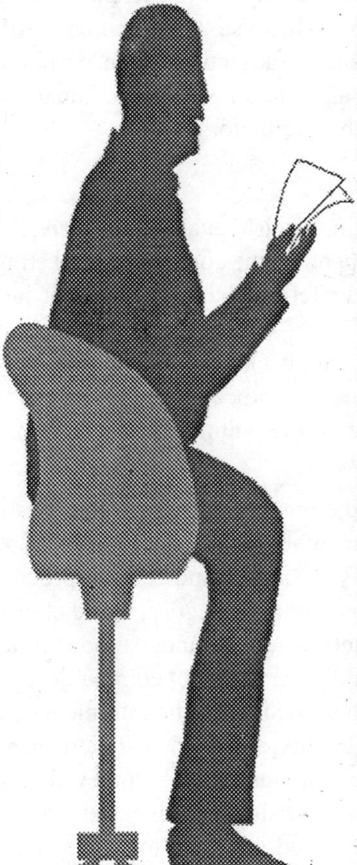

## LEARNING OBJECTIVES

- *Channels of Distribution: An Introduction*
- *Types of Intermediaries/Channels*
- *Importance of Channels*
- *Channel Development*
- *The Role of Marketing Channels: Channels Functions, Channel Flows and Channel Levels*
- *Channel Design Decisions*

## TYPES OF INTERMEDIARIES/CHANNELS

Intermediaries can be broadly categorized in three categories as follows, on the basis of the criteria like ownership rights and the possession of the goods.

- **Merchants:** These are the intermediaries who take title to the merchandise and resell the merchandise, generally having the physical possession of the goods. Some of these types of intermediaries are wholesalers and retailers. They sell the merchandise and earn profit.
- **Agents:** These are the intermediaries, sales agents, brokers, auctioneers, etc., who may have the possession of the goods or may not have the possession of the goods, but in no case will have the title to the merchandise. They are the intermediaries who search for buyer and seller together, bring buyer and seller together or may negotiate the sale transaction on behalf of the seller.
- **Facilitators:** These are the intermediaries who assist in the distribution process of the merchandise. In this process, they may have physical possession of the merchandise in certain cases or may not have physical possession of the merchandise, but in no case will have title to the merchandise or negotiate purchase or sales transaction. Transportation companies, independent warehouses, banks, advertising agencies, insurance companies, etc., are some of the intermediaries in the category of the facilitators.

### The Importance of Channels

A marketing channel system decisions affects the other marketing decisions also, and therefore are among the most critical decisions. Channel choices themselves depend on the company's marketing strategy with respect to segmentation, targeting, and positioning. Marketing channels must not just see markets but they must also make markets as one of the chief roles of marketing channels is to convert potential buyers into profitable customers. In addition channel decisions include relatively long-term commitments with other firms as well as a set of policies and procedures. Marketers in the present dynamic market should adopt the holistic perspective and ensure that marketing decisions in all these different areas are made to collectively maximize value.

In managing the intermediaries, the firm must also decide on the emphasis given to the 'push' versus 'pull' marketing strategy. A 'push' strategy uses the manufacturer's sales force, trade promotional money, or other means to induce intermediaries to carry, promote, and sell the product to end-users. This strategy is appropriate where there is low brand loyalty in a category, brand choice is made in the store, the product is an impulse item, and product benefits are well understood. While, in the 'pull' strategy the manufacturer uses advertising, promotion, and other forms of communication to persuade consumers to demand the product from intermediaries, thereby, induce the intermediaries to order it. 'Pull' strategy is appropriate when there is high brand loyalty and high involvement in the category, when consumers are able to perceive differences between brands, and when they choose the brand before they go to the store. Marketing activities directed towards the channel as part of 'push' strategy are more effective when accompanied by a well-designed and well-executed 'pull' strategy that activates consumer demand. On the other hand, without at least some consumer interest, it can be very difficult to gain much channel acceptance and support.

## Channel Development

Any new firm generally starts the local operation of selling the merchandise in a fairly limited market, using existing intermediaries. The number of such intermediaries is usually limited to the few manufacturers' sales agents, a few wholesalers, several established retailers, a few trucking companies, and a few warehouses. For such firms, deciding the best channels might not be a problem but the problem is faced in convincing the available intermediaries to carry and handle the firm's merchandise line. Thus, the success of the firms on this front would assist the firm to determine whether the firm might branch into new markets and use different channels in different markets. The variety of the channels to be adopted by the firm may gradually change from one market to the other, from one locality to the other, from one product category to the other product category, from one country to the other country. The firm might sell directly to retailers in smaller markets and through distributors in larger markets. The firm in rural areas, might work with general goods merchants while deal with limited-line merchants in urban areas. In one part of the country, it might grant exclusive franchises; in another, it might sell through all outlets willing to handle the merchandise. In one country, it might use international sales agents; in another, it might partner with a local firm. For the international players, the criticality of the decision increases as the shopping habits of the customers' vary by countries. Many retailers channel design illustrated that exemplifies the same. Retailers, namely, Germany's Aldi, the United Kingdom's Tesco, and Spain's Zara, while entering in the new market have redefined their channel distribution strategy to certain extent, enabling better tailoring of their image to local needs and wants. While, there are also the retailers in the global market who have largely stuck to the same selling formula irrespective of the geographical differences, although have sometimes encountered trouble in entering new markets such as Eddie Bauer, Marks & Spencer, and Wal-Mart. Thus, the channel system of any firm evolves as a function of local opportunities and conditions, emerging threats and opportunities, company resources and capabilities, and other factors.

Many companies in the present scenario have started using such hybrid channels, with many successful companies multiplying the number of 'go-to-market" or hybrid channels in any one market area. The company, while adopting hybrid channels must assure its effective working all together and whether it matches with each target customer's preferred ways of doing business. The features of the channel system sufficing the channel integration expectation of the customers are as mentioned below:

- the ability to order a product online and pick it up at a convenient retail location;
- the ability to return an online-ordered product to a nearby store of the retailer;
- the right to receive discounts and promotional offers based on total online and offline purchases, etc.

To illustrate, ICICI Bank targets four different kinds of market segments in rural markets, namely, rich, small and medium enterprises, the middle-class, and the low-income group, for which the ICICI Bank uses a combination of hybrid channels such as branches, franchisees, kiosks, and microfinance institutions.

Also, the channel design system of HP company exemplifies the same. It has used its sales force to sell to the large accounts, outbound telemarketing to sell to medium-sized accounts, direct mail with an inbound number to sell to small accounts, retailers to sell to still smaller accounts, and the internet to sell specialty items. Also in order to tap its staples' markets it has used its traditional retail channel as well as other mediums like direct-response internet site, virtual malls, and thousands of links on affiliated sites are also used by this company.

## THE ROLE OF MARKETING CHANNELS: CHANNELS FUNCTIONS, CHANNEL FLOWS AND CHANNEL LEVELS

Producers or manufacturers delegate some of the selling job related to the produced merchandise to the various types of intermediaries enabling the producers to gain effectiveness and efficiency. Delegation refers to the "relinquishing some control over how and to whom the products are sold". The key role of the marketing channel is to perform the work of moving goods from producers to consumers. The intermediaries with their contacts, experience, specialization, and scale of operation makes possible the wide availability and accessibility of the merchandise to the target markets. Moreover, it also overcomes the time, place, and possession gaps that separate goods and services from those who need or want them. Thus, the various functions performed by the intermediaries offer the firm the synergistic effect, i.e., actually more than the manufacturers and producers can achieve independently. The key functions performed by the various categories of intermediaries are explained below:

### I. Functions of Intermediaries

- **Information:** Intermediaries like merchants and agents gather various information about potential and current customers, competitors, and other actors and forces in the marketing environment that are of crucial importance to the producers and suppliers of the various products. This information is also of equal importance and sought by the potential consumers of the target markets, which in the absence of the intermediaries would become hectic session of the information surfing for the particular product and product-related information.

- **Disseminating:** The intermediaries not only gather the information but also develop and disseminate such persuasive communications to stimulate purchasing to the other interested groups, ultimately serving the purpose of being the intermediaries and collecting the information. Ultimately, gathering of the information accomplishes its purpose of meeting the sales target of the merchandise, if and when the related information is disseminated as and when sought for by the sources authorized for such information flow.

- **Negotiating:** The role of the intermediaries like agents and auctioneers is to finalize the sale transaction by negotiating on the price and other related terms obstructing the finalization of the sale transaction, thus, assist the actual transfer of ownership or possession as the case may be.

- **Ordering:** Intermediaries, wholesalers and retailers do purchase the merchandise from the manufacturers in bulk and small quantity respectively, and resell the produces to the potential consumers of the target markets. With this service provided by the intermediaries, it also assists the potential consumers to avail and access the product required, without placing the purchase orders directly with the manufacturers.

- **Financing:** Intermediaries, like wholesalers also acquire the funds required to finance inventories at different levels in the marketing channel, through the banks and other financial institutions, for the purchasing of the produces.

- **Risk:** The intermediaries like, insurance companies, banks, del credere agents and others do assume the risks involved in the distribution of the products from the particular destination or party to the another destination or party in the flow of the movement of the produces ultimately. Thus, intermediaries smooth the flow of the merchandise by controlling the degree of the uncertainty involved in the distribution.
- **Storing:** The intermediaries desiring to stock the produces in bulk necessarily have to be equipped by well structured warehouses. The intermediaries should assure the successive storage and movement of the physical products, for which various wholesalers as well as the independent warehouses perform an active function for the same.
- **Payment:** Various banks and financial institutions enable making the payment of the bills and movement of the currencies from one party to the other. Not only the aforementioned intermediaries, but also some of the wholesalers, assist the purchase/sale transaction, by providing the credit facilities and the instalment mode of the making the payments to the buyers by the manufacturers, or wholesalers or the retailers or the end-users.
- **Title:** The final stage of movement of the goods is from the manufacturer to the end-user, i.e., through the transfer of the ownership rights from the purchaser to the buyer, the end-user. The final destination of the transfer of the title to the goods and the obstacles in the movement of the goods are thereby are streamlined to oversee actual transfer of ownership from one organization or person to another.

## II. Channel Flows

The various key functions performed by the different intermediaries, constitute the different flow of the constituents of the sale transaction as well as the produces. In all, it results into forward flow, backward flow as well as the two-way flow. Backward flow refers to flow of activity from customers to the company while forward flow refer to the flow of the activity from company to the customer and, the two-way flow refer to the flow of activity from both the directions, i.e., from company to customer as well as from customer to company.

The functions, namely, physical, title and promotion constitutes a forward flow of activity from the company to the customer, while some other functions, namely, ordering and payment, constitute a backward flow from customers to the company, and the functions, information, negotiation, finance, and risk taking, occurs in both the directions. These flows can be understood individually and not from just one diagram as it increases complexity. These five flows are diagrammatically represented below:

### 1. Physical Flow

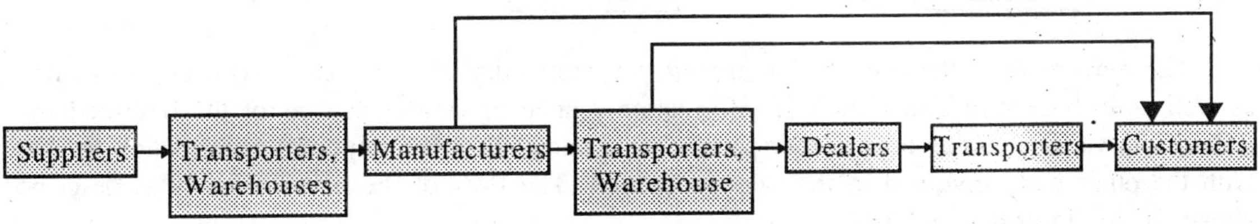


A manufacturer selling the physical goods will require at least the above mentioned three to four intermediaries. As it is not possible to move the physical goods from one place to another without the support of any transportation services, the role of this intermediary is mentioned in the physical flow of the goods at all the points wherever the movement of the physical possession of the goods is involved. Also, generally, the goods physically from the suppliers, through transportation to the manufacturers, get it processed, move from the manufacturers as the finished products through transportation and warehouses services to the dealers, who further moves the same to the customer, again through the transportation services. This is the forward flow of the activity as described in the diagram of the 'Physical Flow' above.

### 2. Title Flow

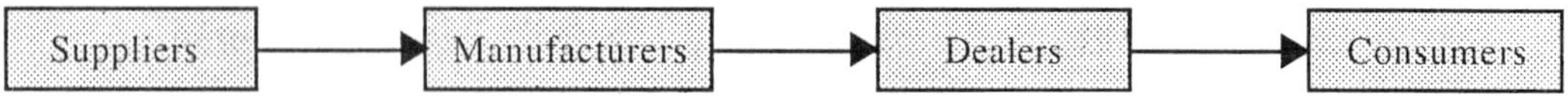


When the goods move physically from one party to another, it is not necessarily that this physical movement of the goods is accompanied by the movement of the title of the goods. The title of the goods is moved when the goods are purchased by one party to another party that is from suppliers to the manufacturer, from manufacturer to dealers and dealers to the customers. The other intermediaries like transporters and warehouses as mentioned in the physical flow, may possess the goods physically but in no case will have the ownership rights on those goods. The title flow is as described above in the diagram 'title flow', which is the forward movement of the activity.

### 3. Payment Flow

The movement of the goods physically involves various parties, intermediaries in the activity, but the 'payment flow' moves among the parties involved in the movement of the title to the goods, connecting each party with the other through the flow of the payment with the help of the banking services. Here, the payment flow refers only to the movement of the payment among the parties having the right to the ownership to the distribution of the goods. The 'Payment Flow' is as described above in the diagram, which is the backward flow of the activity.

### 4. Information Flow

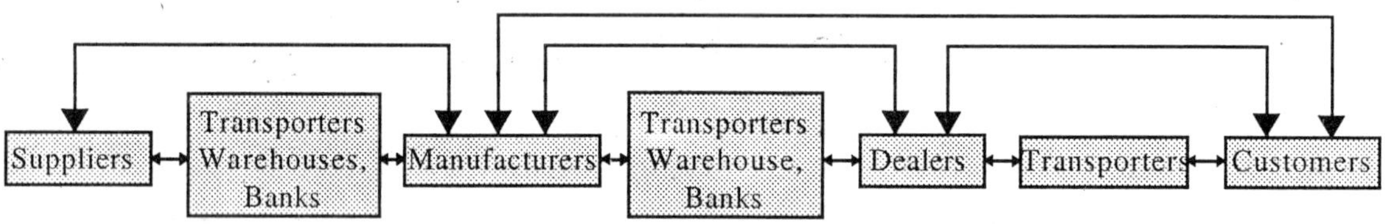


The movement of the information among the intermediaries flows two ways, i.e., in forward as well as in backward direction. The information related to various aspects of the intermediaries flows from various parties to the other parties, each party has some important information to share with the other party involved in the sale transaction. The flow of the information is as described above in the 'Information Flow'.

**5. Promotion Flow**

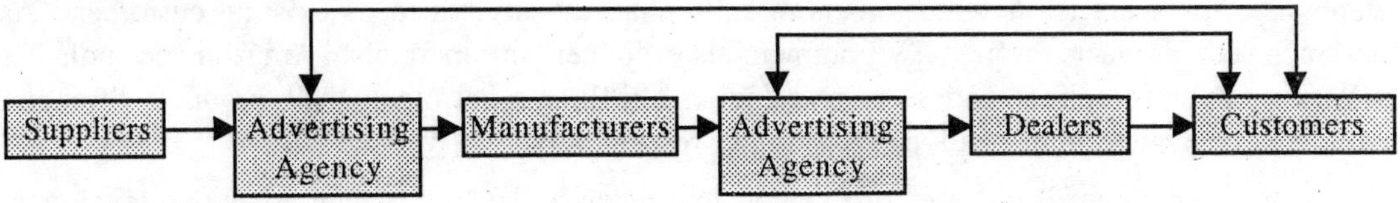


The manufacturer often undertakes various promotional efforts to promote the produces in the market, attracting a large number of the potential consumers by attracting large number of the middlemen to make product available to the end-users. The manufacturer may adopt the **'Push Strategy'** or the **'Pull Strategy'**. Push strategy of the promotion refers to the influencing and persuading the middlemen to carry the company's product, to carry more of the company's product, thus safeguarding the shelf-space for the company's products. While, 'Pull Strategy' focuses on the first level communication about the product-related information and promotional campaigns directly to the customer, and the customers themselves inquire about the product with the dealers for its purchase. The same idea of the varied promotional strategies, with the help of the services of the advertising agencies as practised is described in the diagram above, 'Promotion Flow'.

Channels normally describe a forward movement of products from source to user, but there are also reverse-flow channels. These are important in the following cases: (1) to reuse products or containers (such as refillable chemical – carrying drums); (2) to refurbish products (such as circuit boards or computers) for resale; (3) to recycle products (such as paper); and (4) to dispose of products and packaging (waste products). Several intermediaries play a role in reverse-flow channels, including manufacturers' redemption centres, community groups, and traditional intermediaries such as softdrink intermediaries, trash-collection specialists, recycling centers, trash-recycling brokers, and central processing warehouse.

A manufacturer selling a physical product and services might require three channels: a sales channel, a delivery channel, and a service channel. Some of the common features in various functions of the channels are that, they use up scarce resources, their performance can be enhanced by specialization and they can be shifted among the other channel members. Moreover, the producer's cost and prices are lower when some functions of the intermediaries are shifted by the manufacturers, but the intermediary does adds a charge to cover its work, as applicable. When, in case, the intermediaries are more efficient than the manufacturer, prices to the consumers are lower, generally. Also, in case, where consumers perform some functions themselves, they should be provided an opportunity to enjoy even lower prices. Thus, changes in channel institutions largely reflect the discovery of more efficient ways to combine or separate the economic functions providing assortments of goods to target customers.

## III. Channel Levels

The producer and the final customer are part of every channel. We will use the number of intermediary levels to designate the length of a channel. In the figure below, several consumer-goods marketing channels of different lengths are mentioned.

A zero-level channel (also called a direct marketing channel) consists of a manufacturer selling directly to the final customer. The major examples are door-to-door sales, home parties, mail order, telemarketing, TV selling, internet selling, and manufacturer-owned stores, Eureka Forbes sales representatives sell their products door-to-door; Tupperware representatives sell kitchen goods through home parties; Otto Burlington sells its products through mail order; ICICI Bank uses the telephone to prospect for new customers or sell enhanced services to its existing customers; Asian Sky Shop sells products through TV commercials or longer "infomercials"; Amazon and India Times sell their products online; and Bata and Indian Oil/Bharat Petroleum sell products through the manufacturer-owned stores and petrol pumps, respectively.

A one-level channel contains one selling intermediary, such as a retailer. A two-level channel contains two intermediaries. In consumer markets, these are typically a wholesaler and a retailer. A three-level channel contains three intermediaries.

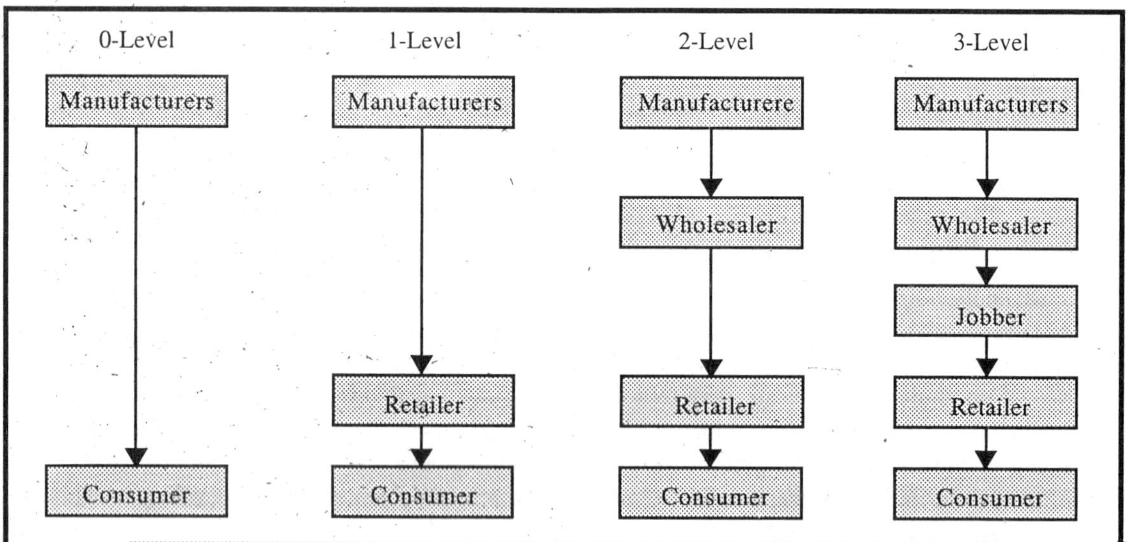


*Fig. 10.1(a): Consumer Marketing Channels*

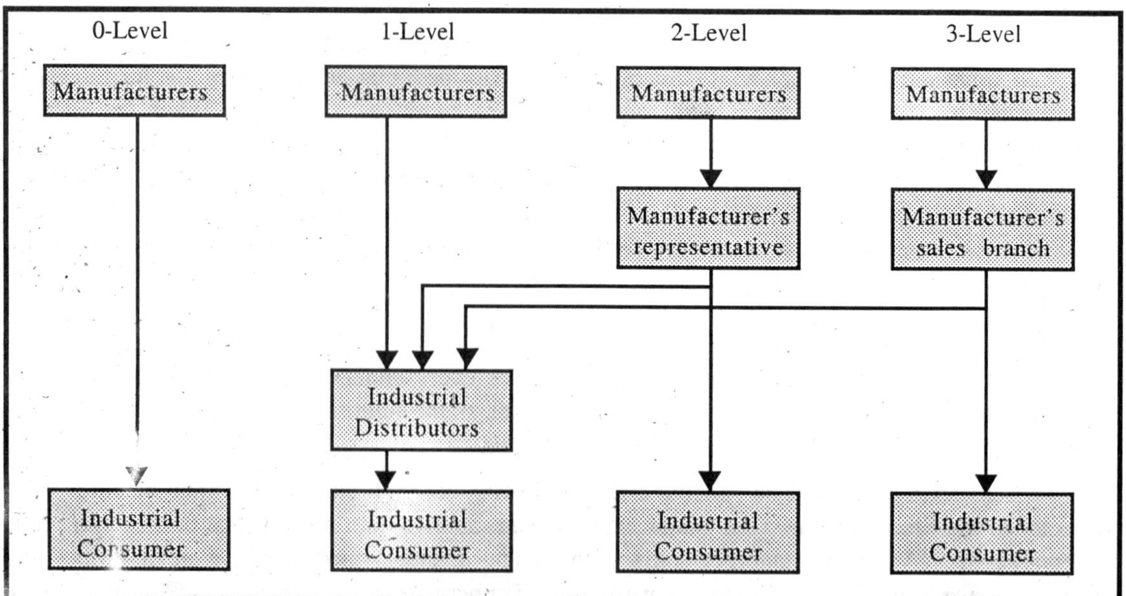


*Fig. 10.1(b): Industrial Marketing Channels*

Figure (b) shows channels commonly used in B2B (Business-to-Business) marketing. An industrial-goods remanufacturer can use its sales force to sell directly to industrial customers; or it can sell to industrial distributors, who sell to the industrial customers; or it can sell through manufacturer's representatives or its own sales branches directly to industrial customers, or indirectly to industrial customers through industrial distributors. Zero-, one-, and two-level marketing channels are quite common.

### Service Sector Channels

Marketing channels are not limited to the distribution of physical goods. Producers of services and ideas also face the problem of making their output available and accessible to target populations. For example, schools develop "educational-dissemination systems" and hospitals develop "health-delivery systems", thus, figuring out agencies and locations for reaching the population, spread out over an area. Marketing channels also keep changing in personal marketing. Besides live and programmed entertainment, entertainers, musicians, and other artists can reach prospective and existing fans online in many ways, by creating their own websites, social community sites such as MySpace, and third-party websites. Service industries such as banking, insurance, travel, and stock buying and selling are enriched and operating with the new channels, and the development of internet and other advance technologies.

## CHANNEL DESIGN DECISIONS

Whether to select a channel for making the product available to the end-user is not a question for the marketing activity of any marketer, but how should this channel be organized and what should be this channel system, comprising of how many number of intermediaries to meet the customers' desired service output levels, and degree of terms and conditions involved in the contract agreement, formally or informally with the various decisions, are the effort worth to be analyzed by the marketer while designing the marketing mix strategy, thereby, performing the marketing activities. Among the various considerations for designing a marketing channel system, Analyzing Customer Needs, Establishing Channel Objectives, Identifying Major Channel Alternatives and Evaluating the Major Channel Alternatives are the crucial decisions to be taken by any marketer. The steps for channel design decisions are explained below:

**1. Analyzing Customers' Desired Service Output Levels:** Channels or the intermediaries are basically making the desired product available to the consumer conveniently, in the expected quantity, at expected price, out of the maximum possible product varieties and so on. The ultimate objective of the channel is met by the marketer only if the expectations of the desired output levels of the intermediaries by the customers are accomplished. Thus, marketers must design the marketing channel after understanding the service output levels desired by the target customers. The five service outputs as produced by the channels are explained below:

(a) ***Lot Size:*** It refers to the number of units of the particular product item permitted by the channel to a typical customer to purchase on one occasion. Thus, it provides the customers with an opportunity to purchase the product in lot size as desired by the customers.

(b) ***Waiting and Delivery Time:*** The general common characteristic of all the customers is that they increasingly prefer faster and faster delivery channels, with minimum waiting time for the receipt of the goods. One of the purpose of using the services of the intermediary is delivering convenience in the product acquisition/purchase by the customer, however, is highlighted here.

*(c)* ***Spatial Convenience:*** It refers to the expansion of the intermediaries substantially and thereby increasing the distribution outlets of the company and the reach of the products of the company. To illustrate, Bata and Exide Batteries, in the last few years have increased their distribution outlets by expanding their intermediaries substantially to access the products of the company.

*(d)* ***Product Variety:*** It refers to the product assortment breadth provided by the marketing channel. Customers prefer to purchase from the channel having the wide product assortment providing the wide product choice to the customers, as more choices increase the chance of finding what they need.

*(e)* ***Service Backup:*** It refers to the add-on services, like, credit, delivery installation, repairs, etc., provided by the channel. The greater the service backup, the greater the work provided by the channel. For customers of certain products like, vehicles, electrical products and gadgets, the add-on services are inevitable. Also, the provision of such add-on services by the intermediaries maintains and enable in sustaining the functional performance of the product.

But, the designer of the marketing channel that provides greater service outputs is accompanied by the increasing channel costs, resulting into rise in the price for the customers. The marketer considering the varied services output levels of the target customers should not ignore the other side of coin that different customers have different service needs. To illustrate, the success of discount stores indicate that many consumers are willing to accept smaller service outputs if they can save money.

**2. Establishing Objectives and Constraints:** The targeted service output levels by the marketers are stated in the form of the channel objectives by the marketers. But at the same time, the companies should also have clear outline of the limitations or the constraints to accomplish the predetermined objectives. For any marketer, whatsoever be the competitive conditions, the channel institutions that provide desired levels of service outputs without compromising their functional tasks to minimize total channel costs, remains the sole important objective for designing channel design system.

Channel objectives vary with product characteristics like; perish ability; bulky products; standardized and non-standardized products; installation and maintenance services and high-unit-value products. To state, perishable products require more direct marketing, while for the bulky products, such as building materials, require channels that minimize the shipping distance and the amount of handling. For the products that are non-standardized, such as custom-built machinery and specialized-business forms, are generally sold directly by company sales representatives, while the products requiring installation or maintenance services such as heating and cooling systems, are usually sold and maintained by the company or by franchised dealers. Certain high-unit-value products, such as generators and turbines, are often sold through a company sales force rather than intermediaries.

Also, the channel objectives by the marketers must be adapted by considering the larger marketing environment which also affects the channel objective consideration. During the depressed economic conditions, producers usually opt to move their goods to market using shorter channels with reduced or without services, and thus reducing the final price of the goods. Legal regulators and restrictions also affect channel design. In most countries, the law looks unfavourably on channel arrangements that substantially lessen competition or create a monopoly.

A number of other factors that affects channel objectives are the competitors' characteristics, intermediaries' characteristics, legal characteristics, country's characteristics as well as the company characteristics as a whole with the products' characteristics affects the channel objectives selection.

**3. Identifying and Evaluating Major Channel Alternatives:** Companies can choose from a wide variety of channels for reaching customers, namely, sales forces; agents; distributors; dealers; direct mail; telemarketing and the internet. Each channel has some strengths as well as weaknesses. To illustrate, to handle complex product characteristics and transactions, sales forces are very suitable, but they are expensive as compared to the internet, which is much less expensive but is not as effective as the other complex products. On the other side, the company gains sales by using the services of the distributors, but at the cost of losing the direct contact with the customers. While, manufacturers' representatives are able to contact customers at a low cost per customer as the cost is shared by the several clients, but in this type of the channel alternative the selling effort per customer is less intense as compared to that made by the company sales representatives.

With most companies using the hybrid channels, the problem has become more complex as the underlining idea is that each channel reaches a different segment of buyers and delivers the right products at the least cost but, the failure of this objective, in any case, results into channel conflict and excessive cost.

A channel alternative is described by three elements: the types of available business intermediaries, the number of intermediaries needed, and the terms and responsibilities of each channel member.

## A. Types of Intermediaries

Various types of intermediaries are identified by the firm to carry-out its channel work, both the common traditional intermediaries adopted by most of the similar product supplying companies as well as the modern innovative channels. To illustrate, direct distribution by the use of mobile vans by the state government was made to make the subsidized foodgrains available to the remote villages, which was later altered slightly with the help of the available insight on tribal customer buying behaviour, these vans started distributing foodgrains by visiting periodic markets (hoofs), and agricultural markets (mandis) with a substantial reduction in the distribution costs. Other such innovative marketing channels are, India Times webmarketing site and ITC's e-Choupal. Sometimes, a company opts for the new or unconventional channel as the company experiences difficulty, or increased cost, or ineffectiveness of working with the dominant channel. By introducing and following the innovative channel for distribution the company enjoys the advantage of the facing less competition in the initial phase of distribution through such an innovative channel of distribution. In India, direct selling of vacuum cleaners and Aqua Guard water purifiers by Eureka Forbes exemplifies the same.

## B. Number of Intermediaries

There are three strategies available for the companies to take decisions on the use of a number of intermediaries at each channel level, namely, exclusive distribution, selective distribution, and intensive distribution. Each of these strategies describes the total number of intermediaries set by the marketers/company through which the product or the merchandise is to be made available to the customers. These strategies are explained below:

**Exclusive Distribution:** It refers to the strategy of the company to severely limit or restrict the number of intermediaries. When the producer wants to maintain control over the service level and outputs offered by the resellers, exclusive distribution strategy is appropriate. Thus, the producer hopes to obtain more dedicated and knowledgeable selling from the intermediaries by granting exclusive distribution strategy. Exclusive deals between suppliers and retailers are becoming a mainstay for specialists looking for an edge in a business world that is increasingly driven by price. It includes exclusive dealing arrangements and therefore, considerable closer partnership between seller and reseller is inevitable in this type of distribution strategy. This type of strategy is generally suitable in the distribution of new automobiles, some major appliances, and some women's apparel brands. When the legendary Italian designer label Gucci realized about its stained image severely due to overexposure from licensing and discount stores, it decided to end contracts with third-party suppliers, control its distribution, and open its own stores to bring back some of the lustre, exemplifies the shift to the exclusive distribution strategy.

**Selective Distribution:** It refers to the strategy of the company, whereby, a company relies on more than a few but less than all of the intermediaries willing to carry a particular product. It is suitable for established companies and for those new companies seeking distributors. The company does not have to experience panic of managing too many outlets; and can successfully gain adequate market coverage with more control and less cost as compared to the intensive distribution.

**Intensive Distribution:** It refers to the placing of the goods or services in as many outlets as possible by the manufacturer. This strategy is generally used for items such as snack foods, soft drinks, newspapers, candies and gum, products the consumer seeks to buy frequently or in a variety of locations. For example, Western Union in Pakistan has outlets throughout the country. Another example is Titan watches in India sells its watches through seven different channels, namely, World of Titan, Time Zone, Valuemart outlets, Sonata stores, Titan Signet Club, Tanishq boutiques, and private mustier and outlets. These channels — some of which are only present in selected cities provide Titan with a wide coverage, cover different price points, and target different segments of customers. It helps Titan generate sales volume while protecting its brand image at the same time.

Manufacturers are constantly tempted to move from exclusive or selective distribution to more intensive distribution to increase coverage and sales. This strategy may help in the short-term, but it can hurt long-term performance. Intensive distribution increases product and service availability but and also encourage retailers to compete aggressively. Price wars can then erode profitability, potentially dampening retailer interest in supporting the product and harming brand equity. Some firms avoid intensive distribution and do not want to be sold everywhere.

## C. Terms and Responsibilities of Channel Members

Each channel member must be treated respectfully and given the opportunity to be profitable. The main elements in the "trade-relations mix" are price policies, conditions of sale, territorial rights, and specific services to be performed by each party.

(i) **Price Policy:** It refers to the establishing of the price list and schedule of discounts and allowances that intermediaries see as equitable and sufficient by the producer.

(ii) **Conditions of Sale:** It refers to the payment terms and producer guarantees. Most producers grant cash discounts to distributors for early payment, or a guarantee against defective merchandise or price declines. Such type of guarantee against price declines gives distributors an incentive to buy larger quantities.

(iii) **Distributors' Territorial Rights:** It defines the distributors' territories and the terms under which the producer will enfranchise other distributors. Normally, distributors expect to receive full credit for all sales in their territory, whether or not they did the selling. Also, in the franchised and the exclusive-agency channels, mutual services and responsibilities must be spelled out very carefully. To illustrate, McDonald's provides franchisees with a building, promotional support, a recordkeeping system, training, and general administrative and technical assistance. In turn, franchisees are expected to satisfy company standards for the physical facilities, cooperate with new promotional programmes, furnish requested information, and buy supplies from specified vendors.

## 1. Evaluating the Major Alternatives

Each channel alternative needs to be evaluated against economic, control, and adaptive criteria.

**Economic Criteria:** Each channel alternative will produce a different level of sales and costs. Firms will try to align customers and channels to maximize demand at the lowest overall cost. Clearly, sellers try to replace high-cost channels with low-cost channels as long as the value added per sale is sufficient. As an example of an economic analysis of channel choices, consider the following situation. Suppose a Delhi-based branded furniture manufacturer wants to sell furniture in the southern markets. The manufacturer has to decide between two alternatives: 1.Hiring 10 new sales representatives who will operate from offices in Bangalore, Chennai, and Hyderabad, receiving a base salary plus commissions, apart from company meeting the expense of setting up the office-cum-residence for these employees. 2. Using a Bangalore-based industrial distributor dealing in furniture with offices in Chennai and Hyderabad. The distributor has 30 sales representatives, who would receive commission based on their respective sales.

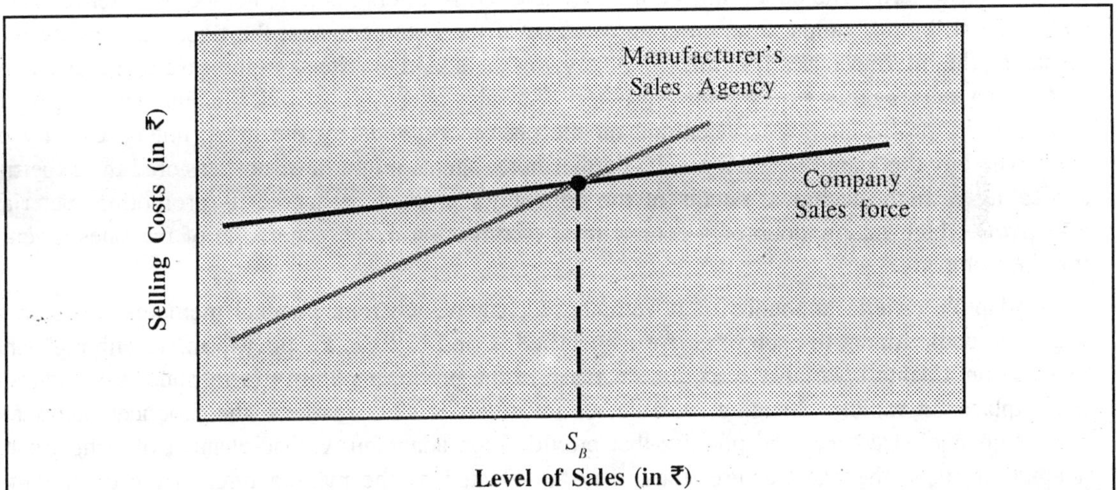


The first step in the analysis is to estimate what sales are likely to be generated by a company sales force or a sales agency. On one hand, a company sales force is better trained to sell the company's products enabling them to concentrate on the company's products. The company's sales force will make aggressive efforts because each representative is aware of the fact that their future depends on the company's success. While, on the other hand, the sales agency has 30 representatives, not just 10; it may be just as aggressive as a direct sales force, depending on the commission level, better received by customers as more independent agency, benefitting the company with its extensive contacts and marketplace knowledge. These are some of the factors to be considered by the marketer and required to be analyzed further for formulating a demand function for the two different channels, in the example.

The next step is to estimate the costs of selling different volumes through each channel. In the figure given above, although the fixed costs of engaging a sales agency are lower than those of establishing a new company sales office, its costs rise faster through an agency because sales agents get a larger commission than company salespeople, should be noted by the marketers.

Thereafter, the final step is comparing sales and costs. As mentioned in the figure above, there is one sales level (SB) at which selling costs are the same for the two channels. The sales agency is thus, the better channel for any sales volume below $S_{B,}$ and the company sales branch is better at any volume above $S_{B,}$ Given this information, it is not surprising that sales agents tend to be used by smaller firms, or by large firms in smaller territories where the volume is low.

**Control Criteria:** The control criteria for the selection of the intermediaries refer to the extent to which the selected intermediary permits the company, the producer to exercise its control, in spite of the considerable role of the direct contact with customers performed by these intermediaries. The hold of the producer on the intermediary, the company sales force, is maximum as compared to the sales representatives hired by the manufacturers' sales agency, with regard to various aspects of making the products available to the consumers. Moreover, the company sales force is exclusively performing the task of promoting the company's own image and the products related thereby.

**Adaptive Criteria:**The adaptive criteria in the selection of the intermediaries refer to the degree of flexibility permitted to the manufacturer/producer by the particular intermediary, with respect to the future changes in the distribution system characteristics. The characteristics of the distribution system refer to terms and conditions on the payment terms, pricing policy, number of intermediaries with the distributor's rights, discontinuing of some of the intermediaries, the fixed cost involved in managing the intermediaries if at all, etc. Analyzing the adaptive criteria in the case being discussed here, using sales agency poses control problem. As sales agency is an independent firm seeking to maximize its profits, it may concentrate on the customers who buy the most, not necessarily on those who buy the manufacturer's goods. Furthermore, agents might have not mastered the expertise of dealing with the technical details of the company's product or handle its promotion materials effectively which may undoubtedly control their contribution in the generation of the sales revenue for the company.

Adaptive criteria announce of developing a channel, wherein, channel members make some degree of commitment to each other for a specified period of time, keeping in mind, although, that these commitments invariably lead to a decrease in the producer's ability to respond to a changing marketplace. In rapidly changing, volatile, or uncertain product markets, the producer needs and prefers channel structures and policies that provide high adaptability. The channel offering greater adaptability is to the manufacturer thus, may be selected by the manufacturer in the competitive, dynamic marketing environment.

## SUMMARY

'Channels' refers to the links between the manufacturers and the consumers, a set of intermediaries performing a variety of functions. They are the set of pathways followed by the product or service after production, culminating in purchase and use by the final end-user.

The companies in the present dynamic market must build and manage a continuously evolving and increasingly complex channel system and value network. Intermediaries can be broadly categorized in three categories, namely, Merchants, Agents and Facilitators, on the basis of the criteria like ownership rights and the possession of the goods. A marketing channel system decisions affects the other marketing decisions also, and therefore are among the most critical decisions. In managing the intermediaries, the firm must choose between the push versus pull marketing strategy. The key role of the marketing channel is to perform the work of moving goods from producers to consumers. The intermediaries with their contacts, experience, specialization, and scale of operation makes possible the wide availability and accessibility of the merchandise to the target markets. Moreover, it also overcomes the time, place, and possession gaps that separate goods and services from those who need or want them. Thus, the various functions performed by the intermediaries offer the firm the synergistic effect, constituting the different flows of the constituents of the sales transactions as well as the produces, namely, the forward flow, backward flow as well as the two-way flow. The number of intermediaries decides the levels of the flow. Among the various considerations for designing a marketing channel system, Analyzing Customer Needs, Establishing Channel Objectives, Identifying Major Channel Alternatives and Evaluating the Major Channel Alternatives are the crucial decisions to be taken by any marketer.

## CASELET 1

### How Carmax is Transforming the Auto Business

For years, buying a used car was dangerous and risky business; used-car salesmen were stock figures in comedy routines. Then CarMax emerged to change the face of the industry and its standards. Circuit City, a major retailer of electronic products, started CarMax, the Auto Superstore, in 1993. The first superstore opened in Richmond, Virginia, where its headquarters are located, and CarMax is now the nation's leading specialty retailer of used cars; it operated 50 used-car superstores in 24 markets. CarMax also operates 12 new-car franchises, which are integrated or co-located with its used-car superstores.

What is so special about CarMax? The company locates it used-car superstores, each carrying around 500 cars, on large lots on the outskirts of a city near a major highway. Customers enter an attractive display room, where a sales associate finds out what kind of car they want and then escorts them to a computer kiosk. Using a touch screen, the associate retrieves a full listing of the cars in stock that meet the customer's criteria. A colour display of each car can be shown along with the vehicle's features and its fixed selling price. The company has over 15,000 cars in all, nearly every make and model.

There is no price negotiation. The salesperson, paid a commission on the number of cars sold rather than their value, has no incentives to push higher-priced cars. The customer is informed that CarMax mechanic have carried out a 110-point inspection and made any necessary repairs beforehand. Furthermore, a car buyer receives a 5-day moneyback guarantee and a 30-day comprehensive warranty. If the buyer wants financing, the CarMax associate can arrange it in 20 minutes. The entire process typically takes less than one hour.

The company's niche has been to focus on the used-car market. Given that today's cars are better and have longer life expectancies, many buyers now prefer to save money by buying a used car, and the substantial growth of cars leasing has greatly inflated the supply of used cars.

Banks are more willing to offer low-cost financing for used cars, especially when research revealed that default rates were lower for used-car buyers. Finally, dealers have reported earning a higher profit on used cars, up to $100 more than for a new car.

CarMax has been very successful in achieving even greater margins: The company's average selling price for a used vehicle is $ 15,000 and its average profit margins is 13 per cent, compared with industry averages of $ 13,650 and 11 per cent, respectively. Although the major auto makers experienced a decline in sales and profitability in 2003 with new cars, CarMax experienced sales and revenue growth.

### Questions

1. How was the CarMax formed?
2. Review the channel design system of the CarMax?
3. Suggest the unconventional channels for the products of the CarMax.

## ........ QUESTIONS FOR DISCUSSION

### Descriptive Questions

1. Define channels of distribution. Discuss with suitable examples the functions of the channels of distribution.
2. Discuss different types of channels, levels and flows, in detail, giving suitable examples.
3. Discuss the various steps involved in the channel design decisions in detail with suitable examples.

### Assignments

(a) Visit the distributor of the product in your city or area, and make the report of the various terms and conditions applicable to their contract of distributorship.

(b) Review the process of getting dealership, distributorship or agency of the product of your choice.

### Objective Questions

1. ________ refer to the links between the manufacturers and the consumers,
2. ________ are a set of intermediaries performing a variety of functions.
3. ________ are also called as the intermediaries or the middlemen,
4. ________ comprise and the entire flow, the movement of the goods from the manufacturer to the consumers.
5. ________ are the intermediaries who take title to the merchandise and resell the merchandise, generally having the physical possession of the goods.
6. The intermediaries, sales agents, brokers, auctioneers, etc., are called as ________ types of intermediaries.
7. ________ who may have the possession of the goods or may not have the possession of the goods, but in no case will have the title to the merchandise.
8. ________ refers to the, "relinquishing some control over how and to whom the products are sold".
9. ________ refers to flow of activity from customers to the company.
10. ________ refers to the flow of the activity from company to the customer.
11. ________ refers to the flow of activity from both the directions, i.e., from company to customer as well as from customer to company.
12. ________ is also called a direct marketing channel
13. ________ consists of a manufacturer selling directly to the final customer.

14. A ________-level channel contains one selling intermediary, such as a retailer. A two-level channel contains two intermediaries, typically, wholesaler and retailer in consumer markets.
15. ________ refers to the strategy of the company to severely limit or restricts the number of intermediaries.
16. ________ refers to the strategy of the company whereby a company relies on more than a few but less than all of the intermediaries willing to carry a particular product.
17. ________ refers to the placing of the goods or services in as many outlets as possible by the manufacturer.
18. ________ refers to the establishing of the price list and schedule of discounts and allowances that intermediaries see as equitable and sufficient by the producer.
19. ________ refers to the payment terms and producer guarantees.
20. ________ defines the distributors' territories and the terms under which the producer will enfranchise other distributors.
21. The ________ criteria for the selection of the intermediaries refer to the extent to which the selected intermediary permits the company, the producer to exercise its control, in spite of the considerable role of the direct contact with customers performed by these intermediaries.
22. The ________ criteria in the selection of the intermediaries refer to the degree of flexibility permitted to the manufacturer/producer by the particular intermediary, with respect to the future changes in the distribution system characteristics.

**Ans:** **1.** Channels, **2.** Channels, **3.** Channels, **4.** Channels, **5.** Merchants, **6.** Agents, **7.** Agents/Facilitators, **8.** Delegation, **9.** Backward flow, **10.** Forward flow, **11.** Two-way flow, **12.** Zero-level channel, **13.** Zero-level Channel, **14.** one, **15.** Exclusive distribution, **16.** Selective distribution, **17.** Intensive distribution, **18.** Price Policy, **19.** Conditions of sale, **20.** Distributors' territorial rights, **21.** control, **22.** adaptive

☺ ☺ ☺

CHAPTER 11

# Advertising

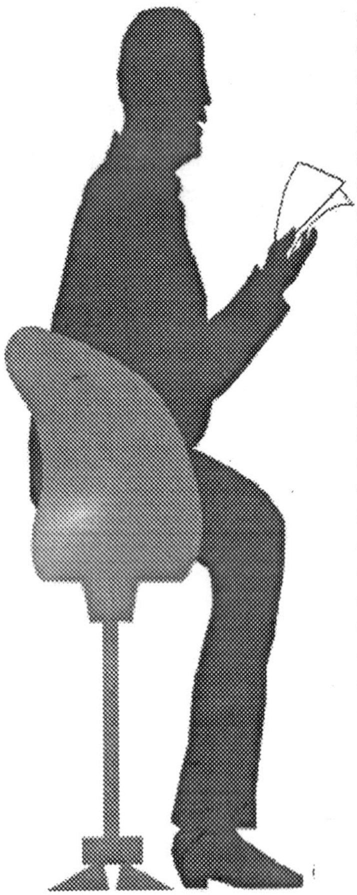

## LEARNING OBJECTIVES

- *Advertising: An Introduction*
- *Setting the Objectives*
- *Deciding on the Advertising Budget*
- *Message Decisions*
- *Media Decisions*
- *Measurement Decisions*
- *Summary*
- *Key Terms*
- *Caselets*
- *Descriptive Questions*
- *Assignments*
- *Objective Questions*
- *References*

## ADVERTISING: AN INTRODUCTION

Advertising is any paid form of no personal presentation and promotion of ideas, goods, or services by an identified sponsor, with the specific objective. Advertisements can be the cost-effective way to disseminate messages, be it building a brand preference or educate people. Although today's media environment is challenging, good advertisements can pay-off.

The development of an advertisement programme starts with the identification of the target markets and buyer motives followed by the five major decisions known as "the five Ms", which are mentioned below:

- **Mission:** What are our advertising objectives?
- **Money:** How much company spends on advertisement?
- **Message:** What message to be sent by the company?
- **Media:** What media should we use?
- **Measurement:** How should we evaluate the results?

These decisions are summarized in the diagram given below:

## SETTING THE OBJECTIVES

An advertising goal (or objective) refers to the specific communications task and achievement level to be accomplished with a specific audience in a specific period of time. The decisions on target market, brand positioning, and the marketing programme source the determination of the advertising objectives. The advertising objective should emerge from a thorough analysis of the current marketing situation. If the product class is mature, the company is the market leader, and brand usage is low, the objective is to stimulate more usage. If the product class is new, the company is not the market leader, but the brand is superior to the leader, then the objective is to convince the market of the brand's superiority. Advertising objectives can be classified according to whether their aim is to inform, persuade, remind, or reinforce, which corresponds to the different stages in the hierarchy of effects of the promotional messages. These different advertisement objectives are explained below:

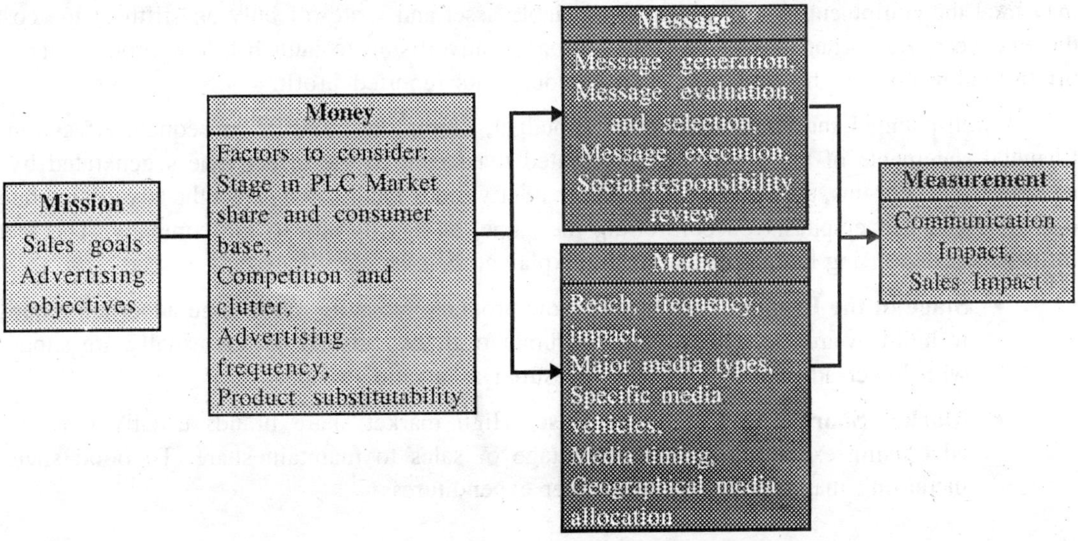

- **Informative Advertising:** Informative advertising aims to create brand awareness and knowledge of new products or new features of existing products.
- **Persuasive Advertising:** Persuasive advertising aims to create liking, preference, conviction, and purchase of a product or service.
- **Comparative Advertising:** Comparative advertising aims to make an explicit comparison of the attributes of two or more brands. It becomes more effective when it obtains cognitive and affective motivations simultaneously, accompanied by the consumers processing advertisement in a detailed, analytical mode. A study indicated that people in Asian countries, especially China and India, unlike people in Europe and America, prefer "explicit, verbally expressed communication of the brands", their characteristics, and how they compare *vis-a-vis* competing brands.
- **Reminder Advertising:** Reminder advertising aims to stimulate repeat purchase of products and services, reminding the target market about its long period association with the delivering functional benefit through the particular brand of the product. Such advertisements are also telecasted for reminding the target marketing about certain seasonal or on-occasion products.
- **Reinforcement Advertising:** Reinforcement advertising aims to convince current purchasers that they made the right choice. Such advertisements targets to dilute the dissonance level of the consumer in relation to various aspects of the purchased brands, may be, price, functions, colour or such other.

## DECIDING ON THE ADVERTISING BUDGET

Advertising is the sea of the budget absorption, and therefore, a company should keep a check on the spending for the advertisements. Some critics comment that large consumer-packaged-goods firms overspend on advertising as a form of insurance against not spending enough, and industrial companies underestimate the power of company and product image building and thus, underspend. Although, advertising is treated as a current expense, part of it is really an investment in building brand equity and customer loyalty. When a company spends ₹ 50 million on capital equipment, it may treat the equipment as a five-year depreciable asset and write-off only one-fifth of the cost in the first year. But, when it spends ₹ 50 million on advertising to launch a new product, it writes off the entire cost in the first year, which reduces its reported profit.

A well-planned and realistic advertising budget, keeping in mind its consequent effects on the financial statements of the company, contributed maximum to the effectiveness generated by the advertisement. For this, the company should consider various factors that affect the advertising budget decisions and can emphasis on controlling the same, as appropriate to the company. The factors influencing advertising budget decisions are explained below:

- **Stage in the Product Life Cycle:** New products typically merit large advertising budgets to build awareness and to gain consumer trial. Established brands usually are supported with lower advertising budgets, measured as a ratio to sales.
- **Market Share and Consumer Base:** High market share brands usually require less advertising expenditure as a percentage of sales to maintain share. To build share by increasing market size requires larger expenditures.

- **Competition and Clutter:** In a market with a large number of competitors and high advertising spending, a brand must advertise more heavily to be heard. Even simple clutter from advertisements, not directly competitive to the brand, creates a need for heavier advertising.
- **Advertising Frequency:** The number of repetitions needed to put across the brand's message to consumers has an obvious impact on the advertising budget.
- **Product Substitutability:** Brands in less-well-differentiated or commodity-like product classes (beer, soft drinks, banks, and airlines) require heavy advertising to establish a differential image.

## MESSAGE DECISIONS

In designing and evaluating an ad campaign, marketers employ both art and science to develop the message strategy or positioning of an advertisement. Advertisers go through three steps:

(a) Message Generation and Evaluation,

(b) Creative Development and Execution,

(c) Legal and Social Responsibility Review.

**(a) Message Generation and Evaluation:** Also, many of today's automobile ads have sameness about them, like car drives at high speed on a curved mountain road or across a desert, which results in forming a weak link between the brand and the message. Advertisers are always seeking 'the big idea" that connects with consumers rationally and emotionally, sharply distinguishes the brand from competitors, and is broad and flexible enough to translate to different media, markets, and time periods. Fresh insights are important for avoiding the use of the same appeals and position as others. Here a USP (Unique Selling Proposition) is required to be developed as it builds a distinctive image of the brand in a cluttered environment.

A good ad normally focuses on one or two core selling propositions. As part of refining the brand positioning, the advertiser should conduct market research to determine which appeal works best with its target audience and then prepare a creative brief typically covering one or two pages. This is an elaboration of the positioning statement and includes: key message, target audience, communications objectives (to do, to know, to believe), key brand benefits, supports for the brand promise, and media.

How many alternative ad themes should the advertiser create before making a choice? The more ads themes explored, the higher the probability of finding an excellent one. Fortunately, the expense of creating rough ads is rapidly falling, thanks to computers. An ad agency creative department can compose many alternative ads in a short time by drawing from computer files containing still and video images.

Marketers can also cut the cost of creative drastically by using consumers as their creative team, a strategy sometimes called "open source" or "crowd sourcing".

**(b) Creative Development and Execution:** The impact of an advertisement not only depends on what it says, but often more importantly, how it says it. Execution can be decisive. Execution of the ads refer to the format elements, fonts size, message framing, the animated characters, celebrity endorsing, scientific and technical evidence, and such other woven in the advertising message, through the effective media. Format elements such as ad size, colour, and illustration also affect a print ad's impact. Larger ads gain more attention, though not necessarily by as much as their difference in cost. Four-colour illustrations increase ad effectiveness and ad cost. New electronic eye-movement studies show that consumers can be led through an ad by strategic placement of dominant elements.

**(c) Legal and Social Responsibility Review:** Advertisers and their agencies must take care that advertising does not overstep social and legal norms. Public policy makers have developed a substantial body of laws and regulations to govern advertising.

Under the Indian law, advertisements for alcoholic beverages and cigarettes are not permitted on television. However, indirect advertising (or surrogate advertising) is permitted in print and outdoor advertisements for these product categories. Similarly, infant food advertising is not acceptable, and there are also restrictions on advertisements targeted at children. Advertisements of pharmaceutical products that promise cure, diagnosis, and treatment are governed by the Drugs and Cosmetic Act, 1940, and the Drugs and Magic Remedies (Objectionable Advertisements) Act, 1954. As per the law, no advertisement should promise magical cure for any ailment or disease, and the rules specify the diseases and ailments that cannot be advertised promising cure or remedies. Rules also prohibit any advertisements that offend morality, decency, and religious susceptibility of the audience. In addition, as per the advertising code specified by the Advertising Standards Council of India, women must not be portrayed in a manner that emphasizes passive, submissive qualities that encourage women to play subordinate or secondary roles in the family, and in the society. There are also some ethical dilemmas regarding the use of children in advertisements.

Several acts and laws in India govern the conduct of business in general and advertisements in particular. The Monopolies and Restrictive Trade Practices Act of 1969 specifies that any misleading, false, and wrong representation either in writing or in oral form (in advertisements, warranty, guarantee, etc.), that causes actual or intended injury or loss to consumers is considered to be an unfair trade practice.

The Advertisements Standard Council of India (ASCI), a self-regulatory voluntary organization formed by the advertising industry, provides basic guidelines for ensuring fairness in advertising, and has mechanisms to safeguard against misleading messages. Any individual or organization can file complaints against specific advertisements and ASCI, through due processes, can pass directives on the complaints. Consumer protection organizations also play a significant role in ensuring that advertisements do not make misleading or false claims. In addition, the Consumer Protection Act of 1986 recognizes the rights of consumers, and provides remedial action when consumer rights are violated.

## MEDIA DECISIONS

After choosing the message, the advertiser's next task is to choose media to carry it. The steps in reaching to the media decisions are as explained below:

(a) Deciding on desired reach, frequency, and impact

(b) Choosing among major media types

(c) Selecting specific media vehicles

(d) Deciding on media timing

(e) Deciding on geographical media allocation

## (a) Deciding on Reach, Frequency, and Impact

Media selection is finding the most cost-effective media to deliver the desired number and type of exposures to the target audience. What do we mean by the desired number of exposures? The advertiser seeks a specified advertising objective and response from the target audience — for example, a target level of product trial. This level depends on, among other things, level of brand awareness. Suppose the rate of product trial increases at a diminishing rate with the level of audience awareness, as shown in Figure 11.1 (a). If the advertiser seeks a product trial rate of P, it will be necessary to achieve a brand awareness level of A*.

The next task is to find out how many exposures, E*, will produce a level of audience awareness of AT. The effect of exposures on audience awareness depends on the exposures reach, frequency, and impact:

***Reach (Rd):*** The number of different persons or households exposed to a particular media schedule at least once during a specified time period. Reach is most important when launching new products, flanker brands, extensions of well known brands, or infrequently purchased brands; or going after an undefined target market.

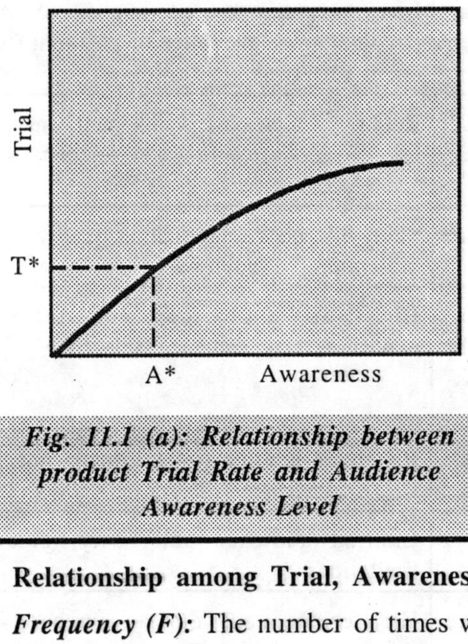


*Fig. 11.1 (a): Relationship between product Trial Rate and Audience Awareness Level*

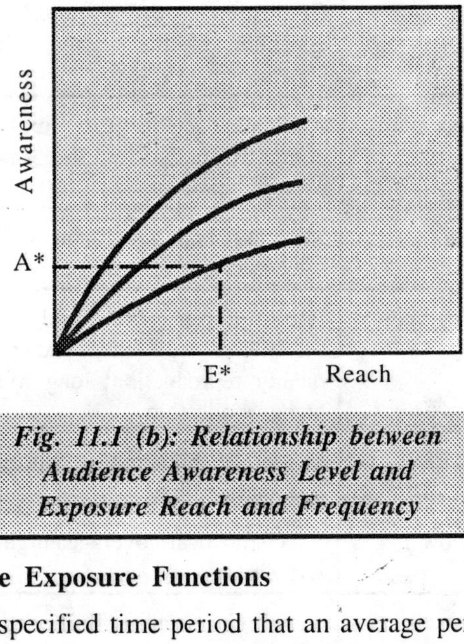


*Fig. 11.1 (b): Relationship between Audience Awareness Level and Exposure Reach and Frequency*

**Relationship among Trial, Awareness, and the Exposure Functions**

***Frequency (F):*** The number of times within the specified time period that an average person or household is exposed to the message; frequency is most important where there are strong competitors, a complex story to tell, high consumer resistance, or a frequent-purchase cycle.

***Impact (I):*** The qualitative value of an exposure through a given medium (thus a food ad in Good Housekeeping would have a higher impact than in *Fortune* magazine)

The table above describes the relationship between audience awareness and reach. Suppose the planner has an advertising budget of ₹ 10,00,000 and the cost per thousand exposures of average quality is ₹ 5. This means it can buy 20,00,00,000 exposures (₹ 10,00,000 ÷ [₹ 5/1,000]). If the advertiser seeks an average exposure frequency of 10, it can reach 20,00,000 people (20,00,00,000 ÷ 10) with the given budget.

Many advertisers believe a target audience needs a large number of exposures. Others believe that after people see the same ad a few times, they either act on it, get irritated by it, or stop noticing it. Another reason for repetition is forgetting. The higher the forgetting rate associated with a brand, product category, or message, the higher the warranted level of repetition. However, advertisers should not coast on a tired ad but insist on fresh executions by their ad agency.

## (b) Choosing among Major Media Types

The media planner must know the capacity of the major advertising media types to deliver reach, frequency, and impact. The profile of the major media types is as explained in the table given below:

**Table 11.1:**

| Medium | Advantages | Limitations |
|---|---|---|
| Newspapers | Flexibility; timeliness; good local market coverage; broad acceptance; high believability | Audio presentation only; lower attention than television; no standardized rate structures; fleeting exposure |
| Television | Combines sight, sound and motion; appealing to the senses; high attention; high reach | Long ad purchase lead time; some waste circulation; no guarantee of position; Costs could run away |
| Direct mail | Audience selectivity; flexibility; no ad competition within the same medium; personalization | Relatively high cost; "junk mail" image |
| Radio | Mass use; high geographic and demographic selectivity; low cost | Short life; poor reproduction quality; small 'pass-along" audience |
| Magazines | High geographic and demographic selectivity; credibility and prestige; high-quality reproduction; long life; good pass-along readership | High absolute cost; high clutter; fleeting exposure; less audience selectivity |
| Outdoor | Flexibility; high repeat exposure; low cost; low competition | Relatively high cost; "junk mail" image |
| Yellow Pages | Excellent local coverage; high believability; wide reach; low cost | Limited audience selectivity; creative limitations |
| Newsletters | Very high selectivity; full control; interactive opportunities; relative low costs | High competition; long ad purchase lead time; creative limitations |
| Brochures | Flexibility; full control; can dramatize messages | Overproduction could lead to runaway costs |
| Telephone | Many users; opportunity to give a personal touch | Relative high cost unless volunteers are used |
| Internet | High selectivity; interactive possibilities; relatively low cost | Relatively new media with a low number of users in some countries |

**Marketers decide on the various types of media, by considering the following variables:**

- **Target Audience:** A target audience media habits should be researched. For example, radio and television are the most effective media for reaching teens.
- **Product Characteristics:** Different media types offer itself for varied potentials for demonstration. The extent to which the demonstration, visualization, explanation, believability, and colour, are important for an ad of the particular brand, depends on the various product characteristics. For example, for the ads of women's dresses, the effect of the coloured ads is relatively higher than the black and white coloured ads. But, the high-tech products demanding dynamic presentation using digital cameras, printers, or cell phones can be more effectively demonstrated on the television.
- **Message Characteristics:** Timeliness and information content does influence media choices. A message announcing major sale tomorrow will require radio, TV, or newspaper, while the message containing a great deal of technical data might require the use of specialized magazines or mailings.
- **Cost:** Different media offers a varied range as per the financial budget of the company, which also varies on the basis of the time, day, space, length of the content, the animated characters, etc. In general, television is very expensive, whereas newspaper advertising is relatively inexpensive. What counts is the cost per thousand exposures. Given the abundance of media, the planner must first decide how to allocate the budget to the major media types. Consumers are increasingly time starved. Attention is a scarce currency, and advertisers need strong devices to capture people's attention.

## Other Alternative Advertising Media Options

In recent years, researchers have noticed reduced effectiveness for television due to increased commercial clutter, increased "zipping and zapping" of commercials and lower viewing owing to the growth in cable and satellite TV and DVD/VCR5. Furthermore, television advertising costs have risen faster than other media costs. Many marketers are looking for alternative media, some of them are described below.

Place Advertise or Out-of-home Advertising is a broad category including many creative and unexpected forms to grab consumers' attention. The rationale is that marketers are better off reaching people where they work, play, and, of course, shop. Some of the options include billboards, public spaces, product placement, and point of purchase:

- **Billboards-hoardings:** Billboards have been transformed with the colourful, digitally produced graphics, backlighting, sounds, movement, and unusual three-dimensional images. Billboards-hoardings, as they are refined to in South Asia – at traffic junctions and highways are an important reminder medium. Most of the outdoor hoardings were hand-painted earlier; but of late, hoardings are vinyl-printed making for better reproduction of the pictures and messages. Electronic display boards are being increasingly used for outdoor hoardings. The cost of rentals for hoardings varies significantly across cities, and also in locations within the cities.

  In India, for example, the total size of the outdoor media is estimated to vary between ₹ 70 and 100 billion, which is estimated to be twice as large as radio advertising. The outdoor media in India accounts for approximately 5 per cent of the total media spent.

- **Public Space:** Public space advertisers are placing ads in unconventional places such as movies, airlines, lounges, sports arenas, office and hotel elevators, and other public places. Transit ads on buses, subways, and commuter trains, around for years, have become a valuable way to reach working women. "Streez furniture", bus shelters, kiosks, and public area are another fast-growing option. Even advertisers can buy space in stadiums and arenas on garbage cans, bicycle racks, parking meters, airport luggage carousels, petrol pumps, shops signage, train tickets as well as supermarket floors.

- **Product Placement:** Product placement has expanded from movies to all types of shows. Sometimes placements are the result of a larger network advertising deal, and the other times they are the work of small product-placement shops that maintain ties with prop masters, set designers, and production executives.

  FedEx received a great deal of favourable exposure from the movie Castaway, starring Tom Hanks as a marooned FedEx employee. In one of the popular Hindi films, *Chalte Chalte*, the hero, played by Shah Rukh Khan, acting as a truck driver, endorsed Castro, while in another Hindi film, *'Hum Tum'* about more than seven brands were placed at different points. This form of obtaining exposure to brands by placing them in films is a new trend in India.

  Marketers are finding inventive ways to advertise during real-time television broadcasts. Sports fans are familiar with virtual logos networks add digitally to the playing field. Such ads although invisible to spectators at the event, are just like painted-on logos to home viewers. Ads also appear in best-selling paperback books and movie videotapes. Written material such as annual reports, data sheets, catalogues, and newsletters increasingly carries ads. Advertorials are print ads that offer editorial content reflecting favourably on the brand and are difficult to distinguish from newspaper or magazine content. Many companies include advertising inserts in monthly bills. Some companies even mail CDs or DVDs to prospects.

- **Point Purchase:** There are a number of ways to communicate with consumers at the point of purchase (P-O-P). In-store advertising includes ads on shopping carts, cart straps, aisles, and shelves, various promotion options such as in-store demonstrations, and live sampling, etc. Some supermarkets are even selling floor space for company logos and experimenting with talking shelves. P-O-P radio provides FM-style programming and commercial messages to thousands of food stores and drug stores nationwide.

### (c) Evaluating Alternative Media

Advertisers now target even virtually a few spare minutes or even seconds of the consumers, no matter any where they are. The main advantage of non-traditional media is that they can often reach a very precise and captive audience in a cost-effective manner, if the message is simple and direct. In fact, outdoor advertising is often called the "15-second sell". It's more effective at enhancing brand awareness or brand image than creating new brand associations. The challenge with nontraditional media is demonstrating its reach and effectiveness through credible, independent research. Unique ad placements designed to breakthrough clutter may also be perceived as invasive and obtrusive. Consumer backlash often results when people see ads in traditionally ad-free spaces, such as in schools, on police cruisers, and in doctors' waiting rooms. But consumers must be favourably affected in some way to justify the marketing expenditures for nontraditional media. Some firms offering ad placement in supermarket checkout lines, fast-food restaurants, physicians' waiting rooms, health clubs, and truck stops have suspended business, in part because of a lack of consumer interest. But there will always be room for creative means of placing the brand in front of the consumers.

## (d) Selecting Specific Media Vehicles

The media planner must search for the most cost-effective vehicles within each chosen media type. In making choices, the planner must rely on measurement services that provide estimates of audience size, composition, and media cost. Audience size has several possible measures which as briefed below:

- **Circulation:** It refers to the number of physical units that carries the advertisement.
- **Audience:** It refers to the number of people exposed to the vehicle. But, if the vehicle has pass-on readership, then the audience is larger than circulation.
- **Effective Audience:** It refers to the manner of people with target audience characteristics exposed to the vehicle.
- **Effective Ad-exposed Audience:** The number of people with target audience characteristics who actually saw the advertisement.

Media planners calculate the cost per thousand persons reached by vehicle to the target customers. A full-page colour advertisement in *The Times of India*, Delhi edition, for example, costs ₹ 1,600 per column centimetre — a common unit of measurement of advertisement space in print media — or a full-page advertisement of 1,700 column centimetre costs ₹ 2.72 million. With an estimated readership of 2.8 million people, the cost of exposing the ad to 1,000 persons is then approximately ₹ 0.60 per unit of column centimetre, or a total cost of ₹ 970 per thousand people. The same ad in *Hindustan Times*, Delhi edition, may cost ₹ 1,800 per column centimetre, or ₹ 3.06 million for a full-page advertisement of 1,700 square column centimetre, and reach 2.6 million persons at a cost of ₹ 0.70 per unit of column centimetre or a total cost of ₹ 1,170 per thousand readers. The media planner ranks each publication (newspapers in this example) by cost-per-thousand for reaching target customers. The publications themselves often put together a "reader profile" for their advertisers, summarizing the characteristics of the newspaper's readers with respect to age, income, occupation, education, leisure activities, and similar segment characteristics.

Marketers need to apply several adjustments to the cost-per-thousand measure. Some of them are mentioned below:

- **First, They Should Adjust the Measure for Audience Quality:** For a baby lotion ad, a magazine read by one million young mothers has an exposure value of one million; read by one million teenagers, it would have an exposure value of almost zero.
- **Second, Adjust the Exposure Value for the Audience Attention Probability:** Readers of *Vogue* may pay more attention to ads than the readers of *Newsweek* do.
- **Third, Adjust for the Magazine's Editorial Quality (Prestige and Believability):** People are more likely to believe a TV or radio ad and to become more positively disposed toward the brand when the ad is placed within a programme they like.
- **Fourth, Adjust for the Magazine's Ad Placement Policies and Extra Services:** It refers to the media providing various policies and extra services such as regional or occupational editions and lead-time requirements.

Media planners are increasingly using more sophisticated measures of effectiveness and employing them in mathematical models to arrive at the best media mix. Many advertising agencies use a computer program to select the initial media and then make further improvements based on subjective factors.

### (e) Deciding on Media Timing and Allocation

In choosing media, the advertiser faces both a macro scheduling and a micro scheduling problem, as explained below:

- **Macro Scheduling:** The macro scheduling problem involves scheduling the advertising in relationship to seasons and the business cycle. Suppose 70 per cent of a product's sales occur between June and September. The firm can vary its advertising expenditures to follow the seasonal pattern, to oppose the seasonal pattern, or to be constant throughout the year.
- **Micro Scheduling:** The micro scheduling problem calls for allocating advertising expenditures within a short period to obtain maximum impact.

*An Illustration:* Suppose the firm decides to buy 30 radio spots in the month of September. The chart below shows several possible patterns. The left side shows that advertising messages for the month can be concentrated ("burst" advertising dispersed continuously throughout the month, or dispersed intermittently). The top side shows that the advertising messages can be beamed with a level, rising, falling, or alternating frequency. The most effective pattern depends on the communications objectives in relationship to the nature of the product, target customers, distribution channels, and other marketing factors.

The timing pattern is influenced by three factors:

- Buyer turnover expresses the rate at which new buyers enter the market; the higher this rate, the more continuous the advertising should be.
- Purchase frequency is the number of times during the period that the average buyer buys the product; the higher the purchase frequency, the more continuous the advertising should be.
- The forgetting rate is the rate at which the buyer forgets the brand; the higher the forgetting rate, the more continuous the advertising should be.

In launching a new product, the advertiser must choose among continuity, concentration, fighting, and pulsing, explained below in detail:

- **Continuity:** It means exposures appear evenly throughout a given period. Generally, advertisers use continuous advertising in expanding market situations, with frequently purchased items, and in tightly defined buyer categories.
- **Concentration:** It calls for spending the entire advertising budget in a single period. This makes sense for products with one selling season or related holiday.
- **Flighting:** Flighting calls for advertising for a period, followed by a period with no advertising, followed by a second period of advertising activity. It is useful when funding is limited, the purchase cycle is relatively infrequent, or items are seasonal.
- **Pulsing:** A Pulsing is continuous advertising at low-weight levels reinforced periodically by waves of heavier activity. It draws on the strength of continuous advertising and flights

to create a compromise scheduling strategy. Those who favour pulsing believe the audience will learn the message more thoroughly, and at a lower cost to the firm.

### (f) Deciding on Geographical Media Allocation

A company must decide how to allocate its advertising budget over space as well as over time. The company makes "national buys" when it places ads on national TV networks or in nationally circulated magazines. It makes "spot buys" when it buys TV time in just a few markets or in regional editions of magazines. These markets are called areas of dominant influence (ADIs) or designated marketing areas (DMAs). Ads reach a market 40 to 60 miles from a city centre. The company makes "local buys" when it advertises in local newspapers, radio, or outdoor sites.

## MEASUREMENT DECISIONS

Advertisers measure the communication effect of an advertisement, on the basis of the various criteria, like, Ads' potential effect on awareness, knowledge, preference or sales effect. Measuring the effectiveness of the communication, often takes the form of the "Communication Effect Research", also called as the 'Copy Testing'. It seeks to determine whether an ad is communicating effectively or not. Marketers should perform this test, both, before an ad is put into media and after it is printed or broadcast. There are three major methods of pretesting, namely the consumer feedback method, the portfolio test methods and the laboratory test methods.

- **The consumer feedback method asks consumers questions such as these:**
  1. What is the main message you (respondent) get from this ad?
  2. What do you think they want you to know, believe, or do?
  3. How likely is it that this ad will influence you to undertake the action?
  4. What works well in the ad and what works poorly?
  5. How does the ad make you feel?
  6. Where is the best place to reach you with this message?
- **Portfolio Tests:** Portfolio tests ask consumers to view or listen to a portfolio of advertisements. Consumers are then asked to recall all the ads and their content, aided or unaided by the interviewer. Recall level indicates an ad's ability to stand out and to have its message understood and remembered.
- **Laboratory Tests:** Laboratory tests use equipment to measure physiological reactions-heartbeat, blood pressure, pupil dilation, galvanic skin response, perspiration-to an ad; or consumers may be asked to turn a knob to indicate their moment-to-moment liking or interest while viewing sequenced material. These tests measure attention-getting power but reveal nothing about impact on beliefs, attitudes, or intentions.

## SUMMARY

Advertising is any paid form of no personal presentation and promotion of ideas, goods, or services by an identified sponsor, with the specific objective. The development of an advertisement programme starts with the identification of the target markets and buyer motives followed by the five major decisions known as "the five Ms", namely, Mission; Money; Message; Media and Measurement. An advertising goal (or objective) refers to the specific communications task and achievement level to be accomplished with a specific audience in a specific period of time. Advertising objectives can be classified according to whether their aim is to inform, persuade, remind, or reinforce, which corresponds to the different stages in the hierarchy of effects of the promotional messages.

Various factors affecting the advertising budget decisions, are, stage in the product life cycle, market share and consumer base, competition and clutter, Advertising frequency and product substitutability.

Message decision involves the following three steps:

- Message Generation and Evaluation
- Creative Development and Execution
- Legal and Social Responsibility Review.

After choosing the message, the advertiser's next task is to choose media to carry it. The steps in reaching to the media decisions are as explained below:

(a) Deciding on desired reach, frequency, and impact

(b) Choosing among major media types

(c) Selecting specific media vehicles

(d) Deciding on media timing

(e) Deciding on geographical media allocation

Advertisers measure the communication effect of an advertisement, on the basis of the various criteria, like, Ads' potential effect on awareness, knowledge, preference or sales effect. Measuring the effectiveness of the communication, often takes the form of the "Communication Effect Research", also called as the 'Copy-Testing'. There are three major methods of pretesting, namely the consumer feedback method, the portfolio test methods and the laboratory test methods.

## CASELET 1

### Playing Games with Brand

Given the explosive popularity of video games with younger consumers, many advertisers have adopted an "If you can't beat them, join them" attitude. Online games have wide appeal. Fifty-eight million people were thought to have played in 2002, and half are women with an average age of 28. Women seem to prefer puzzles and collaborative games, whereas men seem more attracted to competitive or simulation games. A top-notch "advergence" can cost between $ 1,00,000 and $ 5,00,000 to develop. The game can be played on the sponsor's corporate homepage, on gaming portals, or even at restaurants. The NTN iTV Network is an out-of-home interactive entertainment and sports games in approximately 3,600 North American hospitality locations such as Applebee's, Bennigan's, TGIFriday's, and others.

7-Up, McDonald's, and Porsche have all been featured in games. Honda developed a game that allowed players to choose a Honda and zoom around city streets plastered with Honda logos. In the first three month, 78,000 people played for an average of eight minutes. The cost per thousand of $ 7 compared favourably to a prime time TV commercial cost per thousand of $ 11.65. Marketers collect valuable customer data upon registration and often seek permission to send e-mail. Of game players sponsored by Ford Escape SUV, 54 per cent signed up to receive e-mail. The US Army has also employed games in its marketing arsenal. Recognizing that 90 per cent of the target audience was online at least once a week, the US Army decided to make its Website the centrepiece, a game titled "America's Army: Operations" which half a million people play each weekend. The army also sponsored a NASCAR car and toured black colleges and high schools with an Army of One Hummer fitted with a basketball hoop and blaring hip-hop. A TV campaign, over 2,01,000 leads were generated on the toll-free phone number. Overall, the campaign almost doubled the number of leads and produced higher-quality applicants in terms of aptitude tests and college experience.

### Questions

1. Discuss the objective of the advertisements discussed in the above case.
2. Identify and comment on the various advertising decisions involved in the above-mentioned case-study.

## ........ QUESTIONS FOR DISCUSSION

### Descriptive Questions

1. What is the meaning of an 'Advertising'? What are the various advertising decisions, explain in brief.
2. Explain the objectives of advertising?
3. Discuss steps involved in the Message decisions in detail, with the use of appropriate examples.
4. Discuss steps involved in the Media decisions in detail, with the use of suitable examples.
5. Write a short note on the Measuring the Advertisement Effectiveness.
6. Write a short note on the characteristics and limitations of the major media types.

### Assignments

(a) Identify the innovative advertising media effective in your city or your area, along with the details of the company and its products highlighted, and make the presentation of the same.

(b) Select two advertisements of your choice, and comment on the execution style of that advertisement.

### Objective Questions

1. ________ is any paid form of no personal presentation and promotion of ideas, goods, or services by an identified sponsor, with the specific objective.
2. ________ refers to the specific communications task and achievement level to be accomplished with a specific audience in a specific period of time.
3. ________ type of advertising aims to create brand awareness and knowledge of new products or new features of existing products.
4. ________ -type of advertising aims to create liking, preference, conviction, and purchase of a product or service.
5. ________ type of advertising aims to make an explicit comparison of the attributes of two or more brands.
6. ________ type of advertising aims to stimulate repeat purchase of products and services, reminding the target market about its long period association with the delivering functional benefit through the particular brand of the product.
7. ________ type of advertising aims to convince current purchasers that they made the right choice.
8. ASCI refers to ________.
9. The number of different persons or households exposed to a particular media schedule at least once during a specified time period is called as ________.

10. The number of times within the specified time period that an average person or household is exposed to the message is called as _________.
11. The qualitative value of an exposure through a given medium is called as _________.
12. _________ refers to the number of physical units that carries the advertisement.
13. _________ refers to the number of people exposed to the vehicle.
14. _________ refers to the manner of people with target audience characteristics exposed to the vehicle.
15. The number of people with target audience characteristics who actually saw the advertisement is called as _________.
16. The _________ scheduling problem involves scheduling the advertising in relationship to seasons and the business cycle.
17. The _________ scheduling problem calls for allocating advertising expenditures within a short period to obtain maximum impact.
18. _________ means exposures appear evenly throughout a given period.
19. _________ calls for spending the entire advertising budget in a single period.
20. _________ refers to the advertising for a particular period followed by the period with no advertising, followed by the second period of advertising activity.
21. _________ refers to the continuous advertising at low-weight levels reinforced periodically by waves of heavier activity.
22. Communication Effect Research is also called as _________.
23. _________ or _________ seeks to determine whether an ad is communicating effectively or not.

***Ans:*** **1.** Advertising, **2.** Advertising goal (or Advertising objective), **3.** Informative, **4.** Persuasive, **5.** Comparative, **6.** Reminder, **7.** Reinforcement, **8.** The Advertisements Standard Council of India, **9.** Reach, **10.** Frequency, **11.** Impact, **12.** Circulation, **13.** Audience, **14.** Effective Audience, **15.** Effective Ad-exposed Audience, **16.** macro, **17.** micro, **18.** Continuity, **19.** Concentration, **20.** Flighting, **21.** Pulsing, **22.** Copy Testing, **23.** Communication Effect Research, 'Copy Testing'

## References


- Kotler P. and Keller K; 2006; *Marketing Management*; 12th Edition; p. 443 and p. 539; Pearson-Prentice Hall; Delhi;
- Philip Kotler; 2004; *Marketing Management*; 11th Edition; Pearson Education


☺ ☺ ☺

Chapter 12

# Marketing Research

**LEARNING OBJECTIVES**

- *Research*
- *Types of Research*
- *Meaning and Definitions of Marketing Research*
- *The Growth of Marketing Research*
- *Scope of Marketing Research*
- *The Marketing Research Process*
- *Limitations of Marketing Research*
- *Threats to Marketing Research*
- *Criteria for Good Research*

## INTRODUCTION: RESEARCH

Research is an activity related to any problem or an opportunity and it is carried out with the help of other managerial tools. In other words, research means to find out what is already in existence but not known to us or the organization. The researcher conducts the research to identify and analyze any problem or an opportunity. The problem or an opportunity might exist but the researcher has to identify and to analyze it in meaningful terms. The main objective of research is to solve problems. Three important things are included in research, *viz*., problem, collection and gathering of data, and detailed study of the problem. It means that,

- There must be a problem or an opportunity to conduct the research.
- For solving the problem, a data of information should be gathered together through various sources of data collection and application of the scientific method.
- To systematically and intensively study the problem, to get the more complete knowledge about the problem.

### Types of Research

Research can be classified into two broad categories:

1. Basic Research
2. Applied Research

**1. Basic Research:** Basic research is also called as the 'fundamental research', 'theoretical' research or 'pure' research. It aims at expanding the frontiers of knowledge and does not directly involves pragmatic problems. It means that this type of research has general usage or this type of research is carried out for the whole universe. The essence of the basic research is that it addresses itself to more fundamental questions and not to the problems with immediate commercial potential.

**2. Applied Research:** Applied research is also called as the 'decisional research'. It is carried out with the aim of finding out alternative solutions to the problem or for guiding a specific decision. Unlike, basic research it is prompted by commercial considerations and it is carried on for specific problem, therefore, its results are private.

Applied research can be divided into two categories:

*(a)* ***Problem-solving Research:*** It is concerned with a particular issue or a problem. It is usually proprietary in character. It means that such a research is undertaken within a firm or by an outside consultant on its behalf.

*(b)* ***Problem-oriented Research:*** It is concerned with a class of issues or problems in which various firms may be interested. For example, when the research is concerned with the applied problems of the conceptual aspects.

## MARKETING RESEARCH: MEANING AND DEFINITION

Marketing research does not address itself to basic or fundamental questions, it does not qualify as basic research. On the contrary, it tackles problems which seem to have immediate commercial potential. In this context, marketing research should be regarded as applied research. It can be categorized in both, problem-solving and problem-oriented types of applied research.

Marketing research has been defined differently by different scholars.

The most widely used definition of marketing research is that of the American Marketing Association, which defines it as, "Marketing research is the systematic gathering, recording, and analyzing of data about problems related to marketing of goods and services".

According to Green and Tull, "Marketing research is the systematic and objective search for and analysis of information relevant to the identification and solution of any problem (i.e., specific marketing situation) in the field of marketing".

According to Philip Kotler, Marketing research is defined as, "the systematic design, collection, analysis, and reporting of data and findings relevant to a specific marketing situations facing the company".

Marketing research is a systematic and objective study of problems pertaining to the marketing of goods and services. Marketing programme starts from identifying and creating needs; segmenting, targeting and positioning the heterogeneous needs, and not even ends, until customers' needs are satisfied effectively and efficiently, consistently and continuously, better than the competitors by the marketers. Marketing research is also the starting point of the marketing management and perform as the base of the marketing efforts throughout. It may be emphasized that it is not only restricted to any particular area of marketing, but is applicable to all its phases and aspects. Marketing research is the fundamental function linking the consumer, customer, and public to the marketer through such information which is used to identify and define marketing opportunities and problem; generated, refine, and evaluate marketing actions; monitor marketing performance; and improve understanding of market as a process. Marketing research provides the requisite timely and accurate information for making marketing decisions by reacting to the marketing opportunities and problems.

## THE GROWTH OF MARKETING RESEARCH

Over the past several decades, there has been a gradual development in the field of marketing research. The first evidence of formal research techniques being employed could be traced as far back as 1824. However, for almost one century, thereafter, marketing research developed rather slowly and sporadically. It was only from 1910 that it made rapid strides.

Following factors contribute to the growth of marketing research:

**First,** as a result of large-scale productions, producers do not have direct contact with the consumers. This leads to problems in marketing of goods. It is necessary for a manufacturer to know the potential areas where his goods could be marketed, the probable demand for the same and the extent of profitability and competition. This is possible only when a systematic investigation is undertaken.

**Second,** there has been a shift from seller's to a buyer's market. This necessitates a better understanding of buyer behaviour. This aspect is studied in marketing research.

**Third,** the emergence of specialists such as statisticians, psychologists and behavioural scientists in a fairly large number has also enhanced the importance of marketing research in no small measure. These specialists have helped in the development of marketing research as a separate discipline and strengthened its techniques.

**Fourth,** the increasing use of computers has further contributed to the growth of marketing research.

**Finally,** changes in the composition of population, particularly the shift from the rural to the urban areas, has widened the scope for the marketing of various types of goods and services in the urban areas.

## SCOPE OF MARKETING RESEARCH

According to Green and Tull, "Marketing research is the systematic and objective search for and analysis of information relevant to the identification and solution of any problem (i.e., specific marketing situation) in the field of marketing". The purpose of the marketing research can be drawn as given below:

(a) The identification of the marketing problem or the marketing opportunity

(b) The determination of the magnitude of the such problem

(c) The determination of the required information

(d) The determination of the methods for the obtainment of the information

(e) The collection of the information from the various sources of the information

(f) The application of the specific analytical techniques for evaluation of the alternative solutions

(g) The selection of the appropriate course of action or the prospective opportunity

(h) The presentation of the findings of the research through the appropriate type of the report, along with the suggestions on the implications of the decision making

(i) The follow-up for the implementation and action on the findings and the feedback on the research.

On the basis of this, it can be said that, there are many kinds of marketing research, which may be based on either the nature of the problem or the purpose of the study which serves in a decision making process, or on the kinds of the techniques used in the variety of the marketing activities.

The scope of the research is as wide as that of the marketing, and it also further widens the boundaries of the marketing activities, which involves the various research areas, ranging from the framing of the decisions on the marketing plan and implementation to the determination of the marketing mix strategy, which involves research in various marketing mix tools, i.e., product, price, place or promotion in general, or, the detail investigation on each of the element of the various marketing mix tools, and other, which are explained below:

**1. Consumer Behaviour Research:** This category of research involves the research into the various areas of the consumer behaviour, which are directing the marketing activities of the researcher. It involves, the marketing research in the area of the consumer behaviour in general, and the specific research areas, such as the measuring or assessing the preferences; the perceptions; the attitudes; the satisfaction; the factors affecting the purchase of the products; the post-purchase decisions; the adoption process by the consumer; the patterns of the consumers learning, and their motivational aspects, etc.

**2. Sales and Market Research:** This areas of the marketing research focuses on the size and the magnitude of the demand for the product of the company, along with the duration of the demand for the same. The trends in the sales revenue of the company or the influence of the market related factors on the product sales; review of the competitors performance and offerings; preparation of the market profile; market share analysis; market segmentation identification; market testing; identification of the future need and the emerging needs, etc.

**3. Product Research:** It involves research into various areas of the product mix, such as the line, levels, width, and variant of the product; product-line stretching decisions; branding and positioning decisions; packaging and labelling decisions, as well as the new product development decisions; analysis of the product life cycle stages and the research into the effectiveness of the various marketing strategies of the various product life cycle stages.

**4. Price Research:** The research into this marketing mix tools, involves, the research into the effects of the price and quality perceptions; the pricing methods; the reference price factors; the responses to the price changes; profitability analysis; the break-even price determination, etc.

**5. Channel Design Decisions Research:** It involves the research into the convenience aspects of the offering. The various marketing research areas involved therein are selection of the appropriate channel alternative; the performance of the various intermediaries; the studies on the various international marketing channels, i.e., direct marketing channel and the indirect marketing channel, etc.

**6. Promotional Research:** The promotion mix comprises of the sales promotion, personnel selling, direct marketing and advertising. Each of these tools can be selected for the detail research into it further, such as, the effectiveness of advertisement of the consumers recall ability; the impact of the sales promotion campaign; the copy and concept testing; the recognition testing; the research into various media decisions; the comparative study of the factors affecting the sales force motivation and their performance; the preferences of the consumers on the various direct marketing channels; the response study of the consumers for the selected sales promotional message, etc.

Thus, marketing research is a very diverse function.

## THE MARKETING RESEARCH PROCESS

Marketing research specifies the information required to address various marketing issues; designs the method for collecting information; manages and implements the data collection process; analyses the results; and communicates the findings and their implications.

The marketing research process involves a number of interrelated activities which overlap and do not rigidly follow a particular sequence. A researcher is often required to think few steps ahead. This is because the various steps are interwoven into each other and each step will have some influence over the following step. In marketing research, even though the focus is on one particular step, other interrelated steps or operations are also being looked into simultaneously. As one activity or operation is completed, the focus naturally shifts from it to the subsequent one, i.e., the focus is not concentrated exclusively on one single activity or operation at any particular point of time.

Effective marketing research involves the six steps which are described below:

### Step 1: Formulating the Research Problem

It is the first and the most important step in applied research. Poor defined research problems in applied research will not yield useful results, as it cause confusion and do not allow the researcher to develop a good research design. It is rightly said that "a problem well defined is half-solved". For identifying the research problem, symptomatic situations should be studied. There are three categories of symptomatic situations, namely, over difficulties, latent difficulties and unnoticed opportunities.

- Overt difficulties are those which are quite apparent and which manifest themselves. For example, decline in sales experienced by the firm for sometime, is considered as the over difficulty as decrease in the sales figure can be assessed, and becomes quite apparent from the books of accounts of that firm.
- Latent difficulties are those which are not so apparent and which, if not checked, would soon become evident, and affect the organization's performance adversely. For example, although evident decline in sales from the books of accounts, but the reason behind these declining sales may by hidden, like demoralized sales staff, inefficiency of the dispatch department to meet the delivery dates of orders, or the mistakes on the part of the accountant in recording the transactions and receiving of the bills. All these reasons for the decline in sales may surface after an investigation into an apparent overt difficulty.
- Unnoticed opportunities indicate the potential for growth in a certain area of marketing. The marketing environment is dynamic, offering diverse opportunities wrapped with varied intensity of the risk factors. Such opportunities are not clearly seen and some effort is required to explore them. Effective marketing environment scanning does benefit the firm, through marketing research.

There is no concise prescription for recognizing problems from the varied marketing situations. But, a person with an inquisitive nature and the necessary background would recognize a problem or an opportunity in less time. After identifying various problems or opportunities, the researcher then has to identify the problems or opportunities that are to determine priorities in the light of their importance to the organization, as dealing with all the identified problems or opportunities at a particular time may not be possible on account of limited finances and time constraints. The selection of the problem should justify the commitment of resources allocated for the research process by the researcher. Thus, the problem which gives the maximum net value of research should be selected.

Once the problem is selected, a good deal of care on the part of marketing researchers will be required to formulate research problem precisely. Formulation of the problem implies a clear statement or definition of the problem.

A complete problem definition must specify each of the following:

1. **Unit of Analysis:** The individuals or objects whose characteristic are to be measured are called the units of analysis. The units always identify subjects to be studied. It is necessary to be defined. Consider, for example, the statement — "Men's dress buyers in Vadodara stores on August 30, 2010". This specifies a particular universe, provided that clear definitions are given for 'Men's dress buyers', with reference to the buyers' only, irrespective of whether it is purchased by men or women, whether the local men's dress buyers or by areas of the Vadodara City, men's dress buyers from the Vadodara old city area or, buyers from any other specific areas, etc., as well as 'Vadodara stores', with reference to whether stores are to be categorized in various types on the bases of the factors like establishment, annual sales, total number of visitors, locations, etc.
2. **Time and Space Boundaries:** Time boundaries refer to the time which is to be considered for the research to be undertaken on the subject's unit of analysis. For example, in the above example, the specific date is given, the men's dress buyers on 30th August, 2010 in the Vadodara stores is dictated.

Space boundaries refers the extent to which the subject are considered with respect to its entire universe. In other words it refers to the 'universe' of the subjects involved in the research problem. To illustrate, in the above example, 'Vadodara stores', refers to all the stores in the city, and men's dress buyers refers to all those buying men's dress, irrespective of whether it is purchased by a men or a women.

F. E. Brown comments that marketing managers run the risk of making the right decision at the wrong time. Marketing executive, who ignores the fact that opportunities are transient and assumes a static environment, is doomed to failure. From this point of view, it is essential that the marketing manager and researcher decide upon the suitable time reference for the decision.

3. **Characteristics of Interest:** Characteristics of interest refer to both the 'results' that are of concern to management and the 'variables' that are to be tested for their relationship to the results. The characteristics of interest can be style and colour preferences, buying behaviour, personality traits, etc.

4. **Environmental Conditions:** It may be emphasized that the problem definition in marketing research is a step towards identification and structuring of the management's question. The most important objective of problem definition, however, should be to answer the right question. The irrelevant factors not required to be studied or those that are ignored for the purpose of the study, and the environmental conditions thus formed for this purpose should be specified by the researchers at this point of time.

5. **Hypothesis Development:** Once the problem of the research is defined, the researcher focuses on the hypothesis development. Thus, before going for the next stage, it is worthwhile to briefly mention the development of hypotheses. A hypothesis is a proposition which the researcher wants to verify. There may be several competing hypotheses, which may be either specified with the problem definition or implied. The objective of the research is to select among the possible hypotheses and to test them empirically with the help of statistical tools in order to ascertain whether they are true or false. Those hypotheses which are found true by the researcher before undertaking the research, there is no need whatsoever to undertake research including those hypotheses. However, it is not necessary that every marketing research study must have a hypothesis, although the formulation and testing of hypotheses are important in research. For example, the studies in which the researchers are only interested in knowing factual information, formulation and thereby testing of hypothesis is not required.

   The vigilant formulation of the research problem may support the research staff in providing a sense of direction. It makes research both meaningful and economical as it specifies the precise scope of the problem. Further, problem formulation, by setting out assumptions, provide an idea of the environment in which the research is to be undertaken, maintains the focus of the problem, thus, avoids confusion to the researcher as well as the reader. Problem formulation indicates the limitation of research which enables to view it in a proper perspective.

## Step 2: Developing the Research Plan

Developing the research plan calls for decisions on the research design, data sources, research approaches, research instruments, sampling plan, and contact methods.

**1. Research Design:** A good research design that answers the questions put earlier and which is appropriate in achieving the objectives of the study should be selected, as the extent to which the research projects are specific-detailed, varies from one research project to the other. Research design can be broadly exploratory, descriptive or causal.

- ***Exploratory Research Design:*** Exploratory research emphasize on the real nature of the problem. It suggests possible solutions or new ideas for the problem or opportunity emphasized in the research problem. An exploratory research focuses on the discovery of ideas and is generally based on secondary data. It is generally a preliminary investigation without any rigid design as the researcher engaged in an exploratory study may have to change his focus according to the emergence and identification of new ideas and relationship among the variables.
- ***Descriptive Research Design:*** The objective of the descriptive type of research design is to ascertain magnitudes. Exploratory research design does not have any concrete structure, unlike descriptive research studies, which are well-structured. A descriptive study is undertaken when the researcher wants to know the characteristics of certain groups such as age, sex, educational level, income, occupation, etc.
- ***Causal Research Design:*** When the researcher is interested in knowing the cause and effect relationship between two or more variables, a causal research is undertaken. Thus, causal research studies are based on reasoning along well tested lines.

As there are several alternative methods for solving a particular problem, similarly, it should be noted that there is no one 'best' research design. It is through experience that one is able to select the most appropriate research design. The research, therefore, in the hunt for the 'ideal' research design, should not be delayed.

**2. Data Sources:** The researcher can gather secondary data, primary data, or both.

Secondary data are data that were collected for another purpose and already exists somewhere. Primary data is freshly gathered for a specific purpose or for a specific research project. Researchers usually start their investigation by examining secondary data to see whether the problem can be partly or wholly solved without collecting costly primary data. Secondary data provides a starting point for research and offer the advantages low cost and ready availability. Primary data is collected when the needed data do not exist or is outdated, inaccurate, incomplete, or unreliable, the researcher will have to collect primary data. Some primary data collection is involved in most of the marketing research projects.

**3. Research Approaches:** Primary data can be collected in five ways: through observation, focus groups, surveys, behavioural data, and experiments.

(a) ***Observational Research:*** This method suggests that data is collected through one's observation. Fresh data can be gathered by observing the relevant factors and settings. If the researcher is keen observer with integrity he would be in a position to observe and record data faithfully and accurately. The responses recorded through observation method are more accurate and realistic, providing more objective picture of the respondents' observable (external/overt) behaviour.

For example, instead of asking respondents about their current behaviour, marketer/ researcher may observe it (respondents' movements in the shop; the product display which made them to stop at; eye movements of the shoppers/respondents, etc.), and record the observations.

There are several methods of observation of which any one or a combination of some of them can be used by the observer. Thus, there are structured or unstructured methods, disguised or undisguised methods, or observations made in a natural setting or laboratory setting, direct-indirect observations, or human-mechanical observation.

While the observational method may be suitable in case of some studies, several things of interest such as attitudes, opinions, motivations and other intangible states of mind cannot be observed. Only the current behaviour of the person or group of persons can be observed, and that too becomes difficult when there is a large number of people are to be contacted. Certain other difficulties that come in the way of accurate observation and cause it to become distorted are inadequacies of sense organs of an observer, interdependence of observation and inference and effects of interaction between the observer and the observed.

*(b)* ***Focus Group Research:*** A focus group research is a gathering of six to ten people who are invited to spend few hours with a skilled moderator to discuss a product, service, organization or other marketing entity or with the objective of understanding group dynamics or the behaviour of the respondents (consumer/customer). For this the moderator needs to be objective, knowledgeable on the issue, and skilled in group dynamics, to record the discussion through note taking or on audio or on videotape. Generalizations of the findings of the focus group respondents' responses by the researcher should be avoided as it resembles very small non-random sampling size. Participants are normally paid a small sum for attending. The meeting is typically held in pleasant surroundings and refreshments are served.

It is the method of assisting gathering more information about the particular product or services or marketing issues at the core, as it also yields insight into consumer perceptions, attitudes and satisfaction, enabling to accomplish the objectives of exploratory research design. Consumer goods companies have been using focus-groups for many years, and an increasing number of newspapers, law firms, hospitals, and public-service organizations are discovering their value. With the development of the Web, many companies are now conducting online focus group research.

*(c)* ***Survey Research:*** In marketing research, field surveys are commonly used to collect primary data from the respondents. Surveys are best suited for descriptive research. Companies undertake surveys to learn about people's knowledge, beliefs, preferences, satisfaction, socio-economic characteristics, attitudes, opinions and to measure its magnitudes in the general population. Marketers use survey method for gathering information for making various marketing decisions like planning for product features, message and media decisions for advertising, the preference of the customers/consumers to various sales promotion schemes, the channels of distribution frequently used by the target customers, etc.

Surveys can be personal, telephonic, by mail or by diary. Of these, personal and mail surveys are more frequently used in India. A choice has to be made regarding the type of survey for collecting data. In survey, questions are directly asked to the respondents by using a questionnaire. Information pertaining to, etc., can be gathered by this type of research method.

There are certain advantages and limitations of each type of survey method. Broadly speaking, telephonic survey is suitable when very limited information is to be sought in a short period of time. Moreover, such information should be readily available with the respondents. In contrast, surveys, based on personal interviews are suitable when detailed information is to be collected. Sometimes, a combination of two or more methods could also be used.

(d) ***Behavioural Data:*** Customers leave traces of their purchasing behaviour in store scanning data, catalogue purchases and customer databases. Much can be learned by analyzing these data. Customers' actual purchases reflect preferences and often are more reliable than statements they offer to market researchers. People may report preferences for popular brands, and yet the data show them actually buying other brands.

For example, grocery shopping data show that high-income people do not necessarily buy the more expensive brands, contrary to what they might state in the interviews; and many low-income people buy some expensive brands.

(e) ***Experiments:*** The most scientifically valid research is experimental research. The purpose of experimental research is to capture cause-and-effect relationships by eliminating competing explanations of the observed findings. To the extent that the design and executions of the experiment eliminate alternative hypotheses that might explain the results, research and marketing managers can have confidence in the conclusions. It calls for selecting the matched groups of subjects, subjecting them to different treatments controlling extraneous variables and checking whether observed response differences are statistically significant. To the extent that extraneous factors are eliminated or controlled, the observed effects can be related to the variations in the treatments.

**4. Research Instruments:** Marketing researchers have a choice of three main research instruments in collecting primary data: questionnaires, psychological tools, and mechanical devices.

(a) ***Questionnaires:*** A questionnaire consists of a set of questions presented to respondents. Because of its flexibility, the questionnaire is by far the most common instrument used to collect primary data. Questionnaires need to be carefully developed, tested and debugged before they are administered on a larger-scale.

In preparing the questionnaire, the researcher carefully chooses the questions and their form, wording and sequence. The form of the question asked can influence the response. Marketing researchers distinguish between close-ended and open-ended questionnaire, as the form of the questionnaire also influences the response of the respondents. Open-end questions allow respondents to answer in their own words, often revealing more about what people think, are useful in exploratory stage of research. These often reveal more because respondents are not restricted. While, the close-ended questions pre-specify all the possible answers, provide answers that are easier to interpret and tabulate after respondents have made a choice among them.

One can easily spot many errors in a casually prepared questionnaire. Due care should be taken while framing the questions, in terms of the selection of the simple, direct and unbiased words, appropriate fonts and colour of the wordings, headings and underlining, logical order of the questions, etc. Therefore, it is necessary to design a suitable questionnaire, suiting the research approach, and conduct a pilot study as well as undertake a pretesting of the questionnaire. The pretesting will enable the researcher to realize the shortcomings of his questionnaire. In the light of this 'reaction' of the respondents, coupled with the personal observation of the researcher, the questionnaire should be modified. The steps in the process of designing the questionnaire should be taken into consideration further, for the same.

(b) ***Psychological Tools:*** Marketing researchers can probe a buyer's deeper beliefs and feelings using psychological tools such as laddering techniques, depth interviews, and Rorshach tests. Depth interviewing involves going deeply into the thoughts that an individual may have about a product or services. The late Ernest Dischet was a master of depth interviewing and came out with many surprising findings. Zaltman introduced a psychological instrument called the Zaltman Metaphoric Elicitation Technique (ZMET), which uses metaphors to access nonverbal images. This techniques gets an association that are less likely to emerge during normal interviewing.

(c) ***Mechanical Devices:*** Mechanical devices are occasionally used in the marketing research. Some of such mechanical devices and their use in the marketing research are outlined. Galvanometers measure the interest or emotions aroused by exposures to a specific ad or picture. The tachistoscope flashes an ad to a respondent with an exposure interval that may range, from less than one hundredth of a second to several seconds. After each exposure, the respondent describes everything he or she recalls. Eye cameras study respondents' eye movements to see where their eye land first, how long they linger on a given item, and so on. An audiometer is attached to television sets in participating homes to record when the set is on and to which channel it is tuned.

(d) ***Qualitative Instruments:*** Some marketers prefer more qualitative methods for gauging consumer opinion because consumer actions do not always match their answers to survey questions. New tools such as videos, pagers, and informal interviewing will help marketers overcome the limitations of traditional research methods.

In addition to the new qualitative research tools, marketers have developed the methodologies to help them understand the target consumers. Two of these are Prototype and Articulate interviewing. Customer prototyping attempts to paint a realistic portrait of an individual describing a specifying customer type (for example: ideal customer or "non-user") in qualitative terms. To arrive at prototype, marketers strive to answers questions such as "What is important to this person"? and "How this person does wants other persons to view him or her"? The process is repeated until the prototypes begin to overlap. The areas of overlap describe the marketers' target customers. Articulate interviewing is designed to determine what social values interviewees hold dear by having them talk about broad topics such as their various roles in life and their daily activities. This broad format enables the marketers to draw out relevant information; the interviewee is likely to reveal valuable information regarding core beliefs and other social factor that many influence product decisions.

**5. Sampling Plan:** After designing on the research plan, marketing researcher must design a sampling plan.

Sampling plan involves decisions on Sampling Unit, Sampling Size and Sampling Procedure.

(a) ***Sampling Unit:*** Who is to be surveyed? The answer to this question refers to the decisions on the sampling unit. For this, the marketing researcher must define the target population that will be sampled, so that the information collected is relevant. In other words, it should be collected from those units who are most likely to have information. Once the sampling unit is determined, a sampling frame is developed, so that everyone in the target population has an equal or known chance of being sampled.

(b) ***Sampling Size:*** How many people should be surveyed? Undoubtedly, large sample gives more reliable results as compared to the small samples. The cost of collecting the data and the reliability of information gathered thereby, through large number of samples and that through small numbers of sampling units should be considered, while taking decisions on the sampling size. However, it is not necessary to sample the entire target population or even a substantial portion to achieve reliable results. Samples of less than one per cent of a population can often provide good reliability, with a credible sampling method.

(c) ***Sampling Procedure:*** How should the respondents be chosen? There are two methods of the sampling, Probability Sampling and Non-probability Sampling method. To obtain a representative sample, a probability sample of the population should be drawn. Probability sampling allows the calculation of confidence limits form sampling error. When the cost or time involved in the probability sampling is too high, marketing researchers will take non-probability samples.

**6. Contact Methods:** Once the sampling has been determined, the marketing researcher must decide how the subject should be contacted. The contact methods are discussed below:

(a) ***Mail Questionnaire:*** It is the best way to reach people who would not give personal interviews or whose responses might be biased or distorted by the interviewers. Mail questionnaires require simple and clearly worded questions. Unfortunately, the response rate is usually low or slow.

(b) ***Telephone Interviewing:*** It is the best method for gathering information quickly; the interviewer is also able to clarify questions if respondents do not understand them. The response rate is typically higher than in the case of mailed questionnaires. The main drawback is that the interviews have to be short and not too personal. Telephone interviewing is getting more difficult because of answering machine and people becoming suspicious of telemarketing.

(c) ***Personal Interviewing:*** It is the most versatile method. The interviewer can ask more questions and record additional observations about the respondent, such as dress and body language. Braind Wansink has developed a customer profiling technique based on personal interviews that generation interesting hypotheses which can be further tested or used in communication strategy. At the same time, personal interviewing is the most expensive method and requires more administrative planning and supervision than the other three. It is also subject to interviewer bias or distortion.

Personal interviewing takes two forms. In arranged interviews, respondents are contacted for an appointment and often a small payment or incentive is offered. Intercept interviews involve stopping people at a shopping mall or busy street corner and requesting an interview. Intercept interviews have the drawback of being non-probability samples, and the interviewing must not require too much time.

(d) ***Online Methods:*** There is increased use on online methods. Online product testing is expected to grow and provide information faster than traditional marketing research techniques. A company can include a questionnaire on its website and offer an incentive to answer the questionnaire; or it can place a banner on some frequently visited site such as Yahoo!, inviting people to answer some questions and possibly win a prize. The company can enter a target chat room and seek volunteers for a survey, or sponsor a chat room and introduce questions from time-to-time.

A company can learn about individuals who visit its site by following how they click stream through the website and move to other sites. Computers contain cookies that capture this data. By analyzing the click stream of different visitors, the company can make inferences about consumer behaviour. A company can post different prices, use different headlines, offer different product features on different websites or at different times to learn the relative effectiveness of its offerings.

Not everyone is on the web however, and online market researchers must find creative ways to reach certain population segments. One option is to combine offline sources with online findings. Providing temporary internet access at locations such as malls and recreation centres is another strategy. Some research firms use statistical models to fill in the gaps in market research left by offline consumer segments.

Many companies are now using automated telephone surveys to solicit market research information. One popular approach is to distribute prepaid phone cards as an incentive. A survey is programmed into an interactive call system that not only administers the survey, but also sorts the result vitality in any way the client wants them. When the call users place their free calls, a voice prompt asks them if they would like to gain additional minutes by taking a short survey. Coca-Cola is one of the companies that have used prepaid phone cards to survey their customers.

## Step 3: Collect the Information: (Field Work)

After the research design is determined the next step is the actual data collection. The job of data collection may be done by the research department of the company, or may be subcontracted. The data collection phase of marketing research is generally the most expensive and the most prone to error. In the case of surveys, four major problems arise which are outlined below:

- **Not-at-home:** While data collection, many times it happens that the respondent is not available at home. In such situations, the interviewer must either call back later in case of telephonic interviews or confirm for personal interviews the presence of the respondent at their residence, or otherwise will have to collect the same information from some other respondent.
- **Refusal to Cooperate:** One of the other data collection problems is the refusal of the respondent to cooperate the interviewer, by providing the responses to the questionnaire. The interviewer must develop the skills of motivating the respondents to cooperate and provide the necessary information, generally by disentangling the confusion and hesitation restricting them to respond to provide necessary information.
- **Respondent Bias:** Moreover, the interviewer must also encourage the respondent to provide accurate and meaningful information, which is free from bias, serving the actual purpose of the research. The inaccurate information and biased responses will affect the findings and interpretations of the data, thus collected.

- **Interviewer Bias:** Many a times, it also happens that an interviewer introduces a variety of biases because of their age, sex, experiences, beliefs, perceptions, etc., interfering intentionally or unintentionally in the data collection procedure. An interviewer or the data collector has to be very careful in these contexts, and thus assure the recording of the accurate and to the point responses of the respondents.

The modern economy and digitalized world, has introduced the rapid improvements in the telecommunications sectors, enabling the professional interviewers to collect the data from the centralized location, by asking questions, reading from the monitor, sitting in the booths formed for this purpose. The respondents' responses are typed in the computer by the interviewer, eliminating the procedure of editing and coding, along with the reduction in time and errors, and get the required statistics. Other research firms have set up interactive terminals in shopping centres. Persons willing to be interviewed sit at a terminal, read the questions from the monitor, and type in their answers. Most respondents enjoy this form of "robot" interviewing. Several recent technical advances have permitted marketers to research the sales impact of ads and sales promotion.

## Step 4: Processing and Analysing the Collected Data

The next step after data collection is to aggregate the data in meaningful manner, i.e., by data processing and analysis. Data analysis refers to the process of analyzing the collected data to derive some meaningful information. Data analysis includes consolidation, classification, tabulation and analysis of the data.

The researcher should have a well thought out framework for processing and analyzing data, and this should be done prior to the collection. In order to bring out the main characteristics of the data, number of tables are prepared. It is advisable to prepare dummy tables, as such an exercise would indicate the nature and extent of tabulation as also the comparisons of data that can be undertaken.

One or more of the following four steps are used by the researcher in order to derive meaningful results from the statistical tables:

1. The first step is to tabulate the data and one-way and two-way frequency distributions.
2. The second step is to calculate relevant measures of central tendency as also of dispersion, highlighting the major aspects of the data.
3. The third step is to cross tabulate the data to ascertain some 'useful relationships'.
4. The fourth step is to calculate the correlation coefficient and undertake a regression analysis between variables.
5. The fifth step is to undertake a multivariate analysis. Such an analysis is used to determine important relationships amongst several variables by using variety of techniques.

Thus, adequate thought should be given to the use of particular analytical techniques, while designing a research study. With the emergence of the computer and information technology, many such analytical techniques have proliferated. The researcher now has access to an increasing assortment of techniques and it is desirable to know well in advance as to what analytical techniques are going to be used, so that the data can be collected accordingly.

The researcher should essentially give as much importance to the analysis and interpretation of data as given to the collection of the data, or else the data may be rendered useless resulting in a waste of time and money.

## Step 5: Presentation of the Findings: (Report Presentation)

The next step after the data analysis is the presentation of the research findings that are relevant to the major marketing decisions faced by the management. Once the data have been tabulated, interpreted and analyzed, the marketing researcher is required to prepare his report embodying the findings of the research study and his recommendations and presentation of the relevant research findings. As a poor report on an otherwise good research will considerably undermine its utility, it is necessary that the researcher gives sufficient thought and care to its preparation.

Although report writing needs some skill which can be developed with practise, the researcher should follow the main principles of writing a report. Some of these principles are objectivity, coherence, clarity in the presentation of ideas and use of charts and diagrams. The essence of a good research report is that it effectively communicates its research findings. As management is generally not interested in details of the research design and statistical findings, the research report should not be loaded with such details, otherwise, there is a strong likelihood of its remaining unattended on the manager's desk. In view of this, the researcher has to exercise extra care to make the report a useful and a worthwhile document for the management.

Sometimes, a detailed marketing research study show one or more areas where further investigation is needed. Since research on those areas or aspects could not have been fitted into the original project, a separate follow-up study has attempted.

## Step 6: Follow-up and Making Decisions

The researcher has to make constant follow-up to see that the relevant findings and suggestions of the research conducted has been implemented by the managers or not. The managers who commissioned the research need to weigh the evidence. They know that the findings could suffer from a variety of errors. The marketing managers, when satisfied about the results and the alternative actions thereby provided in the research reports, in accordance to the time, element and other resources, will make necessary arrangements for its execution after approval of the same.

# LIMITATIONS OF MARKETING RESEARCH

However, one should not believe that the marketing research can solve all the problems of marketing, as it is subject to certain limitations which are as explained below:

1. The marketing research has the fragmentary nature, which means that it involves various fragmented steps, which makes the understanding of the overall perspective difficult.
2. Marketing research, being the costly and time-consuming activity, fails to offer quick solutions to urgent problems.
3. The marketing research also becomes too superficial and faulty in many industries when it is used by those who do not have its formal training. Such individuals avoid using detailed investigations and the systematic techniques as they lack time and patience for the same.
4. There is an absence of the meaningful dialogue between the marketing management and the marketing research team.
5. Moreover, as marketing research is not an exact science and it often lacks the accuracy.
6. Analytical tools of the marketing research are still deficient due to which the precise idea on the behavioural studies cannot be drawn.

## THREATS TO MARKETING RESEARCH

The success of marketing research depends upon the cooperation of the public. Unprofessional or unethical marketing research practices may seriously jeopardise the public's willingness to cooperate in surveys. It is, therefore, necessary to ascertain the reaction of the public towards marketing research. George Day, who looked into this issue, identified three major threats to marketing and survey research: (1) excessive interviewing, (2) lack of consideration and abuse of respondents, and (3) the use of marketing research as a sales ploy. It may be noted that these factors pose a threat to marketing research particularly in Western countries, where it is far more developed. In a country like India, marketing research is still used infrequently and as such these threats are almost non-existent.

## CRITERIA FOR GOOD RESEARCH

The criteria for the good research are as given below:

1. The research should be well defined, along with the clear cut purpose in light of the research objectives.
2. The research should not be conducted in the haphazard manner. The research should have the scientific base which is executed in the systematic and organized manner, in the light of the well-designed research procedure.
3. For enabling the systematic research execution, the research plan has to be formulated. The good and appropriate research plan/research design provides the base on which the decisions pertaining to the scope, coverage, sources of data and sampling decisions are made for the execution of the research.
4. The research design and research methodology should be prepared by the researcher, by not only considering the limitations of the research activities but also considering the effects of the limitations on the accuracy and quality of the research activities.
5. There are two sources of collection of data, secondary data and the primary data. In the light of the appropriate, relevant, and adequate secondary data, the research problem has to be identified. The secondary data should be used only after it has been evaluated, in accordance with research to be conducted. The primary data are to be collected by the researcher in the outline provided by the objectives, scope and coverage, research design and research methodology, for the research study.
6. The conclusions and the suggestions provided by the researcher should be confined to the data of the research and the findings of the research.
7. The planning, organization and the execution of the research is also subject to the ethical integrity of the researcher. The data collection and the data interpretation if gets affected by the subjectivity of the researchers' views and preferences, the ultimate purpose of the research will be in vain. Therefore, the researchers' integrity and the reputations is also one of the important criteria for the good research.

## SUMMARY

Research is an activity related to any problem or an opportunity and it is carried out with the help of other managerial tools. The researcher conducts the research to identify and analyze any problem or an opportunity. Thus, three important things are included in any research activity, i.e., there must be a problem or an opportunity to conduct the research; there should be gathering and collection of information through various sources of data collection and application of the scientific method; to study the problem more systematically and intensively, to get the more complete knowledge about the problem. Research can be classified into two broad categories, Basic Research and Applied Research.

According to the American Marketing Association, Marketing Research is defined as, "The systematic gathering, recording, and analyzing of data about problems related to marketing of goods and services". Marketing research is also the starting point of the marketing management and performs as the base of the marketing efforts throughout. In the year 1824, the first evidence of employment of formal research techniques could be traced. But, it made rapid strides from the year 1910.

The marketing research process involves a number of interrelated activities which overlap and do not rigidly follow a particular sequence. The steps in the marketing research process are as mentioned below:

**Step 1** : Formulating the Research Problem:

**Step 2** : Developing the Research Plan:

**Step 3** : Collect the Information: (field work)

**Step 4** : Processing and Analyzing the collected data

**Step 5** : Presentation of the findings: (report presentation)

**Step 6** : Follow-up and making decisions

Moreover, the unprofessional or unethical marketing research practices may seriously jeopardise the public's willingness to cooperate in the surveys. George Day identified three major threats to marketing and survey research: (1) excessive interviewing, (2) lack of consideration and abuse of respondents, and (3) the use of marketing research as a sales ploy. In a country like India, marketing research is still used infrequently and as such these threats are almost non-existent.

## KEY TERMS

- **Research:** Research is an activity related to any problem or an opportunity and it is carried out with the help of other managerial tools.
- **Basic Research:** It means that this type of research has general usage or this type of research is carried out for whole universe. Basic reseach also called as the 'fundamental research', 'theoretical' research or 'pure' research.
- **Applied Research:** Applied research is carried with the aim of finding out alternative solutions to the problems or, for guiding the specific decisions. Applied research is also called as the 'decisional research'.
- **Marketing Research:** Marketing research is the systematic gathering, recording, and analyzing of data about problems related to marketing of goods and services.
- **Overt Difficulties:** Overt difficulties are those which are quite apparent and which manifest themselves.

- **Latent Difficulties:** Latent difficulties are those which are not so apparent and which, if not checked, would soon become evident, and affect the organization's performance adversely.
- **Unnoticed Opportunities:** Unnoticed opportunities indicate the potential for growth in a certain area of marketing.
- **Unit of Analysis:** The individuals or objects whose characteristic are to be measured are called the units of analysis. The units always identify subjects to be studied.
- **Time and Space Boundaries:** Time boundaries refer to the time which is to be considered for the research to be undertaken on the subject's unit of analysis. Space boundaries refers the extent to which the subject are considered with respect to its entire universe. In other words it refers to the 'universe' of the subjects involved in the research problem.
- **Characteristics of Interest:** Characteristics of interest refer to both the 'results' that are of concern to management and the 'variables' that are to be tested for their relationship to the results. The characteristics of interest can be style and colour preferences, buying behaviour, personality traits, etc.
- **Hypothesis:** A hypothesis is a proposition which the researcher wants to verify.
- **Exploratory Research Design:** Exploratory research emphasize on the real nature of the problem. It suggests possible solutions or new ideas for the problem or opportunity emphasized in the research problem.
- **Descriptive Research Design:** The objective of the descriptive type of research design is to ascertain magnitudes. A descriptive study is undertaken when the researcher wants to know the characteristics of certain groups such as age, sex, educational level, income, occupation, etc.
- **Causal Research Design:** When the researcher is interested in knowing the cause and effect relationship between two or more variables, a causal research is undertaken.
- **Secondary Data:** Secondary data are data that were collected for another purpose and already exist somewhere.
- **Primary Data:** Primary data are freshly gathered for a specific purpose or for a specific research project.
- **Observational Research:** This method suggests that data are collected through one's observation.
- **Focus Group Research:** A focus group research is a gathering of six to ten people who are invited to spend few hours with a skilled moderator to discuss a product, service, organization or other marketing entity or with the objective of understanding group dynamics or the behaviour of the respondents (consumer/customer).
- **Behavioural Data:** Customers leave traces of their purchasing behaviour in store — scanning data, catalogue purchases and customer databases, which becomes the behavioural data, for the study of the behaviour of the customers.
- **Questionnaire:** A questionnaire consists of a set of questions along with the alternative responses presented to respondents, with the particular objective. It can be both, open-ended as well as close-ended.

- **Psychological Tools:** Marketing researchers can probe a buyer's deeper beliefs and feelings using psychological tools such as laddering techniques, depth interviews, and Rorshach tests.
- **Depth Interviewing:** Depth interviewing involves going deeply into the thoughts that an individual may have about a product or services.
- **(ZMET) Zaltman Metaphoric Elicitation Technique:** Zaltman Metaphoric Elicitation Technique (ZMET), which uses metaphors to access nonverbal images. These techniques get an associations that are less likely to emerge during normal interviewing.
- **Galvanometers:** Galvanometers measure the interest or emotions aroused by exposures to a specific ad or picture.
- **Tachistoscope:** The tachistoscope flashes an ad to a respondent with an exposure interval that may range, from less than one hundredth of a second to several seconds.
- **Eye Cameras:** Eye cameras study respondents' eye movements to see where there eye land first, how long they linger on a given item, and so on.
- **Audimeter:** An audiometer is attached to television sets in participating homes to record when the set is on and to which channel it is tuned.
- **Articulative Interviewing:** Articulative interviewing is designed to determine what social values interviewees hold dear by having them about broad topics such as their various roles in life and their daily activities.
- **Interviewer Bias:** Many times, it also happens that an interviewer introduces a variety of biases because of their age, sex, experiences, beliefs, perceptions, etc., interfering intentionally or unintentionally the data collection procedure.
- **Data Analysis:** Data analysis refers to the process of analyzing the collected data to derive some meaningful information. Data analysis includes consolidation, classification, tabulation and analysis of the data.
- **Channels:** 'Channels' refers to the links between the manufacturers and the consumers, a set of intermediaries performing a variety of functions. They are also called as the intermediaries or the middlemen, and the entire flow, the movement of the goods from the manufacturer to the consumers, consisting of the various intermediaries is called as the 'Channels of Distribution' or 'Trade Channel'.
- **Merchants:** These are the intermediaries who take title to the merchandise and resell the merchandise, generally having the physical possession of the goods.
- **Agents:** These are the intermediaries, sales agents, brokers, auctioneers, etc., who may have the possession of the goods or may not have the possession of the goods, but in no case will have the title to the merchandise.
- These are the intermediaries who assist in the distribution process of the merchandise. In this process, they may have physical possession of the merchandise in certain cases or may not have physical possession of the merchandise, but in no case will have title to the merchandise or negotiate purchase or sales transaction.
- **Push Strategy:** A push strategy uses the manufacturer's sales force, trade promotional money, or other means to induce intermediaries to carry, promote, and sell the product to end-users.

- **Pull Strategy:** Pull strategy the manufacturer uses advertising, promotion, and other forms of communication to persuade consumers to demand the product from intermediaries, thereby, inducing the intermediaries to order it.
- **Delegation:** Delegation refers to the, "relinquishing some control over how and to whom the products are sold".
- **Backward Flow:** Backward flow refers to flow of activity from customers to the company.
- **Forward Flow:** Forward flow refers to the flow of the activity from company to the customer.
- **Two-way Flow:** The two-way flow refer to the flow of activity from both the directions, i.e., from company to customer as well as from customer to company.
- **Zero-level Channel:** A zero-level channel (also called a direct marketing channel) consists of a manufacturer selling directly to the final customer.
- **One-level Channel:** A one-level channel contains one selling intermediary, such as a retailer.
- **Two-level Channel:** A two-level channel contains two intermediaries, typically, wholesaler and retailer in consumer markets.
- **Exclusive Distribution:** It refers to the strategy of the company to severely limit or restricts the number of intermediaries.
- **Selective Distribution:** It refers to the strategy of the company, whereby a company relies on more than a few but less than all of the intermediaries willing to carry a particular product.
- **Intensive Distribution:** It refers to the placing of the goods or services in as many outlets as possible by the manufacturer.
- **Price Policy:** It refers to the establishing of the price list and schedule of discounts and allowances that intermediaries see as equitable and sufficient by the producer.
- **Conditions of Sale:** It refers to the payment terms and producer guarantees.
- **Distributors' Territorial Rights:** It defines the distributors' territories and the terms under which the producer will enfranchise other distributors.
- **Control Criteria:** The control criteria for the selection of the intermediaries refer to the extent to which the selected intermediary permits the company, the producer to exercise its control, in spite of the considerable role of the direct contact with customers performed by these intermediaries.
- **Adaptive Criteria:** The adaptive criteria in the selection of the intermediaries refer to the degree of flexibility permitted to the manufacturer/producer by the particular intermediary, with respect to the future changes in the distribution system characteristics.
- **Advertisement:** Advertising is any paid form of number of personal presentation and promotion of ideas, goods, or services by an identified sponsor, with the specific objective.
- **Advertising Goal (or Advertising Objective):** An advertising goal (or objective) refers to the specific communications task and achievement level to be accomplished with a specific audience in a specific period of time.

- **Informative Advertising:** Informative advertising aims to create brand awareness and knowledge of new products or new features of existing products.
- **Persuasive Advertising:** Persuasive advertising aims to create liking, preference, conviction, and purchase of a product or service.
- **Comparative Advertising:** Comparative advertising aims to make an explicit comparison of the attributes of two or more brands.
- **Reminder Advertising:** Reminder advertising aims to stimulate repeat purchase of products and services, reminding the target market about its long period association with the delivering functional benefit through the particular brand of the product.
- **Reinforcement Advertising:** Reinforcement advertising aims to convince current purchasers that they made the right choice.
- **ASCI:** The Advertisements Standard Council of India.
- **Reach:** The number of different persons or households exposed to a particular media schedule at least once during a specified time period.
- **Frequency:** The number of times within the specified time period that an average person or household is exposed to the message.
- **Impact:** The qualitative value of an exposure through a given medium.
- **Circulation:** It refers to the number of physical units that carries the advertisement.
- **Audience:** It refers to the number of people exposed to the vehicle.
- **Effective Audience:** It refers to the manner of people with target audience characteristics exposed to the vehicle.
- **Effective Ad-exposed Audience:** The number of people with target audience characteristics who actually saw the advertisement.
- **Macro Scheduling:** The macro scheduling problem involves scheduling the advertising in relationship to seasons and the business cycle.
- **Micro Scheduling:** The micro scheduling problem calls for allocating advertising expenditures within a short period to obtain maximum impact.
- **Continuity:** It means exposures appear evenly throughout a given period.
- **Concentration:** It calls for spending the entire advertising budget in a single period.
- **Flighting:** Flighting refers to the advertising for a particular period followed by the period with no advertising, followed by the second period of advertising activity.
- **Pulsing:** A pulsing is continuous advertising at low-weight levels reinforced periodically by waves of heavier activity. It draws on the strength of continuous advertising and flights to create a compromise scheduling strategy.
- **Communication Effect Research or Copy Testing:** Communication Effect Research, also called as the 'Copy Testing'. It seeks to determine whether an ad is communicating effectively or not.

## CASELET 1

### General Mills, Inc. (A)

During August 1984, the executives of General Mills, incorporated (hereafter referred to as GM), were facing a number of very important decision. This was normal, as it had been the past forty years, while GM was developed from the largest flour miller in the United States to a huge diversified company. During the fiscal year that ended on May 26th, 1985, GM achieved a sales volume of nearly $ 4.3 billion (a rise of 4 per cent from the previous year.) Its profits were slightly lower to year.

At that time GM had proliferated into six major fields. One was food manufacturing, within which were several groups, including its original flours. Its largest success was in semi-processed foods, which included cake mixes, ready-to-eat cereals, and instant potatoes (GM being a top company in each of these lines). Other product-lines included restaurants, specialty retail stores, fashion garments, and creative products (toys, games, and crafts). In 1984 GM was preparing to narrow its product-lines radically.

Food manufacturing also included a number of other lines, one of which was snack foods. In that category were "wholesome snacks". There GM faced strong rivalry, as its 1985 annual report to stockholders referred to this line as a "most competitive product category in 1985". Here, too GM was a leader, as indeed it should have been since GM had created ten years before.

The granola bar is a cereal-based confection bar. It was just a miniscule product category until General Foods introduced its granola bar under its name of "Nature Valley". The product was immediately popular, and strong rivalry began when Quaker Oats invaded the field with its bar, which also enjoyed instant popularity. As these brands slugged it out, the total sales in this category were rising at an amazing 35 per cent annually. However, in 1984 sales growth tapered off to 10 per cent.

That was the only one of the adverse situations that GM faced in the wholesome snacks category. Competition was intensifying, as nine new competitors entered this market in 1984. As a consequence, prices slipped. New types of bars were entered, including Quaker Oats with a bar dipped in chocolate, Ralston Purina adding marchmallows, and Pillsbury partly substituting milk for granola. Also, it was reported that many consumers were switching to crunchier snacks, such as, gourmet popcorn and rice-based snacks, that had fewer calories than granola.

GM at that time was fighting to hold its market leadership. Sales were rising slightly, but profits were declining in the wholesome snacks line as GM began to spend heavily on it. Some steps taken to prop up Nature Valley Chewy Granola bars, GM's best selling item, included the addition of three new flavours. Its "Dandy" bars were new and just achieving national distribution. GM innovated too with its "Fruits Corners", a fruit roll-up granola bar, that Sunkist was countering.

The glut in granola bars faced 1984 was just one of the chaotic grocery product categories in that year. Most lines were affected to some degree. As *The Wall Street Journal* has pointed out that the food industry has been stung by a series of failed diversification efforts, into everything from "restaurants to toys", and a "new-product frenzy" was sweeping the industry.

With population growth at a reduced rate, food firms felt compelled to create new specialty grocery products to take market share from the rivals.

## Questions

1. What appear to have been major corporate-wide decisions that GM faced to which marketing research would have contributed substantially?
2. Also suggest some decisions needing marketing research help, relative to the "healthful snacks" category.
3. For each of the decisions that you have given, tell in very definite terms how marketing research would enable a better decision to be made.

## ........ QUESTIONS FOR DISCUSSION

### Descriptive Questions

1. Define research and marketing research.
2. Define marketing research and discuss the step of problem formulation in the in the process of marketing research in detail.
3. What are the different types of research and discuss the growth of marketing research in detail.
4. What are the various steps in the marketing research process. Discuss the various research approaches in detail.
5. What are the various sampling decisions involved in the marketing research process.
6. Write a short note on the types of the research designs.
7. Write short notes on the following: (a) Questionnaires, (b) Survey Method, (c) Observation Method

### Assignments

(a) Prepare a detailed report on the various types of marketing research firms in India and review of the marketing research projects with any two of them.

(b) Review the marketing research report of the company of your choice and present the findings of the same marketing research report, along with an outline of the marketing research process followed by the company.

### Objective Questions

1. ________ is an activity related to any problem or an opportunity and it is carried out with the help of other managerial tools.
2. ________ is the type of research with general usage.
3. ________ is the type of research carried out for whole universe.
4. ________ is also called as the 'fundamental research'.
5. ________ is also called as the 'theoretical' research.
6. ________ is also called as the 'pure' research.
7. ________ is carried with the aim of finding out alternative solutions to the problems or, for guiding the specific decisions.
8. ________ is also called as the 'decisional research'.
9. ________ is the systematic gathering, recording, and analyzing of data about problems related to marketing of goods and services.
10. ________ difficulties are those which are quite apparent and which manifest themselves. (Overt/Covert)
11. The ________ difficulties are those which are not so apparent and which, if not checked, would soon become evident, and affect the organization's performance adversely.
12. ________ indicate the potential for growth in a certain area of marketing. (Overt/Covert/Latent/Unnoticed Opportunities)

13. The individuals or objects whose characteristic are to be measured are called the ________.
14. ________ refer to the time which is to be considered for the research to be undertaken on the subject's unit of analysis.
15. ________ refers the extent to which the subject are considered with respect to its entire universe.
16. A ________ is a proposition which the researcher wants to verify.
17. ________ explains the real nature of the problem.
18. ________ suggests possible solutions or new ideas for the problem or opportunity emphasized in the research problem.
19. The objective of the ________ type of research design is to ascertain magnitudes.
20. A ________ study is undertaken when the researcher wants to know the characteristics of certain groups such as age, sex, educational level, income, occupation, etc.
21. When the researcher is interested in knowing the cause and effect relationship between two or more variables, a ________ is applicable.
22. ________ are data that were collected for another purpose and already exist somewhere.
23. The fundamental functions linking the consumer, customer, and public to the marketer through information is called as the ________.
24. ________ provides the requisite timely and accurate information for making marketing decisions by reacting to the marketing opportunities and problems.
25. The first evidence of formal research techniques being employed could be traced as far back as in the year ________.
26. ________ comments that marketing managers run the risk of making the right decision at the wrong time.
27. ________ research design do not have any concrete structure.
28. The ________ types of questions prespecify all the possible answers, provide answers that are easier to interpret and tabulate after respondents have made a choice among them.
29. ________ involves decisions on Sampling Unit, Sampling Size and Sampling Procedure.
30. ________ are gathered for a specific purpose or for a specific research project.
31. Customers leave traces of their purchasing behaviour in store scanning data, catalogue purchases and customer databases, is called as the ________ data.
32. A ________ consists of a set of questions along with the alternative responses presented to respondents, with the particular objective. It can be both, open-ended as well as close-ended.
33. ________ involves going deeply into the thoughts that an individual may have about a product or services.
34. ________ uses metaphors to access nonverbal images. These techniques get associations that are less likely to emerge during normal interviewing.
35. ________ measure the interest or emotions aroused by exposures to a specific ad or picture.
36. ________ flashes an ad to a respondent with an exposure interval that may range, from less than one hundredth of a second to several seconds.
37. ________ study respondents' eye movements to see where their eye land first, how long they linger on a given item, and so on.
38. An ________ is attached to television sets in participating homes to record when the set is on and to which channel it is tuned.
39. ________ type of interviewing is designed to determine what social values interviewees hold dear by having them about broad topics such as their various roles in life and their daily activities.
40. ________ refers to the process of analyzing the collected data to derive some meaningful information.
41. Data analysis includes ________, ________, ________ and analysis ________ of the data.

42. ________ refer to the links between the manufacturers and the consumers,
43. ________ are a set of intermediaries performing a variety of functions.
44. ________ are also called as the intermediaries or the middlemen,
45. ________ comprise and the entire flow, the movement of the goods from the manufacturer to the consumers.
46. ________ are the intermediaries who take title to the merchandise and resell the merchandise, generally having the physical possession of the goods.
47. The intermediaries, sales agents, brokers, auctioneers, etc., are called as ________ types of intermediaries.
48. ________ who may have the possession of the goods or may not have the possession of the goods, but in no case will have the title to the merchandise.
49. ________ refers to the, "relinquishing some control over how and to whom the products are sold".
50. ________ refers to flow of activity from customers to the company.
51. ________ refers to the flow of the activity from company to the customer.
52. ________ refers to the flow of activity from both the directions, i.e., from company to customer as well as from customer to company.
53. ________ is also called a direct marketing channel.
54. ________ consists of a manufacturer selling directly to the final customer.
55. A ________ -level channel contains one selling intermediary, such as a retailer. A two-level channel contains two intermediaries, typically, wholesaler and retailer in consumer markets.
56. ________ refers to the strategy of the company to severely limit or restricts the number of intermediaries.
57. ________ refers to the strategy of the company whereby a company relies on more than a few but less than all of the intermediaries willing to carry a particular product.
58. ________ refers to the placing of the goods or services in as many outlets as possible by the manufacturer.
59. ________ refers to the establishing of the price list and schedule of discounts and allowances that intermediaries see as equitable and sufficient by the producer.
60. ________ refers to the payment terms and producer guarantees.
61. ________ defines the distributors' territories and the terms under which the producer will enfranchise other distributors.
62. The ________ criteria for the selection of the intermediaries refer to the extent to which the selected intermediary permits the company, the producer to exercise its control, in spite of the considerable role of the direct contact with customers performed by these intermediaries.
63. The ________ criteria in the selection of the intermediaries refer to the degree of flexibility permitted to the manufacturer/producer by the particular intermediary, with respect to the future changes in the distribution system characteristics.
64. ________ is any paid form of no personal presentation and promotion of ideas, goods, or services by an identified sponsor, with the specific objective.
65. ________________ refers to the specific communications task and achievement level to be accomplished with a specific audience in a specific period of time.
66. ________ type of advertising aims to create brand awareness and knowledge of new products or new features of existing products.
67. ________ type of advertising aims to create liking, preference, conviction, and purchase of a product or service.
68. ________ type of advertising aims to make an explicit comparison of the attributes of two or more brands.

69. ________ type of advertising aims to stimulate repeat purchase of products and services, reminding the target market about its long period association with the delivering functional benefit through the particular brand of the product.
70. ________ type of advertising aims to convince current purchasers that they made the right choice.
71. ASCI refers to ________.
72. The number of different persons or households exposed to a particular media schedule at least once during a specified time period is called as ________.
73. The number of times within the specified time period that an average person or household is exposed to the message is called as ________.
74. The qualitative value of an exposure through a given medium is called as ________.
75. ________ refers to the number of physical units that carries the advertisement.
76. ________ refers to the number of people exposed to the vehicle.
77. ________ refers to the manner of people with target audience characteristics exposed to the vehicle.
78. The number of people with target audience characteristics who actually saw the advertisement is called as ________.
79. The ________ scheduling problem involves scheduling the advertising in relationship to seasons and the business cycle.
80. The ________ scheduling problem calls for allocating advertising expenditures within a short period to obtain maximum impact.
81. ________ means exposures appear evenly throughout a given period.
82. ________ calls for spending the entire advertising budget in a single period.
83. ________ refers to the advertising for a particular period followed by the period with no advertising, followed by the second period of advertising activity.
84. ________ refers to the continuous advertising at low-weight levels reinforced periodically by waves of heavier activity.
85. Communication Effect Research is also called as ________.
86. ________ or ________ seeks to determine whether an ad is communicating effectively or not.

***Ans:*** **1.** Research, **2.** Basic Research, **3.** Basic Research, **4.** Basic Research, **5.** Basic Research, **6.** Basic Research, **7.** Applied Research, **8.** Applied Research, **9.** Marketing Research, **10.** Overt, **11.** Latent, **12.** Unnoticed opportunities, **13.** units of analysis, **14.** Time boundaries, **15.** Space boundaries, **16.** hypothesis, **17.** Exploratory Research Design, **18.** Exploratory Research Design, **19.** descriptive, **20.** descriptive, **21.** causal research design, **22.** Secondary data, **23.** Marketing Research, **24.** Marketing Research, **25.** 1854, **26.** F.E. Brown, **27.** Exploratory, **28.** close-ended, **29.** Sampling Plan, **30.** Primary data, **31.** Behavioural, **32.** questionnaire, **33.** Depth interviewing, **34.** (ZMET) Zaltman Metaphoric Elicitation, **35.** Galvanometers, **36.** Tachistoscope, **37.** Eye cameras, **38.** audiometer, **39.** Articulative, **40.** Data analysis, **41.** consolidation, classification, tabulation analysis, **42.** Channels, **43.** Channels, **44.** Channels, **45.** Channels, **46.** Merchants, **47.** Agents, **48.** Agents/Facilitators, **49.** Delegation, **50.** Backward flow, **51.** Forward flow, **52.** Two-way flow, **53.** Zero-level channel, **54.** Zero-level Channel, **55.** one, **56.** Exclusive distribution, **57.** Selective distribution, **58.** Intensive distribution, **59.** Price Policy, **60.** Conditions of sale, **61.** Distributor's territorial rights, **62.** control, **63.** control, **64.** Advertising, **65.** Advertising goal (or Advertising objective), **66.** Informative, **67.** Persuasive, **68.** Comparative, **69.** Reminder, **70.** Reinforcement, **71.** The Advertisements Standard Council of India, **72.** Reach, **73.** Frequency, **75.** Circulation, **76.** Audience, **77.** Effective Audience, **78.** Effective Ad-exposed Audience, **79.** macro, **80.** macro, **81.** Continuity, **82.** Concentration, **83.** Flighting, **84.** Pulsing, **85.** Copy Testing, **86.** Communication Effect Research, 'Copy Testing'.

☺ ☺ ☺

CHAPTER 13

# Production Management

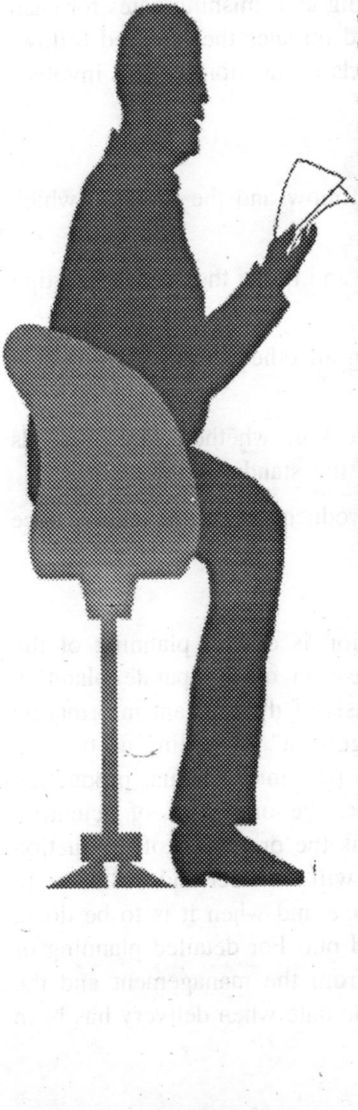

LEARNING OBJECTIVES

- *Production Planning and Control*
- *Inventory Management*
- *Materials Management*

## PRODUCTION PLANNING AND CONTROL

The control of production is one of the important problems of production management. The plant is organized and operated primarily with the object of and is also spoken of as manufactuer of goods. In productive enterprises, it is essential that production is carried out in the best manner at the lowest cost and the goods are of right quality and are produced at the proper time. The management will have to take all possible steps to see that the plans, chalked out by the Planning Department are properly adhered to and the standards set are attained and improved. This is precisely the function of production control. Production is thus concerned with direction and guiding production along the lines set by the Planning Department. It is the means by which actual performance of the productive apparatus is constantly evaluated in the light of plans formulated by the planners. Obviously the fundamental object of production control is "that the product shall be produced in the best and the cheapest method, that it shall be of the required quality and that it shall be produced at the right time". To achieve these objectives the management plans production in advance of operations, sets the exact route or path of each individual item or part, fixes the starting and finishing dates for each item, assembly or finished product releases the necessary orders, and initiates the required follow-up to ensure the smooth functioning of the enterprise. In other words production control involves the following steps:

(i) Planning of the productive operations in detail.

(ii) Routing, i.e., laying down the path which the work will follow and the order in which various operations will be carried out.

(iii) Scheduling, i.e., establishing the amount of work to be done and fixing the time for starting and finishing each operation.

(iv) Dispatching, i.e., the issuing of necessary order and taking all other steps to ensure that the time targets set in the schedules will be achieved.

(v) Follow-up or checking the progress, i.e., taking steps to check-up whether work proceeds according to plans and how far there are variances from the standards set earlier.

(vi) Inspection, i.e., conducting occasional check-ups of the products to ensure maintenance of high standards of quality.

These steps are described below:

**Planning:** The first important step toward control of production is careful planning of the operations in advance of actual production. This involves the creation of a separate planning department that will chalk out a programme of production on the basis of the relevant information available. As has been observed in the chapter on "Scientific Management" the setting up of such a department and the preparation of the planning function from the function of actual production in the workshop are important innovations made by F.W. Taylor, the originator of scientific management. In fact, it will be no exaggeration to refer to Taylor as the originator of production control too. Taylor visualized that those in the planning department will consider and decide as to what work is to be done, how it is to be done, where it is to be done and when it is to be done, while those in the shop will see to it that these decisions are carried out. For detailed planning of operations, the planning department will receive full information from the management and the engineering department as to the quantity required to be produced, the date when delivery has been promised to the customers and the necessary engineering and drawing specifications. On the basis of such information, the planning department will proceed to prepare chart and written plans which will form the core of the programme of production control.

**Routing:** As has been mentioned above the planning department is concerned with the selection of the path or route over which each piece is to travel in being transformed from raw material into finished product. This is referred to as "Routing". Routing includes the planning of where and by whom work shall be done, the determination of the path that work shall follow and the necessary sequence of operations. The object of routing is to find out the best and cheapest sequence of operations so that those working in the shop are instructed to carry the work through the workshop in a systematic and economical manner. In some cases, it suffices the case of products requiring more detailed planning, the particular machines and processes to be used in production are also to be prescribed. In the routing of the most comprehensive type, however the sequence of detailed operations to be performed, the set-up of the special fixture, special tools to be used for each operation, and the feed and speed for each tool are also specified. The route clerk who is entrusted with the task of routing in the planning department can succeed at the job only if he has the complete knowledge of the product, the manufacturing processes and the capacity and characteristics of every machine. The following considerations must be kept in view while preparing a route card showing the route of the materials through various processes:

(i) The machine in the plant should be operated at their full capacity.

(ii) Where accuracy is important, the product should pass through work stations which are manned by the ablest of the personnel.

(iii) The route indicated in the card should be the shortest and the most economical of all possible routes.

**Scheduling:** After the route clerk has laid the path to be followed by product through various machines and processes, the next step in production control would be the preparation of a schedule showing the time that will be needed for the production of the article at each stage. This will involve the preparation of a timetable indicating the total time needed for the manufacture of a product as also the time expected to be spent at each machine and process. Scheduling is thus, "the determination of the time that should be required to perform each operation and also the time necessary to perform the entire series as routed, making allowance for all factors concerned". The term can be clearly understood with the help of an analogy. A person intending to travel (say, by rail) has first to select the route which will suit him best out of the various alternative routes available. That may be called routing. The next step for him will be to find out the time which the train will take for reaching each station on the selected route. On the basis of the information, he can prepare a schedule for his own guidance indicating the train's timetable of arrival and departure from each station. Generally, timetable or time-schedules of this kind are prepared and supplied by the railway authorities. Applying this analogy to the case of manufacturing unit the time schedule will show when the product will enter to particular process and when it will leave the same for another process. In this manner the total time for the entire process of production will be determined.

In preparing schedules the persons concerned will have to take into consideration the various types of orders on hand and the dates by which their completion has been promised. Some orders may be such that will require overtime work of special handling because completion is not possible according to the delivery dates set for them in the regular course of production. Such rush orders will naturally receive top priority. The regular orders on the other hand can be finished within the stipulated time in the regular course. These orders will, however, generally receive preference of the repair orders on goods already sold. Three types of schedules may be prepared as a part of a programme of production control: (a) Master schedule indicating the date on which the various jobs are to be completed. (b) Operation schedule asking the total time required to do a piece of work with a given machine or process. (c) Daily operation schedule showing the time required to do each detailed operation of a given job with a given machine or process. The master schedule is a kind of control board and can be regarded as the key schedule recording the entire activity throughout the plant. The other two are refinements of this schedule. It will be seen that scheduling is a difficult though important process, and requires the collection of data which may not always be easily available.

**Dispatching:** Having drawn the proper route for the product (routing) and the timetable of production, the process of production planning will be more or less complete. The next logical step would be to proceed to execute the plan. Dispatching (literally meaning – sending something toward a particular destination) is the name given to all such steps as are meant to give effect to, and implement the programme of production chalked out by those responsible for routing and scheduling in the planning department. It is the function of initiating production according to plans. The following steps have to be taken to perform the function of dispatching in the manufacturing plant:

(i) The procurement of necessary tools, jigs and fixtures before they are actually required by the workmen so that the work may not be delayed due to the nonavailability or delay in obtaining them.

(ii) Giving the workmen the necessary work orders instructions, drawings, etc., for initiating the work.

(iii) Maintaining a record of the time of starting and completing each operation.

(iv) Moving the work after completion to the next process or machine on the route.

For the purpose of dispatching an order box is kept near each workmen. It may have not less than two compartments — the first containing the work order instruction card, etc., the second holding instructions, etc., for collecting tools, jigs, etc., for the next job. The moving of material to and from machines and processes may be entrusted to a 'move man' who will act under a 'move order'.

**Follow-up and Checking Progress:** The functions discussed in the foregoing pages are concerned more with production planning then with the function of control. As has been observed earlier, the control function of management is concerned chiefly with an appraisal and evaluation of the results achieved against the standard of performance set by the plans. It is equally concerned with locating deficiencies in actual working of the organization and taking the necessary corrective steps to set things in order. Production plans require significance only when they are supplemented by steps meant to expedite work. In continuous process industries, the function of those responsible for the follow-up of production would consist in avoiding bottlenecks in production and taking prompt remedial action to remove them if they interfere with the production. In job-lot production expeditors and stock chasers may pursue the product through various stages exhorting and enabling those engaged in production to avoid delays and complete the work according to schedule. The function of follow-up or expediting will also be responsible for the maintenance of proper records of work and the delays and bottlenecks. Such records can be used in future to control production.

**Inspection:** Production control is introduced not merely to ensure that the goods will be produced on time, but is also meant to see that the goods produced are of the right quality. This is done through inspection of the products manufactured. Since the purpose of inspection is to compare the products with the standards of quality set earlier it too can be regarded as an effective agency of production control. One way of inspection is to examine the quality of finished products at the end of the process of production. But this may involve too much of wastage in the form of rejected products. To minimize the rejection of defective products, inspection may be conducted at every stage of production. Also, materials may be inspected against certain established standards and so may machines and tools be inspected to find out their performance and accuracy. Inspections may be made either in respect of samples selected at random or of each particular product. (i.e., cent per cent inspection). The inspectors may inspect materials semi-finished and finished products either at the work bench or in special laboratories or testing rooms.

**Requirements for Production Control:** From the above description of the various functions of production control it is evident that any scheme of production control will require the following for its successful operation:

(i) Complete information relating to engineering special tools and times and costs of previous performances.

(ii) Accurate and up to date information about the stores which are to be used.

(iii) Knowledge of work-in-process.

(iv) Data on power speeds and feeds of all machines and on the most effective forms of cutting tools, etc.

(v) Records of the best performances on similar work with best combination of tools, feeds and speeds.

(vi) Careful instructions to the workmen, following up and correction of short schedule, and inspection of all tools and appliances.

**Advantages:** Production planning and control yield a number of advantages some which are summed up as under:

**(i) Efficient Service:** It ensures better service to the customers by enabling production to be conducted in such a way that the products can be delivered on promised dates, in the absence of such control the firm may not be able to honour its commitments on time with the result that the customers may be put to a great inconvenience.

**(ii) Avoidance of Rush Orders:** By planning production and controlling its time aspects, production control reduces the number of rush orders and overtime works plant.

**(iii) Avoidance of Bottlenecks:** The work-in-process does not get accumulated because production control maintains an even flow of work.

**(iv) Inventory Control:** It leads to a better control of the raw materials inventory because the operations and their requirements are thoroughly planned.

**(v) Economy in Production Time:** It reduces the loss of time by the workers waiting of materials and causes improvement in plant morale.

**(vi) Equipment Utilization:** It makes for the most effective use of equipment.

# INVENTORY CONTROL

Inventory control means control over materials lying in store. Inventory control keeps continuous track of inventories. But it is not merely recordkeeping. Inventory control aims at the following triple objectives: (1) never runout of anything (out of stock), (2) never build-up a very large inventory, i.e., having much of anything on hand (unwanted stocks), and (3) never send out too many small costly orders for more, i.e., never pay high prices and incur high freight because of buying in small quantities. Too many small orders also involve recurrent clerical work. We lose quantity discount also. You must avoid hand-to-mouth buying or making. Effective inventory control can assure at least 10 p.c. savings in our total investment.

Too much inventory is painless — even pleasant. Production is continuous. Customer is happy. Everyone is happy. Even then it is bad, because of inventory is locked-up and hence, it is very costly. The basic savings and the costs and capital needs associated with large stocks.

## Objectives of Inventory Control

1. We have to reduce to the minimum idle time due to shortage of materials and spare parts. Neither man nor machine should have idle time due to lack of materials.
2. Similarly, we have to offer maximum service and satisfaction to our customers with regard to fulfilling the due dates strictly as per orders. The sole aim of a business is to create and retain customers.
3. At the same time we are interested in minimizing capital investment and cost of storage.

Better sales through improved service to customer lower costs through smoother production operations and lower investment needs through reduced inventories are not doubt legitimate aims of any business. But they are usually in conflict. The best inventory control recognizes the conflict and forces a business, which balances or reconciliates the objectives and then assures faithful compliance with the balance arrived in day-to-day operations. Please note that efficient inventory control cannot eliminate business risk but it certainly can reduce it. We can only assess risk, plan a strategy and accept the risk on most favourable terms. Production planning and control, purchasing plan and inventory control go hand-in-hand to achieve overall basic company goals. Systems approach emphasizes integration and coordination of all subsystems of a business enterprise.

## Importance of Efficient Inventory Control System

1. An efficient inventory control system minimizes the possibility of delay in production. There is no danger of closure of plant, unemployment, lower dividend and replacement of management — a dark picture resulting out of poor inventory control.
2. It helps a company to secure many economies. For instance, no duplication in ordering, better use of available materials by interdepartmental transfers, economies due to bulk purchases such as low freight, higher discount, lower price, less clerical work, etc.
3. It is necessary for efficient accounting system, particularly for material aspect of cost accounting.
4. It discourages dishonesty, e.g., stealing material from the plant.

5. It expedites preparation of financial statements.
6. Losses, damages, deterioration of materials can be minimized.

We can have careful material handling.

## Functions of Inventory Control

With particular reference to a commercial or merchandising concern, e.g., a big wholesaler or a large retail establishment, the following are the typical functions of inventory control.

1. Keeping the stock of goods at the most appropriate level at all times so that the requirements of sales department can always be fulfilled.
2. Maintaining capital investment in stocks at a minimum desirable level, without sacrificing the main interest of trading.
3. Protecting the stocks from losses and damages due to improper handling, pilferage or unauthorized removal from the store.
4. Receiving and recording of all goods routed in the store and keeping up to date trace of every outgoing item.
5. Indexing of all items of stock for their quick location. This is done through identifying marks, labels and Bin Cards.
6. Up to date inventory records must show the quantity and value of all goods in the warehouse, all receipts and deliveries made from the warehouse and the points at which replenishment of stocks become necessary by ordering new stocks.

In manufacturing, the bulk of purchasing is the procurement of raw or semi-finished materials needed for processing. In addition we need tools, supplies of consumable goods, machines, etc. In contrast, merchandising firms buy finished goods for resale along with supplies for daily operations and equipment. The procurement of materials in manufacturing or in merchandising, however, creates similar problems in inventory control.

## The Flow and Pricing of Inventories

**Pricing of Materials Issued:** Inventories do change, deteriorate, and become less desirable. Hence, there is the problem of inventory flow, which management has to face. There are five alternatives of pricing materials that are issued:

**1. First-in-first-out (FIFO):** The material which flows in first is the first to flow out. Older stocks are to go first. The materials are issued at the price of earliest goods lying in stock. Such a pricing is suitable in a falling market when the prices are falling continuously.

**2. Last-in-first-out (LIFO):** The material which flows in last is the first to flow out. Latest consignment will go first. The issue price is fixed at the price of the latest stock. Such a pricing is preferred when the market is rising and prices are continuously going up.

**Example: Rising Prices in the Market**

| In | Out | Balance | Price | Transaction |
|---|---|---|---|---|
| FIFO Method | | | | |
| | 00 | | | |
| 50 | | 50 | 50 Paise | + ₹ 50.00 |
| 100 | | 150 | 75 Paise | + ₹ 75.00 |
| | 60 | 90 | 50 at Paise 50<br>10 at Paise 75 | – ₹ 32.50 |
| LIFO Method | | | | |
| | 00 | 50 Paise | + ₹ 25.00 | |
| 50 | | 50 | 75 Paise | + ₹ 75.00 |
| 100 | | 150 | 75 Paise | + ₹ 75.00 |
| | 60 | 90 | 60 at 75 Paise | – ₹ 45.00 |

**Analysis:** FIFO Method. Since prices are rising we can pay at least the most recent price of 75 paise per unit for the next purchase or ₹ 45 to replace the units sold. This same amount of material was priced out at ₹ 32.50; so we have wiped out ₹ 45 minus ₹ 32.50; or ₹ 12.50 of any profit we might have anticipated by the act of replacing the inventory. It is not a very profitable transaction.

## MATERIALS MANAGEMENT

All goods between the receipt of raw materials and the dispatch of final products to customers are termed as materials. Inventory (all classes of materials including finished goods) is money temporarily in the form of raw materials components parts, supplies, in-progress goods and finished products. But it is not like money in the bank. In reality it is money on which you pay interest. You do not earn interest on this money. Bank deposit of ₹ 1,000 after a year may be worth ₹ 1,100. But inventory in the store of ₹ 1,000 worth may be worth ₹ 825 after deducting carry-over charges of ₹ 175 for one year. The carry-over charge includes interest rent, insurance and establishment charge. Under normal circumstances carry-over charge is a positive cost. On an average carry-over cost is estimated at 15 p.c. to 20 p.c. of inventory value per year. In simple terms materials management is a process in which an organization involves in planning, organising, scheduling and controlling (inventory) of all the important elements which play a crucial role in the production function in an organization. It plays a decisive role as the core-competence and strength of an organization depends upon its production capability.

An organization is now regarded as a structured process or a system having a mechanism of inflow-process-outflow. It has a dynamic nature and it is a subsystem of its own environment which provides inputs and demands output. The systems approach emphasizes integrated interrelated character of its components which constantly interact with one another for accomplishing common objectives. People and things (materials) are two most important resources in charge of management of any enterprise. Materials do not involve human factor and cannot offer resistance against change or control, whereas men involve human factor and management of people is definitely much more complicated than the management of materials.

Materials management and control can make necessary arrangement to ensure supply of proper quality and quantity of all materials as and when needed in the process of production at a minimum cost. It also looks after storage and inventory controls. Business deals with six Ms: (1) Men (2) Money (3) Materials (4) Machines (5) Management, and (6) Markets. These resources are required in each area of management: (1) Production (2) Marketing (3) Finance (4) Personnel, and (5) Purchasing.

Materials constitute an important item in the total mix of resources. Substantial part of the total capital or investment is locked up in materials. On an average the material content is about 60 p.c. of production cost in the USA, Japan and India. A recent survey by the Reserve Bank of India pointed out that about, ₹ 200 crore was locked up in inventory in the public and private sectors. If we can reduce our inventories through better materials management even by 20 p.c. we will release about ₹ 250 crore working capital in our business system.

As material control and management is definitely simpler than that of management and control of human resources, modern management has started taking great interest in materials management.

Materials management can have total integrated approach for the entire company. We can have materials flow system with comprehensive and feasible controls right from the procurement of materials till the final goods reach in the hands of consumers or users.

Our economics system based on monetary exchange has three distinct flows: (1) Goods flow (2) Money flow, and (3) Information flow. We can see these three flows continuously in the circle of exchange, *viz.*, market. They are circular flows. When goods flow is balanced by money flow, we have economic stability — neither inflation nor deflation. Every enterprise must develop and establish a good information system interrelating continuously the material flow and money flow. Information flow enables management to maintain effective control over both material flow and money flow. In fact, all managerial decisions in purchasing; selling, financing, producing and in administering the business are invariably based upon information. At present, computers enable the enterprise to build-up up to date information system. Management Information System (MIS) is essential.

## IMPORTANCE OF MATERIALS MANAGEMENT

There are only two fundamental inputs in which management is primarily interested:

1. Men, and 2. Materials. Management is equally interested in optimizing the use of both these resources. However, from management point of view, materials management offers greater promise as a cost reducing device. Better and scientific management of materials can not only bring about substantial cost savings but also result in improved production capacity of plants, saving of labour time, reduction in inventories, reduction in storage space, reduction in damage to materials, smooth flow or production, easier production control, reduced employee fatigue and so on.

In India, we have adopted planned economic development at an accelerated rate under our Five-Year Plans since 1951. Planned development requires optimum utilization of available scarce resources and prevention of all types of wastes. We are required to import many raw materials, capital goods and supplies from abroad. These large imports need ample foreign exchange resources. Under controls on foreign exchange and imports and under heavy import duties we are complied to adopt scientific system of management and control of our materials — both imported as well as home-produced materials. We are literally living in the era of shortages of all kinds of materials and supplies particularly under inflationary conditions for the last two decades. Under such circumstances, materials management is a boon to our economy and it can yield rich dividend much more easily and without inviting resistance like human resources.

## Scope of Materials Management

'Materials management is concerned with planning, and directing and controlling the location, movement and timing of the various flows of commodities (goods flow) used in and produced by a business enterprise' (Bethel).

Production planning breaks the product into materials and parts. This is the starting point of materials management. Production planning has also to determine the needs of supplies and equipment items required for the manufacturing process. Thus, materials supplies, (consumable items) and equipment required to produce a final product constitute the beginning of the materials management in the case of an industrial company either for producer goods or for consumer goods. Thereafter, materials management is a running partner of production control till the product is manufactured. Then, it becomes the logistic branch of the production function. Flow of goods from the manufacturer to the ultimate consumers also becomes an integral part of materials management. At each stage in the process of marketing we have the movement of goods. In a sense entire marketing is basically materials management under the integrated or systems approach to business. In reality, responsibilities of integrated materials flow system and materials management end when the correct finished product in proper condition, quality and quantity is in the hands of ultimate consumer or user of the product.

## Flow of Material

### Classes of Materials

In the materials flow system we have: Raw materials, parts, in-process materials, supplies and equipment items. These are demanded by manufacturers and processors. Finished goods: These are demanded by customers in the market to satisfy their needs and desires.

1. **Raw Materials:** They are the materials used in the product which is in an unprocessed condition. E.g., cotton, jute, leather hides, iron and steel, chemicals.
2. **Purchased Parts:** They are items used in the assembly of the product, e.g., bolts, nuts, screws, etc.
3. **In-process Materials:** They are called works-in-process inventories. They are semi-manufactured goods demanding further processing, e.g., shoe upper cut from leather.
4. **Finished Products:** These are goods fully manufactured, inspected and ready for dispatch to a customer, e.g., finished pair of shoes, decorated flower-pot, ready-made garments, etc.
5. **Supplies:** These are consumable goods used in the process of manufacturing, e.g., stationery, pencil, oils, grinding wheels, files, etc.
6. **Equipment Items:** These are our physical facilities and fixtures, fittings and such other expendable parts of machines.

## SUMMARY

Production is thus concerned with direction and guiding production along the lines set by the Planning Department. It is the means by which actual performance of the productive apparatus is constantly evaluated in the light of plans formulated by the planners. Obviously the fundamental object of production control is "that the product shall be produced in the best and the cheapest method, that it shall be of the required quality and that it shall be produced at the right time".In other words production control involves the following steps:

(i) Planning of the productive operations in detail.

(ii) Routing, i.e., laying down the path which the work will follow and the order in which various operations will be carried out.

(iii) Scheduling, i.e., establishing the amount of work to be done and fixing the time for starting and finishing each operation.

(iv) Dispatching, i.e., the issuing of necessary order and taking all other steps to ensure that the time targets set in the schedules will be achieved.

(v) Follow-up or checking the progress, i.e., taking steps to check-up whether work proceeds according to plans and how far there are variances from the standards set earlier.

(vi) Inspection, i.e., conducting occasional check-ups of the products to ensure maintenance of high standards of quality.

Inventory control means control over materials lying in store. Inventory control keeps continuous track of inventories. But it is not merely recordkeeping. Inventory control aims at the following triple objectives: (1) never runout of anything (out of stock), (2) never build-up a very large inventory, i.e., having much of anything on hand (unwanted stocks), and (3) never send out too many small costly orders for more, i.e., never pay high prices and incur high freight because of buying in small quantities. Too many small orders also involve recurrent clerical work. We lose quantity discount also. You must avoid hand-to-mouth buying or making. Effective inventory control can assure at least 10 p.c. savings in our total investment.

All goods between the receipt of raw materials and the dispatch of final products to customers are termed as materials. Inventory (all classes of materials including finished goods) is money temporarily in the form of raw materials components parts, supplies, in-progress goods and finished products. But it is not like money in the bank. In reality it is money on which you pay interest. You do not earn interest on this money.

Materials management can have total integrated approach for the entire company. We can have materials flow system with comprehensive and feasible controls right from the procurement of materials till the final goods reach in the hands of consumers or users. There are only two fundamental inputs in which management is primarily interested:

1. Men, and 2. Materials. Management is equally interested in optimizing the use of both these resources. However, from management point of view, material management offers greater promise as a cost reducing device. Better and scientific management of materials can not only bring about substantial cost savings but also result in improved production capacity of plants, saving of labour time, reduction in inventories, reduction in storage space, reduction in damage to materials, smooth flow or production, easier production control, reduced employee fatigue and so on.

# CASELETS 1

## 1. What shall We Do?

Roy and Friends Plastics (Pvt.) Ltd. is a new company in plastics business. Its experience of past two years in the business has not been happy. The management of the company finds that the company is facing some of the burning problems such as: (a) machine costs are rising (b) some of the machines remain idle, some are overworked while others are underworked (c) orders are delayed in execution (d) the finished goods are piling up in the godown, and (e) some of the valued customers have threatened to leave the firm in case they are not given goods in time. The management wishes you to outline a production plan for overcoming these problems and ensuring maximum efficiency. What corrective steps will you suggest and why?

## 2. Play it Yourself, Now

The management of Great India Cloth Mills (Pvt.) Ltd., finds that the company's customers are not satisfied with the services of the company and have threatened to leave the company in case they are not supplied goods in time. The company, however, is known for its fine quality goods. The General Manager, Mr. C.V. Thomas, calls the sales manager, Mr. A.C. Dey, and asks him why his department was not functioning well. Mr. Dey explains that his department was making the highest competitive sales in the market but deliveries were delayed because production department was not coping with them. Mr. Thomas, then calls the Production Manager, Mr. Krishan Dubey, and enquires why his department was not doing well. Mr. Dubey clarifies that his department was working to its fullest capacity. The situation leads to a state of confusion. Then, a management consultant, Mr. L.C. Chunawala, is called and he discusses the entire problem with the three managers. Assume the role of these four persons and outline the essence of their discussion.

## 3. What shall We Do?

The Greenfields Tractor India Ltd., manufactures tractors and also spare-parts. In spare parts division, they carry 35 types of product-lines. The manufacture of spare parts is subcontracted to small units. Of late the cost of carrying inventories is found to be rising. The management of the company wishes you to chalk out a suitable Inventory Policy so as to minimize the cost without facing stock-outs. How will you go about?

### Questions

1. Discuss the various steps in production control.
2. Discuss briefly the objectives of inventory control.
3. What do you mean by "Materials Management" Discuss its importance and scope.

## ........ QUESTIONS FOR DISCUSSION

1. Discuss the various steps in production control.
2. Discuss briefly the objectives of inventory control.
3. What do you mean by "Materials Management" Discuss its importance and scope.

# Part-III
# Portfolio Management

Chapter 14 : The Portfolio Management and Stock Exchanges

CHAPTER 14

# The Portfolio Management and Stock Exchanges

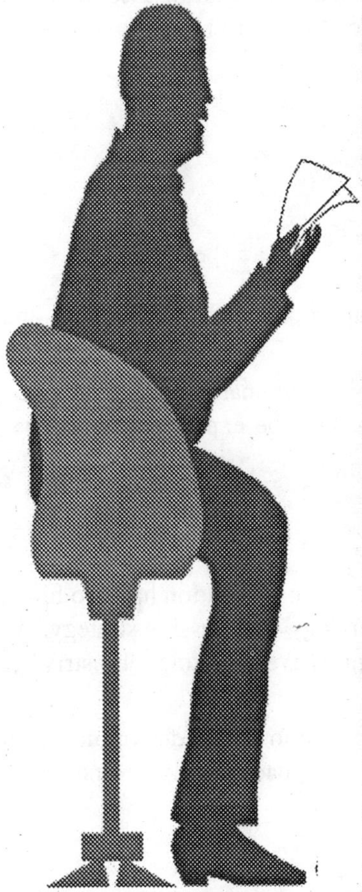

**LEARNING OBJECTIVES**

- *Concept of Portfolio Management*
- *Security Analysis*
- *Securities Market*
- *Functions of Stock Exchange*
- *Importance and Services*
- *Trading Settlement*
- *Buying and Selling of Shares*
- *Role of SEBI*

## PORTFOLIO MANAGEMENT

Portfolio management is also to be referred as Investment Management in which a company decides its optimal financial mix on the basis of following broad categories:

- Specification of the investment objectives and constraints.
- Choice of asset mix.
- Formulation of the portfolio strategy.
- Selection of securities.
- Portfolio execution.
- Portfolio revision.
- Performance evaluation.

In simple terms, portfolio management is a process in which an organization tries to proportionately choose variety of options available for the choice of the right kind of asset mix and allocation of its financial resources and decides how much of your portfolio is to be invested in each of the following asset categories:

- Cash.
- Bonds.
- Stocks.
- Real Estate.
- Shares and Other Securities.

The thrust area of portfolio management is to determine the appropriate mix of "Bonds" and "Stocks" in the portfolio.

Portfolio management is to specify the investment policy which summarizes the objectives, constraints and preferences of the investors. The investment policy may be expressed as follows:

- Financial objectives of an organization and its requirement.
- Risk tolerance level.
- Investment constraints and preferences.

Investment objectives are expressed in terms of returns and risk. An organization has two broad choices available with respect to portfolio strategy, *viz.*, an active strategy or a passive strategy. An active strategy is followed by most investment professionals and aggressive investors who strive to earn superior returns, after adjustment to risk.

A passive portfolio strategy calls for creating a well-diversified portfolio at a predetermined level of risk and holding it relatively unchanged over time, unless it becomes inadequately diversified or inconsistent with the investors risk-return preferences.

## STOCK EXCHANGE

According to the Securities Contracts (Regulations) Act, 1956 (India), "It is an association, organization, or body of individuals, whether incorporated or not, established for the purpose of assisting regulation and controlling business in buying, selling and dealing securities".

Securities include:

1. Shares, stocks, bonds and debentures issued by the companies.
2. Government securities and bonds issued by semigovernment units.

The market for outstanding securities is referred to as the secondary market, or, more popularly as the stock market. In other words, stock exchange is the market, wherein, the industrial securities are bought and sold, under the code of rules and regulations.

It thus, provides capital to industry, commerce and government.

Presently, Indian stock market comprises of twenty-three stock exchanges. The most important of them are National Stock Exchange and Bombay Stock Exchanges. The Securities Exchange Board of India (SEBI) is the regulatory body which supervises the operations of the stock market in India.

## Functions of Stock Market

The stock exchanges constitute an organized market, wherein the securities issued by the Indian companies and Central and State Government are traded. A well-ordered stock market performs the several economic functions as discussed below:

1. **Measure of Safety and Fair Dealing:** The stock exchanges operates under a regulatory framework, and thus, are approved by the Central Government. For listing the securities on the stock exchanges, the companies/government/or the units are required to meet the criteria as outlined by SEBI. This ensures the reasonable safety to the investors. Moreover, the competitive conditions for the transactions are also fair enough to all the interested groups.
2. **Act of Magic:** The stock exchanges plays the role of the magic stick of the magician. The stock exchanges are operating under the regulations of the SEBI, ensures fair dealing, easily convinces the interest of the general public to invest in the securities listed by the companies.

   The requirements of the funds for company are long-term, while most of the investors are interested in the short-term of medium-term investments. But the companies are assured about the availability of the funds by listing securities on Stock Exchanges. The entire system of the market (stock market) is designed in a way that enables the negotiability and transferability of the securities. Thus, the companies are in a position to manage its long-term capital requirements.
3. **Guidance on the Cost of Capital:** Companies can raise capital through various sources. Some of these sources involves heavy burden of interest payment in addition to repayment of the principal amount. Moreover, balancing the debt and equity ratio as well as the cost of capital, becomes the prior responsibility for the manager managing companies' capital. Raising capital by issuing shares, debentures, bonds, etc., is comparatively desirable for the companies. For calculating the cost of capital, market values of the securities of the company can be obtained from the stock market quotations.
4. **Inducement to the Companies to Raise their Standard of Performance:** The company's performance is reflected in the market price of the equity stock of the company listed on the stock exchanges. This has direct relationship with the persuasive power of the companies' securities on the investors. Undoubtedly, the performance becomes more 'visible' in the eyes of the public, through stock exchanges.

Moreover, as referred in the prior points, the companies need to meet the criteria of the SEBI, to list the securities on stock exchanges. This also provides direct inducement to the companies to raise as well as popularize their performance, among various interest groups.

5. **Flow of Capital to the Most Profitable Channels:** The flow of the savings in the form of investment would not have been transformed into the capital, in the absence of the regulated stock exchanges and stock market. Moreover, the savings are more productively utilized when the investors invest in the companies' securities. Also, the investors will invest in those companies' securities, which promise the most profitable investment opportunities. It is but obvious, that such companies, in order to satisfy the expectations of the investors and to retain the trust of the investors, will also invest the capital raised in the projects accomplishing their objectives.

Thus, capital formations by capital flow as well as the maximum returns on the capital thus invested from, the most profitable channels would not have been possible without the functions performed by the stock exchanges.

## Services by the Stock Exchanges

The services hidden in the functions performed by the stock exchanges are explained below:

**1. Continuous Marketability to the Securities:** The functioning of the stock exchange is such that provides the continuous scope for trading on the securities. These are the ready and steady outlets for purchasing and selling the securities, and thus stimulate the larger income. Any change in the market value of the securities listed on the stock exchanges can be monitored continuously, and the probable profit or the probable loss, can be visualized, in respect of the securities held or intended to be held by any investor. Thus, stock exchanges provide continuous marketability and price continuity to the investors interested to trade or the players familiar in this game.

**2. Proper Direction to the Flow of Capital:** Stock exchanges are the sensitive barometer of the business activity. The price quoted for different securities implies their relative profitability as well as probability. The rule "Higher the listed price indicated the higher performance of the companies, as well as the promising opportunities", guides the investor. Thus, the securities with greater market standing attracts more investors, in other words the flow of capital is thus directed to the securities with higher market standing, which investors are expecting and hoping to be fulfilled even in future.

**3. Higher Distribution of New Securities:** For listing their securities on stock exchanges a company requires to fulfil the criteria determined by the regulatory body. The functioning of the stock exchanges is also under the strict observation of the various authorities. Thus, the magic of stock exchanges attracts and convince higher number of investors, and higher public response. The securities listed on stock exchanges are more acceptable as well as fetch higher market value. Moreover, costs of underwriting such issues are also relatively less.

**4. Ensures Safety of Funds:** Obviously, with the stock exchanges coming under the direct monitoring of the SEBI rules and regulations, the companies' can relatively convince and attract the investors on one side and the investors are assured of the companies' authenticity. Moreover, the probable opportunities offered by the listed securities can also be probed, ensuring the returns on the investments to the investors, which directly affects/assures the concerned companies with availability of funds. Also, there is check on overtrading, illegitimate speculations and manipulations, thus, assures fair dealings to all the interested groups. Thus, stock exchanges ensure safety of funds, not only to the companies and investors, but to all the players in the secondary market.

**5. Mobilization of Savings:** The uncertainties to the considerable level, the risk factor in terms of fraud listings and illegal performance of the stock exchanges are tapped under the regulations and the monitoring of the SEBI. This has increased the number of investors contributing in this process of capital formation. The savings of the general public and others are converted into investments through various securities' investment, these investments are accepted as the capital by the companies and further invested into various productive projects yielding high returns thereof, and thus the capital formation cycle continues.

But, in the absence of the regulated stock exchanges it would have been difficult for the companies to convince and attract the savings for being converted into investments.The investors, the general public would have made savings out of the cycle of capital formation, or unproductive investment having negligible returns, which would have not accelerated the mobilization process.

Thus, stock exchanges help in the mobilization and facilitate capital formation and assist the economic growth.

**6. Mirror of Business Cycle:** Two of the important stock exchanges in India, NSE and BSE, are on the topic of the discussions. Nifty falls by 50 points and BSE closed at 4,000 points is the news headlines. The only reason is that at this stock exchanges, the market prices of the listed securities of the companies reflects the performance of the companies, which forms the trend line or the graph on the concerned stock exchanges, showing the overall picture of the various economical giants. The performance of the companies in return also depends on the stock exchanges for the availability of the funds/capital, thereby on the investments.

The investments are again dependent on the economic conditions of the country as well as the expected boom or depression in the economy. The falling market prices of the securities listed indicates the depression in the economy, while the increasing in the investments reflects the booming economy. But, the role of inflation and deflation and the company's hidden objectives must be analyzed with great care in such evaluation.

## Benefits Provided by the Stock Exchanges

The functions performed and the services rendered by the stock exchanges can also be understood from the perspective of its benefits to the various sections/sectors in the economy. The benefits of stock exchanges are discussed below from three perspectives:

1. **Benefits to the Investors:** Ensures about the authenticity of the listed securities, as it is permitted for listing after being evaluated by the stock exchange authorities and the functioning of the stock exchanges are monitored by SEBI.
   - Guides investors on the choice of securities to be traded, which is provided by the trends of dealings.
   - Ensures liquidity of the securities.
   - Information of the value of the securities through daily quotations of listed securities.
   - Undue fluctuations in securities' prices are avoided by the balancing operations of the speculators (bulls and bears).
   - Ensures safety of funds.
2. **Benefits to the Companies:**

   (a) High distribution of the Securities

   (b) Continuous Marketability of the Securities.

(c) Credit standing and goodwill of the company increases.

(d) Quicker and better convincing and attracting the investors.

(e) Ensures safety of funds.

(f) Guidance on the cost of capital

3. **Benefits to the Community/Society:**

(a) Ensures safety of funds to the investors, to the companies and the society as a whole.

(b) Inculcates the saving habits and facilitates for capital formation.

(c) Capital formation and mobilization becoming possible.

(d) Providing medium for evaluating value of different securities.

(e) Flow of capital to the most profitable channel.

(f) Mirror of business cycle.

## TRADING AND SETTLEMENT

The listed securities on the stock exchanges, its trading as well as the settlement have passed through various changes with the development of the technology, increasing interest of the investors and the requirements for amending the rules and regulations of the stock exchanges, thereby keeping a check on the entire functioning of the stock exchanges as well as the players of this game. The picture of trading and settlement of the securities before as well as at present is explained below:

### Trading

Each stock exchange has certain listed securities and permitted securities, which are traded on it. Only the members of the exchange have the authority and are entitled to the trading privileges. Investors interested in buying or selling securities should place their orders with the members of the exchange.

There are two ways of the trading:

**1. Open Outery System:** Till 1994, trading on the stock market in India was based on the Open Outery System. This is the traditional method of trading in the securities. Here, the trading is organized on the floor ring, having trading posts for different securities, the brokers, the jobbers and various interest groups/investors who bring it (the trading floor) alive. In this system traders literally shouts and resort to signals on the trading floor at the trading posts.

The member or his representative, who wishes to buy or sell the securities, reaches the trading post where the intended securities are traded. He then comes in contact with the other interested parties transacting for the securities. Buyers make their bids and the sellers make their offers and the deal is finalized by bargaining, after mutually agreeing upon the price bids. Thus, there is actually a vibrant atmosphere in this system, the role of bulls and bears in this system, and the extent of speculation created have at times depressed and thrown many of the investors out of the ring, forever.

**2. Screen-based System:** With the establishment of the National Stock Exchange (NSE) in 1994, India entered the era of screen-based trading. As a result of the initiatives taken by SEBI, within a short period of time compared to the other countries, all the stock exchanges in India were renowned by the screen-based system.

Rightly said, "Technology has its own way of pushing colourful traditions and practices into oblivion (forgetfulness)". The screen-based system replaced the vibrant open outery system by the computer screen. It enables large number of participants, geographically separated, to trade simultaneously at high speed. The participants can get the full view of the market and the updated information, and transparent audit trials, thus raises the confidence of the interested groups in the system.

The screen-based system adopted in India is referred to as the open Electronic Limit Order Book (ELOB) market system. Trading through this system includes:

**(a) Placing the orders on the computer — Limit order/Market order.**

In case of the **"Limit order"**, the buyer or the seller have to prespecify the price limit to buy or to sell, whatever the case may be. In case of purchasing the shares the limit order implies the maximum price limit, above which he/she will loose the interest of purchasing the securities, and *vice versa* in case of selling the securities.

E.g.: Purchase 40 shares of Reliance at ₹ 600 per share, if the price is more than ₹ 600, then don't purchase, thus ₹ 600, is the maximum price limit.

In case of the **"Market order"**, the order of buying or selling the securities at the best prevailing price in the market is made. A market order to sell will be finalized at the highest bid price and the market order for the purchase of the share will be finalized at the lowest bid price.

**7. Computer matches the mutually compatible orders on the price-time priority — price is given preference over time:** Mr. A made the purchase order for shares at ₹ 600, earlier than Mr. B. But, Mr. B made the purchase order for shares at ₹ 650, seller will be giving preference to Mr. B as he is ready to pay higher price, this is price-time priority.

**8.** Moreover, the list of unmatched order is displayed on the screen, in the limit order book, which is open for inspection to all traders.

## Settlement

**1. Physical movement of the Securities — Dematerialized mode:**

(a) **Traditionally,** trades in India were settled by physical delivery. There was the physical movement of the securities, from seller to seller's broker, from seller's broker to purchaser's broker (through the clearing house of the stock exchange), and from purchaser's broker to the purchaser. Further, the purchaser has to pledge the securities with the transfer agents of the company and the process of transfer take one to three months. This had further led to high paper cost, and created bad paper risk, including the transfer charges and the uncertainty factor.

(b) **Transactions in the developed countries** are settled mainly through electronic delivery facilitated by depositories to overcome the problems of the physical transfers and the cost thereby.

"A depository is an institution which dematerializes physical certificates and the effect of transfer of ownership is made through electronic book entries".

(c) In order to enable **dematerialized trading system in India,** Central Government circulated the Depository Ordinance in 1995, which was followed by the Depositories Act, 1996. Each depository has to be registered with the Securities and Exchange Board of India.

The National Securities Depositories Limited (NSDL) was the first depository in India, set up in 1996, followed by Central Securities Depositories Limited (CSDL).

Initially, investors were given a choice to continue the physical delivery of securities or opt for the dematerialized mode of the transfer, but, later with regulations of SEBI it was made compulsory. It means that if one wants to buy or sell shares on any exchange, you have to do it only in the dematerialized form.

Investors willing to join the depository mode are required to register with the agents of the depositories, i.e., to open the "Demat Account" with the agents of the depositories. For example: agencies like banks, financial institutions, and large brokerage firms.

**2. Settlement:**

(a) **Weekly Account Period Settlement System:** Share transactions in India were also settled on the basis of the weekly account period. (BSE account period from Monday to Friday and on the NSE account period from Wednesday to Tuesday). It means that the purchases and selling transactions during the account period were settled at the end of the week, and the actual transfer of securities and the amount was the difference thus arrived. But this system led to uncontrolled speculative activity and periodic market crisis.

For example: Suppose if you have purchased 200 shares of Reliance at ₹ 4,000 a share on Monday and sold 100 of the shares at ₹ 4,500 a share on Friday. Here, you were suppose to take the delivery of only remaining 100 shares by paying ₹ 3,50,000 (Purchase consideration – 8,00,000 and Sale consideration – 4,50,000) at the end of the account period.

(b) **Rolling Settlement System:** In rolling settlement system, purchase and selling of the securities was done virtually and not in reality, but for which the account was maintained by both the parties, broker as well as investor. In this account, the details of the transactions were recorded, as if the transaction has actually taken place. The purchase or sale of securities continue as specified by the investor, until and unless, any of the party (Broker or investor), demands for settlement of the account. On demanding, from either of the party, the balance amount was then transferred along with the number of shares, to the concerned party.

(c) **Intra-trade:** In case of intra-trade, the person trading has to settle the transaction on the same day. It means, for example, if the shares are purchased in morning at a particular price, then the same shares are to be sold in the evening at the price prevailing in the market of those securities. The license of the broker, not following these rules, of its selected settlement options, will be cancelled or forfeited by the stock exchange authorities.

This, settlement can be on "t + 2" or "t + 5", basis also, where, t = trade and +2 or +5 specifies the day after the trade has been taken place. Most of the dealings are settled on "t+2" basis.

(d) **Delivery Based:** Many of the investors prefer the pattern of "delivery based", for their transaction in the securities. Here, the person is not compelled to sell-off the securities within the time limit declared in advance, but it is at his own discretion, to sell or to buy the securities.

## BUYING AND SELLING SHARES

**Procedure of Buying and Selling of Shares involves the three basic steps:**

1. Locating a Broker.
2. Placement of Order.
3. Executing the Order.

Traditionally, the investors or the person trading or intending to trade can do so only with the help of the members authorized for same, i.e., brokers and others. But, with the introduction of technological developments on the Indian stock exchanges the picture has changed. **Today, the person can trade in securities by various modes:**

A. Trading through Brokers (Traditional Method and Modern Method)

B. Internet Trading

— Through banks

— Through trading firms

The procedure of buying and selling of shares by various modes is explained below:

### A. Buying and Selling of Shares Through Brokers

**1. Locating a Broker:** Typically, shares are brought through the share broker, who is a licensed member of a recognized stock exchange. Here, locating a broker is the base for buying shares. Make primary evaluation of the references of the persons recommended by family members, friends and neighbours. The broker should be able to render prompt and efficient service and protect client's interest.

If satisfied, the client registration form as well as a member-constituent form for doing the business with the broker should be submitted. Broker charges commission for the services provided to the clients.

**2. Placement of Order:** The next step is to place the order. It is but obvious that the clear details about the number of shares, price at which the shares are to be purchased and the name of the company should be provided to the broker. At present, all the transactions at stock exchange are settled through depository, therefore, opening a Demat account with the authorized agent of the depository is must, before placing the order.

Either limit order or market order can be placed. In case of limit order, one has to make clear whether the limit order is to be considered valid for a day (Day limit order), or a week (Week limit order), or a month (Month limit order), or is an open order. Open order will be valid until it is executed or cancelled.

While placing market order, one has to specify only about the quantity/number of the shares and the company's name. Placing the market order is advisable when the client have knowledge about the market prices of the securities in which interest is shown. Those who place market order essentially requires/demands liquidity from the market.

**3. Execution of Order:** On receiving the order, broker will feed the same on his terminal. Once the order is executed, the broker informs the client and sends a "contract note" as a proof of the execution of the transaction. Thus, "contract note" is the documentary evidence of the transaction, which should be preserved for the tax and other purposes.

After receiving the "contract note", client has to make payment for the purchase including the commission within the stipulated time period, when received by broker; he will transfer the securities to the client's depository account. Thus, the transaction is completed.

**Selling of the Shares:** Here again the procedure is same, starting with locating the broker, placing the sale order, either limit order or market order, and the broker executing the order as per the details provided. After executing the order he releases the "contract note" with a cheque after deducting his commission. The same when deposited in the bank, the securities sold are transferred from the client's depository account (Demat account of client) to broker's depository account (Demat account of broker). Thus, the sale transaction is completed.

## B. Internet Trading

**Internet Trading Through Banks:** From February 2000, stock trading through internet was introduced in India thus, another mode of the trading was introduced, online trading through banks authorized for the same. In this case, apart from having computer, a modem, and a telephone and internet connection, one has to open with the authorized banks, for the purpose, a savings account, Demat account as well as the securities trading account. These banks through securities trading account feed on the client's computer terminal thus authorized (NSE/BSE). The procedure for purchase and selling of the securities is changed here. The client does not have to give details about the securities to be purchased/sold to the broker but, through the securities trading account password can get the terminals of the stock exchanges (NSE/BSE), can trade and monitor the ups and downs in the stock market. Any transaction of either purchase or sale, when placed, will be confirmed by the receipt from the concerned bank under the depository services provided by them.

**Internet Trading Through Trading Firms:** Currently, ICICI Web trade, ShareKhan, Kotakstreet, Geogit Securities, and Invest Mart provides the services of Internet trading, and thus manages the portfolio of the investors.

For internet trading through this mode, one has to get registered as a client with the internet broker, apart from having a computer, a modem, and a telephone connection. One has to keep a minimum deposit in the bank account with the internet broker, which the broker can directly debit and credit. For example: For trading through ICICI Web trade, one should open bank account as well as the Demat account with the ICICI Bank.

Rest of the procedure remains same; here one has to place the order with internet broker and accordingly carries out the trading.

**Conclusion:** Thus, convenient trading is evolving on Indian stock exchanges, and the purchase/selling of the securities can be carried out either through brokers or internet brokers or online trading (through bank, without broker).

## SUMMARY

- Investment management, also referred to as portfolio management, is a complex process or activity that may be divided into several broad phases such as specification of investment objectives and constraints, choice of asset mix, formulation if portfolio strategy, selection of securities, portfolio execution, portfolio revision, and portfolio evaluation.
- Investment objectives are expressed in terms of return and risk.

- The conventional wisdom on stock-bond mix says that higher tolerance for risk and longer investment horizon imply a greater allocation to stocks compared to bonds and *vice versa.*
- Here two broad choices are available with respect to a portfolio strategy that is an active strategy and a passive strategy. An active strategy is followed by most investment professionals and aggressive investors who strive to earn superior returns, after adjustment for risk.
- A passive strategy calls for creating a well-diversified portfolio at a predetermined level of risk and holding it relatively unchanged over time, unless it becomes inadequately diversified or inconsistent with the investors risk return preferences.
- People trade in shares and securities for cognitive and emotional reasons.

## ........ QUESTIONS FOR DISCUSSION

1. Discuss the benefits provided by stock exchanges.
2. Examine the services and importance of stock exchange.
3. "Portfolio management is a process in which an organization tries to proportionately choose variety of options available." Explain this statement.
4. Explain the benefits of stock exchange with reference to various stakeholders.
5. Write a note on trading and settlement procedure.
6. A _____________ is an institution which dematerializes physical certificates and the effect of transfer of ownership is made through electronic book entries.
7. A ___________ strategy calls for creating a well-diversified portfolio at a predetermined level of risk and holding it relatively unchanged over time, unless it becomes inadequately diversified or inconsistent with the investors risk return preferences.

*Ans:* **6.** Depository, **7.** Passive.

☺ ☺ ☺

# Part-IV
# Office Management

CHAPTER 15

# Office Management

## LEARNING OBJECTIVES

- *Introduction*
- *Meaning of Office and Office Management*
- *Importance of Office and its Functions*
- *Historical Developments*
- *Factors Contributing the Growth of Office Work*
- *Office Systems, Routines and Procedures — Concept, Objectives*
- *Advantages and Limitations of Systems and Procedures*
- *Filing: Meaning and Essentials,*
- *Advantage and Disadvantages of Filing*
- *Objectives and Methods of Filing*
- *Indexing — Meaning, Objectives, Advantages and Disadvantages*
- *Essentials of Indexing Types of Indexing*
- *Office Machines and Equipments*
- *Types of Office Machines*
- *The Changing Office Scene*
- *Secretary: Meaning, Types,*
- *Scope and Functions of a Secretary*
- *Qualifications of a Secretary*
- *Changing Role of a Secretary*
- *Chapter Summary*

## INTRODUCTION

The 21st century office will be an electronic wonderland where extensive paper-based routine work will be replaced by result-oriented and advanced information technology. Office automation, with its micro-circuitry and visual display screens, is surely to take over the old and wornout methodology in office management. Within the next few years, office information system would be installed and developed to such an extent that it would replace the desk, the typewriter, the filing cabinet and the plethora of paperwork.

With the fast developments and advances in the field of science and technology the manufacturing techniques have undergone a rapid change. The economies of large-scale production has brought into being a number of multinational business organizations. The ever-widening markets also pose a challenge to the organization. Moreover, modern management has to take into account the emerging human relations in business. All this information can be tackled only if adequate information is available. An efficient and effective organization and management must possess all the information it needs to enable it to come to a variety of decisions. To retain information, to analyze it and furnish it to the management, are the basic functions of modern office. Information management has gained more attention in preference to the older one "Office Management". The reason is that information management connotes more precisely the activities performed by a modern office.

## MEANING OF OFFICE

The dictionary meaning of the term 'Office' is a place where business is carried on. Traditionally, an office is a place where clerical work is performed and where all kind of paperwork (letters, correspondence, files, records, etc.), is maintained and dealt with.

Handling of mail, correspondence, recordkeeping, payments, receipts, execution of orders, collection, processing and communication of information, framing of business policies are some important activities handled by the office.

- "It is a central place where all sorts of clerical work are done to coordinate and control the affairs of the whole organization."
- According to Mills and Standing Ford "The office is the administrative centre of a business. The purpose of an office has been defined as providing of a service of communication and record".
- An office is the place where the control mechanism for an enterprise is located, where records are initiated for communication, control and efficient operations of the enterprise.
- "An office is a place where work in connection with the preparing and furnishing of information is done."
- "The act of collecting, storing and distributing information comprise the functions of the office."
  — *George R.Terry*
- "An office is a place where business is transacted or professional services are available".
  — *Random House Dictionary*

It may be noted that these definitions emphasize "paperwork" as the main and perhaps the only function of an office. However, in modern business, the term office is used in a broader sense. The modern approach view office as a function rather than a particular place. When an office is regarded as a function, "It can plan, organise, coordinate, standardize and supervise paperwork, wherever it is done and whoever does it.

According to Leffingwell and Robinson, "The essential feature of the office is the work itself, not who does it or where it is done. If it is the office or clerical work in one place, it is the office or clerical work everywhere regardless of where the work is done or who does it".

In other words of Charles O Libbey: "The office is not in one place, no matter how much we centralize its services, there will still be office work at the point of use. Some enterprises are almost all office. The activities of the office do not, constitute a function, they are parts of all functions".

To conclude, it may be said that an office refers to the functions performed by a certain set of people rather than the place where clerical work is done and the act of collecting, processing, storing and distributing information comprise the functions of an office.

## MEANING OF OFFICE MANAGEMENT

The term "Office Management" means the technique of controlling an office in order to achieve its purpose which is possible only when the office is well organized and managed. Office management is concerned with the people who work in the office. Office management is concerned with the planning, organizing, co-coordinating, directing and controlling the efforts of office staff towards specific objectives.

According to J.C.Denyer, "office management is primarily concerned with the organization of an office in order to achieve a specified purpose and to make the best use of personnel by using the most appropriate machines and equipments, the best possible methods and by providing the most suitable environment".

In the words of Mills and Standing Ford, "Office management may be defined as the art of guiding the personnel of the office in the use of materials, methods, machines and equipment appropriate to their environment in order to achieve its specified purpose".

One of the functions of the management is to organize or arrange the office and to lay down methods to get things done, so that it may achieve its objectives. The manager has to see that human and material resources are properly utilized. The manager should also lay down the procedures or systems for the office. Management should see that the work is performed properly in the office.

### Importance of Office

An office is an important and indispensable part of every organization. Be it a government institution, trading or manufacturing organization, a hospital or an educational institution, an office is vital for its functioning. The office act as a storehouse and nervous system of every operation. A well managed office is an indispensable aid to management. It helps the management to plan its operations intelligently and to put them in action competently. The office coordinates all activities of the business. Without an efficient and an organized office business activities cannot be carried through systematically.

The modern office serve as an: (a) Information centre, (b) an intermediary, (c) a co-coordinator, (d) a service centre, (e) an administrative nerve centre, and (f) as a control centre.

Leffingwell and Robinson have summed up the importance of an office thus "A well organized office make it possible for the management to plan its operations intelligently, to put its plans into effect surely, to follow their progress currently, to determine their effectiveness promptly, to appraise their results without delay and coordinate all the activities of the business".

The main purpose of an office is:

1. To direct and coordinate the activities of the various departments
2. To plan the policies of the business and ensure their implementation
3. To handle inward correspondence
4. To maintain accounts, statutory and non-statutory books, etc., of the business

Some of the office activities are: (a) processing incoming and outgoing mail (b) dictation, (c) transcription, (d) typing, (e) printing, (f) copying (g) filing, (h) records retrieval, (i) records disposal, and (j) communication.

## Hstorical Developments

The following technological developments made during the last 150 years that have led to the evolution of the modern office:

1870: First commercial typewriter introduced

1880: Alexander Graham Bell invented telephone

1920: Electric typewriter introduced

1930: Important machines like duplicators, dictaphones, intercoms developed

1950: Calculators, computers, copying machines, addressographs, and franking, tabulating and accounting machines developed.

1961: Memory electronic typewriters launched

1964: Word processing equipments, cash registers, etc.

1970: Introduction of digital networks, Local Area Networks (LAN)

1980: Computerized telephone networks, picture phones, etc.

1990: Personal computers, microprocessing equipments, electronic mail, fax machines, modems, pagers, cellular phones, internet system, etc.

## Factors Contributing to the Growth of Office Work

According to Leffingwell and Robinson: "Office work is concerned with records and statistics, with communication, with computing, with planning and scheduling. Every office task comes within the scope of one or the other of these activities. "With the growth of industrial revolution and expansion of economic activities, the quantum of office work has increased manifold."

In addition, the following factors have also contributed to the growth of office work:

1. Increase in size and complexity of modern business caused the growth of office work.
2. Need of proper and timely information on all aspects of the business operations so as to arrive at intelligent decisions.
3. Recognizing the indispensability of research and development activities for survival and growth in modern times, business houses are increasingly having R&D in such aspects

of markets, products, manufacturing process, etc. As a result additional paperwork is required.

4. The ever-increasing information demands of governments are also continuously causing growth of paperwork.
5. With the increase in number and size of service activities like banking, insurance companies, advertising mail order houses, etc., with which a particular business has to deal, office work has grown considerably.
6. A large amount of growth of office work occurred because of failure to modernize and simplify office practices in keeping up with time and changing requirements of the office.

## Office Functions

The functions of modern office may be classified into two categories:

I. Basic functions or routine functions, and

II. Administrative management functions

### I. Basic Functions

According to Terry, "The act of collecting, processing, storing and distributing information comprises the basic function of the office". According to Mills and Standing Ford, "The purpose of the office has been defined as the providing of a service communication and record".

Denyer, however says: "The basic function of an office can be said to receiving, recording, arranging (and analyzing) and giving of information. In the work of an office, be it sales, purchasing, personnel or even the drawing office, it has seen that this is done most of the time. In fact, a leading spokesperson of the institute of office management has referred to the office manager as the "Information Manager".

The basic functions of the office may be analysed under the following headings:

**1. Receiving Information:** Information relating to the activities of an organization may be received from a variety of sources, which may be internal sources or external sources. From internal sources, information may be received from various departments, divisions or sections of the organization. From external source, it is received from suppliers, customers, visitors, other organizations, government departments, etc., examples of the form in which information is received are letters, telephone calls, orders, invoices and reports on the various activities of a business.

**2. Recording Information:** The object of keeping record is to make information readily available to the management whenever required. For this purpose the information that is received is converted into some form of written record. The records that are normally kept in a business office include financial and cost accounts, orders, progress of work, hours worked by employees, correspondence, etc. While some records are required to be kept by law, some others should be kept to meet the needs of the management in planning and controlling the business.

**3. Arranging Information:** The information acquired by an office is rarely in the form in which it is given out; facts have to be gathered from various sources and calculations, tabulations, etc., have to be made. An office is required to submit information in the form which best serves the purpose of the management, and this is a function of the highest importance which must be carried out by a properly trained staff. Examples of arranging information are preparing invoices, payrolls, cost accounting statements, statistical statements and reports.

**4. Giving information:** An office furnishes information from its records as and when it is required by the management. The information required by the management may be of a routine nature or of a special nature, and may be supplied verbally or in writing. Examples of given information are: orders, estimates, invoices, progress reports, statement of accounts, statistical and financial statements, and instructions issued on behalf of the management. All this work involves typing, duplicating, telephoning, mailing, teleprompting, etc.

## II. Administrative Management Functions

Apart from the basic functions of an office, there are certain administrative management functions which have to be performed for the smooth functioning of an office. These functions are:

(a) **Management Functions:** For the efficient functioning of an office, the management functions include: (a) Planning, (b) Organising, (c) Staffing, (d) Directing, (e) Communicating (f) Controlling, (g) Coordinating, and (f) motivating. Office work has to be properly planned and then organized and executed according to the plan. A proper control must be exercised over office activities, and the affairs of the different individuals and department in the organization must be coordinated.

(b) **Public Relation Functions:** An office has not only to maintain cordial relations with other departments in the organization but also with outsiders. It has, therefore to perform public relation function as well. Good public relation enhances the goodwill and reputation of the organization. Public relations include the reception service, the liaison service provided by the organization.

(c) **Instituting Office Systems and Routines:** Systems and routine indicate a planned and systematic approach to the problems of management. A system may be regarded as a planned approach to the attainment of desired objectives. An office routine may be defined as a series of steps in the performance of office work, each step in the series being performed in the same order and in the same way every time. A procedure is a planned sequence of operations for the handling of recurring business transactions uniformly and consistently. Office systems, routines and procedures, etc., should be developed to ensure an uninterrupted and smooth flow of office work so that it may be efficiently performed.

(d) **Retention of Records:** Office records include correspondence, letters, invoices, orders, financial and cost records, reports, statistical records, minutes, etc. These records have to be retained for future reference. Apart from maintaining records, which is a basic function, an office has to perform functions like those of filing and indexing and the preservation of outdated records.

(e) **Safeguarding Assets:** It is the function of the office to safeguard the assets of the organization, which may be fixed assets like building, plant and machinery, office equipment, lightning and air-conditioning equipments, or which may be movable assets like furniture, typewriter, calculating and accounting machines, equipment of various types or which may be in the form of cash, title deeds, securities and documents, etc. Vital records such as major contracts must be properly protected, cash must be held in safe custody or in bank, stock records must be properly maintained and deficiencies may be immediately brought to the notice of the management, fixed assets should be protected against hazards of fire and theft through insurance policies and by other means.

(f) **Form Designing and Control:** Since the office work is mostly paperwork, office forms are extensively used to perform the recording functions of the office, "A form is a standardized record which is used to accumulate and transmit information for reference purpose". Office forms serve as a storehouse of information. It is the task of the management to design, standardize, produce and control the forms to be used in the office as well as the other departments of the organization.

(g) **Stationery and Supplies Control:** Office work requires the supply of office stationery of suitable quality and in adequate quantity. It is the duty of the office to carefully procure and maintain an adequate supply of stationery items. Since stationery is a very costly item these days, it should be bought at competitive prices in economic order quantities; reasonable levels of stock must be maintained and made available at all times; and it should be issued only against authorized requisitions and stored scientifically to avoid damage, loss or deterioration.

(h) **Selection and Purchase of Office Appliances:** Office work also requires adequate equipment and machines like furnitures, fixtures, telephone, intercom systems, Dictaphones, calculators, accounting machines, filing cabinets and drawers, typewriters, duplicators, computers, etc. It is the duty of the office manager to purchase the right type of machines, equipment and furniture and also to maintain these in efficient working order. The office appliances should be suitable, simple to operate, flexible and adaptable.

(i) **Personnel Function:** The efficiency of the office depends on the personnel manning it. The personnel should be scientifically recruited and trained, and assigned work after a proper appraisal. The personnel function, performed by the personnel department, is generally assisted by the office. The office manager must make a provision of adequate and trained staff to ensure the systematic, timely and efficient performance of office work. Job evaluation and merit rating is periodically done; the staff should receive reasonable remuneration and should be properly motivated to attain the best performance. Opportunities for betterment and promotion should be made available to the office staff.

(j) **Controlling Office Costs:** With the adoption of scientific method for office management, a modern office is further supposed to discharge the functions of "controlling office costs". This may be done by:

(a) Mechanization of the office

(b) Adopting time and labour saving devices in the office

(c) Analyzing the existing office routine and adopting improved ones.

## OFFICE SYSTEMS, ROUTINES AND PROCEDURES — CONCEPT, OBJECTIVES

**Office System:** It may be noted that most of the office work is composed of a pattern of office systems, procedures and methods. A "system" is a planned approach to the activities needed to attain desired objectives. Specifically, a system may be defined as a group of interrelated and interdependent parts operating in sequence according to predetermined plan, in order to achieve a goal or series of goals. According to Terry, "a system is a network of procedures which are integrated and designed to carry-out a major activity". An office system is a standard sequence of operations in a particular business activity (e.g., paying of wages, sales, invoicing, etc.), and is concerned with how these operations are performed as well as where and when they are performed.

The term system refers to a complete picture of the personnel, forms, records, machines and equipments involved in completing a major phase of office work. For instance, there is sales system which involves the forms, personnel, equipments and records which are necessary to complete a sale from the time an order is received up to the time the goods are shipped and payment is received. A similar system is developed for handling purchases.

Another example is the system for approving credit risk in a business organization. The general objective is to screen out the prospective credit buyers who are unable or unwilling to pay and to encourage those who would pay. A sequence of steps therefore established, i.e., application is taken in a specially designed form, applicant is interviewed, his references are checked and then it is decided whether to grant credit and if so, how much and then notify the applicant accordingly. The whole sequence of steps are called a system which is followed in essentially the same pattern for each new credit.

**Procedure:** "Office procedure or office routine are a series of steps to be taken for doing a particular work in the office as per the office systems". According to Nuner and Keeling "the term procedure or routine signifies a planned sequence of operations for handling recurring business transactions uniformly and consistently".

Carl Heyel describes "a procedure is a series of logical steps by which all repetitive business action is initiated, performed, controlled and finalized. A procedure establishes what action is required, who is required to act and when the action is to take place. Its essence is chronological sequence and its implementation is translated into results or action, "For example, in a sales system, the receipt of a purchase order may involve a procedure. For each operation, within a procedure there is a method for accomplishing a particular phase of the work.

According to Milton Reitzfeld: "Success in business, government and non-profit ventures is determined by the maximum utilization of people, information and resources". Such utilization can be achieved only through the development, installation and supervision of appropriate systems and procedures.

**Method:** "A method is a manual or mechanical means and devices by which each operation is performed". For each operation within a procedure, there is a method for accomplishing that phase of work. For instance, in an "order processing procedure" there is a method for acknowledging the incoming order, checking the credit status of the customer, preparing the sales invoice and distributing the copies of the invoice. A method is thus concerned with "a sequence of motions used in performing an operation and with the specific equipment".

Some of the common office systems and procedures applicable to every office are:

(i) Dictation and transcription

(ii) Filing

(iii) Inter-office communication

(iv) Duplicating and reproductive services

(v) Mailing — incoming and outgoing

(vi) Telephone and Telegraph services

## Objectives of Systems and Procedures

(i) To bring efficiency in the utilization of the organizational resources

(ii) To control operating costs and to improve operating efficiency by avoiding wasteful movements, delay and uncertainty

(iii) Well designed system help to achieve the objectives of the organization

(iv) To assist in carrying out the various functions of the organization

## Advantages of Systems and Procedures

1. Systems and routines provide an orderly plan of action to perform an activity. Every employee is instructed to follow a definite track. It minimizes waste motions, delays and errors in the smooth flow of work.
2. If identical procedures are followed for similar work throughout the office, uniformity would be achieved and the duplication of various routine would be avoided.
3. Systems and routines bring about an economy in office operations, because unnecessary operations are eliminated and wastage of any nature is controlled.
4. Responsibility can be fixed for each employee, for each is assigned a particular job.
5. Through systems and procedures, office personnel can perform their job independently and with confidence.
6. Systems ensure better control of work. They fix the responsibility in performing the operation. Any inconsistency or deviation is made known easily which facilitates control by the management. Many system do have inbuilt mechanism of control.
7. Good system provides for coordination of different procedures necessary to perform the work. They can also serve as a basis of achieving coordination among different sections of the organization.
8. Tool of training system can be used in training the new and existing employees. Employees can be easily made to understand about the details of their job, if they know the system and the relationship of their jobs to various systems. The management need not supervise every activity closely. Only the exceptional matters are reported to the management. So, management can concentrate on strategic issues.

## Limitation of Office Systems and Procedures

Office systems and procedures suffer the following limitations:

1. **Limitations of Planning:** The effectiveness of a system depends on planning. Therefore, a system must be planned by doing a sufficient groundwork and it must be given a trail before it is put into practice. A system must be kept up to date because it may become obsolete because of changes in the organization.
2. **Rigidity:** Strict adherence to the system makes it inflexible and unworkable. A system should leave something to the discretion and judgement of the personnel responsible for its application. Systems need to be changed from time-to-time to meet the changing environments of business. Certain systems have to be modified keeping in view the demands

of other systems which operate in an organization. Further, system must be integrated to achieve the desired objectives.

3. **Expensive:** The efficiency of the system should be evaluated by making a cost-benefit analysis of it. A system should bring economy and should not result in an increased cost of office operation. The repetitive use of a system adversely affects its efficiency in a large measure. On the other hand, frequent changes in the system on the basis of current needs may impose the burden of a great expenditure on the organization.

## IMPORTANCE OF OFFICE RECORDS

The term Record refers to any written matter or document prepared for possible future uses. It may take the form of a letter, notice, circular, invoice, voucher, picture, chart, diagram, statement, registers, and books of account, tapes and microfilms. It constitutes some of the tangible evidence of operations or transactions of an enterprise. There are different types of records like correspondence records, accounting records, purchase and sales records, personnel records, legal records, administrative records and other records like survey reports, office diaries, visitor's book, etc. For planning, policy making, coordination and control functions, management can be provided with necessary information only if past and present records are preserved properly and located promptly. Filing helps to arrange the files in proper order and indexing helps to locate it.

## FILING DEFINITIONS

Filing is the process of arranging and storing records so that they can be located whenever required. It performs a library function by storing the records for future reference.

G.R.Terry has defined filing as the placing of documents and papers in acceptable containers according to some predetermined arrangement so that any of these may be located quickly and conveniently, whenever required.

According to Zane K.Quible "Filing is one of the activities in the records management programme which involves systematically classifying, coding, arranging and placing of records in storage."

### Essentials of a Good Filing System

A good filing system is one that can be depended upon for accuracy and which produce the information whenever required. The following are the essentials of a good filing system:

1. **Simplicity:** The filing system should be simple to understand and easy to operate. It should be understandable by any person without any special training or knowledge of filing.
2. **Rapidity of Filing:** The filing system adopted should be such that it does not consume much time to file the letters. This is possible only when the system followed is simple.
3. **Accessibility:** The filing system should be such that any file can be picked up from the cupboard and replace it back without loss of time. The filing department should be at such a place, so that it may be easily accessible to every department.
4. **Economy:** The filing system should be economical as regards labour, equipment and overhead. The filing system adopted should consume minimum space or storage. So, to achieve this objective, old files, which are no longer in use, should be destroyed to create space for new files. Some files have to be maintained for a very long time period such as service records of employees.

5. **Safety:** Care should be taken that the files which have to be preserved for a longer period of time should not be damaged by insects, fire, dust, theft, etc.
6. **Flexibility:** The filing system of the office should be so organized that it can be expanded in future as every progressive business expands in the future and more work and correspondence will be required. Filing system should also be capable of being contracted so that with the reduction in the volume of correspondence, space may be available for other purposes. It other words, it must be sufficiently adaptable to meet the changing circumstances.
7. **Suitability:** The nature and volume of filing system vary from organization-to-organization. The system of filing should be such that it suits the organization.
8. **Classification:** The filing system should be supported by a proper system of classification. A proper system of classification helps in inserting as well as locating the documents in files. There are many methods of classification such as alphabetical, numerical, alpha numerical, geographical and subject wise classification.
9. **Indexing:** If alphabetical classification is not adopted, office should maintain an index of files. Indexing helps to locate the files easily.
10. **Cross Reference:** Sometimes, a letter can be filed under two different heads. In such a case cross-reference should be given under that head where letter was not filed.
11. **Movement Guide:** Whenever a file or a letter from a file is removed from the filing department, a "Guide" or an "Indicator" should be inserted mentioning the purpose for which the letter or the file was removed and the name and signature of the person to whom it was delivered.
12. **Retention:** There should be some specific records retention policy. The period for which every record is to be kept must be clearly stated. Only live records should be kept in the filing cabinets as space is very costly in these days.

## Advantages of Filing

1. **Ready Reference:** Records contain information and files act as the store house of information facilitating easy and quick reference to the past and present activities of the business.
2. **Safety of Records:** Letters and other documents are put into folders and the folders are kept in cabinets and fire proof almirahs. Filing ensures protections of office records against possible losses or damage caused by the dirt, dust, fire, theft, etc.
3. **Documentary Evidence:** Records serve as documentary evidence in case of disputes. The copies of the original letters filed, if preserved properly, may be produced to settle the claims with different parties. Records can also be produced in a court of law when a party to a dispute resorts to the process.
4. **Prompt Handling of Correspondence:** Filing enables to handle the correspondence without delay. It builds up the reputation of the organization and helps in securing orders.
5. **Statutory Requirements:** Records are kept in compliance with the provisions of various statutes like companies Act, Factories Act, and Income Tax Act, etc.

6. **Barometer of Progress:** Filing makes available the records of previous years and thus helps in comparing the current year's performance with the previous years. Thus, it is an important aid in measuring the efficiency of the enterprise and various departments.

7. **Helps in Policy Formulation and Decision Making:** Filing helps office management in better planning and control of business activity by providing timely and up to date information.

8. **Increased Efficiency:** Filing increases the efficiency of the office in the discharge of the various functions by providing the required information. It makes available to the management the required information with speed and accuracy which is helpful for prompt decision making. Follow-up actions are also taken quickly if records of past correspondence are easily available.

## ORGANISATION OF OFFICE

The filing function should be organised in such a way that it helps in proper maintenance of records. The records should be made available whenever required. The department should be provided with required filing equipments like drawers, cabinets, folders, index cards, etc. The department may be organized either of the two ways: (i) Centralized filing, and (ii) decentralized filing.

### Centralized Filing

A centralized filing system is a system where all the files pertaining to all the department of whole of the organization are preserved in a centralized office which may be called a filing section or recording section under a chief recordkeeper.

This implies that individual departments in the organization need not undertake their own filing work independently. Whenever any department needs any file, it asks the central filing section for it. After referring the file, it is returned back to the central filing section. The purpose of centralizing is to render better and efficient service to all who handle correspondence.

**Advantages**

1. Duplication of records and filing equipments can be avoided.
2. In centralized filing, filing staff are trained and specialized in handling filing activities which helps to reduce operational cost and provide better service.
3. It helps in optimum utilization of space.
4. It is easy to locate the file and cross reference has also become very easy in this method.
5. It ensures better supervision and control over records retention, retrieval, and transfer and disposal activities.
6. In this filing system uniform methods and equipments of filing can be followed.

**Disadvantages**

1. If different departments are located quite far away from the central filing room, then it may take lot of time to get the required file which may cause delay and inconvenience.
2. Maintenance and handling of all information at one place affect the secrecy of confidential matters which may adversely affect the organization.

3. Different department have different needs. Sometimes, it is necessary to have information in different forms such as by the name of the customer in one instance, by location or geographical filing in another.

## Decentralized Filing or Departmental Filing

Under this system, filing is not done centrally at one place. Files relating to different departments are maintained departmentally. Every department installs its own filing system, maintains separate equipments and allocates staff to look after the filing work.

**Advantages**

(a) Papers needed are easily available in the respective units, thus saving a lot of time and effort.

(b) Secrecy of confidential matters can be preserved with great assurance.

(c) It is more suitable to the large organization, where the distances between departmental office and the main office may not permit the quick availability of records from the central filing section.

(d) Departmental staffs have a good knowledge of the nature of records so chances of misfiling and misplacement are minimized.

**Disadvantages**

1. It leads to duplication of space, equipments and supplies. This adds to the cost of filing.
2. The organization does not have the benefit of specialized services which can be provided through centralized filing.
3. Different departments in the organization adopt different filing procedures and methods.
4. Departmental filing may create difficulty when a piece of paper is relevant to more than one department.

## Centralized vs. Decentralized Filing

| | Centralized filing | Decentralized filing |
|---|---|---|
| Location of filing work | In one central filing department | In different sections or departments separately |
| References | Somewhat delayed | Easy and quick |
| Specialized staff | Available | Not available |
| Uniformity | Possible | Not possible |
| Space requirement | Limited | Larger |
| Office cost | Relatively lower | Relatively higher |
| Duplication of records and instruments | Can be avoided | Unavoidable |
| Secrecy | Cannot be maintained | Can be maintained |
| Training of juniors | Not possible | Possible |
| Supervision and control | Better and effective | Loose and difficult |

## Filing Methods

| Old Methods | Modern Methods |
|---|---|
| 1. Metal Holders/Guard Books | **1. Horizontal Filing** |
| 2. Box Files | Flat Files |
| 3. Spike Files | Lever Files |
| 4. Pigeon Hole or docketing | **2. Vertical Filing** |
| 5. Concertina Filing | Suspension Files |
| 6. Press Copy Book | Lateral Files |
| 7. Expanding Alphabetical Cases | Folders |
| | Cabinets |
| | **3. Open-shelf Filing** |

### Old Methods

**1. Metal Holders and Guard Books:** Under this method the papers are held together by metal holders or are pasted in bound books in chronological order. They are both inconvenient and awkward and do not serve any purpose. Therefore, this method is not used by big concerns.

**2. Box Files:** Cardboard boxes, about 3 to 4 inches deep, are used for filing papers. The boxes are fitted with spring clips to hold the papers down in the proper places. Sometimes papers may be placed in manila folders, which may be kept in the box file. Box files are not suitable for permanent storage of papers as and when they get old the hatches may become loose with the result that the papers will no longer remain secure.

**3. Spike Files:** This method uses a spike or a wire fixed to a small wooden stand which may be placed on the desk or may be hung on the wall. The letters, which are intended to be filed, are punched through the sharp point of the spike. They pile up one above the other on the wooden base. This equipment is very cheap and simple one and may be used by small shop vendors. It can be used where letters and other documents, such as water bill, electricity bill, are to be filed for a short period. The limitation of this method is that, the papers accumulate dust and may become illegible and letters can be arranged in chronological order only.

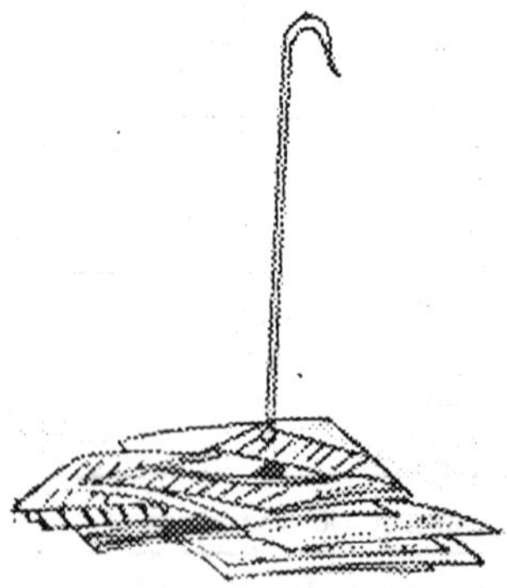

*Spike Files*

**4. Pigeon-hole or Docketing:** Under this system a cupboard is provided. It is divided into number of small compartments, each compartment being allotted to a letter of alphabet. The cupboard is open from one side and the compartments are square holes, also known as pigeon-holes. Sometimes, the papers are just inserted into the compartment, which is marked with the letter of the alphabet corresponding to the first letter of the subject matter. The papers and letters are neatly folded and outside the fold brief particulars are given. The writing of these particulars is known as docketing. The pigeon-hole may be cleared periodically so that letters, which are no longer in use, may be destroyed. This system of filing is suited only for small offices.

*Pigeon-hole Cabinet*

**5. Concertina Filing:** It provides a series of cardboard pockets usually sufficient to permit alphabetical classification and is readily portable. It is suitable for keeping only a small number of papers since its capacity is limited. However, it is said to be an important landmark in the development of vertical filing.

*Concertina Filing*

**6. Press Copybook:** All the letters which are sent out are copied in a book marked for the purpose. The press copybook may be divided either on alphabetical or on geographical basis. One press copy may be allotted for a few letters of the alphabet, like from A to E. The press copybook serves as good evidence for a particular letter having been written on a particular day in the regular course of business. Another way of this system is to take Xerox copy of all letters written and to file these copies in order, in which the letters were written. Such a file is known as "master file".

**7. Expanding Alphabetical Cases:** There are lettered or numbered pockets, in which letters and other papers can be placed alphabetically or otherwise. These cases or pockets can be useful for sorting correspondence or keeping papers together for temporary purposes. For permanent record, this method is not suitable.

## Modern Methods

**1. Horizontal Filing:** Under this method, the files are placed in the folders and these folders are kept in horizontal position. Folders or files containing papers are kept in drawers one upon the other and papers are inserted in the order of the date on which it is received or dispatched. Naturally the latest papers are found on the top. An index is prepared allotting the numbers to the file. Guide cards may also be kept showing the movement of the files.

The horizontal filing method can be: (a) Flat files, (b) Arch Lever files, (c) Shenon files:

*(a)* ***Flat Files:*** These are covers made of card board or thick paper fitted with metal hinges for fastening the papers together. A file is allotted to each customer or subject. All the papers relating to the customers or subject are placed in that file in chronological order (date wise). The letters or papers to be filed are punched and inserted into the metal hinges of the files. Then these files are kept upon each other in cupboards or drawers.

*(b)* ***Arch Lever Files:*** These files are made of very thick cardboard and are fitted with strong metal arches operated by a lever (double spring). If any paper is to be inserted into the file, the lever is moved upwards which will open the metal hinges and after inserting the paper press the lever down. The main advantage of this system is that, a paper can be inserted at any place and can be taken out without disturbing the order of other papers and it can preserve the paper for a long time. These are commonly used in offices; it is very simple, cheap and convenient for filing large number of invoices, delivery notes, letters, replies, etc.

*(c)* ***Shenon Files:*** Papers under this system are attached to hinges of metal drawers which remain inserted in steel cabinets containing 4 to 64 drawers. The drawers can be classified into alphabetical or any other convenient order. The drawers can be brought out of the cabinets and replaced after inserting or taking out papers from the drawers.

### Advantages of Horizontal Filing

(i) It is easy to understand and simple to operate.

(ii) It enables easy reference as the documents are arranged in chronological order.

(iii) It is a flexible system; number of files can be increased or decreased depending on the volume of papers.

(iv) Papers can be inserted or taken out without disturbing the order of the papers.

(v) It can keep all papers in proper order with the help of string fastening device, so misplacement can be reduced.

(vi) This the best flat filing method. In this method, papers remain well protected from theft, insects and dust.

**Disadvantages**

(i) It is not suitable where the volume of papers is very large.

(ii) It requires relatively more space.

(iii) Location of exact paper at short notice is difficult as the files containing papers are placed one above the other.

(iv) In the event of expansion in the volume of papers, the drawers must be reorganized, this is troublesome.

(v) To take out any paper from a flat file, other papers have to be removed first.

**2. Vertical or Upright Filing System:** In this method of filing, the files are placed vertically or in a straight, standing position. Here, the papers or letters remain unfastened as against the flat filing system where they are carefully fastened. This system consists of folders and cabinets.

*Vertical Filing Concertina*

***(a) Suspended Filing:*** Folders are suspended vertically from metal rods fitted across the inside of the drawers. It becomes a visible vertical filing system. Papers are filed in folders, which are placed inside the suspended pockets, each holding a number of folders. The top of each folder is made of metal sheet. Front side of the sheet is used for pasting the title of the paper. Hence, titles of all files can be viewed without touching or shuffling the papers. It keeps the files upright and neat. It gives a speed of reference by index strips on each pocket.

***(b) Lateral File (Filing from Side to Side):*** In lateral filing, files are placed vertically across the width of the cupboard with four or five shelves. The documents are filed laterally along a shelf, the pockets having index strips on the visible ends of the files. It saves 50% space, offers full visibility, has greater filing height, i.e., two metres high with five filing rows, and it is very cheap. In this method, papers after being put in inter-connected folders which have hooks are hung on the railings of shelves in the same manner as cloth hangers are hung in the wardrobes. The top of the folders is fitted with the indicators, which can be adjusted for the required angle of vision.

*(c)* ***Folders:*** The folder consists of manila sheets. The back of a folder is slightly higher than the front part of the sheet. This extended back part of the sheet is used for writing the details like name of correspondent, address, etc. For each correspondent, a separate folder is used. These folders are kept in a standing position in chronological order. Any paper can be taken out or put back without disturbing the other papers.

*(d)* ***Cabinets:*** A cabinet with a wooden or steel drawers are used to preserve the papers. The drawers must be deep enough to place the folders in standing position. The folders are placed vertically in the drawers. Each drawer slides forward and backward so that folders can be taken out and put it back into the drawer. These drawers are fitted with rods, so, sometimes a drawer can be easily suspended from the rod.

**3. Open Shelf Filing:** In this method, files are arranged in open shelves like books are kept in libraries. Generally, the shelves do not have doors but provision can be made for them. The files are arranged in numerical order and the outer edges of the files show the serial number of the file. Open shelf filing permits more visibility, provides compactness and helps in doing the filing work faster and efficiently.

**4. Microfilming:** Microfilming is also a filming method and is becoming popular because of space problem. Under this method record of documents is kept by taking their photographs on very small films. In the film of 30 cubic centimetres, a record of 10 lakh cheques can be kept. The information photographed on a film can be projected on a screen with the help of machine called 'Viewer' or 'Reader'. It is the filing method of the near future. It is gaining importance because it saves office space, paper and overhead expenditure in maintaining huge filling equipment. A microfilm as compared to other method of filing, can record the same information permanently and safely at two per cent of the space, yet it will have the authenticity like the original document.

**Advantages of Vertical Filing**

(i) It facilitates ready reference and thereby saves time and effort.

(ii) It is economical to use as large number of folders can be accommodated in drawers when vertically arranged.

(iii) Files are easily accessible and can be referred to, inserted in, or withdrawn easily and quickly.

(iv) It provides ample scope for expansion.

(v) It ensures safety and security of the office records by means of locking devices.

(vi) It is readily adaptable to the changes in classification as the folders can be arranged alphabetically, numerically or geographically.

(vii) It has wide applicability as it can be used for all types of papers and documents, e.g., orders, invoices, quotation, tenders, circulars, etc.

**Disadvantages**

1. There is a danger of files sagging under other files with the results that they may not become readily available.
2. Papers loosely inserted in folders may be misplaced in wrong folders unless it is done carefully.
3. It needs to be supplemented by the use of flat files for movement of papers from dealing assistants to one or more officers in connection with current matters.

**Horizontal Filing vs. Vertical Filing**

| Points | Horizontal Filing | Vertical Filing |
|---|---|---|
| 1. Arrangements of papers or files | In the flat position, i.e., one upon each other | In the standing or upright position |
| 2. Filing equipments | (i) Flat files, (ii) Arch lever files (iii) Shenon files | (i) folders, (ii) cabinets, (iii) lateral file, (iv) suspended file |
| 3. Misplacement of the papers | No misplacement as papers are fastened by a clip | Possible as papers are kept in loose manner |
| 4. Cost element | Economical, as only file covers are necessary | Costly, as it requires folders, drawers, guide cards, cabinets, cupboards |
| 5. Flexibility | Not flexible, having limited scope for expansion | Flexible as it enjoys scope for expansion |
| 6. Reference | Not easy and quick | Easy and quick |
| 7. Protection of records | Limited protection | Maximum protection due to steel cabinets and almirahs with locking devices. |
| 8. Suitability | For small office | For big offices |
| 9. Requirements | Large space | Limited space |

## INDEXING: MEANING

Indexing is an important component of any systems of records management. It is an essential supplement to a filing system. Index is anything that indicates or points out. It guides as to where the necessary document or detailed information is available. Indexing may be defined as the process of determining the name, subject or other caption under which the documents are to be filed. If the files are arranged alphabetically, chronologically or geographically in alphabetic order, there is no need of having a separate index as the order of files is automatically revealed. But in other cases index must be kept to enhance the utility of filing. Indexing may also be used to store key information regarding any subject in a condensed form. For example, a business house may prepare an index of its regular customers containing their names, addresses, telephone numbers, ledger folios, credit limits, etc. According to George R. Terry "An index is a finding tool. It furnishes the key as to how the materials are arranged." Indexing doesn't mean classification. "Classification" means grouping and arranging papers in different files while "indexing" means making reference to the records filed. The main purpose of an index is to facilitate the location of the required files.

## Objectives of Indexing

1. It facilitates the location of records or files. Index indicates or points out the place where the documents will be found.
2. Lower costs of the records management due to improved efficiency.
3. Indexing also ensures easy and quick cross referencing and thereby saves time and effort.
4. To increase the general efficiency of office work

## Essential of Good Indexing

A good system of indexing should possess the following qualities:

(i) **Simplicity:** It should be simple and easy to operate.

(ii) **Economy:** It should be economical in terms of money, space and efforts.

(iii) **Efficiency:** It should ensure speed and accurate way of locating the files.

(iv) **Cross referencing:** It should ensure cross referring of documents relevant to two or more files.

(v) **Flexibility:** A good indexing system should have sufficient scope for expansion as the records of a firm go on increasing day-by-day.

(vi) **Safety:** Safety of index is required to avoid pilferage of index card and to save it from destruction by dust, insects, rats, fire, water, etc. Index equipment should ensure the safety of records.

(vii) **Conformity with the filing system:** The indexing system should go well with the filing system of the organization.

(viii) **Signalling:** It should provide for suitable plastic or metallic signals. A signal is a metal clip, plastic tub or a thick paper slip which is attached to the exposed edge of a card or file. Its purpose is to draw attention to certain facts recorded on the card. For example, the blue signal on a staff card may indicate that the concerned employee is a member of the staff pension scheme and a red signal may indicate that the concerned employee is a member of the salary linked insurance plan. Signals can also be used to find out folders, cards, ledger folios, etc.

**Cases in which index can be dispensed with**

1. If the files are arranged alphabetically no index needs to be prepared as this method of filing is self-indexing.
2. If the files are arranged alphabetically or numerically, there is no need to prepare separate index, as these files are self-indexing.

## Types of Indexes

Methods of indexing may be classified into the following categories,

1. Ordinary Page or Bound Book Index.
2. Vowel Index

3. Loose-leaf or Vertical Card Index
4. Visible Card Index
5. Visible Loose-leaf Binders
6. Strip Index
7. Wheel Index

**1. Ordinary Page or Bound Book Index:** It consists of a bound book in the form of a register; each page of the book is allotted a letter of an alphabet. Each page has a tab, which indicates the alphabet allotted to it. For example, the name of the companies beginning with letter 'A' can be entered on the page having the tab 'A' in the book. An example of this method is the telephone diary. Page number will be also given in each page of the book.

**Advantages**

1. This system is durable and pages can be maintained easily.
2. It is cheap and is generally not misplaced.

**Disadvantages**

1. The names are entered in order of occurrence, and hence if one has to find any particular name, whole page of the index book has to be referred which is very time-consuming.
2. This system is inflexible, as it cannot be expanded because of limited space in the book.
3. The names of certain companies, which are not in use, have to be deleted from the index book, but it is not possible in this method.

**2. Vowel Index:** Under this method, the pages of the index book reserved for each alphabet are divided into six subsections. Each subsection is reserved for a vowel (A, E, I, O, U, Y). The names of the correspondents are recorded on the page reserved for its initial letter. For example, the name AYUB will be recorded on the page with "A" in the column marked for "Y". This type of index is having very limited use.

**3. Loose-leaf or Vertical Card Index:** Under this system cards, usually of size of 4½ × 3½ are arranged vertically in a drawer. There is a metal rod running through the card at the bottom from one end of the drawer to the other end in order to hold these cards in proper position. It is arranged similar to card index which is arranged in a library. Each correspondent is allotted a card on which the name, full address, the number of file of a customer is entered. To facilitate the tracing of a card, tabs are attached at intervals according to the alphabetical order or "Guide Cards" are inserted to indicate the beginning of cards with the particular of the alphabet. This system may be adopted in the offices to maintain staff records, credit records and so on. Example: Catalogue of books in library.

**Advantages**

1. The cards provide a complete list of the names and addresses of all persons or firms with whom business is transacted.
2. It is flexible. Index cards which are no longer in use can be removed whenever necessary. Similarly, new cards can also be added.
3. If the number of the cards has increased then, additional drawer may be used.

**Disadvantages**

1. The cards can get torn by constant use.
2. It takes more time to locate a particular card.
3. There is a risk of cards being misplaced after it is taken out from the drawer.
4. This system is very expensive as the equipments, cabinet and cards cost more than the book. So, small firms may not adopt this system.

**4. Visible Card Index:** Under this system a series of cards are held in transparent covers and are so arranged so as to overlap so that one line on each card at the bottom is visible and which contains the name of the firm or the subject dealt with on the card. The other portion of the card gives other particulars in detail. These cards are placed in a metal tray. This tray contains about 50 cards and the cabinet may accommodate 6 to 12 such strips of cards and the cards are held in the trays in such a way that the required card can be held in position and at the same time it can be written or withdrawn, replaced or so arranged as may be required. The trays containing the cards are kept horizontally in cabinets or may be attached vertically to a metal stand. The cards are arranged in trays alphabetically or numerically as decided. These cards may be ruled, or coloured to distinguish them from one another or can be arranged according to the size of the drawer.

**Advantages**

1. The required card can be located promptly.
2. Entries in the card can be made without their being removed from the tray.
3. A card can be removed or replaced after the purpose is accomplished.
4. The management can control purchases, production, sales, credit limit, etc., which are available on each card of an individual or firm, etc.

**5. Visible Loose-leaf Binders (Kind of Writing Pads):** When speed in writing is required, loose-leaf binder may be used with advantage. In this case a binder contains thick leaves which are fitted with metal rings and which can be opened or closed by pressing a lever. The book should be of suitable size to hold the master card. The advantage of this binder is that a card can be removed or replaced or another card can be inserted according to need by opening the metal ring and by pressing the lever.

**Advantages**

1. References can be made with greater speed.
2. It is not an expensive method as compared to "Visible Card Index" for which the steel cabinets have to be purchased.

**6. Strip Index:** In a business, where there is need for the list of names of the customers or members such as their telephone numbers, addresses, etc., and information has to be written in one or two lines, then strip index is followed. In this method the numbers are typed on a stiff paper in one line. These strips are placed in alphabetical order in a metal frame in such a way, that they can be easily taken out or replaced. These strips can be fixed on a tray overlapping on each other. Strips, which are no longer in use, can be removed.

**7. Wheel Index:** The latest development in the indexing system where speed and case for reference is of great importance, Wheel index or Rotary index has been adopted. Under this system of index, cards are mounted on the circumference of a wheel, which is placed in a cabinet or desk. Guide tabs indicating the letters of the alphabet are affixed. The wheel rotates on a ball bearing. Thus, when a particular card is required, the wheel is rotated and the desired card may be referred by removing it from the wheel.

**Advantages**

1. When cards are required frequently, this system is adopted.
2. Economy of space.
3. Flexible

## OFFICE MACHINES AND EQUIPMENTS

There are a large number of machines and appliances which may be used for different operations in an office. They make for the accuracy and speed of operations, reduce work tensions and relieve monotony and fatigue.

**Mechanization offers the advantages of:**

(i) Better quality of work, (ii) Lower operating cost, (iii) improved efficiency, (iv) facilitates control, (v) ensures greater accuracy, (vi) Relieves monotony, and (vii) facilitates standardization.

**Its disadvantages are:**

(i) Worker's resist to it,

(ii) Its high cost,

(iii) It is uneconomical,

(iv) It requires specific skills,

(v) It is less flexible,

(vi) There is risk of obsolescence,

(vii) It generates surplus staff,

(viii) It ensures the dominance of the machine,

(ix) It raises problems of noise control and space.

Factors need to be considered while selecting office machines are: (i) ease of operations, (ii) flexibility, (iii) durability, (iv) portability, (v) adaptability, (vi) service, (vii) operating cost, (viii) reputation of the supplier, (ix) styling, and (x) cost.

### Types of Office Machines

(a) Typewriters

(b) Stenographic machines

(c) Dictating machines

(d) Duplicators or duplicating machine

(e) Photocopying machines

(f) Accounting and tabulating machines

(g) Addressing and mailing machines

(h) Punched card machines

(i) Electronic computers

(j) Desktop publishing system

(k) Latest in computers

(l) Miscellaneous Machines: (i) time recording clocks, (ii) payroll machines, (iii) cheque writing machines, (iv) check signing machines, (v) numbering machines, and (vi) impression stamps.

### The Changing Office Scene

Office activities has undergone vast changes in the last five or six decades. A modern office is well planned, well laid out and well organised. The scope of office activities has widened tremendously following the spectacular developments in science and technology, industrialization, transport and communication, etc. These scales have led to an expansion in the scale of production and business activities, to greater governmental and legislative interference and control, and the consequent enlargement of the volume of office work. In today's office activities are performed not by general purpose clerk but by specialized clerks — by receptionists, accountants, clerks, cashiers, stenographers, typists, etc. There is thus a greater division of labour. The old fat leather bound ledgers have been replaced by loose-leaf binders. Filing and indexing techniques have been developed. Departmentalization of office has been effected. A greater and wider use of machines (typewriters, dictaphones, calculators, accounting machines, computers, etc.), is made to save time and labour, work standardization, job evaluation, merit rating and other techniques of personnel management has been practised. Telephones, intercom, telex and other communication devices are used for rapid and global communication. Many large sized offices use computers to handle the enormous volume of work. The use of carbonless copy paper has become very popular. In short, office today is organized on scientific principles and their management and administration is in the hands of highly specialized managers. The term "Office management" is rapidly being replaced by the term "Administrative Office Management" and "Information Management".

## SECRETARY

The word secretary is derived from Latin word secretaries who mean "a confidential officer". The basic idea behind keeping a secretary is that there should be a person who can assist these authorities in carrying out the details of the work so that all matters could be handled in confidence and with utmost efficiency.

According to Oxford Dictionary, "One whose office it is to write for another; especially one who is employed to conduct correspondence, to keep records and to transact various other businesses, for another person or for a society, corporation or public body is a secretary".

According to Concise Dictionary, "A person employed by another to assist him in correspondence, literary work, gathering information and other confidential matters is a secretary".

Webster's New International Dictionary of English Language defines 'Secretary as: (i) one who is entrusted with secrets; (ii) a person employed to attend to orders, letters and the like and to have oversight in a general way of the business connected with these for an association, a public body or an individual; (iii) an officer of the state whose business is to superintend and manage the affairs of a particular department of government and who is usually a member of the cabinet of advisory council of the chief executive; and (iv) one who writes especially that directed by another.'

Under Section 383 A as per Companies (Amendment) Act, 1974, every company having a paid-up share capital of ₹ 25 lakh or more shall have a whole-time secretary, and where the board of directors of any such company comprises only two directors, neither of them shall be the secretary of the company.

## Types of Secretaries

The role of secretarial work in modern times will be clearly understood if secretaries are classified on the basis of their functions and positions. Secretaries may be divided into several categories as follows:

**(i) Private Secretary:** The private secretary is usually employed by an important person to conduct correspondence and do other private and personal work on his behalf. Ministers, Members of Parliament, Administrative officers, Managers, or persons engaged in various professions like doctors, lawyers, architects, etc., have private secretaries. The functions of a private secretary vary according to the nature of work of his employer. However, there are certain routine duties which have to be performed by all private secretaries. These include:

(a) Routine office duties, such as handling mail, conducting routine correspondence, taking shorthand dictation and typing, maintaining accounts and records; and

(b) Receptionists' duties, such as handling telephone calls and visitors or callers, making and recording appointments and engagements of the employer, etc. Under special circumstances, the private secretary may also be required to undertake certain duties of the private nature, such as drafting reports and speeches, handling bank transactions, paying bills, arranging tours, travels, parties, as also making arrangements for meetings.

**(ii) Secretary of an Association or Club:** Secretaries of cultural associations, sports clubs, professional and business associations, trade unions and similar bodies come under this category. Associations, unions or clubs requiring the service of a whole-time secretary usually appoint a paid secretary to conduct the day-to-day activities of the association and act as the agent and adviser of the managing committee. The secretary of an association generally performs the following functions:

(a) As an executive officer, he undertakes all administrative functions such as supervision of the staff, correspondence, maintenance of accounts and records, receipts and payments of cash, preparing statement of accounts and arranging audit.

(b) As the chief officer he supervises and conducts the activities of the club or association — such as registration of new members, collection of subscription and donation, purchase and maintenance of equipment, arrangements for parties and social gatherings.

(c) He arranges all matters connected with the convening and holding of meetings of the general body and the managing committee, such as issue of notices and agenda, seating arrangements, preparation of documents to be placed before the meeting, recording or proceedings, circulation of minutes, etc.

(d) As an agent of the association he acts as the mouthpiece of the managing committee, executes the decisions of the committee, acts as public relations officer, issues press statements, notifications, etc.

(e) As an adviser of the managing committee, the secretary advises the committee on matters relating to framing of rules, actions to be taken for violation of rules, legal matters, etc.

**(iii) Secretary of Cooperative Society:** The secretary of a cooperative society may be appointed as a paid secretary or elected from among the members of the managing committee. The main function of the secretary of a cooperative society is to manage the affairs of the society under the control and direction of the managing committee. He performs more or less the same duties as the secretary of an association. Besides, he is required to maintain proper records and registers in accordance with the rules framed by the government and submit periodical statements and returns to the Registrar of Cooperative Societies. His duties as an agent of the managing committee also involve communication with members, defending and conducting law suits, attending conferences, investigation of matters entrusted to him, etc.

**(iv) Secretary of Government Department:** The civil servants attached to the various ministries of the government and acting as their executive heads are known as Secretaries, e.g., Secretary, Ministry of Home Affairs, or Secretary, Department of Company Affairs, etc. Each of these departments and ministries is in the charge of a minister. When the department and ministry are large, there may be a number of Joint and Additional Secretaries attached to each department. The Secretary as well as the Joint or Additional Secretaries are assisted in their work by a number of Assistant (or Under) Secretaries. The duties of a Government Secretary depend largely upon the size, importance and nature of functions of the department. Thus, the executive and advisory functions of the Secretary of the Education Ministry will obviously be different from those of the Secretary of the Home or Finance Ministry. However, these functions may be generalized as follows:

*(a)* ***Administrative and Executive Functions:*** These include overall control and day-to-day administration of the office, issuing directives, orders and circulars for the guidance of officers and clerical staff, conducting and supervising activities in execution of the normal functions of the department, co-coordinating the activities of the department with those of allied departments, supervising the collection and collation of data for policy decisions, conducting and supervising investigation into special projects, schemes or proposals, etc.

*(b)* ***Advisory Functions:*** These include keeping the minister posted with all developments relating to the functions of the department, advising the minister on all proposals, schemes, and projects, on the need for changes in policy and new policies, and supplying all documents and information for use in Parliament or the Legislative Assembly.

**(iv) Secretary of Local Body:** Laws relating to public bodies (Municipal Corporation, Panchayat, etc.), usually provide for the appointment of a paid secretary to look after their day-to-day affairs. His primary function is that of an office executive. He has to coordinate and supervise all office activities, looking after mails, maintaining records, etc. He also acts as a link between the authorities and staff of the local body. Besides, he has to perform several other functions, *viz.*:

(a) Prepare budget estimates, statement of accounts, annual reports, etc.

(b) Issue notices of meetings, prepare agenda and draft minutes.

(c) Make enquiries on particular matters and report to the local body, and

(d) Undertake special duties which may be entrusted to him.

**(v) Secretary of an Institution:** Social, religious, economic, educational and cultural institutions have often to appoint a secretary who shall be an ex-officio member of the governing body. The secretary of an institution generally performs the following functions:

(a) He issues notices for the meetings of governing body.

(b) He implements the decisions taken in the meetings of the governing body.

(c) He takes the authorities into consultations to solve the problems and difficulties arising in the course of the running of the institution.

(d) He maintains proper books of accounts.

(e) To preserve perfect harmony and coordination with the parent body, i.e., a church or a religious mission.

**(vi) Secretary of Trade Unions:** The labourers establish trade unions to safeguard their interest. Trade unions act as a link between the labourers and employers. Trade unions put forward the difficulties of labourers before the management. Secretary of a trade union establishes coordination and does the necessary correspondence.

**(vii) Secretary of Minister:** Each and every minister appoints a secretary for the smooth running of his affairs known as 'Secretary of Minister'.

**(viii) Secretary of a Joint Stock Company:** The company secretary plays an important and vital role in the affairs of the company. Every company appoints secretary for the smooth running of the work. Company secretary is a link between the shareholders and the directors of the company. The company secretary must be thoroughly conversant with the Companies Act.

Section 2(45) of the Companies (Amendment) Act, 1988, "A company secretary means a person, who is a member of the Institute of Company Secretaries of India, and includes any other individual possessing the prescribed qualification, and appointed to perform the duties which may be performed by a secretary under this Act and any ministerial or administrative duties."

The definition reveals three important facts:

1. Only an individual can be appointed as company secretary and any firm or body corporate cannot be so appointed.
2. The company secretary should either be a person who is a member of the institute of company secretaries of India or has requisite qualification prescribed by the Central Government.
3. The duties of the secretary are ministerial and administrative and not managerial ones, he is not entrusted with the direction, control and management of the affairs of the company.

## Functions of the Company Secretary

**(i) Secretarial Functions:** Secretarial functions can be divided into two parts:

***(a) Pre-incorporation secretarial functions:*** The promoter has to perform many functions before the incorporation of the company. Memorandum of Association and Articles of

Associations are to be filed with the registrar. The secretary helps the promoters in preparing, printing and filing these documents.

***(b) Post-incorporation secretarial functions:*** After the incorporation of the company the secretary has to perform many functions of secretarial nature. In real sense, the entire secretarial practice revolves around the floatation of the company.

***(ii) Non-secretarial functions:*** These functions are generally executed by executive secretary. Directors being affected by the talents, qualification and experience of the secretary can ask the secretary to perform any of the following functions:

(a) Administrative function

(b) Managerial function

(c) Liaison function

(d) Organisational function

(e) Coordination function

(f) Other functions

In brief, the secretary works in the following capacities:

(a) As an agent of the board of directors

(b) As a departmental officer of secretarial office

(c) As a chief administrator

In most of the cases, however, the position of the secretary is that of an office executive, besides, he has also to act as a liaison officer and as an advisor to the management.

As an office executive, the secretarial functions include:

(i) Supervision, coordination and control of clerical work.

(ii) Selection, appointment and assignment of office work to the staff.

(iii) Maintaining office discipline.

(iv) Supervising secretarial work related to meeting, etc.

The secretarial position as a liaison involves such functions as:

(i) Handling staff matters, dealing personally with outside callers.

(ii) Acting as a mouthpiece of the management for communicating their decisions to the staff.

(iii) Maintaining public relations, i.e., keeping the public informed about the activities of the organization.

(iv) Communicating to the management the grievances of the staff, or reactions of the staff to management policies.

The secretary is frequently called upon to perform another important role, that of advisor to the management.

## SCOPE OF COMPANY SECRETARIAL WORK

In the modern era of corporate enterprise, company secretarial work has assumed a great importance in conducting the affairs of a trading or an industrial organization. The scope of secretarial work depends upon the size of the company, the nature of its business and the extent to which the board has delegated its powers to the secretary. In the case of a smaller company secretarial work is more varied and the secretary has to act as an office manager and as an accountant also. In the case of bigger company, the secretary usually will have more and more specialized secretarial work. While the directors are in charge of direction, control and management of a company's business, the secretary is in charge of ministerial (acting as an agent, helping) and administrative functions.

The general duties and responsibilities of the secretary may be classified as follows:

### (i) As to Directors

He has to look after the correspondence with directors, arranging board meetings, keeping minutes and executing the orders and instructions of the board. The secretary is confidential clerk of the board. The brain of the company is the board of directors. The directors contemplate and decide the general policy of management. The secretary acts as ears, eyes, hands and mouth of the company. The board acts through the company secretary. He is the mouthpiece of the board of directors.

### (ii) As to Shareholders

The secretary is the connecting link between the shareholders on the one side and the directors on the other side. The company communicates with the outside world through its secretary.

In general he has to organize and supervise correspondence with shareholders with regard to the following:

(a) Receiving of applications and allotment of shares,

(b) Calls on share,

(c) Forfeiture of shares,

(d) Transfer and transmission of shares,

(e) Dividend distribution,

(f) Notices and circular to members,

(g) Shareholder's meetings-agenda, minutes, voting, etc.

### (iii) As to Management and Administration

The secretary has to organize and control the central office. He is responsible for the proper maintenance of the statutory books and the books of account. He has to meet creditors and the public on behalf of the company. He has to negotiate for the company contracts with the third parties. He has to look after the company's investment and banking account. He has to draft the 'Annual Reports of Directors' and he may be called upon to prepare special secretarial reports on problems of management and administration of the company.

### (iv) As to Company Law and Other Legislations

In the eyes of the company law, the secretary is regarded as one of the principal company officers personally responsible for filing various company returns and statements with the Registrar of the Companies. As per Income Tax Act, he is responsible for collection and payment of income tax from the salaries of the staff and payment of corporation tax. The income tax is also collected from dividends. He is also responsible for verifying the proper stamping of the documents, if required by the Indian Stamp Act, i.e., Transfer Forms.

A secretary is charged with the primary responsibility of ensuring that the documentation of the company is in order, that the requisite returns are made to the Registrar correctly and in time and that the company's statutory books and registers are properly maintained. On all important documents and contracts he is required to give signature, authenticating the documents as true.

Under the Income Tax Act and Indian Stamp Act, he is held responsible for non-fulfilment of the legal provisions. Under the Monopolies and Restrictive Trade Practices Act, Secretary's position is bracketed with that of a manager or director as a principal officer of the company responsible to fulfil the provisions of MRTP Act, 1969. Under many other legislations, e.g., Shop and Establishment Act, Sales Tax Act, Fabrication Act, Criminal Law, etc. Secretary is recognized as the principal authority in regard to administrative requirements of such statutes.

## ESSENTIAL QUALIFICATIONS REQUIRED FOR A SECRETARY

The following essential qualifications are required for the secretary:

1. **Sound Education:** At present, sound education is a passport for entering any professional vocation. The real education combines theory and practice and enables you to develop your mind into a 'logical engine' a reasoning instrument capable of recognizing, analyzing and arranging in their proper order the facts connected with any subject or any problem. The secretary is the chief source of information of the right kind. The top executives cannot find for themselves all that they require to know. They invariably depend on their secretaries who can keep them posted with up to date information — accurate and adequate information.

2. **Specialized Knowledge:** Secretarial profession is a specialized branch of management. The secretary must have necessary qualifications prescribed by usage or by legislation.

A company secretary at present must have qualifications prescribed by the Companies Act, Chartered Secretary or Chartered Accountant (by passing the necessary examination) alone can be appointed as a Company Secretary in future. The Companies Act has given statutory recognition to the specialized character of secretarial profession. The Chartered Institute of Company Secretaries of India, 1 Rani Jhansi Road, New Delhi, is the authority granting necessary status to Company Secretaries in India. It is a statutory body and conducts necessary examinations for granting the legal status to Company Secretaries. A personal or private secretary must have specialized knowledge and reasonable proficiency in the basic subjects, reading, writing (including composition), arithmetic, shorthand and typewriting, taking down letters, either from dictation or from rapid general instruction; composing letters, setting them properly and filing correspondence. The secretary should also have knowledge of bookkeeping, general office routine, postal communications, methods of payment, etc. Shorthand and typewriting are the bread and butter qualifications of a private secretary. A private secretary worthy of name, who cannot write shorthand and who cannot type letters is now unthinkable. Only a stenographer secretary can save the time, labour and energy of the chief who is a man of affairs and who needs secretarial help to cope with his vast amount of work.

**1. Proficiency in Language:** Competence in language and in shorthand is the two indispensable qualifications of a secretary. A good knowledge and command over the language is a fundamental qualification, without which skill in shorthand is of little importance. Simplicity, directness and conciseness should be aimed at while securing proficiency in language.

**2. Knowledge of Human Relations:** A human being cannot be treated like a commodity or a machine. He is a living and animate machine. He has ever-changing mind. He has changing moods, feelings, likings, attitudes and preferences. Each person is unique. Even the twins are not exactly alike in all respects. Each person has also changing social wants. The secretary must recognize dynamic psychological and social wants of the people working under him. He must duly recognize human values, aspirations and expectations. Understanding the feelings, problems and difficulties of the subordinates is necessary for assuring the voluntary cooperation from them in the execution of plans and policies determined by the directors. This is called knowledge of human relations.

**3. Knowledge of Meeting Procedure:** The secretary must have thorough knowledge of law/custom relating to the conduct and procedure at meetings of registered companies, public bodies, cooperative societies and other associations or organizations.

**4. Wide General Knowledge:** Well read and well informed secretary can act as a ready source of general knowledge of his employer. A versatile secretary has multipurpose utility and can give complete satisfaction to his boss.

**5. Legal Knowledge:** A business enterprise is governed by many laws. A secretary must be fully familiar with:

(a) Industrial Laws

(b) Mercantile Laws

(c) Laws of Income Tax and Sales Tax

(d) The Monopolies and Restrictive Trade Practices (MRTP) Act

(e) The Companies Act

(f) The Exchange Control Act, and

(g) The Negotiable Instruments Act.

Preferably a person with a degree in Law is qualified to act as a secretary of any institution or legal body. Degree in Commerce should be supplemented by degree in Law.

**6. Working Knowledge of Commerce and Finance:** A secretary should have specialized knowledge of secretarial practice, office management, machinery of commerce, money market, banking and finance, stock exchange and investment market, foreign exchange market, bookkeeping and accountancy, etc. Hence, a commerce graduate is always preferred for higher secretarial profession.

**7. Winning Personality:** Personality is what makes one human being different from another. Personality is everything you are — what you do and how you do it. It is your impact on other people. A pleasing manner is essential in dealing with people and the more likable you are to people, the smoother will be your path. It is not necessarily what kind of features you have but rather the expression on those features.

**8. Leadership:** As a member of management, the secretary must acquire leadership qualities. Leadership demands winning personality, leadership is essential to perform the role of a manager or an executive. Leadership is defined as the ability to enthuse, to inspire and guide subordinates. The essence of leadership is the ability to get the best out of people working with you, as well as getting them to work as a team instead of as individuals.

**9. Knowledge of Company Law:** A company secretary is expected to have a thorough knowledge of Companies Act and its implications along with the leading case laws. He should possess complete knowledge of the provisions of the Companies Act as regards the procedure of holding company meetings.

**10. Knowledge of Mercantile Law:** The company secretary should possess the knowledge of the laws relating to contracts, sales of goods, carriage of goods, negotiable instruments, insurance, etc. Some knowledge of labour laws and laws relating to patents, trademarks and copyrights may also be of great help to him at times.

**11. Knowledge of Accountancy and Taxation:** As an office executive he must have a basic knowledge of bookkeeping and accountancy as well as the law and practice of income tax, sales tax, etc.

**12. Knowledge of Office Organization and Management:** A company secretary must have a sound practical knowledge of up to date methods of filing, indexing, layout, mechanical devices, methods of recruitment of office staff, assignment and delegation of work, methods of remuneration, etc. Training and experience in office management add to the quality of his functions.

**13. Knowledge of Economics, Banking and Finance:** A company secretary should have knowledge of the law and practice of banking, working of the money and capital markets, methods of financing trade and industry and foreign exchange. He should also know the methods of modern banking and finance so far as it relates to the financing of his company.

**14. Prioritizing Tasks:** It is essential that a secretary be able to organize the work to be done so that the most important tasks are carried out first. The executive knows that smooth office work flow depends on the secretary's ability not only to handle routine matters but also to set-up sensible work priorities — a skill that demands good judgement. The competent secretary knows those matters that can be handled with prior approval of the executive, recognizes the kinds of problems that should be relayed to other executives for action, and knows what material must be sent directly to the executive for whom one works.

**15. Familiar with the Rules and Regulations of a Foreign Country:** Since these companies operate in countries throughout the world, the secretaries to the corporate executives of such firms are involved in planning for international travel by the executives. In addition, a competent executive-level secretary should be sufficiently familiar with pertinent laws and regulations indigenous to a particular country in order to assist a manager in researching, interpreting, and applying them.

Other desirable skills would include a broad background in the customs and history of the country or countries with which the executive deals and the ability to speak at least one foreign language.

**16. The Communication and Retrieval of Information:** The secretary needs to be able to acquire, handle, store, retrieve, and understand varied types of information as rapidly and as efficiently as possible. The secretary's ability to search for information efficiently from the appropriate reference sources can be extremely helpful to the executive. Such information may be acquired manually, mechanically, or electronically. Even in an era of automation, manual techniques of recording data are used on certain business forms and communications, such as purchase orders, cost tickets, expense accounts, and credit memorandums. On such forms the secretary may record information or instructions which are to be conveyed to others within a company or to other organizations. Letters are not only important conduits of information but are also one of the many ways in which the corporate image is projected. Reports are also vital information medium, as they assist in keeping designated persons abreast of past, present, and future management actions. Secretaries may also acquire data orally (as at conferences or meetings or through telephone conversations).

## CHANGING ROLE OF A SECRETARY

The secretary is now much more than a receptionist-cum-typist, for an increasing number of executives expect their secretaries to function as administrative assistants who can relieve them of many routine and some specialized tasks. Of course, the secretary has always been a vital link between those who make management-level decisions and those who react to and implement the decisions. In the present role of administrative assistant, however, a competent and responsible secretary is not only a link between management and line personnel but also a supporting adjunct to the executive.

In the past, many secretaries have been placed in positions of responsibility without being delegated enough authority to carry-out the responsibility. The current global outreach of business and the resultant pressures affecting managers have caused them to rethink the secretarial function and to delegate more responsibility and implementation authority to their secretaries. While the qualifications set down by employers for various job slots vary with the nature of the particular job and with the requirements of each executive, the trend today is toward better-educated secretaries who are willing and qualified to accept and perform with competence as many tasks as can be delegated to them. Some of these tasks are specialized and demanding and require good judgement in their execution; many of them were once considered administrative or executive functions. Additional responsibilities expected of today's administrative secretary might include the following:

1. Preparing rough drafts of executive responses to communications
2. Reading, signing and sending out some executive correspondence
3. Composing speeches, memorandums or reports for the executive to edit
4. Composing articles for publication
5. Editing copy prepared and typed by others
6. Consulting reference sources to obtain information desired by the executive
7. Abstracting information from various sources for the executive's use
8. Setting up meetings and conferences and reminding executives afterward of the tasks delegated to them at these meetings
9. Participating actively in some meetings and chairing certain others
10. Supervising and or training one or more other employees
11. Selecting or recommending office equipment systems and supplies for purchase by the organization.

Such duties clearly indicate that the secretarial function is being extended to encompass many specialized tasks that the executive may delegate. This administrative expansion of the secretarial function is reflected in the definition of a secretary provided by Professional Secretaries International: 'an executive assistant who possesses a mastery of office skills, demonstrates the ability to assume responsibility without direct supervision, exercises initiative and judgement, and makes decisions within the scope of assigned authority'.

Another aspect in the changing role of the secretary is the effect of rapid and continual technological developments especially in office equipment systems. Rather than eliminating secretaries from the office, technological developments have freed them from many time-consuming routine tasks so that they may be better employed in the more specialized areas of office work that have been listed above. For example, a secretary may now retrieve information from a computerized file without having to leave the work station. Desktop and pocket calculators have greatly streamlined and speeded accounting procedures. Sophisticated copying equipment enables secretaries to handle increased paperwork with relative ease. Word processing systems and typewriters with automatic correcting features expedite the processing of written communications. Highly sophisticated telecommunication equipment systems are now available to facilitate and speed up oral business communication, while electronic mail systems facilitate rapid transmission of written business communications. And other electronic devices such as dictation and transcription on machines increase input and output and markedly decrease turnaround time.

A significant result of these technological developments is the division of secretarial careers into what are now generally called administrative support (AS) positions and word processing (WP) positions. In many offices the installation of word processing equipment has effectively created two separate career paths: (1) the administrative secretary, who tends to telephone and mail messages, handles files, and arranges executive travel and meetings, and (2) the word processing or correspondence secretary, whose work centres on activities in the word processing centre. The word processing centre, however, is a far cry from the steno pool of old, where the work was fairly routine. Today a wide variety of advancement possibilities stems from the division of work and the necessity for specialization and supervision.

While not every person will aspire to or reach the rank of executive secretary or word processing supervisor, all members of the secretarial profession can strive to attain a higher level of competence by giving considerable thought to just how far they want to go in the field and how they can improve their skills and general education in order to become more competitive. Self-evaluation is essential for those who aspire to business careers, for those who are already employed as secretaries, and for those who are considering recently into the workforce. In short, one should make a mental balance sheet of one's professional assets and liabilities and then decide how the assets can be improved still further and how the liabilities can be eradicated or transformed into assets. For example, a secretary who is weak in English grammar should give serious thought of taking a course in that subject. A secretary who is unfamiliar with a modern electronic calculator but who has to perform routine accounting functions as a part of a job could ask the company to purchase one and, by learning how to use it efficiently, could save valuable company time. Secretaries working for corporations that are involved in international business operations can improve their professional status and their value to the company by learning a foreign language that might be useful in assisting the executive. In the fast-paced business world of this decade, it is too easy just to keep afloat — to do one's job and keep one day or one hour ahead, rather than to take the time to sit down and evaluate oneself.

This evaluation is absolutely essential and cannot be overemphasized because the competition for jobs and promotions shows no signs of slackening; rather, it is stiffening. An ambitious secretary must have specific career goals and the courage and the competence to attain them.

## SUMMARY

Traditionally, an office a place where clerical work is performed and all kind of paperwork (letters, correspondence, files, records, etc.), is maintained and dealt with. "It is a central place where all sorts of clerical work are done to coordinate and control the affairs of the whole organization." The term "Office management" means the technique of controlling an office in order to achieve its purpose which is possible only when the office is well organized and managed. Office management is concerned with the people who work in the office. The functions of modern office may be classified into two categories: (i) Basic functions or routine functions, and (ii) Administrative management functions. A "system" is a planned approach to the activities needed to attain desired objectives. Specifically, a system may be defined as a group of interrelated and interdependent parts operating in sequence according to predetermined plan, in order to achieve a goal or series of goals. Office procedure or office routine are a series of steps to be taken for doing a particular work in the office as per the office systems. "A method is a manual of mechanical means and devices by which each operation is performed." Index means to point out something. Anything which gives certain information regarding anything is called as an Index. An Index is a kind of "guide" which guides a person as to where the information, in detail, will be available. Filing is the "Systematic preservation of letters, documents, received and copies of those sent out for future reference is known as filing". It is the "process of arranging and sorting the original records, or copies of them, so that, they can be readily located whenever required". In case of very large business organization, a problem arises as to whether filing may be organized departmentally or centrally. A centralized filing system is a system where all the files pertaining to all the department of whole of the organization are preserved in a separate room in a centralized office and consequently any departmental head searching a particular file has to search it from there. Under this system, each department of the organization makes its own arrangements for filing. Every department maintains its own filing equipment and has its own staff to operate the system. There are a large number of machines and appliances which may be used for different operations in an office. They make for the accuracy and speed of operations, reduce work tensions and relieve monotony and fatigue. The word secretary is derived from a Latin word 'secretaries' which means "a confidential officer". The basic idea behind keeping a secretary is that there should be a person who can assist these authorities in carrying out the details of the work so that all matters could be handled in confidence and with utmost efficiency. Functions of a secretary and be divided into secretarial function and nonsecretarial function. As an office executive, the secretarial functions include: supervision, coordination and control of clerical work, selection, appointment and assignment of office work to the staff, maintaining office discipline, supervising secretarial work related to meeting, etc. The secretary has always been a vital link between those who make management-level decisions and those who react to and implement the decisions. Another aspect in the changing role of the secretary is the effect of rapid and continual technological developments especially in office equipment systems. While not every person will aspire to or reach the rank of executive secretary or word processing supervisor, all members of the secretarial profession can strive to attain a higher level of competence by giving considerable thought to just how far they want to go in the field and how they can improve their skills and general education in order to become more competitive.

## KEYWORDS

- Office Management
- Office Routines,
- Indexing,
- Office Machines,
- Office Systems,
- Office Procedures,
- Filing,
- Company Secretary

## ........ QUESTIONS FOR DISCUSSIONS

1. "The office is in many respects the brain of a business organization."Justify the statement by bringing out the functions of modern office
2. Explain the importance of an office to the organization
3. Write the objectives of an office in detail
4. Write short notes on: (a) indexing, (b) filing
5. Explain the essential qualifications required to become a secretary
6. State the role of a secretary in modern management

## Objective Questions

### A. Fill in the Blanks

1. ________ is the process of arranging and sorting the original records or copies, so that they can be readily located when required.
2. A ________ filing refers to a system where all the files pertaining to all department of the organization is preserved in a separate room.
3. ________ is that branch of art or science of management which deals with the efficient performance of office work.
4. Under ________ system small compartments are created, each compartment being allotted an alphabetic letter.
5. Flat and lever files are ________ filing system. (Vertical, Horizontal, Loose-vertical)
6. Folders and cabinets are ________ filing system. (Vertical, Horizontal, Loose-vertical)
7. A good filing system should have a ________ filing department.
8. A good filing system should provide a ________ reference.
9. ________ filing system is also known as docketing filing.
10. ________ means to point out something.
11. Under ________ index system the cards of the size of 4½ ×3½ are arranged vertically in a drawer.
12. Under ________ index system a series of cards are held in transparent covers and are arranged as to overlap on each other.
13. Under ________ system cards are mounted on the circumference of wheel which is placed in a cabinet or desk.

*Ans:* **1.** Filing, **2.** centralized, **3.** Office management, **4.** Pigeon holing, **5.** horizontal, **6.** vertical, **7.** centralized, **8.** cross, **9.** Pigeon holing, **10.** Index, **11.** loose/vertical card, **12.** visible card, **13.** wheel index.

## B. Multiple Choice Questions

1. The main purpose of an index is ________ of files.
   (a) Collection (b) copying (c) locating (d) dispatching
2. Under ________ filing system, a cupboard is provided, which is divided into small compartments and each compartment is allotted a letter of the alphabet.
   (a) Pigeon hole (b) spike (c) vertical (d) horizontal
3. ________ and ________ files are horizontal filing methods.
   (a) Office and Index (b) Suspension and lateral
   (c) Loose leaf and visible card (d) flat and lever
4. ________ and ________ files are vertical filing methods.
   (a) Suspension and lateral (b) flat and lever
   (c) Office and Index (d) Loose leaf and visible card

*Ans:* **1.** (c), **2.** (a), **3.** (d), **4.** (a)

## C. State Whether the Following Statements are True or False. Justify Your Answer

1. A good filing system should be flexible.
2. It is suggested the files should be a self-indexing
3. If the files are arranged in an alphabetical order an index is not needed.
4. An index is anything that indicates or points out something.

*Ans:* **1. True**

The filing system of the office should be capable of expansion at the same time should be capable of contracting by destroying the old files so that new files can be accommodated. An inflexible system is obviously useless after a certain limit is crossed.

**2. True**

So that unnecessary time or labour may not be spent in the preparation of index and then to locate a particular file by referring to the index in the first instance.

**3. True**

It will help in locating the files even when the index is not there provided they are arranged in an alphabetical order.

**4. True**

Indexing means alphabetical or numerical arrangement of papers or files. So, any file can be pointed out easily if indexing is done.

☺ ☺ ☺

CHAPTER 16

# Management Information System

LEARNING OBJECTIVES

- *Importance of Management Information System*
- *Information System Required at Different Levels of Management*
- *Information System and Functional Areas of Management*
- *Positive and Negative Impact of MIS*
- *Changing Role of Information System in Modern Business*

## INTRODUCTION

Information systems play a crucial role in the management of any contemporary enterprise such as a small, medium or large organization; a profit making or a social service set-up; a public or a private sector undertaking; a manufacturing or a service organization; a local or a global corporation; and an upcoming or an established business house. The fast changing scene of liberalization, competition and globalization combined with a never before seen emphasis on quality, timeliness, innovation, customer orientation and efficiency puts a premium on accurate, superfast and timely dissemination of information across the globe. The unprecedented developments in computing and communication technologies have indeed made such demands translatable into realizable goals. Thus, a large portion of the world population has its stake in information systems.

## INFORMATION SYSTEM: MEANING

An information system can be defined as a set of interrelated components that collect (or retrieve), process, store, and distribute information to support decision making, coordination, and control in an organization. In addition to supporting decision making, coordination, and control, information systems may also help managers and workers to analyze problems, visualize complex subjects, and create new products. Information systems contain information about significant people, places, and things within the organization or in the environmental surrounding it.

By information we mean data that have been shaped into a form that is meaningful and useful to human beings. Data, in contrast, are streams of raw facts representing events occurring in organizations or the physical environment before they have been organized and arranged into a form that people can understand and use. For example, supermarket checkout counters ring up millions of pieces of data, such as product identification number or the cost of each items sold. Such pieces of data can be totalled and analyzed to provide meaningful information, such as the total number of bottles of dish detergent sold at a particular store, which brands of dish detergent are selling most rapidly at that store or sales territory, or the total amount spent on that brand of dish detergent at that store or sales region.

Three activities in an information system produce the information that organizations need to make decisions, control operations, analyze problems, and create new products or services. These activities are input, processing, and output. Input captures or collects raw data from within the organization or from its external environment. Processing converts this raw input into a meaningful form. Output transfers the processed information to the people who will use it or to the activities for which it will be used. Information systems also require feedback, which is output that is returned to appropriate members of the organization to help them evaluate or correct the input stage.

For example, an information system for apparel buying, the raw input for an order from retailers consists of item numbers, item description, and amount of each item ordered along with the retailer's name and identification number. The computer processes these data by comparing each item number on the order to item numbers in company's master catalogue and supplying the correct item number where differences are found. The system schedules the shipment of order to retailers, notifying the retailer if an item is out of stock. Shipping documents, invoices, and online reports to the retailer showing delivery date and location of the order in transit become outputs. The system thus provides meaningful information, such as lists of what items a retailer ordered, the total number of each item ordered daily by all retailers, and the total number of each item ordered by each retailer.

## DEFINITION OF MIS

Gordon B. Davis defines Management Information System, as an integrated user-machine system, for providing information, to support the operations, management analysis and decision making functions in an organization. The system utilizes computer hardware and software, manual procedures, models for analysis, planning, control, and decision making, and a database.

Jerome Kanter defines it as "A system that aids management in making, carrying out and controlling decisions".

Management Information System (MIS) is a computer-based system that provides flexible and speedy access to accurate data. The three subcomponents — Management, Information, and Systems — together bring to focus clearly and effectively.

1. Management emphasizing the ultimate uses of such information systems for managerial decision making rather than merely stressing on technology.
2. Information highlighting on processed data rather than raw data and in the context in which it is used by managers and other end-users.
3. Systems emphasizing a fair degree of integration and a holistic view.

An MIS is a set of computer-based systems and procedures implemented to help managers in their crucial job of decision making. The actual process will involve the collection, organization, distribution and storage of organization-wise information for managerial analysis and control.

Management Information Systems (MIS) serve the management level of the organization, providing managers with reports or with online access to the organization's current performance and historical records. Typically, they are oriented almost exclusively to internal, not environmental or external, events. MIS primarily serve the functions of planning, controlling, and decision making at the management level. Generally, they depend on underlying transaction processing systems for their data. MIS summarize and report on the company's basic operations.

MIS usually serve managers interested in weekly, monthly, and yearly results — not day-to-day activities. MIS generally provide answers to routine questions that have been specified in advance and have a predefined procedure for answering them. For instance, MIS reports might list the total pounds of lettuce used this quarter by a fast-food chain or, compare total annual sales figures for specific products to the planned targets. These systems are generally not flexible and have little analytical capability. Most MIS use simple routines such as summaries and comparisons, as opposed to sophisticated mathematical models or statistical techniques.

In order to get a better grip on the activity of information processing, it is necessary to have a formal system which can:

1. Handle large volume of data,
2. Confirmation of the validity of data and transaction,
3. Complex processing of data and multidimensional analysis,
4. Quick search and retrieval,
5. Mass storage,

6. Communication of the information system to the user on time,
7. Fulfilling the changing needs of the information.

The management information system uses computers and communication technology to deal with these points of supreme importance.

## Characteristics of MIS

Jerome Kanter in his work titled *'Management Information Systems'* mentions several characteristics of MIS. Some of them are:

(i) **MIS is Management-oriented:** The designing of MIS takes care of the managers, who meet the information requirement. The development of the system starts after deciding the management needs and keeping in view the overall objectives of the management.

(ii) **Management Directed:** Since MIS requires heavy planning and investment, management is deeply involved in the design, implementation and maintenance of the system.

(iii) **Integrated System:** Five Ms — Men, Money, Materials, Machines, and Methods are the basic resources of management information and is recognized as an important factor and its effective use contributes to the success of the management. MIS is the 'catalyst and nerve centre' of an organization. It has a number of subsystems. In order to make these subsystems effective, it becomes necessary that they have to be viewed as an integrated system, so that the result is balanced. It binds together databases of all subsystems of the business system and through information interchange, integrates the organization.

(iv) **Avoids Redundancy in Data Storage:** Since MIS is an integrated system, it avoids unnecessary duplication and redundancy in data gathering and storage.

(v) **Common Data Flow:** To achieve the objective of integration and to avoid duplication and redundancy in data gathering, storage and retrieval, data capturing is usually confined to original sources and it is done only once. Common data flow tries to utilize minimum data processing effort and strives to minimize the number of outdated documents and reports. This type of integration can avoid duplication and produce an effective MIS. But separate files should be opened which are significant to one application with the use of common data flow.

(vi) **Detailed Planning:** Design and implementation of MIS require detailed planning of such activities as acquisition and deployment of hardware, software, data processing operations, information presentation and feedback.

(vii) **Subsystem Concept:** MIS gives provision for breaking into various subsystems based on the activity as well as the functions of the organization, so that effective implementation of each subsystem is possible at a time.

(viii) **Common Database:** It acts as a master that holds the functional subsystems together. It achieves this aim by allowing access to different master files of data to several functional subsystems. Data requirements for different levels of management also support the need of more than one database, unique databases and common database.

(ix) **Flexibility and Ease of Use:** MIS has been designed flexible enough to accommodate new requirements. The system is easy to operate so that not much computer skills are required on the part of the user to access database for information or for carrying out special analysis of data.

(x) **Computerization:** MIS can be computerized because of its nature as a comprehensive system. This provides speed in creating and accessing files, accuracy, consistency in data processing, reduction in clerical work, avoid human errors, etc.

## Evolution of MIS

The digital computer was primarily designed for scientific calculations. However, ever since the use of computers for the American census in 1954, the commercial applications of computers have far exceeded the scientific applications. It is estimated that the commercial applications account for as high as 80 per cent of the investment in hardware and software. A significant portion of such commercial applications aims at providing some form of information system support to the management of an enterprise.

The concept of MIS evolved over the years. In the fifties and sixties, many organizations realized the potential of computers to process large amount of data speedily and accurately. The accuracy and speed of data processing of the computing equipment of that era far exceeded that of people who used to undertake data processing in those days. Typically, such data processing activities included wage calculation, material accounting, invoicing and billing. Subsequently, with the substantial increase in business, these clerical activities had to be performed very fast, using very large amount of data. Even the use of a large number of personnel to cope with large-scale data processing was ineffective. Increasing the number of workers could speed up processing, but the inherent deficiency of inaccuracy in repetitively performing mundane data processing, which is a characteristic of human beings, could not be improved. Organizations, therefore, visualized in the early computers, which were primarily programmable calculators, a potential to overcome this deficiency. This lead to the activity widely known as Electronic Data Processing (EDP), a term used to indicate the use of computers that used electronic equipment (e.g., vacuum tubes and later on transistors) for processing a large volume data. Obviously, such EDP approach capitalized on the ability of computers to perform accurate processing of repetitive data with practically no signs of fatigue, thus eliminating performance degradation exhibited generally by human beings when confronted with such data processing work.

The focus of EDP was on recordkeeping — an activity that is a statutory requirement in many organizations. The majority of the items whose records had to be maintained were accounting data. So, the finance and accounts departments took early lead in EDP activity. In fact, many EDP departments were under the administrative control of such accounting departments. A classic example of such a situation in the Indian context is the Indian Railways, where EDP departments were under the direct control of the Financial Advisor and Chief Accounts Officer (FA&CAO). A natural extension of such accounting applications was the Payroll and Inventory Control; soon other financial services that were data dominated took to EDP easily. Insurance companies, like the Life Insurance Corporation of India, were the leading examples of EDP pioneers. Triggered by the need, a whole lot of specialized mechanical and electromechanical accessories for the computers were also developed, the chief among them being Card Punch Equipment, Card Readers, Card Sorters, and specialized printing equipment known then as Accounting Machines. The emergence of International Business Machines (IBM) as a huge multinational corporation was a direct fallout of such a momentum in EDP departments.

The next stage of development of MIS was concerned more with insight and analysis that would possibly be provided by the routine availability of such accurate and timely data. In the seventies, the digital computers underwent a fundamental change by the introduction of time-sharing and interactive computing. Such a change along with large availability of discs and the emergence of file processing systems and COBOL programming language saw a discernible shift from data to information. The focus was not merely on processing of data; it was more on the analysis of corporate data. While accuracy and timeliness were important, relevance, analysis and insight became the key words. The emphasis was more on the effectiveness of the analysis of the data rather than on the more efficiency of speedy processing of data. Such a shift in emphasis was first conveyed through the term MIS. Management Information Systems stressed information — often thought to be a refined form of data. The MIS philosophy underlined both the content — information in contrast to data — and the focus of processing.

The eighties saw the Personal Computer (PC) revolution that is continuing today. In the seventies, the top management relied on the staff departments of EDP and MIS to supply the necessary information. Information systems play a key role information re-engineering process. It could redesign a particular activity, a major restructuring of an organization, or a complete transformation of the business goals and processes of an entire organization. Obviously, then, a clear understanding of the organizational structure and processes is called for, before information systems supporting such re-engineering exercises can be redesigned, thus bringing into sharp focus the interplay between information systems and organizational systems.

The knowledge and information revolution began at the turn of the twentieth century and has gradually accelerated. By 1976, the number of white-collar workers employed in offices surpassed the number of farm workers, service workers, and blue-collar workers employed in manufacturing. Today, most people no longer work on farms or in factories but instead are found in sales, education, health care, banks, insurance firms, and law firms; they also provide business services, such as copying, computer programming, or making deliveries. These jobs primarily involve working with, distributing, or creating new knowledge and information.

Knowledge and information are becoming the foundation for many new services and products. Knowledge and information-intensive products such as computer games require a great deal of knowledge to produce. Knowledge is used more intensively in the production of traditional products as well. In the automobile industry, for instance, both design and production now rely heavily on knowledge and information technology.

## Functions of MIS

Management Information System is a combination of computers and procedures for providing information that manager's use in making decisions.

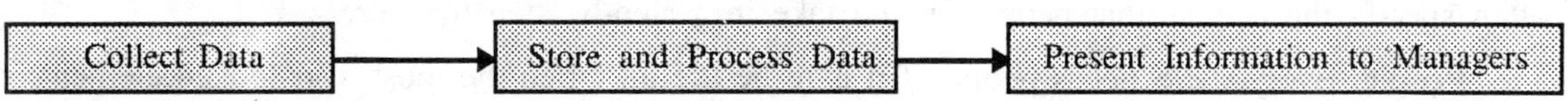


**Collect Data:** Massive amount of information are available to organizations — personnel records, information about customers, information about competitors, sales data, accounting data and so on. The first function of an MIS is to determine the information needed to make decisions and to organize it into a database.

A 'Data Base' is an integrated collection of data stored in one place for efficient access and information processing. Data can be obtained from sources, within and outside the organization. Generally, most data collected for an MIS come from internal sources such as company records or reports and information compiled by managers themselves. External sources include trade publications, customers and consultants.

**Store and Process Data:** After creation of data, a database must be stored and processed in a form useful to managers. Data are generally stored on magnetic tape or hard disks when mainframe computers are used and on hard disks or floppy (soft) disks, when minicomputers are used. The data can be loaded into computers in seconds for easy access by the user.

**Present Information to Managers:** After collection of data, storing and processing of data, the next step is to present the information to managers for their use.

## COMPONENTS OF COMPUTER-BASED INFORMATION SYSTEMS

A computer-based information system (CBIS) is an information system in which the computer plays a major role in collecting, storing and processing data. The purpose of CBIS is to collect, store and disseminate information from an organization's environment and internal operations to support organizational functions and decision making, communication, coordination, control, analysis and visualization.

Such a system consists of the following elements:

**Hardware:** The term hardware refers to machinery. This category includes the computer itself, which is often referred to as the central processing unit (CPU), and all of its support equipment. Among the support equipment are input and output devices, storage devices, and communications devices.

**Software:** The term software refers to computer programs and the manuals (if any) that support them. Computer programs are machine-readable instructions that direct the circuitry within the hardware parts of the CBIS to function in ways that produce useful information from data. Programs are generally stored on some input/output medium — often a disk or tape — for use by the computer.

**Data:** Data are facts that are used by programs to produce useful information. Like programs, data are generally stored in machine-readable form on disk or tape until the computer needs them.

**Procedures:** Procedures are the policies that govern the operation of a computer system. 'Procedures are to people what software is to hardware' is a common analogy that is used to illustrate the role of procedures in a CBIS. For instance, the steps that must be taken to enter a password and log on to a computer terminal are a procedure. The actions needed to restore the computer system to its operational state after a major power failure is another example of a procedure. Procedures often specify the actions that people should take in a step-by-step manner.

**People:** Every CBIS needs people if it is to be useful. Often the most over-looked element of the CBIS, people is probably the components that most influence the success or failure of information systems. Users, programmers, systems analysts, and database administrators are just some of the people associated with computer-based information systems.

## The Need for a Management Information System

Computers are making inroads into every activity of human endeavour. MIS provides balanced perspectives into the applications of computers in the broad areas of business. It is used in oil exploration, space exploration, weather forecasting, market analysis, financial planning, production planning, human resource management, transportation, communication, heavy industry, chemicals, small-scale industry, health care, tourism, hospitality industry, education and research. Thus, a basic knowledge of information systems is almost becoming a generic skill needed by every professional. To the top management, MIS is a tool to gain insight into the overall health of the organization itself.

In a knowledge and information-based economy, information technology and systems take on great importance. Technology-based products and services of great economic value, such as credit cards, overnight package delivery, and worldwide reservation systems, are based on new information technologies. Information technology constitutes more than 70 per cent of the invested capital in service industries like finance, insurance, and real estate.

There are several factors which make such a system more necessary than it was just two or three decades ago. One factor is that managers must deal with a much more complex business environment than that existed before. One of the major reasons for this complexity is increased government regulation, which requires organizations to undertake many activities that were previously unnecessary; usually these involve filing a variety of regulatory reports.

Another reason for this complexity is the wider variety of products and services that organizations offer their customers; managing this greater variety requires more sophisticated information systems. The business environment is not only more complex but also more dynamic. Managers have to make more decisions quickly, and typically less time must elapse between the emergence of a management problem and its satisfactory solution. This is true partly because competitors have learned to adapt more rapidly to their environment. An MIS that provides both sophisticated and timely information is a necessary part of the required adaptation. Indeed, a major trend in information systems is towards developing capabilities intended to facilitate the organization's rapid adaptation to change.

The MIS objective calls for supporting contribution to meet the company's goals. Suppose a company wants to increase its market share from 10 per cent to 14 per cent, it requires numerous information:

(i) How the market is currently allocated?

(ii) What products did each competitor offer to get and hold its share of the market?

(iii) What are the pros and cons of these products?

(iv) To what customer set does each of these products appeal?

(v) How much advertising is spent on each product?

(vi) In what stage of the product life cycle in each product?

Managers now understand and utilize more sophisticated management techniques than their predecessors did. Managers of today routinely use marginal analysis, standard costs, and direct costing as well as traditional full costing, sensitivity analysis techniques, and a variety of other management methods not widely used two decades ago. Applying these techniques requires more sophisticated information than was previously needed, and this in turn requires a more sophisticated information system. Information systems can help companies extend their reach to faraway locations, offer new products and services, reshape jobs and work flows, and perhaps profoundly change the way they conduct business.

The most powerful worldwide changes have altered the business environment are:

- The emergence and strengthening of the global economy.
- The transformation of industrial economies and societies into knowledge and information based service economies.

Today, information systems provide the communication and analytical power that firms need for conducting trade and managing businesses on a global scale. Controlling the far flung global corporation — communicating with distributors and suppliers, operating twenty-four hours a day in different national environments, servicing local and international reporting needs — is a major business challenge that requires powerful information system responses. Because of global communication and management systems, customers now can shop in a worldwide marketplace, obtaining price and quality information reliably 24 hours a day. To become competitive participants in international markets, firms need powerful information and communication systems.

Desktop machines, inexpensive computer-aided design (CAD) software, and computer controlled machine tools provide the precision, speed, and quality of giant manufacturers.

Information immediately accessed by telephone and communications links eliminates the need for research staff and business libraries. Managers can easily obtain the information they need to manage large numbers of employees in widely scattered locations.

Custom manufacturing systems allow large factories to offer customized products in small quantities. Massive databases of customer purchasing records can be analyzed so that large companies know their customers' needs and preferences as easily as local merchants. Information can be easily distributed down the ranks of the organization to empower lower-level employees and work groups to solve problems.

## The Emergence of Digital Firm

The changes we have described represent new ways of conducting business electronically both inside and outside the firm that can ultimately lead to digital firms. Increasingly, the internet is providing the underlying technology for these changes. The internet can link thousands of organizations into a single network, creating the foundation for a vast electronic marketplace.

An **electronic market** is an information system that links together many buyers and sellers to exchange information, products, services, and payments. Through computers and networks, these systems function like electronic intermediaries, with lowered costs for typical marketplace transactions, such as matching buyers and sellers, establishing prices, ordering goods, and paying bills (Bakos, 1998). Buyers and sellers can complete purchase and sale transactions digitally, regardless of their location.

A vast array of goods and services are being advertised, bought, and exchanged worldwide using the internet as a global marketplace. Companies are furiously creating eye-catching electronic brochures, advertisements, product manuals, and order forms on the World Wide Web. All kinds of products and services are available on the Web, including fresh flowers, books, real estate, musical recordings, electronics, and steaks.

Many retailers maintain their own sites on the Web, such as Wine.com, an online source of wine and food items. Others offer their products through electronic shopping malls, such as shopnow.com. Customers can locate products on this mall either by retailer, if they know what they want, or by-product type, and then order the products directly. Even electronic financial trading has arrived on the Web for stocks, bonds, mutual funds, and other financial instruments. Increasingly the Web is being used for business-to-business transactions as well. For example, airlines can use the Boeing Corporation's website to order parts electronically and check the status of their orders.

The global availability of the internet for the exchange of transactions between buyers and sellers is fulling the growth of electronic commerce. **Electronic commerce** is the process of buying and selling goods and services electronically with computerized business transactions using the internet, networks, and other digital technologies. It also encompasses activities supporting those market transactions, such as advertising, marketing, customer support, delivery, and payment. By replacing manual and paper-based procedures with electronic alternatives, and by using information flows in new and dynamic ways, electronic commerce can accelerate ordering, delivery, and payment for goods and services while reducing companies' operating and inventory costs. For example, Drugstore.com operates a virtual pharmacy on the internet selling prescription medicine and over the-counter health, beauty, and wellness products. Customers can input their orders via Drugstore.com's website and have their purchases shipped to them.

## INFORMATION SYSTEM AT DIFFERENT LEVEL OF MANAGEMENT

The main types of information systems serve at different organizational levels are:

**Operational-level Systems** support operational managers by keeping track of the elementary activities and transactions of the organization, such as sales, receipts, cash deposits, payroll, credit decisions, and the flow of materials in a factory. The principal purpose of systems of this level is to answer routine questions and to track the flow of transactions through the organization. How many parts are in inventory? What happened to Mr. Murthy's payment? To answer these kinds of questions, information generally must be easily available current, and accurate. Examples of operational-level systems include a system to record bank deposits from automatic teller machines or one that tracks the number of hours worked each day by employees on a factory floor.

The payroll represents a typical operational system for the financial management. Since such systems must execute accurately, data pertaining to a large number of staff in a timely manner, month-after-month, cost-based efficiency and speed would be major considerations in the design of such a system.

**Knowledge-level Systems** support the organization's knowledge and data workers. The purpose of knowledge-level systems is to help the business firm integrate new knowledge into the business and to help the organization control the flow of paperwork. Knowledge-level systems, especially in the form of work stations and office systems are among the most widely used applications in business today.

**Management-level Systems** serve the monitoring, controlling, decision making, and administrative activities of middle managers. The principal question addressed by such systems is:

Are things working well? Management-level systems typically provide periodic reports rather than instant information on operations. An example is a relocation control system that reports on the total moving, house-hunting, and home financing costs for employees in all company divisions, noting wherever actual costs exceed budgets.

**Some Management-level Systems** support non-routine decision making. They tend to focus on less-structured decisions for which information requirements are not always clear. These systems often answer 'what if' questions: What would be the impact on production schedules if we were to double sales in the month of December? What would happen to our return on investment if a factory schedule were delayed for six months? Answers to these and other questions frequently require new data from outside the organization, as well as data from inside that cannot be easily drawn from existing operational-level systems.

**Strategic-level Systems** help senior management tackle and address strategic issues and long-term trends, both in the firm and in the external environment. Their principal concern is matching changes in the external environment with existing organizational capability. What will employment levels be in five years? What are the long-term industry cost trends, and where does our firm fit in? What products should we be making in five years?

A strategic decision by the production function of the management is, for example, deciding about the location of a new plant. Such a decision requires much of the internal information generated by the tactical system designed to analyze the production bottleneck which is internal to the organization. But a long-term decision like location of a new plant is likely to be influenced far more by environmental information such as changing market, changing technology, changing fiscal and governmental policy, e.g., deregulation and tax incentive for backward area. Obviously, strategic information systems should have a mechanism for scanning and assimilating environmental information which are likely to influence strategic decisions in a systematic way.

Information systems also serve the major business functions, such as sales and marketing, manufacturing, finance, accounting, and human resources. A typical organization has operational, management. Knowledge, and strategic level systems for each functional area. For example, the sales function generally has a sales system on the operational level to record daily sales figures and to process orders. A knowledge-level system designs promotional displays for the firm's products. A management-level system tracks monthly sales figures by sales territory and reports on territories where sales exceed or fall below anticipated levels. A system to forecast sales trends over a five-year period serves the strategic level.

The table summarizes the features of the six types of information systems. It should be noted that each of the different kinds of systems may have components that are used by organizational levels and groups other than their main constituencies. A secretary may find information on an MIS, or a middle manager may need to extract data from a TPS.

| Type of systems | Information inputs | Processing | Information outputs | Users |
|---|---|---|---|---|
| ESS | Aggregate data; external, internal | Graphics; simulations; interactive | Projections; responses to queries | Senior managers |
| DSS | Low-volume data or massive databases optimized for data analysis; analytic models and data analysis tools | Interactive; simulations; analysis | Special reports; decision analyses; responses to queries | Professionals; staff managers |
| MIS | Summary transaction data; high-volume data; simple models | Routine reports; simple models; low-level analysis | Summary and exception reports | Middle managers |
| KWS | Design specifications; knowledge base | Modelling; simulations | Model; graphics | Professionals; technical staff |
| Office systems | Documents; schedules | Document management; scheduling; communication | Documents; schedules; mail | Clerical workers |
| TPS | Transactions; events | Sorting; listing; merging; updating | Detailed reports; lists; summaries | Operation personnel; supervisors |

## Positive and Negative Impacts of Information Systems

| Benefits of Information System | Negative Impacts |
|---|---|
| Information systems can perform calculations or process paper work much faster than people | By automating activities that were previously performed by people, information systems may eliminate jobs |
| Information systems can help companies learn purchase patterns and preferences of their customers | Information systems may allow more about the organizations to collect personal details about people that violate their privacy |
| Information systems provide new efficiencies through services such as automated teller machines (ATMs), telephone systems, or computer-controlled airplanes and air terminals | Information systems are used in so many aspects of everyday life that systems outages can cause shutdowns of businesses or transportation services, paralyzing communities |
| Information systems have made possible new medical advances in surgery, radiology, and patient monitoring | Heavy uses of information systems may suffer repetitive stress injury, techno-stress, and other health problems |
| The Internet distributes information instantly to millions of people across the world | The Internet can be used to distribute illegal copies of software, books, articles and other intellectual property. |

## INFORMATION TECHNOLOGY AND MANAGEMENT PROCESS

Information technology is recasting the management process, providing powerful new capabilities to help managers plan, organize, lead, and control. For instance, it is now possible for managers to obtain information on organizational performance down to the level of specific transactions from almost anywhere in the organization at any time. Product managers at Frito-Lay Corporation, the world's largest manufacturer of salty snack foods, can know within hours precisely how many bags of Fritos have sold on any street in America at its customers' stores, how much they sold for, and what the competition's sales volumes and prices are. This greater availability and detail of information makes possible far more precise planning, forecasting, and monitoring than ever before.

**Planning:** Strategic level planning requires considerable amount of environmental information like shifting markets, changing technology as well as internal information like core competitive strength of the organization. Tactical planning activities such as vendor development, make-or-buy decisions would call for cost and availability information pertaining to materials and production capacities which are internal as well as external to the organization. Operational planning like staff scheduling requires large amount of internal information, e.g., schedules, attendance, up times of equipment.

**Organizing:** Strategic organizing needs external and internal data to decide on restructuring as well as to forge strategic partnerships. Tactical organizing requires changing wage-level data of the organization as well as that of competitors. Operational organizing needs data relating to skills and training requirements of the operational staff.

**Coordinating:** Strategic coordination calls for industry-wise data corresponding to technology availability. Tactical coordination calls for plant-wise and supplier-wise bottleneck data that reflect deficiencies both inside and outside the organization. Operational coordination requires itemized breakup of plant and machinery performance, failures, etc.

**Directing:** Strategic directing functions such as introduction of office automation requires detailed cost-benefit analysis of new technologies. Tactical directing (e.g., innovative marketing strategy) needs detailed market and production data. Operational directing function requires detailed data pertaining to the individual managers skills.

**Control:** Strategic control decisions like total quality management needs detailed performance data and benchmarking data from outside the organization. Tactical control decisions like maintaining steady market share in the medium run would necessitate continuous monitoring of plant data. Operational control may call for techniques of statistical process control which involves the collection of substantial sampling information that must be collected and processed continuously during the entire production period.

In short, each and every area of managerial decision making, be it planning, organizing, coordinating, directing or control, calls for substantial amount of information processing.

## INFORMATION SUPPORT FOR FUNCTIONAL AREAS OF MANAGEMENT

The functional areas of management are: Production, marketing, finance (including accounting), personnel and services. Information support to these functions varies widely from one organization to the other, particularly in countries like India, due to varying levels of development in different sectors of the economy.

**Production:** In manufacturing organizations, the production function occupies a central role. The role of this function is to control the entire production and operation function consisting of the following subareas:

- Design
- Location and layout
- Product design
- Facilities planning
- Operation
- Production planning and control
- Materials management
- Quality control
- Cost control
- Logistic planning.

Information support to the production function has received considerable attention over the years. In the Indian context, large manufacturing companies in the public sector like BHEL had taken an early lead in this area. Globally, detailed operational planning of materials requirements, production scheduling and resource scheduling in an elaborate and detailed manner has received considerable attention in the form of Materials Requirement Planning (MRP) and its ally, Manufacturing Resources Planning (MRP-II).

From an information systems point of view, MRP is a large-scale transaction processing system. It deals with operational data, such as time-phased production schedules, operator and machine allotment, planned order releases, receipt of goods and other related information. It cuts across the production planning, manufacturing, materials management, dispatch and delivery, stores and inspection units, collectively known as manufacturing departments. With the surge in interest in manufacturing activities globally, such innovative ideas like Just-in-time (JIT) philosophy, KANBAN systems of inventory control and Total Quality Management (TQM) are gaining currency in the production management practices. These systems need decision support and executive support systems that deal with the policies and strategies, and not transaction processing systems using large volumes of data. These emerging systems need MRP systems in place to generate the necessary data for higher level planning systems. Though several companies in India have gone for expensive hardware and software to implement MRP, like MANMAN from Digital, the relatively large uncertainty of production and distribution, lack of infrastructure support in the areas of transportation and communication have limited the ability of management of these enterprises to fully exploit the power of such powerful information systems.

Manufacturing and production information systems deal with the planning, development and production of products and services and controlling the flow of production.

**Marketing:** The marketing function in the consumer goods industry has a major component of advertisement and publicity. In engineering units this will consists primarily of the sales function with a large number of subsystems like:

- Sales
- Marketing
- Accounts receivable
- Accounts payable
- Distribution and logistics.

The services sector like hospitals, schools and hotel industry will have varying components of the sales and advertising functions, depending on the nature of its operation and the operating environment.

Marketing, traditionally has not been the major focus of information systems, particularly in India. The early applications have concentrated on sales data processing for recordkeeping and for tax computation, e.g., sales tax, excise duty, which are statutory and needed by governments both at the Centre and in the Sates and Union Territories. In fact, many of these systems are sales accounting systems rather than marketing systems and are primarily transaction processing and office automation systems. Only recently market information systems are emerging, thanks to the ready availability of data generated by market research and media research organizations like IMRB, ORG, etc. Decision support systems that intelligently make use of such market information for strategic market analysis and logistics support are only emerging recently. Software support tools like Market Map, Capitoline, etc., will be of significant help in such analysis. Such decision support tools need sophisticated analytical tools like statistical techniques and simulation. In a vast country like India, communication support to link data from diverse locations is also necessary for national marketing plans to be studied well. In short, sales and marketing information system, helps the firm's to identify customer's for firm's products or services, develop, promote and sell firm's products and services and provide customer support.

**Finance:** In general, the finance and accounting function consists of the following modules:

- General ledger
- Payroll
- Accounts payable
- Cash books
- Reconciliation
- Budget control
- Taxation
- Costing
- Benefits like Provident Fund, Bonus, Gratuity, Pension, and Insurance.

The finance and accounting function was the earliest function that provided data support through EDP systems in the 60s. Typical systems that got implemented were the Payroll and the General Ledger. Over the years these systems have become the mainstay of commercial application of computers. They are characterized by large operational data that must be efficiently processed in a time critical manner. The decisions supported by these systems belong to the programmed category and the information systems to support such decisions were largely transaction processing systems.

This segment represents the largest segment of computer applications. Large organizations in India like LIC, Railways, BHEL, and TELCO are the typical examples that have a tradition of efficiently run accounting and finance systems over the past several years. With emerging financial services markets, niche markets like share accounting, electronic stock exchange trading, etc., have been developed in the country. Banking automation using new technologies like ATM (Automated Teller Machines) and credit cards are the other applications in the financial segment that are emerging as major applications in the Indian context. The related areas of decision support for tax planning and investment planning are also emerging, though rather slowly. The analyst must be very skilled in realizing the differences in information support needed by systems like payroll and the new generation tax planning and stock market analysis systems. Financial and accounting information system keeps track of firm's financial assets and fund flows.

**Personnel and Services:** In general, the personnel function consists of the following modules:

- Recruitment,
- Promotion,
- Retirement,
- Transfers,
- Leave management,
- Training and skill development.

The services module may consist of the following:

- Welfare activities — housing, sports, recreation,
- Utilities like electricity, water supply, and air-conditioning,
- Communication including posts, telephone, fax and e-mail,
- Community living and health care.

Information systems, to support the personnel function, have once again taken the recordkeeping view rather than the decision support view. Particularly in the Indian context, it is limited to creating large databases often of questionable value and accuracy. Decision support systems that use the database of personnel information to make quick estimates of manpower cost, plan future manpower, plan effective manpower deployment, plan training needs, etc., are slowly getting implemented. Exciting ideas like the creation of multimedia databases like personnel records that incorporate signatures and pictures are being introduced to provide effective decision support capability. Personnel (human resource) information system maintain employee records, track employee skills, job performance and training and support planning for employee compensation and career development.

| | **Production** | **Finance** | **Personnel** | **Marketing** |
|---|---|---|---|---|
| Strategies | New plant location | Alternative financing | Welfare policy | Competitor survey |
| Tactical | Production bottleneck | Variance analysis | Performance appraisal | Advertising |
| Operational | Daily scheduling | Payroll | Leave records | Sales analysis |

The main challenges in building and using management information system are:

1. Designing systems that are competitive, efficient and more digitally enabled.
2. Understanding the system requirements of a global business environment.
3. Creating an information architecture and IT infrastructure that support the organization's goals.
4. Determining the business value of information system.
5. Designing system that people can control, understand and use in a socially and ethically responsible manner.

## Imapact of the Management Information System

Since the MIS plays a very important role in the organization, it creates an impact on the organization's functions, performance and productivity.

- With a good MIS support, the management of marketing, finance, production and personnel becomes more efficient.
- The tracking and monitoring of the functional targets becomes easy. The functional managers are informed about the progress, achievements and shortfalls in the activity and the targets.
- The manager is kept alert by providing certain information indicating probable trends in the various aspects of business. This helps in forecasting and long-term perspective planning.
- The manager's attention is brought to a situation which is exceptional in nature, inducing him to take an action or a decision in the matter.
- A disciplined information reporting system creates a structured database and a knowledge base for all the people in the organization. The information is available in such a form that it can be used straightaway or by blending and analysis, saving the manager's valuable time.
- The MIS calls for a systemization of the business operations for an effective system design. This leads to streamlining of the operations which complicates the system design.
- It improves the administration of the business by bringing a discipline in its operations as everybody is required to follow and use systems and procedures. This process brings a high degree of professionalism in the business operations.
- Since the goals and objectives of the MIS are the products of business goals and objectives, it helps indirectly to pull the entire organization in one direction towards the corporate goals and objectives by providing the relevant information to the people in the organization.
- A well designed system with a focus on the manager makes an impact on the managerial efficiency. The fund of information motivates an enlightened manager to use a variety of tools of the management. It helps him to resort to such exercises as experimentation and modelling.
- Since the MIS work on the basic systems such as transaction processing and databases, the drudgery of the clerical work is transferred to the computerized system, relieving the human mind for better work.

## Changing Role of the MIS in Modern Business

Information system has become essential for helping organizations deal with changes in global economies and the business enterprise. Information system provides firms with communication and analytical tools for conducting trade and managing business on a global scale. Information systems are the foundation of new knowledge based products and services in knowledge economies and help firms manage their knowledge assets.

Information systems make it possible for business to adopt more decentralized structures and more flexible arrangements of employees and management. Organizations' are trying to become more competitive and efficient by transforming themselves into digital firms where nearly all core business processes and relationships with customers, suppliers and employees are digitally enabled. The following are the main roles of a management information system:

- The MIS ensures that an appropriate data is collected from the various sources, processed, and sent further to all the needy destinations. The system is expected to fulfil the information needs of an individual, a group of individuals and the management.
- The MIS satisfies the diverse needs through a variety of systems such as Query Systems, Analysis Systems, Modelling Systems and Decision Support Systems. The MIS helps in Strategic Planning, Management Control, Operational Control and Transaction Processing.
- The MIS helps the clerical personnel in the transaction processing and answers their queries on the data pertaining to the transaction, the status of a particular record and reference on a variety of documents.
- The MIS helps the junior management personnel by providing the operational data for planning, scheduling and control, and helps them further in decision making at the operations level for correct an out of control situation.
- The MIS helps the middle management in short-term planning, target setting and controlling the business functions. It is supported by the use of the management tools of planning and control.
- The MIS helps the top management in goal setting, strategic planning and evolving the business plans and their implementation.
- The MIS plays the role of information generation, communication, problem identification and helps in the process of decision making. The MIS, therefore, plays a vital role in the management, administration and operations of an organization.

There is growing interdependence between business strategy, rules, and procedures on the one hand, and information systems software, hardware, databases, and telecommunications on the other. A change in any of these components often requires changes in other components. This relationship becomes critical when management plans for the future. What a business would like to do in five years often depend on what its systems will be able to do. To increase the market share, to become the high-quality or low-cost producer, to develop new products, and for increasing employee productivity depend more on the kinds and quality of information systems in the organization.

A second change in the relationship between information systems and organizations results from the growing reach and scope of system projects and applications. Building and managing systems today involves a much larger part of the organization than it did in the past. As firms become more like 'digital firms', the system enterprise extends to customers, vendors, and even industry competitors, where early systems produced largely technical changes that affected only a few people in the firm, contemporary systems have been bringing about managerial changes (who has what information about whom, when, and how often) and institutional 'core' changes (what products and services are produced, under what conditions, and by whom). As companies move toward digital firm organizations, nearly all the firm's managers and employees — as well as customers and vendors — participate in a variety of firm systems, tied together by a digital information web. For instance, what a customer does on a firm's website can trigger an employee to make an on-the-spot pricing decision or alert a firm's suppliers of potential 'stock out' situations.

The kind of systems build today are very important for the organizations overall performance. Information systems are driving both daily operation and organization's strategy. Powerful computers, software and networks including the internet have helped the organizations to become more flexible eliminate layers of management, separate work from location and restructure work flows, giving new powers to line workers and management. Information technology provides managers with tools for more precise planning, forecasting and monitoring of the business.

## SUMMARY

Information systems plays a crucial role in the management of any contemporary enterprise such as a small, medium or large organization; a profit making or a social service set-up; a public or a private sector undertaking; a manufacturing or a service organization; a local or a global corporation; and an upcoming or an established business house. The fast changing scene of liberalization, competition and globalization combined with a never before seen emphasis on quality, timeliness, innovation, customer orientation and efficiency puts a premium on accurate, superfast and timely dissemination of information across the globe. An information system can be defined technically as a set of interrelated components that collect (or retrieve), process, store, and distribute information to support decision making, coordination, and control in an organization. In addition to supporting decision making, coordination, and control, information systems may also help managers and workers analyze problems, visualize complex subjects, and create new products. By information we mean data that have been shaped into a firm that is meaningful and useful to human beings. Data, in contrast, are streams of raw facts representing events occurring in organizations or the physical environment before they have been organized and arranged into a form that people can understand and use. An MIS is a set of computer-based systems and procedures implemented to help managers in their crucial job of decision making. The actual process will involve the collection, organization, distribution and storage of organization-wise information for managerial analysis and control. The functions of MIS include collect, store, process data and present information to management. A computer-based information system (CBIS) is an information system in which the computer plays a major role in collecting, storing and processing data and transmits information to management. Information technology is recasting the management process, providing powerful new capabilities to help managers plan, organize, lead, and control. MIS plays a very important role in the organization; it creates an impact on the organization's functions, performance and productivity. As companies move toward digital firm organizations, nearly all the firm's managers and employees — as well as customers and vendors — participate in a variety of firm systems, tied together by a digital information web. In a knowledge and information-based economy, management information system plays a crucial role in the overall success of an organization.

## CASELET 1

The Bharat Tyres, a leading tyre manufacturing company manufactures all sorts of tyres to cater to the diverse needs of customers. It has a number of dealers all-over India. The company wants to keep track of every information in the manufacture and sale of tyres. The chief information officer has developed a computer-based information system. The system provides all information like the availability of right quality raw material (correct size of rubber in this case), quality of finished products, quantity of sales at different places by different dealers, etc. The system has helped to increase the production by 20 per cent and also has saved lakh of rupees for the company.

### Questions

1. How the information system has helped the company to increase its profit?
2. What is the information requirement in this case?

## ........ QUESTIONS FOR DISCUSSION

1. Define MIS. Explain the functions of MIS.
2. What is data? How is it different from information?
3. Why are information systems essential in business today? Discuss four trends in the global business environment that have made information system so important?
4. Explain the positive and negative impact of MIS?
5. Identify and describe the four levels of the organizational hierarchy. What type of information system required at each level?
6. What is the relationship between organization and information system? How is the relationship changing over time?
7. How are information systems changing management process?
8. Write a brief note about the key challenges involved in building, operating and maintaining information systems today?

### B. Fill in the Blanks

1. ________ are facts that are used by programmes to produce useful information
2. An ___________ is an information system that links together many buyers and sellers to exchange information, products, services, and payments.
3. ________ is the process of buying and selling goods and services electronically with computerized business transactions using the internet, networks, and other digital technologies.
4. ___________ support operational managers by keeping track of the elementary activities and transactions of the organization, such as sales, receipts, cash deposits, payroll, credit decisions, and the flow of materials in a factory.
5. _____________ serve the monitoring, controlling, decision making, and administrative activities of middle managers.
6. ___________ help senior management tackle and address strategic issues and long-term trends, both in the firm and in the external environment.
7. ________________ formulate operational plans and objectives to implement strategy; make operational decision.
8. ____________ implement operational plans and objectives; make short run decision, transact day-to-day business operations.

9. ___________ formulate strategies, policies, long-term plans and objectives; make strategic decision
10. ___________ are machine-readable instructions that direct the circuitry within the hardware parts of the CBIS to function in ways that produce useful information from data.

*Ans:* **1.** Data, **2.** electronic market, **3.** Electronic commerce, **4.** Operational-level systems, **5.** Management-level systems, **6.** Strategic-level systems, **7.** Middle-level managers, **8.** First-level managers, **9.** Top-level managers, **10.** Computer programs.

## C. State Whether the Following Statements are True or False. Justify Your Answer

1. MIS can only be designed around a computer.
2. Data and information are synonymous.
3. The major purpose of MIS is to store and retrieve data.

*Ans:* **1. False**

Ever since decisions were a managerial action, information on manual and later on unit record machines have given management information system.

**2. False**

Data when processed become information.

**3. False**

The purpose is to provide information for developing decisions regarding the managerial functions of planning and decision making.

## D. Multiple Choice Questions

1. Information systems that monitor the elementary activities and transactions of the organizations are:
   (a) Management-level systems (b) Operational-level systems
   (c) Knowledge-level systems (d) Strategic-level systems
2. Which of the following individuals typically have less formal, advanced educational degrees and tend to process rather than create information?
   (a) Knowledge workers (b) Executives
   (c) Systems analysts (d) Data workers
3. Deciding where to locate new production facilities is an example of a manufacturing and production information system operating at the:
   (a) Operational level (b) Management level
   (c) Knowledge level (d) Strategic level
4. Preparing short-term budgets is an example of a finance and accounting information system operating at the
   (a) Operational level (b) Management level
   (c) Knowledge level (d) Strategic level
5. Tracking employee training, skills, and performance appraisals is an example of a human resource information system operating at the:
   (a) Operational level (b) Management level
   (c) Knowledge level (d) Strategic level
6. Information is:
   (a) Data (b) Processed data
   (c) Manipulated input (d) Computer output
7. Strategic information is needed for:
   (a) Day-to-day operations (b) Meet government requirements
   (c) Long range planning (d) Short range planning

8. Strategic information is required by
   (a) Middle managers
   (b) Line managers
   (c) Top managers
   (d) All workers
9. Tactical information is needed for
   (a) Day-to-day operations
   (b) Meet government requirements
   (c) Long range planning
   (d) Short range planning
10. Tactical information is required by
   (a) Middle managers
   (b) Line managers
   (c) Top managers
   (d) All workers
11. Operational information is needed for
   (a) Day-to-day operations
   (b) Meet government requirements
   (c) Long range planning
   (d) Short range planning
12. Operational information is required by
   (a) Middle managers
   (b) Line managers
   (c) Top managers
   (d) All employees
13. In motor car manufacturing the following type of information is operational
   (a) Decision on introducing a new model
   (b) Scheduling production
   (c) Assessing competitor car
   (d) Computing sales tax collected
14. In a hospital information system the following type of information is strategic
   (a) Opening a new children's ward
   (b) Data on births and deaths
   (c) Preparing patients' bill
   (d) Buying an expensive diagnostic system such as CAT scan

*Ans:* **1.** (b), **2.** (d), **3.** (d), **4.** (b), **5.** (a), **6.** (b), **7.** (c), **8.** (c), **9.** (d), **10.** (a), **11.** (a), **12.** (b), **13.** (b), **14.** (d)

☺ ☺ ☺

# Part-V

# Banking and Negotiable Instrument

CHAPTER 17

# Banking

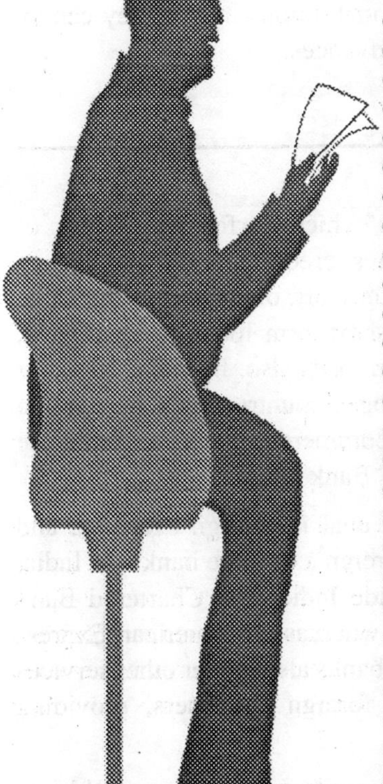

## LEARNING OBJECTIVES

- *Meaning of Bank*
- *Types of Banks*
- *Functions of Commercial Banks*

# BANKING

## MEANING OF BANK

Chamber's Twentieth Century Dictionary defines a bank as an "institution for the keeping, lending and exchanging, etc., of money". Economists have also defined a bank highlighting its various functions. According to Crowther, "The banker's business is to take the debts of other people to offer his own in exchange, and thereby create money". A similar definition has been given by Kent who defines a bank as "an organization whose principal operations are concerned with the accumulation of the temporarily idle money of the general public for the purpose of advancing to others for expenditure". Sayers' on the hand, gives a still more detailed definition of a bank thus: "Ordinary banking business consists of changing cash for bank deposits and bank deposits for cash".

Transferring bank deposits from one person or corporation (one 'depositor') to another; giving bank deposits in exchange for bills of exchange, government bonds, the secured or unsecured promises of businessmen to repay, etc. Thus, a bank is an institution which accepts deposits from the public and in turn advances loans by creating credit. It is different from the public and in turn advances loans by creating credit. It is different from other financial institutions in that they cannot create credit though they may be accepting deposits and making advances.

## TYPES OF BANKS

Banks are of various types which are explained as under:

1. **Commercial Banks:** Commercial banks are those banks which perform all kinds of banking functions such as accepting deposits, advancing loans, credit creation, and agency functions. They are also called joint stock banks because they are organised in the same manner as joint stock companies. They usually advance short-term loans to customers. Of late, they have started giving medium-term and long-term loans also. In India, 20 major commercial banks have been nationalized, whereas in developed countries they are run like joint stock companies in the private sector. Some of the commercial banks in India are Andhra Bank, Canara Bank, Indian Bank, Punjab National Bank, etc.
2. **Exchange Banks:** Exchange banks are those banks which deal in foreign exchange and specialize in financing foreign trade. They are also called foreign exchange banks. In India, these exchange banks have their head offices located outside India. The Chartered Bank and the Grindlays Bank have their head offices in England, whereas the American Express Bank and Citibank have their head offices in the USA. These banks also render other services such as collecting and supplying information about the foreign customers, providing remittance facilities, etc.
3. **Industrial Banks:** Industrial banks are those banks which provide medium-term and long-term finance to industries for the purchase of land, machinery, etc. They underwrite the debentures and shares of industries and also subscribe to them. In India there are a number of financial institutions which perform the functions of industrial banks such as Industrial Development Bank of India, Industrial Finance Corporation of India, Industrial Credit and Investment Corporation of India, etc. Each State in India has its own State Financial Corporation. These institutions are also known as Development banks.

4. **Agricultural Banks:** Agricultural banks are those banks which provide credit to farmers for short-term, medium-term and long-term needs. In India, commercial banks, regional rural banks and Agricultural Cooperative Banks provide short-term loans to farmers. Land Development Banks give medium-term and long-term loans to farmers on the mortgage of their land. The National Bank for Agriculture and Rural Development (NABARD) provides refinance facilities to all types of banks which give loans to agriculturists.

5. **Cooperative Banks:** Cooperative banks are those financial institutions which are organised on the principle of cooperation. They provide short-term and medium-term loans to their members. In rural areas, there are agricultural cooperative banks which accept deposits and give loans to agriculturists, rural artisans, etc. In urban areas, there are also cooperative banks which perform the functions of ordinary commercial banks but give loans to their members only. There is a State Cooperative Bank in every State of India with its branches both in urban and rural areas. Every State Cooperative Bank is an apex bank which provides credit facilities to the Central Cooperative Banks. It mobilizes financial resources from the richer sections of the urban population by accepting deposits and creating credit like commercial banks and borrowing from the money market. It also gets funds from the Reserve Bank of India.

6. **Savings Banks:** Saving banks help promote small savings and mobilize them. They have been very successful in Japan and Germany. In India, post offices act as savings bank.

7. **Central Bank:** The Central Bank is the apex bank in a country which controls its monetary and banking structure. It is owned by the government of the country and operates in national interest. It regulates and issues currency, performs banking and agency services for the state, keeps cash reserves of commercial banks, keeps and manages international currency, acts as the lender of the last resort, acts as a clearing house, and controller of credit.

## FUNCTIONS OF COMMERCIAL BANKS

Commercial banks perform a variety of functions which can be divided as:

1. Accepting deposits;
2. Advancing loans;
3. Credit creation;
4. Financing foreign trade;
5. Agency services;
6. Miscellaneous services to customers.

**1. Accepting Deposits:** This is the oldest function of a bank and the banker used to charge a commission for keeping the money in its custody when banking was developing as an institution. Nowadays, a bank accepts three kinds of deposits from its customers. The first is the savings deposits on which the bank pays small interest to the depositors who are usually small savers. The depositors are allowed to draw their money by cheques up to a limited amount during an week or year. Businessmen keep their deposits in current accounts. They can withdraw any amount standing to their credit in current deposits by cheques without notice. The bank does not pay interest on such accounts but instead charges a nominal sum for services rendered to its customers. Current accounts are known as demand deposits. Deposits are also accepted by a bank in fixed or time deposits. Savers who do not need money for a stipulated period from six months to longer periods ranging up to ten years or more are encouraged to keep it in fixed deposit accounts. The bank pays a higher rate of interest on such deposits. The rate of interest increases with the length of the time period of the fixed deposit. But there is always the maximum limit of the interest rate which can be paid. For instance, the interest rate on fixed deposits over five years is 11 per cent in India.

**2. Advancing Loans:** One of the primary functions of a commercial bank is to advance loans to its customers. A bank lends a certain percentage of the cash lying in deposits on a higher interest rate than it pays on such deposits. This is how it earns profits and carries on its business. The bank advances loans in the following ways:

(a) *Cash Credit:* The bank advances certain loans to businessmen against certain specified securities. The amount of the loan is credited to the current account of the borrower. In case of a new customer a loan account for the sum is opened. The borrower can withdraw money through cheques according to his requirements but pays interest on the full amount.

(b) *Call Loans:* These are a very short-term loans advanced to the bill brokers for not more than fifteen days. They are advanced against first class bill or securities. Such loans can be recalled at a very short notice. In normal times they can also be renewed.

(c) *Overdraft:* A bank often permits businessmen to draw cheques for a sum greater than the balance lying in his current account. This is done by providing the overdraft facility up to a specific amount to the businessman. But he is charged interest only on the amount by which his current account is actually overdrawn and not by the full amount of the overdraft sanctioned to him by the bank.

(d) *Discounting bills of Exchange:* If a creditor holding a bill of exchange wants money immediately, the bank provides him the money by discounting the bill of exchange. It deposits the amount of the bill in the current account of the bill holder after deducting its rate of interest for the period of the loan which is not more than 90 days. When the bill of exchange matures, the bank gets its payment from the banker of the debtor who accepted the bill.

**3. Credit Creation:** Credit creation is one of the most important functions of the commercial banks. Like other financial institutions, they aim at earning profits. For this purpose, they accept deposits and advance loans by keeping small cash in reserve for day-to-day transactions. When a bank advances a loan, it opens an account in the name of the customer and does not pay him in cash but allows him to draw the money by cheque according to his needs. By granting a loan, the bank creates credit or deposit.

**4. Financing Foreign Trade:** A commercial bank finances foreign trade of its customers by accepting foreign bills of exchange and collecting them from foreign banks. It also transacts other foreign exchange business and buys and sells foreign currency.

**5. Agency Services:** A bank acts as an agent of its customers in collecting and paying cheques, Bills of exchange, drafts, dividends, etc. It also buys and sells shares, securities, debentures, for its customers. Further, it pays subscriptions, insurance premium, rent, electric and water bills, and other similar charges on behalf of its client. It also acts as a trustee and executor of the property and will of its customers. Moreover, the bank acts as an income tax consultant to its clients. For some of these services, the bank charges a nominal fee while it renders others free of charge.

**6. Miscellaneous Services:** Besides the above noted services, the commercial banks perform a number of other services. It acts as a custodian of the valuables of its customers by providing those lockers where they can keep their jewellery and valuable documents. It issues various forms of credit instruments, such as cheques, drafts, and travellers' cheques, etc., which facilitate transactions. The bank also issues letter of credit and acts as a referee to its clients. It underwrites shares and debentures of companies and helps in the collection of funds from the public.

## SUMMARY

A bank is an organization whose principal operations are concerned with the accumulation of the temporarily idle money of the general public for the purpose of advancing to others for expenditure. Ordinary banking business consists of changing cash for bank deposits and bank deposits for cash. The bank performs a variety of roles. Credit creation is one of the most important function of the commercial banks. One of the essentials of a sound banking system is to have a high degree of liquidity. One of the primary functions of a commercial bank is to advance loans to its customers. A bank lends a certain percentage of the cash lying in deposits on a higher interest rate than it pays on such deposits. This is how it earns profits and carries in its business. It issues various forms of credit instruments, such as cheques, drafts, and travellers' cheques, etc., which facilitate transactions. The bank also issues letter of credit and acts as a referee to its clients. It underwrites shares and debentures of companies and helps in the collection of funds from the public. Some of the recent changes in the banking sector include Core banking services, Mobile banking, online banking, ATM facilities, and financial advisory services, portfolio management, etc. Such service provided by the banks adds up to its versatility and responsiveness to the changing market.

## CASELET 1

Bangladesh economy has been experiencing a rapid growth since the '90s. Industrial and agricultural development, international trade, inflow of expatriate Bangladeshi workers' remittance, local and foreign investments in construction, communication, power, food processing and service enterprises ushered in an era of economic activities.

Urbanization and lifestyle changes concurrent with the economic development created a demand for banking products and services to support the new initiatives as well as to channel's consumer investments in a profitable manner. A group of highly acclaimed businessmen of the country grouped together to responded to this need and established Dhaka Bank Limited in the year 1995.

The Bank has 55 branches across the country and a wide network of correspondents all over the world. The Bank has plans to open more branches in the current fiscal year to expand the network.

The Bank offers the full range of banking and investment services for personal and corporate customers, backed by the latest technology and a team of highly motivated officers and staff.

In our effort to provide Excellence in Banking services, the Bank has launched fully automated Phone Banking service, joined a countrywide-shared ATM network and has introduced a co-branded credit card. A process is also underway to provide e-business facility to the Bank's clientele through Online and Home Banking solutions.

Dhaka Bank Ltd., is the preferred choice in Banking for friendly and personalized services, cutting edge technology, tailored solutions for business needs, global reach in trade and commerce and high yield on backed by the latest technology and a team of highly motivated officers and staff, the Bank offers full range of banking and investment services for personal and corporate customers.

Responding to the market demand, Dhaka Bank has a complete array of personal banking products and services.

### Questions

1. Is Dhaka Bank is performing all functions of Commercial Banks?

## ........ QUESTIONS FOR DISCUSSION

1. Explain in brief the concept of banking and various types of banks.
2. Explain the various functions of a commercial bank.
3. Write short notes on:
   (a) Overdraft Facility.
   (b) Cash credit.
   (c) Advancing loans.
4. A bank acts as an agent of its customers. Explain this statement.

☺ ☺ ☺

CHAPTER 18

# Negotiable Instruments

## LEARNING OBJECTIVES

- *Definition of Negotiable Instruments*
- *Features of Negotiable Instruments*
- *Types of Negotiable Instruments*
- *Definition of Promissory Notes*
- *Essential Elements of Promissory Notes*
- *Definition of Bill of Exchange*
- *Essential Elements of Bill of Exchange*
- *Distinction Between Bill of Exchange and Promissory Notes*
- *Definition of Cheque*
- *Draw the distinction between Bill of Exchange and Cheque*
- *Features of a Cheque*
- *Marking of Cheques*
- *Crossing of Cheques*
- *Types of Crossing*

## NEGOTIABLE INSTRUMENTS

There are certain documents which are freely used in commercial transactions and monetary dealings. These documents, if they satisfy certain conditions, are known as 'negotiable instruments'. The word 'negotiable' means "transferable from one person to another in return for consideration" and 'instrument' means a "written document by which a right is created in favour of some person". Thus, a negotiable instrument is a document which entitles a person to a sum of money and which is transferable from one person to another by mere delivery or by endorsement and delivery. If the person who signs does so with the intention of obtaining payment of the instrument or acquiring or transferring rights to the instrument, the signature is called an endorsement.

A **negotiable instrument** is a specialized type of "contract" for the payment of money that is unconditional and capable of transfer by negotiation. As payment of money is promised later, the instrument itself can be used by the holder in due course. Common examples include cheques, bank notes (paper money), and commercial paper.

Either wholly blank or having written thereon an incomplete negotiable instrument, thereby gives *prima facie* authority to the holder thereof to make or complete, as the case may be, upon it a negotiable instrument, for any amount specified therein and not exceeding the amount covered by the stamp. The person so signing shall be liable upon such instrument, in the capacity in which he signed the same, to any holder in due course for such amount: provided that no person other than a holder in due course shall recover from the person delivering the instrument anything in excess of the amount intended by him to be paid thereunder.

**Illustrations**

(a) A, the holder of a negotiable instrument payable to bearer, delivers it to B's agent to keep for B. The instrument has been negotiated.

(b) A, the holder of a negotiable instrument payable to bearer, which is in the hands of A's banker, who is at the time the banker of B, directs the banker to transfer the instrument to B's credit in the banker's account with B. The banker does so, and accordingly now possesses the instrument as B's agent. The instrument has been negotiated, and B has become the holder.

The law relating to negotiable instruments is contained in the Negotiable Instruments Act, 1881, which deals with promissory notes, bill of exchange and cheques, as also hundis (a bill of exchange in a vernacular language). It is based, except where conditions in India require a departure, mainly upon the English Law as to negotiable instruments and judicial decisions.

The Act extends to the whole of India. It does not affect any local usage relating to any instrument in a vernacular language. The local usages may, however, be excluded by any words in the body of the instrument (Sec.1).

The Act came into force on first day of March, 1882.

The latest amendment to the Act was made in 1988.

### The Reserve Bank of India Act, 1934

The Negotiable Instruments Act does not affect the provisions of Secs. 31 and 32 of the Reserve Bank of India Act, 1934. The object of Sec. 31 is to prevent private persons from infringing the monopoly of the Government in note issue (paper currency) in India. The provisions of Sec. 31 are as follows:

1. No person (other than the Reserve Bank or Central Government) can draw, accept, make, or issue any bill of exchange, hundi, or promissory note payable to bearer on demand.
2. No person (other than the Reserve Bank or the Central Government) can make or issue any promissory note payable to the bearer of the instrument. This renders the words 'or to bearer' in the definition of a 'promissory note' in Sec. 4 of the Negotiable Instrument Act inoperative. But a bill or a note, on being indorsed in blank, can become payable to bearer on demand. A cheque is also payable to bearer on demand. These are exceptions to the rules as contained in Sec. 31.

Sec. 32 of the Reserve Bank of India Act provides that if anybody issues a bill or note payable to bearer on demand, or a note payable to bearer, he shall be punishable with fine.

## Definition of Negotiable Instrument

A negotiable instrument is a method of transferring a debt from one person to another. The term 'negotiable instrument' as such is not defined in the Negotiable Instrument Act. Sec. 13, however, says that "a negotiable instrument means a promissory note, bill of exchange or cheque payable either to order or to bearer". The definition, as it is, says that a negotiable instrument 'means' and not 'means and includes'. Therefore, any other instrument which satisfies the conditions of negotiability can be added to the list of negotiable instrument.

"A negotiable instrument, may be made payable to two or more payees jointly, or it may be made payable in the alternative to one of two, or one or some of several payees" [Section 13(2)].

The Act, thus, mentions three kinds of negotiable instruments, namely notes, bills, and cheques and declares that to be negotiable they must be made payable in any of the following forms:

(a) **Payable to Order:** A note, bill or cheque is payable to order which is expressed to be 'payable to a particular person or his order'.

(b) **Payable to Bearer:** "Payable to bearer" means 'payable to any person whosoever bears it'. A note, bill or cheque is payable to bearer which is expressed to be so payable or on which the only or last endorsement is an endorsement in blank.

Justice Wills defines a negotiable instrument as "one the property in which is acquired by anyone who takes it bona fide and for value notwithstanding any defect of title in the person from whom he took it". (The Law of Negotiable Securities, 5th ed., p. 5).

According to Thomas, a negotiable instrument is one which is, by a legally recognised custom of trade or by law.

(a) Transferable by delivery or by endorsement and delivery.

(b) Without notice to the partly liable, in such a way that the holder of it for the time being may sue upon it in his own name, and

(c) The property in it passes to a *bona fide* transferee for value free from equalities and free from any defect in the title of the person from whom he obtained it (*Commerce, Its Theory and Practice* by Thomas, 8th ed., p. 629)

This means that the person taking an instrument: (1) bona fide, and (2) for a value known as a holder in due course, gets a good title even though the title of the transferor may be defective. A rough and ready test of negotiability in case of bearer instrument is: Can a good title be acquired through a thief? If yes, the instrument is negotiable.

Negotiable instrument are a special class of contracts.

## Features of Negotiable Instrument

The features of a negotiable instrument are as follows:

**1. Easy Negotiability:** They are transferable from one person to another without any formality. In other words, the property (right of ownership) in these instruments passes by either endorsement or delivery (in case it is payable to order) or by delivery merely (in case it is payable to bearer), and no further evidence of transfer is needed.

**2. Title of Holder Free From All Defects:** A person, taking an instrument bona fide and for value, known as a holder in due course, gets the instrument free from all defects in the title of the transferor. He is not in any way affected by any defect in the title of the transferor or of any prior party.

Negotiability confers absolute and good title on the transferee. It means that a person who receives a negotiable instrument has a clear and undisputable title to the instrument. However, the title of the receiver will be absolute, only if he has got the instrument in good faith and for a consideration. Also the receiver should have no knowledge of the previous holder having any defect in his title. Such a person is known as holder in due course.

*Example.* S sells certain goods to B. B gives a promissory note to S for the price. He refuses to pay the promissory note, claiming that the goods are not according to order. If S sues B on the note, B's defence is good. But if he negotiates the note to H, a holder in due course, B's defence will be of no avail.

*For example,* suppose Rajiv issued a bearer cheque payable to Sanjay. It was stolen from Sanjay by a person, who passed it on to Girish. If Girish received it in good faith and for value and without knowledge of cheque having been stolen, he will be entitled to receive the amount of the cheque. Here Girish will be regarded as 'holder in due course'.

The holder in due course is also not affected by certain defaces, for example, fraud, which might be available against previous holders, provided he himself is not a party to it.

**3. Recovery:** The holder in due course can sue upon a negotiable instrument in his own name for the recovery of the amount. Without giving notice of transfer to the party liable on the instrument to pay.

**4. Presumptions:** Certain presumptions apply to all negotiable instruments, unless contrary is proved. These presumptions are dealt within Secs. 118 and 119 and are as follows:

*(a)* ***Consideration.*** Every negotiable instrument is presumed to have been made, drawn, accepted, endorsed, negotiated or transferred, for consideration. This would help a holder to get a decree from a court without any difficulty.

*(b)* ***Date.*** Every negotiable instrument bearing date is presumed to have been drawn on such date.

(c) ***Time of Acceptance.*** When a bill of exchange has been accepted, it is presumed that it was accepted within a reasonable time of its date and before its maturity. If the time is mentioned as "when convenient". It is not a negotiable instrument.

(d) ***Time of Transfer.*** Every transfer of a negotiable instrument is presumed to have been made before its maturity.

(e) ***Order of Endorsements.*** The endorsements appearing upon a negotiable instrument are presumed to have been made in the order in which they appear thereon.

(f) ***Stamp.*** When an instrument has been lost, it is presumed that it was duly stamped.

(g) ***Holder Presumed to be a Holder in Due Course.*** Every holder of a negotiable instrument is presumed to be a holder in due course (Sec.118) the person who takes a negotiable instrument in good faith and for value is assured of obtaining a good title.

(h) ***Proof of Protest.*** In a suit upon an instrument which has been dishonoured, the court, on proof of the protest, presumes the fact of dishonour, until such fact is disproved (Sec.119)

The above presumptions are rebuttable by evidence. If anyone challenges any of these presumptions, he has to prove his allegation. Again, these presumptions would not arise where an instrument has been obtained by any offence, fraud or unlawful consideration.

### Types of Negotiable Instruments

Negotiable instruments may be:

1. Negotiable by statute or
2. Negotiable by custom or usage.

**1. Instruments Negotiable by Statute:** The Negotiable Instruments Act mentions only three kinds of negotiable instruments (Sec.13). These are: promissory notes, bills of exchange and cheques. These instruments are negotiable by statute.

**2. Instruments Negotiable by Custom or Usage:** There are certain other instruments which have acquired the character of negotiability by usage or custom of trade. In England, for example, the following instruments have been held to be negotiable by custom, *viz.*: exchequer bills, bank notes, share warrants, circular notes, bearer debentures, dividend warrants, and share certificates with bank transfer deeds, etc. The list of negotiable instruments thus appears to be flexible and inclusive. The courts in India usually follow the practice of English courts, in accordance with the character of negotiability to other instruments. Sec, 137 of the Transfer of Property Act also recognizes the negotiability of instruments 'by law or custom'. Thus, in India, Government promissory notes, banker's drafts and pay orders, hundis, delivery orders and railway receipts for goods, have been held to be negotiable by usage or custom.

## PROMISSORY NOTE

A 'promissory note' is an instrument in writing (not being a bank note or a currency note) containing an unconditional undertaking, signed by the maker, to pay a certain sum of money only to, or to order of, a certain person, or to the bearer of the instrument (Sec.4).

A promissory note, referred to as a note payable in accounting, or commonly as just a "note", is a contract where one party (the maker or issuer) makes an unconditional promise in writing to pay a sum of money to the other (the payee), either at a fixed or predeterminable future time or on demand of the payee, under specific terms. A document signed by a borrower promising to repay a loan under agreed upon terms also called note. Secured notes are backed by some type of collateral put forth by the maker, such as real estate or a car.

The person who makes the promissory notes and promises to pay is called the maker.

The person to whom the payment is to be made is called the payee.

In course of transfer of a promissory note by payee and others, the parties involved may be:

(a) **The Endorser:** The person who endorse the note in favours of another person.

(b) **The Endorsee:** The person in whose favors the note is negotiated by endorsement.

Suppose you take a loan of ₹ 5,000 from your friend Ramesh. You can make a document stating that you will pay the money to Ramesh or the bearer on demand. Or you can mention in the document that you would like to pay the amount after three months. This document, once signed by you, duly stamped and handed over to Ramesh, becomes a negotiable instrument. Now Ramesh can personally present it before you for payment or give this document to some other person to collect money on his behalf. He can endorse it in somebody else's name who in turn can endorse it further till the final payment is made by you to whosoever presents it before you. This type of a document is called a Promissory Note.

More recently, however, it has been the maker, not the payee, who has had to take care with promissory notes. Companies have used promissory notes as a tried and true method of raising capital. But whereas, the individual-to-individual note is often a very simple written agreement, the company-to-individual note is usually very complex. It is for this reason that corporate promissory notes are primarily sold not to the general public but rather to sophisticated buyers who are capable of performing their own due diligence. Such notes are usually classified as securities, and anyone trying to sell them on behalf of a company must be registered with the Securities and Exchange Commission or a state equivalent.

*Example:* A signs an instrument in the following terms:

(a) 'I promise to pay B or order ₹'

(b) "I acknowledge myself to be indebted to B in ₹ 1,000 to be paid on demand, for value received."

(c) "Mr. B, I.O.U ₹ 500."

(d) "I promise to pay B ₹ 500 and all other sums which shall be due to him."

(e) "I promise to pay B ₹ 500, first deducting there out any money which he may owe me."

(f) "I promise to pay B ₹ 500 seven days after my marriage with C."

(g) "I promise to pay B ₹ 500 on D's death, provided D leaves me enough to pay that sum."

(h) "I promise to pay B ₹ 500 and to deliver to him my black horse on 1st January next".

Of these only (a) and (b) are promissory notes.

The specimen of a promissory note is given as follows:-

## Specimen of a Promissory Note

₹ 10,000 June 8, 2010

Three months after date, I promise to pay Ramesh or order the sum of ten thousand rupees, for value received.

To,

Ramesh

222, Ashok Vihar

Delhi 110052

Stamp

SD/- Ram

## Essential Elements of Promissory Note

For an instrument to become a promissory note, it must have the following essential elements.

**1. Writing:** The instrument must be in writing. Mere verbal engagement to pay is not enough. Writing includes print and typewriting and may also be in pencil or ink.

**2. Promise to Pay:** The instrument must contain an express promise to pay. A mere acknowledgement of indebtedness or implied undertaking by the use of the word "debt" or "pronote", is not sufficient, although it is valid as an agreement and may be used upon as such. A promissory note is not complete till it is delivered to its payee.

The following instruments signed by A are not promissory notes:

(a) "Mr. B, I.O.U ₹ 100" or "Mr. B, I owe you ₹ 100".

(b) "I am liable to B, in a sum of ₹ 500 to be paid by instalments".

(c) "I am bound to pay the sum of ₹ 500 which I received from you."

A receipt for money, if it does not contain express promise to pay, is not a promissory note.

*Example.* "I of my own free will and accord approached B and borrowed from him the sum of ₹ 100 bearing interest at the rate of 2 per cent. I have, therefore executed these few presents by the way of a promissory note so that if may serve as evidence and be of use when needed." Signed by A, held, the instrument is not a promissory note as it does not contain an express undertaking to pay the amount mentioned in it. [Bal Mukand v. Munna Lal Ramji Lal, A.I.R. (1970) P. &H. 516]

But if the receipt is coupled with a promise to pay, it is a promissory note.

*Example:* "We have received the sum of ₹ 9,000 from Shri R.R. Sharma. This amount will be repaid on demand. We have received this amount in cash." Held, this is a promissory note [Surjit Singh v. Ram Ratan, A.I.R. (1975) Gau.15].

**3. Definite and Unconditional:** Certainty is very necessary in the commercial world. The promise to pay must be depend upon the happening of some uncertain event, i.e., a contingency or the fulfilment of a condition. It must be payable absolutely. If an instrument contains a conditional promise to pay, it is not a valid promissory note and will not become valid and negotiable even after the happening of the condition. [HILL vs. HALFORD].

The promise to pay must be definite and unconditional order or promise for payment. If it is uncertain or conditional, the instrument is invalid.

Thus, the following instruments signed by A are not promissory notes:

(a) "I promise to pay B a sum of ₹ 500, when convenient or able."

(b) "I promise to pay B ₹ 500 by instalments with a provision that no payment shall be made after my death."

(c) "I promise to pay B ₹ 500 when he delivers the goods."

(d) "I promise to pay B ₹ 500 on D's death, provided D leaves me enough to pay that sum." [Robert v. Peake (1757) 97 E.R. 333].

However, the promise to pay may be subject to a condition which according to the ordinary experience of mankind is bound to happen. Thus, a promise (or order, in case of a bill of exchange) to pay is not 'conditional' if:

1. It depends upon an event which is certain to happen though the time of its happening may be uncertain.

*Example:*

A. A promise to pay B a sum of ₹ 500 after the death of C. This is not a conditional promise for it is certain that C shall die.

B. "I promise to pay ₹ 1,000 to B, 30 days after his marriage with C." Signed by A. This is not a promissory note as it is probable that B may not marry C [Beardsley v. Baldwin, (1741) 93 E.R. 1994].

2. The promise is to pay at a particular place or after a specified time.

**4. Signed by the Maker:** The instrument must be signed by the maker, otherwise it is incomplete and of no effect. Even if it is written by the maker himself and his name appears in the body of the instrument, his signature must be there. Signature means the writing of a person's name in order to authenticate and give effect to the contract contained in the instrument. It is at the same time, essential that the mind of the signer must accompany the signature. An agent of a trading firm can sign a promissory note on its behalf [Meenakshi v. Chettiar, A.I.R. (1957) Mad. 8].

**5. Certain Parties:** The instrument must point out with certainty as to who the maker is and who the payee is. Where the maker and the payee cannot be identified with certainty from the instrument itself, the instrument, even if it contains an unconditional promise to pay is not a promissory note. The payee may sometimes be misnamed or designated by description only. In such a case, the note is valid if the payee can be ascertained by evidence (WILLS v. Barret, (1816) 2 Stark 29). As such promissory note payable 'to the manager of certain bank' is payable to a certain person.

Where there are two or more makers, they may bind themselves jointly or jointly and severally. It may be made payable to two or more payees jointly or it may be made payable in the alternative to one of two, one or some of several payees (Sec. 13(2)).

A promissory note cannot be made payable to the maker (promisor) himself. Such a note is a nullity. But if it is endorsed by the maker to some other person or endorsed in blank, it becomes a valid promissory note (Gay v. Landal, (1848) L.T.C.P.286]

The payee must be a certain person. It means that the person in whose favour the instrument is made must be named/described with reasonable certainty. The term "person" includes individual, body corporate, trade unions, even secretary, director or chairman of an institution. The payee can also be more than one person.

**6. Certain Sum of Money:** The sum payable must be certain and must not be capable of contingent additions or subtractions.

The following instruments signed by A are not promissory notes (as the sum payable is not certain):

(a) "I promise to pay B ₹ 1,000, and all the other sums due to him."

(b) "I promise to pay B ₹ 1,000 and the fine according to the rules."

(c) "I promise to pay B ₹ 500, first deducting there out any money which he may owe me."

The sum payable is certain:

1. When it is payable with interest, but if the date of interest is not stated in the instrument, it is not a promissory note.
2. When it is payable at an indicated rate of exchange.
3. When it is payable by instalments, with a provision that on default being made in payment, the balance unpaid shall become due. (Sec. 5, Para 3).

**7. Promise to Pay Money Only:** The payment to be made under instrument must be in the legal tender money of India. If the instrument contains a promise to pay something in addition to money, it cannot be a promissory note. One can't make promissory note on assets, securities, goods/ certain amount of foreign money.

Thus, the following instruments signed by A are not promissory notes:

(a) "I promise to pay B ₹ 200 and deliver one quintal of paddy."

(b) "I promise to pay B ₹ 20 shares and 10 bonds of XY Ltd."

(c) "I promise to deliver B 100 bags of wheat."

**8. Bank Note or Currency note is Not a Promissory Note:** This is because a bank note or a currency note is money or a currency note is money itself.

**9. Formalities like Number, Date, Place, Consideration, etc.:** These are usually found in an instrument, although they are not essential in law. The omissions of the words "for value received", the place where the instrument is made or where it is payable or date (if the date of execution of the instrument can be independently proved) do not invalidate the instrument. The date of promissory note is also not necessary unless the amount is payable at a certain time after date. But it must bear the necessary stamp under the Indian Stamp Act, 1899. The value of stamp depends upon the value of the promissory note and time of their payment. The maker's signature with the date across the stamp cancels the stamp effectively. Although not stamped or inadequately stamped promissory note is invalid, but the amount of loan can be recovered if proved otherwise.

**10. It may be Payable on Demand or After a Definite Period of Time:** The expression on demand means payable immediately or forthwith.

**11. It Cannot be Made Payable to Bearer on Demand:** The Reserve Bank of India Act, 1934 prohibits issue of such promissory notes except by the Reserve Bank of India itself or the Central Government.

Lack of any of the requirements mentioned in Sec.4 will not make a document a promissory note [Bapanna Krishnayya v. Chaparala Baburao. A.I.R. (1977) A.P. 42].

In short, while promissory notes are very useful, valuable, and well-travelled debt instruments, both the maker and the payee are well advised to do their homework when dealing with them.

## BILL OF EXCHANGE

A bills of exchange is an instrument in writing, containing an unconditional order, signed by the maker, directing a certain person to pay a certain sum of money only to, or to the order of a certain person or to the bearer of the instrument. (Sec. 5 of the Negotiable Instrument Act, 1881).

A bill of exchange is an unconditional order in writing addressed by one person to another, signed by the person giving it, requiring the person to whom it is addressed to pay on demand or at fixed or determinable future time a sum certain in money to order or to bearer. (Sec.126).

Bill of exchange is a written order by the drawer to the drawee to pay money to the payee. It is essentially an order made by one person to another to pay money to third person.

At the very outset, the following two facts must be noted:

(i) Although a bills of exchange directing to pay 'only to a particular person' is valid if it satisfies the requirements of the definition but it shall not be a negotiable instrument within the meaning of the Negotiable Instruments Act as its transferability is restricted.

(ii) Although a bills of exchange may be originally drawn 'payable to bearer' but in such a case, it must be payable otherwise than on demand (say, three months after date). In other words, a bill cannot be drawn 'payable to bearer on demand'. If it is 'payable on demand' then it must be made 'payable to order' (Sec. 31 of the Reserve Bank of India Act).

**Parties to a bill.** There are three parties to bills of exchange, *viz*., the drawer, the drawee and the payee.

The person who gives the order to pay or who makes the bill is called drawer. The maker of the bills of exchange is called drawer.

The person who is directed to pay is called the drawee. The person to whom the order to pay is made.

When the drawee accepts the bill, he is called the acceptor.

The person to whom the payment is to be made is called payee.

The parties need not all be distinct person. Thus, the drawer may draw on himself payable to his own order (Sec. 8).

Where the payee named in a bill is a fictitious or non-existing person, the bill is treated as payable to bearer [Clutton v. Attenborough, (1897) A.C. 90]. In some cases, the drawer and the payee or when a principal draws on his agent, the drawer and the drawee may be one and the same person.

The drawer of the payee who is in possession of the bill is called the holder. The holder must present the bill to the drawee for his acceptance.

When the holder endorses the bill, note or cheque, he is called the endorser. The person to whom the bill, note or cheque is endorses is called the endorsee.

When the bill or in any endorsement thereon, the name of any person is given in addition to the drawee to be referred to in case of need, such person is called drawee in case of need (Sec. 7. Para 2). The name of the drawee in case of need may be given in the bill by the drawer at the same time when it is drawn or by some subsequent endorser. The resort is to be had to the "drawee in case of need" only when the bill is dishonoured by non-acceptance or non-payment.

Drawee in case of need. Sometimes the name of another person may be mentioned in bills of exchange as the person who will accept the bill, if the original drawee does not accept it. Since, another person so named is to be approached in case of need, he is known as "drawee in case of need". (Sec. 7).

Acceptor for honour. When a bill of exchange has been noted or protested for non-acceptance or for better security, and any person accepts it supra protest for honour of the drawer or of any one of the endorsers, such person is called an "acceptor for honour" (Sec. 7). Thus, any person may voluntarily become a party to bills as an "acceptor for honour".

### Specimen of Bills of Exchange

Arjun of Delhi buys goods on credit from Krishan of Delhi for ₹ 10,000 to be paid three months after date. Krishan buys goods from Ram of Delhi for ₹ 10,000 on similar terms. Now Krishan may order Arjun to pay the sum of ₹ 10,000 to Ram. The order will be a bill of exchange.

₹ 10,000 New Delhi, January 10, 2010

Three months after date pay to Ram or order of the sum of ten thousand rupees, for value received.

To,

Arjun
235, Subhash Marg,
Delhi-110006

| In case of need with | Accepted | | Stamp |
|---|---|---|---|
| Canara Bank, Delhi | Arjun | Sd/- | Krishan |

## Essential Elements of Bills of Exchange

1. It must be in writing.
2. It must contain an order to pay. For example, words like "Please pay ₹ 5,000 on demand and oblige" are not used. This is not a bill of exchange as it contains a request and not an order.
3. The order to pay must be unconditional.
4. It requires three parties, i.e., the drawer, the drawee, and the payee.

   A bill cannot be drawn on two or more drawees in the alternative, because of the rule of law that "where liability lies, no ambiguity must lie". But a bill may be made payable in the alternative to one of two or more payees. (Sec. 13).

5. The parties must be certain.
6. It must be signed by the drawer, accepted by its drawee.
7. The sum payable mentioned must be certain or capable of being made certain.
8. It must contain an order to pay money.
9. The formalities relating to number, date, place and consideration, though usually found in bills, are not essential in law. But a bill must be affixed with the necessary stamp. Stamping of bills of exchange is mandatory. This is required as per the Indian Stamp Act, 1899. The value of stamp depends upon the value of the bill of exchange and the time of their payment.

A bill as originally drawn cannot be made payable to bearer on demand. It will be seen that the fundamental essentials of a bill enumerated above are more or less similar to that of a promissory note. As such the rules that apply to promissory notes in regard to those essentials in general applicable to bills of exchange as well.

## Distinction Between Bill of Exchange and Promissory Note

(a) In a note there are two parties — the maker and the payee. In a bill, there are three parties — the drawer, the drawee and the payee.

(b) A note contains an unconditional promise to pay. A bill contains an unconditional order to pay.

(c) The maker of a note is the debtor and he himself undertakes to pay. The drawer of a bill is the creditor who directs the drawee (his debtor) to pay.

(d) The maker of a note corresponds in general to the acceptor of a bill. But the maker of the note cannot undertake to pay conditionally, whereas the acceptor may accept the bill conditionally because he is not the originator of the bill.

(e) The liability of the maker of a note is primary and absolute, whereas the liability of the drawer of a bill is secondary and conditional.

(f) A note cannot be made payable to the maker himself, whereas a bill the drawer and the payee may be one and the same person.

(g) A note requires no acceptance as it is signed by the person who is liable to pay. A bill payable after sight or after a certain period must be accepted by the drawee before it is presented for payment.

(h) A note cannot be drawn payable to bearer. A bill can be so drawn. But in no case can a note or bill be drawn 'payable to bearer on demand'.

(i) The maker of a note stands in immediate relation with the payee. The drawer of a bill stands in immediate relation with the acceptor and not the payee.

(j) Certain provisions like: (a) presentment for acceptance (Sec. 61), (b) acceptance (Sec. 75), (c) acceptance for honour (Sec. 108), and (d) bill in sets (Sec. 132) apply to bills but not to notes.

(k) In case of dishonour of a bill either by non-acceptance or by non-payment, due notice of dishonoured must be given to the entire person who are to be made liable to pay. This includes the drawer and the prior endorsers. But in the case of dishonour of a note no such notice is required to be given to the maker (Sec. 93).

(l) Foreign bills must be protested for dishonour when such protested for dishonour when such protest is required by the law of the place where they are drawn (Sec. 104). No such protest is required in case of note.

(m) The maker of a promissory stands in immediate relation with the payee, while the maker or drawer of an accepted bill stands in immediate relation with the acceptor and not the payee (Sec. 44).

The position of the maker of a promissory note also differs from the position of the acceptor of a bill. Promissory note must contain an unconditional promise to pay and therefore the maker who himself is the originators of a note, cannot make it conditional. In the case of a bill of exchange although the drawer, who is the originator of a bill has to make an unconditional order to pay but under Section 86, the acceptor may accept the bill conditionally.

## CHEQUE

Section 6, as substituted by the Negotiable Instruments (Amendment and Miscellaneous Provisions) Act, 2002, defines a cheque as follows:

"A cheque is a bill of exchange drawn on a specified banker and not expressed to be payable otherwise than on demand and it includes the electronic image of a truncated cheque and a cheque in the electronic form."

### Definitions and Types of Instruments under the Cheques Act:

"A cheque is an unconditional order in writing that is addressed by a person to another person (being a financial institution), signed by the person giving it, and requires the financial institution to pay on demand a sum certain in money."

Accorded the extraordinary privilege of being able to receive a better title to a cheque than the person who gave it to him, and to take free from disputes between the immediate parties to the cheque. Cheque must be transferred by negotiation to the holder.

Cheque must be complete and regular on the face of it (note SS.18 and 16 Cheques Act).

A cheque in the electronic form means "cheque which contains the exact mirror image of a proper cheque, and is generated, written and signed in a secure system ensuring the minimum safety standards with the use of digital signature and asymmetric crypto system".

A truncated cheque means a cheque which is truncated during the course of a clearing cycle, either by a clearing house or by the bank whether paying or receiving payment, immediately on generation of an electronic image for transmission. Substituting the further physical movement of the cheque in writing.

"Clearing house" means the clearing house managed by the Reserve Bank of India or a clearing house recognised as such by the Reserve Bank of India [Sec. 6 as substituted by the negotiable instruments (Amendment and Miscellaneous Provisions) Act, 2002].

A cheque is a species of a bill of exchange; but it has the following two additional qualifications, *viz.*

1. It is always drawn on a specified banker, and
2. It is always payable on demand.

All cheques are bills of exchange, but all bills of exchange are not cheques. A cheque must have all the essential requisites of a bill of exchange. It must be signed by the drawer. It must contain an unconditional order on a specified banker to pay a certain sum of money to or to the order of a specified person or the bearer of the cheque. But it does not require the acceptance as it is intended for immediate payment. Delivery of the instrument is essential. Cheque is not complete till it is delivered to its payee. For example, you may issue a cheque in your brother's name, but it is not a negotiable instrument till it is given to your brother.

Cheque is a very common form of negotiable instrument. If you have a savings bank account or current account in a bank, you can issue a cheque in your own name or in favour of others, thereby directing the bank to pay the specified amount to the person named in the cheque.

Therefore, a cheque may be regarded as a bill of exchange; the only difference is that the bank is always the drawee in case of a cheque.

## Usual Form of a Cheque

₹____________

Pay..........................................................................................................................................

..........................................................................................................or bearer

Rupees..................................................................................................

..........................................................................................................

STATE BANK OF INDIA

Jawaharlal Nehru University, New Delhi-110067.

MSBL/97

Cheques are not merely orders to a bank to make a payment, they are transferable orders and, if not marked 'not negotiable', they are negotiable instruments. The Cheques Act, 1986 regulates the transfer of cheques from person-to-person and defines their liabilities to each other. The terminology is slightly confusing; the Act provides for 'transfer by negotiation' even when the cheque is 'not negotiable'. It is not possible to restrict the transfer of a cheque.

## Distinction Between Bill of Exchange and Cheque

1. A bill of exchange may be drawn on any person, including a banker, but a cheque is always drawn on a banker. Thus, all bills are not cheques, whereas all cheques are necessarily bills.
2. A bill must be accepted before the drawee can be called upon to make payment upon it. A cheque requires no acceptance.

3. A bill which is not expressed to be payable on demand is entitled to three days of grace. A cheque is not entitled to any days of grace.
4. A bill may be payable on demand or after the expiry of a certain period after date or sight. A cheque is always payable on demand.
5. A bill must be duly presented for payment to the acceptor or else the drawer of the bill will be discharged from liability. The drawer of a cheque is not necessarily discharged from his liability by delay of the holder is presenting it for payment. He is discharged only to the extent of the damage, if any, suffered by him. For example, by the failure of the bank, the drawer has lost the money which would have otherwise discharged the amount of the cheque. However, where the drawer is so discharged, the payee may rank as creditor of the bank for the amount of the cheque. (Sec. 84)
6. A cheque may be crossed but not a bill.
7. A cheque does not require any stamp, whereas a bill, except in certain cases, must be stamped.
8. The payment of a cheque may be countermanded by the drawer but the payment of a bill cannot be countermanded.
9. A cheque is not required to be noted or protested for dishonour. A bill may be noted or protested for dishonour.

### Features of a Cheque

Let us look into some important features of a cheque.

(i) A cheque must be in writing and duly signed by the drawer.

(ii) It contains an unconditional order.

(iii) It is issued on a specified banker only.

(iv) The amount specified is always certain and must be clearly mentioned both in figures and words.

(v) The payee is always certain.

(vi) It is always payable on demand.

(vii) The cheque must bear a date otherwise it is invalid and shall not be honoured by the bank.

## MARKING OF CHEQUES

A cheque does not require acceptance in ordinary course of business as it is intended for immediate payment. The custom among bankers to mark cheques as 'good for payment' does not amount to an acceptance. Marking is the writing on the cheque by the drawee banker that it would be honoured when it is duly presented for payment. The effect of marking a cheque as good by the drawee banker is that it cannot be countermanded by the drawer subsequently and the payee is certain of getting the money. In India, no such practice of marking of cheques has been established either by judicial decisions or by statutes [Bank of Baroda v. Punjab National Bank, (1944) A.C.176].

Cheques may be marked as good by the drawee banker at the instance of:

1. The drawer, or
2. The holder, or
3. The collecting banker.

1. **Marking at Drawer's Instance:** The maker of the cheque is called the drawer. When a cheque is marked well at the instance of the drawer, the drawee banker earmarks sufficient funds in the account to meet the cheque when it will be presented for payment. The drawer cannot afterwards countermand payment of such cheque. The banker is entitled to dishonour other cheques if their encashment would leave the banker with insufficient funds to meet the cheque marked good.
2. **Marking at Holder's Instance:** When a cheque is marked good at the holder's instance, it is intimation to the holder that at the same time of marking, the banker has sufficient funds of the drawer in his hands. The banker may refuse to honour the cheque when it is subsequently presented for payment if in due course the drawer has withdrawn funds or stopped payment of the cheque.
3. **Marking at Collecting Banker's Instance:** Where a cheque is received by a collecting banker too late for inclusion in the clearing, he may have to safeguard the interest of the customer, present such cheque for marking by the drawee banker. When a cheque is marked at the collecting banker's instance, the marking is treated as 'constructive payment' because the banking custom is that such cheque shall be honoured when it is presented through the next clearing.

## CROSSING OF CHEQUES

There are two types of cheques, open cheques and crossed cheques. A cheque which is payable in cash across the counter of a bank is called an open cheque. When such a cheque is in circulation, a great risk attends it. If its holder loses it, its finder may go to the bank and get payment unless its payment has already been stopped. It was to prevent the losses incurred by open cheques getting into the hands of wrong person that the custom of crossing was introduced. Since open cheque is subject to risk of theft, it is dangerous to issue such cheques. This risk can be avoided by issuing another type of cheque called crossed cheque.

A crossed cheque is one on which two parallel transverse lines with or without the words and Co.' are drawn. The payment of such a cheque can be obtained only through a banker. Thus, crossing is a direction to the drawee banker to pay the amount of money on a crossed cheque generally to a banker or a particular banker so that the party who obtains the payment of the cheque can be easily traced. The crossing compels the holder to present the cheque through a 'quarter of known respectability and credit' and affords security and protection to the owner of the cheque, as the cheque is payable only through a banker.

### Types of Crossing

There are two types of crossing, *viz.*:

1. General crossing, and
2. Special crossing.

Another type of crossing known as 'restrictive crossing' has developed out of business usage.

**1. General Crossing:** A cheque is said to be crossed generally where it bears across its face an addition of:

(a) The words 'and company' or any abbreviation thereof, between two parallel transverse lines, either with or without the words 'not negotiable', or

(b) Two parallel transverse lines simply, either with or without the words 'not negotiable' (Sec. 123).

## Specimen of General Crossing

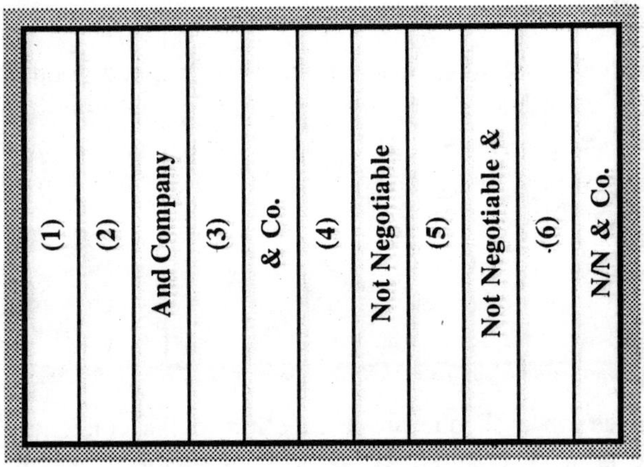


Where a cheque is crossed generally, the drawee banker shall not pay it unless it is presented by a banker (Sec. 126, Para 1).

**2. Special Crossing:** Where a cheque bears across its face an addition of the name of a banker, either with or without the words 'not negotiable', the cheque is deemed to be crossed specially (Sec. 124). Transverse lines are not necessary in case of a special crossing. The payment of a specially crossed cheque can be obtained only through the particular the banker whose name appears across the face of the cheque or between the transverse lines, if any.

## Specimen of Special Crossing

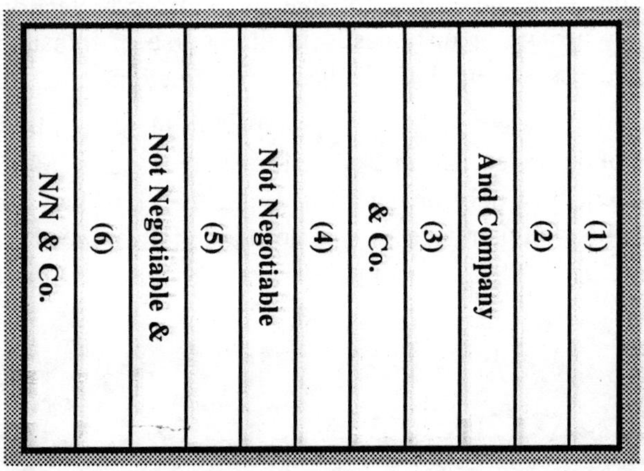

Where a cheque is crossed specially the banker on whom it is drawn shall pay it only to the banker on whom it is crossed, or his agent for collection (Sec. 126. Para 2).

**3. Restrictive Crossing:** In addition to the two statutory types of crossing discussed above, there is another type which has been adopted by commercial and banking usage. In this type of crossing, the words 'A/c Payee' are added to the general or special crossing.

## Specimen of Restrictive Crossing

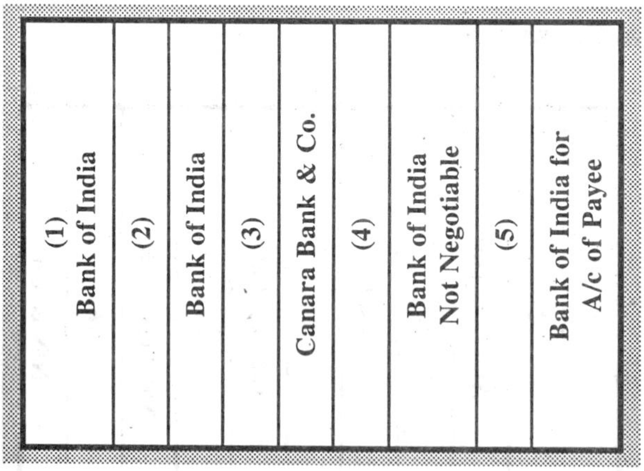


The words 'A/c payee' on a cheque are a direction to the collecting banker that the amount collected on the cheque is to be credited to the account of the payee. If he credits the proceeds to a different account, he is *prima facie* guilty of negligence and will be liable to the true owner for the amount of the cheque. It should however be noted that 'A/c payee' cheques are negotiable'. [British Bank of Middle East v. Almal Bros., 66 CWN 285].

**Not Negotiable Crossing** (Sec. 130). The effect of the words 'not negotiable' on crossed cheque is that the title of the transferee of such a cheque cannot be better than that of its transferor. The addition of the words "not negotiable" does not restrict the further transferability of the cheque. It only takes away the main feature of negotiability. Which is that a holder with a defective title can give a good title to a subsequent holder in due course. Anyone who takes a cheque marked "not negotiable" takes it at his own risks.

The object of crossing a cheque "not negotiable" is to afford protection to the drawer or holder of the cheque against miscarriage or dishonestly in the course of transit by making it difficult to get the cheque so crossed cashed, until it reaches its destination.

Example, we drew a cheque crossed "not negotiable" in blank and handed it to his clerk to fill the amount and the name of the payee. The clerk inserted a sum in excess of her authority and delivered the cheque to P in payment of a debt of her own. Held, the clerk had no title to the cheque and as such P had no better title, and therefore W was not liable [Wilson & Meeson v. Pikering. (1946) K.B. 422].

**Who may Cross a Cheque** (Sec. 126)? A cheque may be crossed by:

1. **The Drawer:** He may cross the cheque generally or specially.
2. **The Holder:** Where the cheque is uncrossed, the holder may cross it generally or specially. Where it crossed generally, he may cross it specially. Where it is crossed generally or specially, he may add the words "Not negotiable".
3. **The Banker:** Where a cheque is crossed specially, the banker to whom it is crossed may again cross it especially to another banker (his agent) for collection.

## SUMMARY

A negotiable instrument is the property which is acquired by anyone who takes it bona fide and for value notwithstanding any defect of title in the person from whom he took it — Justice Willis

The law relating to negotiable instruments is contained in the Negotiable Instruments Act, 1881, which deals with promissory notes, bill of exchange and cheques as also hundis (bills of exchange in vernacular language).

### Characteristics of Negotiable Instruments

1. The property in a negotiable instruments passes from one person to another by a simple process, i.e., by mere delivery if it is payable to bearer, and by endorsement and delivery if it is payable to order.
2. The holder in due course (one who acquires the instrument in good faith and for consideration) gets it free from all defects.
3. He can sue upon the instrument in his own name.
4. The transferee of the instrument need not give notice of transfer to the party liable to pay.
5. Consideration is presumed to have been given for the instrument.

**Presumptions:** The Act lays down a number of presumptions in favour of negotiable instruments. These presumptions are as to: (a) consideration (b) date (c) time of acceptance (d) time of transfer (e) order of endorsements (f) stamp (g) holder in due course, and (h) proof of protest.

**Types of Negotiable Instruments:** Negotiable Instruments may be:

1. Negotiable by statute, or
2. Negotiable by custom or usage.

**"A Promissory Note"** is an instrument in writing (not being a bank note for a currency note) containing an unconditional undertaking signed by the maker to pay a certain sum of money only to, or to the order of certain person, or to the bearer of the instrument (Sec. 4). The person who makes the promissory note is called the maker: the person to whom the payment is to be made is called the payee.

Its essentials: (1) It must be in writing. (2) It must contain an express undertaking or promise to pay. (3) The promise to pay should be unconditional. (4) It must be signed by the maker. (5) The parties, i.e., the maker and the payee must be certain. (6) The sum payable must be certain.

(7) It must contain a promise to pay money. and (8) A bank note or a currency note is not a promissory note.

**Bills of Exchange** is an instrument in writing containing an unconditional order, signed by the maker, directing certain person to pay a certain sum of money, only to or to the order of certain person, or to the bearer of the instrument (Sec. 5). The person who makes the bill is called the drawer. The person who is directed to pay is called the drawee. The person to whom the payment is to be made is called the payee.

A **Cheque** is bills of exchange drawn on a specified banker and payable on demand (Sec. 6). It is a species of a bill of exchange with two additional qualifications *viz.*: (i) it is always drawn on a specified banker, and (ii) it is always payable on demand.

**Crossing of Cheque.** When a cheque bears across its face two parallel transverse lines, the cheque is said to be crossed. The payment of a crossed cheque can be obtained only through another banker. The crossing may be general, special or restrictive. In case of 'not negotiable crossing' the title of the transferee cannot be better than that of transferor.

A cheque may be crossed by the drawer of the holder, or the banker.

## ........ QUESTIONS FOR DISCUSSION

1. Discuss crossing of cheque and types of crossing.
2. On December 31 Rajesh draws a bill at 2 months for ₹ 500 on Kavita. The sum is payable to Mukesh. Kavita accepts the bill. Identify the parties to the bill.

### Questions for Review

1. Write a short note on negotiable instruments.
2. Give three examples of negotiable instruments.
3. Explain in detail the features of promissory note.
4. What is the effect of the words "account payee only" written between crossed lines. Explain.
5. "A bill of exchange must contain an unconditional promise to pay." Do you agree with this statement? Justify your answer.
6. Give the definition of a 'cheque'. How does it differ from a bill of exchange?
7. Distinguish between open cheque and crossed cheque.

*Ans:* **2.** Drawer — Rajesh, Drawee — Kavita, Payee — Mukesh

## Objective Questions

### Fill in the Blank

1. The person to whom the amount mentioned in the promissory note is payable is known as ________.
2. Transfer of a negotiable instrument to another person by signing on it, is known as ________.
3. In a promissory note, the person who makes the promise to pay is called ________.
4. The person who endorses the promissory note in favour of another is known as ________.
5. A promissory note must be signed as per ________ Act.
6. Every negotiable instrument is presumed to have been made, drawn, accepted, indorsed, negotiated or transferred, for ________.

*Ans:* **1.** payee, **2.** endorsement, **3.** maker, **4.** endorser, **5.** Indian Stamp, **6.** consideration.

## Multiple Choice Questions

1. Which of the following is negotiable instrument?
   (a) Currency notes (b) Coins (c) Money orders (d) Cheques
2. The person who makes the promissory note and promises to pay is called the:
   (a) Payee (b) Acceptor (c) Maker (d) Drawee

*Ans:* **1.** (d), **2.** (c)

## Match the Following

| | |
|---|---|
| 1. Crossed cheque | (a) Risk of theft is less. |
| 2. Open cheque | (b) Which can be encashed at the counter of the bank |
| 3. Negotiable Instrument Act | (c) 1881 |
| 4. The Reserve Bank of India Act | (d) 1934 |

*Ans:* **1.** (a), **2.** (b), **3.** (c), **4.** (d).

## True or False

1. A bill of exchange must be accepted by the payee.
2. A bill of exchange is drawn by the creditor.
3. The person to whom payment is to be made in a bill of exchange is called payee.
4. A negotiable instrument does not require the signature of its maker.
5. Stamping of promissory note is not mandatory.
6. The time of payment of a negotiable instrument need not be certain.
7. Transverse lines are not necessary in case of a special crossing.

*Ans:* **1.** False, **2.** True, **3.** True, **4.** False, **5.** False, **6.** False, **7.** True.

☺ ☺ ☺

# Part-VI

# Insurance and ISO 9000

CHAPTER 19

# Insurance and Transportation

**LEARNING OBJECTIVES**

- *Insurance*
- *Concept of Risk*
- *The Ways of Managing Risk*
- *Importance of Insurance*
- *Transportation*
- *Warehousing*

Insurance contracts, to whatever category they may belong, are based on the following fundamental principles:

**1. Utmost Good Faith.** The contracts of insurance are included in the category of the contracts *uberrimae fidai*, i.e., those contracts which require absolute and utmost good faith on the part of the parties concerned. In this respect, such contracts are different from the ordinary business contracts which are based on the rule of *caveat emptor* (let the buyer beware). In an ordinary contract of sale of goods, for instance, the buyer will have no remedy against the seller *and will have to bear the loss.* But in insurance contracts of any kind, each one of the parties is under an obligation to make the fullest disclosure of all such facts which may have some bearing on the decision of the other *part* to enter into such contract. This binding applies particularly to the insured party who is naturally in possession of all material facts relating to his life or property.

**2. Insurable Interest.** No person can enter into a valid contract of insurance unless he had insurable interest in the object or the life insured. If it were not so, and if everyone were at liberty to take out an insurance policy on any object or life in the world irrespective of his insurable interest in it, the contracts of insurance would have been reduced to sheer gambling. In such conditions, insurance contracts would be wagering contracts which are not valid and, therefore, cannot be enforced in a court of law. Simply stated, insurable interest is understood as an interest in the preservation of a thing, or continuance of a life, recognized by law. Whenever such interest in a thing or life has may insure that thing or that life. Essentially speaking, insurable interest is in the nature of pecuniary or financial interest in a life or thing. It follows that one can have an insurable interest only when one would stand to benefit financially by the continuance of the life or object insured, or when, in other words, one would be put to a financial loss by the happening of the event against which a thing or the life of a person has been insured. Moreover, insurable interest is not a mere sentimental interest in the object insured. It is pecuniary interest and it follows that the loss caused by the risk insured against must be capable of estimation in terms of money.

A person has an insurable interest in his own life and there is no limit as regards the amount for which a person may insure his own life. But since insurance of a big sum carries a high premium, the insured would naturally insure him up to an amount for which he can pay the premium regularly and without inconvenience. A person will have insurable interest in the lives of those on whom he is dependent for support or those whose death will mean a financial loss to him. Thus, a husband and wife have insurable interest in each other. A creditor has insurable interest in the life or his debtor to the extent of his debt and can take a policy on his life within that amount.

Insurable interest must be present in the person insured at the time when the policy is taken in case of life insurance. It may or may not be in existence at the time of death of the person whose life is insured. In case of fire insurance, the insured must have insurable interest in the things insured against fire both at the time when the policy is taken and also at the time when the loss is incurred and a claim is filed with the insurer. In all other types of insurance, including marine insurance, the insured has to establish his insurable interest in the insured object at the time when the loss is paid to him on the happening of the event insured against.

**3. Indemnity.** All contracts of insurance, except for life insurance contracts, are contracts of indemnity. The basic purpose of insurance is to transfer the loss of a person to the insurance company which can easily spread it over a large number of policyholders. It is, therefore, necessary that a person gets exactly the same amount as he has lost due to the loss of his goods or damage to his property. For reasons, the insured cannot be permitted to make a profit out of his loss. If the insurance company agrees to pay a fixed sum higher than the amount of loss which the insured may suffer, there will be a constant temptation for him to destroy his goods or property intentionally and thus reap a profit out of insurance. This will be an anti-social act. It is, therefore, a recognized principle of insurance that an insured should be paid only the cash value of his loss in the event of the occurrence of loss and nothing more. To take an example, suppose a person insures his goods against fire for ₹ 20,000. In the course of the year, his goods are destroyed and his actual loss is found to be ₹ 15,000. When, however, the goods or property is insured for a smaller sum than the actual cash value of the actual loss, the insurance company is bound to pay the amount of the policy (assuming there is no average clause) and not the actual loss. This is so because by under-insuring his goods, the insured expresses his intention of transferring only a part of his actual loss to the insurance company. The balance of the loss will have to be met by the insured himself. Thus, if the insured takes a policy of ₹ 10,000 while the actual loss is considered to be worth ₹ 15,000 the company will pay only ₹ 10,000 and no more. In a way, indemnity is connected with insurable interest. An insured cannot recover anything more than the value of his own insurable interest in the subject matter of an insurance contract.

The principle of indemnity does not apply to life and other kinds of personal insurance. In such cases, the loss caused by the death of a person cannot be calculated in terms of money, nor is money any compensation for loss of life. In this category of insurance contracts, therefore, a fixed sum is undertaken to be paid either on the death of a person or after the expiry of a fixed period. In this sense, life insurance contracts may be described as 'contracts of indemnity'.

**4. Subrogation.** The doctrine of subrogation is an extension and a corollary of the principle of indemnity. According to it, the insurer steps into the shoes of the insured and becomes entitled to all 'rights of the insured regarding the subject matter insurance after the claim of the insured has been fully and finally settled. In some cases, there may be a possibility of his getting something in addition to that which he has received from the insurance company. The goods may have been partially damaged or the property may not have been fully destroyed. In such a case, the insured may try to obtain the value of scrap in addition to the money received in settlement of the claim. This will, however, be contrary to the principle of indemnity because the insured will be able to get more than what he has really lost. The doctrine of subrogation comes into operation here. The scrap, or whatever is left of the damaged or destroyed goods or property, will automatically pass into the hands of the insurance company after the payment of the claim under this doctrine.

**5. Contribution.** Sometimes a person may get his goods insured with more than one insurer. This is referred to as 'Double Insurance'. In this event of a loss, the insured will deserve to be indemnified only against the actual amount of loss incurred through the risk insured against. In such cases, the companies concerned will follow the principle of contribution. Each company will contribute that proportion of the loss which the policy issued by it bears to the total amount for which insurance has been effected with all the companies. In case the insured chooses to collect the amount of loss from one particular company or two of them, the paying company or companies can later on adjust accounts with other insurers of the same property by receiving their contributions according to the proportion of their insured amount.

**6. Mitigation of Loss.** When the mishap insured again occurs, it is the duty of the insured to take all such steps to mitigate the loss as would have been taken by anybody who is not insured. The idea behind this principle is that the insured should not become careless and inactive in the event of the mishap merely because the property which is getting damaged is insured; he must, instead.

act like any uninsured prudent man. This does not, in any event, mean that the insured should risk his own life for saving the property which is getting damaged or destroyed. All that is implied is that a reasonable effort towards saving the insured property must be made by the policy holder in the event of the mishap insured against.

**7. *Causa Proxima.*** In those cases where the mishap insured against is the outcome of a series of events the insurance company will meet the loss only if it is definitely established that the said loss was caused directly by an event covered by the policy. What has to be referred to in such cases is not the first of a series of events leading to the mishap but the last one. The maxim in this regard is *'cause proxima non remota spectatur'*, i.e., the nearest or the direct cause and not the remote cause is to be looked to. To take an example, suppose a ship which gets damaged on the high seas is anchored at port of call for repairs. To affect repairs, its cargo of biscuits has to be partly unloaded. If, in this process, the biscuits are damaged, the insurers will not be liable to pay for them because the nearest or the proximate cause of the damage is the mishandling of the cargo which is not covered by the terms of a marine insurance policy. The damage suffered by the ship on high seas is only a remote cause of the damage suffered by the cargo and is, therefore, not to be considered.

**Re-insurance.** Sometimes an insurer may take upon him more liability on account of insured risks than he can conveniently bear. In such a situation, he can transfer the excessive part of such risk to another insurer. For this he will insure that part of risk with another insurer. This is called re-insurance. But re-insurance may not always be affected to spread and share risks with other insurers. Sometimes, an insurer may undertake the insurance of certain risks at a higher rate of premium and may re-insure a part of them with some other insurer at a lower rate with a view to making profit from the difference between the two premiums. It must, however, be remembered that whatever be the purpose of re-insurance, the original contract is never superseded and replaced by the contract of re-insurance. Re-insurance may be affected in two ways:

(i) Facultative re-insurance, i.e., the re-insurance of particular risks by agreement with another insurer.

(ii) Treaty re-insurance, i.e., re-insurance under a treaty by which the re-insurers agree to accept a certain proportion of all risks beyond a certain limit underwritten by the insurers.

According to Section 101 of the Insurance Act as amended in 1961, every insurer must insure with two re-insurance corporations set up by the Government a certain percentage of the sum insured as may from time-to-time be specified by the Government. The percentages are contained in Schedule of the notification issued by the Government on May 24, 1961. The two re-insurance corporations are: Indian Re-insurance Corporation and Indian Guarantee Corporation. The insurers may re-insure the balance of risk, not insured with the re-insurance corporations, with other Indian insurers on a reciprocal basis.

## LIFE INSURANCE

**Introduction.** Generally speaking, life insurance is referred to as 'Life assurance' for the reason that in this case the event insured against is certain to happen though the time when it may happen is rather uncertain. Thus, life assurance differs from other classes of insurance in providing an assured benefit in return for an insurer, in consideration of a premium, paid either in lump sum or in periodical instalments undertakes to pay an annuity or a certain sum of money, either on the death of the insured or on the expiry of a certain number of years. Obviously, if a person dies, the payment will be made to representatives of the deceased. If, however, the money becomes due for payment during the lifetime of the assured, the amount of the policy will be paid to him. Moreover, the assured has to pay a fixed sum by way of premium constantly during the time when the policy is in force.

**Protection with Investment.** Originally, the life assurance contracts were used by the creditors to protect their own interests for short periods as, for example, the insurance of the life of ship's captain while on a specific voyage. In later years, it came to be used on a much wider scale for more varied purposes. In its modern form, the life assurance provides protection against the risk of early death and is at the same time a good investment. Thus, if a person dies before the policy matures for payment, life assurance undertakes to replace income to his dependants. But if the person whose life is insured lives up to the maturity of the policy, life assurance undertakes to replace income to him and his dependants in old age. Thus, on the one side, life assurance help due to the sudden and premature death of their bread-winner; on the other hand, it is one of the best means of saving for investment in the future. In the evening of one's life, when one finds it too late in the day to struggle and work hard to earn for oneself and one's family, the small sums paid to the insurance company by way of premium over a long period of 15 or 25 years grow into a large sum which is a source of great confidence in oneself. The first-mentioned aspect is the feature of protection and the second refers to the prospect of saving for the future. Life assurance is, therefore, not merely a protection against the uncertainty of life; it is an investment, too.

To business, too, life assurance brings some definite advantages. To mention a few of them, life assurance provides protection against the premature death of the important members of the staff, develops loyalty among employees if it is extended to all of them, is an ideal collateral security for securing loans and can be used for the repayment of debts, etc.

## Types of Insurance

- Fire Insurance
- Marine Insurance

# TRANSPORTATION — I

The chief function of physical distribution is to take goods from the places where they are produced to those places where they are to be consumed. This is referred to as the creation of 'place utility'. Transportation performs this essential function of marketing. Proper arrangements for the transportation of products to markets are, of course, vital to the process of marketing. Improvements in transportation and traffic services have always led to a widening of the markets, increase in the scale of production and specialization in industry. Apart from the economic significance of transportation, the social, political and cultural importance of an efficient system of transport is all too well known to be over-emphasized. India's independence movement and the emotional unity among the people –both owe a great deal to railways and motor transport.

Of course, let it be made clear that transportation is not merely a marketing activity. To use economic 'possession utility' and aids manufacturing processes in creating 'form utility'. If production is regarded as the creation of utilities, there can be no objection to regarding transportation as a productive activity. As a matter of fact an article is not fully produced in its broadest economic sense until it is in the hands of the ultimate consumer. From this standpoint also, transport is a productive function.

## General Benefits of Transportation

In specific terms, transport is indispensable for the assembling and dispersal of raw materials and goods. By making possible assembling and dispersal of goods and materials, transport places them in the hands of those who derive greater utility from their possession or consumption than those who possessed them before transportation. It is also through wide dispersal and the consequent extension of the market that transport has enlarged the scale on which production can be carried on. But for transport, the scale of production would have been limited to the quantity which could be locally consumed and this would surely have restricted the size of business concerns to be miniscule. Transportation has made possible the relation, and has also helped in the establishment of big manufacturing enterprises by carrying the raw materials found at different places to their sites. To put it briefly, transportation is the mother of large-scale production. In fact, transportation is among the few important factors which determine the location of any enterprise.

It is the facility of transport that has made possible trade within and between countries and thereby permitted the various regions and countries to specialize in the production of those commodities in which they have comparatively greater advantages.

The benefits flowing from the regional and international division of labour are, therefore also to be put to the credit of transportation.

Transportation has also given a great fillip, to the promotion of several industries producing perishable articles like fishing, dairy farming, poultry farming, and meat packing, and so on. The prosperity of many nations can be ascribed to the export earnings from these industries. Quick means of transport have made possible their transportation to long distances without any fear of their deterioration in transit.

Transportation has exercised a stabilizing influence on the prices of commodities by the movement of supplies to deficient areas, thus matching supplies to demand at different places. Price of a commodity is made uniform throughout the country with the assistance of transportation.

Transportation also benefits the consumers in at least three ways. First, transportation provides them the benefit of diversified consumption, i.e., of consuming a large variety of products which cannot be locally produced. This is made possible by exchange of goods between places through transportation. Secondly, the consumers get the product at lower costs as a result of large-scale production due to extension of the market with the help of transportation. Thirdly, the prices are kept stable by the quick movement of goods from surplus to deficient areas.

The effect of transportation on the sharing of national income in the form of rent, wages, interest and profit is also beneficial. Easy transportation facilities improve the accessibility of distant areas, and thereby increase the rural and urban site rents; they throw open a new vista of opportunities and thus increase interest and profits and the mobility of labour possibly resulting in increased money wages. Since aggregate production and income in any community are boosted by transportation facilities the absolute shares of all factors can grow.

The economic effects of good transportation facilities described above show clearly, how indispensable transport is in an economy, be it capitalist or socialist. The development of efficient, sufficient, reliable, and cheap and coordinate transport facilities should, therefore, be an integral part of economic planning in any country.

**Relative Evaluation of Chief Means of Transport.** If, however, one wishes to choose between the various means of transport, a study of their relative merits will be more relevant. The final choice is to be made after a consideration of four factors, *viz.*, cost, speed, flexibility and regularity of service. In the following paragraphs, the relative position of each means of transport as regards these factors is assessed.

**Cost of Service.** The railways are cheaper means for the transport of bulky and heavy materials over long distances. They possess this advantage for two reasons: First, the requirement of power for traction by trains on smooth rails is lower than that of trucks on roads, Secondly, the railway trains can handle very large volumes of freight at a time. The railways involve a very large amount of fixed expenditure which leads to operation of the principle of diminishing costs as the traffic increases. However, for small consignments over short distances, railway transport is not as economical as the truck transport. The latter involves lesser expenditure by way of packing and handling while the rates of the former are higher as terminal costs, *viz.*: of assembling and disassembling of wagons and unloading, etc., increase for short hauls.

The motor transport is not suited to the carriage of bulky articles of small value over long distances because of the very limited carrying capacity of a truck, the high cost of fuel and the poor capacity of such traffic to bear high transport charges. The water transport, especially where it is natural and the speed is allowed to be slow, is eminently suited to the carriage of bulky and heavy materials and machinery, for it is the cheapest means. The air transport is the costliest means, and as such, its use is restricted to the transport of valuable articles or spare parts of machinery urgently needed.

**Speed of Transport.** Over short distances, motor transport has the merit of being faster than the railway transport. This is because the carrying capacity of a truck is much smaller than that of a full train with a large number of wagons. The loading and uploading and the assembling of wagons take much time in case of railways, thus placing motor transport in a superior position as regards speed over short hauls. Over long hauls, however, the railway transport is potentially speedier means because it enjoys exclusive track and as such can run at higher speeds. Even faster than the railway transport, and in fact the quickest means, is the air transport. It is quickest not only because it is the speediest but also because it adopts the shortest route flying over dense forests, high mountains and wide oceans and rivers. The water transport lags behind all other means of transport in the matter of speed and as such in unsuitable for perishable articles.

**Flexibility of Service.** The railway transport facilities are available only between certain definite places and the goods have to be carried to the railway station. In other words, railways are not able to pick-up a major part of their traffic directly at the point of production and deliver at factory warehouses or at the point of consumption. The motor transport, however, is not bound down between any fixed points. It is flexible and can provide its services between any two points in the country, if necessary from door-to-door, on difficult gradients or poor roads. It is particularly suitable for special jobs, e.g. pick-up and delivery in small lots, carrying traffic between places not directly connected by rail and providing services to off-rail points. It is also flexible as the trucks may be loaded at a time convenient to its character. The air and transport are both inflexible as they are available only between certain points. The water transport serves a limited area but is indispensable for foreign trade between countries having no common land frontiers.

**Regularity of Services.** In this respect, the railway transport stands first in rank as if follows a regular schedule and is unaffected by weather conditions. Thus, rendering dependable service. The motor transport may or may not follow some schedule but it is somewhat dependant on weather. The air transport is very much affected by weather conditions though there is a regular schedule which is followed in 90% to 95% of the cases. The water transport in not available throughout the year as the water may get frozen or may get dried during certain periods rendering this means unusable.

From the preceding discussion, it is clear that each means of transport is suited only for a certain type of traffic. The railways are suited for carrying heavy and bulky items and for long hauls. The roadways are useful in carrying freight over short distances. The airways are needed for quick transit of light articles having higher values as compared to weight. The waterways are of use in the carriage of heavy and bulky items at very low costs and some other items which can only be brought or sent through them. There is, however, a certain amount of overlapping in the areas of different means of transport and in fact any means of transport does not handle only the type of traffic for which it is most suited.

## TRANSPORTATION — II

### Principles Underlying Rate-making

Like any manufacturer or trader, the transport agencies have also to fix the prices, i.e., the freight rates and fares of their services. In their case, however, the services are rendered under such differing conditions and to such a large variety of traffic that the rate-making is of necessity but a difficult affair. Their rates have to be determined in such a way that the cost will be covered, the traffic will be maximized and burden will be equitably or fairly distributed. At times, there may be certain additional objectives which may be desired to be achieved through rate-making as, for instance, stimulation of foreign trade or relief of urban congestion. The achievement of such objectives will require a certain modification of the rates.

There are three basic theories or principles of rate-making which are carefully considered by all transport agencies while determining the freights and fares. As the various means of transport differ somewhat in regard to the proportion of fixed costs in their total costs, there is some difference in the weight given by them to various theories. In road transport, for instance, the fixed costs form a smaller proportion of the total costs that they do in the railway transport. The result of this is that the road hauliers will adjust their rates more nearly to costs that will be possible by the railways which will have to give more weight to the demand for service. This being understood, it is possible to explain the three principles in terms of the railway transport. To assist assimilation and understanding, it is proposed to explain their meaning or implication, the possibility of their strict application, and their merits and drawbacks in the following pages.

**Cost of Service Principle.** This principle implies that the charges of the railways should be based on the cost incurred by them in providing the service. If the cost of carrying a wagon-load of sugar comes to, say, ₹ 50, then the freight charged must at least cover this amount. If the actual freight charged is less than this amount, the railways will be incurring a loss. Apparently, this principle is quite simple and reasonable. On second thought, however, it becomes clear that it is difficult, almost impossible, to determine the cost which will be relevant for the rate-fixation purposes.

Obviously, the cost of rendering service by the railways is influenced by the following factors, all of which must be considered: (i) ton-miles or passengers-miles covered by the trains; (ii) size of consignments, whether small packets or big bundles; (iii) mode of packing, whether hand or machine pressed; (iv) bulk in relation to weight of the commodity carried; (v) speed and distance of haul; whether by express or slow trains and whether carried for short distance or over long distance; (vi) characteristics of the material carried, whether explosive, perishable or liquid or fragile; (vii) time of demand, whether peak or off-peak demand; (viii) availability of traffic on a particular day; (ix) party responsible for risk of loss in transit; and (x) share of fixed or common or joint costs to be apportioned to a particular haul.

But then the question that arises is: Can accurate figures of true costs which take into account all these factors be determined, and that too in advance of carriage of traffic? The answer is surely in the negative. Can rates, then, be based strictly on cost? No, never. This is what Acworth meant when he remarked, "To claim that rates shall automatically be fixed on the basis of cost of carriage is to claim what is impossible".

To proceed further, let us assume that the cost of each service can be calculated. There is another question to be answered now, namely, 'Are rates based strictly on cost altogether advantageous'? The answer again must unfortunately though it may appear, be an outright 'no'. There are two reasons for this. First, in the conditions of existing capacity not being fully utilized and the best size of the plant not having been attained, rates based strictly upon average total unit cost prevent the movement of paying traffic (i.e., traffic which fetches more than the special or direct or the out-of-pocket cost of its carriage). According to cost of service principle the freight rates on articles of high value relative to weight and bulk will be lowered, those on goods of low value relative to weight will be raised; the traffic of the former type will be increased only marginally (as its demand is less demand is more elastic). Thus, the readjustments of rates according to this principle will reduce the volume of traffic, increase the average total unit cost and make it impossible for railways to operate in some cases. Therefore, the cost of service principle is not wholly advantageous to the railways themselves.

Secondly, the rates based on the cost of services principle will retard a balanced industrial development of the country. The movement of heavy or bulky raw material and the mineral products over long distances which may sometimes be necessary to develop industries in other regions not possessing them, will be discouraged by the heavy rates charged according to cost of service. As a result, industries will be concentrated in a few regions possessing them. This has again economic, social and strategic implications.

In spite of all that has been said above, this principle is useful in two ways. First, it provides a minimum limit for rates below which, it will not be advantageous for the hauler to operate. A freight rate below the special or direct cost of the haul will be uneconomical to the railways as it would gain more by not undertaking that haul. Also, rates charged below even the special cost in utter violation of this whose products are costlier may be encouraged in preference to another with cheaper products because of lower freight rate on the products of the former which outweighs the superior position of the latter industry. Secondly, cost is an important factor in adjusting particular rates so as to equate total revenue to total costs. Though total cost does not definitely fix particular rates, it has a bearing thereon.

To summarise, rates based on this principle cannot be set except arbitrarily. These rates are disadvantageous as they may prevent the full utilization of capacity and check an even development of the country. However, the principle is useful inasmuch as it points out that rates below the special cost are uneconomical and can induce improper development and location of industries. The cost does exercise some influence on rates also.

## STORAGE AND WAREHOUSING

Storage is another essential function of the marketing process. It involves the making of proper arrangements for retaining the goods in a perfect state till they are needed by the consumers and are to be taken to the marketplace. From the point of view of economies, storage results in the creation of both time and place utilities. It enables goods to be made available to buyers wherever and whenever they are in demand. More specifically, it involves the technical process of warehousing and financing. Of these, financing will be dealt with separately in this chapter.

The need for storage is not difficult to understand. In the first place, modern production is carried on in anticipation of demand rather than in response to specific orders of customers. All these goods are, therefore, not sold off immediately. The manufacturer has to make adequate arrangements for storage of his output. Secondly, many of the products are produced seasonably while the demand for them has to be met all the year round. Wheat is harvested mostly as a rabi crop in India in April and May, but it has to be stored to meet the demand all through the year. Thirdly, some products are produced throughout the year thought their demand may arise mainly in a particular season. The woollen cloth and wool are examples of this kind. In such cases, the products have to be stored till the season arrives. Fourthly, raw materials have to be stored to enable mass production like to be carried on continuously. Fifthly, storage makes it possible for middleman like retailers and wholesalers to function. The retailers store goods for the sake of consumers and the wholesalers store goods on a much larger-scale to feed the retailers. Sixthly, goods may also have to be stored for curing or processing. Seventhly, storage of goods becomes necessary also when the prices are going down too low in the market. The agriculturists in India are now able to get better prices for their products because they can store their produce in warehouse and cold storage. Finally, goods may be kept in storage for speculative purpose, i.e., for the purpose of repaving the gains of increased prices in future.

Thus, it may be concluded that storage of goods becomes necessary at almost every step throughout the marketing process. Storage can really be regarded as the function of equalization. In the ultimate run, it tends to adjust the supply to demand so as to equalize them in the interest of the manufacturers, middlemen and consumers.

**Warehouse.** Warehouse is places meant for the storage of products. Storage facilitates are provided generally by three classes of warehouses. (i) Private warehouse, (ii) public warehouse, and (iii) bonded warehouses.

**Private Warehouse.** The private warehouses are owned by big business concerns or wholesalers who use them for the storage of their own stocks. Being privately owned, their maintenance and insurance are the responsibility of their owners. These warehouses have a limited value and utility as business units in general cannot make use of them.

**Public Warehouses.** These are warehouses which are operated for business units in general. They may be owned by somebody or some agency whose sole job consists in providing storage facilities to the public for certain fees or charges. They have to work under a license from the State and are required to conform to certain regulations framed by the Government for them. The public warehouses may be put to diverse uses. Usually, if they are owned by a dock authority, they are used for storing goods which cannot be immediately shipped on reaching the port or which have arrived at the port though the importer is not able to take possession of them immediately. Similarly, they can be used for storing goods which are not immediately to be used after they are ready. The public warehouses provide facilities of storing to all without discrimination and constitute a vital link in the mechanism of the marketing process. They serve a number of useful purposes. Chief among them are:

1. Warehousemen take the responsibility of keeping and storing in order and in perfectly safe custody.
2. Most of the public warehouses are constructed at favourable points both on railway routes and highways, quite often, railway sidings are provided to these warehouses. Similarly, mechanical equipment for handling heavy goods may also be provided there.
3. Small manufacturers who cannot afford to construct private warehouses of their own benefit a great deal by keeping their goods in warehouses situated in the different regions of the country, thus getting the benefit of various regional markets.
4. The receipt issued by such warehouses can be used as a collateral security for obtaining loans during the period when they are lying in storage.
5. Whenever the owner intends to sell his goods, he can take the intending purchasers to the warehouse and get his goods inspected by them. Not only that, the owner can even make his goods into marketable condition by grading, branding and packaging them in the warehouse itself.
6. The owners can keep their stocks in safe custody quite economically. They need not invest and lock-up their capital in constructing or taking on lease buildings for the storage of goods.
7. The public warehouses render a number of essential ancillary services to those who make use of the facilities offered by them. They usually undertake to load and unload goods from ships and railways. They may arrange for cars for the purpose of carrying goods, and for delivery in accordance with the owner's directions.

**Bonded Warehouses.** Bonded warehouses are used by importers of goods for keeping their goods in safe custody at or near the ports. When goods are imported, customs duties have to be paid on them before they can be taken away from the dockyard. But it is difficult for the importers to pay the whole of such duties and get keep their goods in certain licensed warehouses even before the import duties have been paid. These warehouses are called bonded warehouses and the goods deposited with them are said to be 'in a bond'. Such warehouses may be Government-owned or privately-owned, though in the latter case, they are required to work under the supervision and control of the Government. An importer can make use of bonded warehouses by securing the special permission of the customs authorities on a prescribed form of application.

Goods warehoused in bond (i.e., kept in a bonded warehouse) can be branded, blended and packaged in the warehouse itself. This of considerable importance in the case of such goods as is meant to be re-exported. Even otherwise, the buyers can be taken to the bonded warehouses to enable them to inspect the goods there. But the most outstanding advantage of the bonded warehouses lies in the facility which they provide for the payment of the customs duties by instalments. The customs authorities allow the owners to take the goods out in parts after paying duties only on the part withdrawn by them. Thus, import duty has not to be paid on the whole lot of goods all at once but is charged only on the goods actually taken out by the owner.

## ........ QUESTIONS FOR DISCUSSION

1. Discuss the various types of warehouses and bring out their relative importance.
2. Discuss various benefits of warehousing.
3. "The public warehouses provide facilities of storing to all without discrimination and constitute a vital link in the mechanism of the marketing process." Explain this statement with valid examples.
4. If production is regarded as the creation of utilities, there can be no objection to regarding transportation as a productive activity – Elucidate this statement.

## Test Yourself

1. (a) "Life Assurance is both a protection and an investment." Explain.
   (b) Explain what is meant by "insurable interest".
2. Explain the essentials of a valid fire insurance contract. How do these differ from the essential of life assurance contract?
3. Explain the nature and characteristics of insurable interest in different type of insurance, to what extent, if any, do you consider insurable interest exists in the following cases: (a) creditor in the life of his debtor; (b) a husband in the life of his wife; and (c) an employer in the life of his employee?
4. Do you favour nationalization of road transport in India? Give reasons, Discuss the advantages and limitations of road transport in India.
5. Write notes on: (a) Principles of insurance, (b) Regrouping of railways, and (c) Floating policy.
6. Insurance is meant to:
   (a) Prevent specified events.
   (b) Prevent damage to assets from specified events.
   (c) Compensate for losses from specified events.
   (d) Rebuild the lost assets.
7. Insurance compensates losses:
   (a) By replacing the original loss.
   (b) To the full extent of the lost outcome.
   (c) Only to the extent of the insured amount.
   (d) All of the above.
8. Insurance is necessary because:
   (a) Assets depreciate over time and through usage.
   (b) Assets may be damaged by the external causes.
   (c) Assets require regular maintenance.
   (d) None of the above reasons.

***Ans:*** **6.** (c), **7.** (c), **8.** (b)

☺ ☺ ☺

CHAPTER 20

# ISO 9000

## LEARNING OBJECTIVES

- *ISO 9000*
- *General Direction*
- *ISO 9000 and TQM*
- *Objectives of ISO 9000*
- *The ISO 9000 Series*
- *Reasons for Adopting ISO 9000 System*
- *Benefits of ISO 9000 Quality System*
- *Standardization in India*
- *Bureau of Indian Standards*
- *ISI Certification Marks Scheme*
- *General Direction*
- *Objectives of ISI Mark*
- *Standardization in Small-scale Industries*

# ISO 9000

## GENERAL DIRECTION

The system was developed by the International Standards Organization (ISO) for management and control of quality at every stage of production, namely design, development, planning, manufacturing, installation and servicing.

As quality became a major focus of business throughout the world, various organizations developed standards and guidelines. Terms such as quality management, quality control, quality system, and quality assurance acquired different meanings in different countries, within a country and even within an industry. As the European community moved towards the European Free Trade Agreement which went into effect at the end of 1992, quality management became a key strategic objective. To standardize quality requirement of European countries within the common market and those wishing to do business with those countries, a specialized agency for standardization, the International Organization for Standardization (ISO) was found in 1946 and composed of representatives from the national standards bodies of 91 nations. It adopted a series of written quality standards in 1987. This are called the ISO 9000 standards and were revised in 1994. The ISO adopted the ISO prefix in naming the standards. The standards outline the collective plans, responsibilities, procedures and resources which ensure that customer requirements will be met. ISO 9000 provides a starting place for all-encompassing quality efforts. This standard merely stipulates where the documentation is needed to validate processes and approaches. ISO 9000 stands for system standardization and certification rather than product standardization and certification.

ISO (International Organization for Standardization) is a worldwide federation of national standards bodies, at present comprising 140 members, one in each country. The object of ISO is to promote the development of standardization and related activities in the world with a view to facilitating international exchange of goods and services, and to developing cooperation in the spheres of intellectual, scientific, technological and economic activity. The results of ISO technical work are published as International Standards.

'ISO' means equal (Isotherm lines of a weather map show equal temperatures). Organizations certified under the ISO 9000 standard are assured to have quality equal to their peer organizations. The standards have been adopted in the US as the ANSL/ASQC Q 9000-1994 series but are commonly referred to as ISO 9000. The standards are recognized by over 100 countries including India and Japan. In some foreign markets, companies will not buy from non-certified suppliers. Thus, meeting ISO 9000 standards is becoming a necessity for international competitiveness. The standards are applicable to all types of manufacturing and service industries. ISO 9000 certification assures customers that a firm has designed and managed its processes to assure delivery of a quality product.

Industries and business houses engaged in the production and delivery of various kinds of products and services can be grouped under the following four generic categories: Hardware. Software, Processed materials, Services.

The text of these standards released by the ISO central secretarial in Geneva are adapted as the IS 14000 series of standards by the Bureau of Indian Standards (BIS). These standards embody comprehensive quality management concepts and guidance. The control (creation, modification and deletion) of all documents related to quality management is an important requirement of ISO 9000 covering elements such as drawings, specifications, blueprints, work instructions, test procedures, inspection reports, calibration data and quality cost reports. A record retention system should be in place to facilitate the use of documents, which are themselves organized in three tiers: (i) the quality manual, (ii) the work procedures, and (iii) the instructions and data records.

The ISO 14000 family addresses "Environmental management".

This means what the organization does to:

- minimize harmful effects on the environment caused by its activities, and to
- achieve continual improvement of its environmental performance.

## ISO 14000 (EMS) — FAQs

- Assures customers of commitment to demonstrate environmental management
- Improved industry government relations
- Helps in conservation of raw materials and energy
- Reduces incidents that results in liability

The ISO 9000 standards require that third party audits be performed leading to the suppliers becoming certified. This certification is accepted by all customers, eliminating 10 to 20 different audits by many companies interested in doing business with supplier.

**Quality System Certification:** BIS is operating Quality System Certification Scheme against IS/ISO 9000 series of standards. This scheme is governed by the Bureau of Indian Standards Act, 1986 and has been accredited by Raad Voor Accreditatie (RVA), Netherlands. Under this scheme, the capability of supplier of goods or services is certified to IS/ISO 9000 series of standards for ensuring the quality of goods and services satisfying the customer as relevant to the particular contracts entered into between the respective parties.

It is for these reasons that companies in Europe and North America are devoting considerable resources to setting up quality systems and to having these systems externally certified. Furthermore, more and more large corporations and trading houses, anxious to obtain greater assurance of product quality and timely delivery, are demanding certified quality systems from their suppliers.

Before one can consider how to introduce quality systems into companies in developing countries, one must understand nature of their markets, their industrial cultures, and their perceptions of quality, needless to say, these countries do not constitute a homogeneous group. They vary considerably in terms of level of development, political and economic systems, cultural traits and market environments.

A revolution occurred in 1987 in the management of quality worldwide when the International Standards Organization (Geneva, Switzerland) bought out a set of standards pertaining not to the quality of products but rather to the practice of quality assurance methods within a company. Termed as ISO 9000 standards, these proved their value rather quickly and went global. Many countries worldwide, including India have adopted them as their own standards to benchmark quality management practices.

ISO 9000 is a generic name given to a family of standards developed to provide a framework around which a quality management system can effectively be implemented. The ISO 9000 family of standards represents an international consensus on good management practices with the aim of ensuring that the organization can time and time again deliver the product or services that meet the client's quality requirements. These good practices have been distilled into a set of standardized requirements for a quality management system, regardless of what your organization does, its size, or whether it is in the private, or public sector. The family of ISO 9000 standards has been developed by ISO and it is made up of four core standards:

ISO 9000 was originally issued as a series of six internationally agreed upon standards to guide and audit a company's quality management practices. Named as ISO 9000, ISO 9001, ISO 9002, ISO 9003, ISO 9004 and ISO 8402 each standard contains specific guidelines pertaining to a certain segment or quality related activities. These standards are the minimum acceptable level of standards that a supplier's quality management practices should meet, in order to receive the ISO 9000 accreditation or certification. Several additional standards have been issued subsequently by ISO, including a major revision of the original series done in 1947. Today, this series covers such varied activities as designed, manufacturing, software development, service activities, auditing, calibration of equipments and methods for improving quality.

The term ISO 9000 unfortunately has two different meanings: it refers to a single standard (ISO 9000) and it refers to a set of three standards (ISO 9000, ISO 9001, and ISO 9004). All three are referred to as quality management system standards.

ISO 9000 discusses definitions and terminology and is used to clarify the concepts used by the ISO 9001 and ISO 9004 standards. ISO 9001 contains requirements and is often used for certification purposes while ISO 9004 presents a set of guidelines and is used to achieve sustained success.

ISO's purpose is to facilitate international trade by providing a single set of standards that people everywhere would recognize and respect.

ISO 9000 is not a mandatory system nor is it a government regulation. However, it is a very important customer regulation. It provides assurance to a wide variety of customers about an organization's quality assurance methods and quality management practices.

European Economic Community (EEC) was the first to adopt this standard formally as the requirement suppliers should meet in order to do business in Europe. ISO 9000 registration or accreditation is not a permanent certificate. An audit of an organization's quality management system must be done by a competent agency (called the assessor) once in three or six months in order for the organization to retain its accreditation.

Some of the requirements in ISO 9001: 2008 (which is one of the standards in the ISO 9000 family) include:

1. a set of procedures that cover all key processes in the business;
2. monitoring processes to ensure they are effective;
3. keeping adequate records;
4. checking output for defects, with appropriate and corrective action where necessary;
5. regularly reviewing individual processes and the quality system itself for effectiveness; and facilitating continual improvement.

**Example of using the ISO 9000 family of standards**

A metal parts fabricating company, a welfare agency, an electrical appliance manufacturer, a large chemical processing company, a firm of international lawyers, a computer software developer, a bank.

It describes the elements of quality systems. It is the 'top level' quality document and is supplemented by specific procedures which describes business processes to produce quality products and services.

The organization's QA methods are reviewed once in every three years by such an agency. ISO 9000 auditors do not audit the quality of finished product but rather the procedures and methods used in delivering quality. After accreditation, quality assurance becomes system driven and person independent.

According to the International Organization for Standardization (ISO), "TQM is a management approach to an organization, centred on quality, based on the participation of all its members and aimed at long-term success through customer satisfaction, with benefits to the members of the organizations and the societies".

Total Quality Management is, as its name implies, related to the monitoring of quality throughout the organization by everyone in that organization. This means that if problems are spotted during the production process, it is the responsibility of that person to solve the problem before it goes any further through the process. This way, problems should be identified before they ever get near the consumer but if they do, every effort is made to sort out the problem with the minimum of fuss.

## ISO 9000 AND TQM

Companies that have effectively implemented ISO 9000 standards and TQM concepts have dramatically improved their profits and customer retention. ISO 9000 is not TQM, but is a sub-component of TQM and a good start on the TQM path. ISO 9000 is only the minimum required quality standard that a supplier must demonstrate to receive ISO 9000 accreditation. TQM by contrasts is much more comprehensive. TQM links quality to customer satisfaction by requiring action on four essentials:

1. A strong customer orientation (internal and external in all activities in the organizations).
2. Top management's direct involvement in the delivery of quality.
3. Total company-wide participation in the delivery of quality, and
4. The systematic analysis of quality problems focused on continuous improvement of quality performance and prevention of quality problems.

### Objectives of ISO 9000

1. Achieve, maintain and seek to continuously improve product quality (including services) in relationship to requirements.
2. Improve the quality of operations to continually meet customers' and stakeholders' stated and implied needs.
3. Provide confidence to internal management and other employees that quality requirements are being fulfilled and that improvement is taking place.

4. Provide confidence and satisfaction to customers and other stakeholders that quality requirements are being achieved in the delivered product.
5. Provide confidence that quality system requirements are fulfilled.
6. Provide turnkey solution to customer to improve product quality and process efficiency.

### Strategic Objectives of ISO 9000

**Customer Service:** Provide all customers with the best quality products and services possible consistent with their resources and serve as a resource centre to determine customer needs.

**Regulatory:** Design, develop, and conduct courses for personnel working in the worldwide maritime community that meet individual and company simulation, training, assessment and research needs as well as being in compliance with the latest national and international rules, regulations, and guidelines.

**Technology:** Acquire, use, and apply the latest technology and information in the field of maritime training consistent with resources in the development and delivery of simulation, training, assessment and research.

**Ethics:** Conduct all business in an ethical and professional manner sensitive to human needs and social responsibilities in order to achieve our customers' goals and create opportunities for our employees.

**Continuous Improvement:** Identify and examine non-conformities in design, delivery, and customer service to determine processes that require improvement and implement necessary changes to continuously improve.

**Employee Acceptance:** Create and maintain an environment that encourages teamwork, cooperation, initiative, leadership, problem solving, constructive decision-making, and a commitment to continuous improvement.

**Leadership:** Provide expertise and input to industry and regulatory bodies that promotes the improvement of safety at sea, protection of the marine environment, and the overall betterment of the worldwide maritime community.

## THE ISO 9000 SERIES

ISO 9000 consists of:

1. ISO 8402 — terminology standard, provides definitions of all terms, is a comprehensive glossary.
2. ISO 9000 — it describes and clarifies quality concepts and provides guidelines for the selection and use of series of international standards on quality systems.
3. ISO 9001 — it provides a model for quality assurance in design, development, production, installation and services.
4. ISO 9002 — it describes the supplier's required capabilities in production and installation.
5. ISO 9003 — it is a seldom used subset of ISO 9001 and ISO 9002. It applies to companies providing final inspection and test services.

6. ISO 9004 — it describes each of the quality systems elements in ISO 9000, helping companies to understand the entire operation in sufficient detail to select the appropriate elements in designing a quality system for a particular facility.

ISO 9000 is written in general terms to accommodate the full range of activities undertaken by manufacturers and service providers. Companies that achieve quality system registration can look forward to improved relations with customers, better control paperwork and processes and increased marketability for their products and services.

ISO 9001 is the most comprehensive and is the application of the process model at the company level. It outlines quality management activities and requirements during a complete product or service life cycle from design to installation.

The standards for the ISO 9000 family deal with the following areas:

**1. Quality Management Systems:** establishing and monitoring the process whereby product and service quality are maintained.

**2. Management Responsibility:** how the management establishes, maintain, monitor and communicate their commitment to the standards.

**3. Resource Management:** how the business provides the resources — both physical and human – to enable the standards to be met and maintained.

**4. Product Realization Requirements:** how businesses establish and monitor quality from concept to final product or service delivery.

**5. Measurement, Analysis and Improvement Requirements:** how businesses use data to monitor their quality control and how this data is used to improve quality provision.

**Reasons for adopting ISO 9000 system** could vary with the needs of the company. It is also to be noted that a company need not adopt the standard in all the functions at a time; adoption can be in steps or in a particular function (e.g., marketing, manufacturing, finance, projects, etc.), as per the need of the company. Whatever be the mode of adaptation, the standard is considered useful for the following situation:

- Developing a superior quality management system as per ISO 9001 for customer satisfaction and goodwill creation.
- Contractual purposes in transacting business
- Approval of customers for quality capability.
- Third party certification/registration regarding capability of the company for supply of materials and services that can be used as certificate of competency to quality supply materials. This enhances its market image and helps in establishing its credibility among its customers worldwide.

In general ISO 9000 requires:

1. Management that is committed, involved, focused and responsive to the changing market trends.
2. People who are organised, responsible, authorized, competent, empowered, and knowledgeable.

3. Processes that are visible, traceable, consistent, repeatable, measurable and documentable.
4. Documents that are appropriate, relevant, simple, understandable and consistent with the processes in use.

This version of ISO 9000 was successful in instituting a documented quality management system, which provided the much needed confidence between suppliers and buyers with regard to contractual agreement.

## Benefits of ISO 9000 Quality Systems

ISO 9000 quality systems bring various benefits to their users. The primary purposes of an effective quality system are to inspire confidence among customers in a contractual situation. It is also of immense value to the suppliers themselves. Because it enables them to achieve customer satisfaction cost effectively. If all tasks were carried out correctly the first time, there would be no waste, costs would be minimized and profit maximized. An effective quality system confers the following benefits on the supplier:

1. Companies getting ISO 9000 registration has to comply with quality systems as documented by them. ISO 9000 registration means conformity to documented practices (i.e., it conforms the practices specified in a registrant's own quality systems). Thus, it enhances and facilitates trade.
2. It enables them to identify and plan tasks and their methods of performance in order to yield the right results.
3. Since, a company registered under ISO 9000 perceives certain quality systems and achieves increased quality level; it obtains market advantage over competitors.
4. Since a company is registered under ISO 9000 and is fulfilling its various requirements, it should also meet European Union's (European Community) regulation requirements. This helps to obtain trade in Europe.
5. It provides the means for identifying and resolving problems and preventing their recurrence, thereby improving conformance.
6. It enables staff to control their own operations. Thereby reducing firefighting and freeing managers from constant intervention in business operations. This will help to create quality awareness and job satisfaction among employees.
7. It provides a means for documenting the company's experience. This can serve as the basis for training staff and thus for improving their performance.
8. Internally for a company, ISO 9000 registration brings better documentation, greater quality awareness, positive cultural change and increased efficiency and productivity.
9. International customers have started to make ISO 9000 compliance an integral part of their purchase agreements. Customers are using the standards as a way to differentiate the offerings of various suppliers, particularly when products and services are substantially similar. Thus, it improves customer satisfaction and reduces customer quality audits.
10. It generates objective evidence to demonstrate the quality of products and the effectiveness of systems and thus to build confidence among customers.

11. It provides data that can be used to determine the performance level of operating processes and products, and to effect improvements.

12. ISO 9000 provides the foundation for further quality effects and substantial growth in the global market.

    ISO provides foundation for a 'Total Quality Management' programme by concentrating the various processors and procedures, and ensuring that appropriate quality emphasis is established and followed by everyone in the organization.

13. Company seeking ISO 9000 registration has a great deal of flexibility in deciding on the appropriate "Scope" of the registration. Individual product "lines" or functional entities can be separately registered; a single site can be registered; or a division with multiple sites/ locations can also be registered.

Implementing a quality system based on ISO 9000 can help transform an *ad hoc* method of quality control into an organized and cost-effective quality-management system. By combining high quality with low cost, this can give the company a tremendous competitive advantage.

An ever-increasing number of companies all over the world are implementing quality-system standards internally. In addition, the bigger companies are insisting that their suppliers implement certified quality systems. It is therefore imperative for companies in developing countries to adopt quality systems based on ISO 9000. This would greatly help in the improvement of their image, their credibility and their acceptability in international markets, factors essential for success in the export trade.

## STANDARDIZATION IN INDIA

During the last decade, several basic industries and large, medium and small-scale industries have been set-up. Industrial standardization has played a very significant role in the industrial growth through the formulation of specification to establish uniform perspective requirements relating to the characteristics and quantities of constituents and elements which enter into the production of commodities. It has also proved the basis for determining the efficiency, quality, utility, performance and structure of a commodity and made possible the advantage of interchangeability.

THE world now acknowledges that technological progress and innovations are long-term drivers of economic growth, especially in developing country like India. These views were expressed by PJ Thomas, Department of Telecom secretary and chairman Telecom Commission, Government of India while inaugurating the three-day Global ICT Standardization Forum for India (GISFI) Standardization Series Meeting in collaboration with Indian Institute of Information Technology, Allahabad in Ashoka Hotel, New Delhi recently.

New services generated by ICT in the forms of e-commerce, e-finance and e-governance are contributing towards greater economic efficiency while raising the living standard of citizens.

GISFI has been set-up as a public-private partnership, which will include industry, academia, manufacturers, operators, standardization bodies, and the government.

The main objective of GISFI will be to harmonize and unify the standardization efforts within the Indian market and work in close cooperation with all standardization bodies acting as a catalyst for India's growth as a knowledge-based economy. This will also result in improved competitiveness within companies and create conducive investor-friendly environment.

## BUREAU OF INDIAN STANDARDS

The Bureau of Indian Standards (BIS), the National Standards Body of India, is a statutory body set-up under the Bureau of Indian Standards Act, 1986. The Bureau is a body corporate and responsible for formulating National Standards. It comprises of members representing the Industry, Consumer Organizations, Scientific and Research Institutes and Professional Bodies, Technical Institutions, Central ministries, State Governments and Members of Parliament.

Bureau of Indian Standards (BIS) is a national standards body engaged in the preparation and implementation of standards, operation of certification schemes both for products and systems, organization and management of testing laboratories, creating consumer awareness and maintaining close liaison with international standards bodies.

It has 19 branch offices. It also works as WTO-TBT enquiry point for the Government of India recognized the importance of standardization in the rapid industrial development before launching big industrial development plants, the Indian Standards Institution (ISI) now known as Bureau of Indian Standards (BIS) was therefore established in 1947 to ensure the preparation, promotion and general adoption, at national and international levels of standards relating to materials, commodities, structures, practices and operations. As a corporate body, it has 25 members drawn from national and state politics, industry, scientific and research institutions, and consumer organizations. Its headquarters are in New Delhi, with regional offices in Kolkata, Chennai, Mumbai, Chandigarh and Delhi. The institution aims at assisting in the rationalization the efforts of producers and consumers to improve coordinates processes and products. It promotes quality control methods.

The BIS has over the years taken up programmes for the formulation of standards in a big way handled by several technical committees, sectional committees, subcommittees and panels.

Under standards formulation, it is engaged in formulation of Indian Standards for 14 sectors namely chemicals, food and agriculture, civil, electrical, electronics and telecommunications and information technology, mechanical engineering, management and systems, metallurgical engineering, petroleum, coal and related products, medical and hospital planning, textile, transport engineering and production and general engineering, water resources under division councils which have 308 sectional committees working under them. As on 31 March, 2008, 18,424 standards formulated by BIS, are in force. These cover important segments of economy, which help the industry in upgrading the quality of their goods and services. BIS formulates need-based Indian Standards in line with the national priorities as a time-bound programme.

The various committees and councils comprised of representatives of manufacturers, consumers, trade bodies, government departments and other interested concern. The BIS has published over 8,000 standards on various industrial materials, semifinished goods, codes of practice, methods of tests, methods of quality control, and glossaries of terms.

Besides formulating and publishing standards, the BIS initiated a big programme to help industries in the production of goods to the prescribed quality. For this purpose, it operated a "Certification Mark Scheme" which brought manifold advantages to the industry. Any commodity for which an Indian standard has been published is eligible to get the "BIS" mark if the industry has got the necessary facilities for manufacturing quality goods. The BIS charges nominal fees for certification marks, which is stamped on the product by the manufacture. The ISI mark is an assurance on the part of independent party of the quality of the goods. The BIS has given over 1,000 licenses for certification marks under this scheme. The sample inspection of the product is done by it and if any product is found not to be in accordance with the specifications the manufacturer is liable to be panelized. The BIS keeps a continuous watch on industrial commercial concerns to ensure that specifications standards are strictly adhered to. Various Central and State Government purchase organizations have been increasingly adopting the BIS for the purpose of purchases on behalf of their various departments including Defence.

The BIS also play an important role in the international standardization field. It coordinates its activities with those of the international body and takes a leading part in its technical and other work. Its work has been well organized in the international field. As a matter of fact, its Vice-president was President of the International Body, i.e., the ISI, for 3 years.

Bureau of Indian Standards (BIS) came into existence, through an Act of Parliament on 1st April, 1987, with a broadened scope and more powers taking over the staff, assets, liabilities and functions of erstwhile Indian Standards Institution (ISI) with following objectives.

- Harmonious development of activities of standardization, marking and quality certification.
- To provide new thrust to standardization and quality control.
- To evolve a national strategy for according recognition to standards and integrating them with growth and development of industrial production and exports.

BIS is involved in multifarious activities like Standards Formulation, Certification, and Product/ Schemes, Laboratory Services, International Activities, Consumer-related Activities, Promotional Activities, Training Services, Information Services, Sale of Standards and Publications.

In the first phase, BIS has selected the engineering industries for intensifying quality upgradation work and is working very closely with the Confederation of Engineering Industries (CEI). With a view to encouraging manufacturers and service organizations to strive for excellence, Rajiv Gandhi National Quality Award was instituted by the Bureau in 1991. BIS is self-reliant in meeting its non-plan expenditure without any budgetary support from the Government of India. Most of these standards are voluntary in India. Indian standards promotions therefore, have assumed a great significance in our country. Its efforts have therefore been directed towards persuading manufacturers, Government departments, statutory authorities and the consumers to apply or adopt Indian Standards in their own fields of activity.

Marching further ahead on the path of 'total customer satisfaction' BIS had set-up a single window information and SSI Facilitation Cell at its headquarters in New Delhi which became operational since 1997 with the aim of providing variety of information/assistance. A number of entrepreneurs, consumers and professionals visit this centre. To impart training to technical and management personnel from industry, consumer organizations, public sector undertakings, government bodies and developing countries, BIS has established, the National Institute of Training for Standardization (NITS) at NOIDA (UP).

As a result of this, 88% of Indian Standards specification has been adopted as the basis for purchase and other activities by government agencies. Recently, the Government of India had decided that contracts for purchase of its stores will be entered into only for items bearing BIS standard mark in case BIS marked products are not available, items strictly conforming to Indian Standards will be purchased.

BIS technical library is a national resource centre for information on standards and related matters and meets the needs of industry, trade, government, researchers and consumers. It is the largest library of standards in the South Asian Region, covering a floor area of 1,000 square metres. The collection includes about 6 lakh standards from all over the world and 50,000 technical books. The Bureau's library system comprises the Headquarters' Library (New Delhi) and four Regional Office Libraries at Mumbai, Kolkata, Chandigarh and Chennai. BIS has also been designated as WTO/TBT Enquiry Point by the Ministry of Commerce, Government of India under the Technical Barriers to Trade Agreement of World Trade Organization.

BIS has brought out all Indian Standards on CD-ROMs through a franchisee with a view to computerize its sales points as well as to provide standards in electronic form directly to the customers. The product has been well received by the industry and provides excellent full-text searching facility in over 18,000 standards formulated by the Bureau.

BIS has a website with domain name www.bis.org.in. Information of interest to the Indian industry as well as consumers, relating to various activities and schemes of the Bureau, such as certification, standards formation, consumer affairs, various application forms, laboratory services and other support services, is available on the website.

The Product Certification Scheme of BIS aims at providing Third Party Guarantee of quality, safety and reliability of products to the ultimate customer. Presence of ISI certification mark known as Standard Mark on a product is an assurance of conformity to the specifications. The conformity is ensured by regular surveillance of the licensee's performance by surprise inspections and testing of samples, drawn both from the market and factory.

BIS Product Certification Scheme is basically voluntary in nature. However, keeping in view the health and safety of the consumer, it has been made mandatory for 68 items by the government through various statutory measures such as Prevention of Food Adulteration Act, Coal Mines Regulations and Indian Gas Cylinders Rules besides BIS Act. Some of the items brought under mandatory certification on consideration of health and safety are milk powder, packaged drinking water, LPG cylinders, oil pressure stoves, clinical thermometers, etc. As on 31st March, 2008, 20,025 certification marks licenses are in operation under the Scheme, covering about 1,000 different items ranging from food products to electronics.

All foreign manufacturers of products who intend to export to India are required to obtain a BIS product certification license. To facilitate this, BIS launched its Product Certification Scheme for overseas manufacturers in the year 1999.

BIS also runs other certification schemes like IECEE-CB, IECQ and IECEs Schemes of IBC under different provisions.

So far products, such as food additives, steel products, cement, vanaspati and miner's equipment have been brought under mandatory certification. This list may have to be progressively enlarged to meet the growing demand for compulsory marking, where substandard quality had generated considerable public displeasure. There are socio-economic problems in case of items reserved for or predominantly manufactured in the small-scale sector. Bringing a product under compulsory certification would not by itself ensure desired quality levels. A number of steps such as survey of production technology in the units, consultancy for designs, availability of quality raw materials and components, adequacy of testing facilities and a viable plan for quality upgradation are necessary.

their responsibilities to lower level functionaries and freeing them to concentrate on important strategic issues and the improvement of operations.

The adaptation of standardization for large and basic industries though comparatively easy is not so for small-scale industries because the problems of standardization in small-scale industries are somewhat different from those of large-scale industries and therefore the introduction of standardization has to be such that it may not prove uneconomical or unproductive for this sector. The experience of Indian in the field of standardization for the small-scale sector should be of great use to other developing countries. While formulating the standards for such commodities, as are manufactured in the small-scale sector; it is necessary that its representatives are consulted and their guidance sought by the relevant committees of the BIS. A large number of standards have been formulated for the items manufactured by small-scale units. These include items like bicycle components, farm implements, food products, builder's hardware, hospital equipment, sports goods, surgical and medical instruments, etc. Small-scale units have been widely using the BIS certification mark in the past few years. Small-scale ancillary industries also make use of this certification marks. Several industries — machine tools, bicycles, electrical machinery and equipment, automobiles and supply parts and components to the large unit's suppliers continuously follow company standards. For items manufactured by the units the specifications are laid down by large-scale units are for the ancillary units supply parts and components in accordance with these standards.

Several items manufactured by small-scale units have contributed to foreign exchange earnings: and these units have to undergo inspection prior to the export of their products in accordance with the standards precise and for this purpose, which are generally the Indian Standards Specifications. The BIS certification mark has also been recognized 1965, in case of several light engineering products as knives, buckets, lower bolts, wire nails, umbrellas, scissors, electrical cables and conductors, etc. manufactured by these units.,

SSI promotional efforts were started in 1966 by the creation of the National Small-scale Industries Corporation (NSIC) under the National Development Corporation (NDC). Due to operational inefficiency, poor planning and lack of an extension network, NSIC provided little constructive support of small-scale industrial development and was subsequently replaced by the Small-scale Industries Development Organization (SIDO) in 1973.

## SUMMARY

- The ***ISO 9000*** quality management system is an internationally accepted tool for quality assurance practice and customer satisfaction in all areas of business operations.
- ***ISO 14000*** series is a comprehensive quality management concepts and guidance.
- ISO 9000 standards require that third party audits be performed leading to the suppliers becoming certified and this certification is accepted by all customers.
- The ISO 9000 series includes ISO 8402, ISO 9000, ISO 9001, ISO 9002, ISO 9003, and ISO 9004.
- It is the 'top level' quality document and is provided by specific procedures which includes business processes to produce quality products and services.
- **Total Quality Management (TQM)** is a management approach that emphasizes quality. It is concerned with continuous improvement in all work. It does not aim to improve results

by improvements alone, but more importantly, by improving capabilities to produce better results in the future and solve the problems.

- There are various ISO 9000 strategic objectives and reasons for adopting ISO 9000 systems which provide turnkey solution to customer and improve product quality and process efficiency.
- **Standardization** played a vital role in industrial growth through the formulation of specification to establish uniform perspective requirements relating to the characteristics and quantities of constituents and elements which enter into the production of commodities.
- **Bureau of India,** National Standards Body of India, compromises of members representing the industry, consumer organizations, scientific and research institutes, professional bodies, technical institutions, Central ministries, State Governments and members of Parliament.
- BIS ensures the preparation, promotion and general adoption at national and international levels of standards relating to materials, commodities, structures, practices and operations.
- BIS initiated a big programme to help industries in the production of goods to the prescribed quality. For this purpose, it operated a 'Certification Mark Scheme'.
- BIS Product Certification Scheme is basically voluntary and keeping in view the health and safety of the consumer. It has been made mandatory for 68 items by the government.
- **ISI Certification** allows the licenses to use the popular ISI Mark which has become synonymous with quality products for the Indian and neighbouring markets over the past 50 years.
- The objective is to harmonious development of standardization, marketing and quality certification, quality control and growth and development of production and exports.
- **Small-scale Industries** play an important role for economic development. Provide jobs for ever-increasing population and offer many consumer products at moderate rates and perform a vital complementary role as suppliers of components, subsystems, job work and other services to the larger manufacturers.

## ........ QUESTIONS FOR DISCUSSION

1. Explain and discuss ISO 9000 series.

### Questions for Review

1. Explain the quality standards under ISO 9000.
2. What are the reasons for adopting ISO 9000.
3. Explain in detail the various objectives of ISO 9000.
4. Describe the various benefits of ISO 9000.
5. Write a short note on standardization in small-scale industries.

## Objective Questions

### Fill in the Blank

1. ISO 14000 family addresses ________.
   (a) Comprehensive glossary
   (b) Environmental management
   (c) Technical committees
   (d) Technology
2. Bureau of Indian Standards was established ________.
   (a) 1926
   (b) 1937
   (c) 1947
   (d) 1931

*Ans:* **1.** (b), **2.** (c)

### True or False

1. ISO 9000, ISO 9001, ISO 9002, ISO 9003, ISO 9004, and ISO 8402 contain specific guidelines pertaining to a certain segment of quality related activities.
2. European Economic Community (EEC) was the first to adopt ISO 9000 formally as the requirement suppliers should meet in order to do a business in Japan.
3. The BIS has given over 1,000 licenses.
4. With a view to encourage manufacturers and service organizations Rajiv Gandhi National Quality Award was instituted by the bureau in 1990.
5. ISO is a Worldwide Federation of national standards bodies at present comprising 140 members, one in each country.

*Ans:* **1.** True, **2.** False, **3.** True, **4.** False, **5.** True

☺ ☺ ☺

# Further Readings

# Further Readings


- Arun Monnappa and Mirza S. Saiyadain, *"Personnel Management"*, 2nd edition, Tata McGraw-Hill Co. Ltd., New Delhi, pp. 207-231.
- Arun Monnappa and Mirza S. Saiyadain, *"Personnel Management"*, 2nd edition, Tata McGraw-Hill Co. Ltd., New Delhi, pp. 252-275.
- Bill of Exchange Act, 1985 RSC Chapter B-4.
- BIS Annual Report 2006-07.
- Biswajeet - Pattanayak, *"Human Resource Management"*, PHI Learning Pvt. Ltd., New Delhi, February 2010.
- C.B. Mamoria and S.V. Gankar, *"Personnel Management – Text and Cases"*, Himalaya Publishing House, Mumbai, December, 2000.
- C.B. Mamoria and S.V. Gankar, *"Personnel Management – Text and Cases"*, Himalaya Publishing House, Mumbai 2006, pp. 361-402.
- C.B. Mamoria and S.V. Gankar, *"Personnel Management – Text and Cases"*, Himalaya Publishing House, Mumbai, 2006, pp. 432-458.
- C.B. Mamoria and S.V. Gankar, *"Personnel Management – Text and Cases"*, Himalaya Publishing House, Mumbai, 2006, pp. 840-850.
- C.S.V. Murthy, *Management Information System*, 2003, Himalaya Publishing House, Mumbai.
- Clayton Town Site Co. vs. Clayton Drug Co. Supreme Court of New Mexico, USA, 1915, 147 p. 460.
- D.A. Decenzo and S.P. Robbins, *"Personnel/Human Resource Management"*, Prentice-Hall of India Private Limited, New Delhi, 2007.
- David J. Luck and Ronald S. Rubin, 2002; *Marketing Research*; 7th Edition; Prentice-Hall.
- Dr. Nageswar Rao and Dr. R.P. Das, *"Cases in Human Resource Management"*, 1st Edition, Himalaya Publishing House, Mumbai.
- Edwin Flippo, *"Personnel Management"*, McGraw-Hill Company, New York, February, 2002.
- Edwin Flippo, *Personnel Management*, 5th Edition (International student edition), Tata McGraw-Hill Co. Ltd., New Delhi, pp. 203-223.
- Edwin Flippo, "*Personnel Management*", 5th Edition (International student edition), Tata McGraw-Hill Co. Ltd., New Delhi, pp. 249-319.

- G.C. Beri, 2000; *"Marketing Research"*; Third Edition, Tata McGraw-Hill Publishing Company Ltd.
- Gary Dessler and Biju Varkkey, *"Human Resource Management"*, Pearson, Prentice-Hall, New Delhi, November, 2009.
- Gordon B. Davis, Margrethe H. Oslon, *"MIS Conceptual Foundation, Structure and Development"*, 2nd Edition, Tata McGraw-Hill Companies, New Delhi.
- Harold Koontz and Heinz Weihrich (2003); *"Essentials of Management"*; Tata McGraw-Hill Publishing Company Limited, Reprint 2003, New Delhi.
- *http://class.classmatandread.net*
- *http://fliiby.com/get/839943*
- *http://marketingdreams.net*
- *http://nptel.iitm.ac.in/courses*
- *http://www.articlesbase.com/law-articles/what-is-a-promissory-note-425112.htm*l
- *http://www.delsolmedina.com/La%20primera%20letra%20de%20cambio.htm*
- ISO Online – International Organization for Standardization website.
- James A. F. Stoner, R. Edward Freeman, and Daniel R. Gilbert Jr. (2008); *"Management"*; Pearson, Prentice-Hall, 6th Edition, Reprint in 2008.
- Jerome Kanter, *"Management Oriented MIS"*, 3rd Edition, Prentice-Hall.
- John Bratton and Jeffrey Gold, *"Human Resource Management – Theory and Practice"*, 2nd Edition, McMillan Business, pp. 213-236.
- K. Aswathappa, *"Human Resource and Personnel Management"*, McGraw-Hill Companies, 2005.
- K. Aswathappa, *"Human Resource Management – Text and Cases"*, 5th edition, Tata McGraw-Hill Co. Ltd., New Delhi, pp. 238-253.
- K. Aswathappa, *"Human Resource Management – Text and Cases"*, 5th edition, Tata McGraw-Hill Co. Ltd., New Delhi, pp. 547-567.
- Kenneth C. Laudon and Jane P. Laudon, *Management Information System*, 7th Edition, Pearson Education, Asia.
- Kotler, Keller, Koshy, Jha (2009); *"Marketing Management: A South Asian Perspective*", Pearson, Prentice-Hall and Dorling Kindersley (India) Pvt. Ltd., 2009, New Delhi.
- Kotler P. and Keller; 2006; *"Marketing Management"*; 12th Edition; p. 443 and p. 539; Pearson, Prentice-Hall; New Delhi.
- L.M. Prasad (2002); *"Principles and Practices of Management"*; Sultanchand & Sons, Educational Publishers, 2002, New Delhi.
- L.M. Prasad, *"Principles and Practice of Management"*, Sultanchand & Sons, New Delhi, 2007.
- L.T. Gen., H. Lal, *"Trade Support Services"*, *"ISO 9000 Quality Management Systems. Guidelines for enterprises in developing countries"*, International Trade Centre, UNCTAD/WTO Geneva, Switzerland and International Organisation for Standardisation, Geneva, Switzerland, 2004.
- Lamb Hair, McDaniel (2004); *"Marketing"*; Thomson Asia Publisher Ltd., 2004, Singapore.
- Luis R. Gomez-Mejia, David B. Balkin and Robert L. Cardy, *"Managing Human Resources"*, PHI Learning Pvt. Ltd., New Delhi, March 2004.
- M.C. Kuchhal, *"Secretarial Practice"*, 15th Edition, Vikas Publishing House Pvt. Ltd., New Delhi.
- McLean vs. Shields 1 Man. L. R. 278 (1884).

- McPherson vs. Johnston 3 BCR 465 (1894).
- N.D. Kapoor, *"Elements of Mercantile Law"*, 29th Edition, Sultanchand & Sons, New Delhi, 2008.
- N.D. Kapoor, *"Elements of Mercantile Law"*, 31st Revised Edition, Sultanchand & Sons, New Delhi, 2009.
- N. Kumar and R. Mithal, *"Office Management"*, 1st Edition, Anmol Publications Pvt. Ltd., New Delhi.
- N. Kumar and R. Mithal, *"Secretarial Practice"*, 1st Edition, 2002, Anmol Publications Pvt. Ltd., New Delhi.
- *National Portal Content Management Team*, Reviewed on: 02-06-2010.
- P.C. Tripathi, and P. N. Reddy (2008); *"Principles of Management"*; Tata McGraw-Hill Publishing Company Limited, 4th Edition, 2008, New Delhi.
- P.G. Aquinas and S.C. Srivastava, *"Human Resource Management"*, Vikas Publishing House Pvt. Ltd., New Delhi, 2009.
- P. Subba Rao, *"Personnel and Human Resource Management – Text and Cases"*, Himalaya Publishing House, Mumbai, 2008, pp. 133-151.
- P. Subba Rao, *"Personnel and Human Resource Management – Text and Cases"*, Himalaya Publishing House, Mumbai, 2008, pp. 225-246.
- P. Subha Rao, *"Personnel and Human Resource Management – Text and Cases"*, Himalaya Publishing House, Mumbai, 2008, pp.352-364.
- Paul E. Green, Donalds Tull and Gerald Albaum; *"Research for Marketing Decisions"*; 5th Edition (PHI).
- Paul J. Jerome, "Evaluating Employee Performance", Wheeler Publishing, New Delhi, November, 1998.
- Philip Kotler (2003); *"Marketing Management"*, Pearson Education (Singapore) pte. Ltd., 2nd Indian Reprint, 2003, Delhi.
- Philip Kotler, Armstrong (1999); *"Principles of Marketing"*; Ashok K. Ghosh Prentice-Hall Publication, 8th Edition, 1999, New Delhi.
- Philip Kotler (2004); *"Marketing Management"*; 11th Edition.
- Prof. S.A. Sherlekar and Dr. Virendra Sharad Sherlekar (2000); *"Modern Business Organisation and Management"*; Himalaya Publishing House, 5th Edition, Reprint 2000.
- R.K. Chopra and Ankita Chopra, *"Office Management"*, 14th Revised Edition, Himalaya Publishing House, Mumbai.
- Richard L. Daft, *"Management"*, a Division of Harcourt College Publishers, December 2002.
- S. D. Bagade (Shankar D. Bagade), *"Total Quality Management"*, Himalaya Publishing House, Mumbai, 2000.
- S.L. Goel, *"Personnel Administration and Management"*, Sterling Publishers Pvt. Ltd., New Delhi, January 1994.
- S.L. Goel, *"Personnel Administration and Management"*, Sterling Publishers Pvt. Ltd., New Delhi, January 1994.
- S. Sadagopan, *"Management Information System"*, 1998, Prentice-Hall, India.
- Stephen P. Robbins, Mary Coulter, and Neharika Vohra (2010); *"Management"* Pearson, Prentice-Hall, 10th Edition, 2010.
- Sterling Publishers Pvt. Ltd., New Delhi, January 1994.

- Tom Redman and Adrian Wilkinson, *"Contemporary Human Resource Management"*, Third Edition, Pearson.
- Udai Pareek and T.V. Rao, *"Designing and Managing Human Resource System*", 3rd Edition, Oxford and IBH Publishing Company Pvt. Ltd., New Delhi, pp.129-199.
- V. S. Ramaswamy, Namakumari (2002); *"Marketing Management Planning, Implementation and Control Global Perpective Indian Context"*, McMillan Business Books, Third Edition, 2002, Delhi.
- V.S.P. Rao and V. Hari Krishna (2009); *"Management – Text and Cases"*; Excel Books, 1st Edition, Reprint 2009, New Delhi.
- V.S.P. Rao and V. Harikrishna, *"Management – Text and Cases"*, Excel Books, New Delhi, January, 2006
- V.S.P. Rao, *"Human Resource Management – Text and Cases"*, Excel Books, New Delhi, 2005.
- W.S. Jawadekar, *"Management Information System"*, 3rd Edition, Tata McGraw-Hill Companies, New Delhi.
- *www.learnmarketing.net*
- *www.more-for-small-business.com*
- *www.wikipedia.org*
- Y. K. Bhushan (2008); *"Fundamentals of Business Organization and Management"*; Sultanchand & Sons, Reprint 2008, New Delhi.


☺ ☺ ☺

# References

# References

## REFERENCE


Biswajeet - Pattanayak, "*Human Resource Management*", PHI Learning Pvt. Ltd., New Delhi, February 2010.

C.B. Mamoria and S.V.Gankar, "*Personnel Management*" (text and cases), Himalaya Publishing House, Mumbai, December 2000.

D.A.Decenzo and S.P.Robbins, "*Personnel/Human Resource Management*", Prentice-Hall of India Private Limited, New Delhi, 2007.

David J. Luck and Ronald S. Rubin; 2002; *Marketing Research*; 7th Edition; Prentice-Hall of India Private Limited;

Edwin Flippo, "*Personnel Management*", McGraw-Hill Company, New York, February 2002.

*Financial Management* by I. M. Pandey. Vikas Publications. 6th Edition, (2009).

*Fundamentals of Business Organization and Management* by Y. K. Bhushan, Sultan Chand & Sons. 1999, Reprint.

G.C. Beri; 2000; *Marketing Research*; 3rd Edition; Tata McGra-Hill Publishing Company Limited;

Google search.

*Investment Analysis and Portfolio Management* by Prasanna Chandra – March – Tata McGraw-Hill Publications, (2008).

Kotler P. and Keller K; 2006; *Marketing Management*; 12th Edition; P. 443 and P. 539; Pearson Prentice-Hall; Delhi;

Kotler P. and Keller K.; 2006; *Marketing Management*; 12th Edition; p-443 and p-539; Pearson Prentice-Hall; Delhi;

Kotler, Keller, Koshy, Jha (2009); '*Marketing Management A South Asian Perspective*', Pearson Prentice-Hall and Dorling Kindersley (India) Pvt. Ltd., 2009, New Delhi.

L.M. Prasad, "*Principles and Practice of Management*", Sultanchand & Sons, New Delhi, 2007.

Lamb, Hair, McDaniel (2004); '*Marketing*'; Thomson Asia Publisher Ltd., 2004, Singapore.

Luis R. Gomez-Mejia, David B. Balkin and Robert L. Cardy, "*Managing Human Resources*", PHI Learning Pvt. Ltd., New Delhi, March 2004.

P.G. Aquinas and S.C.Srivastava, "*Human Resource Management*", Vikas Publishing House Pvt. Ltd., New Delhi, 2009.

Paul E. Green, Sonald S. Tull and Gerald Album; *Research for Marketing Decisions*; 5th Edition; Eastern Economy Edition (PHI).

Philip Kotler (2003); '*Marketing Management*' Pearson Education (Singapore) pte. Ltd., 2nd Indian reprint, 2003, Delhi.

Philip Kotler, Armstrong (1999); '*Principles of Marketing*'; Ashok K. Ghosh Prentice-Hall Publication, 8th edition, 1999, New Delhi.

Philip Kotler; 2004; *Marketing Management*; 11th Edition; Pearson Education;

Philip Kotler; 2044; *Marketing Management*; 11th Edition; Pearson Education;

*Production and Operations Management* by K. Aswathappa and K. Shridhara Bhat Publisher: Himalaya Publishing House, (2007).

S.L. Goel, "*Personnel Administration and Management*", Sterling Publishers Pvt. Ltd., New Delhi, January 1994.

V.S. Ramaswamy, Namakumari (2002); '*Marketing Management Planning, Implementation and Control Global Perpective Indian Context*', McMillan Business Books, Third edition, 2002, Delhi.

V.S.P Rao and V Harikrishna, "*Management*" (Text and cases), Excel Books, New Delhi, January 2006.

V.S.P Rao, "*Human Resource Management*" (text and cases), Excel Books, New Delhi, 2005.

## Webliography

1. *www.learnmarketing.net*
2. *www.wikipedia.org*
3. *http://nptel.iitm.ac.in/courses*
4. *www.more-for-small-business.com*
5. *http://fliiby.com/get/839943*
6. *http://marketingdreams.net*
7. *http://class.classmatandread.net*
8. *http://www.einsteincollege.ac.in/Assets/Department/Lecturer%20notes/MBA/Security%20analysis% 20and%20portfolio%20management.pdf*
9. *http://www.nls.ac.in/resources/ded/resources/MBL%20II/december2A-%20Gen%20Princiles%20of%20%20Insurance%20Law.pdf*
10. *http://www.investorwords.com/2510/insurance.html*
11. *http://en.wikipedia.org/wiki/Life_insurance*
12. *http://www.nos.org/Secbuscour/cc11.pdf*
13. *http://www.nos.org/Secbuscour/cc10.pdf*
14. *http://www.nseindia.com/content/ncfm/ncfm_CBBM_workbook.pdf*

☺☺☺

# Glossary

# Glossary

**Acceptor:** When the drawee accepts the bill, he is called the acceptor.

**Adaptive criteria:** The adaptive criteria in the selection of the intermediaries refer to the degree of flexibility permitted to the manufacturer/producer by the particular intermediary, with respect to the future changes in the distribution system characteristics.

**Advertisement:** Advertising is any paid form of number of personal presentation and promotion of ideas, goods, or services by an identified sponsor, with the specific objective.

**Advertising goal (or Advertising objective):** An advertising goal (or objective) refers to the specific communications task and achievement level to be accomplished with a specific audience in a specific period of time.

**Agents:** These are the intermediaries, sales agents, brokers, auctioneers, etc., who may have the possession or may not have the possession of the goods, but in no case will have the title to the merchandise.

**Application blank:** It is a printed form completed by job aspirants detailing their educational background, previous work history and certain personal data.

**Applied research:** Applied research is carried with the aim of finding out alternative solutions to the problems or, for guiding the specific decisions. Applied research is also called as the 'decisional research'.

**Arbitration:** It is a process by which unsettled or unresolved disputes can be settled by an outside agency.

**Articulative interviewing:** Articulative interviewing is designed to determine what social values interviewees hold dear by having them about broad topics such as their various roles in life and their daily activities.

**ASCI:** The Advertisements Standard Council of India.

**Assessment centre:** It is the standardised form of employee appraisal that uses multiple assessment exercises such as "in-basket", games, role play, etc., and multiple raters.

**Attitudes:** Enduring and learned tendencies to act in a particular consistent way with regard to a given object or idea.

**Attribute positioning:** A company positions itself on an attribute, such as size or number of years in existence.

**Audience:** It refers to the number of people exposed to the vehicle.

**Audiometer:** An audiometer is attached to television sets in participating homes to record when the set is on and to which channel it is tuned.

**Backward flow:** Backward flow refers to flow of activity from customers to the company.

**Basic research:** It means that this type of research has general usage or this type of research is carried out for whole universe. Basic research is also called as the 'fundamental research', 'theoretical' research or 'pure' research.

**Behavioural data:** Customers leave traces of their purchasing behaviour in store scanning data, catalogue purchases and customer databases, which becomes the behavioural data, for the study of the behaviour of the customers.

**Belief:** A descriptive thought that an individual has about a product, service, or idea

**Benefit positioning:** The product is positioned as the leader in a certain benefit.

**Bill of exchange:** A bills of exchange is an instrument in writing, containing an unconditional order, signed by the maker, directing a certain person to pay a certain sum of money only to, or to the order of a certain person or to the bearer of the instrument. (Sec. 5 of the Negotiable Instrument Act, 1881).

**Bureau of Indian Standards (BIS):** Is a national standards body engaged in the preparation and implementation of standards, operation of certification schemes both for products and systems, organization and management of testing laboratories, creating consumer awareness and maintaining close liaison with international standards bodies.

**Campus placement:** Visiting specific skill institutes to hire graduates.

**Capability:** Developing the technique of utilising the available resources to perform an activity efficiently and within the stipulated timeframe.

**Causal research design:** When the researcher is interested in knowing the cause and effect relationship between two or more variables, a causal research is undertaken.

**Centralized filing system:** A system where all the files pertaining to all the department of whole of the organization are preserved in a separate room in a centralized office and consequently any departmental head searching a particular file has to search it from there.

**Channels:** 'Channels' refers to the links between the manufacturers and the consumers, a set of intermediaries performing a variety of functions. They are also called as the intermediaries or the middlemen, and the entire flow, the movement of the goods from the manufacturer to the consumers, consisting of the various intermediaries is called as the 'Channels of Distribution' or 'Trade Channel'.

**Characteristics of interest:** Characteristics of interest refer to both the 'results' that are of concern to management and the 'variables' that are to be tested for their relationship to the results. The characteristics of interest can be style and colour preferences, buying behaviour, personality traits, etc.

**Cheque:** A cheque is a bill of exchange drawn on a specified banker and not expressed to be payable on demand.

**Circulation:** It refers to the number of physical units that carries the advertisement.

**Collective bargaining:** The term collective bargaining refers to negotiation, administration and interpretation of a written agreement between two parties that covers a specific period of time.

**College placements:** An external search process focuses recruiting efforts on a college campus.

**Communication-effect research or copy-testing:** Communication-effect research, also called as the 'Copy-testing'. It seeks to determine whether an ad is communicating effectively or not.

**Company secretary:** Section 2(45) of the Companies (Amendment ) Act, 1988, "A company secretary means a person, who is a member of the Institute of Company Secretaries of India, and includes any other individual possessing the prescribed qualification, and appointed to perform the duties which may be performed by a secretary under this Act and any ministerial or administrative duties".

**Comparative advertising:** Comparative advertising aims to make an explicit comparison of the attributes of two or more brands.

**Competition:** Competition includes all the actual and potential rival offerings substitutes that a buyer might consider.

**Competitive advantage:** An ability of an organization to perform activities exceptionally well (availing profitable opportunities and thereby maximising returns on investment) and gaining and edge over rivals when competing. To attain competitive advantage, firms need to add value to services and products offered to end customers.

**Computer programs:** Computer programs are machine-readable instructions that direct the circuitry within the hardware parts of the CBIS to function in ways that produce useful information from data.

**Computer-based information system:** A computer-based information system (CBIS) is an information system in which the computer plays a major role in collecting, storing and processing data. The purpose of CBIS is to collect, store and disseminate information from an organization's environment and internal operations to support organizational functions and decision making, communication, coordination, control, analysis and visualization.

**Concentration:** It calls for spending the entire advertising budget in a single period.

**Conditions of sale:** It refers to the payment terms and producer guarantees.

**Continuity:** It means exposures appear evenly throughout a given period.

**Control criteria:** The control criteria for the selection of the intermediaries refer to the extent to which the selected intermediary permits the company, the producer to exercise its control, in spite of the considerable role of the direct contact with customers performed by these intermediaries.

**Core competence:** Activities that the firm performs especially well when compared to its competitors and through which the firm adds value to its goods and services over a period of time.

**Craft unions:** If the workers of the same craft or category of the job form into a union, that union is called Craft Union

**Crossed cheque:** A crossed cheque is one on which two parallel transverse lines with or without the words and Co.' are drawn.

**Data analysis:** Data analysis refers to the process of analyzing the collected data to derive some meaningful information. Data analysis includes consolidation, classification, tabulation and analysis of the data.

**Database:** A 'Database' is an integrated collection of data stored in one place for efficient access and information processing.

**Data:** Data are streams of raw facts representing events occurring in organizations or the physical environment before they have been organized and arranged into a form that people can understand and use.

**Decentralized filing system:** Each department of the organization makes its own arrangements for filing.

**Delegation:** Delegation refers to the, "relinquishing some control over how and to whom the products are sold".

**Demographics:** Objective and easily measurable characteristics of a population such as age, income, education, occupation, sex and marital status.

**Demotion:** Employee movement that occurs when an employee is moved from one job to another that is lower in pay, responsibility and organizational level.

**Depth interviewing:** Depth interviewing involves going deeply into the thoughts that an individual may have about a product or services.

**Descriptive research design:** The objective of the descriptive type of research design is to ascertain magnitudes. A descriptive study is undertaken when the researcher wants to know the characteristics of certain groups such as age, sex, educational level, income, occupation, etc.

**Dismissal:** The termination of the services of an employee as a punitive measure for some misconduct.

**Distributors' territorial rights:** It defines the distributors' territories and the terms under which the producer will enfranchise other distributors.

**Drawee:** The person who is directed to pay is called the drawee.

**Drawer:** The person who gives the order to pay or who makes the bill is called drawer.

**Effective ad-exposed audience:** The number of people with target audience characteristics who actually saw the advertisement.

**Effective audience:** It refers to the manner of people with target audience characteristics exposed to the vehicle.

**Effectiveness:** The extent to which goals have been met.

**Efficiency:** The degree to which operations are carried out in an economical way.

**Electronic commerce:** Electronic commerce is the process of buying and selling goods and services electronically with computerized business transactions using the internet, networks, and other digital technologies. It also encompasses activities supporting those market transactions, such as advertising, marketing, customer support, delivery, and payment.

**Electronic market:** An electronic market is an information system that links together many buyers and sellers to exchange information, products, services, and payments. Through computers and networks, these systems function like electronic intermediaries, with lowered costs for typical marketplace transactions, such as matching buyers and sellers, establishing prices, ordering goods, and paying bills (Bakos, 1998).

**Employee counselling:** The process through which employees are given advice in solving work related as well as personal problems.

**Employee development:** A kind of future oriented training, focusing on the individual growth of the employees.

**Employee leasing:** Hiring permanent employees of another company on lease basis for a specific period as per the leasing arrangement.

**Employee referral:** A recommendation from a current employee regarding a job applicant.

**Empowerment:** Allowing employees more control over what they do on the job.

**Exclusive distribution:** It refers to the strategy of the company to severely limit or restricts the number of intermediaries.

**Exploratory research design:** Exploratory research emphasize on the real nature of the problem. It suggests possible solutions or new ideas for the problem or opportunity emphasized in the research problem.

**Eye cameras:** Eye cameras study respondents' eye movements to see where their eye land first, how long they linger on a given item, and so on.

**Facilitators:** These are the intermediaries who assist in the distribution process of the merchandise. In this process, they may have physical possession of the merchandise in certain cases or may not have physical possession of the merchandise, but in no case will have title to the merchandise or negotiate purchase or sales transaction.

**Federation and confederation:** Industrial Unions, either of the same industry or of the different industry may form into an association in order to improve Trade Union unity/strength. Such a Union of Unions is called Federations. During the critical situations, Unions/Federations in different industries may resort to concerted action without losing their individuality. In such situations, the Federations form into an Association and such an association is called Confederation.

**Feedback:** Output that is returned to the appropriate members of the organization to help them evaluate or correct input.

**Filing:** The systematic preservation of letters, documents, received and copies of those sent out for future reference is known as filing.

**Flighting:** Flighting refers to the advertising for a particular period followed by the period with no advertising, followed by the second period of advertising activity.

**Focus-group research:** A focus-group research is a gathering of six to ten people who are invited to spend few hours with a skilled moderator to discuss a product, service, organization or other marketing entity or with the objective of understanding group dynamics or the behaviour of the respondents (consumer/customer).

**Forward flow:** Forward flow refers to the flow of the activity from company to the customer.

**Fraternal or extra-mural functions:** These functions include providing financial and nonfinancial assistance to workers during the periods of strikes and lockouts, extension of medical facility during sickness and casualties, provision of education, recreation, recreational and housing facility provision of social and religious benefits, etc.

**Frequency:** The number of times within the specified time period that an average person or household is exposed to the message.

**Galvanometers:** Galvanometers measure the interest or emotions aroused by exposures to a specific ad or picture.

**General unions:** If the workers of any industry, any region and of any job or occupation form into one union in order to protect the overall interests of the workers, such unions are called General Unions.

**Globalization:** Viewing the world as a single market for the firm, the process by which expansion takes place across different regions and national markets.

**Grievance processing and handling procedures:** Under which grievances are redressed or dealt with by a correction of the situation or by a channeling up of these "up the line". When a grievance reaches the chief executive officer, it has to be satisfactorily dealt with by him or sent to an outside statutory agency for settlement.

**Hardware:** The term hardware refers to machinery. This category includes the computer itself, which is often referred to as the central processing unit (CPU), and all of its support equipment.

**Holder:** The drawer of the payee who is in possession of the bill is called the holder.

**Holistic marketing:** The HMC is based on the development, design, and implementation of marketing programmes, processes and activities that recognizes their breadth and interdependencies.

**Horizontal filing method:** The papers are inserted in the folders and these folders are kept in drawers in horizontal position, i.e., one upon the other.

**Human resource development:** A planned way of developing individual employees, groups and the total organization to achieve organizational goals in an atmosphere of mutual trust and cooperation.

**Human resource management:** A process of bringing people and organizations together so that the goal of each one is met, effectively and efficiently.

**Human resource planning:** The process of assessing an organization's human resources needs in the light of organizational goals and making plans to ensure that a competent, stable workforce is employed.

**Hypothesis:** A hypothesis is a proposition which the researcher wants to verify.

**Impact:** The qualitative value of an exposure through a given medium.

**Index:** A kind of "guide" which guides a person as to where the information in detail will be available.

**Induction:** A technique by which a new employee is rehabilitated into the changed surroundings and introduced to the practices, policies, and purposes of the organization.

**Industrial unions:** If the workers of different categories form into a union, that union is called Industrial Union. These unions are also called "vertical" unions. The logic behind the formation of these unions is that workers of the same industry have the common bend and they are governed by same rules and regulations and are administered by the same management.

**Information system:** An information system can be defined technically as a set of interrelated components that collect (or retrieve), process, store, and distribute information to support decision making, coordination, and control in an organization.

**Information:** By information we mean data that have been shaped into a firm that is meaningful and useful to human beings.

**Informative advertising:** Informative advertising aims to create brand awareness and knowledge of new products or new features of existing products.

**Input:** The capture or collection of raw data from within the organization or from its external environment for processing in an information system.

**Integrated marketing:** It focuses on integration of the marketing programmes, processes and activities to create, communicate and deliver value to consumers. It concentrates integration among communications, products/services, and channels.

**Intensive distribution:** It refers to the placing of the goods or services in as many outlets as possible by the manufacturer.

**Internal mobility:** The lateral or vertical movement of an employee within an organization.

**Interview:** It is the oral examination of candidates for employment.

**Interviewer bias:** Many times, it also happens that an interviewer introduces a variety of biases because of their age, sex, experiences, beliefs, perceptions, etc., interfering intentionally or unintentionally the data collection procedure.

**ISO 9000 standards:** This standard is the minimum acceptable level of standards that a supplier's quality management practices should meet, in order to receive the ISO 9000 accreditation or certification.

**ISO:** The system was developed by the International Standards Organization (ISO) for management and control of quality at every stage of production, namely design, development, planning, manufacturing, installation and servicing.

**Job analysis:** The systematic collection, evaluation, and organisation of information about jobs.

**Job posting:** It is the method of publicising job openings on bulletin boards, electronic media and similar outlets by a company.

**Knowledge-level systems:** Knowledge-level systems support the organization's knowledge and data workers. The purpose of knowledge-level systems is to help the business firm integrate new knowledge into the business and to help the organization control the flow of paperwork.

**Latent difficulties:** Latent difficulties are those which are not so apparent and which, if not checked, would soon become evident, and affect the organization's performance adversely.

**Lay-off:** A lay-off entails the separation of the employee from the organization temporarily for economic or business reasons.

**Learning:** Process of applying results of past experiences to evaluate a new situation or modify future behaviour.

**Lifestyle:** An individual's pattern of living in the world as expressed by the manner in which he spends money and time on various activities and interests, and the opinion that he holds.

**Macro-scheduling:** The macro-scheduling problem involves scheduling the advertising in relationship to seasons and the business cycle.

**Maker:** The person who makes the promissory notes and promises to pay is called the maker.

**Management information system:** Gordon B. Davis defines management information system, as: An integrated user-machine system, for providing information, to support the operations, management analysis and decision-making functions in an organization. The system utilizes computer hardware and software, manual procedures, models for analysis, planning, control, and decisionmaking, and a database.

**Management:** The process of efficiently achieving the objectives of the organization with and through people.

**Management-level systems:** Management-level systems serve the monitoring, controlling, decisionmaking, and administrative activities of middle managers.

**Market segmentation:** A market segment consists of a group of customers who share a similar set of wants.

**Marketing mix:** It is the process of designing and integrating various elements of marketing in such a way as to ensure the achievement of enterprise objectives.

**Marketing research:** Marketing research is the systematic gathering, recording, and analyzing of data about problems related to marketing of goods and services.

**Marketing:** "An organizational function and a set of processes for creating, communicating and delivering value to customers and for managing customer relationships in ways that benefit the organization and its stakeholders."

**Media advertising:** Inviting applications by placing ads in media.

**Merchants:** These are the intermediaries who take title to the merchandise and resell the merchandise, generally having the physical possession of the goods.

**Method:** A manual of mechanical means and devices by which each operation is performed.

**Micro-scheduling:** The micro-scheduling problem calls for allocating advertising expenditures within a short period to obtain maximum impact.

**Militant or Intra-mural functions:** These functions include protecting the workers interests, i.e., hike in wages, providing more benefits, job security, etc., through collective bargaining and direct action such as strikes, 'gheraos', etc.

**Motivation:** Strong, unfulfilled need which spurs a person to take action for his satisfaction.

**Negotiable instrument:** A negotiable instrument is a document which entitles a person to a sum of money and which is transferable from one person to another by mere delivery or by endorsement and delivery.

**Observational research:** This method suggests that data are collected through one's observation.

**Office management:** Means the technique of controlling an office in order to achieve its purpose which is possible only when the office is well organized and managed.

**Office procedure or office routine:** A series of steps to be taken for doing a particular work in the office as per the office systems.

**Office:** A place where clerical work is performed and where all kind of paperwork (letters, correspondence, files, records, etc.), is maintained and dealt with.

**One-level channel:** A one-level channel contains one selling intermediary, such as a retailer.

**Open cheque:** A cheque which is payable in cash across the counter of a bank is called an open cheque.

**Operative-level system:** Information system that monitor the elementary activities and transactions of the organization.

**Output:** The distribution of processed information to the people.

**Overt difficulties:** Overt difficulties are those which are quite apparent and which manifest themselves.

**Panel interview:** An interview during the course of which, several interviewers take turns in interviewing the candidate.

**Payee:** The person to whom the payment is to be made is called the payee.

**Perception:** Process of selection, organization and interpretation of stimuli into cohesive, coherent picture.

**Personnel management:** It is the most effective use of people to achieve organizational and individual goals. It is a way of managing people to work so that they give their best to the organization.

**Personnel policies:** A set of proposals and actions that act as a reference point for managers in their dealings with employees.

**Personnel procedures:** Action guideline governing the behaviour of employees at work.

**Persuasive advertising:** Persuasive advertising aims to create liking, preference, conviction, and purchase of a product or service.

**Placement:** Actual posting of an employee to a specific job with rank and responsibilities attached to it.

**Political functions:** These functions include affiliating a union to a political party, in enrolling members, collecting donations, canvassing during the election and seeking the help of political parties during the strikes and lockouts.

**Positioning:** Positioning is the act of designing the offering and image to occupy a distinctive place in the mind of the target market.

**Price policy:** It refers to the establishing of the price list and schedule of discounts and allowances that intermediaries see as equitable and sufficient by the producer.

**Primary data:** Primary data are freshly gathered for a specific purpose or for a specific research project.

**Processing:** The conversion, analysis and manipulation of raw data into a form that is more meaningful to humans.

**Product:** As anything that is capable of satisfying customer needs.

**Product life cycle (PLC):** Has to do with the life of a product in the market with respect to business/ commercial costs and sales measures.

**Productivity:** The ratio of an organization's output to its inputs.

**Promissory note:** A 'promissory note' is an instrument in writing (not being a bank note or a currency note) containing an unconditional undertaking, signed by the maker, to pay a certain sum of money only to, or to order of, a certain person, or to the bearer of the instrument (Sec. 4).

**Promotion:** Employee movement from current job to another that is higher in pay, responsibility and organizational level.

**Promotion:** Movement of an employee from a lower level position to a higher level position with increase in salary.

**Psychographics:** The technique of measuring lifestyles using psychographic characteristics such as attitudes, opinions, and interests.

**Psychological tools:** Marketing researchers can probe a buyer's deeper beliefs and feelings using psychological tools such as laddering techniques, depth interviews, and Rorshach tests.

**Pull strategy:** Pull strategy the manufacturer uses advertising, promotion, and other forms of communication to persuade consumers to demand the product from intermediaries, thereby, inducing the intermediaries to order it.

**Pulsing:** A pulsing is continuous advertising at low-weight levels reinforced periodically by waves of heavier activity. It draws on the strength of continuous advertising and flights to create a compromise scheduling strategy.

**Push Strategy:** A push strategy uses the manufacturer's sales force, trade promotional money, or other means to induce intermediaries to carry, promote, and sell the product to end-users.

**Questionnaire:** A questionnaire consists of a set of questions along with the alternative responses presented to respondents, with the particular objective. It can be both, open-ended as well as close-ended.

**Reach:** The number of different persons or households exposed to a particular media schedule at least once during a specified time period.

**Recruitment:** The discovering of potential applicants for actual placement of anticipated organizational vacancies.

**Reference group:** A group that serves as a point of reference or comparison for an individual in the matter of forming value, attitudes or behaviour.

**Reinforcement advertising:** Reinforcement advertising aims to convince current purchasers that they made the right choice.

**Relationship marketing:** It has the aim of building mutually satisfying long-term relationships with key parties – customers, suppliers, distributors, and other marketing partners in order to earn and retain their business. It builds strong economic, technical, and social ties among the parties. Its ultimate outcome is building of a unique company asset called as a Marketing Network.

**Reminder advertising:** Reminder advertising aims to stimulate repeat purchase of products and services, reminding the target market about its long period association with the delivering functional benefit through the particular brand of the product.

**Research:** Research is an activity related to any problem or an opportunity and it is carried out with the help of other managerial tools.

**Research:** Research is an activity related to any problem or an opportunity and it is carried out with the help of other managerial tools.

**Resignation:** A voluntary separation initiated by the employee himself or herself.

**Retirement:** Termination of service on reaching the age of superannuation.

**Retrenchment:** A permanent lay-off for reasons other than punishment but not retirement or termination owing to ill health.

**Secondary data:** Secondary data are data that were collected for another purpose and already exist somewhere.

**Selection:** The process of matching the qualifications of applicants with job needs and choosing the most suitable one.

**Selection:** The process of picking individuals who have relevant qualifications to fill the jobs in an organization.

**Selective distribution:** It refers to the strategy of the company, whereby a company relies on more than a few but less than all of the intermediaries willing to carry a particular product.

**Separation:** A separation is a decision that the individual and the organization should part.

**Social class:** Division in a society comprising people sharing same social status, values, beliefs, attitudes, and exhibiting a distinct preference for certain products and brands.

**Social functions:** These functions include carrying out social service activities, discharging social responsibilities through various sections of the society like educating the customers.

**Software:** The term software refers to computer programs and the manuals (if any) that support them.

**Standardization:** It is the formulation of specification to establish uniform perspective requirements relating to the characteristics and quantities of constituents and elements which enter into the production of commodities.

**Stimulus:** An input to any one of the five senses.

**Strategic-level systems:** Strategic-level systems help senior management tackle and address strategic issues and long-term trends, both in the firm and in the external environment.

**Structured interview:** Interview that uses a set of standardised questions that are clearly job related, asked to all job applicants.

**Style:** Describes the product's look and feel to the buyer.

**Subculture:** Culture within a culture'; distinct groups of people grouped on the basis of nationality, religion, geographic region or race and having their own distinct motives, values and behaviour patterns.

**Suspension:** Prohibiting an employee from attending work and to perform normal duties assigned to him.

**System:** A planned approach to the activities needed to attain desired objectives. Specifically a system may be defined as a group of interrelated and interdependent parts operating in sequence according to predetermined plan, in order to achieve a goal or series of goals.

**Tachistoscope:** The tachistoscope flashes an ad to a respondent with an exposure interval that may range, from less than one hundredth of a second to several seconds.

**Test:** A test is a standardised, objective measure of a sample of behaviour.

**Time and space boundaries:** Time boundaries refer to the time which is to be considered for the research to be undertaken on the subject's unit of analysis. Space boundaries refers the extent to which the subject are considers with respect to its entire universe. In other words, it refers to the 'universe' of the subjects involved in the research problem.

**TQM:** TQM is a management approach to an organization, centred on quality, based on the participation of all its members and aimed at long-term success through customer satisfaction, with benefits to the members of the organizations and the societies.

**Trade unions:** According to Section 2(b) of the Trade Unions Act of 1926, "a trade union is any combination of persons, whether temporary or permanent, primarily for the purpose of regulating the relations between workers and employers, or between workers and workers, and for imposing restrictive conditions on the conduct of any trade or business, and includes the federation of two or more trade unions".

**Transfer:** A lateral movement within the same grade, from one job to another.

**Transfer:** Employee movement that occurs when an employee is moved from one job to another that is relatively equal in pay, responsibility and organizational level.

**Two-level channel:** A two-level channel contains two intermediaries, typically, wholesaler and retailer in consumer markets.

**Two-way flow:** The two-way flow refer to the flow of activity from both the directions, i.e., from company to customer as well as from customer to company.

**Unit of analysis:** The individuals or objects whose characteristic are to be measured are called the units of analysis. The units always identify subjects to be studied.

**Unnoticed opportunities:** Unnoticed opportunities indicate the potential for growth in a certain area of marketing.

**Vertical filing method:** The files are placed vertically or in a straight, standing position. This system consists of folders and cabinets.

**Weighted application blank:** It is the printed form completed by candidates in whom each item is weighted and scored based on its importance as a determinant of job success.

**Work sampling:** A selection device that requires the job applicant to actually perform a small segment of the job.

**(ZMET) Zaltman Metaphoric Elicitation Technique:** Zaltman Metaphoric Elicitation Technique (ZMET), which uses metaphors to access non-verbal images. These techniques get an associations that are less likely to emerge during normal interviewing.

**Zero-level channel:** A zero-level channel (also called a direct marketing channel) consists of a manufacturer selling directly to the final customer.

☺ ☺ ☺